THE INSIDERS' GUIDE TO
Salt Lake CITY

THE INSIDERS' GUIDE TO

Salt Lake CITY

by
Kate Duffy
and
Bryan Larsen

Insiders' Publishing Inc.

Published by:
Insiders' Publishing Inc.
105 Budleigh St.
P.O. Box 2057
Manteo, NC 27954
(919) 473-6100
www.insiders.com

Sales and Marketing:
Falcon Publishing Co. Inc.
P.O. Box 1718
Helena, MT 59624
(800) 582-2665
www.falconguide.com
•

FIRST EDITION
1st printing
•

Copyright ©1998
by Insiders' Publishing Inc.
•

Printed in the United States
of America
•

ISBN 1-57380-050-3

Insiders' Publishing Inc.

Publisher/Editor-in-Chief
Beth P. Storie

President/General Manager
Michael McOwen

Creative Services Director
Giles MacMillan

Director of New Product
Development
David Haynes

Managing Editor
Dave McCarter

Project Editor
Eileen Myers

Project Artist
Bart Smith

Regional Advertising
Sales
Greg Swanson

Local Advertising
Sales
Misty Zemp

Preface

Salt Lake City may be one of the world's best-kept secrets. Though we attract hundreds of thousands of visitors each year, many people seem unaware of this vibrant city, a unique blend of the past and future, situated at the crossroads of the West. First-time travelers to Salt Lake City are at once struck by the harsh topography — the imposing, rugged Wasatch Mountain Range to the east, the thirsty desert to the west — and our four seasons, giving residents the pleasure of climatic variety. Outsiders soon recognize the warmth and generous spirit of the people who reside here, qualities that easily soften the severity of terrain and weather. Travelers also see a Western town with concrete sidewalks where wooden boardwalks once carried people along the main streets of commerce, skyscrapers that have replaced the old general stores and the fine, well-preserved mansions of our founders, fused with modern homes in close-knit neighborhoods framed by lush green lawns and flower gardens.

Utah recently celebrated its sesquicentennial year by paying tribute to the early settlers. One-hundred-fifty years have passed since Brigham Young and his party of Mormon pioneers stood at the clearing on the down slope of the mountain pass declaring, "This is the right place." In celebration of this event, many residents dressed in pioneer clothing, boarded covered wagons and made the trek across the country in honor of their ancestors. They experienced the hardship of the early settler's journey and filled themselves with the vision of those who came before. The pioneers came to the Salt Lake Valley in search of a home in the West, a place of solitude isolated from a world that persecuted them. Meanwhile, so-phisticated men and women in stylish business attire sat in stately board rooms in downtown Salt Lake making plans to throw open the front door of our city, welcoming people from all over the world during the 2002 Winter Olympic Games.

The paradox of our culture never ceases to amaze. In this first *Insiders' Guide® to Salt Lake City* we are excited at the opportunity to share with visitors the treasures of the city, our home and the place we love. We will take you down the back roads of our unique, often contentious past, steer you through the bustling streets to our favorite haunts and dispel the many myths about who we are as people. We hope to astound you with the abundant festivities available in our part of the world, the wealth of our past and the innovative promise of our future as an enthusiastic competitor in the world marketplace. We'll show you where to play in the outdoors and point out the best places for indoor fun. We want you to see Salt Lake as we know it, a place bound by tradition and sometimes hampered by its past, but a place where the future and diverse cultures are now welcome.

We're honored to be your hosts as you travel our highways and byways, break bread at our tables and come to know and appreciate the richness of life in the Salt Lake Valley. Insiders' Publishing Inc. appreciates your thoughts and comments. You may write to us at:

Insiders' Publishing Inc.
P.O. Box 2057
Manteo, NC 27954

We also welcome your comments and suggestions on the *Insiders' Guide Online*[SM] website: www.insiders.com. We'd love to hear from you.

About the Authors

Kate Duffy

Kate Duffy has lived in Salt Lake City on and off since 1953. An admitted adventurer, she has lived in Boston, San Francisco, Louisville, Orlando and Sydney, Australia. She invariably returns to this, the city of her affection, taking comfort from the quotation from J.R.R. Tolkien, "Not all those who wander are lost." She lives with her daughter, Sarah, and two cats, Splendid and Magnolia, amid a treasure of books, artwork, too much furniture and a large collection of Jell-O molds.

At the age of 9 she wanted to be Lois Lane and began her career as a journalist by publishing a neighborhood newsletter, circulation about 40. By age 12 she decided that imitating the character of Perry White would be far better. The discovery of *A Coney Island of the Mind* by Lawrence Ferlinghetti at 13 introduced her to a poetry style that soon gave voice to the characters crowding the various rooms of her expanding mind. *The Evergreen Review* published her first poem at age 15. She has had an eclectic writing career.

A freelance writer who enjoys work that enhances the communities in which she lives, she has published more than 500 feature articles in local, regional and national magazines. Subjects include the arts, public safety, wellness, women and travel. She has worked as an editor and a copywriter, written collateral materials for professional theater, scripted documentaries and dabbled in newspaper reporting. Her real passion is storytelling. She has published poems and short stories in the United States and Australia. Her poetry anthology, *America Dispossessed — Voices of the Homeless*, was produced as poetry theater in the 1993 Utah Arts Festival. After years of sharing special places and well-kept secrets with out-of-towners she is delighted to pass along to a larger audience the Salt Lake City known only to Insiders.

Bryan Larsen

Bryan Larsen grew up in Sandy, Utah, a suburb a few miles south of Salt Lake City. He remembers when open fields and sagebrush-covered hills covered most of Sandy. As a boy he fondly recalls chasing lizards at a wild, overgrown spot where an industrial park now stands. Bryan says the most vivid memory of his youth is accidentally torching this same spot while illegally setting off firecrackers with a few of his rowdy friends. His heart still races whenever he hears the whine of a fire engine.

After winning a high school sports-writing contest sponsored by *TheSalt Lake Tribune*, Bryan was awarded a journalism scholarship to the University of Utah in Salt Lake City. He studied English, wrote for the student newspaper, fitfully protested against various social ills and generally had a swell time. He also penned reams of poetry and fiction, most of which remains unpublished to this day. He is still puzzled by the lack of critical acumen on the part of America's publishing houses.

Out of college Bryan briefly worked as editor of the *Wasatch Wave*, a weekly newspaper in Heber City, Utah. Here two significant events occurred: He learned to write short sentences and he met Doris. But wanderlust conquered romance, and Bryan vowed to see the world. He traveled through the United States, worked at a hotel in Lausanne, Switzerland, and spent a year roaming through Southern France. France taught him to love red wine, crusty bread, long conversations and the meditative value of lazy afternoons with nothing to do. It also made him see with fresh eyes the scenic splendor and artistic richness of his hometown.

After returning from France, Bryan and Doris got married. Since then, he's worked at various magazines and newspapers in the Salt Lake area. He recently finished a seven-year stint as a writer and editor at *WordPerfect Magazine*. Bryan has published dozens of feature articles in national magazines on topics as diverse as fly fishing, women's tennis, home decor, computers and butterfly collecting. Now a freelance writer, he specializes in outdoor topics, travel and the environment. His freelance work has appeared in *Utah Fishing* and the *Sports Guide*.

Bryan lives in Salt Lake with Doris and their two children, Alex and Miranda. In the summer the family explores the canyons of the Wasatch Mountains, the wetlands of the Great Salt Lake and the ghostly red rock country of Southern Utah. During the winter they ski, snowshoe, attend the stirring productions of the Utah Opera and cheer for the Utah Jazz and the Running Utes of the University of Utah. Bryan has seen Salt Lake grow from a quiet town little noticed by the rest of the country to a growing metropolis where the world is welcome — and where you can now get a great cup of coffee. Asked to sum up Salt Lake City, Bryan is quick to reply: "Mountains at your doorstep, world-class music and theater, excellent brewpubs, Karl Malone and John Stockton. Is this a great city, or what?"

Acknowledgments

Kate Duffy

Many thanks to old and new acquaintances and the myriad of Salt Lakers who pointed me in the right direction so this first *Insiders' Guide®️ to Salt Lake City* might reach a righteous conclusion. Thanks to Jason Mathis at the Salt Lake Convention and Visitors Bureau, Shawn Stinson at the Park City Chamber of Commerce/Convention and Visitors Bureau and their various staff for answering tons of questions and providing photos, and to Janice Carpenter of the Utah Travel Council for the generous use of photos. A bundle of thanks to the knowledgeable staff at the Sprague branch of the Salt Lake City Public Library for always knowing where to look and for being eternally nice, and to Jeff Fergus, Joy Burraston and Jim Naccarato at the Wasatch Front Regional Multiple Listing Service for statistics, photos and other important information. Special thanks to publisher Beth Storie for allowing me the opportunity to co-author this exciting project and to Eileen Myers for stepping in as our editor to bring it to fruition. Heartfelt thanks to the special people in my life who lent their support throughout the writing of this book. The folks at Warshaw's Energy Saving Design who generously provided me with a backup office: owner Steve Sundloff, Linda Butler and especially Art Peck. To Robert Simmons and Bob Allen for keeping my car on the road. To Peggy Simmons for stretching my other deadlines and always taking the time to listen. To Wendy Erekson for wise counsel, quick reference, laughter, instructions for keeping balanced and many shades of red nail polish because happy fingers keystroke the best. To Larry Schultz for deeply philosophical conversations late into the night, superb intellect and gentle criticism. To my mother, Juanita Tate, and her husband, Fran, for encouragement and support and to my daughter Amy for her kindness, recommendations, the million favors

she graciously granted and Saturday night time-out with chick movies and good food. My deepest gratitude to my daughter Sarah for being my sidekick and best friend, reminding me to eat and sleep, providing pie for incentive at every deadline, keeping the cobwebs away from my work space and the whirling dervishes when things got too big to fathom. Without her, my co-authorship would not have been possible. This was not an easy project but it was the most fun I've had in a very long time.

Bryan Larsen

Lots of good people have helped bring this book to life and deserve thanks. Co-author Kate Duffy is a walking compendium of knowledge about the Salt Lake area and has provided many invaluable insights and thoughtful suggestions. The helpful staff at the Salt Lake Convention and Visitors Bureau and Utah Travel Council gladly came forth with reams of publications, brochures and other useful material, as did Shawn Stinson at the Park City Chamber/Convention and Visitors Bureau. Shawn possess an encyclopedic knowledge of Park City and was always available to answer an obscure question or offer perspective on Park City's unique heritage. Thanks to Christa Thompson, Kimberly Peterson and Michael Grass for providing help on winter recreation. Shawn McDonough, Rosie Brimhall, Franny Trexler, Robyn Nelson, Tiffanie Sammons, Vickie Nelson, John P. O'Brien, Carol Edison, Paul Pollei and dozens of others all helped me learn more about Salt Lake's happenings, cultural life and special activities. Despite a crushing work load, the staff at the Salt Lake Ranger District offered piles of valuable information and unstinting help. The dedicated employees from the Salt Lake County Parks and Recreation, Salt Lake City Parks and Recreation and Murray City Parks and Recreation were most generous in helping me unravel the complexities of recreation in the Salt Lake Valley. Many thanks to the staff from Antelope Island State Park, who were most accommodating with advice and material. Thanks to Caroline Shaw and Mike Korologos for assistance on the 2002 Winter Olympics. As always, special thanks to my wife Doris, whose proofreading skills, generous spirit and other rare gifts helped me immeasurably, in so many ways.

The magnificent mountains offer many opportunities to enjoy nature.

Table of Contents

Directory of Maps

Salt Lake City & Surrounding Areas

Downtown Salt Lake City

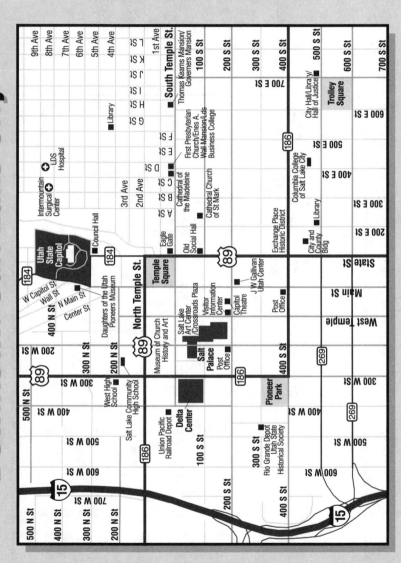

Park City

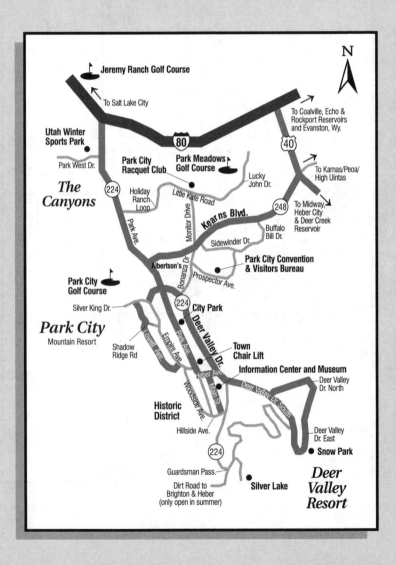

How to Use This Book

We've designed this guide to Salt Lake City to give you the kind of detailed, practical information you need to fill your stay with fun and adventure. This is a hands-on book that you'll want to thumb through, pore over and scribble in. Keep it in your purse or backpack as you saunter about town, soaking up the sights. Each chapter is independent, so you can immediately access information on topics you want to know about — be it a Chinese restaurant, a daytrip to the Great Salt Lake or a fun activity for the kids. If we've done a good job, by the time you go home your *Insiders' Guide® to Salt Lake City* will be dog-eared, coffee-stained and covered with notes. That's what we hope!

We've organized the information so you can quickly understand Salt Lake City and its unique culture. Salt Lake is bounded by two marvelous natural playgrounds, the Great Salt Lake and the Wasatch Mountains. To savor Salt Lake City to the fullest, you should plan a trip to each of these attractions. They are mentioned throughout the book, but the Parks and Recreation chapter gives you the great-outdoors focus, and Sightseeing and Attractions will fill you in on some of the just-for-fun diversions.

Be sure to take a look at our History chapter, which describes in detail the ways in which Salt Lake City has been shaped by the geologic wonders at its borders and by the people who settled here. Are you curious about the Mormons? To get a real sense of the Church of Jesus Christ of Latter-day Saints and its impact on the area, you can read the Close-up in our Area Overview chapter.

You could plan a year's worth of outings around our special events, which you can read about in the Festivals and Annual Events chapter, which is arranged as a month-by-month calendar. Every season has its unique flavor, so try to take in some of these colorful affairs while you're in the area.

And in the event you need medical care while you're here, turn to our Healthcare chapter for a quick reference on hospitals in the Salt Lake Valley.

Salt Lake City and its suburbs fill the Salt Lake Valley, from Temple Square on the north to the suburb of Draper, 15 miles to the south. Salt Lake City proper has about 172,000 people, while the Valley has about 818,860. When we speak of Salt Lake City, we mean the whole Valley, including the nearby canyons of the Wasatch. You'll find that getting around in Salt Lake City is a breeze. The Wasatch Mountains always loom to the east, so you can't get lost as long as you have them in your sights. The roads in the Salt Lake Valley are broad and laid out in a precise, logical manner. When you get the hang of it, you'll agree that navigating the Valley is a snap — except on Interstate 15, which now resembles a war zone because it's being completely rebuilt. You'll want to steer clear of I-15 during your visit — that's what most Salt Lakers do. Read the Getting Here, Getting Around chapter for the complete story.

Most chapters in the book are divided into two parts: a preface, which sums up the flavorful essence of the chapter, and detailed listings for restaurants, hotels or whatever the chapter is about. In some cases, we give you geographic sections as guidelines, and in others, we organize the information into catego-

Photo: Fran Tate

"This is the Place" monument marks the end of the 1,300-mile-long trail
Mormon pioneers traveled to their new home in the Salt Lake Valley.

ries, such as types of cuisine in the Restaurants chapter. The individual write-ups are given alphabetically. The table of contents lists the topics we've covered; look to the index if you need to find a specific listing or a more detailed subject. Insiders' Tips — hints from Salt Lakers in the know — are sprinkled throughout the book, as are Close-ups, which are reports on subjects of special interest, such as basketball star Karl Malone, the film industry or winter safety.

You'll also find a complete section on Park City and its manifold charms. Because Park City is so close to Salt Lake (only 32 miles away) and offers so many exciting things to do and see, we just couldn't leave

it out of the book. You'll find the Park City chapter at the end of the book. It's organized just like the Salt Lake chapters and contains sections on restaurants, accommodations, shopping, nightlife, attractions, history and festivals. You'll definitely want to spend some time in this bustling mountain paradise.

Until March 22, 1998, both Park City and Salt Lake will use the area code 801. Starting March 22, 1998, you'll need to use the code 435 for Park City. Salt Lake City will still use area code 801.

Whether you're planning a business trip, a short vacation or an extended stay in Salt Lake City, we know you'll find this fact-packed guide to be a congenial companion. The city awaits, so mark your favorite chapters and get going!

Brigham Young carried out the most successful colonizing effort in the history of the West. From 1847 to 1857 colonists founded more than 100 Mormon towns. By 1877, more than 300 settlements had been established all over the West.

History

Salt Lake City was founded July 24, 1847, when Mormon pioneers, fleeing religious persecution in the East, first glimpsed the Salt Lake Valley from a nearby mountain pass. Before them spread a valley thick with grass and bisected by streams and rivulets of fresh water. Advance scouts reported no permanent settlements. "This is the right place," said Brigham Young, leader of the Mormons, as he gazed into the valley. "Drive on." Within a year the population of Salt Lake City reached 5,000.

As a planned community, Salt Lake City followed the example of many Western cities. Unlike these cities, Salt Lake was established as a religious haven. Mormon values and beliefs profoundly influenced the cultural and political evolution of the city, and the Mormon influence remains strong to this day. However, even from the earliest days non-Mormons exerted considerable economic and political force. The clash of Mormons and non-Mormons has always been a potent force shaping the city. This unique origin and religious tension has given Salt Lake City its singular character and provided the creative impulse that has made the city what it is today.

The Wasatch Mountains and Salt Lake City

Situated between the desolate splendor of the Great Salt Lake and the alpine crags of the Wasatch Mountains, Salt Lake City is a paradise for lovers of the outdoors. Now light and airy, now dark and brooding, the Wasatch dominate Salt Lake City and have shaped its history like nothing else. Rising on the east 6,000 feet from the valley floor, these mountains grace the city with a stunning skyline of lofty peaks, deep-cut canyons and undulating curves.

The Wasatch, a chain of the Rocky Mountains, have influenced both the economic and aesthetic aspects of life in the Salt Lake Valley. Until recently, the steep slopes yielded valuable minerals and provided timber, building stone and forage for stock. Residents have always counted on the 11,000-foot peaks to gather critical supplies of water. Runoff from the annual deep deposits of mountain snow is stored in reservoirs. Without the snow, Salt Lake would die of thirst.

Just as important, residents have relied on the Wasatch for a daily dose of beauty and for the sense of timelessness so aptly provided by the panorama of mountains in the distance. The slopes and ridges surrounding the valley reflect every whim of nature and every change of weather.

Through time, the Wasatch have seen the ebb and flow of geologic and human history. They have watched the nearby Great Salt Lake swell to fill the Salt Lake Valley, then shrink to a salty puddle in the desert. These mountains have felt hundreds of powerful earthquakes rattle the valley, opening huge gashes in their flanks and sending slabs of rock crashing to the valley floor. They have witnessed prehistoric man wander by in search of woolly mammoth and giant sloth. Native Americans have spent summers hunting deer in their canyons.

Later, trappers slashed their way down the canyons, and settlers on their way to California carved trails under the mountains' peaks. Finally, the Wasatch have seen Mormon pioneers, sustained by deep faith, forge a thriving city out of a desert.

The Geologic Past: Great Salt Lake and Lake Bonneville

Water has played a dramatic role in the evolution of Utah, the second-driest state in the union. As recently as 10,000 years ago — a mere blip in geologic time — an enormous freshwater lake called Lake Bonneville covered much of Western Utah. Visitors to Salt Lake who look at the the city might notice what appears to be horizontal "bathtub rings" that circle the valley. This is no optical illusion. These rings resulted from the sediments deposited by Lake Bonneville as it rose and fell over thousands of years.

Lake Bonneville shaped the physical environment of Salt Lake City in fundamental ways. It deposited the thick layer of fertile soil that sustained the first settlers. The benches and foothills that lead down from the mountains are the former beaches and deltas of this freshwater lake. (In tribute to the geologic fact that these benches are largely composed of sand and gravel, a suburb of Salt Lake was even named Sandy.) The benches provide materials for construction and a favorable area for urban development.

After the last Ice Age ended 10,000 years ago, Lake Bonneville dried up. The Great Salt Lake is the major remnant of this once huge lake. The largest body of water between the Great Lakes and the Pacific Ocean, the Great Salt Lake is more than 70 miles long and 30 miles wide. However, its shores slope so gently that even a small increase in yearly precipitation can completely alter its contours and greatly increase its size. Because of record snowfall between 1980 and 1984, the surface area of the lake increased enormously, flooding highways, destroying cropland and causing concern for the residents of the Salt Lake Valley, who wondered if Lake Bonneville was making a sudden and unwelcome return.

This strange, desolate body of water is a paradox. Its shores are marshy, muddy and dank. Access is difficult. At first glance, its shimmering blue waters dangle the promise of hope and refreshment in a parched land. But the appearance deceives. Since the basin of the Great Salt Lake has no outlet to the sea, over thousands of years mineral salts have accumulated as the water evaporated. As a result the Great Salt Lake is incredibly saline — eight times saltier than the ocean. Its briny water is more poisonous than the alkaline soils that surround it. Other than algae and microscopic life forms, nothing lives in the Great Salt Lake but the brine shrimp, the only organism that has adapted to the unusual water. Clouds of brine flies swarm over the water, feeding on the algae.

Yet its marshy shores abound with life — the lake is an important link in the migratory bird flyway between Canada and Mexico. Millions of birds — avocets, stilts, cormorants, ducks and geese — use the wetlands and bird sanctuaries that have been established on the shores of the lake. Up to a million Wilson's phalaropes (small, dark-winged shore birds) visit the Great Salt Lake in the summer. Biologists have counted as many as 600,000 in one day.

In his excellent book *The Great Salt Lake*, historian Dale L. Morgan sums up the lake this way: "In the end you must take the lake on its own terms — refractory, obstinate, not to everyone's taste. Self-preoccupied, often sullen of mood, yet on occasion yielding itself up with an abandoned beauty that only the desert knows, it is a fit lake for a desert land."

FYI

Unless otherwise noted, the area code for all phone numbers listed in this guide is 801.

Native Americans

The first evidence of human habitation in the Salt Lake Valley comes from excavations in several caves on the west shores of the Great Salt Lake. The bones and tools found in these excavations date back 9,000 to 11,000 years. The denizens of these caves, collectively known as the Desert Culture, were hunter gatherers who roamed the Great Basin in search of food such as roots, nuts and berries, and perhaps a few remaining Ice Age creatures such as the mammoth and the giant beaver.

The Desert Culture lasted until about the fifth century A.D., when the more technologically advanced Fremont and Anasazi cultures replaced it. The Fremont occupied northern Utah and Colorado, while the Anasazi inhabited southern Utah and the Four Corners area. The Fremont were a diverse group of people who made their living in a variety of ways, from hunting and gathering to settled agriculture. Archaeologists believe they hunted for food in the Salt Lake Valley but built few permanent dwellings in the area.

Anasazi is a Navajo word meaning "ancient ones." These unique and resourceful people lived in precarious cliff dwellings high in the remote canyons of the Colorado plateau. To see these dwellings perched amazingly high on remote cliffs is to be astonished by the engineering ingenuity of these people. Many homes seem inaccessible even today with our ropes and rock-climbing equipment.

The Anasazi lived by growing corn and beans in the river bottoms below their homes. They also hunted and gathered available food. Their pottery and basketry are distinctive and skillfully made. Elaborate ruins of the Anasazi still exist in places like Grand Gulch, Utah, and Mesa Verde, Colorado. Throughout the Southwest, archeologists have found Anasazi sandals, pottery, even mummies.

For unknown reasons, both the Anasazi and the Fremont disappeared sometime during the 12th or 13th centuries. Some speculate that a drought forced them to migrate to more promising lands; others think warring tribes compelled them to flee. Many Anasazi habitations appear to be suddenly abandoned. By the time of Columbus, these "ancient ones" had already become the stuff of myth and legend.

Shoshone-speaking Native Americans replaced the Anasazi and the Fremont. These tribes included the Utes, Paiutes, Goshutes and Western Shoshone. When the exploration of the western United States began, trappers and explorers encountered these Native Americans. Since these tribes only sporadically used the valleys along the Wasatch, little conflict occurred with the settlers.

Missionaries, Trappers and Explorers

Spanish explorers, missionaries and trappers all visited the Salt Lake Valley before the Mormon settlement in 1847. In July 1776 two Spanish friars, Father Francisco Atanasio Dominguez and Father Silvestre Valez de Escalante, entered Utah as they searched for an overland route between Santa Fe, New Mexico, and Alta, California. The journals, letters and maps of this expedition afford us the earliest historical descriptions of the people, geography, plants and animals of Utah.

The fathers got as far north as Utah Lake and Utah Valley, about 40 miles south of present-day Salt Lake City. They described the valley as "so spacious, with such good land in beautiful proportions, that in it alone a province like New Mexico can be established and can be maintained here well supplied with every kind of grain and cattle." The Native Americans they encountered in this valley reported the existence of another lake to the north, whose waters tasted noxious and salty. They also described the Native Americans who lived on the marshes of the salty lake. This description is the first written one we have of the Great Salt Lake and the people who lived there.

After the Dominguez-Escalante expedition, the area remained undisturbed until the 1820s, when trappers searching for beaver entered the area. The craze for beaver top hats among gentlemen of merit meant considerable profit for anyone with courage and an adventurous spirit. Those who answered the call were intrepid and hardy souls who explored every stream and lake. They became experts on the geography, climate, and plants and animals of the Intermountain West.

These colorful "mountain men" blazed virtually every route that the stream of settlers heading for Oregon and California later followed. Their knowledge of the area provided critical information for the Mormon pioneers heading to Utah. The best known of the trappers included Jim Bridger, the first man of European descent to see the Great Salt Lake (1824), and Jedediah S. Smith, an energetic explorer who traversed the Great Basin between Utah and California on horseback twice in two years. By 1840, however, the top-hat craze had shifted from beaver felt to silk, and the romantic era of the mountain men came to an end.

After the trappers, other explorers and trail blazers entered Utah and the Salt Lake Valley. Capt. John C. Fremont of the U.S. Army Topographical Corps led two expeditions into

Utah, in 1843-1844 and 1845-1847. His report of 1845 contained enticing descriptions of the lush valleys along the Wasatch range of the Rocky Mountains. Mormon leaders in Nauvoo, Illinois, who were planning their trek west read this report. The information no doubt contributed to their decision to stop in the Salt Lake Valley.

A number of emigrant wagon trains on their way to California also traveled through the Salt Lake Valley. One of these companies was the Donner party, whose story is one of the most tragic in the colonization of the West. The party left the Oregon Trail in 1846, taking the Hastings Cutoff, a supposed shortcut through the Wasatch Mountains. However, the shortcut turned out to be a nightmare of obstacles and thick brush, and the party spent 11 days hacking their way through the mountains. From the Salt Lake Valley the Donner party headed west through the Great Salt Lake Desert, one of the most arid, forbidding places on the continent. Many wagons and stock were lost. Worst of all, when the group reached the Sierra Nevada Mountains they were trapped by deep snows and stranded without food. Many died of hunger; those who lasted through the long, bitter winter did so by resorting to cannibalism. Of the original 87 members of the party, only 47 survived.

Mormon Colonization

The Mormons who settled Salt Lake City 150 years ago were religious seekers looking for a remote place to restore the true kingdom of God and await what they felt was the imminent second coming of Christ. Mormons believed the founder of the church, Joseph Smith, was a true prophet who received direct revelation from God. Smith told his followers that God, Jesus Christ and angels (one of whom was the angel Moroni) appeared to him a number of times, directing him to re-establish the Christian church, which had fallen away from true principles. He called this church the Church of Jesus Christ of Latter-day Saints (LDS), now better known as the Mormon church.

The sacred text of Mormonism is the *Book of Mormon*, which the faithful believe had been directly translated by Smith from a set of ancient records written on golden plates. The *Book of Mormon* narrates the military and religious history of people who long ago lived in the Americas. These early inhabitants had once been Christian, but they had fallen into apostasy and had subsequently been conquered by their enemies. Mormons considered Native Americans, whom they called Lamanites, to be descendants of those conquering peoples.

The Mormon church was founded on the collective principle of group unity over individual desire. Smith opposed religious diversity and the competitive social order that led to disputes and factionalism. He hoped to create a refuge where church leaders would direct all aspects of life for devoted followers. These theocratic principles were maintained by a hierarchy of leaders, which included a First Presidency of three members, a Quorum of Twelve Apostles and a High Council.

Smith wanted to make men more socially and economically equal. He did this by putting into practice a socialistic economic movement known as the Law of Consecration and Stewardship. Smith stated that Mormons were to "be alike . . . and receive alike, that ye may be one." This law required members to sign over to the church their property and any surplus crops. Members would then receive back goods and services according to their needs. The church gave what was left to the poor.

INSIDERS' TIP

The Mormon word for honeybee is "deseret," which symbolizes hard work and industry. Utah's nickname is "The Beehive State," and the motto is "Industry."

The Law of Consecration and Stewardship was only fitfully observed during the early days of Mormonism and was revived for the last time by Brigham Young in the 1870s.

For a number of reasons, including their collectivist economic practices, their success in attracting new members, their belief in the *Book of Mormon* as true scripture, their practice of polygamy and their thundering denunciations of all other churches, the Mormons were persecuted. From New York they were driven to Ohio, then Missouri and Illinois. In Carthage, Illinois, a mob murdered Smith and his brother Hyrum while in jail after being accused of starting a riot. After Smith's murder, Mormons looked to the West as a place of refuge from a corrupt and evil nation.

After reading Fremont's work and other immigrant accounts of the West, new prophet Brigham Young and other Mormon leaders decided that one of the valleys along the western slope of the Rocky Mountains offered them the best chance of isolation and good farming. More or less following the Oregon Trail, the Mormon caravan left the east in April 1847 and arrived in the Salt Lake Valley on July 24 of the same year.

Early Days

The first days in Salt Lake were spent in furious activity. The industrious settlers laid out the city, dammed streams, planted crops and constructed homes. Leaders selected a site for the Salt Lake Temple, which took 40 years to complete. The first winter was mild, but a late spring frost destroyed much of the spring wheat and vegetables. Even worse, hordes of black crickets descended on what was left of the crops. Luckily, when the settlers despaired of saving anything, sea gulls arrived and devoured most of the pests. Mormons consider this intervention by sea gulls a miracle, and in tribute named the sea gull the state bird.

During the first years, theocracy was the prevailing form of government. Brigham Young ruled as both head of the church and state. His loyal followers carried out his wishes in every detail. Young exerted his influence through ecclesiastical units called wards, which are akin to parishes in the Catholic Church. Each ward was presided over by a bishop, who passed on to his members the wishes of Young and other church leaders. Bishops also looked out for their members and made sure their religious, economic and civic affairs were running smoothly.

Young and the High Council soon created a civil unit of government, called the State of Deseret, and sent a petition to Washington asking for statehood. The federal government denied this petition, a precedent that would endure until 1896 when Utah became the 45th state.

Brigham Young also carried out the most successful colonizing effort in the history of the West. From 1847 to 1857 colonists founded more than 100 Mormon towns. By the time Brigham Young died in 1877, more than 300 settlements had been established all over the West. Many of these towns still exist. The colonization system was simple and effective. Faithful members with various skills were called on by church authorities to homestead a certain location, which had usually been scouted out and judged favorably. Members took these callings as revelations from God, so compliance was universal despite the difficulty of leaving home and friends and moving to distant and often inhospitable regions.

The industry, thrift, sobriety and cooperative spirit of the Mormon pioneers quickly paid off. By 1850 more than 5,000 acres were in cultivation. Calvin Taylor, an immigrant on his way to California in 1850, described Salt Lake City in this way: "The Great Salt Lake City is handsomely laid out. . . . The streets are of great breadth and cross each other at right angles, forming large squares which are cut at regular distances by streets of a smaller size, dividing the square into equal parts. . . . To each house is allowed one and a quarter acre of ground which is enclosed and sufficient to produce all the necessary garden vegetables in the greatest profusion, besides a considerable quantity of wheat and corn, quite adequate to the wants of each family."

The U.S. Congress recognized the accomplishments of the Mormons by creating the Utah Territory in 1851. In recognition of the Mormons' political power, President Millard Fillmore appointed Brigham Young governor. At the same

Insider Winnie Burton: More than eight decades in Salt Lake City

Winnie Burton was the first child in her family — Mormon converts of Swedish descent — born in the United States. In her own words she shares memories of her childhood in Salt Lake City, her involvement as a young woman in a union (in a right-to-work state), her views on the 2002 Winter Olympic Games and her perspective, in 1997, on 86 years of change in the Salt Lake Valley.

My parents, Pehr and Emilie Charlott Lindstrom Nilsson, lived in Naffentorp, Bunkoflo, Sweden, where my father was a cabinet finisher in a piano factory. A huge out-migration occurred in Sweden in the late 19th century when labor surpluses forced nearly half the population to relocate throughout Scandinavia and Europe. Some came

to the United States. In May of 1910, my father, who had moved the family to Copenhagen, came to the United States. His journey was sponsored by Mr. Anderson, the Mormon missionary who converted my family to the Church of Jesus Christ of Latter-day Saints. It took six months for my father to establish a home here and earn enough money to bring my mother and four siblings to this country.

I was born Winnifred "Winnie" Elna Nilsson in Salt Lake City on September 25, 1911. I'm sure I was an afterthought, the product of my parent's celebration of their reunion after a long separation. No one in my family spoke or understood English when they arrived but there were many Swedes already living in the Salt Lake Valley who attended the same LDS ward. I didn't speak English until I went to school, but we managed, and eventually we learned the language. It was difficult for my family here because we had no contacts in the United States outside our church and the rest of our family remained in Sweden. In fact, I didn't meet a relative until I was 65 years old when I traveled to Sweden.

Even though my parents were foreigners, I had a good childhood. My parents and siblings worked hard, and the family was well provided for. We never had a car, had to crank an iron pump to get water and had no electrical refrigeration for most of my childhood. I remember the old ice box well. The ice was delivered on a horse-drawn wagon. Fruits and vegetables were also carried on a horse-drawn wagon. The peddlers would load up their wagons with fruit, vegetables and other food items. They became a traveling market. We even had a bakery wagon on a certain day of the week. My mother had never seen a cantaloupe, so one spring day my father told her to watch for the fruit peddler. He bought her a cantaloupe and showed her how to scrape out all the seeds. Later he explained what a watermelon looked like and told my mother to buy one, which she did and cleaned it by scraping out all the seeds, including the red part, which she fed to the chickens. She left the rind for eating.

I saw my first airplane when I was 6 years old [in 1917], on display in a big field near 300 West and 2800 South. People walked for miles or took the streetcar to see it. I also remember seeing my first radio about that time. It was my neighbor's. It had an earphone, and we took turns listening. It wasn't long before everyone had one.

Pioneer Day has always been a big celebration in Salt Lake. Even though the parade is now very big, with a theme each year and many floats, it was quite an event when I was a child. We would go downtown early to get a good spot and watch all the horses

— continued on next page

and the floats which the different LDS wards sponsored. After the parade, which ended in Liberty Park, all the families would head for the park with our picnic baskets and try to find a place to spread our blanket. It was a big community event and we visited with everyone.

The United States entered World War I in 1917 when I was 6 years old. The same year we had a big flu epidemic in Salt Lake City and people had to wear masks tied with strings that wrapped around their ears whenever they went out in public. The schools closed and people everywhere were sick. Three years later our new home burned to the ground and very little was salvaged. In 1923 my father returned to Sweden to serve a mission for the LDS church. My mother went to work for the first time in her life at the American Linen Company to support the family, so I had to do a lot of household chores. After school my responsibility was to make a fire in the stove and start dinner.

In high school I was very busy with academic schooling as well as being active in sports. I participated in running broad jump, track, hockey and even played girl's competitive basketball. I spent a lot of time with my girlfriends in high school. We would take the streetcar downtown and go to Woolworth, Grants and Kress where the sales clerk would be there to help with our selection like they used to do in the big department stores like ZCMI. At that time, all the shopping was in downtown Salt Lake City. During my last year in high school the stock market crashed and the Great Depression began. Times were hard but everyone pulled together because we were all in the same boat. My friends and I used to go roller-skating and ice-skating a lot. Sometimes we went to the ice rinks but we also skated on local ponds because that was free. Churches of all denominations sponsored activities for young people and the LDS wards had movies, dances, plays and hikes in the canyons.

Winnie Burton
Taken about 1917

When times were better, our favorite pastimes were going to the dances at Saltair and Lagoon. We went there on open air trains, the Bamberger Line, because kids at that time didn't have cars like they do now. It was fun. There was more to do than dance. We also went to the Old Mill for dances. Everyone got all dressed up in our best clothes to go to dances at the Old Mill, but all we did there was dance. It was also a real special occasion to go to dinner and dancing at the Roof Garden at the Hotel Utah in those days.

After high school I went to work at the phone company as an operator where I worked eight hours a day, six days a week for $11 per week. It was during the 1930s that the work week was reduced to five days. At the phone company, I sat in a long line with other women operating the switchboard. We were not allowed to talk to each other except on breaks and during lunch. When I first went to work at the telephone company, the women all had to wear gloves and hats. If you didn't wear the hat, you had to carry it in your hand when you were going in and out of the building. One of the prettiest hats I ever had didn't look very good on me, but I carried it and it was quite lovely. We had the reputation in Salt Lake of having the best-dressed people in our downtown in those

— continued on next page

days. People always dressed up to go to the ballet and symphony, too. It was nice. Today, you find people at these events dressed in everything.

This is a very cultural area. I began attending Ballet West's production of *The Nutcracker* around 1945 when Willam Christiansen first brought it to Salt Lake. I've seen it many times since, taken my children and my grandchildren. The arts have been an important part of the city since the early days of the pioneers.

Because I was young and didn't have experience, I got the really bad shifts at the telephone company. Working conditions and arrangements were very hard, especially for women, until the union got involved. I was involved in the union from the beginning, in the 1940s. I was a steward for my section and later ran for and was elected vice president. I held that position for eight years. The phone company was my employer for 30 years, through three husbands — one who became mentally ill after six months of marriage and was permanently institutionalized and two who died — and three children. During that time I received two big promotions. First I was moved from operator to supervisor and later to PBX trainer. I traveled all over the city for 14 years teaching people how to use the different equipment that the telephone company installed. After I retired from the phone company, I worked as a receptionist at Dean Witter for six years.

Since I never had family here, except for my children who were especially important to me, my friends were very important. I made two good friends during my early childhood. One of them passed away in 1986, but the other one is still close to me. When I was 12 years old my friends and I started a sewing club which had its origins in our LDS church Beehive class. There were 12 girls in our neighborhood of the same age. We would get together every other Monday, rotating houses, to do sewing projects. We remained active in the sewing club throughout our teens, and when marriage entered the picture we made sure that our husbands knew that the club was part of the marriage arrangement. When someone moved out of the area — the only reason anyone left the sewing club — a new member was added. The club still meets in the afternoons every other week for sewing and light refreshments. Now the only change in membership occurs when someone dies. There are still six of the original members in the group.

I have seen many changes in the city my 86 years, but the most significant change was during World War II when women began to work. Remington Arms had a big government contract here and they wanted many women to work in the plant making ammunition for the war. The men were already serving in the war, so the women joined the work force. After the war, many of them continued to work. I think that changed things here a great deal, and it has never been the same. Of course many things are different today. The city has spread out in all directions and we have so many hotels and places to shop. People think all this growth is because of the Olympics, but it really isn't. Salt Lake is an important city now and many people come here for business and vacation. The changes are good. I think the Olympics being here is generally a good idea. I just don't know what we're going to do with all those people.

---

time, a number of non-Mormons were appointed to other offices, which led to conflict down the road.

Growth and Conflict

Immigrants recruited from the Mormon church's strong missionary program quickly began flooding into Salt Lake City and outlying areas. By 1870 Salt Lake's population reached 12,800. As the region grew, church leaders emphasized creating a beautiful city: Many elegant homes and building were erected. Shade trees lined the wide, smooth streets, and irrigation canals brought water to numerous orchards and lush vegetable gardens. In 1859 the influential newspaperman Horace Greeley commented favorably on the wide streets and big lots, calling Salt Lake a city of "magnificent distances."

Despite all efforts, however, outside influences began creeping in, which eventually led to the decline of Mormon power and the integration of Salt Lake City into the economic mainstream of American life. From 1849 to 1850, the gold rush brought 25,000 gold-hungry roughnecks through the city. This proved an economic boon for Salt Lake, which had abundant skilled labor and materials but little hard cash. Gold miners willingly paid $200 for a horse that normally sold for $25. Non-Mormon merchants, who first appeared in 1849, quickly prospered. Brigham Young was alarmed at the amount of money going to non-Mormon merchants. He later took steps to make the Saints even more self-sufficient.

Political developments also tied Salt Lake City to the outside world. The announcement of plural marriage in 1852 raised the ire of the nation, and the Mormon question entered national politics. Federal officials wrote letters to President James Buchanan claiming that the Mormons were un-American and antidemocratic.

Buchanan became convinced that the Mormons needed watching. He replaced Young as governor with Alfred Cumming and in 1857 sent an army of 2,500 to assist him. The so-called Utah War began when Brigham Young declared martial law and sent guerillas to harass the approaching army. The bloodless war dragged on for more than a year, with soldiers staying until the start of the Civil War. Economically, Salt Lakers benefited from the presence of these outsiders, but Mormon leaders viewed the Utah War as just one more unjust imposition made by the corrupt outside world.

Mining

More federal troops arrived in 1862 to guard the overland mail and telegraph line that ran through Southern Wyoming. These troops, under the command of Colonel Patrick Edward Connor, were stationed at Fort Douglas, a few miles east of Salt Lake. Connor viewed the Mormons with disdain, calling them "a community of traitors, murderers, fanatics and whores." He allied himself with non-Mormon businessmen and promoted mining as a means of weakening Mormon influence.

Brigham Young strongly opposed mining. "There is no happiness in gold," he told his followers. "We have the real wealth here . . . the good, fine flour, good wheat, horses, cattle, vegetables, fruit, sheep and wool. This is real wealth." It was left up to non-Mormons to exploit the other natural resources. In 1863 Connor's troops discovered gold and silver in the Wasatch Mountains, and by 1864 a mild mining boom had begun.

Mining changed Salt Lake City's economy. It increased the money supply, which stimulated trade, and helped establish the first true banks in Utah, most of which were operated by non-Mormons. Disagreement over the place of mining in Utah's society also spurred the first serious opposition to Brigham Young's leadership. In 1869 several prominent Mormons, among them William S. Godbe and Eli B. Kelsey, were excommunicated from the Mormon church. The "Godbeites," as they became known, believed that Utah's rich mineral resources should be developed by Mormons. They also wanted closer and friendlier ties with the federal officials and non-Mormons living in Utah.

In 1870 the Godbeites and other prominent non-Mormons organized the Liberal Party, a political party opposed to Mormon policies. This political split became a cultural one, which is still prominent today. The conflict resulted in two different school systems, separate

INSIDERS' TIP

Over the years, a body of folklore and strange tales have grown about the Great Salt Lake. Eyewitnesses have reported seeing huge monsters with terrible eyes, schools of whales and whirlpools big enough to suck down a schooner.

neighborhoods and different newspapers. The *Deseret News*, owned and operated by the Mormons, advocated the position of the Saints while *The Salt Lake Tribune*, founded by Thomas Kearns, an Irish Catholic who made a fortune in mining, became the voice of the non-Mormons.

The Railroad

The completion of the transcontinental railroad on May 10, 1869, irrevocably changed the nature of Salt Lake City and Utah. The railroad forever integrated Salt Lake City economically and socially into American society. Access to rail lines spurred mining, manufacturing and other industries needed to supply an expanding economic base.

Over the next 20 years mining towns, fostered by ready rail access, sprang up around Salt Lake City and all over Utah. These rough towns were peopled largely by non-Mormons. As such they were completely different from the tranquil agricultural communities surrounding them. Prostitution flourished and liquor flowed freely. In 1872 the mining town of Alta, Utah, in the Wasatch Mountains, had a population of 8,000 and 180 buildings — 26 of which were saloons.

The railroad and its attendant industries brought various non-Mormon ethnic populations to Salt Lake and outlying areas. Irish Catholics, Poles, Greeks and Slavs entered the state to work on the railroad and in the mills, smelters and refineries. The Mormon population of Salt Lake City dropped from 93 percent in 1867 to about 50 percent in 1891.

The Fight Against Change

Brigham Young and other church leaders strongly opposed these dramatic economic and social changes. In 1866 Young counteracted the influence of non-Mormon merchants and bankers by organizing a boycott. This measure was ineffective, so in 1868 Young created a church-wide cooperative system called Zion's Cooperative Mercantile Institution (ZCMI), which supplied retail stores in every Mormon town with goods. ZCMI worked well. The prices of most goods immediately sank, and ZCMI remains a major retail institution today.

But Young believed he needed to impose a more radical measure to counteract the economic changes unleashed by the railroad. In the 1870s Young undertook to purify and restore Mormon society by creating the United Orders of Enoch, which were essentially a return to the communal ideals set forth in Joseph Smith's Law of Consecration and Stewardship. Young envisioned a fully communal society, where neighborhoods ate together and collectively owned all resources. He and other Mormon leaders dreamed of a day "when there shall be no rich and no poor among the Latter-day Saints; when wealth will not be a temptation; when every man will love his neighbor as he does himself; when every man and woman will labor for the good of all as much for self."

Some smaller communities, such as Orderville and Springdale in Southern Utah, dined communally, consecrated all their property to the Mormon church and generally followed Young's vision. However, most communal organizations never achieved this level of purity and selflessness. Rich Mormons were reluctant to share their wealth. Within a few years all the United Orders disbanded, bowing to many of the same pressures that have led to the demise of other utopian enterprises.

Search for Statehood

From 1870 to 1896 Salt Lake City gradually changed from a communitarian society dominated by one man to a city where the American principles of free enterprise and democracy prevailed. Brigham Young's death in 1877 brought a new generation of leaders to power, ones who eventually realized their concept of a theocracy was doomed.

Polygamy caused the greatest anti-Mormon sentiment among Americans, who viewed the practice as morally reprehensible and demeaning to women. Although many Mormon women defended polygamy, many

FYI

Unless otherwise noted, the area code for all phone numbers listed in this guide is 801.

The Beehive House, built in 1854, was Brigham Young's official residence when he was president of the Mormon church and governor of the territory.

others didn't. In 1876 Ann Eliza Young, one of Brigham Young's numerous wives (whom he had divorced), published her account of life as a polygamist's wife. The book, called *Wife No. 19, or the Story of Life in Bondage*, garnered much national attention, as did as a previous expose, called *Tell It All*, written in 1874 by Fanny Stenhouse, a Mormon who had left the church in 1870.

In 1862, after mounting public pressure, the Republican Congress passed federal anti-Mormon legislation. The Morrill Act prohibited polygamy, disincorporated the Mormon church and restricted the Mormon church's ownership of property to $50,000. Since Lincoln was preoccupied with the Civil War, enforcement was lax. "You tell Brigham Young that if he will leave me alone, I will leave him alone," Lincoln told Mormon representatives.

In 1879 the Supreme Court judged the Morrill Act constitutional. However, the Mormons still refused to give up polygamy, claiming allegiance to a higher law — God's law. Gradually, the federal government tightened the screws on polygamist Mormons. The Edmunds Act of 1882 declared polygamy a felony, disenfranchised polygamists and made them ineligible for office. Hundreds of men and some women were sent to prison. Many received harsh treatment, and others were denied due process of law. John Taylor, Young's successor as president of the Mormon church, went underground in 1885, as did many other prominent Mormons.

As pressured tightened, it became clear that to persist in polygamy would end with the destruction of the Mormon church itself. Prominent Mormon businessmen feared losing their property. A group of young Mormons broke ranks with their elders and called for conformity to federal laws and the end of church control in politics.

Wilford Woodruff, the third president of the Mormon church, knew he had to act. "I have arrived at a point in the history of my life as President of the Church of Jesus Christ of Latter-day Saints, where I am under the necessity of acting for the temporal salvation of the church," he wrote in his journal in 1890. "The United States government has taken a stand and passed laws to destroy the Latter-day Saints upon the subject of polygamy. After praying to the Lord and feeling inspired by the spirit I have issued the following proclamation. . . ."

This proclamation, commonly called the Woodruff Manifesto, urged all Mormons to abide by the marriage laws of the United States. It was approved at the Mormon general conference in October 1890. With its approval, the Mormon church officially abandoned polygamy, and the federal government no longer opposed Utah's enfranchisement. In 1896, Utah, with a population of 150,000, was finally admitted to the Union as the 45th state.

The 20th Century

After 1896 Utah lost its unique position as a functioning theocracy. Mormons no longer dominated politics, and Salt Lake City moved toward a more standard, secular form of government. Mormons still exerted much power, but cultural diversity grew and political debate widened. In many respects, Salt Lake City history in the 20th century reflects the concerns of American society at large.

As the Mormon/non-Mormon split became less of an issue, cooperation among Salt Lakers increased. The city concentrated on improving streets, utilities and public health. In 1911 Salt Lakers adopted a nonpartisan commission form of government that lasted until 1980. From about 1912 to 1930, a coalition of political progressives reformed and cleaned up Salt Lake City. Officials tightened control over prostitution and gambling. Streets and sidewalks were cleaned up and paved. Citizens created a Parks and Playgrounds Association, and the city built a new public library.

Depression and War

Because of Utah's reliance on mining and agriculture, the Depression of the 1930s hit Salt Lake City hard. In 1932 about 35 percent of the work force was unemployed. Bread lines sprang up in Salt Lake, and scores of homeless families camped in vacant lots. Unable to find work, many moved to California and other states.

The New Deal brought the federal government back into Utah, this time with the citizen's approval — Roosevelt and the Democrats were the overwhelming favorite of Utah voters in the 1930s. The New Deal had a lasting effect on Salt Lake City. Many families depended entirely on federal welfare and jobs programs. Workers employed through the Works Progress Administration (WPA) erected several buildings in Salt Lake City. Many still stand, including the Museum of Natural History and Carlson Hall, both on the University of Utah campus.

The New Deal and World War II brought prosperity back to Salt Lake City. During the war the military established Fort Douglas, Hill Air Force Base and other military installations in the Salt Lake area, all of which provided much-needed jobs. Many of these installations remained in operation after the war and contributed to growing postwar prosperity.

The Modern World

After World War II, the city grew quickly. Suburbs and urban sprawl began to touch

Salt Lake in the 1950s. Business in the downtown area declined, so the Mormon church, a major land holder in the downtown area, counteracted by building the ZCMI Center in the north end of downtown Salt Lake. This resulted in a loss of business in the south end, which is now gradually being halted. The military-space industry continued to grow, with a number of companies building guided missiles and rocket engines. These industries still contribute to Salt Lake City's economy.

In the 1960s and 1970s Utah's economy reflected national trends. Many historic buildings were renovated, and new buildings, such as the Salt Palace (now the Salt Palace Convention Center) and Symphony Hall (now Abravanel Hall), went up. The economy gradually shifted from mining and agriculture to tourism. The rest of America discovered Utah's great powder skiing and wonderful slick-rock canyons. In 1995 the International Olympic Committee awarded Salt Lake City the 2002 Winter Olympic Games.

The last decade has brought explosive economic and population growth to Salt Lake City. As in all cities, growth brings both benefits and problems. Salt Lake City now suffers from the same ills that plague many large American cities: strip malls, gridlocked traffic, a serious pollution problem and a dearth of parks and green space. On the positive side, jobs are plentiful and incomes are growing. The area has become a magnet for high-tech industries and intelligent, well-educated workers. Salt Lake sparkles with new buildings and buzzes with excitement. Salt Lakers are bursting with pride over the coming 2002 Winter Olympics Games and the chance to showcase the city they love. And citizens are not sitting back, wringing their hands and doing nothing about the problems—they are attacking these issues with the same confidence and enthusiasm that gave them the vigor and faith to build a thriving city out a desert landscape. The freeway is being expanded, and new parks and trails and being planned and built. Even after 150 years as a city, Salt Lakers are showing that the spirit of cooperation and the ideal of the greater good are still alive, still real and still a force to be reckoned with.

Ours is one of the fastest-growing areas in the country, and during the final countdown toward the dawn of the 21st century, Salt Lake is definitely a city in flux.

Area Overview

Excuse our dust.

Salt Lake City is preparing for the 2002 Winter Olympic Games as well as perching on the brink of a new and exciting era. Ours is one of the fastest growing areas in the country, and during the final countdown toward the dawn of the 21st century, Salt Lake is definitely a city in flux. Filled with great change, both physically and philosophically, the city is spreading its wings, and the mood is electric.

While the city grows, expect a few inconveniences. Traffic jams are regular events because the highway system is being revamped, and hard-hat areas rumbling with cranes and bulldozers create detours for foot traffic from time to time — the price one pays for a civic face-lift. Hotels, office complexes and a new municipal courts building make up just one part of the changing landscape. Single- and multiple-family residential buildings are also springing up all over the Valley. As we prepare for an influx of tourists and families relocating to the area, we'll manage the minor nuisance of growth with the same flexibility and perseverance that has kept us going for 150 years. It may be the '90s, but there's still a strong pioneer spirit igniting the city's flame.

It seemed that it might take forever for the rest of the country to recognize Salt Lake City. A decade ago it wasn't uncommon that the mention of Salt Lake would raise the question, "Where is Salt Lake City?" In the 1980s, airline pilots announcing arrival here joked with passengers, saying, "Welcome to Salt Lake City. Set your watches back 10 years." Perhaps the lack of awareness came from our seeming disinterest in attracting outsiders or, at the very least, being careful about who moved into town. Nevertheless, the city hasn't remained small, nor has it lagged behind in ingenuity or sophistication in technology, or in business or industry. Over the years, Salt Lake has quietly and methodically grown up, taking its place on the national and world stage in medicine, sports, the arts, politics and more. We may still have an old-fashioned small-town friendliness but we're ready to welcome the world. Salt Lake City has been included in *Fortune Magazine's* top-10 list of the best cities in American for business. *Financial World* rates Utah the best fiscally managed state in the nation, and *Western Blue Chip Economic Forecast* and *American Demographics* magazines call the state "one of the top-three economies in the country."

The Salt Lake Valley

Utah ranks 34th in size, fifth in population growth, first in births and last in deaths per 1,000 population in the United States, according to the most recent census. Most of the state's population resides along the Wasatch Front — from Ogden on the north to Provo on the south —

INSIDERS' TIP

Salt Lake City is in the Mountain Time Zone, one hour later than the Pacific Time Zone, one hour earlier then the Central Time Zone and two hours earlier than the Eastern Time Zone.

with the greatest concentrated population living in what is known as the Salt Lake Valley. Salt Lake City makes up a small portion of the Salt Lake Valley with approximately 180,000 residents. The remainder of the Valley's inhabitants reside in Salt Lake County, with a population of approximately 800,000. When Insiders refer to Salt Lake, however, we mean the entire Salt Lake Valley.

Besides Salt Lake City, which has the largest population in Salt Lake County, several other cities are located within the county, including Sandy and West Valley City — the second- and third-largest in population, respectively — and Murray, Midvale, Kearns, South Salt Lake, West Jordan, South Jordan, Draper, Riverton and Magna. We also have neighborhoods within these cities. They include Capitol Hill, Federal Heights, The Avenues, Olympus Cove, Millcreek, Cottonwood, Rose Park, Holladay and Sugarhouse, and there are many more. To get the lay of the land of our neighborhoods, check out our Real Estate and Neighborhoods chapter.

FYI

Unless otherwise noted, the area code for all phone numbers listed in this guide is 801.

The Economy

World Trade Magazine has described

The Mormons

Some think they're quirky while others say they are fanatical. Mormons. Who are they?

If you have never been to Utah and never met a Mormon (a member of the Church of Jesus Christ of Latter-day Saints), you may harbor a few misconceptions

or, at the very least, questions about them. To find out what Mormons embrace in their religion, a tour of Temple Square should be enlightening. There you'll find scads of Mormon missionaries ready and willing to answer your questions about the Mormons' religious beliefs.

Mormons incorporate their spiritual, family, business and social convictions into one package, so to people on the outside it may be difficult to know when the religion ends and the lifestyle begins. We call it the Mormon culture. It should come as no surprise that after 150 years the Mormon influence is still prevalent in Utah, more so in smaller communities throughout the state than in Salt Lake City. After all, LDS leader Brigham Young and his followers, seeking a reprieve from religious persecution, claimed Salt Lake City as a religious community. It should also not surprise anyone too much that while, in theory, there is a separation of church and state, many of Utah's laws reflect the conservative attitudes of the Mormon people. The majority of the state's elected officials are members of the LDS church, but it's more a circumstance of demographics than heavy-handedness.

Some say that everyone who lives in Utah is a Mormon — either a practicing Mormon, a jack-Mormon (nonpracticing) or a non-Mormon. That pretty much tells the tale. Mormons are frequently confused with the Amish, whose members wear plain clothing, travel about in horse-drawn buggies and live a simple life sans modern conveniences such as microwave ovens, TVs and fax machines. While Mormons are often conservative in dress, particularly women — short-shorts, micro-miniskirts and the very visible bustier, à la Madonna, would not be fashion de rigueur among the flock — you'll find Mormons well-dressed and rather stylish.

— continued on next page

Hopsack and gingham frocks are only in vogue here when fashion magazines or Ralph Lauren say so. As to the buggies — pshaw! Mormons ride in style, frequently in minivans to accommodate their large families.

Is it true that Mormons have large families? Yes, indeed. Ours is the highest per capita birthrate in the nation. Many people ask, "Where do these guys keep all their wives?" Mormon husbands only have one wife at a time like everyone else. Polygamy was abolished in 1890. Utah does have polygamists, as many as 20,000, and quite a few live Salt Lake City, but they aren't Mormons. The Mormon church doesn't sanction polygamy, which is a third-degree felony under federal law. Brigham Young had 27 wives, and Archibald Gardner, a prominent Salt Lake Valley businessman in the mid-1800s, had 11, which may lead to the confusion about polygymy.

About those horns. People still ask, "Do Mormons have horns?" Really! We've done extensive research on this one, as with every morsel of this book, but for the life of us we cannot trace the origin of that story. Mormons don't now nor have they ever had horns. Mormon people look pretty much like everyone else. You can often pick out the missionaries who jaunt around town on bikes, most often in pairs. They are usually young men with close-cropped hair wearing dark suits. There's also the telltale Mormon underwear, called garments, visible under lightweight clothing. Mormons take a lot of ribbing about these garments, and well-meaning tourists often ask about the "funny underwear." It's a popular point of curiosity and has to do with their faith. While you're at Temple Square, ask one of the missionary guides. They'll be happy to explain. Unless you are at an exclusive LDS outing, however, Mormons would be hard to pick out in a crowd.

Photo: Salt Lake Convention and Visitors Bureau

A first time visitor to Salt Lake City recently asked us, "Where can I get some Mormon food?" The Dutch oven is the official cooking pot in Utah, but there's no such thing as Mormon food. Mormon families are told to keep a two-year supply of food on hand to sustain them in hard times or for the second coming, and much of that surplus takes the form of wheat and grains that need to be rotated. Families here also have a preponderance of children, so you can bet your calico bonnet that kid food — spaghetti, macaroni-and-cheese and the like — shows up on tables across the Valley more often than California cuisine. You'll also find some of the most sophisticated fare in the country here, and a giant selection of ethnic foods (see our Restaurants chapter).

The monument of Brigham Young welcomes visitors to Salt Lake City and the Morman way of life.

Contrary to the rampant mis-

— continued on next page

conception about alcoholic beverages in the state, you can get a cocktail in Utah. You won't find a bar on every corner, and Mormons don't imbibe. Nevertheless, you can get a mixed drink or a glass of wine here, and Salt Lake and Park City have some great brewpubs (see our Nightlife chapter). Wine connoisseurs might be pleasantly surprised by the selection of more than 2,500 wines at the Utah State Liquor Store's wine store. Several area restaurants have award-winning wine lists as well. For details about our liquor laws, see our Nightlife chapter. If you drop into a practicing Mormon's home, they may offer you a root beer float, a fruit smoothy or some Mormon wine — grape juice and club soda— but never a beer.

Tobacco is another taboo — Mormons don't smoke or chew — and coffee is definitely on the forbidden list. Not to worry, in spite of this edict you'll find a plethora of coffee shops, huts and drive-through cappuccino places that serve a great cup of joe.

All this healthy living falls under the auspices of what the Mormon's call the Word of Wisdom. We won't get into the details except to say that word on the street is that the W of W closely parallels the advice of the surgeon general of the United States and many other health and wellness authorities, but it's been around longer. This may account for the fact that Utah is ranked the healthiest state in the nation.

OK, we admit that some Mormons come off a little radical, a little too straight-laced, maybe even stuffy, and a few well-meaning followers interpret the rules in the extreme. But that seems true of many individuals who hold strong convictions, especially religious ones. For the most part, though, you'll find the Mormon people in the Salt Lake Valley or anywhere in the state friendly, generous, well-educated, industrious and downright nice.

Utah's work force as smart, productive, motivated and multilingual, stating, "They're attracting companies from across the country and around the world." With a strong labor market and one of the youngest work forces in the nation, it has made good business sense for many companies to move to Utah. Productivity is reportedly 25 to 30 percent higher for companies that have operations here. Several factors contribute to this situation. Besides having young, eager employees, the region fosters a strong work ethic — an attribute celebrated in Utah's official emblem, a beehive. This work ethic is generally attributed to two factors: the Mormon religion, which encourages its people to work hard for both family and community, and the weather. In the early days, the seasons waited for no one, and crops had to be planted or harvested by Mother Nature's timetable. Although Salt Lakers no longer depend upon farming for their food supply, the shoulder-to-the-wheel work standard has continued. Ours is one of the healthiest places in the nation, which reduces the over-all absentee rate among workers considerably. In addition, Utah has one of the highest literacy rates in the country and is second in the nation in the number of adults who have completed high school.

Utah's unemployment rate is low — 3.6 percent in 1995, roughly two points below the national average. Across the board the job growth rate has averaged nearly 6 percent per year for nearly a decade. At the close of 1996, jobs in construction had increased by 11.9 percent, services by 7.2 percent, fire service by 7.1 percent, trade by 4.8 percent, manufacturing by 4.4 percent, government by 1.5 percent and transportation, communications and utilities by 4.9 percent. The film industry continues to provide jobs for local workers as well (see the Close-up on Utah's exciting film industry in The Arts chapter). The largest private employers along the Wasatch Front include Brigham Young University, Smith's Food and Drug, Morton International, Matrixx Marketing, Wal-Mart Stores, Albertsons, ZCMI Department Stores, Delta Airlines, Thiokol and United

The Utah State Capitol Building in Salt Lake City was completed in 1915.
The 165-foot-high interior rotunda is made of Georgian marble.
The walls are painted with murals that depict Utah's past.

Parcel Service. Large public employers include the State of Utah, University of Utah (including the hospital), Granite School District, Hill Air Force Base, Jordan School District, Davis County School District, U.S. Postal Service, Salt Lake County, Internal Revenue Service and the Alpine School District.

Wages in Utah in 1994 were more than 15 percent below the national average. This is due in part to the high percentage of women and teens in the workforce and the low union membership in Utah, a right-to-work state. The median household income in Salt Lake City was $22,697 in 1996. That same year, the median household income in Salt Lake County was $33,648.

The tax structure for the area includes a general property tax based on assessed valuations established by elected county assessors. The amount of tax paid is based on the rate of tax applied against valuation. Local entities such as school districts, counties and towns and special taxing districts set these rates. Motor vehicle tax is a uniform property tax of 1.7 percent. State income tax is based on a rate of 7 percent of personal income after deducting half the federal tax. Sales and use tax is applied to retail sales of tangible personal property and select services and the rate varies within each municipality from between 5.87 percent and 6.12 percent. Other taxes include special local taxes for restaurants (1 percent), car-rental tax (3 percent) and tourist tax (10 percent). Corporate franchise tax is 5 percent of the net taxable income with a minimum tax of $100. Utah's free port law is among the most liberal inventory tax laws in the country. Goods used by retailers, wholesalers and manufacturers for processing and sale in Utah are exempt from ad valorem taxes. Salt Lake City, a customs port city, offers a foreign trade zone that allows duties to be deferred or reduced.

The area has two excellent resources for relocating a business or starting a new business in Utah: The Salt Lake Area Chamber of Commerce, 364-3631, at 175 E. 400 S., Salt Lake City; and the Economic Development Corporation of Utah, 328-8824, at 215 S. State Street, Salt Lake City.

The People

Strong family values and a sense of community bound the culture together in the mid-1800s, and little has changed since the Mormon people claimed Salt Lake more than 150 years ago (see the Close-up on Mormons in this chapter). Many cultures joined the Mormons in building the Salt Lake Valley. Our Greek population is the largest between the West Coast and Chicago. Mining attracted many Greek workers to the area in the early 1900s, and their influence is still present in our culture. The railroad brought an abundance of young Japanese men to the Salt Lake Valley in the late 1800s. Several thousand workers and their families settled here and are part of the city's multi-ethnic profile today. Mormon converts from England, Scandinavia and Germany came to Salt Lake City during the early settlement years, blending with the growing community — a trend that has continued throughout our history. In recent years, Mormon converts from the Pacific Islands have arrived in the area, and more Native Americans have moved to Salt Lake City from reservations in the southeast part of the state. All help to create a rich melting pot of heritage and tradition with unique flavors that permeate the cultural arts, religious, business and social scenes.

Several traits characterize the people who live in the Salt Lake Valley. Visitors are often struck by the warmth of the locals, and it doesn't take long to realize that we are an industrious, hard-working lot with a strong spirit of volunteerism. A gracious gesture or

www.insiders.com

See this and many other **Insiders' Guide®** destinations online — in their entirety.

Visit us today!

INSIDERS' TIP

For time and temperature information 24 hours a day, seven days a week, call 467-TIME for a free recorded message.

Climate and Weather

When it comes to Salt Lake's weather, visitors should heed the ancient wisdom of the Boy Scouts: Be prepared. Since Salt Lake lies so far from the moderating influence of the ocean, the weather can dramatically change in a hurry. Storms blow in quickly, and temperatures can instantly plummet. Good weather can return just as fast. But these fluctuations don't occur often enough to put the fritz on any of your outdoor plans. Most of the time, you'll love the weather. With four seasons, Salt Lake boasts of a delightful climate that gives visitors and residents the thrill of spring growth, abundant blue skies and summer sunshine, swirling autumn leaves and snowy — but not too cold — winters.

Because of the varied topography, the Salt Lake area has a number of climate zones. This makes life interesting for residents, who can enjoy different weather by just traveling a few miles. The weather in the mountains at an elevation of 10,000 feet is similar to the climate in Alaska. Frequent storms drench the mountains with 60 to 70 inches of water a year, most of that in the form of snow. Resorts such as Snowbird and Alta commonly receive an astounding 40 feet of dry, powdery snow a year. Such bounty brings hordes of powder hounds to the Wasatch Mountains every winter. (See the Skiing and Winter Sports chapter for more information on skiing in the Wasatch.) Lower

— continued on next page

Photo: Frank Jensen

El Niño often brings heavy winter snows and spring flooding.

down, the semiarid foothills get 20 inches of moisture a year, and the dry Salt Lake Valley only 14 inches. And each year the weather patterns change. Although the total amount of precipitation doesn't vary much, it's impossible to predict when it will come. Sometimes, Salt Lake experiences a snowy winter and a dry spring, while the next year only a few snow storms hit — but spring rains come hard and fast.

The El Niño effect makes Salt Lake's climate even more unpredictable. An El Niño occurs when the water off the South American coast heats up more than usual. The El Niño generally causes wetter and cooler weather in Salt Lake. Serious flooding in the mid-'80s was caused by the El Niño, which occurs every five to seven years.

Whatever the weather, low humidity makes for a comfortable climate, summer and winter. Even though summer temperatures can hit triple digits, the dry air makes it tolerable. In Salt Lake, you'll never say, "It's not the heat, it's the humidity." Winds often blow up the canyons in the day and out of the canyons in the evening, giving relief from hot temperatures.

Spring is the most unpredictable time of the year. A glorious spring morning can quickly give way to a raging afternoon snow storm. Wet, snowy weather can sometimes hang on until May; other years are dry and warm from February on. Balmy late winters tempt gardeners to sow their seeds earlier than usual — but the experienced know that to do so is to invite frozen seedlings in the middle of April.

If you like your weather hot, dry and sunny, you'll love summer in Salt Lake. Temperatures in July and August often reach 100 or more several days in a row. June is usually warm and sunny as well. Summers in Salt Lake stay true to form more than the other seasons. Rain is scarce, except for occasional thunderstorms which rumble and roar, but usually don't even water your lawn. Occasionally a big one will hit, and the gutters will fill and basements flood.

For many people, mellow sunlight, clear days and cool nights make autumn the best season in Salt Lake. Beautiful weather can last for weeks. This is a wonderful time to hike the mountains, explore the Great Salt Lake or take an art tour through Salt Lake's numerous galleries.

Because of Utah's world-class skiing, many people associate winter with Salt Lake City. As mentioned, mountain snows are abundant at the resorts. But in the city itself, about 6,000 feet lower, a storm that dumps 2 feet at Alta may only leave 2 inches at Salt Lake. Unfortunately, high pressure in the winter often causes temperature inversions. During these dreaded events, the temperature in the Valley may stay below freezing for days or weeks. Even worse, the inversion traps pollution in the Valley, which can reach dangerously high levels. When this happens, Salt Lakers will often flee to the mountains for relief from the frigid smog and murky, polluted air.

---

a helping hand is the way of life everywhere in the Salt Lake Valley.

The Quirks

Every city has its quirks and odd customs, and ours is no exception.

The state's liquor laws may be some of the strangest in the country (you can read all about them in our Nightlife chapter). The Utah Indoor Clean Air Act prohibits smoking inside any public building, including restaurants and shopping malls, and within 25 feet of any public building. By law, you can smoke in nonexclusive private clubs, but smoking here is at the discretion of the club.

Utah does not have a blue law, that is, one that restricts businesses from being open on Sundays, but the Mormon church frowns on working on Sunday, so many businesses are closed. In the biannual meeting of the general conference of the Church of Jesus Christ of Latter-day Saints, authorities cautioned that Mormons were becoming too mainstream. Too many cars were seen in parking lots of shopping centers in predominantly Mormon neighborhoods on Sunday, a traditional day set aside for family. That doesn't mean you have to sit around on Sunday twiddling your thumbs in a hotel room. There's plenty to do here seven days a week, but it's always best to check before planning a Sunday outing in the Salt Lake Valley.

The Future

The future of the Salt Lake Valley will always be tempered by its ties to the past. Each new building that claims its place in the cityscape serves as a reminder to Salt Lakers that this once-inhospitable desert valley was prodded into progress by determined forebears. Indeed, many special events occurring throughout the year celebrate this pioneer spirit and history. According to *Adweek Magazine*, Salt Lake City is "poised to become a city of the future." The new take-notice posture is exemplified by the city's successful bid for the 2002 Winter Olympic Games. It took Salt Lake City more than two decades to gain status as a world player, but it has finally arrived (see our 2002 Winter Olympics chapter). The future here is more than a little bit bright, and we embrace this exciting time with open arms.

In the summer of 1997,
the Utah Department of
Transportation started
rebuilding Interstate 15,
scheduled for
completion by 2002.

Getting Here, Getting Around

Salt Lake City is known as the crossroads of the West because of its accessibility by air, rail and ground. The Salt Lake International Airport is closer to the city it serves than nearly any other airport in the country. Two Amtrak routes link East and West by rail. The Utah Transit Authority provides mass transit throughout the Salt Lake Valley. Several taxi, bus and shuttle companies provide door-to-door service to any destination in the area.

In the summer of 1997, the Utah Department of Transportation (UDOT) started rebuilding Interstate 15; it's scheduled for completion by 2002. In addition, many surface roads are also getting a face-lift. Tearing up the highways and surface streets to create a better, safer system with greater access to various parts of the Valley is not unlike telling a kid he has to have his tonsils removed. It's going to hurt a little, but when it's over you'll feel a lot better. Insiders wonder why this entire makeover had to happen all at once, but the Winter Olympics are coming in 2002, and the future has a way of sneaking up on you. In the future, it's a good bet that an ongoing maintenance program for our highways and surface roads will be looked at a little more seriously.

The advantage of all this construction for visitors is that because the city is laid out on a grid system, with many roads running from one end of the Valley to the other — both north to south and east to west — you really don't have to drive on the freeway to get around. You'll have an opportunity to see neighborhoods and places you might have missed if you had taken the interstate. Lucky for you, surface road redos are in the final stages.

Speaking of the future, by the year 2000 commuters can get between Salt Lake City and the mid-Valley and south Valley aboard UDOT's light rail system. The light rail will offer numerous stops and is designed to reduce congestion on the freeway and surface roads, lessen pollution from automobiles and ease parking in the downtown area.

Courtesy on the highway has never been more important than during this construction period. Insiders have taken this project in stride, leaving for their destinations a little earlier and trying to chill out as the traffic backs up for a half-mile. Commuters continue to use the bus system as a welcome alternative to suffering through gridlock behind the wheel of their own cars. Local drivers are notorious tailgaters, and many forget to signal. While driving in the Salt Lake Valley, don't fall into the old "when in Rome" habit. Cool your jets and enjoy the ride. Salt Lake is a great place to visit and we'll get you around to all the sights without too much confusion.

Getting Here

By Air

Commercial Flights

Salt Lake City International Airport
776 N. Terminal Dr. (3700 W.), Salt Lake City • 575-2400

The Salt Lake City airport is ranked the 23rd-largest in the nation for passenger travel and the ninth-largest for international travel. The airport consistently ranks among the most outstanding in the country for on-time arrival and departure schedules as well as for high quality and safe service. The Salt Lake City International Airport was the 1997 recipient of the Federal Aviation Administration's Airport Operations Leadership Award.

Twelve airlines serve Salt Lake City: Alpine Aviation, America West, American, Continental, Delta, Frontier, Mountain Air Express, Northwest, SkyWest/Delta Connection, Southwest, TWA and United. These airlines offer more than 41,885 daily domestic seats and 1,262 international seats for nonstop service to 67 cities. Just 5 miles from downtown Salt Lake City, the airport has two terminals (Delta Airlines is exclusive to Terminal II), five concourses, 68 gates and four runways, and, as airports go, this one is very easy to figure out. Although the airport facility is large, the well-designed open spaces make it easy to find your way around.

Inside the terminal you'll find lots of information desks and plenty of conveniences including a full-service bank for foreign currency exchange and cash machines, a barber and beauty shop, a business center, gift shops featuring Utah souvenirs, newspapers, magazines and sundry items, customs and a duty free shop. You'll also find infant-care stations, lockers, luggage carts and cocktail lounges including Delta Airline's Crown Room. There's a shoe-shine stand, auto rental desks, a ski rental and lots of places to grab a quick meal or a snack. In addition, the airport has an 18-hole golf course south of the terminals with a clubhouse, a pro shop and restaurants. Also available are TDD phones, computer phones, TV chairs (so you won't miss episodes of your favorite program while you wait) and assistance with translation in more than 200 languages.

The Salt Lake International Airport is designed to accommodate physically challenged individuals with accessibility to restaurants, restrooms and parking facilities as well as phone banks, ramps and elevators.

FYI

Unless otherwise noted, the area code for all phone numbers listed in this guide is 801.

Individual airlines provide indoor motorized-vehicle service and other assistance for passengers with special needs.

Utah Transit Authority (UTA) buses leave the airport for the city center every 40 minutes during the day and every hour after 6 PM. The fare is 75¢. The bus stops are found near door No. 2 in Terminal I and door No. 11 in Terminal II. Most downtown hotels and some mid- and south Valley hotels offer courtesy vans. You can arrange for transportation to your hotel at the Ground Transportation Desks or at the direct-line hotel phone banks. Both are at the far end of the terminal's baggage claim areas. You can reach the Ground Transportation Desks by calling 575-2477.

Car rental companies, which are located on the lowest level of the parking terrace, include: Alamo, 575-2211; Avis, 575-2847; Budget, 363-1500; Dollar, 575-2580; Hertz, 575-2683; and National, 575-2277. Long-term parking is provided on the south and west sides of both terminals. The Salt Lake City Airport Authority provides free shuttle service between the parking lots and the terminals. The shuttle runs every five minutes. The short-term parking terrace is directly west of the terminals. The lower level is restricted to hourly parking. The rates are quite reasonable. Short term parking is $1 per hour, 50¢ for a half-hour and $10 per day maximum. Long-term parking is $1 per hour, $4 per day and $20 per week.

Private Flights

The Airport Authority oversees the operation of three general aviation facilities in the area for private aviators.

At Salt Lake International Airport, you can get information on the fixed-base operators offering full services, including aircraft sales and leasing, air-charter service, aircraft parts and maintenance, fuel sales and aircraft storage by calling Hudson General at 539-2805, Million Air Salt Lake at 359-2085 or Salt Lake Jet Center at 595-6438. For hanger rental call 575-2929.

Airport II is in West Jordan at 7536 S.

4470 W. For information call Alta Aircraft Maintenance at 566-8271, Bemis Avionics at 256-3300, Hudson General at 566-4829 or Sky Dive Salt Lake at 255-5867.

American Aviation at the Tooele Valley Airport, 4363 Airport Road, Tooele, 833-9000, can give you information on services in this part of the Valley.

By Road and Rail

Commercial Carriers

Greyhound Bus Lines
160 W. South Temple, Salt Lake City
• **355-9581, (800) 231-2222**

Greyhound provides service to and from most major cities in the country as well as ticketed service to many locations throughout the state. You can wait for your bus in the adjacent coffee shop or in the main terminal but if you are traveling at night, be wary of the neighborhood. The terminal is on the fringe of the city center and not a great place to be in the wee small hours.

Amtrak
320 S. Rio Grande St., Salt Lake City
• **531-0188**

If you chose to ride the rail, Amtrak has two trains arriving in Salt Lake City daily and two departing. Service is between here and Chicago, Illinois, and Oakland, California, with stops between. The terminal is pleasant, and the customer service people are very friendly, but a word to the wise: The train from Chicago arrives very early in the morning — at 12:15 AM — and the Oakland rail gets in at 4:50 AM. Departure times are 1:05 and 5:15 AM, respectively. The Amtrak station is in a marginal part of town with very few services available in the immediate area at those times of day. You can call for a taxi, but don't plan to walk the few blocks to the city center on your own. It isn't safe.

Getting to the Slopes

Several transport companies will meet you at the airport and whisk you directly to the local ski resorts. You can choose from a variety of services ranging from a shared ride to a private limousine — and fares will vary according to how luxurious and private you want the ride to be. We've provided several listings here. You can also check with your reservationist when making accommodation arrangements. Frequently, the resort hotel will set up transportation for you. See our Park City chapter at the end of the book for information on accommodations in that area.

All Resort Express
1221 Sidewinder Dr., Park City
• **(435) 649-3999, (800) 457-9457**

You can get a ride to Park City with this company's regularly scheduled daily service or book a private trip. It also books tours, charters, sightseeing and limousine transportation.

Day Trips Transportation
1950 Woodbine Way, Park City
• **(435) 649-8294, (800) 649-8294**

Day Trips will shuttle you to and from the airport between 6 AM and 2 AM daily any time of the year. There's a three-passenger minimum for private transport. The company also provides sightseeing tours and limousines service.

DLS/Gus Transportation
3939 S. Wasatch Blvd., Holladay
• **277-1214, (435) 649-2077,**
(800) 837-6490

Ride in style in top-of-the-line limousines and luxury sedans, 4x4s, a Suburban or in the company's 15-passenger vans. DLS will take you from the airport to all local ski resorts. Choose from airport meet-and-greet at your gate or private service.

INSIDERS' TIP

If you need transportation from one medical facility to another or from a medical facility to the airport, call Utah Medi-Van Service, 466-4454. It's a wheelchair-accommodating transport service.

Le Bus

542 S. 2165 W., Salt Lake City
• 975-0202, (800) 366-0288

This company provides private group transfers or charters to the ski resorts, or you can book one of their tours to other areas throughout the state.

Lewis Bros. Stages

549 W. 500 S., Salt Lake City • 359-8677, (800) 826-5844

Lewis Bros. offers year-round, door-to-door scheduled airport transports to the ski resorts as well as sightseeing tours and special charters for groups.

Park City Express

2627 W. Kilby Rd., Park City
• (435) 645-7250, (800) 7-AIRPORT

You can arrive in Park City with this company's private, shared, scheduled and meet-and-greet service. It also offers year-round taxi service in Park City and tours, charters, sightseeing and limousine service.

Park City Transportation Services

1555 Lower Iron Horse Loop Rd., Park City • (435) 649-8567, (800) 637-3803

Service is provided to and from the airport and Park City between 5 AM and midnight daily, every 20-minutes during the winter and once an hour during the summer. The company also offers shuttle service to downtown Salt Lake City from Park City.

Powder for the People

1776 Park Ave., Ste. 4, Park City
• (435) 649-6648, (888) 482-7547

Skiers can get to the area's ski resort with Powder for the People. Charter and sightseeing tours are also available. Service is limited during the summer, but regularly scheduled shuttle service is available during the winter.

Rocky Mountain Super Express

60 S. Redwood Rd., Salt Lake City
• 485-4100, (800) 397-0773

You'll find a two-person minimum on pri-

A Visitors Guide to Utahspeak

Most Utahns admit it: We talk funny.

We're even a little proud of our verbal quirks. To a stranger's ear, many of us (even Salt Lakers) sound like Festus on *Gunsmoke* — kind of slow, slurred and drawly. Recently, a spokesman on a Salt Lake radio station advertised a certain kind of "farplace." An out-of-towner may have thought the man was touting a distant vacation spot, but natives knew

he was selling a device that keeps your home warm in the winter. Disk jockeys Bill Allred, Gina Barberi and Kerry Jackson, who host a popular and irreverent early morning radio show on X 96 (KXRK 96.3 FM), often recite hilarious examples of Utahspeak that they're heard or made up. They've even created a "Utahnics" Web page where these priceless phrases are collected. (See below for some examples.)

Utahns drop syllables, combine several words into one, insert syllables where none are needed and inexplicably change the sound of vowels. Thus, fork become "fark," fire becomes "far," born become "barn," board become "bard," spark becomes "spork" and for becomes "fer." Combine the changed vowel with a dropped syllable and you get "fer ignernt," a classic Utahnism that means someone has been rude to you — perhaps a sales clerk who didn't respond quickly enough to your request to "lookit some farmal dresses."

Utahns often insert an extra "t" into words, then hesitate a bit between syllables, such as, "Didja see the new teat-chur? She's purty as a pit-chur." Giddy up, cowboy.

Besides pronouncing words strangely, Utahns also have a special vocabulary, much of it derived from the Mormon religious heritage. Mormons take their religion

— continued on next page

seriously, which is a credit to them, but religious phrases and buzz words are likely to spill over into secular life in both print and conversation. You'll find that Utahns are forever grateful, blessed and humble. You might be startled the first time you hear people calling each other brother and sister. Don't be alarmed: Mormons have big families, but not that big. They're not all related — it's just the traditional way they talk to each other.

Then there's the issue of Utah swearwords. Utahns don't cuss much, but when they do, they're likely to launch verbal hand grenades like "fetch," "shoot," "scrud" and "oh my heck." (Watch out for this one — it indicates extreme anger.) You'll also hear the word "gol" spoken a lot, as in "Gol, VernaLee, wherdja git them gargeous shoes? Fer cuute!"

Various theories have been put forth explaining the origins of Utahspeak. Perhaps it's the combination of peoples from all over the world who moved to Utah to create a distinctive community. Many Utahns trace their ancestry back to Northern Europe, but the mining industry brought in Greeks, Poles, Italians and Americans from the South, all of whom seasoned the linguistic stew. Maybe it comes from the traditional culture of Utah. Even though most Utahns live in crowded cities, conservative, rural politics dominate the state, and the agrarian way of life is much admired and emulated, including speech. In addition, many of Utah's cultural, religious and civic leaders come from small towns, and Utahns revere their leaders like no place else. It's natural for the speaking patterns of the rich and powerful to spread into the general population, which means that everybody ends up talking like a farmer from Southern Utah. Who knows?

Photo: Challenger School

School children learn their three R's — plus a good dose of Utah dialect.

Salt Lakers like to think it's the people from small towns who talk like hicks. The truth is, although our accents aren't quite as broad, to someone from Seattle or Kansas City, Salt Lakers sound like the rubes on Green Acres. We may despair and yearn to speak like Lawrence Olivier, but in the end, what the fetch cunna feller do? Some things you just can't escape.

Here are a few gems from the Utahnics Web Page, created by Bill Allred, Gina Barberi and Kerry Jackson of X-96 FM radio. These examples will help you learn some of the subtleties of Utahspeak.

The granger of Zion Pork zawn spyring (The grandeur of Zion Park is awe-inspiring.)

He was tard cause he got up surly fer the prayed. (He was tired because he got up so early for the parade.)

I went down to the Macey's for a gal na fruit punch anna cord a melk. (We went to Macey's for a gallon of fruit punch and a quart of milk.)

In Store Wores we learn 'bout Dorth Vader 'n' the dork side of the farce. (In *Star Wars* we learn about Darth Vader and the dark side of the force.)

I git a rill wharm fillin' win I go backta muncle's form. (I get a really warm feeling when I go back to my uncle's farm.)

vate airport-to-resort shuttles with this company. It operates daily between 5 AM and midnight.

Highways

Interstate 15 covers the Salt Lake Valley from north to south, connecting Utah with Idaho on the north and Nevada on the south. Interstate 80 crosses the Valley from east to west, connecting the state with Colorado on the east and Nevada on the west. U.S. Highway 89 runs parallel with I-15 from the far northern part of the Valley to Draper, where it runs into I-15. Interstate 215 is the Belt Route that loops around the city between Wasatch Drive to the east, 6600 South to 300 West, connecting with I-80 at approximately 2400 South where it heads back to Wasatch Drive, connecting the loop on the east side of town. I-215 on the west side of town runs south off I-15 near the Salt Lake International Airport, just west of Redwood Road (1700 West) to 6000 South where it makes an eastward jog to join the eastbound loop.

Surface Roads

Many surface roads will take you from one end of the Salt Lake Valley to the other and from one side of the city to the other. During times of freeway reconstruction these city streets provide excellent alternatives to I-15 and I-215, with their traffic jams and construction delays. Many locals actually prefer to use surface roads instead of the freeway most if not all the time. Travel time is generally not more than five minutes longer using the surface roads if you know what you're doing. The highway and grid map at the beginning of the book will help you make sense of everything. It may sound complicated, but once you figure out the system you can get anywhere in the Valley with the greatest of ease. See our

explanation of this grid system in the next section.

For I-15 closures and construction updates call toll-free (888) INFO-I15. For current surface road construction information call 562-6469.

The Grid

Brigham Young did not invent the grid system for laying out city streets but it's amazing how many tourists think this is unique to Salt Lake City. It isn't. You'll find this method of city planning in many Eastern and Southeastern cities. As to the inventor, if memory serves, it was Thomas Jefferson. What is unusual here are the wide streets. Young found wisdom in allowing oxen to make a U-turn in the middle of the street without having to back up, as well as providing room for two teams to go in opposite directions at the same time by making the streets eight rods (132 feet) wide.

If the grid is new to you, here's how it works. The center point in Salt Lake City is the LDS Temple on Temple Square, which is one square block. Each of the city's blocks is 10 acres. The streets around Temple Square are called North Temple, West Temple, South Temple and East Temple — East Temple was later changed to Main Street — and their coordinate is zero. From these streets, the remaining streets are called First North Street or First South Street and so on. They increase in increments of 100, so the next street is Second North Street and so on. Shorthand for this: 100 North, 200 North, 300 North or whichever is appropriate in each direction.

In speaking of them or writing the address, we've dropped the "street." If you are looking for the address 150 W. 300 S., for example, you will find this location 1½ blocks west of Temple Square and three blocks

---

INSIDERS' TIP

You can rent a full-size, fully accessible van with a wheelchair lift, tie down and hand controls for the day or week from Para Quad Marketing Inc. Call 487-0111. To ensure that a van is available, it's best to make reservations several weeks in advance.

Photo: Frank Jensen

Feel the nostalgia of Salt Lake City as you see the sights aboard
a replica of the old Brigham Street Trolley.

south. The address 270 is 2.7 blocks in whatever direction the coordinate bears. Insiders use another shorthand method in speaking of streets too. Instead of 900 South we say 9th South and even reduce that somewhat with main surface roads, simply saying 7th instead of 7th East.

As you venture farther south and west into the Valley you'll find streets with names like Spruce, Twin View or Osage Orange but under the name on each street sign you'll find the numeric coordinate from Temple Square.

This is really easy, honest. East is the easiest bearing to keep as a constant because of the mountains. See that giant range of mountains over there? Not the middle-size mountains or the foothills or the ones way off in the distance — the really big ones right there in front of you. That's the Wasatch Mountain Range, and it's always going to be east of the city.

Getting Around

Once you're here, you have several options available for getting around the city. Downtown Salt Lake is a walking city so if you plan to spend a few days in a hotel in the downtown area you may want to skip the rental car and hoof it to the malls, restaurants, Temple Square and other attractions such as museums, galleries and happenings in the arts during the day. (We recommend riding to your downtown destinations at night.) You can supplement foot travel with cab rides, the Trolley, buses or a classy carriage ride.

If your tootsies aren't up to the challenge or if you want to expand your adventure beyond the downtown area, we have plenty of cab companies downtown and in the mid- and south Valley, a diversified bus system to transport you from one end of the Valley to the other as well as east to the mountain resorts and to special events. If you really must have wheels, you'll find dozens of rental car companies listed in the Yellow Pages under "Auto Renting." The companies with locations at the Salt Lake City International Airport are listed in that section above.

The downtown area has dozens of lots for parking your car. Daily rates average approximately $4. Add a few dollars more for special-events parking during the day and evening. You can also park in metered parking if you can find an empty spot. Meters are good for 30 minutes to one or two hours, and $2 will cover you for a full two hours (they take nickels, dimes and quarters, but no pennies). Don't be tardy, though. The meter brigade doesn't show leniency toward out-of-state violators. You can park free at meters after 6 PM weekdays, all day Saturday with a two-hour limit and all day Sunday with no time limit.

Okay, times a wastin'. There's so much to see and do in the Salt Lake Valley, so grab your *Insiders' Guide*® and let's go.

City and County

Most Salt Lakers cross over the city/county line a dozen times a day without giving it much thought, and most of the time it doesn't matter on which side of the county line you find yourself. The Salt Lake Valley includes the municipalities of Salt Lake City, South Salt Lake City, Murray, Sandy, Midvale, South Jordan, West Jordan, Riverton, Draper and West Valley City. All of these cities are in Salt Lake County. What may seem confusing is that Salt Lake City is referred to as "the city," while the rest of the Valley is referred to as "the county." When Salt Lakers ask if you live in the city or the county, they are really asking, "Do you live, more or less, south of 3000 South?" The boundaries for the city and county are as follows: Salt Lake City is from 2300 North to 2100

South, from approximately 3000 East to 8400 West. Above 700 East the boundary expands to 3300 South. Salt Lake County boundaries run from the southern boundaries of Salt Lake City east to Wasatch Drive, west to 8400 West and south to 17000 South in Draper where it meets the Utah County line.

Salt Lake City and Salt Lake County each provide their own services, and the property tax may be different in the city and county. Emergency services are also provided separately. Fortunately, if you have an emergency, you need only dial 911 from anywhere in the Valley. The dispatch center can identify your location from the call-in number and dispatch help from the appropriate jurisdiction. If, however, you are calling from a cellular phone, it might be a good idea to try to identify your location from a street sign, landmark or something notable. This helps the dispatcher know whether to send help from a city or county provider.

Room tax on hotels and other accommodations also vary slightly across the county line. In Salt Lake City the rate is 10.73 percent, whereas in Salt Lake County, it's 11.23 percent.

Taxi Companies

Cabbing it is sometimes the best way to get around in the Valley if you didn't arrive in the area by car and don't plan to rent one. If you are in the city and need a ride to the airport or other in-town destinations such as restaurants, shopping, businesses or the sights, call City Cab Company, 363-5550; Yellow Cab, 521-2100; or Ute Cab Company, 359-7798. For taxi service in the mid-Valley call MidValley Cab, 562-0100, or Murray Cab Company, 328- 5704. In the southwest part of the Valley, call West Valley Taxicab Company, 328-5705.

INSIDERS' TIP

Emergency Medical Response time in the Salt Lake Valley is 90 seconds or less from the time the call is answered until the proper responder is dispatched. If you need the services of a translator to communicate your situation in as many as 50 foreign languages, add an additional 10 seconds. For emergencies, call 911 anywhere in the Valley.

Carriage Rides

Carriage Connection, 428 W. 200 N., 531-7433 or 363-8687, lets you see the city in high style in a horse-drawn carriage that takes you through the downtown area. You can pick up the carriage at the West Temple entrance to Temple Square daily from 10 AM to 11:30 PM year round. The carriage will also gather you up at your hotel, any downtown restaurant or other location in the city center if you make this arrangement. The 30-minute ride for six or fewer people runs $32. For $45 the carriage will take you through Memory Grove (see our Parks and Recreation chapter).

Public Transit

Utah Transit Authority, 3600 S. 700 W., BUS-INFO takes you to a variety of places, offers specialized services and is an excellent alternative to losing your cool during high-way reconstruction with nearly 150 bus routes throughout the Valley.

Downtown Area Restaurant Trolley, or DART, is a free service that takes diners from participating area restaurants to the Delta Center for Jazz games.

UTA's Flex Tran buses offer paratransit services to individuals with physical disabilities on a preregistration basis. More than 50 percent of UTA's regular buses in the city and county are lift-equipped as well.

UTA provides bus service to Alta, Snow Bird, Brighton and Solitude Ski resorts during the winter. UTA also offers a ride-free zone in the downtown area: If you board and get off the bus within the specified geographic area your ride is free. UTA's Trolley is also a great way to get around in the downtown area.

To get schedules and info on the many bus-ride options through UTA, call the BUS-INFO number. You won't get a recording. The company has live, warm bodies to answer all your questions.

Some people consider Salt Lakers to be among the friendliest people in the world. As far as our hospitality industry goes, you'll find that compliment is well-deserved.

Accommodations

If you've decided to visit Salt Lake City, you're in luck! Our hospitality industry is booming. We have more than 14,000 affordable rooms to meet the needs of every traveler. Rooms in the Salt Lake area are priced below those in comparable cities. For many years, most of our accommodations were in the downtown area. New properties began to pop up near the airport in the '80s as Salt Lake flexed its civic muscles in the convention arena. To keep pace with the region's new status as "the best place in the nation for smart companies to do business" (according to *Forbes*) and in anticipation of the 2002 Winter Olympic Games, new accommodations are springing up across the Salt Lake Valley like an April garden.

We offer a variety of accommodations from budget to luxury, and most of the properties are either brand-new or newly remodeled. Salt Lake's hospitality industry reflects the sophistication of our cosmopolitan community. Still, we haven't gotten too big for our britches with our recent notoriety. Some people consider Salt Lakers to be among the friendliest people in the world. As far as our hospitality industry goes, you'll find that compliment is well-deserved.

Words to the wise: Book early. Convention business and tourism are growing rapidly. Long-established attractions such as the annual July 24 Pioneer Day parade and festivities and our winter ski season can put a strain on availability. Before deciding whether to catch your Zs downtown, in the mid- or south Valley or near the airport, check out the area write-ups here. We've included overviews of hotels, motels and hostels. Extended-stay visitors and skiers, especially, may want to check out the Vacation and Extended-stay Rentals chapter. We have included a chapter on RV parks, and you won't want to miss the Bed and Breakfasts and Inns chapter if you like accommodations with a homey touch.

People don't consider the mountains part of their community in many parts of the country. Ours are so close you can almost touch them, so we've included mountain accommodations in a separate chapter, Mountain Resorts. Park City is the exception — it's an experience unto itself — so we've given Park City its own chapter.

Proprietors of new and remodeled properties, including budget accommodations, have gone out of their way to make business travelers feel welcome in Salt Lake. Many have included such amenities as data port and power stripping, fax machines and copiers, dual phone lines in-room and on the premises. If you have these requirements, ask the reservationist to describe the extent of the hotel's business amenities. Pooch and Kitty are welcome guests in some, but not all, lodging facilities. It's best to ask about pets when you make reservations. With few exceptions, properties have wheelchair-accessible rooms. We've noted those that don't. Smoking and nonsmoking rooms are available in most hotels and motels. We've flagged the few nonsmoking facilities. And nearly all have color televisions and cable; some also offer VCRs, video games and free movie channels, which we note. If you plan to swim during the winter, make sure your hotel has a year-round pool. An airport shuttle is available to and from most downtown hotels but is not always provided to and from mid- and south Valley properties. Ask about transportation when you make reservations if you aren't driving to the area and don't plan to rent a car.

After a busy day of shopping, sightseeing or business you may want to return to your hotel and unwind over a cocktail. Utah's regulations regarding the consumption of alcohol are unique but not too hard to follow once you understand the law. We discuss them at length in our Nightlife chapter. Any person consuming or purchasing alcoholic beverages must be 21 years of age or older.

Smoking is not allowed inside or in the patio area of any restaurant. You also can't smoke in any public building or within 25 feet of any public building, so don't light up in the hotel's lobby.

It would be an impossible task to list all the accommodations in the Salt Lake Valley, but we've included a wide range. The listings are broken out in three areas: Downtown, mid- and south Valley, and the airport. Your itinerary may determine where you want to be in the Salt Lake Valley. The grid explanation in our Getting Here, Getting Around chapter can be a big help in locating your choice of accommodations.

FYI

Unless otherwise noted, the area code for all phone numbers listed in this guide is 801.

Price Code

Each listing includes a dollar symbol indicating a price range for a midweek, double-occupancy one-night stay. Pricing information is offered as a general guideline. When occupancy is high, such as during conventions and holidays, the room rates tend to be higher. On weekends and during high-vacancy periods, the rates are often reduced. All hotels included in this chapter accept major credit cards.

$	Less than $65
$$	$66 to $125
$$$	$126 to $185
$$$$	$186 and more

Reservation Services

**Salt Lake City
Reservation Services**
2812 E. Bijou St., Ste. 202, Colorado
Springs, Colo. • (800) 590-9878

This company books hotels in the Salt Lake City area as well as ski packages and car rentals. The service is free to visitors. For bookings in Utah outside the Salt Lake area, call (800) 557-8824.

Hotels and Motels

Downtown

Close to nightlife, fine dining, shopping, business venues and the arts, the downtown area is the heartbeat of the Valley. From the downtown area you can be on the slopes in about 40 minutes, at the airport in about 10 minutes and to the far end of the south Valley in less than 30 minutes. Many major attractions are within walking distance of downtown hotels.

Best Western Olympus Hotel
$$ • 161 W. 600 S., Salt Lake City
• 521-7373, (800) 426-0722

This is an older, recently remodeled property with 393 big rooms close to the city center. The light and airy lobby has comfortable sofas and a pleasant collection of contemporary artwork. Cafe Olympus serves homestyle cooking throughout the day. Mullboons Restaurant on the 13th floor is a popular Insiders eatery. While you ponder the entrees, the big bowls of shrimp just keep coming (see our Restaurants chapter). The Uinta Room is a pub-style bar on the property. You can relax in the year-round pool and hot tub or work off stress in the fitness room. Laundry facilities are available. Pay-per-view movies are available in all rooms.

Best Western Salt Lake Plaza Hotel
$$ • 122 W. South Temple, Salt Lake City
• 521-0130, (800) 366-3684

A recent makeover inside and out has given this older downtown hotel a new look that blends well with the cityscape. Featuring the second-largest rooms in the city, this 226-room property is quite comfortable. The Family History Library and Temple Square are a crosswalk away. The hotel has a year-round heated outdoor pool and an indoor Jacuzzi. JB's Restaurant, next to the hotel, is open for breakfast, lunch and dinner.

The Carlton Hotel
$ • 140 E. South Temple, Salt Lake City
• 355-3418, (800) 633-3500

This is a good little find if you like smaller

hotels. The Carlton was built in 1935 and continues to offer hospitality in the tradition of Europe's fine independent hotels. It offers 45 newly remodeled, nicely appointed guest rooms. Each has a refrigerator, a reclining chair and a VCR. Free in-room movies are available around the clock. Guests can relax in the hotel's spa and sauna. The Carlton serves a full, cooked-to-order complimentary breakfast and provides free transportation to the airport and the Family History Library. No wheelchair-accessible rooms are available.

Courtyard by Marriott, Downtown
$$ • 130 W. 400 S., Salt Lake City
• 531-6000, (800) 321-2211

The simple, unpretentious decor in this down-to-business hotel is typical of the chain. Designed primarily for business travelers, the 121 rooms are oversized and comfortable. The Courtyard Cafe serves breakfast and dinner, and room service is available. This recently constructed property has an indoor pool and an exercise room.

Crystal Inn
$$ • 230 W. 500 S., Salt Lake City
• 328-4466, (800) 366-4466

Locally owned and operated, the Crystal Inn is a newer hotel with a friendly family feel. The sleek mini-suites have microwaves and refrigerators. All of the hotel's 175 rooms are comfortable and nicely appointed. A complimentary hot breakfast buffet starts the day for guests, or a short jaunt will get you to Denny's Restaurant located behind the property. The hotel has an indoor pool, an exercise facility, a spa and a sauna. Two more of these large yet homey hotels are under construction in West Valley City and Midvale.

Deseret Inn
$ • 50 W. 500 S., Salt Lake City • 532-2900, (800) 359-2170

This 35-year-old, family-owned hotel was recently remodeled. Its 85 guest rooms are comfortably decorated in warm earth tones with subtle hints of the Southwest. This is a quiet spot with beautifully landscaped grounds. The owners pride themselves on providing homey, personalized hospitality. The Deseret Inn doesn't have a pool, but you can relax in the hot tub. Complimentary coffee is served in the lobby sitting area. The hotel has excellent freeway access. Cafe Mediterranean, a local favorite for Mediterranean and vegetarian meals, is on the premises. Local pianists entertain guests throughout the week. See our listing in the Restaurants chapter.

Diamond Inn
$ • 1009 S. Main St., Salt Lake City
• 355-4567, (888) 500-9192

Sixty-two unassuming but pleasant guest rooms provide the essentials for budget-minded travelers at this newly constructed property. There's no glamour here, but it's a great place for a good night's sleep. The pool, hot tub, movie channels, kitchenettes, guest laundry and extended-stay rates make it a good choice for longer stays. Meals are available at the Holiday Inn next door, and Nector's Restaurant is about a block away.

Doubletree Hotel
$$$ • 255 S. West Temple, Salt Lake City
• 328-2000, (800) 222-TREE

The 495 rooms and 19 suites have undergone extensive remodeling in this first-rate hotel. The health facility offers an indoor Olympic-size lap pool, a sauna, massage therapy and a large sun deck. The

www.insiders.com

See this and many other **Insiders' Guide®** destinations online — in their entirety.

Visit us today!

INSIDERS' TIP

The tax on rooms is 10.73 percent in Salt Lake City and 11.23 percent in Salt Lake County. See the Getting Here, Getting Around chapter to determine which side of the county line you're sleeping on.

rooms are nicely appointed. The 17th floor is exclusively for business travelers and fully decked out to provide an office away from home. The secured concierge, or executive, level on the 18th floor serves a complimentary breakfast and offers a discount on cocktails in the evening. Maxi's Fine Dining serves creative American cuisine and specializes in tableside flambé. City Side Cafe is popular with casual diners and serves meals on the patio in warm weather. Club Max is a full-service lounge with a large-screen TV, DJ entertainment and nightly dancing. There's a shoe-shine stand and a Thrifty Car Rental on the site. Underground parking is available.

Econo Lodge
$$ • 715 W. North Temple, Salt Lake City
• 363-0062, (800) 553-2666

Get your car lubed at the Q-Lube on the property at this downtown Econo Lodge. The hotel offers complimentary coffee and a dip in its outdoor pool. The 120 rooms in this older prop-

erty have been nicely upgraded with new furniture and carpet. You can get three squares a day at Frontier Pies Restaurant on the property. Seniors can book a room with large-button phones and big-faced clocks.

Embassy Suites
$$$ • 110 W. 600 S., Salt Lake City
• 359-7800, (800) EMBASSY

The central atrium and the out-of-the-highrise location make this in-town property quite desirable. The hotel offers 241 two-bedroom suites, each with a microwave, refrigerator and coffee maker. All rooms open onto the central atrium. The lobby is roomy and well-furnished. The Embassy has an indoor pool, a whirlpool, a fitness room and guest laundry facilities. Libations can be enjoyed at Clouseaus', a private club. The Plum Restaurant serves three meals a day.

Hampton Inn, Downtown
$$ • 425 S. 300 W., Salt Lake City
• 741-1110, (800) HAMPTON

Low key is Hampton's style. Its 158 new

rooms are tastefully decorated in a comfy urban style. Geared to business travelers, the Hampton Inn has a fitness center, an indoor pool and a hot tub. You can enjoy the complimentary continental breakfast daily. For the rest of your daily bread, Denny's Restaurant is about two blocks away. Upscale yet casual dining is available at the Red Rock Brewery, within walking distance. Several other brewpubs are close by. See the "Brewpubs" section in our Nightlife chapter.

Holiday Inn, Downtown
$$ • 999 S. Main St., Salt Lake City • 359-8600, (800) 465-4329

Several hotels have occupied this building over the years, but the Holiday Inn seems to have made it work best. The 292 spacious rooms have been recently remodeled; upgrades are a constant at this property. There's a full business center on the premises. A year-round pool, a Jacuzzi and a fitness center will keep you in shape. You can also get a workout on the tennis and basketball courts. A large fireplace in the lobby provides a comfortable gathering center for guests. The Main Street Cafe on the property serves breakfast, lunch and dinner in a casual atmosphere. The hotel is about a mile from the city's center.

The Inn at Temple Square
$$ • 71 W. South Temple, Salt Lake City • 531-1000, (800) 843-4668

Graciously appointed with antique furnishings, this newly refurbished 90-room hotel, built in 1930, is reminiscent of an exclusive London inn. Across from Temple Square, the inn is owned by the Mormon church. No smoking is allowed. Guests may use the inn's library and relax in the sitting area with a good book. The Carriage Court Restaurant serves three meals a day except on Sunday when only brunch and dinner are available. No alcohol is served on the premises. Guests receive a free pass to the Metro Sports Club, a block away.

Little America Hotel and Towers
$$ • 500 S. Main St., Salt Lake City • 596-5966, (800) 453-9450

Little America is Salt Lake's top-drawer hotel. The 850 newly remodeled, elegantly appointed guest rooms offer a choice of garden rooms or high-rise suites in the 17-story tower. Tower suites have more than 600 square feet of space including sleeping and living area. A separate, mirrored dressing room opens into the imported-marble bathroom, complete with a step-down, oversize marble tub. The slightly smaller garden rooms feature sitting areas with either a balcony or patio and beautiful views of the gardens and fountain. The decor is French Provincial, and no two rooms are exactly alike. Care has been taken in the choice of colors and fabrics. The result is an elegant, comfortable ambiance.

The spacious lobby has a decidedly European atmosphere. Guests can relax in the sitting area near the massive fireplace or visit the gift shops in the central lobby. Before you leave the hotel, wander the halls off the main lobby and peek at the beautifully appointed meeting rooms. Even the powder rooms are worth a visit: They're posh.

The hotel's legendary Sunday brunch, offered in the ballroom, is expensive but an absolute must-do. The ballroom features massive crystal chandeliers and, when set up for brunch with its elegant chairs around tables with starched white linens, is very impressive. For more information on Sunday brunch see the listing in our Restaurants chapter. The dining room and coffee shop offer the same delicious food in individual servings. Little America has an outdoor pool in the garden area as well as an indoor/outdoor year-round pool on the second floor of the tower. The health club has a Jacuzzi, a sauna, a weight room, stationary bikes, treadmills and dressing rooms. The hotel's staff is friendly, very accommodating and highly professional.

Marriott Hotel
$$$ • 75 S. West Temple, Salt Lake City • 531-0800, (800) 345-4754

First rate! All 515 rooms and six suites are comfy and warmly decorated. This is a nice place for families, skiers and business travelers. The Marriott's premium fitness center has a larger weight room than those at most hotels. The fitness facility includes a whirlpool and indoor and outdoor pools.

The hotel is directly across the street from

Photo: Courtesy Marriott Hotels

Salt Lake City has many hotels to accommodate the needs of travelers.

the Salt Palace, the Salt Lake Art Center and Abravanel (Symphony) Hall to the west, and adjacent to Crossroads Mall. You can shop 'til you drop at Crossroads without ever going outside. Allie's Restaurant in the hotel serves traditional fare. Diners can order breakfast, lunch and dinner from the menu or select from the generous buffet. JW's Steakhouse offers formal dining in the evening. Pizza Hut items are available at the hotel for lunch and dinner. You can enjoy a cocktail or microbrew, as well as lunch or dinner, in Pitcher's, a private club on the premises. The Gourmet Bean Express Kiosk serves gourmet coffee and other light refreshment. The hotel's bustling staff is efficient and courteous.

Peery Hotel
$ • 110 W. 300 S. (Broadway), Salt Lake City • 521-4300, (800) 331-0073

The Peery is a little gem of a hotel built in 1910 by Joseph and David Peery. The city's oldest hospitality provider has 77 charming, attractively restored rooms and a large lobby, all nicely furnished with antique furniture and curiosa. The hotel offers a whirlpool and an exercise facility. Complimentary continental breakfast is served each morning, and room service is available. The Peery Wasatch Pub serves excellent food and brew (see our Restaurants chapter).

Quality Inn, City Center
$$ • 154 W. 600 S., Salt Lake City • 521-2930, (800) 521-9997

You'll enjoy simple, basic lodging at this Quality Inn, just off the freeway. The 311 comfortable rooms, including 64 brand-new ones, have coffeepots, electronic locks and limited cable TV. The guest rooms are on two floors and have interior or exterior entrances. Nearly half the older rooms have been remodeled. The inn includes an outdoor pool and a hot tub. The pool is closed in winter, but the hot tub is open all year. A weight room and laundry facilities are also available. Two restaurants on the property serve food all day. Sophie Garcia's is an Insiders' favorite for Mexican cuisine and is open for lunch and dinner. The 6th Street Diner serves American-style meals for breakfast, lunch and dinner. The Cantina is a private club where you can enjoy a glass of wine or a mixed drink.

Ramada Inn

$$ • 2455 S. State St., Salt Lake City • 486-2400, (800) 611-3400

Smack-dab in the center of the Salt Lake Valley, this new Ramada Inn has 131 rooms, mini- and full-suites. The casual, contemporary rooms are pleasant and get high marks for cleanliness. The hotel has an indoor pool, a Jacuzzi and a small fitness room and offers free HBO. No smoking is allowed in the suites and mini-suites. An expanded complimentary continental breakfast is served to guests daily. Comfy sofas and a 14-foot stone fireplace make the lobby a nice place for congenial conversation. You can get finger-lickin' good chicken at the KFC next door. The Village Inn Restaurant is within walking distance.

Salt Lake City Travelodge

$ • 524 S. West Temple, Salt Lake City • 531-7100, (800) 578-7878

The 60 standard rooms in this motel across from the elegant Little America pale by comparison, but if you are looking for inexpensive accommodations and don't mind the trés basic decor, this is your place. Some of the rooms have been remodeled, but this older property isn't rushing into a face-lift anytime soon. It has an outdoor pool and hot tub. You can eat breakfast, lunch and dinner at Little American or Embassy Suites or walk a block to the Hilton or Quality Inn. The property is very close to the freeway.

Salt Lake Hilton

$$$ • 150 W. 500 S., Salt Lake City • 532-3344

Guests find the Hilton dependable and comfortable. The 351 rooms here have undergone extensive renovation, as has the lobby. Everything is shipshape — a cut above nice — and the friendly service is a constant. The Room at the Top, a private club, has an extensive menu and libations and a great view of

the city. Annabel's is open for breakfast, lunch and dinner with a buffet and a complete menu. The gift shop is always a fun place to browse. Also on the property are several other shops and services, including a fine jeweler, a beauty salon, a Delta Airlines ticket counter, a business center, Ski Utah Inc. and Avis car rental. The fitness center has a licensed masseuse, an outdoor pool and an indoor Jacuzzi and sauna.

Shilo Inn

$$ • 206 S. West Temple, Salt Lake City • 521-9500, (800) 222-2244

Lit up with a red-neon ribbon outlining the exterior of the building, the Shilo is hard to miss after dark. The top floors of this 200-room, newly remodeled hotel offer a great view of the city or the surrounding mountains. All rooms have comfortable furnishings, microwave ovens, refrigerators and VCRs. The hotel provides an indoor pool, a whirlpool, a fitness center and laundry facilities for guests. Duke's Old Fashioned Steakhouse serves a big-affair complimentary breakfast and is open for lunch and dinner every day but Sunday. Duke's also has a bar, so you can wet your whistle. The Downtown Bakery Espresso is open every day for light meals. Both eateries are on the property.

University Park Hotel and Suites

$$ • 480 Wakara Way, Salt Lake City • 581-1000, (800) 637-4390

University Park is a handsome, starkly modern upscale high-rise with 220 rooms including 29 suites. Breakfast, lunch and dinner are served in the Porter House Grill, and lunch, dinner and spirits are available in the Nickelodeon, the hotel's private club. Guests can sun on the deck, work up a sweat in the fitness room or relax in the indoor pool and hot tub. The hotel also has a business center. The secure, quiet parklike setting is 3½ miles from the city's center.

Wyndham Hotel

$$$ • 215 W. South Temple, Salt Lake City • 531-7500, (800) 553-0075

We recently played musical hotels in the downtown area. The Doubletree became the Wyndham, and the Red Lion became the Doubletree. If you arrive at this address thinking you're going to stay at the Doubletree,

you aren't. Quality is still the name of the game at the Wyndham, and the friendly service gets top marks. This great location takes you just a few steps away from the thick of it, but it's still only a block from Temple Square, great restaurants and shopping. You're within walking distance to the symphony, opera, ballet and the Salt Lake Arts Center. The luxury rooms are spacious and nicely decorated. The City Creek Grill on the property serves three good meals a day.

Mid- and South Valley

Closer to the mountains and a better choice for travelers doing business in the midsection and south end of the Valley, this area is about 35 minutes from the airport and 30 minutes to the heart of downtown. For skiers bent on being the first to plow through the powder, staying here keeps you within 20 minutes of the white stuff. Area attractions are within five to 30 minutes. The area has plenty of restaurants, including some excellent kid-friendly establish-

ments, and shopping is plentiful in this neck of the woods.

Best Western Executive Inn
$$ • 280 W. 7200 S., Midvale • 566-4141; (800) 528-1234

The 92 rooms are pretty much industry-standard, but mini- and full suites are available if you need more space. Guests can use the Fountain of Youth Health and Athletic Club, about 3 miles away. The property includes an outdoor heated pool and a hot tub. The Midvale Mining Company Restaurant, about a block away, offers discounts to guests. Meals can be charged to guest rooms.

Best Western CottonTree Inn
$$ • 10695 S. Auto Mall Dr. (120 West), Sandy • 523-8484, (800) 528-1234

A new property with warmly hued, comfortable decor, the CottonTree has 115 rooms. An indoor pool and a hot tub with direct access to the deck are available to guests. Complimentary coffee and a continental breakfast are served daily in the lobby. All guest rooms come with a coffeepot. Guests can do their laundry without leaving the property and iron out the wrinkles in-room (each room is equipped with an iron). The inn has a fitness center where guests can get a good workout. Shoney's Family Restaurant and Village Inn Restaurant are nearby.

Comfort Inn, Sandy
$$ • 8955 S. 255 W., Sandy • 255-4919, (800) 228-5150

The nicely appointed lobby and 98 sleeping rooms here aren't as new as those in the inn's sister hotel, but they've been kept up well. A recent renovation put a fresh look on everything. Some king suites have microwaves and refrigerators. A TV/VCR with satellite reception is in every room. The property has an indoor pool and a hot tub. A complimentary continental breakfast is served daily. The hotel is within walking distance to several fast-food restaurants. Sandy's Station, a private club, is next door. Your room key gets you in, and they serve a nice dinner.

Courtyard by Marriott, Sandy
$$ • 10701 S. Holiday Park Dr. (160 W.), Sandy • 571-3600, (800) 321-2211

This newer facility is four stories high, typical of what you've come to expect from the chain that caters to business travelers. Some of the 124 courtyard rooms have balconies with mountain views. Each of the three suites has a Jacuzzi. Breakfast and dinner are served daily in the Courtyard restaurant, and complimentary coffee is available in the lobby all day. The fireplace conversation area in the lobby provides a pleasant place to chat. The hotel has an indoor pool, a Jacuzzi and a workout room.

Discovery Inn
$$ • 380 W. 7200 S. Midvale • 561-2256, (800) 380-1415

The Discovery Inn has been around for a while, but the current owners are constantly fuss-

FYI

Unless otherwise noted, the area code for all phone numbers listed in this guide is 801.

ing to make the property better. The coffee, served 24 hours a day in the lobby, is freshly ground. The 89 rooms are quite comfy. Nine mini-suites feature microwave ovens and refrigerators. One of the mini-suites has a fireplace. The inn has a hot tub and sauna and a seasonal swimming pool. At the nearby Midvale Mining Company Restaurant, which offers discounts on breakfast, guests can charge meals to their room. More than a half-dozen restaurants are within walking distance. The Utah Transit Authority (UTA) ski shuttle stops across the street. The hotel is exceptionally clean and service-minded, and the beds are great. Devices for the hearing impaired are available at the front desk.

Econo Lodge
$ • 12605 S. Minuteman Dr. (100 E.), Draper • 571-1122, (800) 553-2666

Offering the same amenities as its sister property in town, this newer 55-room Econo Lodge is the top of the line. Guadalahonkey's Mexican Restaurant is about 3½ blocks away (see our Restaurants chapter). Neil's Charcoal Broiler is about the same distance away.

Hampton Inn, Murray
$$ • 606 W. 4500 S., Murray • 293-1300, (800) HAMPTON

This new 65-room Hampton Inn is typical of the chain. You can enjoy the complimentary continental breakfast or hoof it to Denny's Restaurant two blocks away. Several other restaurants are also in the area. See our Restaurants chapter for local favorites. The hotel has an indoor pool, a hot tub and a whirlpool.

Hampton Inn, Sandy
$$ • 10690 S. Holiday Park Dr., Sandy • 571-0800, (800) HAMPTON

This is a nice 131-room Hampton with amenities you expect from this chain. Walk out

INSIDERS' TIP

The elevation of Salt Lake City is 4,300 feet, or 1,320 meters. When you consume alcohol at high altitudes, especially if you're coming from sea level, you can get tipsy very quickly.

the back door to Carvers Restaurant (see our Restaurants chapter) or out the front door to Shoney's Family Restaurant. The inn has an indoor pool and Jacuzzi and pay-per-view cable TV. Guests are invited to enjoy the complimentary continental-breakfast buffet served daily.

Homewood Suites Hotel
$$ • 844 E. North Union Ave., Midvale • 561-5999, (800) CALL-HOME

This new, 98-room, all-suite property offers fully equipped kitchens and a homey environment. The hotel also has an indoor pool, a hot tub and a workout room. All rooms have TV/VCRs. Complimentary continental breakfast and an evening social hour are provided seven days a week. The spacious lobby has a three-story stone fireplace. Chili's Southwest Grill is within walking distance. Extended-stay rates are available.

Quality Inn, Mid-valley
$$ • 4465 Century Dr. (4500 S. and I-15), Murray • 268-2533, (800) 268-5801

At this older, recently remodeled 132-room hotel, guests can play Frisbee or relax on the large grassy area adjacent to the rooms. The inn has a large indoor pool and a hot tub. Some rooms have microwave ovens and refrigerators. A complimentary breakfast is served daily. The hotel is close to restaurants and shopping.

Reston Hotel
$$ • 5335 College Dr., Murray • 264-1054, (800) 231-9710

With a face-lift to the lobby and the 98 rooms (two of them are Jacuzzi suites) in 1997, this property, built in 1985, is fit as a fiddle for the 21st century. New carpets, vanities and bathrooms allow fresh, comfortable accommodations at an affordable price. The lobby is a charmer, with loads of plants and an inviting color scheme of deep forest green, dusty rose and turquoise.

Gourmet coffee is served free in the lobby each morning. The hotel also has an indoor pool and Jacuzzi, room service, expanded cable TV and a very friendly staff. It's close to I-15 and I-215 and minutes away from most area shopping. The 53rd Street Cafe on the property is open for lunch and dinner. You'll find a variety of tasty sandwiches and meat-and-potato specialties, but the homemade soup, muffins and cookies are really noteworthy.

Sleep Inn, South Jordan
$$ • 10676 S. 300 W., South Jordan • 572-2020, (800) 753-3746

If you are familiar with the Sleep Inn chain, this is a cookie-cutter property. The 68 rooms don't offer a lot of embellishment on the standard bed-chair-lamp package, but they are comfortable and accommodating. The Sleep Inn is close to south Valley businesses. Guests receive a complimentary continental breakfast each morning and have use of an indoor pool and a hot tub.

Sleep Inn, West Valley
$$ • 3440 S. 2200 W., West Valley City • 975-1888, (800) 753-3746

This Choice Hotels International property is newer than its sister property in West Jordan and has put a slight spin on the predictable. The 74 rooms are standard enough but include TV/VCRs in the rooms and movies available for rent at the front desk. The property has an indoor hot tub but no pool. The lobby area is larger than most in this chain and has conversation areas on the main floor and in the balcony area that overlooks the main lobby. They serve a nice complimentary continental breakfast daily.

Airport

If you choose an airport accommodation, you can get to the city in 10 minutes and to the airport in three to five minutes. Mid- and south Valley businesses are a short 30- to 35-minute drive. The hotels in this area offer good dining, and several restaurant chains have set up shop nearby to accommodate you. For shopping, a more expanded dining selection and nightlife, you'll want to head for the city or mid- and south Valley. Most area sightseeing and attractions are within 10 to 30 minutes of the airport.

Airport Comfort Inn
$$ • 200 N. Admiral Byrd Rd. (5400 W.), Salt Lake City • 537-7444, (800) 228-5150

A cut above the standard Comfort Inn, this recently remodeled 156-room property has upgraded amenities including hair dryers and coffee makers in each room. The business-class floor is secured. This standout in the chain has higher-quality linens, more comfortable rooms and a tidier face than most. Service is very friendly. An outdoor pool and a spa are available. The Hotel Cafe Restaurant serves breakfast, lunch and dinner.

Airport Fairfield Inn by Marriott
$$ • 230 N. Admiral Byrd Rd., (5400 W.) • 355-3331, (800) 228-2800

The paint is barely dry on this 106-room property, ideal for business travelers. You'll find all the amenities you've come to know at Marriott's Fairfield Inns plus a few surprises. This property has a weight room, an indoor pool and hot tub and a guest laundry. In addition, Perkins Cafe and Bakery is on the property, a first for the Fairfield chain.

Salt Lake Airport Hilton
$$$ • 5151 Wiley Post Way, Salt Lake City • 539-1515, (800) 999-3736

A comfortable hotel near the airport, this 287-room Hilton is newly remodeled in a warm Southwestern theme. A game room, two swimming pools and two Jacuzzis, one inside and one out, will keep you busy when the business day is done. The large fireplace in the lobby is a great gathering spot. Grill 114 serves breakfast, lunch and dinner. Libations are available at the Club 114 bar.

Airport Quality Inn and Suites
$$ • 5575 W. Amelia Earhart Dr., Salt Lake City • 537-7020, (800) 522-5575

The hotel has 167 sleeping rooms and 22 newly upgraded suites. Nice touches include robes, triple sheeting and small kitchenettes. Amelia's Grill and Sitting Ducks, a sports bar, both serve food. Pizza Hut items are also available in the hotel. All rooms have Nintendo. The chic-eclectic style is unusual and quite pleasant. Metal-based chairs in the lobby have a fish-shape frame with comfy pillows and matching glass-topped tables. A local artist designed the unusual bar stools in Sitting Ducks. Hospitality is stressed in every aspect of the hotel's operation. The service is courteous, and the staff go out of their way to accommodate guests' needs.

Days Inn Airport
$ • 1900 W. North Temple, Salt Lake City • 539-8538, (800) 325-2525

For a no-frills good night's sleep within a budget, try the Days Inn Airport, which has 111 rooms in various stages of remodeling. The motel does not have a pool. You can have breakfast, lunch and dinner at nearby Denny's Restaurant.

Fairfield Inn North, Woods Cross
$$ • 2437 S. Wildcat Way, Woods Cross • 298-3900, (800) 228-2800

Built in the fall of 1995, this 80-room property is typical of the Fairfield chain and ideally suited to business travelers. The hotel has three floors of interior-door rooms, serves a free continental breakfast and allows free local phone calls. The breakfast room off the lobby serves free coffee 24 hours a day.

This Fairfield is 8 miles from downtown Salt Lake and 11 miles from the airport. You can grab a meal at the Village Inn, 450 E. 1100 N., North Salt Lake, 292-2922, or at Denny's Restaurant, 2481 S. 800 W., Woods Cross, 292-3177. If you're looking for upscale dining, this hotel is not too far from Christopher's Seafood and Steak House, 370 W. 500 S., Bountiful, 299-9544.

If you're headed north to Ogden or beyond, you can spend a cozy night at the Fairfield Inn, 1730 North Heritage Park, Layton, 444-1600. You'll find the same warm and cozy accommodations as at the North Salt Lake property, but this one has a meeting room.

Holiday Inn, Express
$$ • 2080 W. North Temple, Salt Lake City • 355-0088, (800) 465-4329

Recently taken over by the Holiday Inn, this 92-room property has been fully refurbished. Its Encore Restaurant serves three meals a day. The hotel has an outdoor pool, a Jacuzzi and a small weight room.

Radisson Hotel, Salt Lake City Airport
$$ • 2177 W. North Temple, Salt Lake City • 364-5800, (800) 333-3333

This hotel looked lonely and misplaced when it was built in 1987. The imposing stone building seemed to drop overnight into the middle of the highway that connects the airport to the city. It turned out to be good planning on someone's part. The Old World charm of this hotel is gracious. The Club Room serves a continental breakfast buffet, lunch and dinner. Guests can enjoy a complimentary cocktail at the manager's reception in the evening from 5 until 7 PM. Each of the 127 rooms has a wet bar and a mini-refrigerator. Fifteen rooms are loft suites, and six rooms have gas-log fireplaces. All are well-appointed. The Radisson provides a year-round pool, a hot tub and a fitness room.

Super 8 Motel, Salt Lake City Airport
$ • 223 N. Jimmy Doolittle Rd., Salt Lake City • 533-8878, (800) 800-8000

Close to restaurants at the Airport Hilton, Perkins Restaurant, and Amelia's and Sitting Ducks at the Quality Inn, this 75-room motel has a heated indoor pool, a spa and a fitness room. It serves a complimentary continental breakfast daily. This motel is 75 percent non-smoking.

Hostels and Residence Halls

Many travelers opt for the super savings of hostel-style lodging. Amenities are basic and often call for sharing space, but the extra cash can make it all worthwhile.

Ute Hostel
$ • 21 East Kelsey Ave., Salt Lake City • 595-1645

Close to downtown, this International Youth Hostel has doubles and dorm rooms for less than $20 a night. You get free tea and coffee, linens and a ride to the airport, Amtrak or Greyhound bus station. The hostel has kitchen facilities and offers cheap rates on bike, ski, skate and golf club rentals. The neighborhood is marginal, but the hostel has safe-deposit boxes for your valuables.

University of Utah Residence Halls
Van Cott Hall, University of Utah, Salt Lake City • 581-6611

The Residence Halls offer double and single dormitory-style rooms on a space-available basis for individuals visiting the city on university-related business.

The properties available on an extended-stay basis include apartments, condominiums and homes. Some are new and modern while others are quaint, restored older properties.

Vacation and Extended-stay Rentals

Some visitors stay in the Salt Lake area for longer than the average of three days. Many are here for extended stays — a week, a month, three months or more. Those who come for longer stays do so for many reasons.

Naturally, skiers are a big part of this business. They often like the comforts of an apartment, condo or private home and choose to stay in the Salt Lake Valley rather than in the mountains because the rates are generally lower here. Since the snow is only 20 to 30 minutes away, they can take in the mountains during the day and the city's restaurants, nightlife and the arts at night. It's the best of both worlds.

Business travelers also account for a large portion of extended-stay guests. Salt Lake's business community is growing by leaps and bounds. Many business travelers spend several weeks to several months in the Salt Lake area and choose extended-stay accommodations because they're more personal than hotels.

Extended-stay properties are also ideal for families relocating to the area. Some of the companies we've listed in this chapter can help you find housing near work or schools while you look for a permanent home.

For those with loved ones in the area's medical facilities, extended-stay properties can be an ideal temporary-housing solution. Salt Lake City has two level-1 trauma centers, LDS Hospital and University of Utah Medical Center, in addition to Primary Children's Medical Center with its highly regarded Intermountain Burn Unit facility. Patients at any one of these facilities could be hospitalized for weeks or months.

Several of our other chapters might be of interest to extended-stay visitors. Getting Here, Getting Around will help you maneuver about the city. If you're interested in renting permanently or buying a home, our Neighborhoods and Real Estate chapter will give you the lowdown on communities in the Salt Lake Valley and how much you can expect to pay for your dream home. If you have some time on your hands, peruse our Sightseeing and Attractions chapter for things to do. For dining options and shopping needs, turn to our Restaurants and Shopping chapters. If you are visiting Salt Lake because a loved one is ill or in the hospital, you may find our Healthcare chapter quite informative. Skiers won't want to miss the details we've provided about our winter wonderland in the Skiing and Winter Sports chapter.

The listings in this section include companies that specialize in extended-stay properties. Some companies rent their own properties exclusively and handle not only reservations but also the details, such as buying furniture and making sure linens get changed. Other companies also book properties for private owners. The latter don't usually get involved with the furniture, pots and pans or linens, but they can provide details about the property and take your reservation. Some companies don't own anything. They just book properties for owners who don't have the time or inclination or don't live in the area. Still other agencies manage properties and see to the upkeep. Services vary from company to company, so be sure to find out what you'll be responsible for when you make reservations.

When a listing includes "owner/broker" after the name, it means that one or more of the properties the company manages belongs to them, and besides managing properties — their own and others — they also sell real estate. These agencies are required to indicate that they are a broker of real estate.

The properties available on an extended-stay basis include apartments, condominiums and homes. Some are new and modern while others are quaint, restored older properties. Whatever your needs and preferences, these companies can make your extended stay in Salt Lake City a pleasant one.

Rates vary from approximately $60 per night in the summer and $90 in the winter to $500 per night in summer and winter. Besides the rental fee, some companies charge a cleaning fee. It is fairly easy to book extended-stay accommodations for the summer months, but for winter stays you'll want to book well in advance. Calling in July for reservations for January is not unrealistic.

Children are welcome at most properties, but pets are not always considered ideal guests. Some properties allow smoking while others do not. Unless otherwise indicated, the properties here are wheelchair-accessible, but the extent to which they are accessible may vary. You'll want to check with the agent about these issues when you make reservations. Amenities generally include the basics such as fully equipped kitchens, linens and TV.

A. Ski Adventures
P.O. Box 711088, Salt Lake City, Utah 84171 • 944-4501, (800) 576-0004

This company books accommodations in apartments, condominiums and homes in town and near the ski-resort areas. The properties are

FYI

Unless otherwise noted, the area code for all phone numbers listed in this guide is 801.

of good quality with full amenities, and the rates are reasonable.

Alpine Cottages
164 S. 900 E., Salt Lake City • 533-8184, (800) 733-8184

Alpine Cottages, which is owned and operated by Saltair Bed and Breakfast, consists of three extended-stay units in an older, restored 19th-century home with antique furnishings, fireplaces and a sun deck. Modern conveniences include fully equipped kitchens, cable television, phones and an outdoor hot tub. The hosts offer continental breakfast.

Alpine Executive Suites
164 S. 900 E., Salt Lake City • 533-8184, (800) 733-8184

Also owned and operated by Saltair Bed and Breakfast, these four extended-stay units in a charming older home are equipped with kitchens, furnishings, cable TV and a phone. Off-street parking is available.

Accommodations for Skiers
8016 S. Sunnyoak Cir. , Salt Lake City • 973-2426

Tom and Nancy Kronthaler, skiers themselves, have been accommodating vacationing skiers for many years. One of the few ski-lodging companies that owns and manages its own properties, they offer fully furnished townhouses, from one bedroom to five, located a short distance from all area ski resorts. Packages are available for two to 14 people.

Advantage Accommodations
9013 Huckleberry Court, Sandy • (800) 246-2992

Advantage Accommodations rents well-equipped, fully furnished homes that are clean, modern and well-appointed. Each has a private spa.

Apartment & Condominium Rentals of Salt Lake City
P.O. Box 17294, Salt Lake City, Utah 84117-0294 • 272-0066

The experienced personnel at this com-

Photo: Alan Yorgason

Nestled at the foot of the Wasatch Mountains, Salt Lake City
is a sophisticated and diverse community.

pany can book fully equipped and furnished homes and condominiums for extended-stay visitors in several locations throughout the Valley.

Broadway Tower Executive Suites
230 E. Broadway, Salt Lake City • 534-1222, (888) 801-3572

This 96-room luxury highrise provides excellent accommodations at affordable prices. Suites have all the comforts of home plus maid service, covered parking, exercise facilities and a conference room.

Cottonwood Ski Lodging
3444 Regalia Rd., Salt Lake City • 942-5044, (800) 574-5044

Cottonwood provides accommodations for families and shared housing for ski vacationers.

John Collins, Owner/Broker
P.O. Box 219, Sandy, Utah 84091-0219 • 571-0691

Large, newer, fully furnished three- to six-bedroom homes with full amenities are available through this company. These accommodations are ideal for ski groups and summer vacationers.

The Kimball
150 N. Main St., Salt Lake City • 363-4000

What Kimball offers is, in a word, elegance. The Kimball has fully equipped and furnished studio and one- and two-bedroom units and an ambitious staff to see to your needs during your stay. In an older apartment building near Temple Square, The Kimball has undergone a recent renovation, creating some exquisitely appointed rooms.

Weekly rental rates and timeshare sales are available.

Luxury Ski Accommodations
3588 E. 7800 S., Sandy • 943-0806, (800) 472-4801

All properties are within walking distance to grocery shopping and bus transportation. Three- to seven-bedroom, fully furnished accommodations include wood-burning fireplaces, saunas, private hot tubs, a washer and dryer, microwaves, a TV/VCR with cable and two-car garages. Luxury Ski Accommodations also handles motor-home rentals.

Parkway Suites
3580 W. Parkway Blvd. (2700 S.), West Valley City • 977-0800

Parkway Suites is an extended-stay hotel with fully furnished 800-square-foot rooms with full kitchens. The hotel provides free continental breakfast, an exercise room and laundry facilities and is within walking distance of restaurants and shopping.

Powder Beach Realty
3690 E. Fort Union Blvd., Salt Lake City • 944-9444, (888) 944-9555

Powder Beach Realty rents fully furnished and equipped homes, condominiums, apartments and cabins.

Queen Anne Suites
866 E. South Temple, Salt Lake City • 533-8184, (800) 733-8184

The Queen Anne is a charming remodeled Victorian home with four fully furnished, fully equipped suites each with a TV and phone. You will be close to area hospitals,

---

INSIDERS' TIP

Discount ski-lift tickets are available at most major grocery stores such as Albertson's, Dan's, Harmons and Smith's. You can save a few bucks by buying lift tickets before you get to the resort areas. Ask your accommodations booking company or call the grocery stores directly.

downtown businesses, restaurants, shopping and the arts.

Resort Rentals of Utah
5300 S. 900 E., Salt Lake City • 261-4844, (800) 888-9875

Lodging or complete packages are available in fully furnished suites, condominiums and homes with all amenities. Resort Rentals can arrange ski packages for large groups.

Sugarhouse Village
2012 S. View St., Salt Lake City • 486-9976, (888) 577-8483

Eleven large furnished suites with kitch-

enettes, TV with HBO and complimentary breakfast are available at this centrally located property.

Wasatch Front Ski Accommodations
2020 E. 3300 S., Salt Lake City • 486-4296, (800) 762-7606

This company manages more than 100 rental properties with accommodations available on a nightly, weekly or monthly basis. The company is a subsidiary of Young & Company Real Estate.

There are only three RV parks in the Salt Lake Valley, but together these three parks offer 800 sites, probably enough to get you through the night — and a few extra days if you fall in love with our city.

Campgrounds and RV Parks

If you don't want to stay in a hotel, inn or bed and breakfast, if you like to travel with too many personal belongings to cram into a suitcase, if you like to cook your own meals in your own pots and pans, you probably think the RV experience is heaven-sent. Pets can tag along on the family vacation, and kids often feel more comfortable when their stuff has its own special place. For those who like to wander the countryside without a schedule or map, RV parks are great places to end up, as they can usually be booked on short notice.

There are only three RV parks in the Salt Lake Valley, but together these three parks offer 800 sites, probably enough to get you through the night — and a few extra days if you fall in love with our city. If you're planning to head out to the high country, check out our Parks and Recreation chapter for camping information in the nearby mountains. Are you headed south? Pick up a copy of *Insiders' Guide® to Southwestern Utah* for camping information in Utah's desert and canyon lands.

Camp VIP
1400 W. North Temple, Salt Lake City
• 328-0224, (800) 226-7752

Open year round, this RV park has a lot to offer with 436 sites, most with full hookups including 50-amp power, water and sewer. Some sites have live phone lines for local calls. You'll find a variety of amenities including a heated spa, outdoor adult and kiddie pools, an RV and car wash, laundry facilities, showers, a video arcade, propane, groceries and camping supplies and a business center with a fax, a copy machine and modems. Daily rates for two people during the summer are $23.95 for power and water, $25.95 for a full hookup and $28.95 for a full hookup plus a phone line. Add $2 for each additional person. Winter rates may be higher, but generally not more than $1 or $2. The park also has 40 tent sites that rent for $18.95 per day. Most campsites are in the shade. Discounts are available.

Located 14 blocks from the heart of downtown, Camp VIP isn't in the nicest part of town, but if you want to be in the center of things, this is the place to park your RV.

Lagoon's Pioneer Village RV Park Campground
375 N. Lagoon Dr., Salt Lake City
• 451-8100, (800) 748-5246, Ext. 3100

Lagoon's is 17 miles from the city's center, next to Lagoon A Beach and Amusement Park. Basic hookup, water and electricity or full hookups are available at the 210 sites. The park has three bathrooms with showers and a general store. Mature shade trees keep the area cool in summer, and tent camping is available on the property. The park is within walking distance of the amusement park.

Daily rates for two people with one vehicle are $16 for a basic hookup, $17.50 with electricity, $18.50 for electricity and water and $19.50 for a full hookup. There's no additional charge for children younger than 4, but the charge for each additional person more than 4 years old is $1.25. The fee for additional vehicles is $1.25 per day each.

Park discounts on all-day passports are available to RV park and campground guests. For information on Lagoon A Beach and Pioneer Village, see our Sightseeing and Attractions chapter. Need something special for the kids? Lagoon A Beach and Pioneer Village can fit the bill with many park attractions designed just for little ones. Check them out in our Kidstuff chapter.

The campground is open midspring to midfall, weather permitting. If you're calling from mid- or south Valley use the toll-free number.

FYI
Unless otherwise noted, the area code for all phone numbers listed in this guide is 801.

Mountain Shadows RV Park
13275 S. Minuteman Dr., (100 E.), Draper
• 571-4024

True to its name, this park lies in the shadow of the mountains, 20 miles from the heart of downtown. The view is beautiful and the ambiance serene. The park offers 133 sites with electric and water hookups and many amenities including a pool, hot tub, and basketball court. If you want to relax outside the hubbub of the city, this park is for you.

Laundry facilities are available 24 hours a day. Pets must be on a leash when outside the vehicle. Children must be quiet at all times.

Year-round rates are $21.50 for electricity and water and $23.50 for a full hookup. The park has tent camping at $17.50 per night. Rates include a tow vehicle. Discounts are available.

Mountain Resorts

We don't save our mountain areas just for winter fun. Insiders enjoy Alta, Snowbird and Brighton just as well during the summer months. Alta is situated at the upper end of Little Cottonwood Canyon. The area is laid-back in summer and offers extraordinary skiing in winter. Snowbird is approximately 2 miles west of Alta in Little Cottonwood Canyon and is one of the country's foremost ski areas. The sophisticated resort setting really has a top-drawer feel. Brighton is in Big Cottonwood Canyon. The area was once a summer retreat for wealthy Salt Lakers.

The accommodations in this chapter offer limited wheelchair accessibility, but the resorts will go out of their way to assist individuals with special needs. Please discuss any requirements and special needs when asking about the properties or making reservations.

Price Code

Each listing includes a symbol showing a price range for single occupancy for a one-night stay. Resorts generally charge per person rather than offer a double occupancy rate during the ski season. Peak season is approximately December 20 to January 1 and President's Day weekend in February. The ski season varies each year according to snow conditions. It begins when the lifts open and ends when the lifts close — more or less from Thanksgiving to mid-April.

Because of the variety of accommodations available at each of these locations — everything from dorms to luxury king-size rooms — we have included an average rate during the ski season. You can expect to pay approximately $50 less during the summer at the pricey resorts and less than half at the other resorts that offer accommodations in the summer.

Pricing information is offered as a general guideline. Unless otherwise noted all hotels accept major credit cards.

$	Less than $150
$$	$151 to $275
$$$	$276 to $525
$$$$	More than $525

To get to these resorts, take Interstate 215 south to the 6200 South Exit and turn toward the mountain. To get to Big Cottonwood Canyon, turn left at the 7-Eleven. Go straight ahead at the 7-Eleven to get to Little Cottonwood Canyon.

Check out our Parks and Recreation chapter for more about the summer activities in the mountain resorts. If skiing is your pleasure, look for details in our Skiing and Winter Sports chapter. Park City skiing is covered in the Skiing and Winter Sports chapter, but you'll find summer and winter fun, restaurants, shopping and more in a special chapter on Park City.

Alta

Alta Lodge
**$$ • Little Cottonwood Canyon, Alta
• 322-4631, (800) 707-ALTA**

Wall-size windows provide unbelievable

mountain views in most of the 40 rooms at the Alta Lodge, built in the late '30s by the Denver & Rio Grande Railroad. Corner rooms have two walls of glass, wood burning fireplaces and balconies. Two-bedroom luxury condos are nearby. Summer and winter accommodations are available at this lodge. The food at the Alta Lodge enjoys its own superb reputation. The summer dining room draws Insiders and tourists for romantic dinners or a pleasant repast after a day of hiking or biking. The baked goods here are all too tempting and include a famous rich dark chocolate soufflé with brandied whipped cream. The lodge also serves Sunday brunch.

Alta Peruvian Lodge
$$ • Little Cottonwood Canyon, Alta
• 328-8589, (800) 453-8488

This veteran ski lodge has provided more than 45 years of unsurpassed hospitality. Lodge accommodations vary from dormitories to spacious two-bedroom suites and fit into every budget. Amenities include a heated outdoor swimming pool, heated outdoor therapy pool, indoor sauna, self-service laundry, a best-seller library, nightly movies, 24-hour coffee and tea in the lobby and up-to-date weather reports. Winter rates include daily meals and a lift pass.

Shuttle service is available to Alta's base areas and Snowbird. A delicious complimentary breakfast buffet begins the day for skiers. The lodge dining room serves breakfast and dinner during the ski season and Sunday brunch year round. The Peruvian is 40 minutes from Salt Lake International Airport.

Rustler Lodge
$$ • Little Cottonwood Canyon, Alta
• (801) 733-0190, (800) 451-5223

The lodge offers an elegant yet conge-

FYI

Unless otherwise noted, the area code for all phone numbers listed in this guide is 801.

nial atmosphere for summer and winter guests with skiing right outside the front door. The rooms, including 30 that are new, are comfortably appointed and include men's dorms, small rooms with single beds and a basin, queen and single bed accommodations with private showers and large deluxe rooms with full baths and TV. Guests can watch TV or movies in the gathering area or enjoy the outdoor heated pool. A sauna and Jacuzzi are also available. Extraordinary cuisine is available in the dining room.

Room rates include breakfast and dinner but you are on your own for lunch. The dining room is open to the public for breakfast and lunch, and dinner by reservation only. Shuttle service is available to Snowbird, and a full-service ski shop is on the premises. The lodge is not open during the summer.

Snow Pine Lodge
$ • Little Cottonwood Canyon, Alta
• (801) 742-2000

This small, charming family-run lodge was recently renovated but has been providing accommodations for skiers since 1938. The Western atmosphere is carried throughout the guest areas that include single, queen- and king-size beds and offer full private and shared baths. Dorm rooms are also available. Breakfast and dinner are served in the dining room and are included in the cost of lodging. The cuisine is simple yet quite impressive. The dining room is also open to the public for dinner with reservations. Cocktails are served and the four course fare changes daily. Shuttle service is provided to Snowbird resort. The lodge is open during the winter only. This is a non-smoking facility.

INSIDERS' TIP

Check out Shallow Shaft Restaurant across the road from Alta Lodge, (801) 742-2177, an Insiders favorite eating spot. *Zagat's* has voted their Southwest cuisine the best in the state.

Snowbird

The Lodge at Snowbird,
Inn at Snowbird and
Iron Blossam Lodge Snowbird
**$$$$ • Utah Hwy. 210 • (801) 742-2222,
(800) 453-3000 Snowbird central
reservations**

Sitting side by side in the center of the Snowbird Village, these three complexes offer summer and winter rentals including fully furnished, fully equipped studio, efficiency, one- and two-bedroom condos with extra sleeping room provided in lofts and on sofa beds.

The Cliff Lodge
$$$$ • Little Cottonwood Canyon Rd., Snowbird • 521-6040, (800) 453-3000

OK, they have sleeping rooms, 532 of them, all with a spectacular view. They have food, lots of it, every bite healthy and delicious. But the spa is the thing. Sitting at the top of this 12-story lodge is the 28,000-square-foot Cliff Spa. This is one gracious resort combined with a premier health spa facility. The delicious treatments include everything from therapeutic and shiatsu massage to balneotherapy, salt glows and detoxifying herbal wraps. The spa offers a full-service beauty and skin-care center. Swimming in the rooftop pool, yoga classes and aerobic workouts are available. You can choose one treatment or the works.

Brighton

Silver Fork Lodge Bed & Breakfast
$ • Big Cottonwood Canyon Hwy., Star Rt., Brighton • 533-9977

Eleven miles up Big Cottonwood Canyon, the Silver Fork Lodge is 30 miles from the Salt Lake International Airport, 1 mile below Solitude and 3 miles below Brighton. Julie and Dan Knopp purchased this old bed and breakfast in 1993 and began serious renovation on the well-worn mountain lodge, appreciated by Insiders since 1943. The Silver Fork goes back to the old mining days, about 1856, when its western corner was a small country store.

The rustic lodge features a family room, sauna, satellite TV and a large deck with extraordinary views of Honeycomb Canyon and the Solitude Ski Resort. Seven guest rooms have everything from bunk to king-size beds with private baths. A full breakfast is included. The lodge is open to the public for breakfast, lunch and dinner. In keeping with the mining tradition, they serve sourdough pancakes from a 50-year-old start. Summer or winter, this is a great place to relax and unwind.

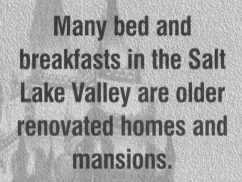

Many bed and breakfasts in the Salt Lake Valley are older renovated homes and mansions.

Bed & Breakfasts and Inns

Not all bed and breakfasts are created equal. Some are traditional, providing sleeping rooms, a gathering place and a continental or full breakfast, with additional amenities such as television. Others take it further and offer expanded services that can include catered luncheons and dinners. All bed and breakfast properties and inns in the Salt Lake Valley are subject to inspection by the Department of Health. Rest assured that if you choose to stay in an inn or a bed and breakfast here, even if it's in someone's home, you won't be sleeping with the family cat.

So what's the difference between a bed and breakfast and an inn in the Salt Lake Valley? Not too much. A bed and breakfast offers private sleeping rooms and a common room, and all serve complimentary breakfasts to their guests. These amenities are standard. Some bed and breakfasts offer extras such as afternoon snacks, wine and hors d'oeuvres in the evening, film and reading libraries and so forth. A few bed and breakfasts have televisions and VCRs in the sleeping rooms, but most don't (in our listings, we indicate the ones that do). An inn, on the other hand, is a small hotel that usually offers many of the same services as a bed and breakfast, including a complimentary breakfast, but has more than 11 rooms. Many inns have restaurants on the properties. Of course, the distinction is not always reflected correctly in the name. We've used them interchangably in the write-ups.

Bed and breakfasts and inns attract a variety of guests. They are wonderful for honeymooners as well as young and not-so-young lovers who want to rekindle the spark of romance. Business travelers find them to be a great alternative to hotel accommodations. Professionals say they are often more productive in a homey environment, and women traveling alone enjoy the safety created by an inn's intimate surroundings. Many bed and breakfasts in Salt Lake offer special accommodations for business travelers such as multi-line telephones in the rooms, fax machines, one-day dry-cleaning service and meeting rooms. Inquire with the innkeeper if you will require these services during your stay.

Many inns and bed and breakfasts in the Salt Lake Valley are older renovated homes and mansions. Because many older buildings have sleeping rooms on the second and third floors, not all are wheelchair-accessible. Ask about wheelchair accessibility and other special needs when making reservations. As dictated by the Utah Indoor Clean Air Act, smoking is prohibited in all bed and breakfasts, although most innkeepers allow guests to smoke outside in specified area.

Pets are generally not welcome guests, and children are not always encouraged because many bed and breakfast don't have places for them to play. Some innkeepers have concerns about the safety of antique furnishings when kids are being kids. In addition, sometimes room occupancy restrictions apply to bed and breakfasts. If the property is a converted older home with small sleeping rooms, the number of people occupying the room may be limited to two. If you are traveling with children and wish to stay at a bed and breakfast in the area, it's best to ask the innkeeper about kids when you make your reservation. We have noted the bed and breakfasts with kid-friendly policies. If one of the bed-

and-breakfast write-ups looks appealing but doesn't specifically say that it is kid-friendly, ask the innkeeper. The age of the children and the number of people in your party may make a difference.

Some travelers who have experienced bed and breakfasts in other parts of the country have complained about the plumbing in older, restored properties. We can't offer any guarantees but we did check out the facilities listed here. Everything seems to flush as it should and there was plenty of water pressure. In some older properties it took the hot water a few minutes to get to the third floor.

The bed and breakfast and inn experience may not be for everyone. For those who enjoy a homelike ambiance and the company of other travelers in a unique setting, this might be the perfect accommodation for you.

FYI

Unless otherwise noted, the area code for all phone numbers listed in this guide is 801.

Price Code

We've provided a dollar-sign code for each accommodation denoting the rate for a one-night double-occupancy stay during the peak winter season. The code is intended as a general guideline based on rates provided by the establishments.

$	Less than $75
$$	$76 to $125
$$$	$126 to $175
$$$$	$176 to $225

Different rooms at the same facility can often vary widely in price. Larger rooms cost more, as do rooms with a private bath. Our pricings reflect the entire range. Some properties offer corporate rates, and others offer packages during the ski season. Unless otherwise noted, all bed and breakfasts and inns in this chapter accept major credit cards.

Perhaps a railroad car is more to your liking. Does a Jacuzzi in a mountain waterfall or sea cave tickle your fancy? If so, you might enjoy one of the 45 theme rooms at the Anniversary Inn's two locations. Snooze in a lush outdoor garden with faux rock walls, climbing vines and vibrant plastic flowers in Victoria's Garden Suite. Hula your head off amid tropical fish and slumber in a cozy grass hut in the romantic South Pacific Suite.

Owners Tom and Dorothy Heers and Bill and Karen Heers dreamed of providing fun and romantic getaway accommodations for couples, a place to rediscover the magic. Thirteen of the rooms are found at the South Temple property, a restored 1895 mansion. The rooms here are tamer than those at the 10th East location. In the Napoleon Room, the namesake's portrait pulls open like a cupboard door to reveal a big-screen TV. They also have a lighthouse room and a room with a bed in a stage coach at this location. You can enjoy the remainder of the rooms at the old Salt City Jail building on 10th East, which was constructed in the late 1800s. Here you can lie back in a round bed inside a mock lighthouse. Overhead, a school of fish swims in an aquarium. You can sleep in a carriage or drift off in a gondola. Get the picture?

All rooms at both locations have private baths and come with in-room stereo, free laserdisc movies and large-screen TV. Complimentary snacks and a continental breakfast are served in the room. No more than two people may occupy a room. Costumes are at the discretion of the guests. The Old Salt City Jail Restaurant at the 10th East property is open for dinner (see our Restaurants chapter). Both locations are close to downtown dining, shopping and nightlife in case you develop a fantasy overload.

Both properties are listed on the National Register of Historic Places.

The Anniversary Inn
$$-$$$$ • 460 S. 1000 E., Salt Lake City • 363-4900, (800) 324-4152
$$-$$$$ • 678 E. South Temple, Salt Lake City • 363-4900, (800) 324-4152

What would it be like to sleep in a tree?

Anton Boxrud Bed & Breakfast
$-$$$ • 57 S. 600 E., Salt Lake City • 363-8035, (800) 524-5511

The second- and third-floor bedrooms are the best part of this charming Victorian bed and breakfast, which was a residence for Anton Boxrud and his wife who immigrated from Norway to Salt Lake City in 1901 and opened a shop that specialized in men's shirts and ladies dresses. Rich polished wood, leaded windows, hand-woven lace and fine linens create a yesteryear setting. The distinctive beds and down comforters are cozy and inviting. Fresh flowers and signature chocolates add a pleasant touch to every room. Specify private or shared bath when you call to make your reservation.

Grandma Gladys's freshly baked cinnamon buns, served at breakfast in the "My Fair Lady" dining room along with stuffed French toast, are another enjoyable aspect of the Anton Boxrud. Freshly ground coffee presented in Bavarian china cups accompanies the baked goods. Guests can socialize in the parlor or formal dining room in the evening and enjoy complimentary snacks and drinks including wine. The pillared front porch is a great place to take in the city on a summer evening or watch the snow fall in winter. The outdoor hot tub lets you unwind after a busy day. City nightlife and restaurants are within walking distance. The Anton Boxrud will arrange luncheons and meals for small gatherings.

The home is listed on the National Register of Historic Places.

The Armstrong Mansion Historic Bed and Breakfast
$$-$$$$ • 667 E. 100 S., Salt Lake City • 531-1333, (800) 708-1333

Former Salt Lake mayor Francis Armstrong built this house in 1893 to fulfill a wedding-day promise to his wife, Isabel. They held many a gala party in this Queen Anne-style Victorian mansion. Fourteen beautifully restored rooms are rich with antique furnishing and curiosa. The building also boasts stained-glass windows, an intricate hand-carved oak staircase

and ornate oak woodwork. The stenciling in the rooms and the carpeting in the parlor and dining room are reproductions of the original patterns found in Mrs. Armstrong's home. The fireplaces in the bedroom and gathering rooms are beautiful, but they are just for show. All rooms have private baths, and all but three have Jacuzzi tubs.

February Interlude, also known as the honeymoon suite, has a spiral staircase leading up into the mansion's corner turret, where the suite's hot tub awaits. The Armstrong serves a full breakfast.

Brigham Street Inn
$$-$$$$ • 1135 E. South Temple, Salt Lake City • 364-4461, (800) 417-4461

When John Pace, a local architect, and his wife, Nancy, purchased this Victorian mansion in 1981, it was in serious disrepair. Built in 1898, the house served as a family residence until 1944. For the next 40 years, several owners operated various businesses here, including a boarding house and an alcoholic rehabilitation center. The 12 designers who worked on the restoration project kept a respectful eye on the design of the original structure. The bird's-eye maple fireplace in the parlor and many doors and windows are original to the home.

Several of the architectural features had a close call prior to the refurbishing. Before the Paces bought the property, a real-estate agent found one of the bedroom's mantels and some doors stacked by the house's back entry. Concerned for their safety, she placed them in a bank vault until the fate of the building was known. Two weeks before the inn opened, they were brought in from the bank and put in place. Almost immediately the mantel and some beveled-glass windows were stolen. The owners scoured the city for a week until they found the items in a local antique store. They had changed hands at

---

INSIDERS' TIP

Bed and breakfast guests can order in from Metro Gourmet Express, 288-4100. Lunch is available from 10 AM to 2 PM weekdays only, and dinner can be ordered from 4:30 to 10 PM. They deliver food from more than 30 Salt Lake restaurants for a small service fee added to the price of the meal.

least four times during the week. The thief is still at large.

Each of the eight distinctly decorated guest rooms has a private bath, and five rooms have fireplaces. The furnishings are elegant yet comfortable. All rooms have cable TV. An impressive grand piano sits in the parlor where local pianists come to play in the evening. The dining room, which features lots of golden oak on the walls, around the windows and in the fireplace mantel, holds a large table for the breakfast buffet. Off-street parking is available. Children are welcome. A 12-block walk puts you in the center of downtown. The home is listed on the National Register of Historic Places.

Castle Creek Inn

$$-$$$$ • 7391 S. Creek Rd. (1300 East), Sandy • 567-9437, (800) 571-2669

The exterior of this lovely inn was completed about 20 years ago. The structure was intended to be a luxury home, but the owner ran out of money before work began on the interior. The house became a local curiosity as it sat vacant for many years. Lynn and Sallie Calder bought the property in 1996 and immediately designed and finished an interior that matched the exterior's grandeur. The 10 suites have a decidedly Scottish feel. Amenities include private baths, fireplaces, telephones, jetted tubs, big-screen TVs with cable and VCRs.

Guests enjoy afternoon tea with fresh-baked pastries upon arrival at this Medieval-style bed and breakfast. A full, complimentary gourmet breakfast, served daily, includes sourdough waffles, quiche, Italian frittatas, stuffed blueberry French toast and white-chocolate cranberry scones.

Grandmother's House Bed and Breakfast

$-$$$ • 6400 S. Holladay Blvd., Salt Lake City • 943-0909, (800) 493-5037

Over the creek and through the woods to this homey bed and breakfast we'll go! A few words about getting to Grandmother's: After crossing the intersection of 6200 South and Holladay Boulevard going south, a large dead-end sign stands as a warning, and you cannot see a thing down the road. Keep going. This is the way to Grandmother's — down a gravel road and across Big Cottonwood Creek on a sturdy metal bridge. Signs are posted along the way.

The gathering area has a TV with VCR, or guests can borrow a book from the family's bookshelf and settle in for a good read. The Sims family, which owns the inn, has a large selection of LDS books and a selection of novels. Grandma and Grandpa, Rowell and Carolyn Sims, raised six children in this home nestled on a large secluded lot in the Holladay/Cottonwood area. When their nest was empty, the Sims converted the family home to a bed and breakfast. They live on the property in a separate part of the home.

This home is as typical a family home in Salt Lake as you'll find. The five guest rooms are pleasant, and each has a distinctive, cozy decor. Three rooms are in the basement. Most have private baths. The furniture doesn't pretend to be anything but comfortable. The beds are quilt-covered, and the little touches are genuine and very grandmotherly. Mature shade trees and pleasant gardens, as well as two patios and a hot tub, grace the grounds. The chicken coup is home to several friendly chickens who provide eggs for breakfast — but will not personally show up in any breakfast entree. A rushing creek provides a soothing background.

The food at Grandmother's House is homestyle and good. Complimentary hot breakfasts include fruit, quiche, German pancakes or strata, bread, cereal and beverages. Veggies or home-baked treats are the afternoon snack. Grandmother's is near two excellent restaurants: The Tuscany (see our Restaurants chapter), which is worth getting gussied up for, but they'll let you in if you go in jeans, and The Cotton Bottom Inn (see our Nightlife chapter), which serves a world-famous garlic burger .

Visiting Grandmother's is like visiting your own grandmother, but you don't have to do the dishes after breakfast. The Sims are a delightful couple. If you feel comfortable in a family environment, you'll enjoy Grandmother's House. Children are welcome.

Saltair Resort: The Grand Lady of the Lake

If you had known this grand resort on the shores of the Great Salt Lake firsthand, or, as some of us did, by our mothers' stories of giggling young women in summer frocks and proper suitors on breezy, star-speckled nights, you would have loved it, too.

Saltair Resort opened in 1893, billed as the Coney Island of the West, where families could enjoy wholesome frolic in the strangely salty water that many considered the eighth wonder of the world. On completion, the pavilion's wings stretched in a crescent shape into the lake, spanning 1,100 feet from end to end. The top of the dome-shaped structure was 100 feet high at the center. Smaller six-sided domes stood at each corner of the massive structure, and beyond that, onion-shaped domes topped double- and triple-story arches wrapped in ornate trellises. A huge central archway welcomed guests inside the pavilion. At night, thousands of small lights outlining the structure created an exciting presence.

More than 100,000 eager visitors flocked to Saltair during its first season. Over the next 25 years attendance reached 450,000 each summer. Guests arrived by train in open cars from Salt Lake City to bob and float in the salty water, ride the Giant Racer roller coaster and dance the maxie, tango and hesitation waltz on the largest dance floor in the world. All was well on the shore of the Great Salt Lake.

Then fire broke out under the grandstand seats of the Hippodrome in 1925 just before the resort was to open for the season. The inferno left most of the resort in ashes

— continued on next page

Photo: Saltair Centennial Station

Bathers at the turn of the century enjoy the briny waters of the Great Salt Lake as the magnificent Saltair Pavilion looms in the background.

— the Giant Racer, merry-go-round, pilings and bathing pier were all that remained. Makeshift repairs were made to open for business that year, but less than one-third of the estimated $500,000 in damages was covered by insurance. Cosmetics covered many charred sections like too much face powder on a toppled society matron. The season faired well enough, and the following year the magnificent resort rallied back to life with bright, new colored trims, pink-orange on its stucco exterior and many new attractions and activities. Prices increased, and the Great Depression approached, but crowds came and bobbed, played and danced once again.

In the mid-'30s Saltair began to import talent from the East — the likes of Eddy Duchin, Xavier Cugat and Harry Owens and his Royal Hawaiians — for longer engagements, and the resort hit its stride over the next decade. Guests now arrived by automobile rather than by train. Artie Shaw took an engagement at the resort. Sodas were 5¢, and beer and sandwiches cost a dime.

But not all was as wonderful as it seemed. Strong winds and salt spray ate away at the resort's paint and wood, and fire again swept through the resort, lashing out at the roller coaster and other rides. The lake began to recede, and bathers now had to be transported to and from the water. Salt Lake City was also growing up, where more sophisticated entertainment opportunities were available for its enthusiastic youth. The thrill of the resort began to fade. World War II brought shortages of all kinds, forcing Saltair to close from 1943 until 1946. The lake's precarious mood swings and the threat of pollution frustrated owners who had spent a bundle on new and improved attractions. Crowds did not throng to the resort as they had in the past. Ownership of the problematic retreat had lost its appeal.

In spite of everything vexing the resort, it opened its 1952 season freshly starched and polished amid rumblings over a proposed $4.2 million state park 4 miles away. Two years later the owners invested $250,000 in an extravagant renovation, but the following year fire struck the resort again, and additional renovation was necessary. For the next two years, The Mills Brothers, Bill Haley and the Comets, Nat King Cole, Stan Kenton and Julie Christy all performed at the resort, and the large crowds of bygone days reappeared. Then a freak accident near the end of the next season — a 75-mile-an-hour gust of wind toppled the Giant Racer — sealed the resort's fate. The roller coaster was not rebuilt, and the following year brought fiscal catastrophe.

In January 1959, nearly 64 years after the resort opened its grounds to an eager crowd, Saltair was given to the State of Utah. No words could describe the sadness of Salt Lakers over the loss of this grand resort better than those of Terrell Dougan in the *Deseret News* July 14, 1975: "Those of us who lived the last years of Saltair still relish it the way New Englanders breathe in the smell of burning leaves in autumn. To us it means racing for the open-air car of the train that went out to Saltair, riding the Giant Racer and screaming all the way, and dancing to Harry James and Louis Armstrong as the waves lapped at the pilings under the biggest outdoor dance floor in the world. And now, years after the grand lady of the lake burned to the ground, new folks or visitors smell that lake wind and say, 'What is that strange sour smell?' We old-timers lick our lips, trying for a taste of salt — that stupid, pecky salt — and maybe trying, too, for a taste of our childhoods."

La Europa Royale

$$$ • 1135 Vine St. (6000 S.), Murray • 263-7999, (800) LA EUROPA

International travelers Tom and Frances Flynn fulfilled their lifelong dream when they created this decidedly European-style inn in the center of the Salt Lake Valley. The invit-ing entrance to this newer Mediterranean/European-style structure offers a glimpse of the elegance guests can expect from this lovely accommodation. The proprietors, who prefer to call their property a small elegant hotel, are very service-minded. The front desk is open every day until they tuck in the last

Photo: Salt Lake Convention and Visitors Bureau

The sea gull, which thrives at the Great Salt Lake, is the state bird and an important part of Utah's early history.

guest. Each of the seven well-appointed rooms has a large whirlpool tub next to a fireplace. A television and VCR are provided in each guest room, and a complimentary video library in the gathering area has movies guests can borrow. Fourteen-inch-thick walls ensure peace and quiet. Towering trees stand guard over the 2-acre grounds. Tom plants 250 flats of annual flowers each season. Guests can wander along the walking path, jog, wiggle a toe in one of two ponds on the property or play a challenging game of croquet.

Breakfasts, business lunches and candlelight dinners are available by special arrangement. The inn serves a complimentary hot breakfast each morning in the atrium next to the marble fireplace or outdoors in good weather. The property is close to several good restaurants for lunch and dinner. During the winter, La Europa guests can be on the slopes in about 30 minutes. Se-

cured ski lockers and boot dryers are provided. The inn also offers an exercise room and laundry facilities.

Log Cabin on the Hill Bed and Breakfast
$$ • 2275 E. 6200 S., Salt Lake City • 272-2969, (800) 639-2969

This charming bed and breakfast is in a log cabin built by legendary Norwegian skier Alf Engen who arrived in the United States in 1929. Engen won many national ski-jumping championships and downhill and slalom events between the early '30s and 1947. He also established a ski school at Alta that he directed for more than 30 years. Set in a natural hollow in the foothills of Holladay/Cottonwood, the inn has a rustic atmosphere that provides a warm welcome in both summer and winter.

The hand-built cabin has four guest rooms.

Special features include down comforters, terry-cloth robes, fresh flowers and private baths. The gathering area has a lovely fireplace that beckons you to curl up with a good book. Afterwards, take a soak in the hot tub under the stars. Breakfast at the Log Cabin is hearty and includes homemade granola, baked goods, fruits and juices. Children are welcome.

Mountain Hollow Bed and Breakfast
$-$$ • 10209 S. Dimple Dell Rd. (3050 E.), Sandy • 942-3428, (800) 757-3428

A roaring fire in the two-story native-stone fireplace is especially inviting on snowy winter nights at this comfortable bed and breakfast. The spectacular mountain views in both summer and winter are breathtaking. Mountain Hollow perpetuates the Old World tradition of comfort and hospitality without being over-the-top. The reading corner in the gathering area is quiet and relaxing. If you forget to bring a book, borrow one from the house library. You can also borrow a video from its extensive collection. It has a game room with a pool table, table tennis and air hockey. The 10-person hot tub is a great place to stargaze or watch a gentle snowfall.

Comfy country or romantic Victorian decor fills the nine sleeping rooms. Snuggle under one of the antique quilts from the inn's large collection. Breakfast is served buffet-style daily. Mountain Hollow is 15 minutes from the slopes of Alta, Brighton, Solitude and Snowbird and 5 to 20 minutes from shopping, dining and entertainment.

Pinecrest Bed & Breakfast Inn
$$-$$$$ • 6211 Emigration Canyon Rd., Emigration Canyon • 583-6663, (800) 359-6663

The massive wrought-iron gates at the entrance to the 6-acre Pinecrest estate belonged to Paramount Studios in Hollywood in the 1930s. The property has formal gardens with a stream and a trout pond. Two of the seven theme rooms are less than a mile up the road away from the main inn. The Oriental honeymoon suite, the pride of Pinecrest, occupies the entire second floor of the main house and overlooks the gardens below. Ming silk couches and furnishings from mainland China set the tone for this extraordinary room. A great collection of Zane Gray short stories along with a 1930s vintage radio that plays Burns and Allen, Jack Benny and Glen Miller are part of the English Library Room. The Holland Blue Room has a collection of antiques from Holland. The Stetson Guest House (filled with Western memorabilia), the Jamaican Jacuzzi Room, the Southwestern Suite and a 1940s-style cabin are nestled among the secluded pines.

You'll enjoy a full breakfast of banana sourdough pancakes, French toast and omelets daily in the dining room or outdoors in summer. Pets are negotiable, and children are welcome.

Saltair Bed and Breakfast
$-$$ • 164 S. 900 E., Salt Lake City • 533-8184, (800) 733-8184

Innkeepers Jan Bartlett and Nancy Saxton are such charming people, it's no wonder half their guests are repeat visitors. The Saltair is the oldest continually operating bed and breakfast in Salt Lake City. It takes its name from the old Saltair Resort near the Great Salt Lake and is listed on the National Register of Historic Places. To find out more about the old Saltair Resort, see the Close-up in this chapter.

The five sleeping rooms in this charming old home range from small and cozy to big and roomy. All rooms have antique brass beds with down comforters and carefully chosen antiques. An intriguing collection of antique lamps deserves a few minutes of study. Some are exquisite and, like the rest of the furnishings, blend well with the style of home. The lady's desk, rocking chairs, the armoire and tables here and there are comfortable and well-preserved. Jan collects pottery, and several of his prize pieces decorate the rooms. Fresh flowers, toiletries and saltwater taffy are provided in each room. Both shared and private baths are available.

The areas on the main floor are filled with memorabilia from old Saltair. Guests are encouraged to play the piano or strum the house guitar in the friendly parlor. Evening snacks are provided. Breakfast in the dining room includes raspberry pancakes, baked goods and Nancy's special breakfast drink, a combination of fruit juice, fresh fruit and yogurt.

Saltair is convenient to shopping, restaurants, the arts, sightseeing and attractions. The proprietors also own and manage three extended-stay properties that offer similar charm: The Alpine Cottages and Alpine Executive Suites are next to the bed and breakfast, and the Queen Anne Suites are about two blocks away (see our Vacation and Extended-stay Rentals chapter).

The Spruces Bed and Breakfast
$$-$$$ • 6151 S. 900 E., Salt Lake City • 268-8762, (800) 820-8762

Built in 1903, this Gothic Victorian was fully restored as a bed and breakfast in 1985. Jared and JaNae Barnes purchased the property in 1995 and have operated it ever since. The bed and breakfast is set amid 16 majestic spruce trees and surrounded by a small quarter-horse ranch. Quail, pheasant, ducks and geese are frequent visitors to the property. A 100-year-old ash tree extends from the main level common area through the ceiling and out the roof next to the second-floor patio. All rooms offer secluded views, and some have private porches. The one-, two- and three-bedroom suites have private baths, cable TV, full kitchens and jetted tubs.

Nutritious in-room breakfasts include fresh-baked bread, yogurt, fresh fruit, muffins and a variety of cereals, bagels, quiche or a breakfast casserole, freshly ground coffee, tea and juice.

The Spruces is about 20 minutes from the downtown area and within 5 to 10 minutes of shopping and restaurants. Children are welcome.

Wildflowers Bed & Breakfast
$$-$$$ • 936 E. 1700 S., Salt Lake City • 466-0600, (800) 596-0009

Set in a residential neighborhood amid some of the city's older homes, this quaint Victorian was built in 1891. The gardens, surrounded by quaking aspen and blue spruce, are vibrant with wild columbine, lupine, wild geraniums, meadow rue and coreopsis. The interior is a delightful step back in time. Hand-carved banisters, stained-glass windows, claw-foot bathtubs, balconies with spindle bands and chandeliers are original to the home. Five well-appointed rooms, named for wildflowers, have private baths. The charming third-floor, king-size attic room, called the Bird's Nest, has a full kitchen.

Your hosts serve a gourmet breakfast on the deck in summer and in the dining room in winter. Guests can relax in the reading room or browse in the gift shop. The art gallery features works by Jeri Parker, a well-known local artist who, along with Cill Sparks, owns Wildflowers. Ski packages are available. Unique shops and restaurants are within walking distance from Wildflowers (see our Shopping and Restaurants chapters). The home is listed on the National Register of Historic Places.

As the population expands and people stream in from all parts of the country, the city is experiencing an explosion of excellent new restaurants.

Restaurants

In food, as in most things, Salt Lake overall is a traditional, comfortable, steak-and-potatoes kind of a place, and many people won't go anywhere without the kids. Therefore, inexpensive chain restaurants, steak houses with huge portions and all-you-can eat diners do a land-office business. While it's true that many Salt Lakers eschew blackened this or balsamic that, mushrooms from Japan or salad greens from Italy, others here appreciate these epicurean pleasures. The city has always had many fine restaurants and great cafes that serve world-class food, and to the inexpressible joy of diners with sophisticated tastes and educated palates, Salt Lake's dining scene is rapidly expanding.

Salt Lake City is one of the fastest-growing metropolitan areas in the nation. With the influx of new residents from all parts of the country, the city is experiencing an explosion of excellent new restaurants. In matters of food, Salt Lakers are becoming more adventurous and willing to spend greater amounts of money on fine dining. We can sample falafel from the Middle East, momo from Tibet and sublime fare from new Italian, Asian and other ethnic restaurants. As it has in the rest of the country, the brewpub renaissance has thundered into Salt Lake and created an entirely new dining and evening-out experience. See our Nightlife chapter for a description of Salt Lake's brewpubs and taverns.

Much of the credit for changing the face of Salt Lake's restaurant scene goes to Gastronomy Inc. This premier restaurant company started in 1978 when it opened the New Yorker, a private club generally acclaimed as the best restaurant in town. Gastronomy now employs more than 700 people and operates several of the finest restaurants and clubs in the Salt Lake area, including Market Street Broiler, Market Street Grill and Club Baci. All of the Gastronomy restaurants offer exciting dining, absolutely fresh ingredients and professional service from top to bottom. Because of religious beliefs, many Salt Lakers don't drink alcohol, coffee or tea. But the devil will have his due, and many residents have a throbbing sweet tooth. In fact, Utah leads the country in per capita consumption of confections and ice cream. This means you'll find great bakeries all over the place, as well as plenty of ice-cream parlors, cookie and donut shops and our full quota of fast-food places.

If you like wine, beer or a cocktail with your meal, you need to become acquainted with Utah's liquor laws, which at first blush seem to be a quagmire of regulations. See the Nightlife chapter for a complete explanation of the rules. Luckily, when it comes to restaurants, the system is relatively simple: Most restaurants have a liquor license, which means you can order a mixed drink, wine or beer — but only if you order food, only if you're 21 or older and only before noon and up to midnight. Unless noted, all restaurants in this section have a liquor license, which means you can order a mixed drink, wine and beer.

To help you find your favorite kind of restaurant, we've organized them by categories, such as diners and cafes, and by cuisine, such as Asian, French, Italian and continental. All restaurants take Visa or MasterCard, and many take others such as American Express or Discover. Smoking is banned in all public buildings, so you can't smoke in any restaurant.

Bon appetit!

INSIDERS' TIP

Don't be surprised to see young children or babies with their parents, even in fine restaurants.

Diners and Cafes

American Grill
$ • 300 S. Main St., Salt Lake City
• 363-6935
$ • 4835 Highland Dr., Salt Lake City
• 277-7082

Arlo Guthrie would love this place — you can get anything you want. Pasta, seafood, sandwiches, great pizzas from the wood-fired oven, you name it, you got it. Try the Szechwan pasta No. 2 or the fresh seafood specials, both much beloved by regulars. They always start you out with hot bread and butter. The casual, 1950s ambiance will make you think you're grabbing a bite with the Fonz. Both locations are open seven days a week for lunch and dinner, with breakfast served on the weekends.

Archibald's Restaurant at Gardner Village
$$ • 1100 W. 7800 S., Midvale
• 566-6940

Local history comes alive at Archibald's, where the memory of polygamist (he had 11 wives) and farmer Archibald Garner is preserved in photos, farming implements and other memorabilia. Since Archibald's occupies a former grain silo, it's a restaurant in the round, which makes for an interesting visual experience. Try the halibut and chips or the prime rib, and be sure to finish your meal with the famous hot apple cobbler. It's open for lunch seven days a week and dinner Monday through Sunday. Sunday brunch is fantastic.

Bill and Nada's Café
$ • 479 S. 600 E., Salt Lake City
• 359-6984

This legendary, always-open Salt Lake eatery attracts an assortment of hippies, students from the University of Utah, out-of-work philosophers, momentarily sidetracked revolutionaries, budding poets and anyone else who's ever wanted to eat eggs and brains and 2 AM. That's right, brains and eggs — probably the best eggs and brains you'll ever eat. (OK, probably the *only* brains and eggs you'll ever eat.) The breakfasts are hearty, the pork chops tasty and the 16-ounce T-bone succulent. You've got your juke box in every booth, your wheel of fortune that picks a lucky winner for a free meal and friendly waitresses. They've been serving up good grub to Salt Lake's hungry eccentrics for more than 50 years. No liquor is available.

Capitol Café
$$ • 54 W. 200 S., Salt Lake City
• 532-7000

Just next door to the Capitol Theatre, this classy upscale bistro is a great spot for dinner before or after the opera. The Capitol Café serves up fresh and tasty California-style cuisine with a Mediterranean influence. The pan-seared crab with arugula is heavenly, and the wonderful bread baked in a wood-fired oven is a meal in itself. You'll enjoy great people-watching through the huge windows that open to 200 South. Add a great wine list and a knowledgeable wait staff and you've got a dining experience worth remembering. If you park at the Bank of Utah Building at 200 South and West Temple, the folks at the cafe will validate your parking. Reservations are recommended.

FYI

Unless otherwise noted, the area code for all phone numbers listed in this guide is 801.

Fiddler's Elbow
$ • 1063½ E. 2100 S., Salt Lake City
• 463-9393

When you need comfort food and nothing else will do, Fiddler's Elbow can fill you up with good home-style cooking at the right price. The lunch and dinner menu are the same and feature great American roadhouse cuisine, such as chicken-fried steak and pork

Photo: Utah Travel Council/Frank Jensen

You can see the city and enjoy people-watching
year round from a comfy horse-drawn carriage.

chops. The smashed potatoes are to die for. They also serve great sandwiches, including a Cajun chicken sandwich and a very good veggie number, plus homemade soups and salads. The dessert menu is awesome. We like the cheesecakes — raspberry, blueberry, plain — and the carrot cake is as good as Grandma's. Fiddler's Elbow features live music on weekends and some week nights (see our Nightlife chapter). It's open seven days a week. You'll find them in the quaint little neighborhood called Sugarhouse.

Grandpa Maddox Restaurant
$ • 1133 W. South Jordan Pkwy., South Jordan • 253-5100

Tasty plates of home cooking await you in this comfortable country setting. With vaulted ceilings, wood beams and two big hearth fireplaces, the setting will make you feel like the lord of the manor surveying your vast fields and the laboring but contented peasants. Everybody likes the steaks and famous fried chicken, and the corn pone, rolls and pies are all freshly baked and delicious. However, you can't get liquor of any kind. Maddox is open for dinner Monday through Sunday and lunch Tuesday through Friday.

Judge Café
$ • 8 E. 300 S., Salt Lake City • 531-0917

Owner Carole Couch knows the formula for a successful cafe: fresh food, a relaxed atmosphere and the friendliest service since Mom sat you down for a peanut butter and jelly sandwich with a glass of milk. Carole makes every guest feel like a personal friend. The Utah Jazz know a good thing when they see it — they've made the Judge Café a home away from home. One or two Jazzmen are always hanging around, and many team members have their pregame dinner here. The breakfasts are satisfying and hearty, the bread fresh and the soups, salads and pastries homemade. An espresso bar will keep you perky. Be sure to check out Carol's collection of basketball shoes and other Jazz memorabilia. The Judge is open Monday through Friday for breakfast and lunch. No liquor is available.

Lamb's Restaurant
$$ • 169 S. Main St., Salt Lake City • 364-7166

Located in the historic Herald Building, Lamb's has been serving up power lunches to the downtown crowd for more than 70 years. It's the oldest restaurant in the city, and nothing in the restaurant has changed since 1938. The long, black marble counter, booths, tables and light fixtures, all still in use today, originally came from a restaurant known as Gunn's Café. The chairs in the main dining room were imported by George Lamb from Vienna in the 1920s, and the fascinating antiques decorating the restaurant have come from all over the world. How about the food? It's American, fresh and abundant. Try the leg of lamb, the French-cut pork chops or — if you're up to it — the tasty liver. The breakfasts are hearty and very popular. Parking is validated down the street at the Crossroads Mall or ZCMI Mall. Lamb's is open Monday through Saturday for breakfast, lunch and dinner.

Park Café
$ • 604 E. 1300 S., Salt Lake City • 487-1670

Overlooking the pond at Liberty Park, the Park Café commands a wonderful view. You'll love the leafy ambiance of the patio, which is always packed in the summer. Diners rave about the breakfasts, including the huevos rancheros, the eggs Benedict and the omelets. For dinner, the chicken dishes and pastas are good choices. The Park Café has a nice selection of locally brewed beers. It's open for breakfast, lunch and dinner seven days a week.

Peery Wasatch Pub and Bistro
$$ • 110 W. 300 S., Salt Lake City • 521-5037

Located in the historic Peery Hotel, this comfortable spot is always delivering something new and creative. The warm and cozy pub atmosphere makes you want to settle down, sip on a hoppy, handcrafted brew and just dig in. Wild mushroom fettuccine is one place to start, as is the smoked pork chop or herb marinated New York steak. They also serve great soups and pastas. You can order from a variety of locally brewed Wasatch beers. It's open for lunch and dinner Monday through Saturday.

Red Butte Café
$$ • 1414 S. Foothill Dr., Salt Lake City • 581-9498

You'll enjoy the Southwestern decor and food of this nicely designed eatery. It specializes in soups, salads and sandwiches, and the daily specials are excellent. The Southwest chicken salad is scrumptious, and the pastries baked on-site are always fresh. Plus, you can splurge and buy a dozen to take home. Red Butte Café is open seven days a week for lunch and dinner and serves breakfast on Sundays.

Ruth's Diner
$$ • 2100 E. Emigration Canyon Rd., Salt Lake City • 582-5807

A great mountain patio and fabulous breakfasts have made this venerable canyon establishment a Salt Lake favorite for decades. The huevos rancheros are sensational, and the chili verde will make your taste buds stand up and do the cancan. The chili rellenos also elicits rave reviews. It's crowded on the weekends, so get there early. The Sunday brunch is especially popular. Ruth's is open for breakfast, lunch and dinner everyday.

Silver Fork Lodge
$$ • Big Cottonwood Canyon Rd., Salt Lake City • 533-9977

If you headed up Big Cottonwood Canyon for some outdoor fun, be sure to stop at this bed and breakfast restaurant for one of the killer breakfasts. The famous sourdough pancakes are as good as advertised, but every breakfast is huge, fresh and delicious. You won't need to pack a lunch after eating one of these monsters. If you're hungry on the way down the canyon, the dinners are just as good. The nightly specials are popular, as is the pepper steak and smoked trout with brie. If possible, eat on the patio — the view of the Wasatch Mountains is stunning, and the hummingbirds will keep you company in the summertime. It's open for breakfast, lunch and dinner seven days a week.

Asian

Bangkok Thai
$$ • 1400 S. Foothill Dr., Salt Lake City • 582-8424

Acclaimed by the local press as the among the best Thai restaurants in Utah, this classy establishment will gladden your heart, fill you with universal brotherhood and make you consider bowing to the many Buddhas adorning the place. You'll feel like the bodhisattava himself as you seat yourself at the polished green marble tables and rest your gaze on the lovely Thai tapestries hanging on the wall. If you sit near the windows on the east side, you'll have a great view of the looming Wasatch Mountains. But you're here to eat, above all. The choices are many: We recommend the honey-ginger duck, Panag salmon and the Great Pad Thai, which is a noodle dish stir-fried with a whole sackful of goodies, like eggs, green onions, shrimp and so on. The restaurant is open for dinner seven days a week and for lunch Monday through Friday. Reservations are recommended.

Cafe Trang
$ • 818 S. Main St., Salt Lake City • 539-1638

All the varied delights of Vietnamese cooking are available at this popular and inexpensive gem of a restaurant. The moderate prices and great food bring a huge crowd of all kinds of people. The menu is huge, but the spring rolls can't be beat and the vermicelli and Shanghai noodles are consistently excellent. The sautéed pork in caramel sauce has elicited numerous yelps of delight from happy patrons. If you're adventurous, ask the waitstaff to select for you: They'll prepare some obscure dish from the Vietnamese countryside you've never eaten and will never forget. Top it off with a rich cup of French-press coffee and you've got an evening to remember. The cafe serves beer only and is open for lunch and dinner seven days a week.

East-West Connection
$ • 1400 S. Foothill Dr., Salt Lake City • 581-1128

Here's another jewel of a Vietnamese restaurant. The look is modern and uncluttered, and the food, perfectly prepared. Try the great lemongrass chicken or beef, the ginger shrimp, halibut in a pot or Look Luck beer, a favorite of regulars. Vegetarians flock here for the extensive offerings. The Vietnamese coffee will stoke your engine for hours. It's open Monday through Saturday for lunch and dinner.

House of Tibet
$ • 145 E. 1300 S., Salt Lake City
• 364-1376

A wonderful new entry in the Salt Lake restaurant scene, the House of Tibet serves food you can't get anywhere else in the state. Owner Nima Lama has created a nice place with a spiritual touch, featuring traditional Tibetan decor like thankas, statues and pictures of the Buddha, as well as jewelry and books by the Dalai Lama. Diners rave about the momo, Tibetan dumplings filled with vegetables or meat; and the phinghsha, bean thread cooked with chicken or beef and eaten with rice. The lamb curry is also fabulous. The lunch buffet gives you an opportunity to try six or seven items, including soup and dessert. You absolutely must try the bocha, the Tibetan national drink, which is buttered and salted tea. It sounds terrible, but it's actually quite tasty. It serves only beer and is open for lunch and dinner seven days a week. The lunch buffet is served on weekdays only.

Kyoto
$$ • 1080 E. 1300 S., Salt Lake City
• 487-3525

Consistently ranked in the local press as the best Japanese restaurant in Salt Lake, Kyoto takes you into the elegant world of classic Japanese cuisine. Your cares will melt away in the serene, minimalist surroundings (polished wood, mellow lighting, rice-paper Japanese screens), characteristic of Japanese architecture. The food is presented so artfully you almost hate to eat it. But, hey, you can't let it sit there forever, so dig in. The tempura is excellent, as is the chicken teriyaki and the sushi, served only on the weekends. For lunch, the wonderful donburi (rice with vegetable tempura and teriyaki chicken) is a must. Kyoto serves wine, beer and great sake, and it's open Monday through Saturday for lunch and seven days a week for dinner. Reservations are recommended.

The Mikado
$$$ • 67 W. 100 S., Salt Lake City
• 328-0929

For some of the best sushi in town, drop into this great restaurant, one of the oldest and best in Salt Lake. The Mikado has served the culinary delights of Japan at the same location since 1958. The Oriental ambiance will settle your nerves and fill you with delight, especially in the private dining room, decorated with rice-paper walls and low tables. You have to take your shoes off and sit on the floor, but that's the fun of it. If you prefer to keep your shoes on and sit in a chair, you can do that, too. But wherever you eat try the sushi or the Mikado mountain trout, grilled and topped with scallops, shrimp, shiitake mushrooms and sautéed with oyster sauce. The soups are also excellent. The Mikado has a complete bar with an impressive selection of Japanese beers and sake. It's open for dinner seven days a week and Monday through Friday for lunch. Reservations are recommended.

Sampan
$ • 675 E. 2100 S., Salt Lake City
• 467- 3663

Although it's small and located in a strip mall, the Sampan cooks up some of the best Chinese specialties around. It'll give you the standard fare, such as lemon chicken or sesame chicken, but if you want, the chef can whip up some more exotic fare, such as duck or strawberry chicken. The pot stickers (dumplings filled with meat or vegetables) go down easy, as well. Sampan serves beer only and is open for lunch and dinner seven days a week.

Shanghai Cafe
$ • 145 E. 1300 S., Salt Lake City
• 322-1841

The menu at this wonderful Vietnamese restaurant is so big it almost overwhelms. Foods are listed by category — beef, pork, vegetables, noodles and so on — which makes things a little easier. We have so many favorites it's hard to select just a few, but the Vietnamese egg roll and barbecue pork are amazing. Although the portions are ample, we get a double order of egg rolls because they're so good. If you are strictly into veggie dishes, the Shanghai won't disappoint. The broccoli and mushrooms with fried noodles is a real treat. The atmosphere is pleasant. Some of the booth benches sag

Photo: Gastronomy, Inc./Market Street Broiler

Fresh seafood in the middle of the desert? You bet! Thanks to Delta Airlines and a conveniently located airport, you can enjoy fresh seafood year round at area restaurants.

a little but are nonetheless comfortable. Ask for a table instead if you have a troublesome back. The waitstaff is very pleasant. Not everyone speaks fluent English, but pointing and nodding works where words sometimes fail. It's open seven days a week.

Continental

Absolute!
$$$ • 52 W. 200 S., Salt Lake City
• 359-0899

Owners Staffen and Kim Eklunt have done the impossible: created an upscale restaurant that everyone feels comfortable in. This is one of the most attractive restaurants in Salt Lake, with mellow dark woodwork, an indoor water-

fall, airy rooms with big pillars and smaller, more-private rooms for intimate dining. The cuisine, Northern European with a Scandinavian touch, emphasizes unique sauces and absolutely fresh ingredients. The toast smogen appetizer can't be beat, and the spinach salad with grilled chicken, strawberries and blue cheese provides an explosion of different tastes. For dessert, you have to have the Swedish ligonberry mousse — it's fabulous. It's open for lunch and dinner Monday through Saturday.

Aerie Restaurant
$$$ • Snowbird Resort, Little Cottonwood Canyon Rd. • 521-6040, (800) 453-3000

Appropriately named for an eagle's nest situated high on a crag or cliff, the Aerie puts you on top of Salt Lake's dining world. Just breathing the bracing mountain air will make you hungry, and your elevated perch commanding a sublime view of granite peaks and rocky cornices is the best accompaniment to great food we know of. From the medallions of foie gras to the rack of lamb and zucchini ravioli, the food is haute cuisine at its loftiest. Naturally, the wine list is extensive. If you're in the area on Sunday during the summer, the Aerie's Sunday brunch is the one Cole Porter sang about. It's the top, it's the Coliseum, it's the — well, you know the words. With ice sculptures as decoration, you'll find smashing sushi, a farmers market of fresh fruit, crepes Suzette à go go and endless trays of every breakfast food imaginable. It's open for lunch and dinner seven days a week. The Aerie is located in the Cliff Lodge (see our Mountain Resorts chapter).

FYI

Unless otherwise noted, the area code for all phone numbers listed in this guide is 801.

Cinegrill
$$ • 344 S. 300 E., Salt Lake City • 328-4900

Redolent of olive oil and garlic, huge and bursting with flavor, the salad at the Cinegrill has been famous among Salt Lakers for 30 years. A fixture for decades at 100 South and 200 East, the Cinegrill moved a few times and was even shut down for a while, but now it's back, as good as ever, and drawing crowds of garlic lovers nostalgic for that old-time taste. The garlic bread, lasagna, spaghetti and Italian sausage are spicy and filling, and you get to eat this comfort food on red-checked tablecloths out of stainless-steel bowls while listening to a jukebox that dates from the 1950s, with music to match. How's that for special? We love this place, as do generations of Salt Lakers. The strains of live piano music drift through the dining room during the evening. It's open for lunch and dinner seven days a week.

The Dodo
$$ • 680 S. 900 E., Salt Lake City • 328-9348

For nearly 20 years the Dodo has keep Salt Lakers happy with its casual elegance and wide choice of exquisite food. The outside patio is a must when the sun shines. Where to start with the food? It's all good, from the famous smoked turkey sandwich to the best soups in town. If you have a sweet tooth (and of course you do, admit it, you naughty thing) you've landed in the right place. The selection is huge, the flavors unique and the decadence complete. The Toll House pie is everybody's favorite, but try the Butterfinger cheesecake, the chocolate macadamia mousse pie or the fantastic Lundigras (chocolate mousse with a marzipan crust). Enough said? It's open for lunch and dinner every night and offers a Sunday brunch. Reservations are recommended.

Little America Hotel and Towers
$$ • 500 S. Main St., Salt Lake City • 363-6781

Sunday brunch is a must-do at Little America. Both the coffee shop and the dining room of this world-class hotel have always served uncomplicated yet delicious food. The dining room's weekday lunch buffet features a salad bar, roast baron of beef and lots of other goodies. The coffee shop has a simple menu featuring soups, salads and sandwiches for lunch and meat-and-potatoes fare for dinner, all reasonably priced.

But the main event is Sunday brunch in the hotel's elegant ball room. It's a tradition among locals. Elegantly presented amid massive crystal chandeliers and a beautiful decor, the food stations include a pastry and bread table with danish pastries, muffins and savory baked goods, and a fresh salad table loaded with fruits and veggies for a build-your-own kind of roughage extravaganza. The omelet, crepes and waffle stations let you be creative. Save some room for the luscious crab legs and delicious hot and cold dishes. You can sample bacon or sausage and eggs, eggs Benedict, and meat and meatless dishes — and the carver is always on duty to present you with a slice or two of turkey, ham or roast baron of beef. You'll find the dessert table inviting with its lovely cakes, pies and exquisite pastries. We generally set aside several hours

to enjoy this delicious treat. Sunday brunch is served from 9 AM to 2 PM. Reservations are required for parties of more than 10.

Log Haven
$$$$ • Millcreek Canyon, 3500 S. Wasatch Blvd. (3000 E.), Salt Lake City • 272-8255

Nestled among pines, waterfalls and wildflowers, Log Haven's spectacular setting in Millcreek Canyon is echoed by the equally wonderful food and service. This is one of Salt Lake's finest restaurants and the place to go to celebrate an important event. Built in 1920, Log Haven underwent a million-dollar renovation a few years ago that enhanced the already beautiful pastoral ambiance. The menu changes frequently, but you can expect perfectly prepared, globally inspired cuisine with Pacific Rim, French and Southwest influences. If it's available, the coriander-rubbed ahi tuna is delectable, as is the lemon-peppered veal porterhouse steak. The wine list is one of Salt Lake's best. Log Haven is open for dinner Mon-

day through Saturday. Reservations are recommended, and valet parking is available.

Metropolitan
$$$ • 173 W. Broadway (300 S.), Salt Lake City • 364-3472

This place is upscale with a vengeance. The modern, minimalist decor — you'll think you're eating in a museum — sets the stage for a superb meal. The wine list is one of the best in Salt Lake. The menu changes weekly, but you'll find some variation of a venison dish, the best angus beef around and stunning seafood. The succulent desserts all are made in-house. The Metropolitan is open for dinner Tuesday through Sunday. Reservations are recommended.

The New Yorker Club
$$$ • 60 Market St., Salt Lake City • 363-0166

This posh, fine-dining establishment in the basement of the old New York Hotel was Gastronomy Inc.'s first foray into the world of dining in 1978, and it's still a standout in superb cuisine and ambiance. The sophisticated dining room is reminiscent of movie-star haunts on both coasts — chic and intimate. Uncommonly beautiful fresh flowers on perfectly starched table linen are a great opening act for the extraordinary food soon to arrive. The club's cafe dining area is a little less formal, but doesn't miss an upscale beat.

Creative fare, fresh ingredients and a great chef are the key ingredients at the New Yorker. The mouth-watering pasta dishes are simply beautiful, but it's a tough decision — they are all so good. Try the lobster fettuccine for a rich treat. Pepper steak with onions, mushrooms and peppercorns in a cabernet sauce served with the New Yorker's own shoestring potatoes and a vegetable is a favorite. Several specials are available each night besides the regular menu items. When it's offered, the pheasant is a good choice, as are the pork medallions, and when in season, their salmon dishes are wonderful. If you don't mind a little heart pounding, finish the meal off with the famous Chocolate Decadence.

The wine list is awesome, and Gastronomy's waitstaff is the best-trained in the city. They make you feel very special. Because this is a private club you'll need to purchase a $5 temporary membership at the front desk before being seated (see our Nightlife chapter for the scoop on liquor laws). It's good for you and your party for two weeks.

The New Yorker is open for lunch and dinner Monday through Friday and for dinner on Saturday. Reservations are essential.

Panache
$$$ • 1306 E. 12300 S., Draper • 523-1400

You'll find the menu at this budding new establishment, opened in December of 1996, upscale progressive American. Pasta dishes are always available, along with prime rib, steaks, seafood and fowl. Try the signature entree, porcini mushroom-crusted veal chops served with Portobello and yam ragout and smoked garlic au jus. The blackened salmon is also delicious, as is the Israeli couscous-crusted venison served with parsnip and roasted-garlic mashed potatoes and root vegetables.

Panache has many daily specials to tempt you. Dessert is also noteworthy. The berries and custard served in a pecan brittle cup is a tasty way to end your meal. Only fresh ingredients are used in the preparation of the restaurant's interesting entrees, and the seafood is flown in fresh daily.

Panache is open Monday through Saturday for dinner and weekdays for lunch. You'll also find them open on Sunday for brunch.

Santa Fe Restaurant
$$$ • 2100 Emigration Canyon Rd., Salt Lake City • 582-5888

Just 10 minutes from the heart of downtown Salt Lake, the Santa Fe offers gorgeous mountain views, a romantic Southwest lodge setting complete with fireplace and outdoor decks for summer supping. The food is exceptional. Try the lamb fillet if price is no object or the more moderately priced pork chops with honey glaze. The Cajun chicken pasta, available for lunch or dinner, is very popular. You can also order delicious freshly made soups and a variety of sandwiches for lunch. Save room for dessert. The Bailey's Irish Cream cheesecake is beyond delicious. Santa Fe is open for lunch Monday through Friday and for dinner on Saturday; it serves a very good Sunday brunch.

French

La Caille at Quail Run
$$$$ • 9565 S. Wasatch Blvd. (3000 E.), Salt Lake City • 942-1751

For a true romantic evening and heavenly luxury in a French country chateau setting, La Caille is the only place to go. Situated on 22 acres of ponds, orchards and vineyards populated by peacocks and lla-mas, La Caille smacks of opulence and European elegance. It's expensive, but the first-cabin service and gourmet fare are worth every penny. You'll be pampered like royalty. The rack of lamb and duck are popular, and you can find any wine you want on the extensive list. It's open for dinner seven days a week and serves brunch on Sundays. Reservations are required.

L' Hermitage

$$$ • 1615 S. Foothill Dr., Salt Lake City • 583-5339

When you put yourself in the capable hands of owner Jean-Jacques Grossi, you'll understand why the French revere food and why French cuisine is the finest in the world. L'Hermitage routinely wins raves for the flawless food and perfect service. You won't have to mortgage the house or sell one of your children, either. The prices are embarrassingly low for food this good. You have to start with pâté, then you can go on to the savory rack of lamb, the beautifully prepared veal, the filet mignon or the salmon served with lobster sauce. L'Hermitage is open for dinner Tuesday through Saturday. Reservations are recommended.

Le Parisien

$$ • 417 S. 300 E., Salt Lake City • 364-5223

For 28 years Max Mercier's Le Parisien has been Salt Lakers' entryway to the culinary delights of French cuisine. Coq au vin, steak au poivre, boeuf Bourguinon, escargot, quiche Lorraine — Le Parisien serves up the tried-and-true favorites and some innovative dishes as well. The salad dressing is famous. At the Parisien you won't find a snooty maitre d' sneering at your clothes and calling you a bumbling rustic in French. Max has created a casual, comfortable place great for the whole family or for meeting friends downtown. You'll pay less here than at other French restaurants around, and the food is just as good. Go ahead, try out your high school French — the Le Parisien folks will love it. It's open for lunch Monday through Saturday and for dinner every night. Reservations are recommended.

Italian

Al Forno's Ristorante

$ • 239 S. 500 E., Salt Lake City • 359-6040

This is an intimate, quiet place that serves consistently good food at moderate prices. The downtown lunch crowd flocks here for the quick service. The grilled garlic bread with olive oil, cheese and tomatoes is popular, as is the polla arolla and prawns topped with cheese. The pasta salads and pizzas are tasty. Al Forno's serves wine and beer and is open for lunch and dinner Monday through Saturday.

Baci Trattoria

$$ • 134 W. Pierpont Ave. (230 S.), Salt Lake City • 328-1500

Gastronomy Inc. does it again with this fine restaurant specializing in unique Italian and Mediterranean cuisine. Located in the heart of downtown Salt Lake, Baci Trattoria draws a young, noisy crowd of downtown professionals who love good food and professional service. The arched ceilings, wall murals painted by local artists, a gorgeous 30-foot wall of stained glass and the long bar draw raves from the crowd. From the roasted chicken, ricotta and spinach-filled cannelloni or the cannelloni de pollo to the wood-fired pizzas, you'll be struck by the innovative combination of flavors and colors. Make sure you try the tasty Italian rolls. Reservations are recommended.

Café Molise

$$ • 55 W. 100 S., Salt Lake City • 364-8833

Intimate and romantic, Café Molise is a perfect place for a tête-à-tête with your lover. Art from local artists adorn the walls, and you can enjoy live jazz on Friday night. But, you'll want to smooch with your friend before you indulge in any of the sensational, garlicky dishes owner Shelly Deproto cooks up from precious family recipes. These recipes come from Molise, a region of southern Italy between the Apennine Mountains and the Adriatic Sea. If people in Molise eat this way every day, it's got to be *la dolce vita* in spades. You won't eat better lasagna anywhere in the world, and the involtini di pollo and pasta with Italian sausage will have you weeping in gratitude. The tiramisu is divine. It's open for lunch and dinner seven days a week, and reservations are recommended.

Cannella's

$$ • 204 E. 500 S., Salt Lake City • 355-8518

This famous little eatery is well-known to locals. You can get lunch here five days a week, but it only serves dinner on Thursday and Friday nights. The Italian salad topped with sausage is noteworthy. The menu also includes lasagne, tetrazzini, manicotti, fettuccine with balsamic vinegar and every other authentic pasta dish under the sun. Desserts here are in a class by themselves. Try the turtle cheesecake or the very moist chocolate beet cake if you fancy a sweet after your meal. On occasion they prepare an outstanding tiramisu. Cannella's is next to Junior's Tavern (see our Nightlife chapter), and seating is first-come, first-served.

Fresco Italian Cafe

$$$ • 1513 S. 1500 E., Salt Lake City • 486-1300

If perfectly prepared Northern Italian cuisine is your weakness, Fresco's is one temptation you won't be able to withstand. Longtime chef Lane Pellinger combines creativity and experience to bring to life wonderfully complex dishes that resonate with flavor. Try the mouth-watering polenta appetizers and minestrone soup. If Lane is serving lamb, do yourself a favor and order it — it's sensational. Couples love this romantic, intimate cottage. Fresco's only has 13 tables, all of which have views of the fireplace. In warm weather, the garden seating is delightful. Fresco's is open for dinner seven days a week, and reservations are recommended. Wine and beer are available.

Michelangelo Ristorante

$$$ • 2156 S. Highland Dr. (1300 E.), Salt Lake City • 466-0961

This may be Salt Lake's finest restaurant. From the elegantly attired, Italian-speaking waiters, the artful ambiance and the exquisitely prepared food, Michelangelo's exemplifies culinary wizardry at its most magical. Seasoned epicures and those familiar with authentic Italian food will flock to Michelangelo's like a second home. Start with the ingredients. Owner Andrea Casella imports just about everything from Italy, and you can immediately taste the difference. Gorgonzola cheese, Parmesan Reggiano, special pasta made with truffles, spices and even fish eggs — you'll have to go to Mr. Casella's native Tuscany to find anything more authentic. Mr. Casella is a true restaurateur, with a family tradition in the business in Italy that goes back generations. He's in his element here, spreading warmth and charm, gesturing wildly and helping patrons enjoy a wonderful evening. The menu is extensive and offers Tuscan delicacies you can't get anywhere else in Utah. Chef Paulo Celeste makes ravishing ravioli, including veal ravioli in walnut sauce and ravioli specials with various subtly flavored pasta and truffles. Mr. Celeste also does wonderful things with steak, basting it in various divine sauces and herbs and making it so tender you can eat it with a fork. Try the sliced New York steak in fresh herbs or the filet mignon with green peppercorns, Dijon mustard and brandy in cream sauce. A perfectly prepared tiramisu with an espresso will top a rare evening. It's open every night for dinner and Monday through Friday for lunch. Reservations are recommended.

Pomodoro

$$ • 2440 E. Fort Union Blvd. (7200 S.), Sandy • 944-1895

Situated in a strip mall in Sandy, Pomodoro's unprepossessing exterior will never make you think you're entering one of the top restaurants in Salt Lake. But it's true: This a superb place and unquestionably the best value for your dollar around. Co-owner Wendy Caron is genuinely warm and friendly and makes you feel at home as soon as you walk through the door. You won't gawk at the furnishings, but you'll enjoy the comfortable ambiance. The food takes center stage here. It's wonderful contemporary Italian fare such as pan-seared salmon on garlic mashed potatoes and homemade sausage linguine with marinara sauce. Pomodoro's recently won an Award of Excellence from the *Wine Spectator*

Magazine for its comprehensive wine list. The dessert menu is splendidly decadent. It's open for dinner Tuesday through Sunday and serves lunch on weekends. Reservations are recommended.

Ristorante Della Fontana
$$ • 336 S. 400 E., Salt Lake City
• 328-4243

For a long, leisurely, six-course meal in a restored old church, come to the Ristorante Della Fontana. With waterfalls, stained-glass windows and handcrafted statutes imported from Italy, the Della Fontana provides a visual treat. Popular with school kids out on a prom date, the elegant atmosphere puts them on their best behavior. The minestrone soup and halibut casserole are delicious. It's open for lunch and dinner Monday through Saturday. Reservations are recommended.

Rino's Italian Ristorante
$$ • 2100 S. 2320 E., Salt Lake City
• 484-0901

Owner Rino DiMeo has pleased legions of Salt Lakers since 1979 with his classic Italian dishes. His obsession with freshness is so great that in the summer he grows many of his herbs and vegetables himself, including Italian parsley, basil, oregano, arugula and Italian tomatoes. You can taste the difference. Everybody loves his combination dish featuring shrimp scampi, fettuccine carbonara and chicken piccata. Finish your meal with the tasty Italian cream-cheese torte tiramisu ("pull me up" in Italian) and somebody will have to do just that to get you out of your chair. The place has a substantial feel, with old paintings and antiques. But you'll want to dine outside in the summer in the vine-covered patio. It's open seven days a week for dinner, and reservations are recommended.

Tuscany
$$ • 2832 E. 6200 S., Salt Lake City
• 277-9919

The northern Italian cuisine isn't the only draw at Tuscany. This charming building with its stone exterior and interior with open-beam ceilings is reminiscent of a big English country cottage. It has housed a restaurant of one kind or another since the 1950s. Set amid lush trees, the location gives patio diners a thicket of foliage to enjoy in summer. For winter dining, the elegant paned windows provide a beautiful view of the overcoat of snow on the trees and a roaring fire in the massive stone fireplace is just the right touch on a nippy night.

Established in 1996, Tuscany is new to our dining scene but the food is wonderful so it should be around for quite some time. The menu ranges from pasta dishes to specialty pizza and more upscale entrees made with chicken, veal or pork. Double-cut pork chops are a popular house specialty, and the pesto-crusted salmon is also a big hit. Tuscany features a sorbet and dessert special nightly — just right for lingering over your romantic repast.

It's open seven days a week for dinner. Lunch is served Tuesday through Friday. Reservations are recommended.

Greek

Hungry I
$$ • 1440 S. Foothill Dr., Salt Lake City
• 582-8600

You're in for a treat if you like Greek food. The Hungry I serves a profusion of delicious roast lamb and chicken dishes, dreamy beef and shrimp creations and a standout salmon specialty wrapped in spinach and phyllo dough. For those who just can't decide, the Hellenic sampler, featuring a little bit of everything is worth its weight in feta. Vegetable dishes are also available if you don't care for meat. Anything to do with eggplant is awesome. This upscale restaurant serves authentic Greek fare, has great ambiance and an attentive waitstaff. You can hear live authentic Greek music on weekends. It's open seven days a week for dinner. Lunch is served Monday through Friday, and brunch is available on weekends. The restaurant is in the Foothill Village Shopping Center. Valet parking is available.

Olympian Greek and American Restaurant
$ • 2181 S. 700 E., Salt Lake City
• 487-1407

Breakfast is served all day, seven days a

week at this very friendly restaurant. It's a local favorite, especially on Sunday morning. Eggs, cooked any way you like them, served with a better-than-average link or patty sausage, thick bacon, ham, pork chops or steak, and your choice of pancakes or toast are always good bets. If you don't mind the calories, we recommend the Belgian waffle topped with fruit and whipped cream. Lunch and dinner are also available. The sandwiches with a Greek salad or thick-cut fries come in all varieties from tuna to Reuben, and full-course meals such as chicken or steak with potatoes and vegetables are down-home good. Your coffee cup will never be empty at the Olympian.

Yanni's Greek Express
$ • 2751 Highland Dr., Salt Lake City • 466-6525

This is a local fast-food Greek restaurant, but it's so out of league with other fast-food chains we had to give it a mention. The gyros have been the best in town for nearly 25 years. The lamb is tender, seasoned just right, and the red and white sauces are thick and yummy. Yanni's Greek rice is heavenly, with a nice hint of lemon. The chicken shish kabob is lean and delicious, especially when served with pita bread and a Greek salad. You can dine in — the restaurant is bright and clean — or take it away. Either way, don't leave without a piece of the baklava for dessert. Yanni's is open for lunch and dinner Monday through Saturday.

Mexican/Southwest

Barking Frog Grille
$$ • 39 W. Market St. (340 S.), Salt Lake City • 322-3764

You'll experience some of the most creative cooking around in this colorful, brightly lit grille. Specializing in Southwestern cuisine, the Barking Frog does amazing things with chiles, salsa, squashes and mole sauce. The grilled salmon with chipolte lime butter and polenta provides an explosion of different tastes, all of which are combined in an eating experience that can only be compared to listening to a symphony. The tortilla shredded chicken soup is another winner, and the barbecued ribs are like none you've ever eaten. Try the grilled bananas for dessert — this is a rare treat in Salt Lake City. Decorated with unusual Southwestern art by local and national artists, the Barking Frog will take all your senses on a wild ride. The Barking Frog is open seven days a week for dinner. Reservations are recommended.

Blue Iguana
$$ • 165 S. West Temple, Salt Lake City • 533-8900

The Cardenas family has spoiled Salt Lakers, and we're very grateful. The Blue Iguana is the upscale sister of their famous Red Iguana (see its separate listing). The menu features regional specialties for south-of-the-border, a be-still-my-heart paella that must be ordered a day in advance, a triumphant chili verde, mole coloradito and a very fine lamb stew. You'll also find more basic favorites on the menu including the ever-dependable enchilada plate served with beans and rice. The restaurant is downstairs in the historic Arrow Press Square, home to various print shops in the early 1900s. The exposed brick and stained glass create a pleasant atmosphere. It's open for lunch and dinner Monday through Saturday. Valet parking is available.

Burrito Baby
$ • 221 E. 300 S., Salt Lake City • 596-9200

Burritos, baby! We're talking the biggest and best around. This small but thriving restaurant is perennially voted the best burrito place by the local alternative press. Wrap your lips around the famous 1-pound burrito and you'll know why — these honeys are full of good things and always fresh. Regulars love the chili verde and the vegetarian burrito, which

Photo: Gastronomy, Inc./Baci Trattoria

Salt Lakers are accustomed to sophisticated cuisine and eclectic ambiance in many restaurants throughout the Valley.

is crammed with rice, beans, lettuce, onions and other tasty items. You can also order many other types and sizes of burritos as well as tacos, enchiladas and so on. It's open Monday through Saturday for lunch and dinner. Takeout is available, but no liquor.

Cenaduria Mexico
$ • 919 State St., Salt Lake City • 359-6326

The whole crew is from down Mexico way, most from Sinaloa, so you know you're getting the real stuff here. The tacos in particular are a great bargain and bursting with chunks of meat. The salsa is piquant, the sauces hot

and the portions generous. The combination plates are popular choices. You can cool your palate with a Dos Equis or a Carta Blanca. It's open seven days a week for lunch and dinner. This is a marginal neighborhood at night.

Guadalahonky's Mexican Restaurant
$ • 136 E. 12300 S., Draper • 571-3838

You'll find this popular Mexican restaurant in the south end of the Valley worth the drive. Bring the whole family — they're very kid-friendly here. Guadalahonky's chili verde wrapped in a flour tortilla is very good. The chimichangas also get raves, especially the vegetarian. Order the chicken or beef smothered in enchilada sauce or pork with chili verde. Can't decide? Try a combination plate. Everything comes with beans and rice. Top off your meal with fried ice cream. You'll be glad you saved room for dessert. It's open seven days a week for lunch and dinner.

La Frontera

$ • 1236 W. 400 S., Salt Lake City
• 532-3158
$ • 1434 S. 700 W., Salt Lake City
• 974-0172
$ • 61 W. 10600 S., Sandy • 553-9500
$ • 3784 W. 3500 S., West Valley City
• 967-9905

For a rousing good time with heaping plates of food and a festive atmosphere, come to La Frontera. You get plenty of bang for the buck at this Salt Lake institution, which serves up a milder, more Americanized version of Mexican food. With its warehouse-like atmosphere and huge space, this is a great place for a big party. The decor is basic, but the prices are rock-bottom, the salsa terrific, and the supply of tortilla chips endless. All locations are open for lunch and dinner seven days a week.

Mr. Sinaloa

$ • 1702 S. State St., Salt Lake City
• 466-9656

Your search for real Mexican food at astonishingly low prices ends here. Owner and chef Jimmy Rosas gives you first-class treatment and heaping plates of food. The corn tortillas are homemade, the tacos fabulous and the chicken mole made from Jimmy's own recipe. Try the menudo and pozole for a new Mexican taste treat. At Mr. Sinaloa, you eat the same food as native Mexicans. You can get domestic and Mexican beer. Mr. Sinaloa is open seven days a week for lunch and dinner.

Red Iguana

$ • 736 W. North Temple, Salt Lake City
• 322-1489

Red Iguana is funky, legendary, a bargain, always crowded and the home of absolutely the most authentic and tastiest Mexican food in Salt Lake. This is the real stuff — not watered down, bland Americanized food. The Cardenas family makes the mole and other sauces weekly right there in the kitchen. This restaurant typifies the difference between family restaurants that serve food made by people who care and the bland food from chain restaurants. Try the killer nachos, the authentic moles or some other adventurous, indigenous dishes from different parts of Mexico, such as the tacos Don Ramon or pumpkin soup. The people-watching here is almost as good as the food. Red Iguana serves beer only and is open for lunch and dinner seven days a week. The neighborhood is marginal at night.

Rio Grande Cafe

$ • 270 S. Rio Grande St. (200 W.), Salt Lake City • 364-3302

Located in the historic Rio Grand train station, the Rio Grande Cafe still rocks on after all these years of serving excellent Mexican food in a sometimes raucous, but always fun, party-like atmosphere. The toy train clicking along the top of the huge, horseshoe shaped bar and the papier-mâché taco lady tell you it's time to let your hair down and get festive. The carnitas are fabulous — the best in town. The Rio Grand taco and the super burrito are also popular. A full bar and nice beer selection let you wash it all down with Margaritas or a cold one. It's open seven days a week for dinner and Monday through Sunday for lunch. The area is marginal at night.

Shallow Shaft Bar and Restaurant

$$$ • Little Cottonwood Canyon Rd., Alta
• 742-2177

If you like your meals served in a pristine mountain setting, you'll want to check out this wonderful restaurant. Zagat's Survey has voted its Southwest cuisine the best in the state. You can begin the meal with grilled prawns or smoked salmon and black-bean quesadilla.

Lamb with ancho-chile sauce or chicken with kiwi tomato salsa are sure bets for the entree. Death by Chocolate is what the restaurant calls its flourless cake made with bittersweet chocolate served on a raspberry mint puree.

The Shallow Shaft is across the road from the Alta Lodge. Don't look for an address — none exists here, but there is plenty of Mother Nature and delicious food. Little Cottonwood Canyon Road dead-ends at the mountain, and the Shallow Shaft is on the left. It's open for dinner seven days a week, more or less, year round. It does take a hiatus between the summer and winter season, so call ahead.

Middle Eastern and Indian

Bombay House
$$ • 1615 S. Foothill Dr. (2000 E.), Salt Lake City • 581-0222

Hankering for vindaloo? Can't live without tandoori chicken or shrimp? Got to have lamb curry? If so, the Bombay House is the place for you. You can have your vindaloo (potatoes and chicken in a tomato curry sauce) as hot or mild as you want. Bombay House doesn't serve beef, of course, but it has an extensive vegetarian menu. The naan (Indian flat bread) is pretty tasty. The atmosphere is elegant, and the food consistently good. You can hear live Indian music on Saturday night. It serves beer and wine and is open for lunch and dinner Monday through Saturday.

Baba Afghan
$ • 55 E. 400 S., Salt Lake City • 596-0786

Owner Kassim, an Afghan native, has quickly made this pleasant little place one of the best ethnic restaurants in Utah. The service is attentive, and the Afghanistan food wonderfully fragrant and spicy but not hot. You can order chicken, lamb and vegetarian dishes. Particularly enticing are appetizers like mantoo, a steamed pastry shell with ground beef and onions; aushak, a kind of ravioli; and showra, which is lamb soup. Among the succulent main courses are the

dwopiaza (lamb and split peas) and koufta challow (meatball, tomatoes and peas). Dozens of other delicious possibilities are available. Try the lunch buffet for a sampler of 18 items. Baba Afghan has won awards in the local press for its superlative cuisine. It's open Monday through Friday for lunch and Tuesday through Sunday for dinner. No liquor is served.

Cafe Mediterranean
$ • 60 W. 500 S., Salt Lake City • 364-4914

First, there's the rum truffle cake. It is a confection worth praise. Light, just the right amount of sweet, a good rum flavor and, ohh, so good. Cap off your entree with this or one of Cafe Mediterranean's other tasty cakes. You'll find a variety of pasta dishes on the menu, as well as lemon chicken, grape leaves and Middle Eastern plates with tabouli, hummus and tahini salad. Other meatless fare includes falafel and wheatmeat veggie burgers. They also serve several varieties of sandwiches including the all-American hamburger.

Cafe Mediterranean is open for lunch and dinner Monday through Saturday. Local musicians who play a variety of musical styles drop in to entertain dinner guests on random nights. The restaurant is next to the Deseret Inn (see our Accommodations chapter).

Cedars of Lebanon
$ • 152 E. 200 S., Salt Lake City • 364-4096

You can surround yourself with the perfumed elegance of the Middle East in this popular restaurant, one of the first Middle Eastern restaurants to open in Salt Lake City. Owner Raffi Daghlian offers a wide variety of vegetarian specialties, including wonderful falafel, chicken shish kebab with cinnamon and Lebanese appetizers like the Baba Gannouj. You can also order savory chicken, lamb and beef dishes. Be sure to check out the swaying sensuality of belly dancing on Friday and Saturday nights. The Moroccan Room, where you sit on luxurious imported rugs, is popular. It's open for lunch and dinner Monday through Friday and Saturday for dinner. Reservations are recommended. It serves beer only.

Sahara
$ • 368 S. State St., Salt Lake City
• 595-6900

As soon as you enter Sahara, you're gently enveloped in the mystery of Middle East. The spell is cast by an intriguing array of rugs, tapestries, ornaments, statues, brass plates, palm trees, even heaps of sand — in fact, you'll wonder if you took a magic carpet ride and ended up in Morocco or Algeria. The spell won't be broken by the food. Originating from various Middle East locations, it's all authentic. You can relish Moroccan couscous or mousaka from Greece. The falafel is wonderful. Whatever you do, don't pass up the lentil soup. Made with chopped spinach, mint, pureed lentils and herbs, its good enough for a full meal. Finish with kenafa (shredded wheat with syrup) and Turkish coffee or mint tea and you'll be giddy enough to write your own 1,001 tales. Sahara is open Monday through Friday for lunch and every day for dinner.

Pizza

Wasatch Pizza Company
$ • 820 E. 3330 S., Salt Lake City
• 466-7777
$ • 820 E. 400 S., Salt Lake City
• 359-2300
$ • 2065 E. 7200 S., Midvale • 942-8720
$ • 4689 S. Holladay Blvd. (2000 E.)
• 278-5999

If you like greasy, fast-food pizzas, you probably won't like the fresh and delicious creations that come from this gourmet pizza company. They proclaim their difference right on the menu: "We're not for everyone," it states. "Wasatch pizza is made for people who want something better." The company uses excellent-quality olive oil and real garlic (not powder), roasts its own peppers and grinds its own rosemary. For vegetarians and cheese lovers, the three-cheese Mount Baldy is a must. Each Wasatch Pizza store has cozy booths where you enjoy your food, or you can order take-out.

Deloretto's
$ • 2939 E. 3300 S., Salt Lake City
• 485-4534
$ • 10600 S. 67 W., Sandy • 576-1240
$ • 2010 S. State St., Salt Lake City
• 485-6615

Hand-thrown, thin-crust New York-style pizza is the specialty at Deloretto's. The calzones are customer favorites. The salads are zesty, and the soups homemade, varied and delicious. A number of vegetarian offerings are available. Deloretto's is open for lunch and dinner every day but Sunday. A young, sassy waitstaff makes dining at Deloretto's a real pleasure.

Gepetto's
$ • 230 S. 1300 E., Salt Lake City
• 583-1013
$ • 2340 E. Murray-Holladay Rd., Holladay
• 272-1061

Located just west of the University of Utah, Gepetto's has been a favorite hangout for students since the late 1960s. It throbs with collegiate energy and rocks with some of Salt Lake's best live music every night, including jazz, contemporary and folk. Gepetto's serves one of the best chef's salads around, as well as 11 different sandwiches, great pizza, pasta and calzones and a nice selection of locally brewed beer on tap. A cozy patio makes dining al fresco a must in the summer. When you're through eating, you can have some fun in the pool room and foosball room. They also have TVs scattered around the place so patrons can watch the University of Utah whup their archrival BYU in football and basketball. It's open for lunch and dinner every day. Check out the Holladay location too.

Litza's Pizza
$ • 716 E. 400 S., Salt Lake City
• 359-5352

When a restaurant stays open for a quarter of a century, you gotta think it's doing something right. Litza's is an old-fashioned pizza parlor where generations of Salt Lakers have hung out and eaten fresh, homemade pizza with a thin crust and heaps of toppings. You can also get excellent calzons, spaghetti and lasagna. It's open for lunch and dinner from

Monday through Saturday. You can't buy beer or alcohol of any kind.

The Pie Pizzeria
$ • 1320 E. 200 S., Salt Lake City
• 582-0193

Located practially next door to the University of Utah, this college hangout has been a local favorite for decades. With dozens of beers on tap and live music on weekends, the Pie is always full of life. Bring some friends — lots of friends — and dig into the giant, 23-inch pizza. Another popular item is the "Zappi," which is kind of like a calzone. The motto is "we stack it high at the Pie," which, as mottos go, ain't half bad. The Pie also serves great salads and soups. It's open for lunch and dinner seven days a week.

Salt Lake Pizza and Pasta
$ • 1063 E. 2100 S., Salt Lake City
• 484-1804

Bliss means settling into your favorite neighborhood restaurant and knowing that no matter what you order, it will satisfy your appetite. Well, if you're in the Sugarhouse area look no further — Salt Lake Pizza and Pasta is exactly what you want. The pine tables, nice carpet and teal-green booths invite you to sit down and stay a while. Thirty-five fabulous locally brewed beers will make any beer lover half crazy deciding which one to choose. After you've got your beer ordered, you'll need food, so try the five-cheese pizza, BBQ chicken pizza or tempting tomato basil linguine. It's all made from scratch and splendidly good. It's open seven days a week for lunch and dinner.

Steaks, Ribs and Seafood

Bubba's BBQ
$ • 4291 S. 900 E., Salt Lake City
• 268-3374

The ribs are tender and smoky, the jambalaya jam-packed with chicken and sausage and the Cajun Creole specialties sizzle with that old-time flavor. So, "put some South in your mouth" and get on down to one of Salt Lake's favorite eateries. It's bright, weird and a lot of funky fun. Caution: Don't try to eat the huge portions at one sitting. Your body will

rebel. It's open for lunch and dinner six days a week.

Carvers
$$ • 10720 S. Holiday Park, Sandy
• 572-5177

Carvers is a civilized and romantic spot that offers fine dining and a choice of intimate rooms, such as the Library, the Studio and the Great Hall. The service is attentive, the prime rib is excellent, and the Beaulieu Vineyards filet mignon, cooked in a burgundy and garlic sauce and topped with goat cheese and mushrooms, is delectable. Carvers offers the best wine list in this part of the Salt Lake Valley. It is open daily for dinner only.

Christopher's Seafood & Steakhouse
$$ • 370 W. 500 S., Bountiful • 299-9544

Although not in the Salt Lake Valley, Christopher's is just a 10-minute drive north up Interstate 15. This elegant but moderately priced restaurant is well-worth the drive. You won't find a better dining experience for the money along the Wasatch Front. The minute you enter Christopher's, you know you're in for a treat. It's light and airy, with exposed wood beams, a classy white-tile floor and what seems like acres of glass.

Christopher's attention to aesthetics is not confined to the setting — the food comes to your table in an explosion of color and design, almost like having Mardi Gras on a plate. And what food it is! The steaks are aged and tender, the seafood fresh and the lamb savory. Regulars go for the 20-ounce porterhouse steak, the prime rib and the New Zealand lamb chops. All the seafood, from the Alaskan halibut to the king crab, is flown in fresh daily and grilled to perfection. Don't leave until you try the fabulous New York cheesecake or the New Orleans bread pudding.

Christopher's is open for lunch Monday through Friday and dinner Monday through Saturday.

Diamond Lil's
$$ • 1528 W. North Temple, Salt Lake City • 533-0547

Famous for steaks and prime rib, Diamond Lil's is Salt Lake's best-known steakhouse. If you like your steaks mammoth and your decor Western, you'll be yodeling with delight and jump out of your chaps when you partake of the grub at this landmark eatery. It's been serving up Billy the Kid filet mignon and Outlaw porterhouse steaks for nigh on 29 years. Your arteries won't thank you, but your taste buds will. It's open for lunch Monday through Friday and dinner Monday through Sunday. The neighborhood is marginal at night.

Mullboons Restaurant
$$$ • 161 W. 600 S., Salt Lake City • 530-1313
$$$ • 6950 S. State St., Midvale • 562-5147

You'll find Mullboons' downtown restaurant on the 13th floor of the Best Western Olympus Hotel. A view of the mountains and cityscape is a great backdrop for the delicious food. Both locations start you off with a large bowl of shrimp on ice while you ponder your entree and await your meal. The bottomless shrimp bowl has always been a big draw at this comfortable, well-appointed eatery. Seafood and steaks are the specialty at Mullboons, and you won't be disappointed if you like your beef thick and juicy.

Open for lunch and dinner Monday through Friday and dinner on weekends, Mullboons also serves a tasty brunch on Sunday. Reservations are recommended.

Old Salt City Jail Restaurant
$$ • 460 S. 1000 E., Salt Lake City • 355-2422

Ever had dinner in jail? This engaging restaurant served as the city's jail house in the late 1800s. The building is now on The National Register of Historic Places. Well-appointed dining rooms set in the cavernous old building provide authentic Old West ambiance. A fresh, well-stocked salad bar provides plenty of greens to get your palate started, and the Old Salt City Jail specializes in prime rib, steaks and seafood, prepared to your liking.

The restaurant is next to the Anniversary Inn. (Check it out in our Bed and Breakfasts and Inns chapter.) Enter the restaurant's parking lot from

500 South and 960 East. The Old Salt City Jail is open for dinner seven days a week.

Redbones
$$ • 2207 S. 700 E., Salt Lake City • 463-4800

For authentic, Memphis-style barbecue, Redbones is the only place in town. Memphis-style barbecue requires hand-rubbing the raw meat with a special dry mix then allowing the flavors to percolate through the meat for at least 24 hours. The meat is then slow-cooked over hickory to achieve the red ring visible in every piece of meat. Sauces are served on the side. Redbones serves pork, chicken and ribs, and it's all delectable. You can also choose from a splendid selection of vegetarian side dishes and a nice variety of beer. The decor at Redbones is classy but casual, with slate walls and granite counters. You'll notice a motorcycle theme — why, we don't know, but it sure revved up our motor. It's open for lunch and dinner seven day a week.

The Roof Restaurant
$$$ • 15 E. South Temple, Salt Lake City • 539-1911

Most people who like good food and a fine dining experience shy away from buffets. The Roof Restaurant is the exception — it's classy all the way, from the elegant linen, silverware and fine china to the positively Rabelaisian abundance and variety of gourmet food. The Roof serves four hot entrees a night, ranging from black-tipped shark to chicken dishes and a seafood medley But that's just the beginning. Every night the tables groan with prime rib, pitted ham, jumbo prawns, hot soups, fresh pasta and a baker's-dozen variety of breads. To end your meal, you can choose from 18 to 24 different sweet creations that basically encompass the entire universe of dessert possibilities.

Because the restaurant is on the 10th floor of the Joseph Smith Memorial Building (the old Hotel Utah), you have terrific view of downtown Salt Lake and Temple Square. Since the building is owned by the Mormon Church, no alcohol, tea or coffee is available. Reservations are recommended.

FYI

Unless otherwise noted, the area code for all phone numbers listed in this guide is 801.

Steak Pit
$$$ • Snowbird Resort, Little Cottonwood Canyon Rd. • 521-6040

Tender slabs of aged beef draw enthusiastic crowds of carnivores to this longtime Salt Lake favorite. You won't taste cutting-edge cuisine here, but if you're hankering for an American-style meat fest, you can't do any better. Steak Pit also serves great seafood, including lobster and Alaskan king crab. It's open for dinner seven days a week, and reservations are recommended. See our Mountain Resorts chapter for information at the resort.

Market Street Broiler
$$ • 260 S. 1300 E., Salt Lake City • 583-8808

Another winner from local restaurateurs Gastronomy Inc., Market Street Broiler combines reasonable prices with professional service and always-fresh seafood. Located in a renovated fire station near the University of Utah, Market Street has an upstairs dining room, a main-floor seating area and a popular outdoor patio. This place is very popular and always packed with nearby residents and students from the University of Utah. Mesquite-broiled fish, famous clam chowder and fresh desserts like chocolate decadence, raspberry almond tarts and fresh fruit pies leave diners groaning in satisfaction. The onion straws are a must. You'll need quick hands and a boardinghouse reach to get your share — those babies go fast! You can also buy fresh fish at the takeout fish market on the premises. It's open for lunch Monday through Friday and dinner every night.

Market Street Grill
$$ • 48 W. Market St. (340 S.), Salt Lake City • 322-4668

The downtown equivalent of the Market Street Broiler, the Grill serves the daily catch flown in on Delta Airlines from all over the country. Fresh salmon from the Pacific Northwest, jumbo prawns from the Gulf of Mexico and lobster from Maine are just a few of the delectable piscine possibilities that await you. With its black-and-white checked floors, blond wood and long counter, this place will remind you of the kind of classy joint where Bogart and Bacall might have broken bread in the 1930s. It gets real noisy here, but at least no one will eavesdrop. Besides the dinner, the Grill has won plaudits for its substantial breakfasts and great Sunday brunch. It's open for breakfast, lunch and dinner daily.

Vegetarian

Long Life Vegi House
$ • 1353 E. 3300 S., Salt Lake City • 467-1111

This family-owned vegetarian restaurant delivers some of the most reasonably price food around. It offers traditional vegetarian fare, as well as vegan dishes, which contain no dairy or egg products. This is favorite hangout for Salt Lake's straight-edged community. The "chicken" dishes are made with fried tofu that is light and delectable. The chicken chow mein, lemon chicken and cashew chicken are tasty. The spring rolls are vegan and scrumptious. Although the service is sometimes slow, don't ever fear your water glass with remain empty for even a second. It gets crowded on weekends. It's open for lunch and dinner every day.

Oasis Cafe
$$ • 151 S. 500 E., Salt Lake City • 322-0404

The patio at the Oasis rivals any in Salt Lake. The feel is light and airy, with delicate fronds and abundant greenery creating a nurturing sanctuary for the soul and a serenely beautiful place to read, relax or sip coffee (French-pressed). And the food at this 2-year-old restaurant. which shares space with the

---

INSIDERS' TIP

If you have a favorite bottle of wine, you can bring it with you to any restaurant. Wine service ranges from $5 to $7, depending on the restaurant.

new age Golden Braid bookstore (see our Shopping chapter), has elevated Salt Lake vegetarian cuisine to another level. A favorite is the coriander-crusted tombo tuna, served with shiitake mushrooms and miso aoli. It's a mouthful, all right. The smoked tofu sandwich is savory and delicate. When soybeans taste this good, who needs meat? The Oasis has a good wine and beer list and is open for lunch and dinner from Monday through Friday. It also serves an excellent brunch on the weekends.

Park Ivy Garden Cafe
$ • 878 S. 900 E., Salt Lake City
• 328-1313

Mira and Mark Machlis run more than just a restaurant. Sure, they have to make a profit to stay in business, but they see their customers as more than just numbers. They want their patrons to be "nurtured as well as nourished." They've accomplished this by creating a leafy haven decorated with three wonderful murals depicting different rain forests of the world. They have comfortable booths in the front and a wonderful outdoorsy sunroom in the back that gives you the illusion of dining al fresco. Just about everyone around has sampled Park Ivy's famous cheesy sun bun, save-the-chicken sandwich or "meat of wheat" hamburger. They also offer yummy vegan (no milk or eggs) cakes and cookies, honey lemonade, true-blue herb tea, organic coffee and Indian chai. The management is enlightened, the service is courteous, and everything is made from scratch. Vegetarian fare doesn't get much better. It's open from Monday through Saturday for lunch and dinner.

Bakeries

Bakers de Normandie
$ • 2075 S. 700 E., Salt Lake City
• 484-1251

Flaky, crusty and soft on the inside, real French bread is tough to find outside La Belle France. Here's one place that comes real close. Bakers de Normandie uses a stone-hearth oven with steam injection for baguettes so real you'll be looking around for the Eiffel Tower. The chocolate-filled crois-

sants are popular, as are the hard rolls and French pastries. It's open Monday through Saturday.

Beau Brummel
$ • 3100 S. Highland Dr. (1200 E.),
Salt Lake City • 486-5908

It's been there for more than 60 years and owned by a couple of different people, but the rich, wonderfully buttery products haven't changed at all. The rum torte has intoxicated generations of Utahns, and the eclairs, napoleons and other French goodies are just as sinfully good. Everything is baked on-site, from scratch, with the best butter, cream and chocolate. It's open from Tuesday to Saturday.

Big Apple Bagels
$ • 3242 S. 3300 E., Salt Lake City
• 485-2968

A few years ago Brackman Brothers Bagels started the bagel craze in Utah. These were the real thing: chewy on the outside and tender on the inside. Unfortunately, after years of success Brackman Brothers has been replaced by bagel chains that produce soft, gooey, salty concoctions more like donuts than bagels. Big Apple Bagels is the exception. This is the best bagel around, and the closest thing to the legendary Brackman Brothers bagel you can find. They'll make you a tasty ham or turkey sandwich, and they also serve great coffee from Seattle's Best Coffee. It's open every day.

The Lion Bread Company
$ • 6960 S. Highland Dr., Salt Lake City
• 943-2264

The heavenly aroma draws you in, and the fragrant French bread keeps you coming back. The Lion Bread Company expertly plays many variations on the French bread theme including rye, sourdough, whole wheat, sourdough-rye and many others. They also specialize in flaky French croissants, fruit-filled puff pastries, cinnamon rolls and muffins. You can enjoy these creations in a small dining area or take them home. They also serve soup, salad coffee and juices. The Lion Bread Company is open Monday through Saturday.

Mrs. Backers Pastry Shop
$ • 434 E. South Temple, Salt Lake City
• 532-2022

Marty Backer can make cake decorations like no one in Salt Lake. He learned the art from his father and specializes in flowers such as daffodils, carnations and poinsettias. His heavenly creations include tarts, tortes, cookies and various other goodies. The place has been around forever — more than 50 years in the same location. It's closed Sundays and Mondays.

Pierre's Country Bakery
$ • 3239 E. 3000 S., Salt Lake City
• 486-0900

Stop in here for a complete line of fine baked goods, including an amazing array of French bread and baguettes. Pierre's has French sourdough, whole wheat, rye, cheese bread, pumpernickel and Italian focaccia. The sweets include croissants bursting with fruit and cream, just to name a few. It's open from Monday to Saturday.

Schmidt's
$ • Trolley Square, 602 E. 500 S., Salt Lake City • 363-5240
$ • 5664 S. Redwood Rd., Murray
• 967-9766
$ • 754 S. State St., in Sears, Salt Lake City • 321-4297

Salt Lakers have relied on Schmidt's for generations to satisfy their cravings for goodies. Each of the three Schmidt's in the Salt Lake Valley offers a delectable bounty of European pastries, torte cakes, napoleons, eclairs, French croissants and marzipan. They also sell great sugar cookies and wedding cakes. It's open seven days a week.

Vosen's Bread Paradise
$ • 249 W. 200 S., Salt Lake City
• 322-2424

New to the Salt Lake bakery scene, Vosen's has quickly become a favorite for its whole wheat bread, seven-grain bread, German hard rolls, pretzels and fabulous German rye bread. Owner Markus Vosen is a certified master baker from Germany, which takes years of apprenticeship and practice to achieve. This expertise shows in his wonderful creations. The pastries are nothing short of exquisite. You won't be able to pronounce their names, but you'll never forget the taste. Markus's famous Beehive cake is delectable, and Vosen's is one of the few places in Salt Lake you can find one. It's open Monday through Saturday.

Delicatessens

Frank Granato Importing Company
$ • 4044 S. 2700 E., Salt Lake City
• 277-7700
$ • 1391 S. 300 W., Salt Lake City
• 486-5643

You'll find Salt Lake's most complete selection of imported Greek and Italian meats, cheese, olives and pasta at this fragrant and friendly place. From prosciutto and taleggio cheese to Italian olive oil and Greek olives, Granato's will have it. This place has been around for more than 40 years, and the friendly folks here know everything about Italian food, so don't hesitate to ask if you want advice on a topnotch recipe for stuffed manicotti or ravioli. They also make killer deli sandwiches you can take home or eat there. It's open Monday through Saturday.

Greek Market
$ • 3205 S. State St., Salt Lake City
• 485-9365

Nothing beats a good Greek salad, with feta cheese and olives, sprinkled with olive oil and eaten with crusty Greek or Italian bread. You can get anything you need to make a good Greek salad and many more Greek specialties at the Greek Market, which has nice selection of cheese, meat and so on. They also serve Greek specialties such as souvlaki, dolmanthes and gyro in a dining room. It's open Monday through Saturday.

Mediterranean Market and Deli
$ • 3942 S. State St., Salt Lake City
• 266-2011

Since 1958 hungry gourmets have made a beeline to Mediterranean for quality imported Greek and Italian food and great sandwiches. They make their own wonderful sausage and carry authentic Parmesan Reggiano cheese, as well as asiago, Romano and dozens of other tasty foodstuffs. They also serve sandwiches in a little cafe on-site. It's open Monday through Saturday.

Siegfried's Delicatessen
$ • 69 W. 300 S., Salt Lake City
• 355-3891

Salt Lake has a large Germany community (around 40,000), and it seems that many of them are either in Siegfried's or Marianne's (see the next listing) spreching Deutsche and procuring their weekly quota of wieners, bratwurst, herring, sauerkraut and many other substantial foodstuffs favored by the German peoples. Siegfried's has an enormous selection of German sausage and cold cuts, many of which are made on-site. Siegfried's also carries Schaller and Webber sausages from New York, German breads, pretzels and pastries. You can shop at Siegfreid's Monday through Saturday.

Marianne's Delicatessen
$ • 149 W. 200 S., Salt Lake City
• 364-0513

Besides a large selection of imported German and European foods similar to Siegfried's, Marianne has a large restaurant that serves excellent German fare like sauerbraten and smoked pork loin. Like Siegfried's, Marianne's makes many of its own sausages and other meat on-site. Marianne's has been around even longer Seigfried's, opening in 1953. They're both venerable, classic delis, bursting with character, great food and topnotch service. Marianne's is open Monday through Saturday.

Ice Cream Parlors

Fendell Ice Cream Company
470 S. 700 E., Salt Lake City • 355-3583

This local treasure opened in Salt Lake in 1910 and moved to its present location in 1957. Today Fendall's is still making delicious ice cream, now under the watchful eye of the founder's granddaughter, Carol, and her husband, Gunther Radinger. The ice-cream parlor serves 40 to 50 flavors of ice cream, but the chocolate varieties are some of the best in town. We don't think anyone can hold a candle to their burnt-almond fudge. The real standout, however, is the spumoni, made with a rum base, nuts and glazed fruit. It's a local favorite. Fendell's is open Monday through Saturday from 9 AM until 5 PM for ice cream to go. With a reservation, larger groups of six or more can enjoy the chilly delights in the front-end dining room.

Red's Frozen Yogurt and Ice Cream
$ • 4991 S. Highland Dr. (1300 E.), Salt Lake City • 278-6148

Hossein Ghandain, the genial proprietor of Red's, believes you should get what you want. That's why he lets you design your own ice cream or frozen yogurt treat the way you want it. He offers tart and sweet frozen yogurt and dozens of flavors of ice cream, all of which you can combine with nuts, candy and fruit to create a treat of unsurpassed lickability. You can also chow down on sundaes, root beer floats, chili, sandwiches and excellent bread-bowl soup. Want coffee or espresso? Red's can do that, as well. It's open every day.

Snelgrove Ice Cream Parlors
$ • 850 E. 2100 S., Salt Lake City
• 485-8932
$ • 605 E. 400 S., Salt Lake City
• 359-4207
$ • 1005 E. Fort Union Blvd. (7200 S.), Salt Lake City • 566-4322

With three locations scattered through the Salt Lake Valley, Snelgrove's reigns as the champ of Salt Lake ice cream parlors. The Snelgrove family has been making ice cream since 1929, and they've been serving up frozen goodies from the 2100 South location since 1930. Generations of families have dropped by the various locations to savor the famous Cashew Conquistador (three scoops of ice cream with cashews) and the Raspberry Hurricane (a raspberry shake with carbonated water), as well as 32 flavors of ice cream and other goodies. They make their own ice cream at the 2100 S. location, using only the finest and freshest ingredients. Ice cream is a family obsession. On a trip to Canada years ago one of the Snelgrove clan stopped in a small diner and sampled a vanilla of unusual tastiness. He asked for the recipe and still uses it for the Canadian Vanilla, a perennial favorite. We bet you'll love it, too. Snelgrove's is open Monday through Saturday.

Salt Lake rocks at night — or at least gently sways.

Nightlife

Whoever said Salt Lake's nightlife is limited to church socials and milk and cookies obviously hasn't taken the time to get out on the streets and see the reality. Salt Lake rocks at night — or at least gently sways. It's true that many Salt Lakers are socially conservative and family-oriented, but Salt Lake is a big place with a healthy population of citizens who enjoy all the pleasures that come with a vibrant nightlife.

With dozens of private clubs, taverns and sports bars, you can find whatever kind of action you want, be it hot blues, country and western line dancing, rock 'n' roll clubs or great pub grub and excellent microbrews. If you like sophistication, moody jazz or a quiet spot for intimacy, you'll easily find plenty to fill the bill.

As in many cities, the biggest change in Salt Lake nightlife in the past 10 years has been the rise of brewpubs. These classy establishments have elevated beer bars to a lofty position. Before brewpubs, Salt Lake beer bars typically drew a motley crowd of working men, college students and hard-core drinkers. The food was bad or nonexistent, and the ambiance decidedly questionable. They weren't the kinds of places you'd take a date or your spouse. Now, brewpubs draw professional people, families, friends and anyone else who likes good food and great beer in a classy setting.

Now, about those Utah liquor laws you may have heard are a bit odd. The legal drinking age in Utah is 21. You can buy "weak" beer (3.2 percent alcohol) at grocery stores, convenience stores and in most private clubs, restaurants and in all taverns. A tavern is an establishment, like a brewpub, that can only sell 3.2 beer. For stronger brew, you have to go a private club or a Utah State liquor store. What is a private club? Glad you asked. It's basically a combination of restaurant and bar that serves liquor by the drink. You can become a temporary member of a private club for $5, which is good for two weeks.

You can order wine, beer and mixed drinks — with or without a meal — at a private club from 10 AM to 1 AM. Wine, beer and mixed drinks can be ordered from noon to midnight at most restaurants — but only if you order food. All the private clubs in Salt Lake City stay open until at least 1 AM, and all provide full bar service. To buy wine and liquor by the bottle, you have to go to a Utah State liquor store.

Utah has some of the strictest drunken driving laws in the country. The legal limit of alcohol in the bloodstream is .08 percent. If you're arrested for drunken driving, your car will be impounded and you'll be put in jail until someone bails you out. If you're convicted of drunken driving, you automatically lose your driver's license, and you'll be levied a large fine — up to $1,000. The bottom line: Just don't do it. If you're too impaired to drive, call a taxi. See the Getting Here, Getting Around chapter for phone numbers of taxis and other private transportation.

By the way, in Utah smoking is only allowed in private clubs — but not all private clubs allow smoking. The best policy is to ask first.

Credit cards are accepted at all taverns, private clubs and brewpubs. Most private clubs that play music have a cover charge.

Brewpubs

Hoppers
7200 S. 890 E., Midvale • 566-0424

Hoppers is the first brewpub to open in the south part of the Salt Lake Valley — a triumphant moment for suburbanites forced to drive 10 miles to downtown for good beer and a real sandwich. From the first day, it was packed with beer lovers and friends out for fun. And for good reason: The building and interior decoration are a delight for the eyes, the sandwiches are tasty and filling, and the appetizers are a meal in themselves. You won't find better or bigger onion rings, and the three-cheese nachos elicit moans of delight. Try the orange honey wheat beer — it's a stunner. Hours are from 11 AM to midnight daily.

Red Rock Brewing Company LC
254 S. 200 W., Salt Lake City • 521-7446

You'll be greeted by an open oven and chickens roasting on a spit when you enter the comfy confines of the Red Rock Brewery. This is the most attractive and best-designed brewpub in Salt Lake. The reddish hues and beautiful setting make for a special lunch or dinner. And all that heat means great pub food, from wood-fired pizzas to sizzling burgers and hefty sandwiches of every variety. You can wash the food down with ales, porters, wheat beers and other specialty beers brewed up whenever the brewmaster fancies. Their Scottish Ale has won recognition at the Rocky Mountain Brewer's Fest. A shaded patio allows you to enjoy your food al fresco in season. Red Rock is open from 11 AM to 1 AM on weekends and 11 AM to midnight on weekdays.

Salt Lake Brewing Company
367 W. 200 S., Salt Lake City • 363-7000

A bit quieter and less crowded than Salt Lake's other brewpubs, the Salt Lake Brewing Company offers a handsome place to quaff a cold one. If you're hungry, Buffalo wings, smoked-chicken pizza and other delectable pub fare will take the edge off. Private rooms add a distinguished touch, and eight nice pool tables add to the fun. Hours are 11:30 AM to 1 AM on weekdays and 11 AM to midnight on weekdays.

Squatters Pub Brewery
147 West Broadway (300 South), Salt Lake City • 363-2739

The original and still most excellent Squat-

ters gave Salt Lake its first brewpub in 1989. Nine years later, it's still crowded, still brewing great beer and still a favorite place for friends to meet, eat and party. You can get scrumptious food from around the world, be it Italian, American or Asian. Taste the fries and chicken wings for a starter. You can choose from seven hand-crafted beers, ranging from pale ales to dark porters and stouts. Try the Millcreek stout — it's creamy, full-bodied and excellent with any food. Squatters is open from 11:30 AM to 1 AM daily.

Desert Edge Brewery
At the Pub, Trolley Square, 602 E. 500 S., Salt Lake City • 521-8917

Since 1972, the Desert Edge Brewery — originally called The Pub — has served the most consistently good and least-expensive sandwiches in Salt Lake. Nothing nouveau, unpronounceable or fancy here — just the freshest bread piled high with the best meat and cheese. Their Reuben sandwich is a masterpiece. The French onion soup and nachos are also highly appreciated. Everything is delivered by a wonderfully cheerful and efficient waitstaff, many of whom have worked here for decades. It didn't take the Desert Edge long to master the art of brewing: Their aromatic, superbly balanced Happy Valley hefe-weizen won the 1996 Gold Award at the Great American Beer Festival as the best wheat beer in the country. Hours are 11 AM to midnight Monday through Wednesday and 11 AM to 1 AM Thursday through Sunday.

Brewvies Cinema Pub
677 S. 200 W., Salt Lake City • 355-5500

Brewvies is the first and only combination brewpub and movie house in Salt Lake. Brewvies features four shows a day, and all shows are $3. You can enjoy local microbrews and eat tasty food while watching great flicks. They're open for both lunch and dinner. It's a

FYI

Unless otherwise noted, the area code for all phone numbers listed in this guide is 801.

INSIDERS' TIP

Check out publications like *The Event* and *Salt Lake City Weekly* for the entertainment schedules of the various bars and private clubs in the Salt Lake Valley.

classy place with comfortable accommodations and a nice atmosphere. The first show starts at 1 PM and the last show starts at midnight. You can find the movie schedule in *The Salt Lake Tribune*.

Taverns

Anchors Aweigh
64 W. 400 S., Salt Lake City • 521-2072

Beer, coffee, espresso, breakfast, lunch — you name it, you can get it at this 24-hour establishment. You'll find cops finishing up their beat, the after-theater crowd and downtown workers crowding Anchors at all hours of the day and night. Beer is available from 10 AM to 1 AM, and the kitchen is open 24 hours a day. Great music and a cool pool table finish up the fun.

Bar-X-inn
155 E. 200 S., Salt Lake City • 532-9114

Want a beer as big as your head? Then order the tankard at the Bar-X. This famous bar, open since 1937, personifies what bars in America used to be: gritty, hard-edged and a refuge for the working man. For years, women didn't dare venture in, but that's changed recently. Still, it's basically a guy's place. You'll see all kinds here, from old men nursing a cold one to frat boys playing pool. No "sissy" microbrews with fancy names at the Bar-X — just ice-cold beer, served fast and furious. Chili dogs are a favorite accompaniment to the beer. Hours are 10 AM to 1 AM daily.

Cotton Bottom Inn
2820 E. 6200 S., Holladay • 272-9830

Sure they have beer — any kind you want — and they have pool tables and a comfortable, homey atmosphere. But the reason people come to the Cotton Bottom Inn is the garlic burgers. They are the Mount Everest of burgers in the Salt Lake area and must be attempted by anyone who appreciates the very best. It's a cool place, and the waitstaff and bartenders are real friendly — even when the joint is jammed, as it often is. The Cotton Bottom is just what a neighborhood bar should be. Hours are from 11 AM to 1 AM Monday through Saturday and 11 AM to 8 PM on Sunday.

Dead Goat Saloon
165 S. West Temple, Salt Lake City • 328-4628

For more than 30 years Dead Goat Saloon has provided Salt Lakers with a rocking atmosphere of nightly live music, satellite TV, great grub and beers galore. The atmosphere of this basement bar is one of uninhibited revelry — get down, party and have some fun. It's a favorite hangout of University of Utah students and athletic teams. You simply must order the Goat Burger. Although it's actually just a hamburger, it's still terrific. Pool tables, darts and pinball give you options for your nightly amusement. The Dead Goat is open from 11:30 AM to 2 AM Monday through Friday and 6 PM to 2 AM Saturday and Sunday.

Iggy's Sports Grill
677 S. 200 W., Salt Lake City • 532-9999

All things sporting set the tone at Iggy's Sports Grill. Sports buffs will go gaga over a gargantuan big-screen TV that measures 100-inches by 111-inches. It's the biggest around. If you can't find a seat anywhere near the mammoth screen, 21 other TV monitors will allow you to catch the big game. If you're watching sports, you've got to be drinking beer, right? Well, Iggy's gives you 47 choices of delectable brew, including two specialty beers made just for them: Iggy's crimson ale and blueberry hefe-weizen. You can enjoy the beer with pasta, roasted chicken or Iggy's specialty: a 1-pound burger. Spend some time looking at all the cool sports memorabilia, including a suit signed by Mohammed Ali. Iggy's is open 11:30 AM to midnight Monday through Saturday and 10:30 AM to 9 PM on Sunday.

Lazy Moon Pub
32 Exchange Place (355 S.), Salt Lake City • 363-7600

This casual place is a great spot for a sandwich, gourmet pizza or plate of pasta, washed down by a beer from one of Utah's microbreweries. The food transcends typical pub fare — everything is fresh, made from scratch, and nothing is deep-fried. Try the pasta de luna, with spinach fettuccine topped with garlic cream sauce, sun-dried tomatoes and Greek olives. It's yum. The Blue Moon nachos draw raves from finger-food aficionados. You can dine on the patio and hear live music from time to time. Hours are from 11:30 AM to midnight on weekdays and 11:30 AM to 1 AM on weekends.

Junior's Tavern
202 E. 500 S., Salt Lake City • 322-0318

Junior's may be a bit worn around the edges, but it has character. You'll see real people, with a crowd that mixes the urban down-and-out with college kids and local professionals. Junior's has been serving cold beer and hot blues and jazz on the great sound system for 23 years. You can munch on pickled eggs and hot dogs, play pool and drink Guinness on tap. An amazing collection of beer cans lines the walls. Hours are from noon to 1 AM daily.

www.insiders.com
See this and many other
Insiders' Guide® destinations
online — in their entirety.
Visit us today!

Slider's Pub and Grill
3505 S. Redwood Rd., West Valley City • 956-0270

This place is one of the few good pubs in the southwest part of Salt Lake Valley. Seven televisions let you keep current with sporting events while you sip one of the several excellent microbrew or domestic beers on tap. The food is great — you'll love the 8-ounce New York steak for only $6.95. The burgers are giant, and the halibut fish and chips tasty. And they have growlers (half-gallon jugs) of microbrew to go. They're open 11 AM to 10 PM Sunday through Thursday and from 11 AM to 11 PM Friday and Saturday.

Fiddler's Elbow
All-American Roadhouse
1036 E. 2100 S., Salt Lake City • 463-9393

Fiddler's Elbow is the kind of place where Americans used to eat before fast-food franchises took over and gave us the dismal homogenized cuisine that only 2-year-olds can tolerate. At Fiddler's Elbow you can get real mashed potatoes, chicken-fried steak, meatloaf and chili — food that tastes good and will stick to your ribs. Thirty beers give you choices from the palest ale to the darkest stout. Live rocking roadhouse piano music on

Tuesdays and Thursdays completes the down-home feel. Hours are 11 AM to 11 PM Monday through Thursday, 11 AM to 1 AM Saturday and Sunday and 11 AM to 10 PM on Sunday.

Tap Room
2168 S. Highland Dr. (1200 E.), Salt Lake City • 466-0974

The Tap Room is possibly the world's smallest bar — it seats maybe 25 people. Still, it's a Salt Lake institution that's been around for more than 50 years. Owner Manny Daniels is there every day, as he has been over the past half-century, exuding courtly friendliness and recounting amusing anecdotes with a friendly wink. At the Tap Room you can always get in a conversation and learn what people think are the vital issues around town. They serve domestic beer only, with peanuts and potato chips. It's open from 9 AM to 1 AM daily.

Private Clubs

Ashbury Pub
22 E. 100 S., Salt Lake City • 596-8600

The Ashbury Pub offers the complete package, from live music every night to a giant TV screen and satellite dish. If you can't find something to do, you're probably just in a bad mood and should go home. Dig the wild '60 and '70s rock 'n' roll posters on the walls — hey, baby, they're playin' your song. Order the Hummingbird, a concoction of rum, triple sec, banana liqueur and God knows what else, and you'll be flapping your wings in delight. Their motto is "where psychedelic meets psychorelic." If you can figure out what that means, let us know. Hours are 11 AM to 1 AM daily, and the cover varies from $3 to $5, depending on the band.

Burt's Tiki Lounge
726 S. State, Salt Lake City • 521-0572

If you're homesick for Hawaii, Burt's Tiki Lounge will take you back to paradise — slightly off kilter. With a grass ceiling and pictures of the Pope, JFK and Elvis, you know you've hit

Photo: Gastronomy, Inc./Market Street Oyster Bar

Salt Lakers love to power lunch or unwind at the end of a busy day at one of the area's private clubs. Visitors are always welcome with a guest membership.

the mother lode. At Burt's you're bound to meet someone weird and wonderful. Every night except Sunday, you can hear music that ranges from jazz, blues to whatever else is available. Try their specialty drinks — the helpful waitstaff can steer you in the right direction. Hours are from 5 PM to 2 AM daily.

Bricks
579 W. 200 S., Salt Lake City • 328-0255

Bricks is one of Salt Lake's premier dance clubs, and with more than 28,000 square feet of space, there's plenty of room to strut your stuff. The place is flat-out huge. Along with dancing, an upscale lounge and a sports room round out the festivities. Depending on the night, you might

even run into an occasional drag queen show or other off-the-wall extravaganza — it's that kind of place. Dancers can cool off with microbrews on tap and Bricks tea, which is like Long Island iced tea, but with fruit juice instead of Pepsi. Hours are from 9:30 PM to 2 AM daily. The cover varies from $5 to $6.

Cabana Club
31 E. 400 S., Salt Lake City • 359-6271

A Salt Lake tradition since 1940, the Cabana Club attracts adults looking for a civilized place for fine dining and intimate conversation. You can listen to the jazz magic of vocalist Peggy Rose on Wednesdays from 7 PM to 10 PM and on Saturdays at 8 PM and 10 PM. The club serves lunch and dinner Monday through Saturdays. You can always count on the chef to whip up steaks, seafood and pasta with an innovative flair. An added bonus is free valet parking daily from 5 PM. The Cabana Club is open from 11:30 AM to 11 PM Monday through Saturday. They're closed Sunday.

Club 90
150 W. 9065 S., Sandy • 566-3254

This huge club seats a whopping 400 people, many of whom have been coming back since the place opened in the late 1970s. Even though it's cavernous, the friendly service makes Club 90 feel like your favorite neighborhood bar — although there just aren't many bars in Sandy to compare with it. Lunch (including a daily special) and dinner are served seven days a week. If you drop in on a Monday for lunch, the famous steak sandwich is mandatory. On Sunday nights you can get a 16-ounce T-bone steak dinner for the amazingly low price of $5.95. How can you beat that? You can enjoy your beef on a patio with a great view or in an upscale dining atrium. For after-dinner amusement, you'll find a game room with darts, video games and five pool tables. Hours are 10 AM to 1 AM on weekdays and 11:30 AM to 1 AM on weekends.

Club D V 8
115 S. West Temple, Salt Lake City • 539-8400

Expect high-energy and full-throttle fun when you visit this four-story dance club. You can find action on all the levels, be it good beer, pulsating lights and the heavy beat of live music or even a fast game of pool. You'll find all kinds of folks, from the suits and ties to tattooed twentysomethings. Those younger than 21 can dance on the first floor. Beer and finger foods are available. Hours are 9:30 PM to 1:30 AM daily. The cover varies from $1 to $5.

D.B. Cooper's
19 E. 200 S., Salt Lake City • 532-2948

For upscale fine dining, a sophisticated ambiance and quiet elegance, D.B. Cooper's can't be beat. *Salt Lake Tribune* staffers love this place, and they'll tell you D.B's serves a great martini. D.B. Cooper's specializes in gourmet Mediterranean and Greek fare and wild game in season, including free-range Cornish game hens. The pasta dishes are also excellent. Cigar smokers are welcome, and you can listen to live jazz or piano every night. Hours are 11:30 AM to 1 AM daily.

Green Street Social Club
602 E. 500 S. Trolley Square, Salt Lake City • 532-4200

Everything is topnotch at this longtime favorite Salt Lake hangout in historic Trolley Square. Superb appetizers, a patio where you watch the summer twilight crawl up the face of the Wasatch Mountains and great live music have made it a classic club since it opened 19 years ago. Green Street has won numerous awards among Salt Lake's alternative press, from best bartenders and waitresses to best lunch. Their specialties include the halibut fish and chips and the pot roast. Try the Green Street coffee, an intoxicating blend of coffee, bourbon, Kahlua and Amaretto. Another favorite is the Steamy Orgasm, a titillating mixture of coffee, O'Darby's and Kahlua. In the summer the Green Street lemonade goes down smooth. Green Street is open from 11:30 AM to 1 AM Monday through Saturday and 11 PM to 12:30 AM on Sunday.

Lumpy's Social Club
3000 S. Highland Dr. (1200 E.), Salt Lake City • 484-5597

Lumpy's bleeds red — on big-game nights hundreds of University of Utah boosters don their red clothes and head for Lumpy's to root on the running Utes. They even run busses to and from games at the

---

INSIDERS' TIP

Beer lovers won't want to miss the annual Utah Brewers' Festival held at the Gallivan Utah Center, 36 E. 200 S. You'll be able to sample dozens of brews from Utah's microbreweries. Tasty pub food helps you enjoy these exquisite, handcrafted beers.

University of Utah. The place is big and loud, with dozens of TV monitors, five big-screen TVs, great food, a game room and local microbrew beer. If you want to get in a discussion with knowledgeable fans, this is the place. Sunday brunch is a big affair here. Hours are from 11 AM to 1 AM daily.

Manhattan Club of Salt Lake
5 E. 400 S., Salt Lake City • 364-7651

This venerable establishment caters to every dance crowd, from ballroom dancers on Saturday night to disco fans on Monday. Wednesday nights draws an alternative crowd for '80s music. If hiphop is your thing, a DJ will spin those records on Thursday. Lunch is served every day, and weekends offer fine dining. You can quench your thirst with the potent Jolly Rancher, a mixture of Malibu rum, Midori and soda water. Hours are from 11 AM to 1 AM Monday through Saturday. They're closed Sunday.

New Yorker Club
60 Market St. (340 S.), Salt Lake City • 363-0166

Rated No. 1 in the Salt Lake area by the 1997 Zagat Survey of Rocky Mountain Restaurants, the New Yorker is the crème de la crème of Salt Lake dining and nightlife. You have three choices here: a bar; a formal, high-class, expensive restaurant; and a more casual cafe. The cafe serves traditional dishes such as pizza, pasta and salads. The restaurant, more elegant but more pricey, serves succulent and perfectly prepared dishes such as venison, lamb and pork loin. The fresh seafood rivals any in the country. If you're a people watcher, you'll spot many of Salt Lake's ruling class planning their next coup while enjoying the luxurious ambiance. Lunch is served Monday through Friday from 11:30 AM to 2:30 PM. Dinner is served from Monday through Thursday from 5:30 to 10 PM and Friday through Saturday from 5:30 to 11 PM.

Port O' Call
400 S. 78 W., Salt Lake City • 521-0589

Truly an isle in a storm for fun-seeking Salt Lakers, Port O' Call makes sure you get what you want. With 26 TVs and satellite access, you can see virtually any televised sporting event on the planet. When the TV pales you can play pool or video games, and when that gets boring you can shake a leg to live entertainment on Wednesday, Thursday, Saturday and Sunday. For the unattached, it's a great place to meet singles. They have all kinds of food and an amazing selection of beers. Port O' Call hosts a huge St. Patrick's Day party on the Saturday before St. Patrick's Day. They're open every day of the year, from 11 AM to 2 AM. The cover charge for live entertainment is $3.

Room at the Top
Salt Lake Hilton, 150 W. 500 S., Salt Lake City • 532-3344

For a great view and a delightful, low-key atmosphere, you can't beat this classy establishment. The daily lunch and dinner specials are a must, and the Sunday brunch is one of the best around. Thursday through Sunday jazz music by Dave Compton and his son, Adam, creates a mood of meditative elegance. For jazz lovers, their Jazz at the Hilton series downstairs in the ballroom has been a godsend. The chicken cashew salad is tasty, and the ultimate meltdown Margarita will have you speaking Spanish in no time. Hours are Monday through Friday from 11:30 AM to midnight, Saturday from 5 PM to midnight and Sunday from 10 AM to 10 PM.

Safari Club
765 S. West Temple, Salt Lake City • 530-0707

Hey mon, you want reggae and nothing else? Bob Marley on the walls watching your every move? If so, take a trip with the Safari Club. You can mellow out with live reggae

---

INSIDERS' TIP

Servers and bartenders in Salt Lake make only about $3 to $4 an hour and rely on tips to make a livable wage. You should tip at least 15 to 20 percent for good service.

bands and eat Caribbean and Cuban food. Hours are 7 PM to 2 AM Monday through Sunday, except Tuesday, when it is closed. The cover charge is $5 to $10, depending on the band.

Sandy's Station
8925 S. 255 W., Sandy • 255-2289

For country line dancing and good times with a Western flair, bring your partner to Sandy's Station. Live Western bands from Thursday through Saturday pack the huge 40-foot-by-80-foot dance floor with a throbbing mass of fun seekers. Just watch out for the spurs and you'll be all right. The place might get a bit rowdy at times, but that's part of the fun. Between dances see if you can identify the various species of animal heads on the wall. Bottled beer and a full bar are available. Hours are 4 PM to 1 AM Monday through Saturday and 4 PM to midnight on Sunday. You'll pay a $5 cover charge on Friday and Saturday.

Sun Club
200 S. 700 W., Salt Lake City • 531-0833

A favorite among the Salt Lake gay and lesbian populations for 16 years, this legendary club is always packed with contented patrons, be they gay, straight or whatever. What keeps 'em coming back for more? Maybe it's the knowledgeable bartenders, the great patio, a throbbing dance scene or the fact that the Sun is the landing pad for Salt Lake's dharma bums, on-the-edge artists and resident beatniks. If you want funky, crazed and colorful, the Sun will deliver, in spades. It's open daily from noon to 2 AM.

Spanky's Pool
45 W. Broadway (300 S.), Salt Lake City • 359-1200

Pool and live rock 'n' roll is what Spanky's is all about. A variety of hot bands Wednesday through Saturday keeps the large crowd on their feet. You can't get food there, but you can get 62 or so kinds of beer and other specialty drinks. The waitstaff is friendly and full of fun. Besides being a great nightspot, Spanky's also supports Utah culture by displaying the work of local artists on the downstairs lobby walls — an unusual gesture that allows a different kind of crowd than your typical art lovers to see paintings, photography and other varieties of local art. More Utah businesses of all kinds should follow Spanky's enlightened example. Hours are 8:30 PM to 12:30 AM daily. For live music, the cover varies from $3 to $5.

Totem's Private Club and Steakhouse
538 S. Redwood Rd., West Valley City • 975-0401

You'll be impressed with the decor and service at this club. The Western lodge atmosphere is sophisticated but with a whoop-and-holler flair. It's big as all outdoors — how about 19,500 square feet with over 23,500 linear feet of 10-inch lodge-pole pine? Big enough fer ya? The cafe is open for breakfast and serves great bacon and eggs and omelets. The Totem's lunch buffet is a must for lovers of variety. For $6.95, it's a great deal. You can dance to live Western music Thursday through Saturday. Hours are Monday through Saturday from 10:30 AM to 1 AM and Sunday from 11 AM to 10 PM.

The Westerner Club
3360 S. Redwood Rd. • 972-5447

This enormous Western club can pack 800 to 900 people on their huge dance floor — one of the biggest around. You'll rub elbows with country line dancers of every age, race, religion, political persuasion and preferred style of country attire. It's sheer down-home, drink-it-straight, bottoms-up fun. A grill turns out steaks, sandwiches and chicken dishes. Hours are 6 PM to 1 AM daily, and the cover varies from $1 to $3.

INSIDERS' TIP

For a break from the bar scene, try an evening of gallery hopping. Every third Friday of the month various Salt Lake art galleries sponsor a Gallery Stroll from 6 to 9 PM. See the Arts chapter for more information.

Zephyr Club

301 S. West Temple, Salt Lake City
• 355-2582

The Zephyr Club put Salt Lake City on the national music map. The list of prominent performers who have played here range from great blues artists like Koko Taylor and John Mayall to superb folk acts like Emmylou Harris and top jazz performers like Charlie Hunter. You'll love the elegant, casual ambiance. It's simply the best place in Salt Lake to hear great music. The cover charge ranges from $3 to $7. Call for a lineup of acts and showtimes.

Coffee Shops

The Coffee Garden

900 S. 900 E., Salt Lake City • 355-3425

This is a superb place to kick back and relax. Lounge chairs, sofas and tables scattered about beg you to sip your coffee or tea and forget your troubles. The Coffee Garden serves Seattle's Best Coffee and tea from the Republic of Tea. The Coffee Garden serves sandwiches and salads, and every Monday they bake up a big batch of yummy scones. Hours are 6 AM to 10 PM Sunday through Thursday and 7 AM to 11 PM on Friday and Saturday. On Sunday they're open from 8 AM to 10 PM.

A Cup of Joe

353 W. 200 S., Salt Lake City • 363-8322

You'll find a sassy city atmosphere here, with fresh-roasted coffee and a plethora of reading material. The youthful waitstaff can be a bit testy at times, but since they're all actually budding poets, artists and so on, it's best to be patient with them. The people-watching is great through the big windows facing 200 South — you'll see all kinds. For poetry in your face, come to the poetry slams the third Saturday of every month. For refreshment, an espresso bar, tea, Italian sodas and baked goods are available. They're open from 7 AM to 12 AM Monday through Saturday and 9 AM to 2 PM Sunday.

Salt Lake Roasting Company and Cafe

320 E. 400 S., Salt Lake City • 363-7572

When you open the door of this Salt Lake institution, you know you're in for a treat — the rich aroma of roasting coffee hits you right in the face. Salt Lakers yearning for a great cup of coffee have headed for the Salt Lake Roasting Company since 1981. Owner John Bolton deserves credit as the first man to believe that Salt Lakers needed — and deserved — a real cup of coffee. He's made Salt Lake a better place. The coffee roaster is right out in front so you can watch the weird-looking machine do its thing. It's fascinating. They offer a full espresso bar and serve lunch and dinner. The pastries are made on the premises and are some of the tastiest in Salt Lake — especially the triple chocolate torte. Hours are 6:45 AM to midnight Monday through Saturday.

Comedy Clubs

The Comedy Circuit

10 North Main St., Salt Lake City
• 561-7777

Nothing makes you feel better than a good belly laugh, and nobody provides more laughs than the Comedy Circuit. The shows are 8 PM on Tuesday, Wednesday and Thursday; 8 and 10:45 PM on Friday; and 9 PM on Saturday. The Tuesday, Wednesday and Thursday shows cost $10.75, and the Friday and Saturday shows, $13.75. Finger foods and beer are available.

David's Comedy Shop

2324 S. Redwood Rd. • 972-9688

David's is a combination private club and sometime comedy club. The comedy is limited to the winter months, and only on Saturday night. The rest of the time it's an upscale, quiet place that serves excellent steaks and halibut and a variety of drinks. Hours are from 11 PM to midnight daily.

Albertsons®

FOOD & DRUG

- 370 East 200 South — Salt Lake City
- 1785 Murray - Holladay Road — Salt Lake City
- 898 East 3300 South — Salt Lake City
- 1638 South 9th East — Salt Lake City
- 2040 South 2300 East — Salt Lake City
- 3865 South 2300 East — Salt Lake City
- 140 North 900 West—Salt Lake City
- 200 West 500 South— Bountiful
- 84 West Parrish Lane — Centerville
- 1212 East Draper Pkwy — Draper
- 3555 West 3500 South — Granger
- 3871 West 5400 South — Kearns
- 6989 South 1300 East — Midvale
- 5570 South 900 East — Murray
- 755 East 9400 South — Sandy
- 1825 West 4700 South — Taylorsville
- 9000 South Redwood Road — West Jordan
- 3420 South 5600 West— West Valley City
- 1760 Park Avenue — Park City

- 3945 Washington Boulevard — Ogden
- 2044 Harrison Boulevard— Ogden
- 5691 S. Harrison Blvs. — Ogden
- 2076 North Main Street — Layton
- 912 North Fairfield Road — Layton
- 1900 West 5651 South — Roy
- 135 East Main — American Fork
- 1585 N. State Street — Orem
- 25 West Center— Orem
- 2255 North University Parkway — Provo
- 560 West Center — Provo
- 652 North 800 East — Spanish Fork
- 905 South Main — Cedar City
- 853 South Bluff Street — St. George
- 49 East 400 North — Logan
- 1323 Dewar Drive — Rock Springs
- 170 West 200 North — Kaysville
- 915 West Redcliff Drive — Washington

Shopping

Warm up those wallets, and get that plastic ready for the quick draw: The Salt Lake Valley has eight malls and shopping centers, not to mention a profusion of one-of-a-kind shops, where you can spend, spend, spend.

You'll find sophisticated designer clothing, handmade imported clothing and wearable art here, plus Western-style duds and togs for tykes. Collectibles and lots of regional wares, from jewelry to quilts, fill the shelves of our specialty stores. And if your tastes run to antiques, consider that some of the pieces available here have traveled across the plains with Mormon pioneers. We offer reading matter for every kind of bookworm, local and regional artwork and an awesome thrift-store scene. From one end of town to the other, whatever you're looking for you are likely to find it somewhere in the Valley.

Business hours vary, so you may want to peruse the stores' hours-of-operation notices carefully. Most stores in the area's shopping malls are open from 10 AM to 9 PM Monday through Saturday and from noon to 5 PM on Sunday. The ZCMI Center and all ZCMI stores are closed on Sunday. Some specialty shops stay open until 9 PM on weekdays and Saturday, while others close at 5 or 6 PM. Many shops have Sunday hours, usually 1 to 5 PM, but not all stores are open on Sunday. Quite a few antique stores and smaller boutiques set their hours according to the weather, placement of the moon or whatever strikes their fancy. Don't rule them out, just call ahead. It's always best to check out the exact hours for a store or shopping mall before you plan a shopping trip in the Salt Lake Valley. We've provided the phone number in each listing. During the holidays, from Thanksgiving to Christmas eve, most mall and many other stores have extended hours.

In this chapter we've provided an overview of Salt Lake shopping opportunities, but there are so many wonderful things to buy we only have room for the tip of the iceberg. Also see our Arts chapter for creative possibilities from artists' galleries. Museum gift shops are another source of interesting items (see our Sightseeing and Attractions chapter). And don't overlook the wonderful shops described in the shopping section of our Park City chapter. Listed below are the shopping spots we consider the best of the best.

Malls and Shopping Centers

We have all the clone stores found in malls across the country as well as a few that will be new to Easterners venturing West for the first time. A few major department stores may be new to visitors as well. Zions Cooperative Mercantile Institution (ZCMI) began in Salt Lake City in 1868. Today, this Mormon church-owned department store offers upscale clothing for the entire family plus china and crystal, furniture, cosmetics and much more.

Nordstrom is well-known to shoppers in the western part of the country, but if you are visiting from the East and have never heard of "Nordies," here's the lowdown. The department store chain is known for its service, high quality, sophisticated clothing and equitable exchange policy. The parent store, known affectionately to Insiders as "Mother Nordstrom," is in Seattle, Washington. You might compare Nordstrom to Dillard's, with a fresh Western attitude. Mervyn's of California is also a popular store in the western states and is on a par with JCPenney.

With that orientation, let the shopping begin.

Cottonwood Mall
4835 S. Highland Dr., Salt Lake City
• 278-0416

ZCMI and JCPenney anchor this mall that has loads of free outdoor parking and more than 150 stores and restaurants. Shapiro's is a local favorite for fine leather luggage and accessories. Wasatch Pendleton is a great stop for wonderful Pendleton wool clothing and blankets. Eclipse has great imported batik ladies clothing, and the Accessory Depot usually has great finds in their jewelry department — lots of liquid silver and stones. LaBathtique can enhance your bath's decor with lots of shower curtains, towels, soaps and other accessories many of which smell very good. Paper ala Carde has unusual greeting cards, and you'll find skis and sporting good at Pederson's, a popular store with Salt Lakers. Nizhoni Trading Company offers a good selection of Indian handmade jewelry, pottery, kachina dolls, music and more.

The chains are well-represented here, too: The Gap, The Limited, Victoria's Secret and The Express all have shops at Cottonwood, and B. Dalton has a great bookstore in the south end of the mall. You can snack on pastries or get a full meal at one of several restaurants in the food court. ZCMI has a deli-style eatery on the third floor. It serves a truly delicious, very uncomplicated hot dog along with soups, salads and sandwiches.

Crossroads Plaza Shopping Center
50 S. Main St., Salt Lake City • 363-1558

Crossroads is across the street from the ZCMI Center downtown and houses nearly 150 store, kiosks and eateries. The anchor stores are Nordstrom and Mervyn's. You'll find well-known shops like Crabtree and Evelyn, The Gap, Baby Gap, Rag Baby, Nature Company, Frederick's of Hollywood, The Limited, Country Seat, The Bombay Company and more. The Tinder Box specializes in fine tobaccos but also has a wonderful selection of music boxes, figurines and gift items. Haroon's is a favorite source of very pretty, flowy, gentlewomen's clothing imported from all over the world. Other standouts include the Accessory Depot, another great place to buy imported women's clothing; JMR Chalk Garden, which carries funky high-end clothing and accessories for men and women; Tabula Rasa, a good choice for cards, journals, stationery, incense and other fun stuff; and Salt Lake-based Glifx, a great find, where you can buy anything from wind chimes to Zen rock gardens. Waldenbooks has a nice store in the mall, and the food court offers numerous choices from sushi to pizza.

FYI

Unless otherwise noted, the area code for all phone numbers listed in this guide is 801.

The mall has a covered parking garage and three cinemas, and all stores give a two-hour validation with your purchase. Crossroads is adjacent to the Marriott Hotel.

Foothill Village Shopping Center
1400 S. Foothill Dr., Salt Lake City
• 582-3646

This east side shopping center has fewer than 75 stores, but with ZCMI II as the anchor, it's worth a visit. You won't find too much formula shopping here. Foothill has several locally owned shops not found in malls or other places in the city. A trip to Bill Loya Fine Women's Apparel provides insight into why many Salt Lake women are so well-dressed. This is a quintessential specialty store with an emphasis on American designers. The clothes are pricy, but you get what you pay for: top quality. Raymond's apparel fits the needs of the country club and jet set to a fare-thee-well. Besides this location, Raymond's has another store on South Temple (you'll find details in the "Unique Clothing" section later in the chapter). Foothill also has the very popular Sports Den for skis, snowboards, mountain bikes, in-line skates and better sportswear. While you're store hopping, take a break at Starbucks. Besides the to-die-for apparel found at Foothill there's a treasure of a bookstore called A Woman's Place; it has a great selection of books and a wonderful staff (for more information, see the listing below under "Bookstores"). Park free in the outdoor lot as well as in a covered parking garage.

We would be remiss not to mention the Sundance Catalog Store next door to the shopping center at 1460 S. Foothill Drive, 581-9711. Items that appear in the extraordinary mail-order catalog, distributed throughout the country by Robert Redford and friends from the Sundance Institute, are available in the store. You'll find men's and women's clothing, jewelry and shoes as well as household items and furniture — all in a Southwestern theme. If you're looking for unique gifts or something special for yourself, you'll really enjoy this place. Bob won't be there to help you, but the friendly staff is the next-best thing. The sales are amazing!

Fashion Place Mall
6200 S. State St., Salt Lake City
• 265-0504

Dillard's, Nordstrom, Sears and ZCMI anchor Fashion Place. You'll find the tried-and-true, such as Eddie Bauer and A.K.A., Ann Taylor, The Gap, The Limited, The Express, Victoria's Secret, Lane Bryant, Foot Locker, the Sock Box, Spencer Gifts, Radio Shack, a large well-stocked Body Shop and a big Waldenbooks. The Nizhoni Trading Company sells local handmade Indian jewelry and pottery. Fashion Place doesn't seem like a big mall, but the 90 stores and 20 places to feed your face always fill the bill. There's plenty of free outdoor parking. Ross Dress for Less can be found in the northwest corner of the large parking lot.

South Towne Center
10450 S. State St., Sandy • 572-1516

More than 130 shops and eateries provide plenty of spending opportunities in this new mall anchored by JCPenney, Mervyn's, Dillard's and ZCMI. There's a Pier 1 Imports outside the mall, and inside you'll find shoe stores, specialty shops like Bath and Body Works, Cutlery Corner and the Candle Shop.

Tux and Tails can supply duds for your next black-tie affair. Enjoy Wear, Copper Rivet, Mr. Rags and Miller Stockman are ready to cover your back for less formal occasions. B. Dalton Booksellers has a nice store for bookworms, and you can choose from two card shops for greeting cards and stationery. South Towne has plenty of service stores to snap your picture or style your hair, and nine jewelry stores will put rings on your fingers and bells on your toes. There's a theater complex with 10 screens and plenty of free outdoor parking.

Trolley Square
602 E. 500 S., Salt Lake City • 521-9877

The 10-acre block now known as Trolley Square served as the city's fairgrounds until 1908 when Union Pacific Railroad magnate E.H. Harriman snapped up the site for his state-of-the-art trolley car system. To house the trolleys, the unusual mission-style car barn was erected. By 1914 more than 144 trolleys served the Valley from this location. Service was discontinued in 1945, and the old decaying car barn, vacant for many years, narrowly escaped the wrecking ball in 1972. Relics from the turn-of-the-century were rescued from other buildings throughout the city and used in constructing the unique stores in this festival marketplace. Trolley Square is registered as a historic site by the state of Utah.

At the east entrance to the square an old 97-foot-high water tower that once held 50,000 gallons of water for use in case of fire is lit up with neon at night to help you find your way. You'll find two floors of specialty shopping here. The Chalk Garden is the anchor store in "Trolley," and it's so delectable you'll be glad you stopped in. Upscale women's and men's clothing, elegant shoes and accessories are just part of the Chalk Garden experience.

The main event, especially for browsers, is the jewelry counter at the front of the store. Drooling is permitted if you don't make a spectacle of it. You'll find lovely antique jewelry pieces, well-crafted replications, antique and new "things" you can't possibly manage without: teapots, picture frames, silver tea service, cache boxes and much more. Some items are quite pricey, but others are very reasonable.

Trolley is also home to Clog Corner, The

Basket Loft — loaded with wonderful baskets and home furnishing — and standards like Williams Sonoma, Laura Ashley, Nicole Miller and Ann Taylor. There's also Talbot's, The Limited, The Express, Banana Republic and Oxford Club Polo. Air Apparent sells all types of kites, and Fowl Weather Friends has tons of ducks — from decoys to artwork. Don't miss Haroon's on the upper level for wonderful imported ladies clothing. Elegant linens are available at European Linens and Design, and B. Dalton Booksellers has a small, well-stocked store.

This shopping center has nearly 90 shops, 20 restaurants and a theater complex with four screens. You can park outdoors on ground level near the shops if you can find a spot. Failing that, you'll find ample parking underground at Trolley or in the lot across the street south of the square. Metered parking is also available on the street surrounding Trolley Square. Unless you opt for a meter, parking is free.

Valley Fair Mall
3601 S. 2700 W., West Valley City
• 969-6211

More than 100 stores and restaurants provide a wonderful shopping and eating experience in this west side mall. JCPenney, ZCMI and Mervyn's anchor the mall. There are shoe stores, men's and women's and kids clothing shops, craft and game stores, jewelers and a host of shops such as Prints Plus, All Around Balloons, the Christmas Cottage (featuring wonderful Christmas decorations year round), Great Expectations (for moms-to-be) and GNC. Tie One On at the tie store or get a photograph to remember at The CoverLook. Mall planners didn't overlook your occasional need for the predictable, so you'll find all the chain stores you've come to know and love. There's plenty of outdoor parking and a cinema with nine screens.

ZCMI Center
36 S. State St., Salt Lake City • 579-6000

ZCMI is the largest store in its namesake mall, featuring more than 3,000 brand names including clothing for the whole family and everything you could possibly need to outfit a well-furnished home. The bakery and candy department in the basement should not be missed. The pastries and breads are beautiful, and if you're a chocolate lover be prepared to indulge your sweet tooth. The store's deli, also in the basement, serves a lite fare. The Tiffin Room has been serving lunch to shoppers in a more formal setting for more than 50 years.

The modern ZCMI Center mall has two stories and more than 60 specialty shops and kiosks in addition to a food court, a bank, a United Airlines ticket office, a U.S. Postal Service site and a covered parking terrace. You'll find tons of things to buy including candles, clothing, shoes, lingerie, jewelry and food. Mr. Mac, a locally owned men's clothing store, is the home of the affordable two-pair-of-pants suit. You won't want to miss the Mormon Handicraft store on the upper level. It has some of the most extraordinary handmade quilts this side of Amish country.

Deseret Book has a large store with an enormous selection of LDS and other book titles (check this store out in our "Bookstore" section later in the chapter). The ZCMI Center is closed on Sunday and closes two hours earlier than most malls and shops on Saturday evening. There's plenty of parking in the covered parking terrace, and all stores provide two-hour validations with purchase.

Factory Outlet Mall

Factory Stores of America
12101 S. Factory Outlet Rd., Draper
• 571-2933

Anchored by the Vanity Fair outlet, this small 33-store indoor outlet mall houses Kay-Bee Toy and Hobby, Adidas Shoes, Casual Corner, Corning Revere and Danskin stores, to name a few. It's an unassuming shopping experience that doesn't require a lot of time. If you want to make a day of your sojourn to the south end of the valley, plan a trip to Kennecott Utah Copper open pit mine about 15 minutes away. Finish the day off in the south end of town with a great meal at Guadalahonkeys Mexican Restaurant (good food for the whole family) or Panache, if you are sans kids. You'll find Kennecott listed in the Kidstuff chapter under "Ohhh!".

Gifts and Specialty Items

The Blue Cockatoo
1506 S. 1500 E., Salt Lake City
• 467-4023

This charming little shop sells jewelry of all kinds including handmade pieces and some very nice commercially made items. Pottery from local artists and potters around the world is certain to get your attention with its intriguing designs. The shop sells handmade decorative tiles, wood carvings, animals, bowls, fossils, watercolors and artistic odds and ends. The items are affordable, and the shopping experience at The Blue Cockatoo is always a pleasure — but never on Sunday.

Cahoots Cards and Gifts
878 E. 900 S., Salt Lake City • 538-0606

A trip to Cahoots is always a good mood elevator. The store caters to the alternative lifestyle — gay, lesbian and transgender — but also has an ample supply of merchandise for straight folks. The greeting cards are some of the funniest in town and appeal to all lifestyles and all occasions. T-shirts are usually a great find here. Some carry a social message and many poke fun at local politics and social situations. The store carries not-so-traditional postcards and adult novelties as well as a sophisticated selection of fine home accessories including ironwork, blown glass and pottery. You can buy Go Girl CDs here with hot music from the New York and LA scene. The bookstore in the back room has a great selection. For details, see the listing under "Bookstores" later in the chapter. Cahoots is open seven days a week.

Dog's Meow
2045 E. 3300 S., Salt Lake City
• 468-0700

A great boutique with fun stuff for felines, canines and humines. The shop has dog and cat accessories including pet carriers, bowls, quality toys, speciality foods and herbal treats. It specializes in very uptown collars made of nylon in various patterns such as chili peppers and art deco designs and leather collars from Germany. Humans will find lots of petlover collectibles like etched-glass items, jewelry, T-shirts and framed pictures. If you need a gift for a furry friend back home, this is the place to shop. It's open Monday through Saturday.

Felt Buchorn
445 E. South Temple, Salt Lake City
• 532-1131

The beautiful china, crystal and collectibles found in this store make gift giving an elegant affair. You'll find Royal Copenhagen, Lladro and Hummel as well as and Bing and Grondahl Christmas collectibles year round. The store has fine-quality stationery and invitations, and Felt Buchorn is one of the very few stores in Salt Lake that carries fine-quality linen, cotton and embroidered handkerchiefs. A small thing, but you just never know when a delicate hankie might be the perfect gift. The children's department carries a line of plush toys, stuffed animals and puppets as well as Beatrix Potter and other designs in children's china collectibles. The store, which is open Monday through Saturday, has served the Salt Lake Valley for more than 40 years.

Gentler Times Quilt Shop
4880 S. Highland Cir., Salt Lake City
• 277-9233

This shop is in an old house built in the 1870s and is a pleasant place to shop. Antique quilts with traditional patterns from the late 1800s to 1930s in good condition are a specialty. You'll also find a few rare Amish quilts from time to time and new quilts from India made of quality fabric, craftsmanship and design. Books on quilt making and its history are also available. The shop sells new fabrics, patterns and quilt-making supplies. Classes are available in making quilts and dolls. The glassware, primitive art and other well-chosen items in the store make interesting gifts. The shop is closed on Sunday.

Kismet Belly Dance Boutique
1760 S. 1100 E., Salt Lake City
• 486-7780

A belly dance supply store and a whole lot more in Salt Lake City? Yes! Kismet sells belly-dancing costumes, music and accessories. The store has a big selection of large and small scarves — from glittery to metallic — for dancers and those who live on the wild side. It also has some very unusual Peruvian and Egyptian earrings. Classes on belly dancing are available, and Kismet hosts an annual belly-dance festival in mid-August each year. It's a big event that attracts dancers and spectators from all over the country (read more about it in our Festivals and Annual Events chapter). Kismet is open Monday through Saturday.

Lost Arts
4835 Highland Dr., Salt Lake City
• 278-9505

This shop on the upper level of Cotton-wood Mall features gifts, books, music, art-work representing more than 140 local artists and a tea bar. Who could ask for anything more? The paintings, sculpture and pottery are created by area artists and reflect contemporary introspection. Some of the jewelry is simple, making use of silver and stones common to the area. Other pieces are more sophisticated in materials and design. The crafts-manship is excellent. Additional jewelry pieces can be ordered from the artist through store. The young staff is knowledgeable, energetic and always makes you feel welcome. They also know a lot about herbal tea. Lost Arts is open seven days a week.

Madre Tierra
4694 Holladay Blvd., Salt Lake City
• 277-7141

This little treasure of a shop has a large selection of jewelry from Latin America and New Guinea including necklaces and chokers, bracelets, anklets and earrings. Most are silver, and some have precious and semiprecious stones. Many of the styles are pre-Colombian from Peru. Prices range from affordable to expensive. The store features handicrafts including Zapotec weaving from Mexico and traditional weaving from Bolivia, Peru and Ecuador along with indigenous clothing and articles made from hand-loomed cloth. If you like unusual gifts or want to spoil yourself with something unique, Madre Tierra is worth a visit, and its open Monday through Saturday.

Tea and Trumpets
1515 S. 1500 E., Salt Lake City
• 487-0717

Teapot collectors and connoisseurs of fine tea are bound to love this place. You'll find a large selection of teapots including Brown Betty's and children's tea sets plus tea cozies, trivets, specialty jams, creamers and lots of teas. You won't walk out with just tea things though. The store also offers fresh-baked goods and food items. The carrot cake may have been inspired by angels (see the "Sweet Things" section in this chapter for more details on the delicious baked goods here). Everything in the shop is good, and you can take away foods for a picnic in any of the local parks (see our Parks and Recreation chapter for nearby spots). While you are in the area of 15th and 15th, as Salt Lakers call this neighborhood, check out the great frame shop next door to Tea and Trumpets. It's called The Framery and carries great prints, local artwork and reasonably priced frames. The King's English bookstore is on the other side of T and T (see the "Bookstores" section). This shop is closed on Sunday.

T.P. Gallery
252 S. Main St., Salt Lake City
• 364-2961

Looks are deceiving. This is not a museum. It's actually a store filled with exquisitely crafted Native American items. You'll find locally and regionally made work including traditional basketry, drums, tribal rugs and weaving, jewelry, pottery, wood and stone carvings, animal and bird fetishes and many beaded items from moccasins to bags and key rings. The store carries artwork including paintings in watercolor, oil and sand. The jewelry is primarily silver with a variety of stones including turquoise, coral, malachite, lapis, black onyx and more. T. P. has belt buckles, rings, earrings, bracelets and necklaces in designs such as squash blossom, butterfly, lightning, scenery and cluster petit-point. There is so much to choose from here. The work represents the

Historic Trolley Square offers a wealth of sophisticated shopping, great dining and loads of entertainment for the whole family.

tradition and culture of Navajo, Paiute, Ute, Goshute, Zuni, Hopi, Crow, Sioux, Cherokee, Apache and Papago people. T.P. Gallery is closed on Sunday.

The Quilted Bear
145 W. 7200 S., Salt Lake City
• 566-5454
1172 E. Brickyard Rd., Salt Lake City
• 466-0052

Small "villages" within the stores display the large selection of handmade items including decorations for your home and gifts for every occasion. Beautiful wood and metal crafted items, pottery and ceramic, dried flowers and floral arrangements, year-round Christmas decorations and handmade clothing and quilts are available at both locations. The small selection of antiques features furniture, glassware, pottery and other collectibles. Plan to spend a little time here. There's so much to

see. Browsing is free, and most of the items are reasonably priced. The shop is closed on Sunday.

The Southwest Shop
914 E. 900 S., Salt Lake City • 531-8523

As the name implies, you'll find gifts, furniture, folk art, jewelry and other interesting stuff in a Southwest motif. The shop, which carries Kilim rugs and Soleri bells, is in the neighborhood called Ninth and Ninth (900 S. and 900 E.) close to other fun shops such as Floribunda, just up the street at 920 E. 900 S., where you'll find wonderful one-of-a-kind gifts. Starbucks is on the west corner. Southwest shop is closed on Sunday.

Under the Sun
301 E. 1700 S., Salt Lake City • 466-1357

This local artisan center has a bit of everything, including unique handcrafted gifts, cards, clothing, jewelry, candles, stained glass and pottery, bottles, handmade papers, jewelry, wind chimes and more. The shop has wearable arts and takes custom orders for clothing. Under the Sun is closed on Sunday.

Clothing for the Whole Family

Unique and Funky Stuff

Bizarre Bazaar
1957 E. Murray Holladay Blvd., Holladay • 278-3334

The Bazaar has a good selection of well-made imported clothing and accessories for women from tie-dye to batik. Apparel here is designed to be eclectic and loose fitting, which means it covers a multitude of food sins and looks quite stylish at the same time. Thin people look nice in it, too. The accessories and jewelry are just right for the unique fashion statement you'll make after a visit to Bizarre Bazaar. It is across the street from the north side of the Cottonwood Mall. The shop is open Tuesday through Saturday.

Chameleon Artwear
875 E. 900 S., Salt Lake City • 363-6463

The clothing in this lovely shop is imported, very beautiful and quite unusual. You won't find these items anywhere else in the city. The jewelry selection is striking and includes some unique Tibetan prayer boxes, stones and silver. You will find Chameleon in the Ninth and Ninth area (900 S. and 900 E.) The shop has wonderful sales and a nice layaway plan if you're on a tight budget. Sorry guys — no menswear here, but you can shop for a special lady. She'll be very impressed. The shop is closed on Sunday.

Dancing Cranes Imports
2120 S. 1100 E., Salt Lake City • 486-1129

You'll find a large selection of handcrafted imported tie-dye, batik, woven and silk clothing for men and women in this giant shop, but you have to look closely at each item to make certain the craftsmanship is worth the money. Quality varies from piece to piece. The store also has a large selection of jewelry including silver, beads and stones. Dancing Cranes has meditation tapes and CDs, drums and other wonderful musical instruments, incense, a nice selection of happy- and serious-face Buddhas and gobs more great stuff. It's a fun shop in the center of Sugarhouse and worth visiting. It's open seven days a week.

Gaia
241 E. 300 S., Salt Lake City • 532-4242

Remember the '60s? Tie-dye, candles, doorway beads. Visit Gaia and step back nearly four decades. This tiny shop is a peace emporium like you'd find in the Haight-Ashbury years ago. Some of the clothing is imported from Indonesia, India and Guatemala. The jewelry is fun, and you'll find loads of bumper stickers, stickers for all occasions, rainbow flags and posters in this blast-from-the-past shop. You can drop in seven days a week.

Nativo
353 W. 200 S., Salt Lake City • 531-8555

Words almost fail to describe this great shop, but that's our job so we'll give it a go. Nativo is a creative store. It sells one-of-a-kind contemporary clothing items and separate pieces that work alone or together. When you wear clothing from this shop you'll look casual yet sophisticated, making a personal statement without looking like you're sporting a neon sign. The jewelry selection is well-chosen. These are investment pieces with a unique look and time-honored craftsmanship. The home furnishings in this shop are uniquely

---

INSIDERS' TIP

Now that you have all kinds of wonderful furniture and collectibles for your home, how do you make it all work? Genius Loci Feng Shui can help create harmony and balance in your personal environment. Call (800) 515-2272.

crafted and will set your decor apart from others. A visit to Nativo will set everything straight, and you'll be glad you took the time. Visit the Park City store for an even bigger selection (see our Park City chapter). The shop is closed on Sunday.

Traditional Garb

Old Navy
634 E. 400 S., Salt Lake City • 322-1566
Of course this is a chain, but we have to mention it because of the large selection of overalls — maybe the biggest in the city. We're thankful the store seldom runs out and the price is always right. Old Navy also has shirts, skirts, pants, shorts, undies, sleepwear and, to keep your feet happy in the summer, fluorescent Jellies. The baby clothes are true-to-size and really cute. The clerks walk around with head sets to communicate with other clerks instead of rushing around asking questions while you're left hanging. What a nifty idea! The store is a few doors down from a wonderful Barnes and Noble bookstore. There's plenty of free parking, and Old Navy is open seven days a week.

Raymond's
350 E. 100 S., Salt Lake City • 364-4377
1400 Foothill Drive • 581-1107
Raymond's has been dressing the well-dressed woman in Salt Lake for more than 60 years. The clothing is uncommon, perfect for the stylish casual occasion or an elegant black-tie affair. The price tag reflects the fine craftsmanship and high-quality style and fabrics in Raymond's clothing. Accessories are always available to complement the wardrobe. The store caters to good taste and refinement as few others do. Raymond's is closed on Sunday.

Richelle's Shoes and Designer Fashions/Dustin's Menswear
4699 S. Highland Dr., Salt Lake City • 272-3111
Salt Lake has some nice boutiques for pricy sophisticated fashion hounds, but Richelle's and Dustin's have gone beyond the norm to bring the best designer apparel to our Western metropolis. Besides your favorite designer clothes not found in other stores here, the shop carries some great accessories. Shoes, however, are the big event. The selection is large, the styles are wonderful, and until the store opened we could only fondle the pages of Vogue and dream.

The layout in the store is very pleasant, and it is also — bless their thoughtful, fashion merchandising-minded hearts — quite spacious. Richelle's has the best of the best for women, and Dustin's has everything every well-dressed guys could want. The sales people will make you feel very special, and when you're spending the kind of money it takes to have a truly satisfying shopping experience here, that's important. The shop is near the Cottonwood Mall. Parking is free and plentiful right outside the front door. You can get your fill of designer delights Monday through Saturday.

Utah Woolen Mills
59 W. South Temple, Salt Lake City • 364-1851
Ohhh! The woolens have been glorious in this shop for nearly 100 years. Men's and ladies suits and overcoats are the specialty, but the shop carries other items as well, such as boiled-wool jackets, Austrian sweaters, blankets, hats and a line of custom-made jewelry. The clothing is expensive, but anything you purchase here is an investment — well-tailored and meant to last a long time. The store is west of the Crossroads Mall parking-ramp entrance on the South Temple side of the mall. This store is open Monday through Saturday.

Small Fry Apparel

Baby Heirlooms
3142 S. Highland Dr., Salt Lake City • 483-2211, (800) 340-8838
From newborn to size 4 toddler, the clothes for little boys and girls at this charming store are pricey and worth every penny. The Allison Rose collection of vintage-look baby dresses is, in a word, precious. The little mister will look spiffy in one of the shop's three-piece outfits with tie or suspenders. The store has christening clothing to make baby look regal

and plenty of layettes for gift giving. Other treasures include hard-to-find Reed and Barton silver service for children and a good selection of very unusual tranquility mobiles. The full-bodied puppets are adorable, and so are the wooden toys. The Kouvalias line of wooden toys from Greece are colorful, and the pull toys are highly creative. Heirlooms has more than eight styles of baby books, first-year calendars, photo albums, note cards, announcements and thank-you cards. If you want your tyke or a special baby in your life to have the very best, you'll find it at this delightful store. It's open Monday through Saturday.

Briar Lane
2240 E. Murray Holladay Rd., Holladay
• 273-7788

Briar Lane carries children's specialty clothing from more than 400 children's designers including Flapdoodles, My Boy Sam, JM Originals and Romantic Baby in sizes 0 to 14 for girls and 0 to 12 for boys. The store has a great gift section filled with stuffed animals, art supplies, hair accessories and kid's cooking accessories. Briar Lane also carries Mustela, a cosmetic line for children. The shop is open Monday through Saturday.

The Brown Eyed Susan
425 E. 100 S., Salt Lake City • 355-8650

An old mansion listed on the National Register of Historic places makes an interesting setting for this lovely children's store. Three floors of top-of-the-line European-designed children's clothing and shoes for boys and girls represent the best of the best for youngsters in the Salt Lake Valley. The store also carries some adult sizes. For children's clothing or gift items, this shop is a must-do. It's closed on Sunday.

Four and Twenty Sailors
2645 E. Parleys Way, Salt Lake City
• 485-2951

This friendly, service-oriented shop for kids carries finer American and European designer clothing in classic styles. The owner has gone to great lengths to create a grownup shopping experience for small girls and boys, giving them separate departments. The store has mother-daughter matching outfits and layettes

and features an impressive line of pretty baby items from a 102-year-old French knitting mill. All the better brands are represented including Petit Bateau, Nautica and Tommy Hilfiger Boys. Sizes range from infant to preteen. This shop is one of the best places to buy little girls' hand-smocked dresses. They are closed on Sunday.

Cowboy Up: Western Wear

A A Callister
3615 Redwood Rd., Salt Lake City
• 973-7058

Headquarters for great Western hats, boots and clothing in the Salt Lake Valley, this store has it all. For horsing around, you'll find saddles, tack, feed and farrier equipment. A A Callister can outfit the most discriminating cowperson with complete outfits from all the top Western-wear lines such as Tony Lama, Justin, Levi Strauss, Wrangler, Carmen Roper and Pan Handle Slim. The store is closed on Sunday.

Shepler's Western Wear
5584 Redwood Rd., Salt Lake City
• 966-4200

This is the world's largest retail and catalog Western-wear store with midrange-priced apparel for the whole family. Shepler's is the only carrier of Lucchese boots in the Salt Lake Valley. The store also has a nifty gift department. You can cowboy up here seven days a week.

Thrift Stores and Consignment Shops

Assistance League of Salt Lake
2060 E. 3300 S., Salt Lake City
• 484-3401

This charitable organization was chartered by the National Assistance League in 1977 to assist and guide men, women and children in need of care and/or assistance either spiritually, materially or physically. Many of the programs sponsored by the league are supported through the sale of clothing and other items in the thrift shop. And what a thrift shop it is! In the basement of this eastside building you'll find great bargains on gently worn expensive designer clothing. All those high-end fashions purchased in specialty shops throughout the Valley have to go somewhere when they retire, and the Assistance League gets a good portion. If you love thrift shopping and want the best, this is the place. The shop is open Tuesday through Saturday.

Bag Lady Boutique
880 S. 900 E., Salt Lake City • 363-4102

A generous supply of well-cared-for tie-dye and funkier clothing seems to find its way to the Bag Lady. You can also get some mainstream designer items for women at great prices. It's worth a stop. If you want to consign clothing, call ahead to see which days they take in merchandise. You can shop here seven days a week.

Cassandra's Closet
4227 S. Highland Dr., Holladay
• 278-5446

Salt Lake's first consignment store, Cassandra's Closet is jammed with mostly high-end clothing in excellent condition. The space is small, but you'll find some very expensive designer clothing at great prices, so don't be shy about elbowing your way in. It's open Monday through Saturday.

Deseret Industries
131 E. 700 S., Salt Lake City • 532-6201
3602 S. 7200 W., Salt Lake City
• 250-4262
4485 S. Main St., Salt Lake City
• 262-6467
727 E. 9400 S., Salt Lake City • 255-8399
2234 S. Highland Dr., Salt Lake City
• 486-3474
743 W. 700 S., Salt Lake City • 579-1200
7839 S. Redwood Rd., Salt Lake City
• 561-1681
4660 S. 400 W., Salt Lake City
• 963-3907

The thrift stores operated by the Mormon church, known to locals as the D.I., are part of the overall welfare program designed to provide jobs for church members who are otherwise unable to find employment. It employs many people with disabilities and provides a storehouse of goods for needy Mormon families while at the same time providing low-cost goods to the community.

The D.I. is one of our favorite thrift stores. Sure, you'll find lots of things you would never take home, but many things you would. Designer clothing occasionally shows up in the racks of well-worn polyester. An Escada jacket in like-new condition for $6 is a good example. The home-furnishings departments are treasure troves for collectors. A Nippon china plate at 50¢ is a good example. The used-furniture department often produces antique pieces, although many stores sell these items on a bid basis. That's fun, too. You can buy a sofa for about $35 at the D.I. Choices range from the occasional shell-back beauty with frieze upholstery in remarkable condition to the boxy, brown-plaid number your grandmother had in the family room for too many years. It's hit or miss, but D.I.-ing is a fun pastime if you love bargains. It's open Monday through Saturday.

Garp's Mercantile
627 S. State St., Salt Lake City
• 537-1357

Garp's is so big you feel like you're in an airplane hanger, but it's also chock-full of interesting old luggage, jewelry, records, books and lots of secondhand clothing for men and women. Most of the items are in good condition, and you can find some great bargains on designer jackets, sweaters, suits and formal wear. The store has a small selection of good-quality vintage clothing and some '60s and '70s frocks that make you want to run out and get a bouffant hairdo. Garp's racks also bulge with '80s clothing that might be good investments if the styles come back into fashion, as they tend to do. Garp's is fun and worth an hour or so rooting through racks. It's is open Tuesday through Saturday.

Grunts and Postures
779 E. 300 S., Salt Lake City • 521-3202

Grunts has a personality unlike any other thrift shop in town. It specializes in men's and women's vintage clothing from the '50s and before, although you will find some '60s and '70s garb as well, but it also has a line of new fashions from LA. You'll find unusual jewelry, hair dyes in your favorite neon colors and miscellaneous gift items. Grunts has one of Salt Lake's best selections of unusual, artistic and often dark-humored postcards. The shop is in an old grocery next to a Laundromat. If you happen to visit on a day when the window dressing includes a large selection of brassieres and girdles from the 1940s, don't be put off. Everyone here has a deliciously offbeat sense of humor. Grunts has everything from the common to the bizarre.

Kid to Kid

1984 E. Murray-Holladay Rd., Salt Lake City
• 273-0282
792 E. 9400 S., Sandy • 572-2144
10366 S. Redwood Rd., South Jordan
• 253-4436
2632 W. 3500 S., West Valley City
• 969-7711

This chain of stores selling lightly used children's clothing, toys and baby equipment is worth a mention because of the savings on necessities and niceties you'll find here. The stores stock a wide selection of kids clothes in good to excellent condition at very reasonable prices. The styles are current, and toys and equipment meet government safety standards. Look for Baby GAP, Jimboree and Oshkosh brands at these stores. The shop also carries used maternity clothing. It's open Monday through Saturday.

Name Droppers

2350 E. Parleys Way, Salt Lake City
• 474-1644

It's nothing but the best for this shop. The owners are very choosey about the clothing they take in, and the customers are grateful. Some of the stock comes from Los Angeles so you can find once-around items that are new to Salt Lake. Gently worn Isaac Mizrahi at a great price is a common find here as well as designer wear by Donna Karan, Calvin Klein Collection, DKNY, Anne Klein, Dolce Gabana, Anna Sui and Armani.

The store also carries new last-season merchandise including a hefty selection of Barry Bricken, Tommy Bahama, Ellen Tracy, Dana Buckman, Seattle Gear, Yves St. Laurent and more. Name Droppers has a small selection of secondhand furniture, some of which is unique and worth taking home. The mother-daughter duo who own the shop are very savvy about fashion. The store is closed on Sunday.

> **FYI**
>
> Unless otherwise noted, the area code for all phone numbers listed in this guide is 801.

Ritzi Rags and Ritzi Babes

4000 S. Highland Dr., Salt Lake City
• 278-8819

This is a small, often cramped store with a rather run-of-the-mill collection of clothing, but it makes our list of places to scout for bargains because the prices are so low. You won't find a wealth of high-end designer threads here, but you can usually find something serviceable at big savings. The infant-to-preteen section has some good buys, too. You can shop at Ritzi Monday through Saturday.

Salvation Army

1232 S. State St., Salt Lake City
• 355-1937
421 W. 300 S., Salt Lake City • 596-1709
4055 W. 5415 S., Kearns • 967-6134
655 E. Center, Midvale • 566-5403

At the "Sally" you'll find used furniture and clothing in various states of repair as well as bric-a-brac that isn't much to write home about. However, on occasion, you will also find a treasure — like a 1950s chrome dinette set in mint condition for less than $75 — that makes your trip to the Salvation Army worthwhile. The thrift store at 421 W. 300 S. is in a marginal

---

INSIDERS' TIP

Rock hounds, listen up! The best little rock shop in town is the Vug, 235 E. 3400 S., 521-6026. You'll find crystals, gems, minerals and fossils plus tools, books and a very knowledgeable shopkeeper.

part of town, but if you are feeling brave and its daylight, you may want to check the some-times-plentiful selection of vintage clothing. It's open Monday through Saturday.

Stork Exchange
3257 E. 3300 S., Salt Lake City • 485-8870

Do you ever wonder where all those expensive kids clothes go when they're outgrown? Look no further. The Stork Exchange was one of Salt Lake's original consignment stores for children and has made a name for itself with affordable children's clothing from such fashion notables as Ralph Lauren, Laura Ashley, Baby Cary, Carriage Boutique and several French labels, just to name a few. You'll also find some less-expensive brands in the used department as well as a line of new clothing. Sizes range from infant to 10.

This fresh, cheerful boutique carries new toys, books and gifts, slightly used baby furniture and equipment and used maternity clothing. It also has new all-terrain stroller/joggers. Stork Exchange is the Modella rental and retail outlet in Salt Lake City for breast pumps and equipment. The owner is very particular about the quality and condition of the clothing taken on consignment, so you won't be disappointed. You can shop here Monday through Saturday.

Antiques, Unique Furniture, Collectibles and Other Neat Stuff

Salt Lake City has hundreds of antique stores and shops that sell unusual, hard-to-find items that aren't 100 years old — the age at which "old" becomes "antique" — but don't fit in the thrift section because of their high quality or distinctive nature. We don't have enough space to include them all so we've focused on the best of the best and presented a broad range of merchandise plotted on a cross section of locations throughout the Valley.

In addition to antiques, we've included some wonderful furniture stores that sell new and very unique furniture. You'll also find a shop or two in this listing selling merchandise that can only be described as Neat Stuff.

A C Emporium
4348 S. 900 E., Salt Lake City • 281-8175

This mid valley antiques source is really two shops in one. One owner specializes in cookie jars and glass items from the '30s and '40s, and the other features Oriental items such as screens, tea carts, handcarved furniture pieces, figurines of Satsuma and Buddha and a collection of cloisonné. You'll also find a good selection of new handmade porcelain dolls.

Afterglow and Lyn Anne's Antiques
4844 S. State St., Salt Lake City • 263-2293

This shop has the largest selection of old glassware and dishes in town including Depression glass, Murano Italian crockery, bottles, dinnerware and Austrian and German painted plates. They also carry linens from the 1940s. You'll find postcards, books, quality costume jewelry from the '50s and '60s and vintage clothing and hats. You won't find furniture here, but if you like crocheted items for tables, clothing and accessories, this shop is a rich source.

Anthony's Antique Center
401 E. 200 S., Salt Lake City • 328-2231
Anthony's Broadway Warehouse
307 E. Broadway (300 S.), Salt Lake City • 521-5256

A well-known actress who lives in the area recently commented that there was no other place in Salt Lake like Anthony's. She's right! The Antique Center has a huge selection of French antiques, African pieces, American furniture, fireplaces and fencing and some new furniture items jam-packed into a stunning store that used to be a Baptist church. Three floors in this restored Georgian building offer lighting, furniture, eclectic items, fine paintings, quality bronzes, fountains, stained glass and the largest selection of armoires west of the Mississippi, ranging in price from several hundred dollars to $30,000.

Tony Christensen, the proprietor, has a keen sense of design integrity, quality materials and workmanship. He can educate any buyer about period, style, woods and other materials, techniques and the aesthetics of decor. He's not afraid to mix periods, and his dissertations on the similarities between art deco and French empire pieces or mixing modern styles with late-1800s pieces is worth the trip downtown. Furniture from the Antique Center and Warehouse can be seen in some of the finest homes in Bel Aire, Chicago, Rancho Santa Fe and Aspen, and he recently supplied several antique architectural pieces to a restaurant in Madrid.

The Broadway store is the larger of the two, with nearly 30,000 square feet of space, and is a mature antique shop with a good reputation. You quickly can spend a lot of money here, but you'll be pleased at the value you receive in return. If you don't have a bulging wallet, stop by anyway — the stores have finds for every budget. The smaller Second South store has some beautiful pine furniture and architectural pieces including Mormon pine and European antiques and reproductions at more affordable prices than you might imagine.

Anthony's is closed on Sunday.

Antique Shoppe
2016 S. 1000 E., Salt Lake City • 466-2171

If you're looking for old wicker pieces you may find them at this shop, where unique items have included wicker sleeper sofas and rocking chairs. You'll also find glassware, turn-of-the-century oak furniture, old pictures, old Limoges and Royal Doulton pieces, dolls, oak wall phones and costume jewelry. The shop has some better jewelry including watches, but you have to ask to see the selection, which is not on display. Prices are fair, and the inventory is of fairly high quality.

Antiques Gallery
217 E. 300 S., Salt Lake City • 521-7055

One of the best selections of "smalls" can be found in this antique gallery which houses the wares of up to 20 antique dealers. You'll find great stuff here including fine estate jewelry from heirloom and Victorian morning pieces to gold filigree rings and pins. Costume jewelry from the '40s and '50s is abundant, and you can occasionally find jewelry from the 1920s. Pottery collectors will want to

visit the gallery for primarily American art pottery pieces from older firms dating from the 1800s to 1940.

Glassware includes a well-chosen assortment of Ruby Red glass, flow blue, Depression glass and everything from Cambridge to Red Rock crystal. One dealer specializes in older fishing gear, and another in telephones from the '30s to the '50s. A few pieces of furniture can be found in the gallery, mostly from the 1950s. If you are a Haywood-Wakefield fan, you will be pleased at the inventory. Prints and textiles are also available, and you'll find a good selection of ladies vintage dresses, Victorian lace-up and button-front shoes, hats and handbags. Antiques Gallery is a great place for gifts and souvenirs.

Antoinette's
247 E. 300 S., Salt Lake City • 359-2192

This shop specializes in fine estate jewelry including white gold and platinum filigree wedding sets, Victorian hair jewelry, cuff links, lockets, old marquisette pieces and a good selection of cameos from the 1800s and early 1900s in angel skin, coral, stone and shell. Antoinette's also has candles, Mormon pioneer quilts and lots of Hummel, Lladro, Royal Doulton and Limoges. We found the prices to be very reasonable.

Arsenic & Old Lace /Briar Patch Antiques
407 E. 300 S., Salt Lake City • 322-5234

Arsenic and Old Lace is in the upstairs part of this charming downtown store in an old home. The linens, lace, patchwork quilts, vintage clothes and antique wedding gowns are lovely to look at, and the owner can share interesting tidbits about her inventory. Briar Patch, on the main floor, has an impressive selection of cut glass and china, crystal goblets, small furniture pieces, picture frames, some older original artwork, gold and silver jewelry including watches and pendants and quality costume jewelry. The shops are small but lots of fun to visit.

Buffalo Antiques Mall
4854 S. State St., Salt Lake City • 263-9050

Sixteen dealers sell their wares from this

antique mall in the mid valley. You'll find a general line of antiques and collectibles in addition to old toys and advertising materials such as posters, signs and light-up clocks. One dealer specializes in glass, and another in primitives. The furniture is a mixed bag dating from the Victorian era to the 1940s.

C. Hruska & Company
1325 Foothill Dr., Salt Lake City
• 582-5235

This store sells new and interesting furniture and gifts, including some extraordinary iron canopy beds, iron tables and lamps.It's a fun place to shop if you don't have a limit on your credit cards. It's open every day but Sunday.

Campo
2855 Highland Dr., Salt Lake City
• 485-1240

Inside this big, mustard-yellow store set on a knoll at the south end of Sugarhouse, you'll find a huge selection of truly praiseworthy Mexican colonial and rustic furniture and accessories. The prices are very reasonable, and each piece has an individual look to complement any decor. They keep regular hours and are closed Sunday.

Carmen Miranda's
270 S. 300 E., Salt Lake City • 359-7741

Want to stroll down memory lane? Drop by Carmen Miranda's and check out the antique and collectible advertisement paraphernalia, especially the porcelain signs and Coca-Cola and other beverage dispensing machines from the '40s and '50s. All machines are in working condition; some are in original condition, and others have been restored. Other soft-drink faves represented are 7-Up, Nehi, R C Cola and Dr Pepper. The shop also has oil cans and oil products related to automobiles plus a variety of oil signs in porcelain or painted metal. You can also choose from a large selection of art deco and chrome kitchen items, funky '50s household gadgets and beverage serving pieces. The store also specializes in vintage and costume jewelry from the 1800s to the 1970s. Prices are reasonably retro, too.

Circa
635 S. State St., Salt Lake City
• 532-2542

Walk through the door and you get a sense that creativity is the operative force in this antique store. Unlike other shops that sell antiques in as-is condition, Circa gives everything a face-lift before it hits the floor. You'll find some exquisite sofas with carved ball feet and Victorian styling, refinished and reupholstered in fashionable tones and high-quality fabrics.

And Circa doesn't skimp in the upholstery department: Many sofas and chairs are finished off nicely with bullion trim. You'll see period fabrics as well as contemporary patterns on old sofas and chairs. The wood furniture may be painted or may be restored to original condition, depending on what works with the piece. Prices are in the high range. This is an excellent place to get ideas if you are a do-it-yourselfer. In the back of the store is a bin with bolts of remnant upholstery fabric — definitely not your run-of-the-mill stuff — priced to be affordable. The large showroom has furniture and collectibles and is a grand place to wander around for an hour or so. Circa is closed Sunday.

Copper Cowboy Antiques
268 S. 300 E., Salt Lake City • 328-4401

Collectors of 1950s copper figurines with a Western motif will think this is cowboy heaven. You'll also find American oak furniture and many Western items including ropes, bits, saddles and old-style log furniture. Copper Cowboy does restoration and repair work on antique furniture, too.

de Conde's Interior Design Showroom
270 E. 100 S., Salt Lake City • 355-1727

You can do a lot of damage to your budget in this store. It's not that the items are outrageously priced, although this is not a low-end furniture store. It's just that the store has so many exquisite pieces to choose from. The 35,000-square-foot showroom in Salt Lake's old film row has an exclusive selection of fine furniture, antiques and accessories not to be missed if the best quality and style is on your decorating mind. They're closed Sunday.

Distelfink Antiques
2182 Highland Dr., Salt Lake City
• 487-5084

Distelfink has the largest collection of old linen in the Western United States. The huge selection of estate bedding including quilts, shams and crocheted spreads comes from all over the country. The pièce de résistance is table linen. You will also find china sets, children's vintage clothing and a broad range of furniture from Victorian oak to country pine. For many years locals knew this shop as the Sugarhouse Antique Mall as well as Distelfink's. The shop is the same, but the Sugarhouse name has been dropped. The address above is new, just north of the old location. The shop also offers caning and wicker repair.

Ec-lec-tic
380 W. Pierpont Ave., Salt Lake City
• 322-4804

Shopping at Ec-lec-tic on Saturday or any other day of the week is a local tradition. The selection of furniture styles, including art deco and Victorian, is awesome. The chrome tables, lamps with banded shades, rugs and other accessories are enough to make a decorator drool. Everything in the store is from the '50s or older, and the styles cover the design gamut, hence the store's name. You'll find a good selection of higher-end vintage clothing, hats, handkerchiefs and gloves for ladies and tuxedos, handpainted ties and bow ties for gentlemen.

The jewelry is remarkable, too: a costume collection that includes lots of nifty rhinestone stuff and a number of marked collector pieces including those by Eisenberg and Miriam Haskell. Martini sets from the '50s, Depression glass, Fiesta ware and other china and glassware are usually available. Doll collectors can often find Madame Alexander and Efanbee dolls here.

You'll also find older luggage in good condition, linens, knickknacks and other cool stuff. If you love 1950s retro, you'll think you've stumbled into a shrine to pop culture. This store has one of the best selections of that genre in town. It's closed Sunday.

Elemente
353 W. Pierpont Ave., Salt Lake City
• 355-7400

This funky store is always a pleasure to visit. The shop doesn't specialize in anything in particular, but it does carry a variety of first-class older furniture in noteworthy styles, mostly from the 1900s. You'll find plenty of artwork, small collectibles, lamps and other goodies for the home too numerous to mention. A trip to the basement is like a visit to Grandpa's cellar. Walk gingerly — it's pretty packed but worth the effort. You never know what you'll find tucked away in the corner. Elemente and Ec-lec-tic are at the end of the street in a section of downtown called Art Space. For more information on this artists' haven, see the Arts chapter.

Form and Function
3232 S. Highland Dr., Salt Lake City
• 467-3131

Form and Function is wall-to-wall in unique furniture for individualists. The sofas, chairs, occasional tables, media centers, bedroom and dining room suites, barstools, lighting and provocative accessories are just for openers. If you like unusual, contemporary accessories you'll find them here. The store has a lot to offer the home decorator who wants atypical furniture and accessories. Form and Function is open Monday through Saturday.

Gingerbread Antiques
14 E. 8720 S., Sandy • 255-5666

Antique sewing items displayed here include sewing tools, gadgets, needle holders, piece goods, shuttles (bobbins for older sewing machines), darning eggs and pin cushions. The shop also carries linens, glassware, postcards, pictures and furniture from small table-and-chairs sets to large dressers, cupboards and desks.

Honest Jon's Hills House Antique Gallery
126 S. 200 W., Salt Lake City • 359-4852

Honest Jon's has been selling antiques in Salt Lake for more than 25 years. The store specializes in 19th-century and turn-of-the-century antiques such as rare museum-quality furniture. You'll also find a general line of collectibles here. The store is housed in an old home listed on the National Register of Historic Places.

Jitterbug Antique Toy Dealers
243 E. 300 S., Salt Lake City • 537-7038

The kid in everyone will find the perfect vintage toy in this shop specializing in 1950s tin windups, Tonka trucks, tractors, Tootsie Toys, marbles and Doepke toys. A limited selection of G.I. Joe and Barbie dolls are available, too. If trains are your passion, Jitterbug sometimes has Lionel, American Flyer and the occasional Marx. You will also find some large Keystone pieces from the '30s and earlier. Remember the old cowboys? The store has Hopalong Cassidy, Roy Rogers and Gene Autrey toys.

Doll dishes from the '20s and earlier along with cooking stoves and doll houses in good to excellent condition are waiting to go home with you. In addition to toys, you will find some unusual kitchen items, utensils and primitives such as coffee grinders and butter molds. The down side of a visit to Jitterbug is that it's hard not to squeal with delight when you walk in the door.

Olympus Cove Antiques
179 E. 300 S., Salt Lake City • 532- 1070, (800) 284-8046

Discontinued china and crystal patterns are the specialty at this 25-year-old antique store. Olympus Cove focuses on Lennox, Spode, Haviland, Wedgewood, Fostoria, Franciscan and Royal Doulton, but you will find other fine manufacturers represented as well. The selection of handpainted plates and gift items is impressive. Prices are well-below most replacement companies, and the shop will ship pieces to you anywhere in the world.

Rustica
3007 S. Highland Dr., Salt Lake City • 485-3643

The buyers for Rustica travel to remote villages throughout the world for unique handcrafted furnishings including rustic pine, wrought iron and accessories. You'll find everything from hefty armoires to small benches. The selection is notable and worth checking out. Stop by any day but Sunday.

Salt Lake Antiques
279 E. 300 S., Salt Lake City • 322-1273

European antiques are the feature here, but the store isn't limited to items from across the pond. In this 23,000-square-foot shop you will find lots of armoires, wardrobes, dining sets, dressers, buffets and cupboards as well as some interesting small items. The shop carries old windows, carpets and rugs, artwork and tons of collectibles such as art glass, china sets, clocks, figurines, candlesticks, ivory pieces, pottery, boxes and tins. The jewelry selection is interesting; expect some unusual pieces among the collection.

Sandy Antique Mall
8672 S. State St., Sandy • 568-9840

Most of the 20 dealers here have a mixed selection of midpriced antiques and collectibles. One dealer specializes in antique papers, another in old glass, and another in oak furniture. If you are in the south end of the Valley and need a one-stop antique fix, you might find this place a satisfying experience.

Bookstores

New Books

A Woman's Place
1400 Foothill Dr., Salt Lake City • 583-6431

This is *the* women's bookstore in Salt Lake City. The shop has a women's studies section with books written for, about and by women as well as a large selection of mysteries by women authors. Allow time to browse through the fiction, poetry and other works all carefully chosen for our female population.

A Woman's Place has an active schedule of author readings and signings, and many of the visiting writers such as Gloria Steinem draw standing-room-only crowds. You'll also find journals, greeting cards, note cards and a selection of gifts made by women. The artwork decorating the walls was created by local women artists. Books by men are given space on the shelves, and men do shop in the store, but the bookseller takes especially good care of the intellectual, creative and personal growth needs of women in the community.

You can shop here seven days a week.

Aswattha (Tree of Knowledge)
4700 S. 900 E., Salt Lake City • 268-3841

You'll find something for nearly every taste among the books, gifts and treasures in this little shop in Ivy Place. Health and healing books, tomes on personal growth, shamanism and spirituality are just for starters. The shop also has incense, herbs, crystals, jewelry, ceramics, candles and new-age music. If you are interested in hypnotic visualization, you'll find tapes for it here.

B. Dalton Bookseller
Cottonwood Mall, Salt Lake City
• 278-2624
Trolley Square, Salt Lake City • 532-7107
Valley Fair Mall, West Valley City
• 967-3361
South Towne Mall, Sandy • 571-6077

B. Dalton Booksellers has stores in four of the Salt Lake Valley shopping malls and is ready to put you together with the book of your choice from an enormous selection of titles. Each of the stores has a friendly and capable staff. If they don't have your title they can usually get it within a few days. All locations are open seven days a week.

Barnes and Noble Booksellers
2236 S. 1300 E., Salt Lake City
• 467-1181
612 E. 400 S., Salt Lake City • 524-0089
5928 S. State St., Murray • 266-0075
7119 S. 1300 E., Midvale • 565-0086
10180 S. State St., Sandy • 233-0203

This book store chain has made a big impression on Salt Lake readers. The discounts it offers on all books makes reading new titles and books you've always wanted to own very affordable. Besides books, Barnes and Noble also offers a series of literary events such as book discussion groups, poetry readings and

access to national and local authors through book signing and seminars; call 464-3142 for a schedule of activities at each store. The bookstore's fund-raising book fairs support local nonprofit literary groups. Young readers can take advantage of children's programming (see the "Chill" section of our Kidstuff chapter). One of the nicest things about Barnes and Noble, books aside, is the comfy seating throughout the store so you can preview books before you buy. The store actually encourages you to get to know the book before you take it home. The Fourth South store downtown, the Midvale store on 7119 South and the Sandy store on 10180 S. State Street have multimedia centers with videos and music to purchase and an in-store cafe for coffee, tea and other civilized refreshments. They are open seven days a week.

Bibliotect
329 W. Pierpont Ave., Salt Lake City
• 236-1010

A wonderful bookstore and more, Bibliotect sells volumes on architecture and art. Don't pass this shop up. You'll also find an impressive art gallery inside the store which features contemporary cutting-edge work by local artists. The bookstore holds poetry readings and other art-oriented events. You may want to check them out in the Arts chapter, too. The shop is closed on Sunday.

Book Warehouse
12101 S. Factory Outlet Dr., Draper
• 572-6464

You'll find thousands of titles on a wide variety of topics in this outlet store. Some books are discounted up to 75 percent off the publisher's retail price. If you are planning a trip to the outlet mall and love books, stop in and check out the selection. The store is open seven days a week.

Borders Books and Music
50 S. Main St., Salt Lake City • 355-6899

Crossing the threshold into Borders is like slipping into a comfortable sweater. The ambiance is warm and inviting, the book and music selection beyond generous, and you know intuitively you're going to enjoy your time here. On the South Temple side of Cross-

roads Mall, Borders has 25,000 square feet on two levels and more than 100,000 book titles. The store is also a catalog leader in classical and jazz music as well as a great source for *Billboard* top 50 hits. Besides the tons of books to browse — settle into one of the soft browsing benches just for that purpose — and the ample selection of music that floats nicely throughout the terra cotta-colored interior, Borders has a charming cafe with a floor-to-ceiling window looking out on Temple Square.

Here you can enjoy a good international newspaper over a cup of coffee and pastry or a light lunch such as soup of the day in a bread bowl. Borders is truly a mind-expanding experience, and no one seems to mind if you pop in for a book and end up hanging out for four or five hours. It's open seven days a week.

Cosmic Utah
258 E. 100 S., Salt Lake City • 328-3300

Cosmic is your comic-book store and more. The main attractions here are current editions and some 10- to 15-year-old issues, plus silver- and golden-age comics. The shop also sells role-playing games, board games, Japanamation videos, collectible card games, some action figures and toys, and general gaming related hobby supplies. Cosmic Utah is open seven days a week.

Deseret Book
Cottonwood Mall, Salt Lake City
• 278-2661
1110 E. Fort Union Blvd., Sandy
• 561-8777
796 E. 9400 S., Sandy • 571-7761
2274 S. 1300 E., Salt Lake City
• 466-2669
ZCMI Center, Salt Lake City • 328-8191
Outlet Store, 2150 W. 1500 S., Salt Lake City • 578-3369
South Towne Mall, Sandy • 572-6050
Valley Fair Mall, West Valley City
• 969-6288
3843 W. 5400 S., Kearns • 967-3884

Deseret Book's roots go back to a pioneer company established in 1866. Concerned that the young people in the isolated Intermountain West were in need of uplifting literature, George Q. Cannon and Sons began publishing and distributing books and magazines for local readers. In 1900 the Mormon church-owned *Deseret News*, which operated a competing publishing company and retail book business, purchased Cannon's firm and renamed it Deseret News Bookstore. This company merged in 1919 with the Deseret Sunday School Union Bookstore, another church-owned company, and the new enterprise was called Desert Book Company. The retail division's flagship store on State Street is in the same location as

George Q. Cannon and Sons' original business.

Today, Deseret Book has 32 retail outlets in Utah, California, Idaho, Oregon, Arizona, Colorado, Nevada and Texas. You will find an enormous selection of LDS books and products in the Salt Lake Valley stores as well as trade books on topics ranging from contemporary issues to fiction, cookbooks, humor and children's and young-adult titles. Deseret Book is an active participant in programs related to community literacy and participates in an annual read-a-thon in which hundreds of children spend a day reading books in malls where Deseret Book stores are located. For their participation, the company contributes books to elementary school libraries.

The stated philosophy of Deseret Book is to support the mission of The Church of Jesus Christ of Latter-day Saints by providing scriptures, books, music and other quality products that strengthen individuals, families and society. All locations are closed on Sunday.

Fertile Ground
274 E. 900 S., Salt Lake City • 521-8124

If you ever need to chill, head for Fertile Ground. Browse a while and enjoy the serene atmosphere. Take in the wooded sanctuary and a gift and book store while sipping a calming cup of tea on the house. Among the shop's merchandise are symbolic jewelry, books, tapes, CDs, drums rattles, smudge sticks and incense. The artwork — Goddess, Celtic, Native American and Egyptian — is inspiring. Fertile Ground also has drumming circles. The shop is open Monday through Saturday.

Frost Bookstore
1320 Foothill Blvd., Salt Lake City • 582-8428

We've been popping into Frost's for books and stationery for nearly four decades. You'll find approximately 20,000 titles and a good selection of books by local authors. This shop specializes in a quick turnaround on book orders, usually one to three days. If you need large quantities, the shop can accommodate that in a hurry, too. Frost's is open Monday through Saturday.

Genesis Books
248 E. 3900 S., Salt Lake City • 268-1919

You'll find a large selection of motivational and informative books at Genesis including titles on eating disorders, child abuse, drug and alcohol recovery, emotional recovery, spiritual enlightenment and self-help. In its gift line, Genesis offers choices such as angel items, candles, T-shirts, mugs and games with an inspirational or teaching message. The ever-expanding line of metaphysical books and materials is also recommendable. Genesis is open Monday through Saturday.

Golden Braid Books
151 S. 500 E., Salt Lake City • 322-1162

Salt Lakers call the Golden Braid their sanctuary in the city. Besides the thousands of volumes on metaphysics, philosophy, psychology, consciousness building, holistic health, alternative lifestyles, Native American studies and fiction to wander through and ponder, you'll find a good selection of music (the store has two listening stations) and a great selection of gifts from around the world.

Feeling a little harried? This is a good place to go to get away from everything. The staff is friendly, knowledgeable and unobtrusive, and you'll always find some little thing to read or take home to a friend that makes life seem a whole lot better. The Golden Braid offers free lectures on Monday nights on topics ranging from meditation to feng-shui and astrology to eco-psychology.

While you're here, visit the shop's Oasis Cafe for a tasty snack or a soothing cup of tea (see our Restaurants chapter). They're open seven days a week.

Gypsy Moon Emporium
1011 E. 900 S., Salt Lake City • 521-9100

For seekers of ancient ways, this cozy shop in a Victorian-era house is certain to please. You will find books on mythology, Celtic mysteries and art, Arthurian legends, folk and fairy tales, fantasy, lunar lore, Goddess and olde religions. The shop also sells cards, candles, incense, oracles and jewelry including Goddess and symbolic pieces. The music selection offers space, Celtic, pagan folk and other genres. Need supplies for a personal ritual or celebration? Gypsy Moon has what it takes to enhance your seasonal or lunar celebration including custom-made robes and cloaks. This is the place for lunar charts and calendars. If you like the TV program *Roar,* you will probably love this shop. Gypsy Moon has been serving Salt Lakers since 1986. It's closed Sunday.

The King's English
1511 S. 1500 E., Salt Lake City
• 484-9100

Serious bookworms haunt this Insider's pick because of the owner's devotion to good books; the friendly, knowledgeable staff; and the impressive, in-depth selection of fiction, poetry, mystery and children's books. The store offers frequent book readings by well-known authors, book groups and discussions and other literary-oriented activities. *Inkslinger,* the store's quarterly newsletter, is full of great information about who's writing what, what books Western authors are reading, great new books worth mentioning, best sellers, current events, scheduled activities and much more.

The King's English has been stimulating the minds and imaginations of readers in the Valley for more than 20 years and has earned its reputation as the best of the best. If you have young readers, don't miss the scoop on The King's English kid scene in our Kidstuff chapter under "Chill." The store is closed on Sunday.

Media Play
7170 S. 1000 East, Midvale • 568-0220
5546 S. Redwood Rd., Taylorsville
• 968-6404

Besides computer software, video games and music, you'll find tons of books — 40,000 to 50,000 titles — and a knowledgable staff at these two Media Play locations. The store does special orders at no charge. You can drop by seven days a week.

Natural Resources Map/Bookstore
1594 W. North Temple, Salt Lake City
• 537-3322, (888) UTAH-MAP

If you need direction, chart a course to this amazing map and book store. Hiking, biking, fishing, hunting, geological and U.S. Forest Service maps are only the beginning. Compasses and other great gadgets are also available. The store is open Monday through Saturday.

Seagull Book and Tape
1720 S. Redwood Rd., Salt Lake City
• 972-2429
242 E. 6400 S., Murray • 261-5434
1961 Murray-Holladay Blvd., Salt Lake
City • 424-0918
1629 W. 9000 S., West Jordan • 568-0444
5730 S. Redwood Rd., Taylorsville
• 969- 7477

If you are looking for LDS books, tapes, scriptures and other materials like CTR (Choose The Right) rings, Seagull has a big selection at discounted prices. Most LDS products are available at the store's several locations. All locations are open Monday through Saturday.

Waking Owl
208 S. 1300 E., Salt Lake City • 582-7323

Near the University of Utah, Waking Owl sells textbooks for a limited number of classes plus a good selection of liberal reading materials on cultural theory, literature, architecture, Utah and the West. The store has a quarterly newsletter, Friday-night discounts, readings by visiting authors, book groups, greeting cards and great prices. Relax in the at-home ambiance, where you can sink into one of the inviting sofas or chairs while you peruse a selection or study the work by local artists hanging on the walls.

Parking for the Waking Owl leaves a little to be desired: There are two spaces in the back of the store in the alley, and the rest is catch-as-catch-can off-street. Don't be discouraged, however; even if you have to walk a block or so, the store is worth it. The Waking Owl is closed Sunday.

Waldenbooks
Crossroads Mall, Salt Lake City
• 363-1271
Fashion Place Mall, Murray • 262-9921
South Towne Mall, Sandy • 572-1952

If you are out and about mall shopping and need a book, stop by one of these Waldenbooks locations. The service is friendly, and the selection is uniformly far-reaching. Waldenbooks has all the latest best-sellers, a great assortment of nonfiction — including computer handbooks and travel guides — and much more. the Fashion Place Mall store has a Waldenkids section for small fry.

You can order your selection if you don't find it on the shelf. All locations are open seven days a week.

Sam Weller Bookstores
254 S. Main St., Salt Lake City • 328-2586
8191 S. 700 E., Sandy • 566-0219

You may hear this store called Zion's Book Store or Sam Weller's Zion's Book Store. To locals it's just Sam Weller, a three-generation family-owned bookstore and local institution. After he returned from World War II, Sam took the store over from his father.

Today, Sam's son, Tony, is the general manager, but for those of us who have been around a while, it's always "Go see Sam Weller." The store specializes in the needs of readers to whom social and cultural works are important. You'll find books on almost everything here, and especially if you are looking for Mormon books, Western Americana and Native American books, you won't be disappointed.

The downtown store has more than 30,000 square feet of space packed to the rafters with reading material. The used-book selection is awesome — the biggest between Denver and the West Coast — and the prices are reasonable. Sam Weller also has a rare-book section and offers a search service for rare and out-of-print books. The Wellers are well-connected and respond quickly. They are closed Sunday.

Used Books

All of the shops in this section are closed on Sunday.

A-Better Book
1450 S. Main St., Salt Lake City
• 487-2766

You'll find many rare and out-of-print books as well as old books still in print in this shop specializing in LDS literature.

The Book Attic
Paperback Exchange
1212 W. Center St., (800 W. 7720 S.), Midvale • 562-2086

If you love romance novels, the kind written by Nora Roberts, Sandra Brown and Elizabeth Lowell, you'll find them here. The shop has more than 200,000 used paperback books. In addition to romance titles you can shop for Western, science fiction, historical and horror novels by mainstream authors. Many titles are available within 30 days of paperback release. If you are a collector of out-of-print romance novels, this is your bookstore. You can also rent audio books at the Book Attic.

Central Book Exchange
2017 S. 1100 E., Salt Lake City
• 485-3913

This is Salt Lake's original paperback book exchange with more than 30 years experience. If you like to read on the cheap you'll find hundreds of thousands of titles to devour on a budget. Take in $10 (retail price) worth of books and get $7 worth of new books for 25¢ per title. High-demand books are sold outright for half the retail price. The store has lots of romances, Westerns and mystery novels plus a lot more from mainstream writers.

Experienced Books
2150 S. Highland Dr., Salt Lake City
• 467-0258

This shop is like a miniature library of new and almost forgotten titles. The resident cat will acknowledge your presence with a nod but won't get in your way as you make your rounds through two floors of books on everything from art to Zen. Some of the sections are very cramped, but if you

From clothing and furniture to unexpected treasures,
shopping in Salt Lake is always an adventure.

don't mind walking through a maze to find what you are looking for you'll enjoy Experienced. Maybe the maze-like setup is for the cat.

Fifth World Books
419 E. 2100 S., Salt Lake City • 486-6437

One of Salt Lake's best-kept secrets is in an old bungalow across the street from St. Ann's School west of 700 East. The intimate ambiance of this three-room bookstore is part of the draw. So is the cat and the proprietor, Robert Furmage, a philosophy teacher at the University of Utah, translator and published poet. The rooms are chock-full of classics representing most genres. This is a scholarly store, an interface between literature and philosophy, with many volumes on religion, poetry, philosophy, literature, the occult and related topics. If you're looking for something special in a used-book store, put this on your must-do list.

The Paperback Trader
3526 S. 2820 W., West Valley City • 966-8156

This small paperback bookstore with approximately 50,000 books has been around for more than 17 years. Titles are traded at 80 percent of the cover price plus a 50¢ cash fee per title. Most of the authors are mainstream, but the store has a good selection of not-so-well-known authors as well. If you have the need to read in the midwest part of the Valley, stop by.

Good Things to Eat

Across the Valley you'll find supermarket chains like Albertson's, Dan's Foods, Harmon's, Macey's and Smith's offering a full complement of every imaginable grocery store item. You'll find them listed in the Yellow Pages under "Grocers Retail." Also worth mention because they stand alone as great places for gourmet grocery shopping and high-quality meats are Kap's Kitchen and Pantry, 6151 S. Highland Dr., 273-0123 and Snider's Bros. Meats, 6245 S. Highland Dr, 272-6469. In this listing we've provided a brief peek into the world of imported-food shops, divine produce markets and organic and natural food markets. The listings here wouldn't be complete without a nod to some of our favorite bakeries, for as you will learn when you come to know us, we love our sweets.

From the Earth

The Downtown Farmers Market
300 S. 300 W., Salt Lake City • 359-5118

In addition to selling Intermountain-grown fresh fruits and vegetables, fresh flowers and plants, cheese, meat, handcrafts with an organic theme, fresh-baked goods, honey, jam, salsa and candies, the Farmers market has a great story. Among the 60 vendors who sell their wares in Pioneer Park, you'll find a group called Wasatch Community Gardens, a nonprofit organization that maintains organic gardens within the city.

Well, there's a little more to it than that. Among the several projects Wasatch is involved with is fund-raising to provide for inner-city gardens and save some existing gardens from an untimely demise. Its famous "Save the Tomato Garden" campaign recently raised enough money to permanently secure the Grateful Tomato Garden at 800 S. 600 E. Organizers also work with at-risk kids who learn responsibility, commitment and cooperation by growing, selling and donating the produce to the local food bank. More than 200 inner-city children ages 4 to 17 are part of the program each season.

Shopping at the Farmers Market is a satisfying experience: You get fresh local produce and other goodies, interesting conversation and an opportunity to participate in the community. The market is open Saturdays between mid-July and mid-October, from 8 AM to 1 PM.

Good Earth Natural Food Market and Deli
7206 S. 900 E., Salt Lake City • 562-2209

Bulk herbs and dietary supplements are the specialty of this health-oriented grocery store and more. Organic produce, all natural groceries, vegetarian "meat" products and fresh juices are always in good supply. The store also has a large selection of books on health-related topics.

Liberty Heights Fresh
1242 S. 100 E., Salt Lake City • 58-FRESH

Where to begin? If an ample selection of well-chosen, truly gorgeous produce and fresh flowers is the thing that make your socks roll up and down, you will appreciate Liberty. The tiny store also has European breads, fresh fruit juice, imported and domestic cheese and packaged specialty food. Funky ambiance — the building was once a gas station and garage — designer food and, oh, a great coffee bar: You get the picture. Go to Liberty. You'll enjoy the moment. It's closed Sunday.

Wild Oats
812 E. 200 S., Salt Lake City • 355-7401
2454 S. 700 E., Salt Lake City • 359-7913
4695 S. Holladay Blvd., Salt Lake City • 278-8242

Salt Lake Valley shoppers have been trying to get used to the name change — it was called New Frontiers for about 20 years — but by any name this is still a great market. All three locations offer fresh organically grown produce, hormone-free meats, quality dietary supplements and delicious deli foods. The meat departments make their own sausage including Cajun, lamb curry, chicken-spinach-Parmesan, chicken-lemon-pepper, Italian and more. The store sells raw honey from a large vat, fresh nuts, grains and other food in bulk and tofu cheese. The milk case is loaded with alternative to cow's milk, but the cow is represented as well. The folks here are well-informed

INSIDERS' TIP

If you're a pipe lover, Jeanie's Smoke Shop, 156 S. State Street, can provide you with fragrant tobacco and stogies. Jeanie's has been around for 50 years and is a Salt Lake institution. The original Jeanie is still at the helm.

and very friendly. Wild Oats is open seven days a week.

Ethnic Foods

Frank Granato Importing Company

1391 S. 300 W., Salt Lake City • 486-5643
4040 S. 2700 E., Salt Lake City • 277-7700

Go to either of these two Italian markets for Italian cooking supplies. This is essential! You'll find everything you need for true Italian cuisine: flavored vinegars, including imported Balsamic; salami and other meats; cheeses such as fresh ricotta and mozzarella, wonderful Parmesan and hard-to-find manchago; olives stuffed with garlic, anchovy, onion and almond and those delicious marinated olives with pits; pasta and sauces; extra-virgin pure olive oil that Granato imports; and fresh truffles in summer and winter, personally dug up by those nice pigs in Italy — they run $200 a pound. While shopping in Granato's take time to indulge in a savory sandwich from the deli counter. The aroma in the stores is so captivating you won't want to leave (see our Restaurants chapter). Both locations are closed Sunday.

India Unlimited

1615 S. Foothill Dr., Salt Lake City • 583-3300

In addition to ready-to-eat vegetarian meals and Ayurvedic herbs, this store is well-stocked with canned and package foods, curry and other spices that may be hard to find in a standard grocery. You will also find books, including a few good cookbooks, and everything you need to prepare a wonderful meal with an authentic Indian flavor. The shop is closed Sunday.

Oriental Food Market

667 S. 700 E., Salt Lake City • 363-2122

This fabulous Oriental market stocks more than 1,000 different food items including rices, spices and specialty items plus cooking equipment. The staff is great about answering questions, giving tips and filling in the blanks if you are experimenting with a new type of cooking for a healthier diet. The shop is closed Sunday.

Sweet Stuff

Mrs. Backer's Pastry Shop

434 E. South Temple, Salt Lake City • 532-2022

Birthday parties and weddings seem incomplete without one of the beautiful cakes from Mrs. Backer's. They have been a tradition since 1942. Everything in this store is pretty and delicious. The hot-cross buns are a great treat in the spring. The bakery is closed Sunday and Monday. (See our Restaurants chapter.)

Beau Brummel Bakery

3100 S. Highland Dr., Salt Lake City • 486-5908

This shop is also known as Glaus French Pastry Shoppe and they have been baking goodies for more than 60 years. You'll find cookies, Danish, cakes and other tempting treats along with bread and rolls. Everything is worth it's weight in calories, but Beau Brummel has three standouts that we can't live without: cream-cheese Danish, Swedish limpa bread and chocolate rum cake. If you could only choose one item to be stranded on a desert island with, go for the rum cake. It's that good. You can buy it by the slice, wedge or entire cake in several sizes. The shop is closed Sunday and Monday.

Brumby's

224 S. 1300 E., Salt Lake City • 581-0888

This standout offers a variety of lovely edibles, but when you start day dreaming about the little tarts with fruit and glaze and the petit chocolate eclairs, it's time for a Brumby fix. The pastries are small so you don't have to stop at one. Wasn't that thoughtful of the pastry chef? Brumby's is open seven days a week.

Great Harvest Bread Company

905 E. 900 S., Salt Lake City • 328-2323
4667 S. 2300 E., Salt Lake City • 277-3277

The bread in this bakery is its calling card. Whether you like it sliced thick or thin or like to tear bites off the loaf with your bare hands you'll love all the bread offered here. They have white, harvest wheat, cinnamon and other varieties, and the pastries are also very good. Just don't leave without the bread. The shop is closed on Sunday.

Scandia Kaffe House
1693 S. 900 E., Salt Lake City • 467-0051

One word: marzipan. This is the place for marzipan cakes. You won't find better anywhere in the city. The shop also sells a variety of other sweets including napoleons, eclairs, Danish pastries and cookies. The macaroons are excellent. You can also get a nice breakfast or lunch. Scandia is closed Sundays.

Tea and Trumpets
1515 S. 1500 E., Salt Lake City • 487-0717

You can drop in for a piece of cake or a call 24 hours in advance to order a whole cake from this wonderful place. Angels must oversee the baking of these delicacies because they are heavenly light, and they definitely lift your spirits. The carrot cake is superb, as is the Bavarian spice. You can also get chocolate or white cakes with butter cream, fudge or German-chocolate icing and delicious fillings that go way beyond these pedestrian depictions. T and T has outrageous cheesecakes; if you order a whole cake you can specify honey or sugar as the sweetener.

Sporting Goods

Angler's Inn
2292 S. Highland Dr., Salt Lake City • 466-3921
8925 S. 255 W., Sandy • 566-3929

If you're an angler, you won't want to miss this well-known shop. You'll find everything from tackle to good advice on the best fishing holes and tall fishing tales. Salt Lakers never head for the stream without fist stopping at Angler's Inn. It's closed Sunday.

Black Diamond Equipment Limited
2092 E. 3900 S., Salt Lake City • 278-0233

This store carries a full line of gear for rock climbing, backpacking, mountaineering and back-country skiing. The service is friendly, and the staff takes a personal interest in your needs. The store is closed on Sunday.

DaleBoot USA
2150 S. 300 W., Salt Lake City • 487-3649

Do your feet hurt after a day on the slopes? DaleBoot is the only alpine ski boot manufacturer in the United States. The company makes custom-fit, high-end performance ski boots in sizes 4 to 14, A to EEE widths. You can order boots with cuts for larger calves as well. Visit the retail store or shop by mail. Your tootsies will thank you.

Evolution Ski Company
790 W. 1700 S., Salt Lake City • 972-1144

This local company manufactures handcrafted alpine, telemark and norpine skis. It also sells fat and parabolic skis, marker bindings and EVO sportswear and offers complete ski tune-up and repair. The store is closed on Sundays.

Kirkham's Outdoor Products
3125 S. State St., Salt Lake City • 486-4161

Wow! What a store. Kirkham's is an A-to-Z source for camping and backpacking gear, cross-country skiing and climbing equipment. The store specializes in tents, sleeping bags, accessories and quality sports clothing.

REI - Recreational Equipment Inc.
3285 E. 3300 S., Salt Lake City • 486-2100

The outdoor specialists at this great store can set you up with bikes for all terrains, camping equipment, canoes, packs, tents, sleeping bags, hiking gear, alpine and cross-country skis, and climbing gear. You'll also find boots and clothing at REI, plus helpful information and awesome sales. If you're looking for equipment to do the outdoors right, this is the place to shop.

Salty Peaks Snowboard Shop
3055 E. 3300 S., Salt Lake City • 467-8000
684 E. Union Sq., Sandy • 523-8686

This store, owned and operated by experienced snowboarders, has been serving Salt Laker's for more than 10 years. In addition to having the best selection in town of the latest snowboarding equipment, the store does repairs, and the owner and staff have their fingers on the pulse of this increasingly popular sport. If you need gear for the slopes or advise on where to go, drop by one of their two locations (they're closed Sundays). The Snowboard Museum is on display at the 33rd South location.

Uinta Golf
560 E. 2100 S., Salt Lake City • 487-8233

Golfers flock to this one-stop shop from all points in the Valley. From equipment to snappy golf duds to how-to books and videos, it's all here. Check them out before you head for one of our beautiful golf courses. You'll find them listed in the Parks and Recreation chapter and our Park City chapter. Uinta Golf is closed on Sundays.

Wild Rose Mountain Sports
702 Third Ave., Salt Lake City • 533-8671

The folks at this bicycle shop are very helpful and knowledgeable. Although the space is small, you'll find everything you need in the way of bikes for dirt and pavement, parts, repairs, accessories, clothing and footwear. You'll find Kona, Litespeed, Bianchi, Marin, Ibis, Proflex, Jamis, Slingshot, Eisentraut and Salsa well-represented in this store. Watch for great sales on equipment here. It's closed Sundays.

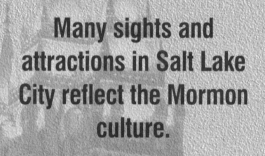

Many sights and attractions in Salt Lake City reflect the Mormon culture.

Sightseeing and Attractions

It isn't surprising that many sights and attractions in Salt Lake City reflect the Mormon culture. Temple Square, which attracts more than 4 million visitors each year, Pioneer Trail State Park, Deseret Village and This Is the Place Monument are rich in Mormon history. A visit to these attractions is a good way to get to know the Mormon people better.

In this chapter we have covered the attractions and sights that most visitors are likely to find interesting — museums, monuments, historic sites, an amusement park, gardens, a zoo and even an aviary — but other chapters include attractions you'll want to add to your itinerary, too. The Kidstuff chapter fills you in on wet and wild stuff for kids and adults and some excellent spots where families can enjoy a good time together. Our Parks and Recreation chapter describes activities available in the canyons and natural playgrounds of the area. For those who are attracted by the area's famous ski slopes, see the Skiing and Winter Sports chapter.

Park City, a 30-minute drive from the heart of the Salt Lake Valley, has lots to see and do. Because Park City is an attraction unto itself, we've devoted a whole chapter to this mountain resort. The Daytrips chapter provides information on a couple of nearby locations worth visiting. If you plan to extend your visit to cover more of the state, you won't want to be without one of our newest books in the series, *Insiders' Guide® to Southwestern Utah*. Its chapters on Parks and Other Natural Wonders and the Grand Canyon's North Rim provide some awesome information on these areas.

There's plenty to keep you busy while you visit Salt Lake City, so slip into some comfortable shoes, grab your *Insiders' Guide®* and head for the attractions.

Beehive House
67 E. South Temple, Salt Lake City
• 240-2671

Built in 1854, this gracious adobe-brick home topped by a beehive (symbol of thrift and industry) served as Brigham Young's official residence when he was president of the Mormon church and governor of the territory. Restored with furnishings of the period, you can get a glimpse of the bedrooms, toys used by Brigham Young's dozens of children and the home school and eating areas shared by his large family. The home is on the National Register of Historic Places. Year-round tours are available at no cost and run approximately 30 minutes. Hours are 9:30 AM to 6:30 PM during the summer, but the house closes at 4:30 during the winter. Saturday hours are 9:30 AM to 4:30 PM year-round. Sunday hours are 10 AM to 1 PM.

Brigham Young Monument and Eagle Gate
Intersection of Main St. and South Temple and State St. and South Temple

The monument and the Eagle Gate, serve as important reminders of the city's beginnings. The Brigham Young Monument showing Young with his hand outstretched was displayed at the 1893 Chicago World's Fair. It stood on Temple Square until 1897 when it was moved to the present site. The names of the 140 men, three women, two children and three black slaves, referred to as "colored servants," who accompanied Young to the Salt Lake Valley appear on the side of the monument. The monument also pays tribute to the Native Americans and fur trappers who preceded the Mormons into the valley.

The 6,000-pound Eagle Gate with its 20-foot wing span once stood watch over Brigham Young's Lion House residence and served as the gateway to City Creek Canyon Road near Young's home. The original gate, built in 1859 of wood, is now an exhibit in the Pioneer Memorial Museum. The newer version was expanded over the years to accommodate wagons, trolley cars and eventually automobiles. Both are worth a look and a snapshot.

Catholic Cathedral of the Madeleine

331 E. South Temple, Salt Lake City
• 328-8941

Money to build the Romanesque sandstone cathedral, dedicated in 1909, came from Bishop Lawrence Scanlin and wealthy Catholic families who had made their fortunes in mining. Bishop Scanlin, an Irish immigrant, is buried beneath the altar. The interior, which was not completed until 1926, has beautiful stained-glass windows and intricately carved angels above the confessionals. The cathedral is on the National Register of Historic Places. The structure recently underwent a multimillion dollar renovation. It's open to the public daily from 8 AM to 9 PM. Free tours are conducted on Tuesday, Friday and Sunday at 1 PM.

Church Office Building

50 E. North Temple, Salt Lake City
• 240-3789

This 28-story high-rise is the headquarters for the Church of Jesus Christ of Latter-day Saints (Mormons) and is partially open to the public.

FYI

Unless otherwise noted, the area code for all phone numbers listed in this guide is 801.

Two observation decks on the 26th floor offer visitors a spectacular view of the Salt Lake Valley. Free tours are held Monday through Saturday during the summer from 9 AM to 5 PM and during the winter Monday through Friday from 9 AM to 4:30 PM.

The City and County Building

451 S. State St., Salt Lake City
• 533-0858, 535-6333

Set in the middle of 10 acres on a grassy square originally known as Washington Square, the gray sandstone Romanesque building, completed in 1889 and restored 100 years later, today houses the offices of city government officials. In 1847 the square served as a campsite for arriving pioneers, and the square was later used as a hay market and a roundup point for cattle drives. The building is on the National Register of Historic Places and is open to the public from 8 AM to 5 PM Monday through Friday. The Heritage Foundation provides free tours on Tuesdays at noon and Saturdays at 10 AM.

Daughters of the Utah Pioneers

300 N. Main St., Salt Lake City
• 538-1050

Sometimes called the Pioneer Memorial Museum, the proper name of this site is as it's listed above. The Utah Daughters of the Pioneers built this museum to house memorabilia of the Mormon pioneers. The building is a replica of the early Salt Lake Theater built in 1861. The theater was demolished in 1928, but the museum has the red-velvet seats, the theater's curtain and costumes used by the performers. In addition, the museum has a large collection of artifacts, photographs and maps that document the pioneers' history from 1847 to 1869.

This is a great place to bring kids. For de-

INSIDERS' TIP

The Heritage Foundation, 485 N. Canyon Road, has information and maps for self-guided tours of several of the city's historic districts including Capitol Hill and the downtown area. Call them for details at 533-0858.

tails on what gets the little one's attention in the museum, see the Kidstuff chapter. The museum is open year-round from 9 AM to 5 PM Monday through Saturday. Admission is free, but donations are appreciated.

Gallivan Utah Center Plaza
36 E. 200 S., Salt Lake City • 532-0459

Land forms, artwork and a variety of activities combine to help this friendly plaza in the heart of the city live up to its nickname, "Salt Lake's Outdoor Living Room." The outdoor chessboard has 2-foot-tall pieces. The thought-provoking artwork includes the Wildlife Wall, a collection of 48 bronze panels created from the work of four dozen 1st graders, and the Story Wall, which features 80 2-foot-square bronze panels depicting Native American legends surrounding the sunken lawn area. A pedestrian bridge constructed of glass blocks filled with sand and soil creates a constantly evolving span of color as light and shadows fall on the glass. A pond at the center doubles as an ice-skating rink in winter.

The Gallivan Center hosts several annual music concerts including the ever-popular Twilight Series. You can check this out in our Festivals and Annual Events chapter. The Media chapter will direct you to local newspapers with calendars for ongoing activities, and our Kidstuff chapter will fill you in on the wonderful children's programs and activities available here.

Family History Library
35 N. West Temple, Salt Lake City • 240-2331

The Church of Jesus Christ of Latter-day Saints founded the Genealogical Society of Utah in 1894 to gather records that help people trace their ancestry. The first library was opened in 1938, and later the society began preserving records on microfilm. Today, 250 microfilm camera operators record birth, marriage, death, probate, immigration, military and other records in 53 countries.

Visitors to the Mormon church's new Family History Library can explore the world's largest collection of genealogy information including 2 million rolls of microfilmed records with more than 2 billion names, 400,000 microfiche and 250,000 books. With the help of more

than 2,650 satellite libraries in 64 countries, the Family History Library is constantly expanding the collection. Most records date from the mid-1500s to 1920. Who knows? You might be related to royalty.

If this massive storehouse of information is a bit overwhelming, check out the FamilySearch Center in the Joseph Smith Memorial Building. This is a good place for beginners, a little like Genealogy 101. Hours for the Family History Library are Monday 7:30 AM to 6 PM and Tuesday through Saturday until 10 PM. There is no cost to use the library.

Hansen Planetarium
15 S. State St., Salt Lake City • 538-2104, (800) UTAH-NET

One of the world's most innovative planetariums, Hansen Planetarium is housed in a building that was once home to the Salt Lake City Public Library, which acquired the territory's original 1,000-volume library with funding from the U.S. Congress. The Beaux-Arts structure was constructed in 1905 of oolite limestone. The building is on the National Register of Historic Places. The planetarium offers two floors of exhibits including a moon rock. The domed theater features star shows and laser/music shows. For more details on the activities and events at the planetarium, see this listing in the Kidstuff chapter. Hours are Monday through Thursday 9:30 AM to 9 PM and until midnight on Friday and Saturday. Admission for the Star and Science Shows is $3.50 for children and seniors and $4.50 for teens and adults. Laser Music Concerts are $5 for children younger than 12 and seniors and $6 for teens and adults. Late Night Laser Concerts are $7.50.

Hogle Zoo
2600 E. Sunnyside Ave. (800 S.), Salt Lake City • 582-1631

More than 1,300 animals live at the Hogle Zoo, including big cats, elephants, hippos, bears and many other animals the zoo likes to call ambassadors of their species. Besides big animals, the zoo has lots of little ones including several varieties of monkeys. Many baby animals are born at the zoo each year. Spring is a big season for babies. The Small Wonders Barn allows children to interact with smaller animals.

Exotic birds and plants live in the zoo's solarium; butterflies flit around the butterfly house in the spring and summer. Kids will especially enjoy Hogle Zoo's Discovery Land (see our Kidstuff chapter for details).

A tour of the grounds is easily managed aboard a small replica of an 1869 steam engine. Everyone will appreciate getting off their feet for a few minutes. Families can picnic in the pavilion or snack at the concession stand.

Hogle Zoo is open every day of the year except Christmas. Hours are 9 AM to 6 PM. Admission is $5 for adults and $3 for children ages 4 to 14 and senior citizens. Kids younger than 4 get in free. Family membership is $50 per year. Strollers are available for rent for $3 a day.

Joseph Smith Memorial Building
15 E. South Temple, Salt Lake City
• 240-1266

This building, with its beautiful interior marble floors and columns, used to be the Hotel Utah. From 1911 to 1987 it was the city's finest hotel. A recent $45 million renovation readied the property for offices which Mormon church leaders now occupy as well as providing a showcase for church history. Tours are available Monday through Saturday 9 AM to 10 PM during the summer. Winter tours are Monday through Saturday from 9 AM to 9 PM.

A 53-minute film called *Legacy*, depicting the history of the church and the westward trek of Mormon pioneers, is on view daily on the second floor of the building. Admission is free, but tickets are required and are available in East Hall in the northeast end of the lobby. Hostesses are on duty to give directions if you get lost.

The FamilySearch Center, located in the Joseph Smith Memorial Building, is the appetizer leading up to the Family History Library. There is no charge to search for your ancestors in the 133 family research workstations which have access to the Family History Library's data base. If you're a genealogy junkie, you may want to skip the center and head for the main library. See the Family History Library listed above.

The Joseph Smith Memorial Building also has two restaurants open to the public. The Garden Restaurant, with its retractable glass skylight and blooming bougainvillea, is open for lunch from 11 AM to 4 PM daily and for dinner from 5 to 10 PM in the summer (until 9 PM in the winter). The Roof Restaurant serves an evening buffet daily from 5 to 9 PM in the winter and until 10 PM during the summer. See our Restaurants chapter for more information.

www.insiders.com

See this and many other **Insiders' Guide®** destinations online — in their entirety.

Visit us today!

Lagoon Amusement Park
375 N. Lagoon Dr., Farmington
• 451-8000, (800) 748-5246

Today's lively Lagoon Amusement Park, which boasts 35 rides and a water park, had its beginnings in the late 1800s when a number of resorts sprang up along the shores of the Great Salt Lake. One of them was the original Lagoon, then called Lake Park. In 1893 the lake began receding, and the resort was moved 2½ miles inland to its present location. The name was changed to reflect the new location on the banks of a 9-acre lagoon. Crowds rode from Salt Lake to Lagoon on the Bamberger Railway for rowing, swimming and dancing. A roundtrip ticket cost 25¢˘.

The park's first thrill ride, Shoot-the-Chute, began operation several years later. In 1906 the merry-go-round with 45 hand-carved horses was delivered, and in 1921 the wooden roller coaster was built. Lagoon built a million-gallon pool and filled it with water said to be "fit to drink" in 1927. During the '30s and '40s, the dancing pavilion featured the likes of Artie Shaw, Benny Goodman, Duke Ellington, Count Basie and Glen Miller.

The train stopped running in 1952 as more guests preferred to arrive by automobile. In October 1953 fire swept through Lagoon's midway destroying everything in its path. The carousel was saved by keeping a constant stream of water pouring over its roof. Lagoon was rebuilt that same year and has continued to expand ever since. Today visitors enjoy the rides and water park plus live entertainment, shops, games and food. In addition, the park now offers visitors a look at the Old West in its Pioneer Village.

Photo: Salt Lake Convention and Visitors Bureau

It took 40 years to complete the Salt Lake Temple, which stands as a worldwide symbol of the Morman faith.

For details on the amusement park, the water park — Lagoon A Beach — and Pioneer Village see these listings in the Kidstuff chapter. Daily individual passports good for the entire day are $25.95 for people 51 inches high to 59 years of age. Kinders 4 years old to 50 inches tall get in for $19.95. Toddlers younger than 3 and adults older than 60 can stay at the park all day for $12.50. Season passports for a family of four are $239.80. The passport includes rides, Lagoon A Beach, Pioneer Village and entertainment. Lagoon is open May through October.

Lion House
63 E. South Temple, Salt Lake City
• 363-LION

A lovely home next to the Beehive House, the Lion House held the overflow of Brigham Young's large family. The Lion House is now used as a restaurant called the Pantry and for catered dining and receptions. Our Kidstuff chapter has details about the wonderful parties for children at the Lion House.

Museum of Church History
45 N. West Temple, Salt Lake City
• 240-3310

Across from Temple Square, the museum houses historical artifacts, memorabilia, art and photographs from Mormon history. Temporary exhibits showcase Mormon culture around the world. Hours are 9 AM to 9 PM Monday through Friday and 10 AM to 7 PM Saturday, Sunday and holidays. It is closed New Year's Day, Easter, Thanksgiving and Christmas. Admission is free.

Old Deseret Village
2601 Sunnyside Ave. (800 S.), Salt Lake City • 584-8391

This living historic village was created to show the everyday life of the pioneers who lived in the Salt Lake Valley from 1847 until the railroad arrived in 1869. Everywhere you turn, people in historic dress conduct routine activities from pioneer days while sharing the pioneers' stories with visitors. You can visit the homes, schools, churches and cultural sites of the early settlers and watch them make adobe brick, haul water or travel to a social in a horse-drawn wagon.

The village offers many special events throughout the year including sheep shearing in early April; a lace-making and handiwork day and a spinning bee in June; a quilting bee, an herb day and harvest days in August; an apple harvest and a pumpkin patch in October; butchering day and a pioneer children's winter day in November; Christmas tours in December; and a New Year's Eve Dance. The village has a ZCMI store like the original ZCMI, an ice-cream saloon, a furniture store and cabinet shop featuring Mormon furniture, Jerusha's Bookstore with a large selection of books on Utah and unusual gifts and Colorado Stables where you can book wagon and sleigh rides and chuck wagon dinners.

Admission to Old Deseret Village is $5 for individuals ages 12 to 61 and $2 for children ages 3 to 11 and senior citizens 62 and older. A family pass for two adults and four or more children is $18. Hours are 11 AM to 5 PM Tuesday through Saturday and until 8 PM on Thursday. The village is closed Sunday and Monday.

Red Butte Garden and Arboretum
300 Wakara Way (2250 E.), Salt Lake City
• 581-IRIS

Nature lovers will enjoy this ever-changing natural attraction with gardens and 100 acres of natural trails. The glass-walled, two-story Visitor Center is the gateway to the garden and a great place to view the city and surrounding mountains. The Sego Lily Fountain and sandstone benches with etchings of 52 Utah wildflowers in the Courtyard Garden provide an excellent gathering place for relaxation and people watching.

The Four Seasons Garden offers spectacular views of the city and color contrast with the dense patterns of dwarf and evergreen trees during all four seasons. Herbs, medicinal plants and fragrances are found in the Terrace Garden. Plants, used for centuries to flavor food, provide sweet scents and heal common ailments are grown here. The Floral Walk offers a colorful stroll through blossoms and foliage to the display gardens on the lower creekside, which includes the Dwarf Conifer Cove and Waterfall Display Garden of perennials.

The Water Pavilion Garden is a show-

Photo: Utah Travel Council

The 6,000-pound Eagle Gate in the heart of downtown has a 20-foot wing span.

case for aquatics, day lilies and ornamental grasses. Beyond the display gardens you'll find the Wildflower Meadow and the Oak Tunnel that lead to the native riparian areas, lush with streamside plants and abundant wildlife.

Red Butte Gardens offers several wonderful programs and a hiking trail gentle enough for children (see our Kidstuff chapter). You might enjoy the summer concerts in the Garden.

Admission is $3 for adults and $2 for kids, students and seniors. Children younger than 4 and Red Butte Garden members get in free. Summer hours (May to September) are 9 AM to dusk. Winter hours (October to April) are 10 AM to 5 PM. The site is open seven days a week.

Social Hall and Heritage Museum
39 S. State St., Salt Lake City • 321-8700

This was the first public building in Utah and the first playhouse west of the Missouri River. A glass enclosure displays the walls of the original building along with artifacts and historical information. Hours are Monday through Friday from 5 to 11 PM and Saturday until 8 PM. Admission is free.

Temple Square
50 W. South Temple, Salt Lake City • 240-2534, (800) 537-9703

Temple Square is like Salt Lake City's centerpiece at the banquet of religious history of the early Mormon settlers. This spectacular city block, surrounded by granite walls between North, South and West Temple and Main Street, takes up 10 acres in the heart of Salt Lake City. In fact, you can see the original surveyor's marker in the southeast corner of the square, indicating the exact center of the city.

The exquisite grounds of Temple Square provide one of the city's best gardens during the summer. Nearly 300,000 small lights adorn the square during the winter months. The square has two visitors centers, on the north and south sides.

Free guided tours are available every 10 minutes during the summer and every 15 minutes during the winter, leaving from the flag pole at the west end of the square between the Temple and Tabernacle. The tours last approximately 45 minutes. Summer hours for the square are 8 AM to 9 PM. Winter hours are 9 AM to 8 PM. There is no admission charge.

Temple Square is the setting for several buildings of importance to the Mormon culture, and most are open to visitors. You can marvel at the magnificence of the exterior of the Mormon Temple on Temple Square, built between 1853 and 1893 from local granite. The golden angel Moroni, an important figure in the history of the Mormon church, sits on top of the temple, blowing his horn. The temple plays an important role in the life of Mormons. Here, faithful members who live according to the teachings of their church participate in sacred ordinances such as baptism and marriage. This is the only Mormon church building that is not open to the public.

Assembly Hall, 240-3323, is a charming building constructed in 1880. Today it is home to the Temple Square Concert Series held Friday and Saturday from 7:30 to 8:30 PM throughout the year. An expanded schedule is included during the Christmas holidays with performances nightly except Sunday and Monday evenings. Visiting performers from all over the world, including military bands and choruses as well as individuals, present classical programs in the hall. During the holidays, high school and college choruses and other performers present more than 300 programs. Some summer programs incorporate a lighter concert flavor, including show tunes.

The Tabernacle, 240-4872, built in 1863, houses the magnificent 11,623 pipe organ considered by many authorities to be one of the finest musical instruments in the world. When Werner von Braun, the German scientist who came to the United State to work on the moon science program, was asked to name the greatest thing he had ever done, he didn't say putting a man on the moon. He said it was playing the organ in the Tabernacle on Temple Square. The dome-shaped Tabernacle building is so acoustically superior that a pin dropped at one end can be heard clearly at the other end 170 feet away. The Tabernacle is home to the world-renowned Mormon Tabernacle Choir (see our Arts chapter).

This Is the Place
State Park Monument
2601 E. Sunnyside Ave. (800 S.), Salt Lake City • 584-8392

This marks the western end of the 1,300-mile (2,090 km) Mormon Pioneer Trail. It was from here that Brigham Young and his party first viewed the Salt Lake Valley. The visitors center has three floors of exhibits and information. The monument and visitors center are open free to the public year-round from 9 AM to 7 PM daily.

Tracy Aviary
589 E. 1300 S., Salt Lake City • 322-BIRD

This wonderful aviary opened in Liberty Park in 1911 with monkeys as the only residents. Deer soon arrived followed by other animals and some feathered friends. It soon became Liberty Park Zoo. The Happy Family Building was constructed in 1915 with 35 peacocks, 50 pheasants, 19 ostriches, one turkey, a family of ducks and a hundred or so rabbits and guinea pigs in residence.

By 1934 the animals were ready for larger quarters and the zoo was moved to its present location at 2600 E. Sunnyside Avenue. James Hogle donated the land for what is now called Hogle Zoo. Russell Lord Tracy donated 200 birds to the city from his personal collection in 1938, and the Tracy family donated money for construction of the building on 4 acres in the park. By the time of Tracy's death in 1945, the aviary was home to more than 800 birds, some of them rare to the area.

The aviary had also expanded to include seven more acres. The emphasis also began to shift from a place simply to admire beautiful birds to include a sanctuary for endangered birds. The aviary is now considered one of the finest displays of American birds in the country. You can take a walking tour through a world of more than 1,000 birds including an Andean condor with an 11-foot wing span, ever-colorful Chilean flamingos, parrots who provide song and conversation, dancing pelicans and a raven who plays practical jokes. See the Kidstuff chapter for hours.

Utah Museum of Natural History
250 S. 1300 E., University of Utah
• 581-6927

This impressive museum offers a look at the natural landscape in the state, beginning in prehistoric times with fossils and dinosaurs. You can view more than 30 Jurassic dinosaur skeletons and Ice Age fossils. The museum interprets archaeological and paleontological sites in the region and shows the geology, biology and mineralogy of the area with displays on gems, minerals, plants, animals and early inhabitants. It has a vast collection and display of Native American artifacts.

This place is a special treat for kids. The museum has gone out of its way to make the displays both educational and child-friendly. Kids are going to love digging for dinosaur bones (see our Kidstuff chapter). Admission is $3 for adults and $1 for children.

Utah State Capitol
400 N. State St., Salt Lake City
• 538-3000, (800) 538-1563

Completed in 1915 of Utah granite, this structure is considered one of the finest examples of Renaissance Revival architecture in the United States. The rotunda reaches 165 feet at its highest point and is centered by a 6,000-pound chandelier held by a 7,500-pound chain. The domed ceiling is painted with sea

gulls in flight. Although the gulls appear small from below, some are rendered with 6-foot wing spans. The interior marble is light in color and had striking patterns.

Utah's history is depicted in large canvasses and murals in the rotunda and lunettes on each end of the Great Hall. The first floor of the Capitol building has dozens of interesting exhibits including a race car that set the land speed record on the Bonneville Speedway. The gardens around the Capitol are arranged in patterns similar to Native American weaving designs.

The building is open to the public daily from 6 AM to 8 PM in the summer and from 8 AM to 6 PM during the winter. Free guided tours are available every half hour on Tuesday, Wednesday and Thursday from 9 AM to 3 PM and during the summer from 10 AM to 3 PM.

Wheeler Farms
6351 S. 900 E., Salt Lake City • 264-2241

Sariah Wheeler and her husband, Henry, set up housekeeping in the Victorian home at Wheeler Farms in 1886. The *Biographical Record of Salt Lake City*, published in 1902, stated "[The Wheeler house] . . . consists of ten commodious rooms, and the entire structure was planned by Mrs. Wheeler and reflects great credit upon her knowledge of architecture, as it is not only homelike and convenient, but one of the prettiest little farmhouses to be found in the country."

Sariah lived on the farm with her husband until her death in 1928. Henry continued to work the farm until his death in 1943. Several families owned the property until 1976, when it was purchased by the state and opened as a living historic farm.

Wheeler Farms hosts a variety of family activities and events throughout the year. Visitors can tour the home, see historic farming demonstrations and do chores as part of the interactive program offered here. The price of admission is $2 for children ages 3 to 12. Children older than 12 and adults to age 65 pay $3. Senior citizen pay $2. Children younger than 2 are admitted free. Admission includes a tour of the house and a wagon ride around the property. For more information on Wheeler Farms, see the Kidstuff chapter.

Many families find that
the best way to keep a
big bunch busy in both
summer and winter is to
enjoy the great
outdoors.

Kidstuff

We've got kids. Lots of them. Utah has the highest per capita birthrate in the nation, and most of the population lives along our Wasatch Front. With so many little people we've become quite creative when it comes to Kidstuff. Many families find that the best way to keep a big bunch busy in both summer and winter is to enjoy the great outdoors. You will find a bazillion outdoor places to have fun with kids in the Parks and Recreation and Skiing and Winter Sports chapters in this book.

We couldn't possibly list all the things kids can do in the Salt Lake Valley, but we have included a generous measure of the very best. We've grouped them by attitude, listing the fun spots alphabetically within the sections. For example, "Get Wild" covers our amusement parks and adventures for big and little thrill seekers. In "Get Wet" you'll learn about the area's sophisticated swimming holes. The section called "Oooh!" lists venues such as museums and the planetarium — places that'll elicit ooohs from everyone. Parents with hungry kids should check out the "Stuff Your Face" section for local kids' favorite food joints. "Taste This" covers the sweet side of life in the Valley, namely candy factories. And "Touch This" hooks you up with hands-on and interactive activities especially for children. The "Chill" section is loaded with interesting things for kids to do that don't require a lot of locomotion. We've also listed some annual events you won't want to miss in the "Please, Can We Do It Again?" section. The "Campy Kidstuff" and the "White Stuff" sections provide a list of summer camps plus ski instruction and activities just for kids in the winter. If you have kids, this is the place!

Get Wild

Lagoon Amusement Park
375 N. Lagoon Dr., Farmington • 451-8000, (800) 748-5246

Are we there yet? Just 17 miles north of downtown, kids can get thrills and chills at the biggest amusement park in the mountain west. Lagoon has more than 35 rides and hundreds of games, attractions and activities. For thrills try the Skycoaster that travels at speeds of up to 80 mph. The Colossal Fire Dragon, at a height of 85 feet, covers 3,000 feet of track in a minute and 45 seconds. Dragster fun is awesome in the Top Eliminator that goes from zero to 75 mph in 2.8 seconds. Lagoon's Sky Scraper Ferris wheel whips skyward to 150 feet. Had enough? Wait. There's more! The park's 60-foot-high wooden roller coaster, built in 1921, covers 2,500 feet of track and moves at a speed of 45 mph.

Want more nostalgia? Ponies and a menagerie of tame animals make up Lagoon's carousel, built in 1893. The hand-carved animals are irresistibly charming. Many have glass eyes and are bedecked with jewels. Need to chill? Lagoon has plenty of rides for not-so-thrill-minded youngsters. The park also offers a variety of games and other attractions.

Daily individual passports are $25.95 for people 51 inches to 59 years of age. Kinders, 4 years old to 50 inches tall, get in for $19.95.

Toddlers younger than 3 and adults older than 60 can stay at the park all day for $12.50. A season passport is $65.95 for an individual and $239.80 for a family of four. The passport includes rides, Lagoon A Beach, Pioneer Village and entertainment. Parents with small children can rent a stroller for $8.50 per day.

Lagoon is open May through October. See the "Oooh!" and "Get Wet" sections in this chapter for information on Pioneer Village and Lagoon A Beach fun. You'll find more on Lagoon in the Attractions and Sightseeing chapter.

Salt Lake County Equestrian Park
10800 S. 2200 W., South Jordan • 254-0106

Imagine the fury of a *Ben Hur* chariot ride, steam pouring from the horse's nostrils as the big beast rushes through the cold winter air. You can see something like that and a lot of other horsing around at this wonderful equestrian park in the south Valley. There is plenty of flat track and barrel racing as well. Jumping stock and other events are held year round.

Admission for quarter-horse racing is $4 for adults and free for children. Admission for all other events is free. Hours are 9 AM to 6 PM Monday through Saturday. This park is closed on major holidays.

The Sports Park
8695 S. Sandy Pkwy., Sandy • 562-4444

Batter up! Seven batting cages with a variety of speeds make for a perfect pastime for those with their eyes on the major or little leagues. Future racecar drivers will enjoy the five go-cart tracks, a big hit with kids who aren't yet old enough to drive. The park also has two 18-hole miniature golf courses. The video arcade is great for hours of indoor fun. Food is available for the but-I'm-really-hungry crowd.

Hours vary according to the season. The price of a pass is $5.95 for kids 3 years old to 46 inches tall. The pass includes a game of miniature golf, four rides and two tokens redeemable at the concession stand. The $14.95 pass, for children more than 46 inches tall and adults, includes a game of miniature golf, four track

rides and four tokens redeemable at the concession stand. Pay-per-play tickets are $4.25 for adults and $3.85 for children 12 and younger. A game of miniature golf costs $4 for adults and $3 for children 12 and younger.

Utah Fun Dome
4998 S. 360 W., Murray • 265-3866

Is this kid heaven? A whopper of an indoor entertainment mall, this nationally acclaimed attraction will keep your kids busy all day with thrill rides — including an indoor roller coaster — activities and games. There's bungee jumping for the very brave, or the slightly crazy. Kids can work themselves into a frenzy with laser tag. The two miniature-golf courses, a 30-lane bowling alley plus roller skating ought to burn off some excess energy. Whew! How about a big challenge with the newest in arcade redemption games such as Skee Ball or Smokin' Token. More points equals more tickets, which can be redeemed for prizes such as stuffed animals, bicycles, jewelry, pens and pencils.

The Dome has bumper cars for kids who need to safely work out a sibling dispute. You'll also find an F-D1 motion simulator that simulates motion by moving to a picture on a 3D movie screen. There's also live entertainment on stage.

Naturally, any kid who plays this hard will work up an appetite. The Fun Dome's got it covered. There are restaurants that serve pizza, or salads, sandwiches and burgers. You can fill the kids up on plenty of our local specialty: ice cream is available at the Fun Dome's Ice Cream Parlor.

There's no entrance fee, and all attractions are individually priced. Hours vary, so call for details.

Get Wet

Lagoon A Beach
375 N. Lagoon Dr., Farmington • 451-8000, (800) 748-5246

Six acres of beachfront in the middle of the desert? How'd they do that? Lagoon A Beach has 550,000 gallons of water to splash in, float on and slide through, so get ready to get wet! Two activity pools offer something for everyone. A tropical oasis with an aqua lagoon encircled by crystal waterfalls, misty tunnels and hot tubs is the lazy way to enjoy the afternoon. The nearby kids' activity pool has a castaway island-of-fun with tunnels, bridges, slides and a giant spouting volcano. Water guns are available for squirting friends.

For thrill seekers Lagoon A Beach has serpentine slides that drop 56 feet from a tower, twisting and splashing to the bottom. The 65-foot free-fall slide makes you feel like you're plummeting straight down, but it glides you gently to a stop in the splash pool below. Two hump slides plunge nearly 70 feet straight down, splashing you to a stop like a human tidal wave. Go tubular on four tube slides or ride the rapids in a river tube.

Beach bunnies can soak up the rays on the sun deck, play beach volleyball or stuff themselves with munchies from the specialty food court.

All-day and season passports are available. Refer to Lagoon Amusement Park in the "Get Wild" section of this chapter for details.

Raging Waters
1200 W. 1700 S., Salt Lake City • 972-3300

Another big water adventure! Raging Waters has food, fun and more than 30 water slides (including the high speed Shotgun Falls and the vertical drop Acapulco Cliff Dive) to keep everyone busy. The Waima Wave is the world's only water roller coaster. Wide-eyed water babies can dip, dive and plunge like never before. Little surfers can challenge the waves with more than 500,000 gallons of liquid delirium in the Wild Wave body-surfing pool. What kid wouldn't love some prehistoric playmates? Dinosaur Bay has active volcanos and tons of prehistoric water fun.

The park is open from May to summer's end. Early season discounts are available. Regular admission is $13.95 for adults and teens and $9.95 for juniors, ages 3 to 11. Children 2 and younger and seniors 60 and older get in free. Hours are 10:30 AM to 7:30 PM. The evening special, 4 PM to 7:30 PM, is $7.95.

Oooh!

Daughters of Utah Pioneers Museum
300 N. Main St., Salt Lake City • 538-1050

This is a fascinating place for kids. We'll start with the museum's gigantic doll collection. The docents aren't sure how many they have, but there are walls and walls of dolls. Pioneer dolls, dolls from all over the world in their native costumes, and character dolls made from almost everything you can imagine, including apples, pears, walnuts and more. Each doll has been donated, and the museum's docents can provide information on their history and origin.

The museum's stuffed, two-headed lamb draws quite a bit of attention and so do the Victorian pictures made out of human hair. Now that's a curious find. Swords and guns are an additional attraction. The collection of antique farm equipment and horse racing buggies will intrigue the youngster in everyone. The museum also has an interesting display that includes baby buggies, an army wagon, a washing machine and three furnished rooms including a parlor, bedroom and pioneer kitchen — without a microwave in sight.

During the Mormons' trek to the Salt Lake Valley, many people had to lighten their load. They buried their heavy pianos along the trail, hoping to return for them later. Many of those pianos, including one buried in a tin box and another wrapped in a buffalo skin, are on display. The museum is good for hours of genuine Ooohs.

It's open year round, Monday through Saturday, from 9 AM to 5 PM. Admission is free, but donations are appreciated.

Fort Douglas
32 Potter St., Salt Lake City • 588-5188

Built in 1862 to ensure that the mail and stagecoach line had safe passage en route to California and, unofficially, to allow the government to spy on the Mormons, Fort Douglas also headquartered the Ninth Army Command during World War II. Deactivated in 1991, the fort was turned over to the University of Utah. Young visitors like this adventure's authenticity. It covers several generations of military history. Five styles of military architecture — including officer's quarters built in the 1870s from red sandstone quarried in nearby Red Butte Canyon, stone barracks and administration buildings that date from 1900 to the 1930s — and the cemetery set the stage for bygone activities at Fort Douglas.

The Fort Douglas Military Museum on the south side of the fort's parade ground, east of the University, exhibits the fort's role in history. Special maps and activity sheets are available for kids. This museum is open year round, Tuesday through Saturday. Hours are 10 AM to noon and 1 to 4 PM. Admission is free.

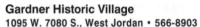

Gardner Historic Village
1095 W. 7080 S., West Jordan • 566-8903

Archibald Gardner, a Mormon pioneer and polygamist, built a water-powered saw mill in 1853 on the site where the Gardner Historic Village now stands. He replaced the saw mill with a flour mill in 1877. A mattress factory, a woolen mill, a broom factory and a button factory soon followed on the surrounding land. As business blossomed, so did the Gardner family. His 11 wives gave him 47 children who, in turn, produced 270 grandchildren. The village has a fun museum with memorabilia about the mill, Gardner and his wives. More than a dozen shops sell furniture, accessories, collectibles and one-of-a-kind items.

Archibald's Restaurant is an Insiders' favorite for Sunday brunch (see our Restaurants chapter). Children's events such as the Scarecrow Festival in the fall and Pony Days during the summer are scheduled throughout the year. Events vary, so call for details. The village is 15 minutes south of downtown on the road to the Bingham Copper Mine and is open year round. Admission is free.

Hansen Planetarium
15 S. State St., Salt Lake City • 538-2104, (800) UTAH-NET

This kid-friendly planetarium is a heavenly place. Children are encouraged to touch and play with scientific stuff in the planetarium's interactive exhibits. A simulated space flight to the stars and beyond lets them explore the cosmos indoors during the planetarium's star shows. Choreographed animated laser light beams boogie to the beat of popular music during laser music concerts including Beatles Laser, Laser U2 Squared, Laser Fest Classic Rock (with music from Yes, Queen and Boston), Laser Zeppelin and Laser Floyd Shines On. Musical selections change every 90 days. Classes in astronomy that cover the stars and planets are available for children of all ages during the summer.

The planetarium is open Monday through Thursday 9:30 AM to 9 PM and until midnight Friday and Saturday. Sunday hours are noon to 5:30 PM. Admission for the Star and Science Shows is $3.50 for children and seniors and $4.50 for teens and adults. Laser music concerts are $5 for children younger than 12 and seniors and $6 for teens and adults. The late-night laser concerts are $7.50.

Hill Aerospace Museum
7961 Wardleigh Dr., Roy • 777-6868

Off we go into the wild blue yonder. Everything a kid ever wanted to know about airplanes is on display at the Hill Aerospace Museum, which has more than 57 aircraft spanning aeronautical evolution from the 1930s to present. Housed inside a 52,000-square-foot building or on the 36 adjacent acres, the exhibit includes F-15 and F-16 fighter planes, a Navy fighter plane, the SR-71 Black Bird spy plane plus rockets, bombs, missiles and a ton of other neat stuff. The museum also has aircraft artwork and uniforms and flight suits that date back to World War I. The museum is open seven days a week, except holidays. Hours are 9 AM to 4:30 PM, Monday through Friday and until 5:30 PM on Saturday and Sunday. Admission is free.

Kennecott Utah Copper Bingham Mine
Copperton • 252-3234

One of the largest open-pit copper mines in the world, the excavated hole is a half-mile deep and 2½ miles across and looks like a giant amphitheater that could seat more than

Kids enjoy Huck Finn Days and many other activities at historic Wheeler Farm.

9 million people. Standing on the visitors observation deck, the large work trucks below look like small Tonka toys in this immense earthen cavity. More than 5 billion tons of material have been removed from the mine to produce in excess of 12 million tons of copper.

Exhibits at the visitor's center provide information on the history, geology and production of the mine. This is an awesome hole in the ground — well-worth seeing. You can take a picnic and stop for lunch at Copperton Park. It's open to visitors from April to October, 8 AM to 8 PM daily. Admission is $3 per car and $2 per motorcycle. Fees are donated to nonprofit and charitable organizations. The mine is 22 miles from downtown. Take Interstate 15 to the Midvale Exit (7200 S.). Go south to 7800 S. then west to the old Bingham Canyon Road (Utah Highway 48). From there, follow the signs to the mine.

FYI

Unless otherwise noted, the area code for all phone numbers listed in this guide is 801.

Pioneer Village at Lagoon
375 N. Lagoon Dr., Farmington • 451-8000, (800) 748-5246

Make-believe villains can get locked up in the old-time jailhouse here, or sit tall like well-heeled city folks while they ride a horse drawn carriage through the streets of Pioneer Village. Gunfights are reenacted on Main Street, using fake bullets, of course. The log flume ride provides plenty of old-fashioned fun for young wannabe pioneers. The village has several historic buildings including a drug store, an old school house, post office and an early soda fountain. One of the best firearms museums in the country is here. The museum includes many early guns made by the famous John Browning and features his tools and work bench. See the "Get Wet" section of this chapter for Lagoon A Beach fun and the "Get Wild"

section for information on Lagoon Amusement Park. You'll find more on Lagoon in the Attractions and Sightseeing chapter.

Tracy Aviary at Liberty Park
589 E. 1300 S., Salt Lake City • 322-BIRD

This is America's only public bird park with more than 1,000 birds representing more than 240 species. The "Birds of a Feather" show is presented daily during the summer. The Lory Feeding Exhibit allows little bird watchers to feed more than 100 brightly colored Lory birds.

Summer hours for the aviary are 9 AM to 6 PM Monday through Friday and until 4 PM on Sundays and holidays. Winter hours are 9 AM to 4:30 PM. The bird shows are at noon and 2 PM on weekdays, with an additional 4 PM show on weekends and holidays. Find out more about Tracy Aviary in the Attractions and Sightseeing chapter.

Stuff Your Face

Chuck A Rama
744 E. 400 S., Salt Lake City • 531-1123
2960 Highland Dr., Salt Lake City • 487-0879
4150 S. Redwood Rd., Salt Lake City • 967-0300
6363 S. State St., Salt Lake City • 262-9233

This is the local kids' pig-out palace. Chuck A Rama has been serving buffet-style food to the community for more than 30 years, and it does it up in grand style. Small people with big appetites can choose from approximately 45 food and salad items including such kid cuisine as macaroni and cheese, fried chicken and a mountain of Jell-O. Go ahead — eat all you want. Gulp down a variety of beverages — there's no limit. Dessert is the highlight of the meal: 16 mouth-watering choices includ-

---

INSIDERS' TIP

Near Tracy Aviary at Liberty Park is a small amusement area with a Ferris wheel, a carousel and a playground with kid-safe equipment guaranteed to tire out your kids and give you a few quiet moments of sitting time. The old-fashioned snow cones at the concession stand are very refreshing.

ing several kinds of brownies, cakes, Rice-Krispy treats, pudding and self-serve soft ice cream.

Chuck A Rama is open from 11 AM to 9 PM Monday through Saturday and until 8 PM on Sunday but closed Christmas day. Kids are charged by their age: Children ages 4 to 12 are charged 50¢ per year of age for lunch and 60¢ per year for dinner. Anyone younger than 4 eats free. For adults lunch is $5.99 and dinner is $7.49. Sunday prices are $7.49 all day. Lunch is served until 3:59 PM.

The Old Spaghetti Factory
5718 S. 1900 W., Salt Lake City • 966-2765
Trolley Square, 602 E. 500 S., Salt Lake City • 521-0424

Both locations have an eclectic flavor, with antiques and a big red trolley car in the middle of the restaurant. An odd assortment of furniture includes benches that were once church pews and old bed steads made into seating for two. They serve more than 10 varieties of spaghetti, so your bambini will love this place. The atmosphere is relaxed and very kid-friendly.

The children's menu offers plain tomato-sauce or meat-sauce spaghetti as well as macaroni and cheese, priced from $2.95 to $3.75. The adult fare — or larger portions and more variety for hungry youngsters — ranges from $4.50 to $8.25.

Tony Romas — A Place for Ribs
895 E. Fort Union Blvd., Midvale • 566-7427
352 Trolley Sq., Salt Lake City • 537-7427
10261 S. State St., Sandy • 495-0702

Some of the food is really messy, so naturally kids love it here. Popular small-fry menu items include Roma Ranger Ribs, chicken strips, burgers, cheese pizza and grilled cheese sandwiches. The special appetizer menu for kids features finger veggies for dipping. Most little ones go for the Dirt Cup from the kid dessert menu: chocolate pudding with crushed Oreo cookies, topped with gummi worms. Yuck! OK, we know it's a chain but Tony Romas is a favorite kid's pick. It's open Monday through Thursday 11 AM to 10 PM, Friday and Saturday until 11 PM and Sunday noon to 9 PM. Prices range from $2.99 for

sandwiches and burgers to $4.99 for Roma Ranger Ribs.

The Lion House
63 E. South Temple, Salt Lake City • 363-5466, (800) 546-4449

If you are planning a birthday party, consider the charming Pioneer birthday party presented at the historic Lion House. The party room is decorated with child size antiques and other period furniture. Little girls get to wear pioneer hats, and the honored birthday girl wears a tiara, of course. Boys wear coonskin caps. Children learn how their pioneer counterparts used to play, and games such as "button, button" and "I'm going across the plain and I'm taking . . ." are lots of fun. The Lion House hostess reads a story about a pioneer child that'll capture everyone's attention. Young guests get a chance to pull taffy the old-fashioned way, and everyone gets to take a piece home. Cake and ice cream are served, and the birthday child opens presents that have been held in an old wash tub. The honoree takes home a special gift, a stuffed lamb for the boys and a porcelain doll for the girls. Treats to take home include typical pioneer goodies such as sunflower seeds and raisins and a sugared sea gull. Kids who attend birthday parties at the Lion House remember them fondly for years.

Taste This

Taffy Town
55 W. 800 S., Salt Lake City • 355-4637

Two cute characters, Tug and Stretch, take kids on an animated tour of the candy factory and show how our world-famous taffy is made. This is a fun place to visit, and little people get free samples. You'll know you're at Taffy Town by the huge, colorful letters on the building.

Peppermint Place
155 E. 200 N., Alpine • (801) 756-7400

About 30 minutes from downtown, south on I-15, the Peppermint Palace, an outlet store for a unique candy manufacturing facility, puts their candy-making operation on display from a large observation deck that allows visitors to watch several kinds of candy being made. Peppermint Palace has hand-dipped chocolates, nut brittle, 24 candy stick flavors, chocolate-covered potato chips and 15 kinds of licorice. If you are on your way to a destination south of the south Valley, this is an interesting stop. Warning: You will not get out of here without buying several sweet treats, available in the gift shop. The production staff is ready to call it a day by 2 PM, so visit early. The factory opens at 10 AM.

Touch This

Wheeler Historic Farm
6351 S. 900 E., Salt Lake City • 264-2212, 264-2241 camp information

What's it like to work on a farm? City dwellers and their country cousins really get into the chores on this interactive working farm. Little farmers can pet the animals and pick up a few tips from the historic farming demonstrations. Hay rides are available in summer and sleigh rides are a wonderful treat in winter. Throughout the year the farm hosts special events such as the teddy bear Victorian tea, an ice cream social, musical events and breakfast with Santa.

The price of admission is $2 for children between the ages of 3 and 11 and senior citizens. Children 12 and older and adults to age 65 pay $3. Children younger than 2 are admitted free. Admission includes a tour of the farmhouse and a wagon ride around the property.

Wheeler Farm has a weeklong summer camp for children ages 8 to 11. Call for information.

Utah Museum of Natural History
250 S. 1300 E., University of Utah • 581-6927, 581-4887 summer field adventure

Young excavators usually take the experience of digging for Mastodon bones very seriously. They can touch a Columbian mammoth skull and get a glimpse of prehistoric life in Utah. They learn how much care is required during excavation by carefully removing chocolate chips from cookies and watch archeologists uncover fossils through a large glass window.

Kids figure out that this is a very cool place as soon as they enter. Al, the talking dinosaur, will introduce himself on their arrival. Many of the artifacts and exhibits here are especially geared toward children. The dinosaur exhibit includes more than 30 different Jurassic dinosaur skeletons and Ice Age fossil mammals, including two allosaurs, a camptosaurus and a stegosaurus. Throughout the year the museum hosts special programs for youngsters and sponsors hands-on projects that focus on ways to be gentler with Mother Earth. Programs such as Science Carnival encourage kids to learn more about human physiology, physics, optics and sound, and temporary exhibits such as To See the Sea let kids in on the exciting world of the deep ocean with photographs, informative texts, relics and equipment used to capture the essence of the underwater world. This museum, with six major galleries that house permanent geology, paleontology, anthropology and biology collections offers a treasure chest of opportunity for young people to learn and to have fun.

Admission is $3 for adults and $1 for children. Call for information about the museum-sponsored summer field adventures for kids. More information about the Utah Museum of Natural History is included in our Attractions and Sightseeing chapter.

Hogle Zoo
2600 E. Sunnyside Ave. (800 S.), Salt Lake City • 582-1631

What an adventure! More than 1,300 animals live at the Hogle Zoo. All the regulars are there: big cats, elephants, hippos, bears and many other animals the zoo likes to call ambassadors of their species. Kids can see the giraffes up close and personal from a special balcony. Besides big animals, the zoo has lots of little ones including several varieties of monkeys. Many baby animals are born at the zoo each year. Spring is a big season for babies. The Small Wonders Barn allows children to interact with smaller animals. Exotic birds and plants live in the zoo's solarium; butterflies flit around the butterfly house in the spring and summer.

Kids will especially enjoy Hogle Zoo's Discovery Land. The Knoll and Burrow section lets curious youngsters go underground to see what it's like to be a burrowing animal. They'll pop up in the marmoset exhibit. In Desert Canyon, kids will learn about the influence plants and animals have on different environments. The Fort in the Forest features a tree slide and covered boardwalk. A tour of the grounds is easily managed aboard a small replica of an 1869 steam engine. Everyone will appreciate getting off their feet for a few minutes. Families can picnic in the pavilion or snack at the concession stand. The Safari Sleepover is just one of many programs the zoo has for children.

Hogle Zoo is open every day of the year except Christmas. Hours are 9 AM to 6 PM. Admission is $5 for adults and $3 for children ages 4 to 14 and senior citizens. Kids younger than 4 get in free. Family membership is $50 per year. Strollers are available for rent for $3 a day.

Children's Museum of Utah
840 N. 300 W., Salt Lake City • 322-5268

The Children's Museum focuses on teaching kids while they play. A cockpit from an airplane and the front end of a red diesel truck get their attention as soon as they walk in the door. The museum is hands-on, so children can play here to their heart's delight. The Kid's Town grocery store, gas station and ATM machine all have gadgets that adults use in everyday life. This is a great way to find out what the grown-up world is all about.

Busy young visitors can put on a puppet show or freeze their shadow on the wall. Buzzing bees can be observed in a hive behind clear glass. What would it be like to see the world sitting down in a wheelchair? An obstacle course lets kids find out as they move through, opening a door, getting a drink of water and looking out the window. Budding artists can draw, paint and do craft projects in the museum's art project area. The doll and multicultural art exhibits change regularly. Magicians, clowns, artists and other special visitors are frequent hosts for story and activity times.

The hours are 9:30 AM to 5 PM, Monday through Thursday and Saturday. Admission is $3 for children and adults. Kids younger than 2 get in for free. On Friday nights the museum is open until 8 PM and everyone older than 2 gets in for $1.50. An adult must accompany children younger than 14.

KidSpace
20 W. South Temple, Salt Lake Art Center • 328-4201

Kids can really get to the art of the matter at KidSpace. A visit to the center's current exhibit will generate plenty of questions and spark their boundless imaginations. Eager little masters can get ready to create in one of the KidSpace work stations devoted to the concepts of the displayed work. Kidspace provides tons of fun materials, ranging from paint to collage to clay, to encourage a variety of experiences and expressions with media. This is a great hands-on experience.

The center is open to children ages 2 to 15. An adult must accompany all children. Hours are Thursday, Friday and Sunday from 1 to 4 PM. KidSpace is open on Saturday from 10 AM to 4 PM. Admission is free, but a suggested donation is $1 for each child and $2 for each adult. For more information about educational programs for adults and current exhibits, see the Salt Lake Art Center in The Arts chapter.

Chill

A Woman's Place Bookstore
1400 Foothill Dr., Salt Lake City • 583-6431

What a great idea! A Woman's Place Bookstore has a mother and daughter reading program for moms and girls (ages 9 to 14). Designed to provide quality time and a common ground, the readings and discussions revolve around titles such as *To Kill a Mockingbird*, *A Tree Grows in Brooklyn* and

INSIDERS' TIP

Get around in style and see the local sights aboard a trolley car. Ride the Discover Trolley! Between June and October the trolley runs on Weekdays and Saturdays from 10 AM to 6 PM. For more information, call BUS-INFO.

The Secret Garden. Call for more information. See the write-up for A Woman's Place in our Shopping chapter for information about its extensive selection books for grownups.

Barnes and Noble Booksellers
2236 S. 1300 E., Salt Lake City • 467-1181
5928 S. State St., Murray • 266-0075
7119 S. 1300 E., Midvale • 565-0086
10180 S. State St., Sandy • 233-0203
612 E. 400 S., Salt Lake City • 524-0089

Every Saturday is story time at all Barnes and Noble bookstores throughout the Salt Lake Valley. Some programs include characters in costume, activities and games. Kids think this is great fun. Barnes and Noble also has book clubs for kids, including the American Girl Club, and other special programs. Call 464-3142 for a recorded message that provides locations, hours and details of weekly events. For more information about the myriad of books and programs available for adults, see our Shopping chapter's "Bookstores" section.

The Children's Bookshelf at Ivy Place
4700 S. 900 E., Ste. 26, Salt Lake City • 281-4828

Books, books and more books for little book worms. The Children's Bookshelf has story time for young children on Thursdays. They stock a great selection of children's titles including award-winners and classics. Tea parties at the bookstore are a special treat, especially for birthdays. Young guests dress up, play make believe and have fashion shows. After story reading they have tea (strawberry lemonade) served with tea cakes and teapot shaped cookies. The store carries a line of book accessories including Curious George, Winnie the Pooh, Beatrix Potter and Madeline toys. Hours are 10 AM to 6 PM, Monday through Saturday.

The Children's Hour
928 E. 900 S., Salt Lake City • 359-4150

Books from this store are hand-selected to reflect the owner's and staff's favorites. They have a large selection of award-winning and classic volumes for children of all ages. The store also carries a line of children's clothing and jewelry plus other items that are a big hit with little girls. They offer book clubs and classes during the summer for children ages 3 to 8, with separate classes for elementary school-age children. Author and character visits are frequent happenings throughout the year. Writing classes are available to elementary school children. Hours are 10 AM to 6 PM, Monday through Saturday .

Gallivan Center
36 E. 200 S., Salt Lake City • 532-0459

Something is always going on at the Gallivan Center downtown, and kids are usually a big part of the activities. Year round art adventures are held every Tuesday. Each project is different, ranging from ceramics to watercolors. The cost is $1 per participant for children 3 and older. An adult must accompany children.

Many programs center around the pond/ice-skating rink in both summer and winter. The rink is open to skaters from mid-November to mid-March. During the winter holidays kids participate in the Holiday Countdown activities beginning the day after Thanksgiving with "Lights On" — when all the Christmas lights downtown are lit up for the first time — through Christmas. Children can visit Santa and deliver their wish lists in person. Carolers provide music of the season around the ice rink during the day and in the evening. A Summer Social in July features a watermelon bust and games, and no one wants to miss the fall Fish Fest. The ice rink becomes a pond and youngsters are invited to try their luck at catching one of the 2,000 stocked trout. A fishing etiquette program must be completed before children are permitted to fish. Call for details.

The King's English
1511 S. 1500 E., Salt Lake City • 484-9100

The King's English has been a favorite bookstore with Salt Lakers for more than 20 years. The young reader's and little listener's book section is filled to the brim with best-selling, award-winning and classic children's

FYI
Unless otherwise noted, the area code for all phone numbers listed in this guide is 801.

The first thrill ride opened at Lagoon Amusement in 1906. More than four generations of kids and their parents have enjoyed the fun at Lagoon.

books for all ages including fiction and nonfiction. They also have books-on-tape, videos, CD-ROM, games and activity books. Story time is every Saturday for pre-school to elementary-aged children. They have reading programs for older kids too. One of the most exciting aspects of their children's programming is the opportunity they provide for their young clientele to meet and interact with the many local and national authors and illustrators who regularly visit for book readings and signings. The annual Kid's Day in June, in conjunction with the neighborhood Arts Festival, is always a big hit. Their *Kid's Inkslinger*, a children's newsletter that comes out twice a year, is full of great information including reviews, recommendations and the scoop on the best new books on the market. The store is open Monday through Saturday 10 AM to 9 PM and Sunday 11 AM to 5 PM. The King's English also has a large selection of books for grown-ups. For more details see the Shopping chapter under "Bookstores."

Red Butte Garden and Arboretum
300 Wakara Way, University of Utah Research Park • 581-IRIS

This is a natural way to chill out after all those wild rides and twister slides. The Garden offers an ever-changing display of growing things on hundreds of acres of natural and mountain trails. The Courtyard Garden is a quiet place to gather. Etchings of 52 Utah wildflowers decorate the sandstone benches near the Sego Lily Fountain.

There's a kid-tested hiking trail about 0.5-mile long that even the smallest children can manage. Young nature lovers will be intrigued with a series of ponds and waterfalls that enhance the Red Butte Canyon watershed. The arboretum staff plants unusual flora along the path and throughout the Garden to test their adaptability to the climate. Trees along the trail are part of a living laboratory. Red Butte Garden hosts a variety of children's programs and nature outings. The Saturday morning summer concert series for kids is very popular with Salt Lakers.

Admission to the Garden is $3 for adults and $2 for kids, students and seniors. Children younger than 4 and Garden members get in for free. Summer hours (May to September) are 9 AM to dusk. Winter hours (October to April) are 10 AM to 5 PM. The Garden is open seven days a week.

Salt Lake City Public Library
Main Branch, 209 E. 500 S., Salt Lake City • 524-8200

Our kids are big library users. Throughout the year the Salt Lake City Public Library System provides a variety of free programs for children, including outdoor survival guides, home-alone safety programs, reading marathons and much more. All locations have weekly preschool story times for children ages 3 to 5. The children's department at the main library also offers weekly Internet training for children and their parents. No registration is required. The summer reading program, June through mid-August, is open to kids of all ages and features fun themes such as Summer Reading Safari and Readers of The Round Table. The Kid's Catalog, an interactive computer program, makes finding books, videos, CDs, cassettes and CD-ROMs easy for even the youngest readers. For more information on programs and hours contact the main branch of the library.

Salt Lake County Library System
2197 E. 7000 S., Salt Lake City • 943-4636

The County Library System has several story time programs. Toddler time is a big hit for little ones ages 2½ to 3¼ years. Preschoolers, ages 3¼ to 5, get a big kick out of their story time, too. The County Library sometimes schedules family story time and, on occasion, they have a baby story time for wee ones. Special programs that feature magicians, puppet shows, storytellers and authors are part of the young people's programming. Most branches in the county are open Monday through Thursday from 10 AM to 10 PM and Friday and Saturday from 10 AM to 6 PM.

Please, Can We Do It Again?

The Nutcracker
Ballet West • 50 W. 200 S., Salt Lake City • 355-2787, 355-ARTS

This wonderful ballet is an absolute Salt Lake tradition! The best thing about this annual holiday production is the children, both the dancers and those in the audience. Nearly 300 children perform in this classic ballet first choreographed by Ballet West's founder, Willam Christiansen. The ballet made it's American debut in San Francisco in 1944. With the assistance of his Russian friends, George Balanchine and Alexandra Danilova, who recalled the treasured ballet from their childhood memories, Christiansen created an extraordinary work which has brought joy to locals since 1955.

Young people sit wide-eyed in the audience as the Sugar Plum fairies, toy soldiers and other wonderful characters bring the story of the Nutcracker to life. Many adults and children who have seen the ballet year after year anxiously await the entrance of Mother Buffoon and the little Buffoons, who quickly scatter about the stage from under her wide skirt. The giggles from the audience are delicious. *The Nutcracker* has evening and matinee performances during December. Prices

---

INSIDERS' TIP

Want to party on the wild side? Hogle Zoo has a special kid's birthday-party package. Kids get a sack lunch with a hot dog, animal cookies and a drink in a souvenir cup. A train ride rounds out the trip. Oh, yes. You get to visit the animals. Call 582-1631, Extension 684, for details.

range from $10 to $45. Call for ticket information.

Ballet West's Deer Valley Dance Camp offers a weeklong program with dance instruction in ballet, creative dance and jazz for children ages 9 to 14. Call 323-6900 for details. Also look for Ballet West in our Arts chapter.

Utah Arts Festival
Triad Center, Salt Lake City • 322-2428

This festival is an anxiously awaited annual event in Salt Lake. The organizers go all out every year to make this a great hands-on kid experience. The recent "Planet Discovery . . . the Art Garden" celebrated bugs, plants, birds, weather, trees and grass with arts projects such as create-a-critter, a recycled objects activity. Young participants had the opportunity to rake in a life-size Zen garden, create a giant pinwheel garden and make small bugs from rocks to take home for their own garden.

The enthusiasm and creativity of the festival's staff and many project coordinators is awe-inspiring. If you are in Salt Lake in late June, don't miss this event.

Children younger than 12 are admitted to the Utah Arts Festival free. Adult admission is $5. Adults 60 and older get in for $2. The event is held at the Triad Center in downtown Salt Lake, on South Temple between 300 and 400 West. You can write to the Utah Arts Festival at 500 N. 168 W. Pierpont Avenue, Salt Lake City, UT 84103. For more information on this event, see the Utah Arts Festival listing in the Festivals and Annual Events chapter.

Campy Kidstuff

Youth Theater Camp
P.O. Box 3119, Park City, UT 84060
• (435) 649-9371

Park City Performances presents summer programs for preschool through high school-age children. Programs are designed to help children develop creativity as well as acting skills. Instruction covers makeup, costumes, sets and acting. The advanced theater camp requires an audition/interview and focuses on acting technique. The regular camp is for beginners and the Treasure Trunk camp is for children in preschool through grade 2. Each camp runs for two

weeks and ends with a performance for friends and family. Programs run from approximately mid-June to late July, and camps overlap. This is a great place for young aspiring thespians.

Bernie Solomon Camps
2416 E. 1700 S., Salt Lake City • 581-0098

The Jewish Community Center offers day-camp programs for children ages 2 to 13. Activities include supervised swimming, horseback riding, nature studies, rock climbing and tennis. Besides the camp's regular activities, the center offers specialized programs that focus on either the arts or sports. Camping programs and three-day field trips are also available. Two days per week programs are available for children ages 2 and 3. Children older than 3 can attend full-time. The center is open Monday through Thursday from 9 AM until 4 PM and on Friday until 3 PM.

Membership at the Jewish Community Center is open to everyone. Members receive reduced tuition rates and have priority sign-up for the summer camps. Summer camps run from mid-June to mid-August.

Junior Jazz Camp
301 E. South Temple, Salt Lake City
• 325-2500

This 3-day basketball camp for children ages 8 to 17 teaches sportsmanship and the finer points of basketball. Kids get instruction from professional basketball players including members of the Utah Jazz. Four camps are available between late June and mid-July.

Theater Schools
1901 South Campus Dr., Rm. 1169, Salt Lake City • 581-6984

Sponsored by the University of Utah, this program is for children ages 8 through 18 who are seriously interested in the performing arts. Classes for children ages 8 to 12 run from mid-June to the first week in July, and classes for children ages 13 to 18 run from early July to mid-August. The program concludes with a student performance.

University of Utah Youth Institute
1901 South Campus Dr., Rm. 1169, Salt Lake City • 581-6984

The University of Utah-sponsored sports

camps teach swimming, diving, golf, horseback riding, martial arts, rock climbing, tennis, gymnastics and more to children ages 4 to 17.

Virginia Tanner Creative Dance Programs
1033 E. 300 S. • 581-7374

The intellectual, physical and creative aspects of dance movement are taught to children ages 3½ to 18. Children study by age in small supervised groups. Year-round programs run on a semester basis, and summer programs are five weeks long. Some sessions conclude with performances.

White Stuff

Most of the area's ski resorts have wonderful winter programs for kids. For more details, please call the individual resorts. Don't forget to check out the Skiing and Winter Sports chapter for more information about the resorts.

Alf Engen Ski School
Little Cottonwood Canyon, Alta Ski Area • 742-3042

Kids ages 4 to 12 who take ski lessons at the Alf Engen Ski School in Alta learn ski etiquette and get excellent ski instruction. The program is fun, and students are treated to an ice cream party on Friday afternoons. Prices range from $25 for a 2-hour session to between $63 and $93 for full day sessions. Costs vary according to skill level and whether a lift ticket is included (since some families ski on a season pass). Lunch is provided for full-day sessions. Hours are 9 AM to 4:30 PM. Lessons begin at 10 AM and children are encouraged to arrive by 9:30.

The Alta Children's Center
Little Cottonwood Canyon, Alta Ski Area • 742-3042

Licensed for children ages 3 months to 12 years, this day-care center has fun activities including snow play when the weather permits. The center is open daily from 8:30 AM to 5 PM. Reservations are encouraged.

The Children's Center
2250 Deer Valley Dr. S., Salt Lake City • (800) 424-DEER

The newly expanded Child Care Center at the Deer Valley Resort is a state-licensed day-care center for children ages 2 months to 12 years. The program includes art projects, story time, indoor and outdoor play and other entertainment. Lunch is provided.

Prices are $68 for children 2 to 24 months and $55 for children ages 2 to 12. Hours are 8:30 AM to 4:30 PM daily during the ski season.

Kinderski
Little Cottonwood Canyon, Brighton Ski Resort • (800) 873-5512

The Kinderski program at Brighton helps young skiers ages 4 to 7 learn the basics and improve their technique. Private lessons are available for children under the age of 4. The cost is $50 for one hour of instruction. The cost of the group lesson for children ages 4 to 7 is $25 for 2 hours and $39 with lunch. The full-day rate including lunch is $59. Lessons begin at 9:45 AM and 1:30 PM. Equipment rental is $8 per day. Kinderski is not a day-care facility. Inquire about their ski rental packages for children.

Deer Valley Ski School
2250 Deer Valley Dr. S., Salt Lake City • (800) 424-DEER

This program for children ages 3½ to 12 provides ski lessons in a safe and fun environment. Children are placed in groups with others of the same ability level. Special activities include the Snow Safari Terrain Garden; the Antler Cup, a race where everyone wins; an Adventure Pin program that helps young people explore the mountain, with a special sticker for each new adventure; and the Enchanted Forest program where kids learn the secrets of fun and safe skiing on new trails.

Rates are $87 per day for the Adventure Club for children in the 1st grade through age 12; $87 for the Reindeer Club, age 4 to kindergarten; $92 per day for the Bambi Club, ages 3 and 4; and $92 for the Fawn Club for kids 3 years old who are not potty-trained. Lunch, lessons and a lift ticket are included in the price.

Hours are 10 AM to 3:45 PM for the Adventure and Reindeer clubs and 9 AM to 4 PM for the Bambi and Fawn clubs. All programs are available seven days a week during the ski season.

Park City Ski School
1435 Lowell St., Salt Lake City
• (800) 227-2SKI

Kinderschule & Mountain Adventure for ages 3 to 6 combines ski instruction with a fun indoor recreation. The daily lessons are geared to beginners and advanced skiers. All-day and half-day sessions are available; reservations are required. The facility also offers a Youth School for children ages 7 to 13.

Cost of the program is $79 per day for the Kinderschule and Mountain Adventure or $220 for three days and $341 for five days. Prices include lunch and group instruction. The six-hour Youth School group instruction is $77.50 per day or $221 for three days and $355.50 for five days, including lunch. All 3-year-olds must be potty-trained. Private lessons are available for $75 for 3-year-olds until they are ready for group lessons. Hours are 10 AM to 4 PM daily during the ski season.

Moonbeam Ski Academy
Little Cottonwood Canyon, Solitude Ski
Resort • 534-1400, Ext. 5730

Solitude's Moonbeam Ski Academy provides specially designed learning programs for kids ages 4 to 12. The instruction includes skiing basics and fun activities. The troll-themed children's ski school has its own surface lift. Reservations are suggested.

Snowbird Ski School
Snowbird Ski Resort • (800) 385-2002 for
children's ski school; Ext. 5026 for child
care

The Snowbird ski program for children ages 3 to 5 years and Youth Super Classes for ages 5 to 15 help kids learn and master the skills of skiing and snowboarding. The Kids Ski Free program for kids 12 and younger makes the ski school an even better deal. Snowbird's state-licensed camp and nursery offers exciting activities and quality supervision for children ages 6 weeks to 3 years in the nursery and ages 3 to 12 years in the camp. Cost is $40 per day, $160 for five days and $520 for 20 days. Multiple-children discounts are available.

In-room babysitting for guests at Snowbird Resort can be booked through Camp Snowbird. The cost is $72 per day and $335 for five days. There's a charge of $1 per hour for each additional child.

Salt Lake residents love to party, and the area has enough cultural diversity to provide an abundance of happenings throughout the year.

Festivals and Annual Events

Salt Lakers are always celebrating something, from art and culture to local traditions or national events. We're a pretty conservative bunch, so you won't usually find the crazed, naked madness of a Mardi Gras or the frenzy often reached at festivals in other cities. Many events are oriented around families, and you'll always see a lot of kids around. Still, you'll find a rich variety of people in Salt Lake, and some events, such as the St. Patrick's Day Parade and the Belly Dance Festival, can really rock on. But no matter whether it's prim and proper or wild and crazy, residents love to party, and the area has enough cultural diversity to provide an abundance of happenings throughout the year.

Salt Lake is growing rapidly, and new events are springing up as different traditions, ways of life and cultures take hold. Skiing and other winter recreation consume a lot of time in the winter for locals and visitors alike, so you'll find that most events take place in the spring, summer and fall. We've listed events by month, in order of occurrence. Unless noted, admission is free to all events. All admission prices mentioned were for 1997, but 1998 prices probably won't have changed much.

For the latest on what's going on, check out *The Salt Lake Tribune's* "Calendar" section each Friday or the "Today" section of the *Deseret News*, also published on Fridays. Alternative publications such as the *Salt Lake City Weekly*, the *Event Newspaper* and *Catalyst* also provide good information on events and festivals. You can also get timely updates from the Salt Lake Convention and Visitors Bureau, 521-2822, or the Utah Travel Council, 538-1030 or (800) 200-1160.

January

First Night
Downtown Salt Lake City • 359-5118

Like many cities across the country, Salt Lake has started observing New Year's Eve with a nonalcoholic, community-oriented celebration of the arts. You'll find dozens and dozens of performances that celebrate the arts in all their diversity. If you've got the urge to groove (and shame on you if you don't on New Year's Eve), the Last Dance Masquerade ball is where you can get funky. Don't miss the Outrageous Parade, where creative accessories such as hats, foghorns and flashing lights are put to uses never dreamed of. At midnight a fireworks extravaganza welcomes in the new year.

February

Chili Open Golf Tournament
6351 S. 900 E., Wheeler Historic Farm, Murray • 264-2212

Golf in February? In Utah? If you've ever been seized by a sudden and inexplicable longing to hit a golf ball out of a snow bank instead of a sand trap, you've come to the right place. The Rotary Club of Utah sponsors this annual bit of weekend lunacy, which draws hundreds of slightly demented links men and women to the several par 3, nine-hole courses specially designed for this event. When your hands lose feeling, a bowl of hot chili will restore life. The entry fee is around $30, with proceeds going to local charities.

March

St. Patrick's Day Parade
Main St., downtown Salt Lake City
• 521-5708

Ireland's patron saint always finds a green welcome, a river of Guinness and a huge crowd at the annual Hibernian Society's St. Patrick's Day parade, which always takes place on the Saturday before St. Patrick's Day. Sometime referred to as the gentile (non-Mormon) Days of '47 parade, this is fast becoming one of the most extravagant and wildest outdoor events in Utah. Everyone has a splendid time, with singing, dancing and all variety of eccentric parade entries. Many of the spectators dress up in weird attire, so sometimes it's hard to tell the spectators from the parade. Actually, the spectators often are the parade!

A popular attraction is the beehive float, which pokes fun at Utah's unofficial hairdo. Other floats gently satirize local political or cultural controversies. In 1997 the parade had 150 entries.

> ## FYI
> Unless otherwise noted, the area code for all phone numbers listed in this guide is 801.

April

Mountain Man Rendezvous
Antelope Island at the Great Salt Lake
• 773-2941

The annual Mountain Man Rendezvous takes place at Antelope Island, a Utah state park where the rocky cliffs and grassy plains remind you of the African veldt. The two-day event features camping, mountaineering and other traditions from the early 1800s. The Fielding Garr Ranch House is open for tours during the Rendezvous. Built in 1848, the house is the oldest building in Utah still on its original foundation. Admission is $6 per vehicle.

To get to Antelope Island, take Interstate 15 north of Salt Lake and drive west from Exit 355.

Buffalo Barbecue
2375 E. 3300 S., Christ United Methodist Church • 486-5473

If the tulips are blooming, it's time once again for Boy Scout Troop 410's annual two-day buffalo feast. Ranch-raised and grain-fed buffalo will delight your palate. No — it doesn't taste just like chicken. Cost for adults is $8.50 per plate; children younger than 11 eat for $5. Take-out is available. All proceeds are used for Scout outings and projects.

May

Beach Fest Saltair
Beach at Great Salt Lake • 972-7836

This all-day event, sponsored by Salt Lake County early in the month, includes K-9 Frisbee, kite flying, disc golf, coed volleyball, a sand sculpture contest and barbecue. If you've never been to the Great Salt Lake, this fest will be a great introduction to the unique body of water. Since you can't sink in the Great Salt Lake's saline water, catching a wave really does mean you're sittin' on top of the world.

Midvale Cinco de Mayo Parade and Celebration
7400 S. 700 W., Midvale's City's Main St.
• 565-3759

The many Cinco de Mayo celebrations around the world commemorate Mexico's victory over French troops at the Battle of Puebla on May 5, 1862. Even though Mexico lost that war, the Mexican victory over a strong French army has always been a cause to celebrate Mexican cultural identity and community. At this Midvale City celebration, a tradition for more than a decade, the Mexican penchant for good times and festive music is evident. The parade winds down Midvale's Main Street and ends up at Midvale City Park (7500 S. 450 W.) You'll likely encounter Mexican dancing, a horse show, ballet folklorico as well as great food, crafts and games.

Asian Pacific Festival
100 S. West Temple, Salt Palace
• 467-6060

Since 1977, Asians in the Salt Lake area have celebrated their traditions, diversity and

Photo: Utah Travel Council

Nearly 300,000 tiny lights sparkle on Temple Square during the holidays.

culture at the Asian Pacific Festival. Events typically include drum and martial arts exhibitions, food booths, music and dancing. The children's activity center and art display are always popular. Tea drinkers can sip a variety of blends and watch an elegant, ancient Japanese tea ceremony unfold. Admission to this one-day event is $3 for adults and $1 for children.

Living Traditions
450 S. 200 E., Washington Square at the Salt Lake City & County Building
• 533-5760, 596-5000

Want to see the grace of a Peruvian dancer, the hallelujah shout of a gospel choir or the delicate artistry of Armenian needlework? The Living Traditions Festival offers all this and more. For 12 years this popular weekend outdoor festival has honored the folk and ethnic arts of Salt Lake City. While wandering the various booths and exhibits, you'll participate in the traditional rituals, artistic celebrations and daily tasks of Utah's many cultures. In addition to crafts, you can feast on a wide variety of tasty foreign foods, including Lebanese kiibe (beef and spinach pita), El Salvadoran pupusas (corn tortillas stuffed with melted cheese), Scottish shortbread, Phillipine lumpia (vegetarian egg rolls) and other exotic delicacies. We get hungry just writing about it. It's held in midmonth.

Salt Lake City Classic
New route starts in 1998 • 972-7839

This 21-year-old classic race, held at the end of the month, is a favorite of Salt Lake runners. With the construction of light rail down Salt Lake's Main Street, 1998 runners will compete on a new course. With 10K and 5K distances and more than 100 categories, this race draws thousands of top local runners and weekend warriors.

Some of the more interesting categories have included the 5K Clydesdale category for women more than 140 pounds and men more than 200 pounds and the 5K costume competition. You'll have a blast running with people dressed up like Porky Pig , Minnie Mouse and

Count Dracula. Past winners of the 10K have included well-known runners Marty Liquori, Paul Cummings and Henry Marsh. Preregistration for the race is $16.

For the past few years, festivities have begun with "Classic Pasta at the Plaza" the evening before the race at the Gallivan Center in downtown Salt Lake (36 E. 200 S). Local restaurants serve their best carboload pasta dish and one dessert for moderate prices, usually less than $10. Free concerts and a waitstaff obstacle-course race round out the festivities.

June

Gina Bachauer Piano Competition
123 W. South Temple, Abravanel Hall
• 521-9200

June is piano month in Salt Lake, which means that some of the most prodigious young musical talent in the world convene at Salt Lake to test their mettle. The International Competition is the major event. It takes place every four years; the next round is in 1998. The other competition is the Junior International Festival and Competitions, which takes place three out of four years. Both competitions offer dazzling musical virtuosity and insightful interpretation of the world's great piano music. Ticket prices vary from $8 to $100, depending on how many competitions you want to attend.

KRCL Day in the Park
2100 S. 1300 E., Sugarhouse Park
• 363-1818

Radio station KRCL 90.9 FM sponsors this laid-back outdoor festival on a Saturday in mid-June. KRCL is Salt Lake City's only nonprofit, community-oriented station. Run largely by volunteers, the station plays wonderful alternative noncommercial music of all persuasions.

The station also fosters community involvement and gives a voice to the minorities, such as gays, lesbians and others. Their annual Day in the Park is the station's way of showing appreciation to listeners. You'll hear the Grateful Dead, see aging hippies in tie-dyed T-shirts and experience a drum circle. Veggie burgers, sunshine, hackey sack, live music and Frisbees are de riguer. It's great fun with great people.

Gay Pride Day Parade and Festival
Washington Square at the Salt Lake City & County Bldg. • 539-8800

Gays and lesbians celebrate their culture and achievements at this fun-filled parade and festival. Salt Lake City's Gay Pride Day is held to honor the memory of the 1969 Stonewall riots in New York City. The three-day riot has been called the defining moment of the gay-rights movement and began after New York police tried to close down The Stonewall Inn in Greenwich Village.

The parade starts at the Utah State Capitol and follows Main Street to Washington Square. Dykes on Bikes usually lead the parade, followed by floats and horses from the Utah Gay Rodeo Association. Thousands of marchers fill the streets, some outrageously dressed in feather boas or as drag queens, some in normal attire. At Washington Square, you can enjoy informational booths, great live music and food.

Oldies Fest
1700 S. West Temple, Franklin Quest Field • 468-2560

Fans of that old-time rock 'n' roll take over Franklin Quest Field in this tribute to legends of the past. In 1997 the event included the Drifters, Gary Lewis and the Playboys, Little Christy, Leslie Gore, Peter Noone and Tommy James. Come on down and get nostalgic. Tickets in 1997 were $10 for adults and $5 for children younger than 12. The affair lasts all day.

Olde English Festival
261 S. 900 E., St. Paul's Episcopal Church • 322-5869

The Utah chapter of the Society for Creative Anachronism puts on this one-day festival, where you may see Norman knights flailing at each other with enormous broad-swords. Members of the Society are devotees of the Middle Ages and adopt personas from different places and times of that epoch. These personas revive various traditions of the Middle Ages — jousting, chivalrous interludes and so on. Singers, dancers, fortune tellers, artisans and food vendors, all in period costumes, provide other diversions.

St. Paul's Church provides an attractive and reasonably convincing historical background. You don't have to be in costume to come, and you don't have to fight.

Utah Scottish Festival and Highland Games
32 Potter St., Ft. Douglas, University of Utah • 295-1356

The kilts come alive at this annual celebration of Scottish culture, with booths, athletic events, traditional dances and much bag-piping. The athletic tournaments reenact the ancient Scottish games of 1,000 years ago, where warriors were selected for battle on the basis of their strength and skill in competition. The contests include the caber (tree trunk) toss, the sheaf toss and the hammer throw. Admission is $5.

Saturday's Voyeur
138 W. 500 N., Salt Lake City • 363-0526, 355-ARTS

If you really want the lowdown on Salt Lake City, don't miss the Salt Lake Acting Company's annual production of *Saturday's Voyeur*. Since 1978, theatergoers have howled in their seats at this raucous parody that pokes fun at local politicians and notoriety, the predominant culture and anyone else whose had the misfortune to fall from grace publicly. If it was stupid, a little too righteous or just an ongoing sore spot with residents, SLAC lights it up and delivers it with neon, full-tilt irreverence. The song and dance numbers are Broadway caliber with a local twist, costumes are usually outrageous, and the cast always delivers noteworthy performances. Writers Nancy Borgenicht and Allen Nevins spiff up Voy-

---

INSIDERS' TIP

Something's always going on at the Gallivan Center in downtown Salt Lake City. Call 532-0459 for information.

eur each season with current material and fresh frolic so you can always count on being on the inside track.

The show runs from mid-June to September. Tickets are $26.50 for regular seats and $29.50 for cabaret seating. (Cabaret seating means you can bring a picnic basket full of delicious fare and your favorite beverage and sit up front.) If you're a SLAC season subscriber, you can purchase as many tickets as you like for $24 each. *Voyeur* is enormously popular with locals, so call ahead for tickets. Check out SLAC's regular season in the Arts chapter.

Westfest
3100 S. 5600 W., Centennial Park
• 963-7753

West Valley City is a city of 100,000 just a few miles south and west of Salt Lake City. Westfest celebrates the formation of West Valley and its rapid growth as a city. The tradition at Westfest is family entertainment, with lots of food, carnival rides, a parade, talent shows and firework displays.

Juneteenth Festival
36 E. 200 S., Gallivan Center • 532-0459

This festival started in Texas in 1865 and commemorates the day black slaves were told of Lincoln's Emancipation Proclamation — two years later than slaves in the rest of America. Normally held June 19 — hence the nickname — it's a nationwide festival where everyone has a chance to participate in black culture through song, food, crafts, arts and history. Utahns have observed this festival for more than 20 years. Great music always fills the air, and you can enjoy a great variety of delicious food.

Utah Arts Festival
55. S. 300 W., Triad Center • 322-2428

This four-day artistic extravaganza, the biggest arts festival in the area, is brimming with treats for the eyes, ears and taste buds. Dozens of visual artists showcase every variety of artistic expression, from basket making and glasswork to furniture and jewelry. With the rich abundance of offerings, you're bound to spot some objet d'art you simply can't live without. Prices are generally very reasonable.

Performance artists shake things up with periodic poetry readings, drumming exhibitions, portrait sculpture or traditional Celtic music. Every year dozens of special interactive art projects are planned just for kids, so don't leave them behind. Special artists are featured every year, such as Kurt Wenner, one of only 12 people to hold the title of Master Street Painter. Using his own handmade pastels, Wenner creates amazing baroque-style, three-dimensional art that looks like a scene out of Dante or the Bible. Wenner's style is called anamorphism, and it combines architectural elements with illusionist painting. The effect is stunning — as you approach his work, you seem to be peering into a new world, and as you move around and change perspective, the painting seems to change before your eyes.

Be sure to bring your appetite — savory delights are available in every ethnic variety imaginable, from pot stickers to Navajo tacos. After you've spent the day soaking up the art scene, you can enjoy nationally known musical performers like Michelle Shocked, Luther Allison, Laurie Anderson or the Five Blind Boys. Something is always shaking, and Salt Lake's biggest street party is sure to light your fire.

Admission is $5, free for children 12 and younger. See our Kidstuff Chapter.

Come Alive after 5
36 E. 200 S., Gallivan Center • 532-0459

Hot town, summer in the city, Wednesday night: It all adds up to free music at the Gallivan Center. Musical stylings run the gamut from rhythm and blues to jazz and salsa. There's no better way to perk up this traditionally dull evening. Food and beverages are available. You can even buy beer! Bring a blanket to spread out on the grass.

You'll love the kick-back-and-have-fun feeling and the great mix of local and national acts. Concerts take place on selected Wednesday nights from late June through September.

July

Obon Festival
Salt Lake Buddhist Temple, 211 W. 100 S.
• 363-4742

For Buddhists, the Obon is a time of welcoming souls to the living world as well as a

Photo: Utah Travel Council

The Days of '47 Parade is one of the biggest events of the year in Salt Lake City and is the second-largest parade in the United States.

memorial service for the dead and an acknowledgment of the power of the dead ancestors over the living. The highlight of this festival is the Bon Odori, or Bon Dancing, which is performed by women dressed in traditional kimonos. Many of the dancers use round fans, folding fans, kachi kachi (finger clickers) and special Japanese towels. In addition to dancing, you'll find exhibitions of Japanese drumming, along with Japanese and American food. Members of the temple give tours of the Hondo (main temple) and explain the temple's symbolism.

Independence Day Festivities
Various sites in and around Salt Lake

As in any city, Salt Lakers love to celebrate the fourth with oodles of food, marching bands, booths, fireworks, parades, dancing and what have you. The *Salt Lake Tribune* and *Deseret News* list all the events in the area with complete details, so you can choose the level of celebration you want — from huge, stereophonic fireworks to small-town breakfasts and parades. Most of the smaller cities in the Salt Lake Valley put on some kind of show. Before you go, read our Getting Here, Getting Around chapter to find out how to navigate the Salt Lake Valley.

You can start the day at Murray Park, 5109 S. State Street, 264-2507, for a flag ceremony and a hearty but inexpensive breakfast, followed by a daylong parade capped with fireworks.

In Magna's Copper Park, 8900 W. 2600 S., you can relish a good old-fashioned chuckwagon breakfast, a baseball game, hourly entertainment and fireworks.

Riverton City pulls out all stops at their shindig, with a 10K race, free swimming, a carnival and fireworks. It's all happening at the city park, 12800 S. 1300 W., 254-0704.

The city of Sandy puts on a really big show with concerts and folk dancers, games and rides. You can participate in a variety of Sandy activities at Jordan High School, 95 E. 9880 S., 568-2900.

At Granite High School, 3300 S. 500 E., 483-6000, South Salt Lake puts on fireworks, food booths and entertainment.

West Jordan does a little something extra with a fourth of July rodeo, parade and carnival. You can enjoy the fun at Main Park, 7900 S. 2200 W., 569-5750.

Salt Lake City offers one of the biggest fireworks displays in the valley at Sugarhouse Park, 1330 E. 2100 S., 972-7800. The Utah Symphony often provides patriotic musical accompaniment to the exploding fireworks.

Twilight Concert Series
36 E. 200 S., Gallivan Center • 532-0459

It's Thursday night, you've been on your feet all day, you're tired and hungry, the summer evening spreads out against the sky as the soft twilight descends, and the blue haze of the Wasatch makes you think about sitting down and having some fun — so what ya gonna do? We think you should consider the Gallivan Center for great, free music.

We're talking top-flight talent here — the legendary Robert Earl Keen, Alison Brown Quartet, Tim & Molley O'Brien and the O'Boys, and Kim Richey are just a few of the top-notch, footstompin' acts that bring thousands of people downtown to enjoy this great concert series. Concerts start at 8 PM. They take place on Thursdays from the mid-July through mid-August.

July 24th Pioneer Day

July 24, 1847, is the day the Mormon pioneers first entered the Salt Lake Valley (see our History chapter for more information). It's a state holiday, and many businesses and government agencies close. The following are the main events you'll want to see.

Days of '47 Parade
Starts at Main St. and South Temple • 560-0047

This parade is one of the largest and oldest in the United States, with numerous floats, bands, horses, clowns and other entries. The entire downtown area shuts down while this parade goes by. It's televised throughout the Intermountain West on a number of local television stations. A crowd of up to 150,000 people lines the parade route early in the morning for the best seats, so get there early — real early. The parade starts at 9 AM. Also, it can be brutally hot in Utah in July, so bring a hat and sunscreen.

Many local residents have made a tradition of camping out in downtown Salt Lake City the night before the parade, creating a festival atmosphere. You'll see a lot of gingham dresses, bonnets, covered wagons and the like.

Days of '47 All Horse Parade
Starts at South Temple and West Temple • 295-4840

Saturday before July 24th More than 1,200 horses parade through downtown Salt Lake City streets in a dazzling display of equine finery and acrobatics. This all-horse parade, one of the largest in the country, has been a Salt Lake tradition for 37 years. It happens on the Saturday before the 24th and traditionally kicks off Utah's Pioneer Days celebrations.

Days of '47 World Champion Rodeo
301 S. West Temple, Delta Center • 250-6832

You'll be hollering "Ride 'em cowboy!" at this huge rodeo — and it's a big 'un. More than $140,000 in prize money is offered, and every big-name bronco buster shows up to test some of the orneriest stock in the country. Bull riding, calf roping, bronco busting, steer wrestling and wild cow milking are all part of the show. Tickets are $8 and $12, and all seats are reserved, but seats may be available on the day of the event — unless it's sold out.

Desert News Marathon and 10K Race
Starts in Parley's Canyon, east of Salt Lake • 468-2560

This marathon, which celebrates its 29th year in 1998, starts in the mountains and follows the route of the Mormon pioneers. It ends at Liberty Park, 700 E. 1300 S. The 10K race joins the marathon at the 20-mile mark.

FYI

Unless otherwise noted, the area code for all phone numbers listed in this guide is 801.

INSIDERS' TIP

If you're interested in Western crafts and folkways, plan on attending the Utah State Fair or the Salt Lake County Fair, where you can learn about all manner of pioneer activities.

Runner's World Magazine named the 10K race one of the fastest in the world.

Jazz and Blues Festival
Snowbird, Little Cottonwood Canyon • 355-2787

Smokin'! That's the only way to describe the music you'll hear at this down-and-dirty celebration of jazz and the blues — America's most important contributions to world music. Since 1987 this gorgeous setting in the Wasatch mountains has witnessed some of the most potent blues in the world: John Mayall, Coco Taylor (Queen of the Blues), Coco Montoya and Little Milton. Jazz legends who have wowed the crowd include Charlie Byrd, the Ray Brown Trio, Herbie Mann and Mose Allison.

Even though the atmosphere is electric and the playing hot, you'll be at 9,000 feet and outdoors, so bring a sweater — it gets mighty cool at night. You'll have plenty of room to boogie, and refreshments are available for a post-dance cool down. But don't celebrate too much — the drive down the canyon is dark, windy and steep.

Ticket prices range from around $22 to $60.

August

Belly Dance Festival
1300 E. 700 S., Liberty Park • 486-7780

Celebrate the sensual side of life by watching the graceful eroticism of belly dancing. Since 1980 this outdoor festival, sponsored by Kismet Dance Company and the Salt Lake Arts Council, has grown from eight dancers and a record player to the largest outdoor Middle Eastern dance festival in the nation. Hundreds of dancers from all over the world come to Salt Lake to participate in the dances and take workshops.

After your head is spinning from the throbbing music and undulating women, you can partially regain your senses by indulging in Mideastern and Greek food and wandering through a bazaar of items from India and the Mideast. We never miss this one. The festival goes on for a weekend. (See our Shopping chapter for more about Kismet Dance Company.)

Salt Lake County Fair
5177 S. 200 E., Salt Lake County Fairgrounds, Murray • 262-0812

Big crowds turn out for this event, which includes a parade, rodeo, 4-H horse show and carnivals. The demolition derby is a big favorite. Nightly fireworks cap off a day of fun and entertainment.

Oktoberfest
Snowbird, Little Cottonwood Canyon • 521-6040

We're not quite sure why it's called Oktoberfest (maybe because Augustfest just doesn't have quite the ring) but it's still loads of fun. Bracing air, superb Bavarian cuisine, some great locally brewed beers and the granite precipices of the Wasatch make for a day you'll never forget. Take a hike while you're there — several wonderful trails take off right from the pavilion. If you decide to ride the tram to Hidden Peak, you might see some mountain goats cavorting in the rocks. Many people take the tram up and hike down. Count on a couple of hours to make it down from the top.

September

Greek Festival
279 S. 300 W., Hellenic Memorial Cultural Center • 328-9681

The Greek Orthodox community of Salt Lake always throws a great bash at this annual festival of Greek culture. The emphasis here is on food — you can get a great heaping plateful of Greek delicacies for less than $10. It's all amazingly good, from the Greek chicken to the pastitsio to the spanakopites. And who could leave without sampling the honey-basted baklava, the buttery koulouria or the apricot and raspberry pasta fluera? Certainly not us. The food is enough to draw most of Salt Lake's gourmands, but you'll also enjoy folk dancing, Greek music and booths. Admission is $2, $1 for kids younger than 12. You can enjoy the festival on the weekend following Labor Day.

Utah State Fair
155 N. 1000 W., Utah State Fair Park • 538-8400

Kids go crazy looking at rabbits, geese

and pigs the size of Volkswagens at the biggest fair in Utah. More than 300,000 people attend this event. You can see all the usual demonstrations, displays, pie-baking contests, carnivals and crafts. Entertainers such as Kathy Mattea and Eddie Rabbit are big attractions.

Admission is $6 for adults, $4 for kids ages 16 to 6 and free for 5 and younger. The fair always takes place the first Thursday through Sunday following Labor Day.

October

Bison Roundup
Antelope Island at the Great Salt Lake
• 773-2941

When your friends ask what you did in Utah, you can casually lean back, tell them about the nice, clean city and the mountains, then slip in, "And, oh yes, we helped round up a herd of about 700 buffalo. Quite amazing beasts. Big as a small car. Run like the wind and can turn on a dime. Succulent dining, as well." Yep — this is a real Western adventure, which is attracting growing interest by people fascinated by these, huge, legendary animals.

Antelope Island's herd of 700 buffalo is one of the largest free-roaming herds in the nation. More than 450 people on horseback and a few in trucks round up the beasts into a corral, where they are tested for health problems and vaccinated. A hundred or so are then sold off. The purpose of the roundup is to cull the herd and keep it from damaging the sensitive island ecology. (If you're wondering why it isn't called Buffalo Island, it's because explorers Kit Carson and John C. Fremont shot an antelope on the island in 1845. In gratitude for the meat, they named it Antelope Island. Antelope disappeared from the island in the 1930s, but were reintroduced in 1993.) Caution: Buffalo weigh up to 2,000 pounds and can run 30 mph. Never approach one in the wild. They are fierce, unpredictable and dangerous.

To get to Antelope Island, take Exit 355 off Interstate 15 north of Salt Lake and head west.

November

Lighting of Temple Square
50 W. South Temple, Temple Square
• 240-4377

Temple Square blazes to life in a dazzling display of Christmas wizardry that draws thousands of people every year. Some 300,000 lights festooned along trees, shrubs, sidewalks and walks begin to sparkle just after dusk, to the cheers of the assembled throng. It's a splendid moment of seasonal magic. Visitors can also enjoy Christmas music and a life-sized creche, with narration of the traditional Christmas story. The lights go on the Friday after Thanksgiving and blaze away until the New Year.

Festival of Lights
6351 S. 900 E., Wheeler Historic Farm, Murray • 264-2212

Tractor-drawn wagons take visitors on a 20-minute tour of the grounds of this historic farm in Murray, where more than 50 displays using 100,000 lights illuminate the landscape. Lights form the shapes of farm animals, trains, fountains and a toyland fantasy. Santa's workshop, featuring St. Nick himself, is the last stop. Since the tour is outdoors, you should dress warmly. Admission is $2 per person or $7 per family. You can enjoy the fun from the end of November through the New Year. (See our Kidstuff and Sightseeing and Attractions chapters.)

December

Festival of Lights
6351 S. 900 E., Wheeler Historic Farm, Murray • 264-2212

And the folks at Wheeler Historic Farm said let there be light — and you know the rest. See the November listing for details.

Nutcracker
50 W. 200 S., Capitol Theatre • 323-6922, 355-ARTS

This holiday classic has been a 40-year tradition in Salt Lake City. Ballet West and members of the Utah Symphony team up for spectacular performances of this favorite. (See our Kidstuff chapter for the history of this event.)

Festival of Trees
100 S. West Temple, Salt Palace
• 534-4777

Utahns love the holidays, so this festival draws a big crowd every year. You'll see hundreds of ornately decorated trees, wreaths and spiffy gifts created by both local and out-of-state craftspeople. Fans of Martha Stewart will feel right at home. Proceeds from this event go to the Primary Children's Medical Center. Admission is $3 for adults, $1.75 for children. This festival starts the first week in December and lasts through the month.

Dickens' Festival
155 N. 1000 W., Utah State Fair Park
• 943-1829

This annual festival offers booths of Christmas bric a brac, lighted villages, ceramics, jewelry, quilts and toys. Fortune tellers, magicians and jugglers animate the crowd. Don't be surprised if you meet Tiny Tim, Oliver Twist or Scrooge himself. You can hear holiday music and eat a variety of Christmas treats, such as hot roasted chestnuts and steaming cinnamon buns. Admission is $5 for adults and $3 for kids. Children younger than 5 are admitted free. The festival runs from the end of November through the end of December.

Visitors are frequently struck by the depth of our arts community — the many small groups that have endured for decades and new, highly promising performing groups that carry on the creative tradition.

The Arts

The cultural arts are woven tightly through the fabric of the unique culture in the Salt Lake Valley. They are part of the flesh and bone, the blood and breath of our city — among the many components that make our eyes widen, feet shuffle and hearts beat.

From the earliest days, the arts have been an integral part of our way of life. Brigham Young told his followers to "go to the dance, study music, read novels . . . and add fire to your spirits." The nation's first state arts council was organized here in 1899, and the Mormon's communal way of life fostered groups whose talents were enjoyed by one and all. Today, our symphony, opera and dance companies have taken their place on the world's stage to receive serious acclaim. Brigham Young would be proud.

But there's a great deal more here than big productions and guest artists on the world art scene. Visitors are frequently struck by the depth of our arts community — the many small groups that have endured for decades and new, highly promising performing groups that carry on the creative tradition. Local artists portray the struggles of living in a city dominated by one religion. They are frequently a solitary lot who rehearse within the private studios of their soul, take risks and sometimes elicit controversy. You'll find their work in galleries, museums, restaurants, coffeehouses and libraries throughout the city.

Writers, too, have come to express personal journeys in poetry and prose. The community has reared several well-known authors whose exquisite passages have attracted national and international acclaim. The Writers at Work program, held annually in Park City, provides an opportunity for local writers to work with nationally recognized, award-winning authors, playwrights and poets (see the "Arts and Annual Events" section of the Park City chapter). Local poets often read their work in coffeehouses around town (see our Nightlife chapter). The Media chapter will put you in touch with the publications offering a calendar of events. Check these out to find theatrical readings of new plays by local playwrights.

Music and theater have long been a staple in our community. The city offers an impressive spectacle of musical talent from classical to jazz, presented in a variety of venues. We've listed quite a few in this chapter. Some of the music scene is covered in our Nightlife chapter, and you'll find more information on musical performances in the Festivals and Annual Events chapter.

One of Brigham Young's first mandates on settling the Salt Lake Valley was to build a theater. The early settlers loved theatrical performances, especially musicals, and the tradition has lived on for well over a century. Although you're likely to visit during a run of *The Sound of Music* somewhere in the Valley, our diverse theatrical community has impressed national critics with the works of local and nationally known playwrights. You'll find everything from vaudevillian farce to innovative American contemporary productions, controversial experimental works to the classics. Even our community theaters are a cut above their peers across the country.

Performing spaces are sometimes at a premium, but as an industrious and thrifty culture we have carved niches, preserved the old and erected new venues for our thriving arts scene. Don't be surprised to find world-class chamber choirs, small orchestras and jazz bands performing in churches, parks and various halls; or that their ticket outlet is a local ice cream parlor. Theater and dance companies with stellar reputations sometimes shift around the city like gypsies for lack of a permanent home, presenting their work in local bars and temporary quarters as they become available.

Many of our arts organizations have permanent homes and frequently offer their facilities to other organizations for performances and concert series. The Capitol Theater at 50 W. 200 S. — now home to the Utah Opera, Ballet West and Ririe Woodbury Dance Company — was once called the Orpheum Theatre, built in 1913 by a vaudeville theater chain. It was used as a movie theater in 1927 and had various tenants until 1976 when it was restored to near original condition. The distinctive Renaissance granite and marble facade with two large cherubs is quite beautiful. The building is on the National Register of Historic Places.

The former Church of Jesus Christ of Latter-day Saints 19th Ward House at 168 W. 500 N. is now home to the Salt Lake Acting Company. This remarkable building is a combination of several architectural styles. The Byzantine "onion" dome atop the chapel's entrance is classic. This building is also on the National Register of Historic Places.

Abravanel Hall at 123 W. South Temple was built in 1976 as part of a bicentennial arts complex. This hall is home to the Utah Symphony and is often the location for other group's musical performances. The Jewett Center at Westminster College 1840 S. 1300 E. is the setting for many theatrical and musical performances. Various locations on the campus of the University of Utah, including the Museum of Fine Arts at 1530 E. S. Campus Drive, provide a venue for local performing arts organizations. Salt Lake's First Presbyterian Church, 12 N. C Street, was built in 1906 in a Scottish-influenced Gothic Revival style of red sandstone quarried in nearby Red Butte Canyon. It is a frequent location for musical performances by prestigious local groups. Its beautiful interior is enhanced by stained-glass windows.

Our newest venue is the Rose Wagner Performing Arts Center at 138 W. Broadway (300 S.). Once home to Wagner Bag Company, this exciting space presents work by a myriad of Salt Lake City performing-arts companies. The center includes a 150-seat black-box theater, three rehearsal/classroom studios, technical and dressing areas and office space for the resident companies, which include Repertory Dance Theatre, Gina Bachauer International Piano Festival and other tenants.

Brigham Young may have been the pioneer of all pioneers, forging out a community and building a strong arts scene in the Salt Lake Valley, but today, the city's arts pioneer is a sculptor-turned-developer named Stephen Goldsmith. His vision for a multi-ethnic, mixed-income village-within-a-city began simply enough in 1979 when he couldn't find affordable living and studio space and knew other artists were in the same situation. His first success in converting old abandoned property for use by artists crystallized several years later when Artspace opened its doors at 333 W. Pierpont Avenue in the renovated Eccles-Browning Warehouse. Built in 1910, the space became home and studio to 35 artists from a variety of disciplines along with several offices and shops. Recently, Goldsmith completed Artspace II in the same neighborhood with 53 living-working spaces housed in the four-story California Tire and Rubber Company, built in 1915, at 353 W. 200 S. Although the plan was initially devised only as a means to provide low-cost housing and studio space to local artists, something miraculous happened in this rundown slum turned bohemian/Soho neighborhood in the heart of the city as the Goldsmith plan took shape. Other artistic concerns (including the Dolores Chase Gallery), restaurants and nightspots began to open in the area. Goldsmith's dream includes the future development of a 140-unit affordable housing development, a community child-care facility, a small theater, restaurants and a farmer's market and grocery.

The arts reach out to all people in the Valley — the wealthy, poor, young and young at heart. As a community, we embrace them, and they in turn embrace us with the extraordinary gift of art unequaled by other cities the size of Salt Lake.

Local newspapers are among the best sources of information on what's going on in the arts. Both daily papers run a calendar in the arts and entertainment sections. We also consume the weekly entertainment papers from cover to cover, and many refrigerator

FYI

Unless otherwise noted, the area code for all phone numbers listed in this guide is 801.

doors throughout the Valley are cluttered with arts calendars. You can find out which papers offer the best information on the arts in our Media chapter.

The Salt Lake Gallery Association sponsors a Gallery Stroll on the third Friday of each month from 6 to 9 PM. The participating galleries stay open late, and some provide entertainment on Stroll nights during the summer. We've noted the galleries that participate in the Stroll in the individual listings; you can pick up a map at any of the galleries taking part or call the Salt Lake Art Center at 328-4201.

Many arts offerings in the Salt Lake Valley are free. Ticket prices for performing arts events vary depending on whether you purchase a single ticket or a season subscription, when available, the day of the week and seating. We've included general pricing information based on the 1997-98 season, but it's a good idea to check with the organization because ticket prices usually increase a little each season. Don't forget to ask about discounts for senior citizens, students and groups.

It would be an impossible task to list all the organizations in the arts community here, but we have included quite a few. It is our hope that you will enjoy and appreciate them as much as locals do.

Theater

Babcock Theater
300 S. 1340 E., Salt Lake City • 581-6961

Downstairs from Pioneer Theatre Company at the University of Utah, the Babcock Theater presents a regular season of five dramatic productions from September through June. Although the work consists of student productions, it should not be dismissed as gawky amateur fare. Many Salt Lakers who enjoy the theater in other parts of the country consider the work here to be of professional caliber and compare performances favorably with Pioneer Theatre. The cast consists of university students. The designers are generally graduate design students. Directors are graduate students in their last year, university faculty or guest directors from Los Angeles and New York.

The 135-seat proscenium-stage theater offers an intimate setting for work like Anton Chekhov's *The Cherry Orchard*. The company also presents Shakespeare and one musical production every other year. Each year in the early fall it stages a Greek play, off-premises at Red Butte Gardens. In keeping with tradition, the performance is presented at dawn. If you are interested in exceptional theater, the Babcock is a worthy consideration.

Single tickets are $8 and $9. A season subscription is available for $35.

Desert Star Playhouse
4861 S. State St., Murray • 266-7600

For nearly a decade the Desert Star Playhouse has been presenting live musical comedy melodrama in this 250-seat theater. The company of eager actors spoofs traditional productions with its own brand of parody. Interpretations of well-known or well-intentioned farce include *Holmes and Watson*, *Phantom of the Opera* — not to be confused with *The Phantom of the Opera* — *Hillbillies 90210* and *Space Wars 2002* — *A Space Odyssey of Olympic Proportion* — *May the Farce Be with You*. Besides the regular six-show season, Desert Star presents a Christmas production taken from such classics as *White Christmas* and *It's a Wonderful Life*.

The fun includes cabaret seating with tables for up to five people, pizza, ice cream desserts and a free basket of popcorn. There's a honky-tonk piano to set the mood, and audience participation in sing-alongs is encouraged. The theater's season runs year round.

INSIDERS' TIP

Several radio stations offer excellent jazz programming and information on the jazz music scene. Steve Williams is an institution on KUER-FM weeknights from 9 PM until 1 AM. The Public Radio Station programs 50 hours of jazz music a week. Check out the listing in our Media chapter.

Single tickets are $10 for adults and $6 for children younger than 13. They offer no senior citizen discount. You can purchase a six-show season pass for $50. The same pass is available for $35, but you can't attend Friday and Saturday performances. A six-show family pass for five people is $150 for any performance days.

Grand Theatre
1575 S. State St., Salt Lake City
• 957-3322

Presented through the public information office and in association with the fine art's department at Salt Lake Community College, the Grand Theatre presents six shows in its regular season, from late August through June. In addition, students perform in the well-received Gilbert and Sullivan Festival during the summer. The 1,140 seat theater houses performances of Broadway musicals with live orchestras and critically acclaimed local talent.

Single ticket prices range from $6 to $13. Season subscription prices range from $22 to $52.

Hale Centre Theatre
2801 S. Main St., Salt Lake City
• 484-9257

The Hale is Salt Lake's premier family theater. The company mounts seven productions a year during its regular season including such classics as *Forever Plaid*, *Arsenic and Old Lace* and *The Sound of Music*. The annual production of *A Christmas Carol* is always a sell-out.

Prices for single tickets range from $8 to $13 depending on the day of week and whether the production is a musical or comedy. Subscriptions are available for the season for $58 and $70.

Lab Theater
204 Performance Arts Building, University of Utah, Salt Lake City
•581-6961

The performers and directors at this small black-box theater present avant-garde work that is sometimes controversial, and they're not afraid to take risks. The 10 to 12 experimental works per year have a fleeting one-week run, and the theater has only 60 seats, but the students pack a lot of creativity and talent into the work. It is worth seeing.

Directed primarily by faculty members and M.F.A. students from the university's theater-direction program, the work includes plays by Bertolt Brecht and Sam Shepard and poetry theater by William Butler Yeats. Performances sell out quickly. If you're interested, you might want to call ahead for tickets, which cost $5.

Pioneer Theatre Company
300 S. 1340 E., Salt Lake City • 581-6961

This memorial to the old Salt Lake Theater built by Mormon pioneers was established in 1962. Headquartered on the University of Utah campus, the company became the first fully professional theater in the Intermountain West in 1986 under the theater's first artistic director, New Yorker Charles Morney. Since then, Pioneer Theatre Company has grown artistically and now enjoys national acclaim. The company operates with a budget of more than $2 million and draws actors, designers and directors from New York, Los Angeles and Utah. Traditional and contemporary plays such as *Sweeney Todd*, *The Miracle Worker* and *A Streetcar Named Desire* make up the company's seven-show season, which runs September to June.

Season subscriptions are available from $88 to $193. Single tickets prices range from $14 to $32.

The Salt Lake Acting Company
138 W. 500 N., Salt Lake City • 363-0526, 335-ARTS

For three decades, The Salt Lake Acting Company, known as SLAC, has produced the best of contemporary American plays, including regional and world premieres, and works by Utah writers of national caliber. *Angels in America, Parts I and II*, *Beast on the Moon*, *Napoleon's China*, *Winter of the Deer* and many other award-winning works are still part of the SLAC tradition.

In the early days SLAC held performances in a church basement, striking the set each night and setting up the following evening. Its foray into professional theater included *Viet Rock*, *Hair* and *Godspell*, highly controversial productions for Salt Lake City in the early 1970s. The venue changed and so did the times, but SLAC persevered, offering brilliant plays like *Who's Afraid of Virginia Woolfe?*, *Fool for Love*, *The Foreigner* and *La Cage Aux Folles* to audiences hungry for theater out of the mainstream.

SLAC found a permanent home at the Marmalade Hill Center in the historic Capitol Hill District and continues to plunge toward to the edge season after season with works such as *M Butterfly*, *The Heidi Chronicles*, *The Lisbon Traviata* and *Nixon's Nixon*. SLAC is recognized locally, regionally and nationally for theater of the highest order. In addition to its regular season of five plays that runs from September to June, SLAC has presented *Saturday's Voyeur*, a musical satire of political and cultural life in Utah, for the past 20 years. This hysterical don't-miss event is enormously popular with Salt Lakers and a great way to get the inside scoop on local politicians and prominent figures.

Tickets for *Saturday's Voyeur* range from $26.50 to $29.50. Some cabaret seating is available for this production. Single tickets for all other performances are $12.50 to $24.50. Subscription prices range from $84 to $114 and include tickets to *Voyeur*.

Theater League of Utah
419 E. 100 S., Salt Lake City • 355-5502, 355-ARTS

Nearly a decade ago when Theater League of Utah set up shop in Salt Lake City, ready to present touring Broadway shows to an already culturally rich community, we all said, "We'll see." We're a sophisticated cultural arts city for our size but could it, would it, support a Broadway series?

The answer was clear when *Les Miserables* arrived. Theater League of Utah had not anticipated the response and was not technologically prepared for the onslaught of callers wishing to purchase tickets by phone. The reaction was so unprecedented in a market the size of Salt Lake that the producers ran a full-page ad in *Variety*, with a story and a photo showing the half-mile-long line of people wrapped around a city block eager to buy tickets.

Les Mis ran for 15 weeks and was seen by more than 240,000 locals. *Phantom of the Opera*, *Cats* and many other productions have enjoyed long runs and continue to excite our audiences. The company presents five regular productions each season beginning in the fall with three additional productions such as the critically acclaimed Australian production *Tap Dogs*. In addition, Theater League of Utah has hosted a half-dozen Equity Fights AIDS cabaret performances where touring actors choose and perform their own material.

Season subscriptions are available from $97.50 to $225. Single tickets are available for some shows and range from $25 to $60.

Dance

Ballet West
50 W. 200 S., Salt Lake City • 355-ARTS

Considered one of the country's leading ballet companies, Ballet West has continued to surprise and inspire audiences with unparalleled performances of classical and modern ballets for more than 40 years. As the internationally celebrated dance company moves toward its half-century mark, its performances embrace the innovative works of new choreographers and pay tribute to long treasured classical ballets.

Under the guiding hand of its new artistic director, Jonas Kage, a native of Stockholm, Sweden, the company's 1997-98 season featured eight masterpieces by choreographer George Ballanchine, *Leaves are Fading* (choreographed by Antony Tudor) and a light-hearted but poignant ballet choreographed by Paul Taylor entitled *Company B*. A mixed program entitled *Pointe/Counterpoint* featured three very different approaches to dance with "In and Out," "Bach Moves" and a vital and energetic ballet entitled "Rapture" by the highly acclaimed choreographer Lila York. Audiences also enjoyed world class performances of *Anna Karenina*, *Sleeping Beauty* and, of course, Ballet West's annual holiday sell-out, *The Nutcracker*.

Season ticket prices range from $34 to $242. Single tickets cost $10 to $60. Tickets to

Dreamkeepers

To celebrate Utah's 100 years of statehood in 1997, the Utah Opera commissioned an operatic work with librettist Aden Ross and composer David Carlson, marrying words and music to tell the story of Utah's history. The tale doesn't focus on wagons and pioneers who sought freedom from religious persecution in the newly settled Salt Lake Valley. Nor does it center on the mines or railroad that created the state's early economic base. Ross dug deeper, to the root of Utah's heritage and the indigenous people for whom the state is named.

Close-up

After four years of collaboration, *Dreamkeepers* emerged as an impressive new American opera with approachable music and a heartening story. Ross, a local poet and playwright known for her feminist bent, gave her leading lady the upper hand "without the usual operatic ending — a woman who dies by strangulation or jumping off a parapet." Carlson's score was precise and true to the history of the Ute people as well as to Ross's characters.

Dreamkeepers is the story of a contemporary Ute Indian woman, Ela Colorow, on a voyage of self-discovery. Ela returns to the reservation from the big city where she is studying to be a veterinarian. While attending to her dying grandmother, who represents tradition and the old ways, she comes face to face with the paradox of

— continued on next page

Photo: Bob Clayton

The extraordinary costumes and set compliment the Utah Opera Company's production of Dreamkeepers celebrating 100 years of Utah's statehood.

culture balanced unsteadily on both sides of her world. The conflict is heightened by the presence of Adam, an Anglo doctor working on the reservation — her love interest — and the dark and penumbral Sloane, who represent the most savage and unwholesome aspects of the non-Ute world.

Ela descends into the Spirit World — her unconscious mind — to confront the demons who war within her, pitting her tribal history against her modern-day identity. When Adam is seriously injured in a car crash, Ela goes within herself again, realizing that the only medicine that will save him comes from her power as a Ute healer.

Carlson's music sets a respectful pace for the tale with elements of Native American music captured by Ute drums and rasps and a specially made flute that simulates the sacred Ute eagle-bone whistle. Much attention was paid to the authenticity of the Ute people's depiction in demeanor, costuming and set design. Careful selections and simulations were incorporated to avoid sacrilege. Company director Anne Ewers, Ross and Carlson worked closely with the Ute tribal council, securing their permission to make the tribe the focus of the celebratory opera and ensuring the accuracy of their depiction. According to Ewers, the Ute council told her, "This is the first time someone has come to give us something, not take something away."

Dreamkeepers was well-received by local audiences when it debuted in January 1996 and was graciously reviewed by out-of-town opera critics including *The Wall Street Journal's,* who wrote, "Dreamkeepers drew strength from Ms. Ross's intelligent, singable text, which, despite the occasional political mouthful . . . captured the cadence of speech and the poetry of feeling."

The New York Times reviewer wrote, "It would be easy to purse your lips at Carlson's unashamedly neo-romantic musical language, but more profitable to note that he handles his chosen idiom with unobtrusive technical skill — pace, dramatic shape, balance; all are persuasively handled — and he writes for voice and large orchestra with total confidence."

Dreamkeepers was dedicated "To all our tribes and the dreams which connect us."

The opera is presently touring throughout the United States. The Utah Opera's director has made a commitment to ensure continuing development of the operatic art form and felt it important to enliven the American opera scene and visibility for the Utah Opera with this world premiere. Ewer believes that living art form relates to contemporary issues and the expression of modern ideas. *Dreamkeepers* accomplished the goals of the company and set down a recorded history of our heritage in beautiful operatic form.

The Nutcracker go on sale to the public in November and cost from $10 to $45. For more information on *The Nutcracker*, see our Festivals and Annual Events and Kidstuff chapters.

The Children's Dance Theatre
1033 E. 300 S., Salt Lake City
• 581-7374, 355-ARTS

The Children's Dance Theatre took "roots and wings" from Virginia Tanner, a choreographer, teacher and writer who, during the 1940s, found her calling teaching and training children. The Children's Dance Theatre has toured nationally and internationally presenting many innovative children's dance programs. Though Tanner died in 1979, the company and her spirit live on in the instruction of more than 800 children each year and the staging of a major performance each spring. Tanner believed in teaching the whole child the discipline and freedom of dance movement to enable them to get in touch with their own creativity.

The annual spring performance is held at the Capitol Theater. Tickets are $8 to $24.

Repertory Dance Theater
138 W. 300 S., Salt Lake City • 534-1000

Housed in the recently dedicated Rose

Wagner Performing Arts Center, RTD, as it is known, has been performing classical and contemporary modern dance since 1966. The company was created through a cooperative effort between the Rockefeller Foundation, the University of Utah and the local community. It was the first professional modern dance repertory company established outside New York City. RDT fills a unique role in preserving and presenting treasured American works of art through a living library of historically significant choreographed and commissioned new works by both established and emerging choreographers. The company celebrates the ethnic influences of Utah's minorities through its historic programs.

RDT has been a prominent company in the National Endowment for the Arts' dance touring program. The company has danced at Riverside Church in New York City, at the Smithsonian Institute and has toured throughout the United States and abroad.

Throughout the year the company features three guest artists in performances. Fall and spring programs are presented at the Capitol Theater. Summer and winter programs are performed at the Rose Wagner Center. In addition, the company presents children's programs and holds workshops and classes for high school students and other members of the community.

Ticket prices range from $5 to $22 for adults for all venues. Discounts for senior citizens, children younger than 13 and groups can reduce the cost of a ticket to as little as $3.50.

Ririe Woodbury Dance Company
50 W. 200 S., Salt Lake City • 323-6801, 355-ARTS

This extraordinary dance company became an institution in the city soon after its inception in 1964. What began as a troupe of professional dance performers and teachers has become a nationally renowned modern dance company whose innovative approach

has uplifted and enlightened audiences for more than three decades.

While assisting Alwin Nicholais at the Tyrone Guthrie Theater in Minneapolis in 1968, the Minnesota Arts Council invited Joan Woodbury to dance at four area colleges. The performance had to be prepared in one week. She and partner Shirley Ririe choreographed a zany — and well-received — performance and lecture demonstration for the Minnesota tour. It was eventually presented at the first U.S.-Canadian dance conference in 1971.

While performing at The Space in New York, members of the National Endowment for the Arts saw Ririe Woodbury's performance and accepted the company for the endowment's Artists In Schools and Dance Touring programs. These prestigious programs offered new full-time touring opportunities as a national company.

The company was the first to perform in Karl Marx Stadt (now Chemnitz) in the former Soviet Union and the first in the former East Berlin. It has performed or conducted residencies in such places as China, South Africa and Puerto Rico. The company performed a benefit fund-raiser for 70,000 Bosnian war refugees in the young republic of Slovenia.

In addition to its regular season of performances in Salt Lake City's Capital Theater the company conducts workshops for dancers of all age and experience levels and educators including a Drug and Violence Prevention Through Dance workshop. Ririe Woodbury's annual season begins in late August or early September and runs through June. Workshops are scheduled during the summer months.

Tickets for Ririe Woodbury performances range from $10 to $25 per performance, with discounts of up to 50 percent for senior citizens and students. No discount is offered for children, but they can use the student discount. Season subscriptions are available from $43 to $64.

INSIDERS' TIP

The first Wednesday of a theatrical run is preview night at some theaters. Tickets usually cost less. While all the bugs may not quite be worked out, this is a good way to see great theater on a budget. Some theaters offer matinee performances on Sundays at a reduced ticket price.

Music

Abramyan String Quartet
660 11th Ave., Salt Lake City • 355-4543

Founded in 1993, this string quartet performs the entire spectrum of the quartet repertoire from classical to contemporary. Abramyan has been hailed by local critics as the area's premier resident string quartet, and its work is considered innovative and stimulating by Salt Lake City audiences. The internationally acclaimed musicians have made a special commitment to bring music to underserved audiences in schools and outlying towns as well as to audiences in the local area. All of the musicians are members of the Utah Symphony. The group presents a series of classical performances in town at the First Presbyterian Church, 12 N. C Street, and frequently appears at the Cathedral of the Madeleine, 331 E. South Temple. They also appeared in other series in the Salt Lake area and tour internationally.

The quartet's performances are free at both churches.

American West Symphony
1950 E. Browning Ave., Salt Lake City • 583-7653

This 85-member community symphony, under the direction of Joel Rosenburg, is a musical force to be reckoned with in the Salt Lake area. Critics have praised the symphony, and Salt Lakers regard the musicians as consummate professionals. The symphony's four concerts a year are free of charge in the Assembly Hall on Temple Square.

Gloriana
2492 W. 6255 S., Salt Lake City • 424-1678, (800) 568-0681

The 30 voices in this chamber choir, under the direction of Deuane Kuenzi, have established themselves as one of the premier performing ensembles in the United States. With performances at the White House, the Kennedy Center, the Washington National Cathedral, the Lincoln Center, the Austrian Millennium Celebration and on tour in Brazil as guests of the Brazilian Office of Cultural Affairs, Gloriana has made a significant impression on the musical world. Their compact disc has been aired on more than 75 classical radio stations nationwide and has been distributed in more than 28 countries. The choir will also record 10 compact discs over the next six years featuring the music of Norman Luboff.

The New York Times praised the choir, saying, "A Gloriana concert is not a performance, it is an event." Local critics cite the ensemble's interesting exploration of existing repertory and see them as "among this planet's greatest vocal forces."

Gloriana performs four or five concerts a year at St. Marks Cathedral, 231 E. 100 S. You can call the number above for other performance schedules. Students and senior citizens can hear Gloriana for $5. The adult ticket price is $8.

Intermountain Classical Orchestra
470 S. 700 E., Salt Lake City • 355-3583

Don't hang up when someone answers the phone, "Fendal's Ice Cream." This is the ticket outlet for the orchestra and the best place to get information about performance schedules. Jeff Manookin conducts this young but highly regarded professional chamber orchestra whose 30 musicians present five concerts a year during the September-to-May season. The work features an innovative classical repertory. Venues vary but the orchestra can usually be seen at the First Presbyterian Church, 12 N. C Street.

Tickets are $10 for adults and $7.50 for students and senior citizens. You can buy a season subscription to the orchestra's performances for $35 ($25 for students and seniors).

Jazz Arts of the Mountainwest
3617 Astro Cir., Salt Lake City • 277-2056, (801) 479-6172

Most of the jazz venues locally offer sporadic performances, but the music is alive and well, and JAM has its finger on the pulse. They even publish a newsletter that you can get by writing to the address above (the ZIP code is 84109). The strength of JAM's movement to support and promote live performances of jazz and related music is Jerry Floor, a local musician and leader of the 20-piece Jerry Floor Band. The band has been a staple for Salt Lakers who love jazz for more than two decades. You can sit in on the band's rehearsals in the back room at Alan Weight Music Studio, 955 E. 900 S., 322-5103, every other Saturday morning around 9 or 9:30. It isn't Preservation Hall, but the music's great. The Phoenix Jazz Band also rehearses here on Thursdays at 7 PM. This is a remarkable group of old-timers — senior citizens who still practice their craft as jazz musicians.

Jazz music can be heard in many local clubs including the Zephyr and D.B. Cooper's. The Hilton Hotel sponsors a memorable jazz series once a month that you won't want to miss if you're in town. Tuesday is jazz night at Cup a Joe. Check out the annual Snowbird Jazz and Blues Festival in the Festivals and Annual Events chapter.

In the Media chapter, look for locations to get local entertainment newspapers like the *EVENT* and *City Weekly*. They offer a lot of information on the local music scene. You have to dig a little to find the locations for jazz performances, but you'll be pleasantly surprised at what the city has to offer.

The Mormon Tabernacle Choir
Temple Square, Salt Lake City
• 240-3221

The Tabernacle is home to the world-renowned Mormon Tabernacle Choir, which broadcasts live from Temple Square every Sunday. The Tabernacle Choir's first radio broadcast — with the organ, choir and announcer all sharing one microphone — was transmitted on July 15, 1929. After more than 65 years and 3,500 broadcasts, the choir's *Music and the Spoken Word* program is heard worldwide through more than 1,500 radio, television and cable stations each week. The choir, which tours the world from Japan to Mexico

Utah's Film Industry

Lights, camera, action! Utah has an illustrious history with the making of motion pictures, dating from the early 1900s. The first film was shot here in 1908, but the first documented film, *Covered Wagon* (one of the most successful silent films in history) was made in Utah in 1922. Fans of Westerns will recognize the stunning red-rock country of Moab and Monument Valley that provided such magnificent backdrops for so many of these classics including renowned director John Ford's *Stagecoach* and *Drums Along the Mohawk* made in 1939 and *She Wore a Yellow Ribbon*, filmed in 1949.

Close-up

Other films shot in Utah in the early days included *My Friend Flicka* with Fred MacMurray and Roddy McDowell (1943) and *Sergeants Three* with Frank Sinatra and the Rat Pack (1963). Robert Redford starred in *Jeremiah Johnson*, shot along the Wasatch Mountain Range in 1972, and made the *Electric Horseman* in St. George in 1979. Clint Eastwood starred in the *Outlaw Josie Wales*, filmed in Utah in 1975.

Ford believed the narrative of film was driven by the dramatic landscape — and Utah has landscape galore. Our diverse geography offers film makers many opportunities for scenes of deserts, snow-capped mountains, red buttes, rural farm and Western-style towns, cosmopolitan cities and 1950s suburban settings. Besides all that, our four stellar seasons allow film makers to capture the essence of climate and environment any time of year.

In recent years, however, Utah has gone from being just another pretty face to a being a hub of highly skilled local talent. The pool of trained technical people, actors and support services can't be beat. Stephen King's TV mini-series *The Stand* was filmed here in the early '90s, as was Ridley Scott's classic film *Thelma and Louise*, and the memorable final scenes from *Independence Day* were filmed on the Salt Flats near the Great Salt Lake. The feature film *Con Air* was filmed in Salt Lake and Ogden in the 1996-97 production year.

— continued on next page

Photo: Courtesy CBS TV

Angels watch over Utah's growing film industry. Roma Downey, Della Reese and John Dye of the CBS TV series *Touched by an Angel,* shot in Salt Lake City.

In 1997 film production revenue added $132.2 million to the state's coffers. Out-of-state productions such as *Touched by an Angel*, a weekly CBS TV series, are shot on location in Salt Lake City, and the popular *Promised Land* series is filmed in Salt Lake and St. George, in the southwest part of the state. These add significantly to the state's income and provide regular jobs for many locals. In addition to feature films, in the 1996-97 production year 11 TV movies, 11 mini-series or parts of other network series (including *Walker, Texas Ranger*), 96 commercials, stills, videos, documentaries and catalogs were produced in Utah, many in the Salt Lake area. If you travel around the city or state you might recognize that our mountains and red rocks appear in several automobile commercials.

Local film companies have also made an impressive name for themselves and contributed significantly to the local economy as well as garnering national and international awards. With a culture that embraces outsiders, an aggressive film commission, the success of the Sundance Film Festival in Park City (see the "Arts and Annual Events" section of our Park City chapter), plenty of locations from which to choose and a growing stable of homegrown industry professionals, Utah's future in the film industry looks bright.

and from Russia to the Hollywood Bowl, has performed at four U.S. presidential inaugurations.

Organ recitals in the tabernacle are open to the public Monday through Saturday from 12 to 12:30 PM and from 2 to 2:30 PM June through September. Sunday recitals are from 2 to 2:30 PM. Visitors can also attend choir rehearsals at the tabernacle on Thursday from 8 to 9:30 PM. Broadcasts on Sunday morning are open to the public as well from 9:30 to 10 AM. Guests must be seated by 9:15 AM. All events are free.

Prevailing Winds Wood Quintet
2105 E. Donegal Cir., Salt Lake City
• 467-3155

This woodwind quintet, which features a

flute, oboe, clarinet, bassoon and French horn, is prominent on the local music scene. *The Salt Lake Tribune* music critic said "[they] offer world-class music making." Prevailing Winds, under the direction of Scott Harris, is a young and thriving organization that plays everything from Bach to Beethoven, as well as world premieres of new composers both local and from Los Angeles.

The group presents four formal concerts during its season, which runs from September through May. The venues vary, so check local newspapers for listings or call the number above. Tickets are $10 for adults and $6 for students and senior citizens.

Salt Lake Children's Choir
1033 E. 300 S., Salt Lake City • 537-1412

This wonderful children's choir has performed and recorded with the Mormon Tabernacle Choir and the Utah Symphony. Many of the choir members have recorded music for Walt Disney Productions, CNN and CBS TV. The children, who range from age 8 to 15, rehearse weekly for the two or three major concerts they perform each season and the numerous satellite performances given throughout the Valley.

Under the direction of Ralph Woodward, the children's choir has been presenting the works of the great masters along with outstanding ethnic music from around the world for nearly two decades. The focus is on the classics, but the children and director enjoy exploring other music so long as it's compatible with high choral standards and uses the young voices to their advantage. The choir's

FYI

Unless otherwise noted, the area code for all phone numbers listed in this guide is 801.

emphasis is on development of the natural voice.

The Salt Lake Children's Choir has been heard on Public Radio International, and the 90 children in two ensembles continue to impress audiences locally and outside the area.

The choir is regarded as one of the finest ensembles of its kind in the nation and is widely admired for its pure, beautiful sound and the versatility of an outstanding repertoire.

You can hear the Salt Lake Children's Choir at various locations throughout the city including Abravanel Hall, 123 W. South Temple. Many performances, including the annual Christmas concert at the Cathedral of the Madeleine, 331 E. South Temple, are free. Tickets for other concerts range from $3 to $8.

Utah Chamber Artists
97 Birch St., Midvale • 255-2233

These artists present a four-concert series in Salt Lake at various locations including the First Presbyterian Church, 12 N. C St., and Abravanel Hall, 123 W. South Temple. The vocal ensemble has been acclaimed as one of the most remarkable choirs in the West. The choir has toured six cities in the Holy Land and recorded a compact disc in Tel Aviv featuring John Rutter's *Requiem*. They have been heralded as a vital part of the nation's cultural scene and continue to expand their audience.

Season subscribers can purchase tickets to all four concerts for $38 for adults, $30 for senior citizens and $25 for students. Single tickets are $15 for adults, $12 for senior citizens and $10 for students.

INSIDERS' TIP

On Tuesday and Friday evenings June through August, you'll enjoy lively entertainment suitable for the whole family at Brigham Young Historical Park on the southeast corner of Second Avenue and State Street in downtown Salt Lake. Sponsored by the Temple Square concert series, performances range from Tongan dancers to Broadway and country and western music. The performances are free. To find out what's happening, call 240-3323.

Utah Opera
50 W. 200 S., Salt Lake City • 355-ARTS

The inspiration for the Utah Opera, like many of our arts organizations, was the dream of one man, nurtured by a community and culminating in a successful, world-class opera company. In this case, the man was Glade Peterson, a farm boy from Fairview, about 100 miles south of Salt Lake City. He was a leading tenor with the Zurich Opera in Switzerland and was a guest performer in many European houses before returning to his roots. Petersen brought the opera company to prominence before his death in 1990.

Following a nationwide search for his successor, the company employed Anne Ewers, a well-known stage director for opera in the United States and Canada and former director of the Boston Lyric Opera. She has further guided the Utah Opera to great heights on the national scene. In spite of its sophistication, the grandeur of its productions and a hefty budget, the company has graciously reached out to the masses with programming and education that touches the spirit of all people in the Valley.

The Utah Opera performs four operas during its regular season between mid-October and late May. It sponsors a young artists program that provides training in all areas of operatic art. The company also travels throughout the state bringing opera to children in public schools.

In celebration of Utah's centennial in 1997, the Utah Opera commissioned a new opera as part of its contribution and tribute to the arts. See the Close-up, "Dreamkeepers," in this chapter for more information.

Single ticket prices range from $12 to $55. You can purchase a season subscription for $40 to $164.

Utah Symphony
123 W. South Temple, Salt Lake City
• 533-6407

Our symphony is the 12th-largest orchestra in the United States. It's first season in 1940 consisted of five concerts performed by 52 part-time musicians. Today the orchestra has 83 full-time musicians and presents more than 250 performances annually both at home and abroad.

The orchestra emerged from the Utah State Sinfonietta, a Works Progress Administration ensemble created in 1935. In 1947, Music Director Laureate Maurice Abravanel guided the Utah Symphony from relative obscurity to national and international prominence. In addition to transforming a community orchestra into one of national celebration, Abravanel was considered one of the outstanding interpreters of Gustav Mahler, and his Mahler recordings on the Vanguard label are still considered classics. He was also a member of the board of the National Endowment of the Arts and artist-in-residence at the Berkshire Music Center at Tanglewood. Abravanel retired as conductor of the symphony in 1979, the same year the impressive hall that bears his name was constructed. Abravanel Hall is hailed by musicians and acoustical engineers as one of the finest concert halls in the world.

The orchestra performs 18 pairs of classical concerts at Abravanel Hall each year and participates in a variety of other programs including a summer concert series at The Canyons ski resort in Park City, a Youth and "Finishing Touches" Series and a Chamber Orchestra Series. In addition, it presents Christmas concerts, the annual New Year's Eve in Symphony Hall, Irish Night and the Symphony Entertainment series — a winter pops series that continues to grow each year. The symphony provides music for hundreds of ballet and opera productions and performs with the Mormon Tabernacle Choir. Each year the orchestra gives approximately 65 concerts in Utah schools.

Single-ticket prices range from $12 to $35 per performance. Series tickets range from $172 to $504.

Visual Arts

Galleries

Art Access Gallery
339 W. Pierpont Ave., Salt Lake City
• 328-0703

Solo and group exhibitions of contemporary artists are presented throughout the year at Art Access. The gallery gives priority to exhibits that include artists from underserved communities or those who have an educational focus. Hours are Monday through Friday from 10 AM to 5 PM. Art Access participates in the Gallery Stroll.

Bibliotect
329 W. Pierpont Ave., Salt Lake City • 236-1010

This is a delicious place to visit. The gallery features contemporary, cutting-edge work by emerging and established local artists. It also has a great bookstore. The gallery holds loosely scheduled art talks, poetry readings and special events related to the arts and participates in the monthly Gallery Stroll. To get more details on the wonderful selection of books at Bibliotect, check out the listing in the Shopping chapter under "Bookstores." Hours are 9 AM to 6 PM Monday through Saturday.

Brushworks Gallery
175 E. 200 S., Salt Lake City • 363-0600

Brushworks has been at the same location for more than 20 years, and although its approach to the art scene is quite low key the gallery is well-respected. Local artists with a traditional style are the mainstay of the four yearly exhibitions. If you enjoy landscapes in oils and watercolors you'll be delighted with the gallery and its representation of well-known local painters whose work is abundant elsewhere but not locally. This is a Gallery Stroll participant. Hours are 9 AM to 6 PM Monday through Friday.

Cordell Taylor Studio Gallery
575 W. 200 S., Salt Lake City • 355-0333

Ask anyone in the local art community about provocative new work and Cordell Taylor's name is bound to be mentioned. This exciting sculptor has created an alternative space with studios that he shares with painters and other sculptors, and a gallery area that presents the work of young unknown artists with excellent skills. In the space that operates under the name Surface at the same location, you'll find installations, readings, film and performance art. If you appreciate insightful new work with an enormous amount of creative energy, you'll want to pay a visit to the gallery. Hours are 10 AM to 5 PM daily during the week or by appointment. You will usually find them open during the Gallery Stroll.

Dolores Chase Fine Art
260 S. 200 W., Salt Lake City • 328-2787

This wonderful gallery offers a variety of work ranging from lithographs and etchings to sculpture and paintings by contemporary artists. The small gallery cafe sells espresso, cappuccino and Italian sodas. Exhibits rotate monthly with one to four featured artists in the main gallery and other artists featured in auxiliary spaces. Hours are Tuesday through Friday from 10 AM to 5 PM and Saturday from 1 to 4 PM. Dolores Chase participates in the monthly Gallery Stroll.

Finch Lane Gallery/Art Barn
54 Finch Ln., Salt Lake City • 596-5000

The Finch Lane Gallery and Park Gallery on the lower level of the Art Barn are administered by the Salt Lake City Arts Council and feature work by emerging and established artists. Exhibits include work by two or more collaborating artists or disciplines, installations, new technology or innovations or ethnic or multicultural subject matter. Hours are Monday through Friday 9:30 AM to 5 PM and Sunday from 1 to 4 PM. The gallery is open during the Gallery Stroll.

Glendinning Gallery
617 E. South Temple, Salt Lake City • 236-7555

Housed in the Glendinning Mansion, this gallery is administered by the Utah Arts Council. It exhibits artwork from the council's traveling exhibition program, historical art exhibits and selections from the state art col-

---

INSIDERS' TIP

Take a piece of Salt Lake's fine-arts scene home as a reminder of your visit. Most galleries and museums in the Salt Lake Valley have gift shops that sell a variety of work by local artists.

Photo: Utah Travel Council

Ballet West is one of America's leading ballet companies. Repertoire includes full-length classical and modern ballets as well as original works.

lection, established in 1899. Hours are Monday through Friday from 9 AM to 5 PM. Glendinning participates in the Gallery Stroll on occasion, depending on their current exhibition.

LeftBank at Pierpont
242 S. 200 W., Salt Lake City • 539-0343
The LeftBank at Pierpont was established to provide a forum for art that's on the cutting edge. Exhibitions include installation and performance art and experimental work in more standard media such as painting and sculpture. Artists are represented individually or in groups with exhibits running from one week to one month. The gallery has more than 12,500 square feet of space with 13-foot ceilings and an unfinished cement floor that allows artists to create and exhibit large works. Opportunities for artists to work in collaborative theater, film, dance and two- or three-dimensional visual media are also available. Hours are Wednesday through Saturday 5 to 9 PM. The LeftBank is open during the Gallery Stroll.

Marble House
44 Exchange Pl., Salt Lake City • 532-7332
This daylighted three-story gallery created within the brick shell of a 19th-century printing plant on historic Exchange Place showcases an outstanding collection of original artwork. The gallery features Utah artists and those from throughout the country in the 6,000-square-foot space. The work includes oil, watercolor, limited editions, prints, pottery and sculpture. Hours are Tuesday through Friday from 11 AM to 4:30 PM. Marble House is open during the Gallery Stroll.

Phillips Gallery
444 E. 200 S., Salt Lake City • 364-8284

Phillips has been a Salt Lakers' favorite gallery for more than 30 years. It represents regional artists working in contemporary and traditional styles in all media including oil, acrylic, metal, paper, wood and photography. The gallery also features a selection of fine crafts from throughout the country. Phillips participates in the monthly Gallery Stroll and hosts seven shows each year with revolving group shows in the lower gallery.

You can buy art supplies and get custom framing in the store next-door to the gallery. Hours are Tuesday through Friday from 9:30 AM to 6 PM and on Saturday until 4 PM. The owners follow a European tradition, closing the gallery for about a month each summer to take a holiday. The dates vary from year to year but you are most likely to find them away during August.

Reparteé Gallery
39 S. Main St., Salt Lake City • 364-4809

The gallery is an authorized Greenwich Workshop Dealer, specializing in fine limited-edition prints, watercolors, oils, alkyds, Prismacolors and gouaches by Western artists. You'll find a unique selection of pottery and bronze pieces and a large selection of original artwork. This 1,750-square-foot gallery is located in the ZCMI Center and is open during the Gallery Stroll. Hours are Monday through Friday 10 AM to 9 PM and until 7 PM on Saturday.

Southam Gallery
50 E. Broadway (300 S.), Salt Lake City • 322-0376

The gallery specializes in traditional landscapes, including impressionist stylings and representational styles by Utah and national artists. Southam is a participant in the monthly Gallery Stroll. Hours are Tuesday through Saturday from 11 AM to 5:30 PM.

Tivoli Gallery
255 S. State St., Salt Lake City • 521-6288

Housed in the historic Rex Burlesque Theatre building, this 25,000-square-foot gallery is one of the largest fine-arts galleries in Salt Lake City. Works include a selective collection of 19th- and 20th-century American and European paintings and a wide selection of pieces by early and contemporary Utah artists. Hours are Monday through Friday 10 AM to 5 PM and Saturday by appointment. Tivoli participates in the monthly Gallery Stroll.

F. Wexler Gallery
132 E St., Salt Lake City • 534-1014

This is a combination art gallery, interior design service and furniture store. It features the work of local artists including painters, sculptors and potters. Hours are Monday through Friday 9 AM to 5:30 PM.

Williams Fine Art
60 E. South Temple, Salt Lake City • 534-0331

Williams specializes in early Utah artists and living contemporary artists with a representational rather than abstract style. The work of individuals and groups is exhibited throughout the year in the 1,500-square-foot space in the lobby of the Eagle Gate Plaza. Hours are Monday through Friday from noon to 5 PM. Williams participates in the Gallery Stroll during the holidays only.

Museums

The Chase Home Museum of Utah Folk Art
1150 S. 600 E., Salt Lake City • 533-5760

Housed in the historic Chase home in the center of Liberty Park, the museum's displays include quilts, ethnic arts, rugs and other crafts. The museum is open weekends from mid-April through mid-October noon to 5 PM and daily from Memorial Day through Labor Day from noon to 5 PM. Admission is free.

INSIDERS' TIP

Most public libraries in the Salt Lake Valley exhibit the works of local artists.

THE ARTS • 189

Rio Grande Railroad Depot/Utah State Historical Society
300 Rio Grande St., Salt Lake City
• 533-3500

The depot houses local artwork and exhibits dealing with Utah and local history. The library has records, photographs and artifacts from Utah's past. The Historical Society is open from 8 AM to 6 PM Monday through Friday and from 10 AM to 3 PM on Saturday. The library is open Tuesday through Friday from 10 AM to 5 PM and until 2 PM on Saturday. Admission is free.

The Salt Lake Art Center
20 S. West Temple, Salt Lake City
• 328-4201

The Salt Lake Art Center is the only visual-arts organization in the area dedicated to contemporary artists and issues. It presents approximately 12 changing exhibits each year including four major exhibitions in the main gallery and eight smaller ones that focus on local and regional artists in the street level gallery. The exhibits in both galleries feature the talent of extraordinary artists who examine issues ranging from the treatment of AIDS patients and victims of breast cancer to issues of ecological and environmental activism. Many of the works examine more personal issues of self, gender and identity in a complex society. The Art Center provides programming for children in KidSpace. For details on this impressive hands-on program see the listing in our Kidstuff chapter.

Adult programming includes a regular series called ART TALKS. These informal gallery discussions on current exhibitions are given by artists, curators, art administrators, and performers. They are held on Wednesday evenings from 7 to 8 PM in conjunction with new exhibitions in the main gallery. ART TALKS are free to the public.

The Art Center School has been part of the Center's programming since its inception in the 1930s. The school provides a curriculum in photography and ceramics for all skill levels. In addition to regular classes, special workshops on various topics in both media are frequently offered.

The Art Center participates in the monthly Gallery Stroll. The galleries are open Tuesday through Saturday 10 AM to 5 PM, Friday until 9 PM and Sunday 1 to 5 PM. Admission to the galleries is free but a donation is appreciated.

Utah Museum of Fine Arts
1530 E. South Campus Dr., Salt Lake City
• 581-7332

On the campus of the University of Utah, this museum is one of the Salt Lake Valley's principal cultural resources, with collections encompassing 5,000-year-old Egyptian art, Italian Renaissance paintings, European and American art from the 17th century to the present, Oriental art, Navajo textiles and African and pre-Colombian artifacts. The museum offers tours, gallery talks and lectures and is host to traveling exhibits and concerts. Hours are Monday through Friday 10 AM to 5 PM and Saturday and Sunday from noon to 5 PM. Admission is free.

Film

Utah Film and Video Center
20 S. West Temple, Salt Lake City
• 534-1158

The center was established in 1979 to promote and support media arts. The annual Short Film and Video Festival is a summer highlight in mid-June and attracts a wide audience. The national competition showcases film and video works of up to 30 minutes in length in all styles, forms and genres. You can view documentary, narrative, experimental and animated film in the small theater. The young media arts category for film and video makers 18 and younger is usually quite remarkable. Friday-night screenings of innovative film and video works and lectures by visiting artists are great ways to spend an evening if you enjoy film. The "media center," as it's called by locals, is open from 10 AM to 5 PM Monday through Friday and later on presentation evenings. You'll find the center on the main floor in the north wing of the Salt Lake Art Center building.

A 30-year quest for Olympic gold had finally panned out, and a crowd of 40,000 at the City and County Building in Salt Lake City gave voice to the triumphant joy of an entire state.

2002 Winter Olympics

On June 16, 1995, the International Olympic Committee selected Salt Lake City as the site of the XIX Olympic Winter Games to be held February 8 to 24, 2002. A 30-year quest for Olympic gold had finally panned out, and a crowd of 40,000 at the City and County Building in Salt Lake City gave voice to the triumphant joy of an entire state. The roar reverberated throughout Salt Lake City as the streets overflowed with jubilant citizens celebrating this historic event.

Salt Lake had bid to become the site of the Olympic Winter Games five separate times. The city was rejected by the U.S. Olympic Committee as the candidate in 1976 and 1992. As the U.S. choice, Salt Lake was rejected by the International Olympic Committee for 1972 and 1998. Persistence paid off, and the 2002 bid proved victorious. Salt Lake needed 46 votes out of the 90 IOC members voting to win. It got 55 on the first ballot — an impressive total and an overwhelming victory for the many Utahns who had spent decades on the effort. The other cities competing were Sion, Switzerland, which received 14 votes, Osterlund, Sweden, also with 14 votes, and Quebec, Canada, with seven votes.

The Olympic Games

As with so many modern ideas and institutions, the Olympic Games began in Greece. The Greeks from Homer on were passionately interested in athletics and warfare, and athletic contests as training for war formed a fundamental part of Greek life. Early in Greek history, athletic games came to be the most important element of religious festivals that grew out of the Greek sense of their own unity as a people with a common way of life. The Olympic Games were one of four great pan-Hellenic religious festivals that included the Pythian, Isthmian and Nemean games. All of these festivals were well-established by the middle of the sixth century B.C. The Olympic Games honored Zeus, the supreme Greek god, which made them the most important festival in Greece.

The Games were famous throughout Greece, and winners were honored wherever the Greek language was spoken. They were held every four years at Olympia, the sacred shrine of Zeus, from 776 B.C. (and probably far earlier) until 261 A.D. During the Games a truce was declared throughout Greece. The original competition consisted

INSIDERS' TIP

Norwegian skier Stein Eriksen won the gold medal in the giant slalom and the silver medal in the slalom at the 1952 Games in Oslo, Norway. Eriksen went on to become a legendary ski instructor, as well as a noted bon vivant and raconteur. He was instrumental in developing the Deer Valley ski resort and now works as director of skiing.

of footraces, the pentathlon and wrestling. Eventually, horse racing, chariot racing, the long jump, discus throwing, boxing and other sports were added. One popular event was the pancration, a brutal form of wrestling where an opponent could be subdued by kicking, arm twisting or strangulation. Only biting or poking out an opponent's eye were prohibited. The victor's prize for winning an Olympic event was a wreath of wild olive from a tree sacred to Zeus, but a winner could also expect rich gifts from his city state upon his triumphant return home.

As the influence of money and commercialism grew in the Olympics, people lost respect for them and their influence waned. Finally, the Christian emperor Theodosius declared the Games a pagan cult in 391 AD and abolished them. For 1,500 years the Olympic Games remained only a ghostly memory, an obscure footnote in history texts. During the 19th century archeologists began excavating Olympia, eventually unearthing dozens of statues, temples and shrines, including the famous statue by Praxiteles of Hermes holding the infant Zeus on his arm. Olympia was also the home of a gold and ivory statue of Zeus sitting on a throne, the masterpiece of the great Athenian sculptor Pheidias and one of the Seven Wonders of the ancient world. However, this statute was destroyed by an earthquake in the 6th century B.C. and is only know by representations on coins of the Greek city state Elis.

These exciting discoveries, along with a growing interest in amateur athletics as a fine way of creating hale, hearty and morally upright young people, led to the modern Olympic movement. In 1893 a wealthy French nobleman named Baron Pierre de Coubertin organized an international conference at the Sorbonne in Paris where representatives from dozens of nations studied the feasibility of reviving the Olympics. The conference passed a resolution declaring that "sports competitions should be held every fourth year on the lines of the Greek Olympic Games and every nation should be invited to participate." In 1896 the first modern Summer Games were held, appropriately, in Athens, Greece. The first modern Winter Games were held in Chamonix, France, in 1924.

The Olympic Village and Stadium

An estimated 4,000 athletes, coaches and trainers are expected to attend the 2002 Games. This contingent will live in an Olympic Village to be built on 70 acres on Fort Douglas, an old U.S. Army base on the University of Utah campus. The University of Utah campus is about 2 miles east of downtown Salt Lake City. You can learn more about the University of Utah in the Education chapter. The state of Utah will build new housing for the Olympics, and the buildings will belong to the University of Utah.

The village will be just a few minutes from downtown Salt Lake City and the Salt Lake International Airport and no farther than an hour's drive (in normal traffic conditions) from any venue. IOC guidelines require that no venue be more than 62 miles from the Olympic Village. However, millions of spectators, athletes and journalists will descend on Salt Lake during the 17 days of the Games, so traffic conditions will be as far from normal, as imgainable. If fierce weather descends, it might take hours to get to any venue.

Salt Lake Organizing Committee

The 2002 Winter Games are managed by

FYI

Unless otherwise noted, the area code for all phone numbers listed in this guide is 801.

INSIDERS' TIP

The first toboggan run was built in St. Moritz, Switzerland, in 1884.

the Salt Lake Organizing Committee (SLOC), a nonprofit, tax-exempt organization set up under Utah law. A board of trustees with 33 voting members governs the SLOC. The board includes the president and executive director of the USOC, as well as IOC members from the United States. A 15-member executive committee of the board of trustees coordinates the affairs of the board of trustees. This committee approves plans, policy and budgets before they are submitted to the board of trustees for approval or rejection. The chairman of the board of trustees is also the chairman of the executive committee. This person governs the activities of SLOC, making sure that the policies set forth by the board of trustees are followed by employees and officers of SLOC.

The number of employees of SLOC is expected to grow to 600 over the next few years. Volunteers are important to the Olympic effort, and SLOC estimates that 12,000 to 15,000 volunteers will come forward to make the Games a success.

TV Rights and Tickets

Rights to televised Olympic events have garnered big bucks. NBC television paid $545 million for the U.S. rights, the European Broadcast Union paid $120 million for the European rights, and Network Seven TV bought the Australian rights for $11.8 million. Salt Lake City will share the worldwide revenues with the IOC and the U.S. revenues with the USOC.

The SLOC estimates that 2 million tickets will be available to the XIX Winter Olympic Games. Prices and other relevant information will be announced in 2000, and tickets will be for sale in the fall of that year. It's expected that the demand for tickets will exceed the supply. The SLOC will handle all ticket sales domestically, and overseas sales will be handled through National Olympic Committees.

Venues and Games

The 2002 Winter Olympic Games will be held at nine separate sites in the Salt Lake area. Competition is scheduled for 70 medal events. First we'll look at the mountain sites and the events scheduled there, then we'll look at the city sites and events. Although no major changes in venues are expected, some events could be shifted around to different sites than those listed below. For a complete description of the mountain sites, read the Skiing and Winter Sports chapter. You can find information on how to get to the various sites in the Getting Here, Getting Around chapter and the Park City chapter.

Outdoor Venues

Deer Valley Ski Area

Deer Valley is just southeast of Park City, about 33 minutes from the Olympic Village. Eight events will be held here, including men's and women's slalom and combined slalom, and men's and women's freestyle moguls and freestyle aerials.

Slalom skiing involves racing through a gated course against the clock, with speeds reaching 60 to 70 mph. The course must have 55 to 75 gates for men and 40 to 60 gates for women. The gate poles are plastic and have a spring at the bottom so they tip over when they're hit. A competitor's body can knock down the gate, but both skis must pass through it or the skier is disqualified. Slalom skiing has been an Olympic event since the first modern Winter Games in Chamonix, France, in 1924.

In the mogul event, competitors ski down a bumpy hill (the bumps are called moguls) and must undertake two jumps and other airborne acrobatics. Competitors earn points for style, speed, aggressiveness and difficulty of maneuvers. Aerial competitors must jump from ski platforms of varying heights

INSIDERS' TIP

The origins of the ski jump date back to games children played on skis in Northern Europe.

and configurations and perform flips and twists. Points are awarded for takeoff, height and length of jump, form and landing. Mogul skiing was added at the 1992 Games in Albertville, France, and aerials were added at the 1994 Games in Lillehammer, Norway.

Competition at this site will go on for eight days. The spectator capacity is expected to be 20,000 people, with 10,000 seated and 10,000 standing.

Park City Mountain Resort

This resort is in the heart of Park City, about 30 minutes from the Olympic Village. Six events will be held here: the men's and women's giant slalom, men's and women's snowboarding half-pipe and the snowboarding giant slalom.

Giant slalom competition is like slalom, but the course is faster and longer and the gates farther apart. The giant slalom began as an Olympic event in the 1952 Olympics in Oslo, Norway. In the giant slalom snowboard event, snowboarders are timed racing through a gated course, much like the skiing giant slalom. The half-pipe event takes place on a course shaped like a pipe cut in half lengthwise. Competitors jump, spin and twirl in midair to earn points. They're judged on form, rotation, height and similar factors. Snowboarding is a new event at the Winter Games, introduced at the 1998 Games in Nagano, Japan.

Competition at this site will go on for six days, with spectator capacity pegged at 20,000 — 10,000 seated and 10,000 standing.

Snowbasin Ski Area

Snowbasin is 17 miles east of Ogden, Utah, which is about 45 miles north of Salt Lake and about 55 minutes from the Olympic Village. See the Daytrips chapter for the lowdown on the Ogden area. Snowbasin is the site of six events: the men's and women's downhill, men's and women's combined downhill and the men's and women's super G giant slalom.

The downhill is the fastest and most thrilling alpine event, with daredevil racers speeding down a course with a vertical drop of 800 to 1000 meters for men and 500 to 800 meters for women. Speeds during the downhill reach 70 to 80 mph, so spills and injuries are common. The course usually has jumps and tight turns. The downhill has been an Olympic event since the 1924 Games.

In the super G, skiers race down a course through a series of gates, similar to the slalom and giant slalom, but the course is steeper and longer, and the gates are farther apart. It can be described as a combination of the downhill and giant slalom. Competitors race down the hill in wide, swooping turns performed at high speed with balletic grace. Winners for both the downhill and super G are determined in one run. The super G slalom was added at the 1982 Games.

Competition at Snowbasin will last six days, and planned capacity for spectators for the downhill and super G giant slalom is 40,000 (20,000 seated and 20,000 standing).

Winter Sports Park

You'll find this facility a few miles north of Park City and 31 minutes from the Olympic Village. This new, 387-acre park offers a 15,000-square-foot day lodge, a 750,000-gallon pool for summer training of aerials and freestyle skiing and five Nordic winter ski jumps of 10, 18, 38, 65 and 90 meters. A 120-meter Nordic ski jump is being built. It also has a 1,335-meter bobsleigh and luge track with five start areas, a refrigeration plant and a timing tower. Ten events are scheduled for this facility: two-man and four-man bobsleigh, men's single and double luge, women's single luge, individual and team K120 (large hill) ski jumping, individual K90 (normal hill) ski jumping and Nordic combined K90 individual and team ski jumping.

The thrilling bobsleigh event is a spectator favorite. These fiberglass-reinforced, metal-chassis sleighs rocket down the track at breakneck speeds — often more than 100 mph. The running push start by the brakeman often determines the winner of the race. The bobsleigh event has been on the official Olympic program since the 1924 Games in Chamonix, France. In the luge race, competitors lie face-up on the luge, which is a kind of high-speed sleigh, and steer with their legs as they hurtle down the ice. The luge reaches top speeds of 70 mph or more. Like the bobsleigh, the successful start of the luge often determines the winner. The luge is a dangerous event, and injuries are common. The luge was added to the Olympics at the 1964 Games in Innsbruck, Austria. Competition for the bobsleigh and luge is slated for nine days with a planned capacity for spectators of 14,000.

In the ski jump, each contestant has two jumps and is awarded points for style, distance and form. Skiers jump from normal hills (K90) and large hills (K120). Competitors land in the telemark position, with one ski in front of the other, knees bent and arms straight out. Jumpers used to keep their skis parallel during the jump, but that changed in 1988 when J. Bokloeg of Sweden assumed a V position with his skis and found it added extra lift. The normal hill ski jump has been part of the Winter Olympic Games since the beginning. The large hill jump was added during the 1964 Games. The Nordic combined merges ski jumping and cross-country skiing. Competitors ski jump from a normal hill then cross-country ski on a 15-kilometer course. Competition for ski jumping and Nordic combined ski jumping will last five days. Spectator capacity is 20,000 (10,000 seated and 10,000 standing).

See the Kidstuff chapter and the Parks City chapter's "Sightseeing and Attractions" section to find out how noncompetitors can use the park for summer and winter fun.

Soldier Hollow in Wasatch State Park

Soldier Hollow is 2 miles southwest of Midway in Heber Valley, about 17 miles southwest of Park City and 50 minutes from the Olympic Village. Cross-country and biathlon competitions are scheduled here. The number of events here has not yet been determined, but the cross-country events will be a mixture of classical and free technique races ranging from distances of 5 kilometers to 50 kilometers. Both men's and women's cross-country events will be staged. Classical cross-country competitions require skis to be parallel on flat terrain, with skis apart in a diagonal pattern on uphill terrain. Free techniques allow any type of stride. Cross-country events have been part of the Olympic Games since 1924.

The biathlon is combination of cross-country racing and rifle shooting. Biathletes use the free technique and shoot a small-caliber rifle (5.6 mm) using both prone and standing positions. Scoring is based on skiing speed and shooting accuracy. Normal biathlon events for men are 20-kilometer individual, 10-kilometer sprints and 7.5-kilometer relays in teams of four. Women compete in 15-kilometer individual, 7.5-kilometer sprint and 7.5-kilometer relay in teams of four. The biathlon became an Olympic event in 1960. The number of competition days and planned number of spectators for the cross-country events and biathlon have not yet been determined.

Indoor Venues

The Ice Sheet at Ogden

You can watch the curling competition

---

at this Ogden venue, 45 minutes north of the Olympic Village (see our Daytrips chapter for more about Ogden). Both men and women's curling events will be held. Curling is an obscure Scottish pastime first added as an Olympic event at the 1994 Games in Lillehammer, Norway. Each curling team has four players, and each player takes turn pushing a 20-kilogram granite stone towards a 6-foot-radius circle called a "house." The object of curling is to place this stone as close to the center of the house as possible. As one player pushes the stone, another gives it a spin, or "curl," hence the name. The other two players are equipped with brooms they use to sweep the ice in front of the moving stone in order to control its speed and direction. After each team has delivered 16 stones, the team with the stone closest to the center wins. Games can last up to 2½ hours, with complicated strategy and tactics — almost like checkers on ice. This event will last for seven days with a planned capacity of 2,000 seated spectators.

Delta Center

Figure skating and short-track speed skating events will take place at the Delta Center, the home of the Utah Jazz. It's in downtown Salt Lake City, only 10 minutes from the Olympic Village. You can read more about the Delta Center in the Spectator Sports chapter. Events scheduled here include men's and women's singles, pairs and ice dance figure skating and men's 500-meter, 1,000-meter and 5,000-meter relay short-track speed skating. The women's 500-meter, 1,000-meter and 3,000-meter relay short-track speed skating event will also be held here.

Figure skating is probably the most popular winter Olympic event, with winners such as Sonja Henie, Dorothy Hamill and Peggy Fleming becoming household names. Contestants in the singles and paired events perform a short program with eight compulsory parts and a free skating program. In the free skating program, skaters perform an original skating program to music they've selected. Ice dancing can best be described as ballroom dancing on ice. This event is made up of three parts: compulsory, where the music and moves are determined beforehand; original dance; and free dance. In the original dances, skaters have to follow rhythms selected beforehand by the officials, but can choose their own music and steps. In free dancing couples choose both the type of music and steps. Figure skating has been an Olympic event since 1924.

Short-track speed skaters compete against each other on an oval track measuring 111.12 meters around. Four racers line up side-by-side at the start of the race and race each other, not the clock. They can pass each other at any time, but can't push. Racers attains speeds of 40 mph and more. Short-track speed skating became an Olympic event at the 1992 Games in Albertville, France.

Ten days of figure skating competition and four days of short-track speed skating will take place. About 14,000 spectators can fit in the Delta Center.

Oquirrh Park Oval

Ten speed-skating events will take place at this venue in the heart of the Salt Lake Valley, only 25 minutes from the Olympic Village (see our Parks and Recreation chapter for information about Oquirrh Park). In speed skating, athletes race against the clock. Events include men's and women's races ranging from 500 to 10,0000 meters. Speed skating has been an Olympic event since the 1924 Games in Chamonix, France. The speed-skating events will go on for 12 days, with a planned spectator capacity of 6,500.

E Center of West Valley City

The E Center is in West Valley City, a few

miles southwest of Salt Lake City and 16 minutes from the Olympic Village. You can read more about the E Center in the Spectator Sports chapter. Men and women's hockey competition will be held here. Ice hockey is a high-speed game with continual action and infrequent interludes of fisticuffs. Ice hockey teams have six players including one goalkeeper, two defense players and three forward players. The ice rink in hockey is surrounded by 1.2-meter high boards. Games consist of three 20-minute periods with two 15-minute intermissions. The purpose of the game is to hit more pucks into the opposing team's goal than they hit into yours. Any player who slashes, trips or roughs up another player is sent to the penalty box, and that player can't be replaced. Men's ice hockey has been an Olympic event since the 1924 Winter Olympic Games in Chamonix, France. Women's ice hockey was added at the 1998 Games in Nagano, Japan.

Many people move to Salt Lake City simply to savor the delights of our outdoor scene. No matter what your outdoor sport is, you'll find a place to do it in Salt Lake.

Parks and Recreation

Salt Lake is a haven for those who love outdoor fun. The nearby 11,000-foot Wasatch Mountains give Salt Lakers a world-class venue for hiking, mountain biking, camping, skiing, rock climbing, snow shoeing and snowboarding. Droves of folks have also taken up the more contemplative activities of watching wildlife and identifying wildflowers. Many people move to Salt Lake City simply to savor the delights of our outdoor scene. You'll find parks aplenty here. If indoor recreation is more to your liking, don't despair — you'll find plenty of recreation centers and gyms where you can swim, pump iron or shoot some hoops.

In this chapter we'll first look at parks and recreation centers, then we'll dive into the fabulous outdoor opportunities available in Salt Lake and the Wasatch Mountains. For information on skiing and winter sports, see the separate chapter that covers those subjects. The Park City chapter adds even more recreation options.

Parks

Salt Lakers love their parks. Whenever there's a glimmer of sun, you can find city residents barbecuing, talking to a long-lost cousin at a family reunion, jogging, playing tennis or just lounging around catching some rays. Despite rapid growth in the past decade, the city and county still offer most folks a place to enjoy themselves. Within the cozy confines of the Salt Lake Valley, you'll find dozens of parks where you can follow your bliss. Following is a description of the most popular and interesting parks and some of their specific features. Entrance to all parks is free, but if a park has a swimming pool, you'll pay a fee to swim. Fees are also charged for reserving a pavilion or picnic area for large groups. These fees differ for each park and the size of the group. Parks open at dawn and close at 10 PM, and alcoholic beverages are prohibited.

Dimple Dell Regional Park
10400 S. 1300 E., Sandy • 483-5473

This exciting natural park covers 644 acres and follows a natural corridor linking the foothills of the Wasatch with the Salt Lake Valley. Most of the park, which opened about five years ago, has been designated as an Urban Natural Area and Wildlife Preserve. The park features a 7-mile trail that starts in the foothills and ends at the Jordan River. Unfortunately, several roads interrupt the trail. Plans are afoot to build crossings, but it will take time and money. Planners hope this trail will one day be linked with other urban natural trails, such as the Bonneville Shoreline Trail and the Jordan River Parkway. This is a popular spot for horseback riding and an excellent area to observe native plants and watch birds and other wildlife. Deer often visit here in the winter.

International Peace Gardens at Jordan Park
1000 S. 900 W., Salt Lake City • 972-7860

What a stunning spot this is! This park combines a playground and tennis courts along with the singular beauty of the International Peace Gardens. Spread along the banks of the Jordan River, these gardens, statues and structures are dedicated to peace and universal brotherhood. The Gardens were started in 1939 by the Salt Lake Council of Women. Of special interest are the Danish gardens, which feature a Viking burial mound as well as a mermaid statue that's a replica of the original Hans Christian Anderson statue in the Danish Harbor. It's one of only four such replicas in the world. The Preaching Buddha of the Indian display shows great peace and spiritual beauty.

FYI

Unless otherwise noted, the area code for all phone numbers listed in this guide is 801.

Mormon leader Brigham Young's estate and was purchased by Salt Lake City in 1880. It's a popular spot for various events and festivals, such as the annual Belly Dancing Festival in August (see our Festivals and Annual Events chapter). The park draws an eclectic mix of Salt Lakers from different ethnic and professional backgrounds. Bird fanciers will flock to the privately operated Tracy Aviary, which harbors a wealth of rare and interesting avian life, including a fascinating display of exotic parrots (see our Kidstuff and Sightseeing and Attractions chapters). A fee is charged to play tennis and swim.

Jordan River Parkway
Jordan River through the Salt Lake Valley (700 W. to 100 W.) • 972-7860

The various government entities in the Salt Lake Valley have lagged behind other cities in creating parkways and walkways that follow rivers, valleys or other geographic features. The Jordan River Parkway is a wonderful exception. The parkway follows the gentle contours of the Jordan River through most of the length of the Salt Lake Valley — about 10 miles. You can canoe or fish in the river or jog, bike or Rollerblade along the pathway that borders it. If you're lucky, you might spot a beaver, a fox or a stately blue heron cavorting in the water or surrounding woods. Pavilions, playgrounds and picnic areas are found every mile or so. The Parkway is accessible to the disabled and has barrier-free areas.

Liberty Park
1300 S. 600 E., Salt Lake City • 972-7860

One of the oldest and biggest parks in the city, Liberty Park offers two playgrounds, a jogging and walking path, tennis courts, a swimming pool, horseshoe pits and some of the largest and stateliest cottonwood trees in Utah. The 110-acre park was originally part of

Memory Grove
370 N. Canyon Rd. 54 E., Salt Lake City • 972-7860

This secluded park covers both sides of Canyon Road in lower City Creek Canyon, south of the State Capitol. Dedicated to Utah's war dead, the area is scattered about with monuments, including a World War I cannon, name plaques inscribed with casualties of World War II and a lovely replica of the Liberty Bell. You can enjoy lovely gardens, ponds, and walking and jogging paths. A marble meditation chapel sits on a hill.

Murray City Park
5109 S. State St., Murray • 264-2614

Led by visionary former mayor Lynn Pett, Murray City has built a number of great parks and created strong, community-wide programs in recreation and the arts. Their effort and concern shows in this delightful park. From playgrounds, a swimming pool, an ice-skating rink and a jogging path, this park has it all. Cottonwood Creek meanders through the park, offering fishing and plenty of hungry

INSIDERS' TIP

Golfers visiting from sea-level regions love Salt Lake Valley courses. The thinner air of our mountain valley gives your drive an extra 20 to 40 yards distance. But don't start thinking you're Tiger Woods: The blazing Great Basin sun and low humidity dry out the greens, making them hard and fiendishly tricky, so you'll probably gain back the stroke you lost from that booming drive.

ducks to feed. Even more interesting is the John M. Hardle Memorial Arboretum, one of Utah's few arboretums, where you can view dozens of species of fascinating trees and shrubs, both native and non-native. A pathway winds through the park, with stone benches where you can rest. All trees are marked and identified. The Bristlecone pine is particularly worth looking at, since members of this species can live for 5,000 years, which makes them the oldest living organisms on earth. You can get a brochure that describes the trees from the Murray City Parks Department at 330 E. Vine Street, which is in the middle of Murray Park. During the summer you can watch plays and concerts in the park's amphitheater. The cost for these events is $5 for adults and $4 for children.

Oquirrh Park
5624 S. 4800 W., Salt Lake City
• 966-4229

This 50-acre complex has caught Olympic fever and is buzzing with excitement. Park officials are spending $40 million to build a new hockey rink and cover the existing 400-meter speed-skating oval and hockey rink. All three facilities will be used in the 2002 Winter Olympic games. Other facilities under construction include a 50-meter outdoor pool complex, an indoor climbing wall and a gymnasium with weight-lifting and aerobics rooms. Existing facilities include eight lighted outdoor tennis courts, swimming pools, lighted basketball and volleyball courts. Call for fees and hours.

Sugarhouse Park
1300 E. 2100 S., Salt Lake City
• 483-5473

With rose gardens and other extensive garden plots, Sugarhouse is one of the prettiest parks in the area. It's a treasure for those who live near it, with gorgeous views of the mountains, rolling hills, large open tracts of lawn and beautiful stands of blue spruce, the Utah state tree. Because of its size and lack of development, walkers and joggers crowd the jogging path, which winds its way around the perimeter of the park. Pavilions, volleyball courts and two playgrounds complete the park. The unob-

structed views make this one of the best places in Salt Lake for a picnic.

Recreation Centers and Amateur Sports

Salt Lake County Parks and Recreation maintains 12 recreation centers and fitness centers throughout the Salt Lake Valley. These facilities are safe, well-equipped and nicely maintained. The recreation centers provide game rooms, gymnasiums, racquetball and tennis courts, fitness facilities, swimming pools and so on. The centers also serve as community education centers where citizens can take classes in a variety of subjects, such as arts and crafts, aerobics, dance and karate. All Salt Lake County recreation centers have wheelchair-accessible features. Not all the centers offer the same facilities, and activity fees vary at each center.

In addition to the physical facilities, the centers are staffed with recreation professionals who oversee a mind-boggling array of athletic programs for youth, adult and senior citizens. If you're an amateur athlete, you can find a program or class for whatever you want. For youth, programs in 15 sports are offered, including baseball, flag football, indoor soccer, Junior Jazz basketball, ice hockey, softball, swimming, tennis and track. Adults can choose from baseball, basketball, racquetball, tennis and softball, among others. Senior citizen activities include bingo, ceramics, swimming and therapeutic exercise.

The county publishes an informative, 50-page brochure detailing the many activities and events they sponsor (including fees) and the location and phone numbers of all the parks and recreation centers. It also includes a list of 35 nonprofit sports organizations and their phone numbers. Call Salt Lake County Parks and Recreation at 468-2560 for more information and to request the brochure.

Outdoor Recreation

The Wasatch Mountains

Superb views. Plunging cliffs and rock-ribbed cornices. Snow-fed streams and waterfalls. Fields of lupine and mint, jealously guarded by dancing butterflies. If you like to hike, mountain bike, camp or just picnic, this is the kind of aesthetic bliss you'll find every time you venture into the Wasatch Mountains, just east of Salt Lake. These steep and rugged mountains offer miles of spectacular hiking and biking trails, hundreds of square miles of field and forest and three wilderness areas to wander in. You'll also find numerous camping and picnic areas. Visible from everywhere in the Valley, the Wasatch have molded the nature of Salt Lake both physically and spiritually and lie at the center of its identity as a city.

The Wasatch are cut by a number of canyons, most of which have permanent small streams flowing down them. You'll find most of the recreational possibilities in Little Cottonwood, Big Cottonwood and Mill Creek canyons. Since they're so close to a large population center, these three canyons are heavily used. On summer weekends popular trailheads and campgrounds are filled with cars by 10 AM. Some trails and picnic areas have become heavily impacted from excessive use. Mill Creek Canyon now charges a $2.25 for each car exiting the canyon. Park City is in Parleys Canyon.

To prevent further degradation, everyone who uses these mountains must understand the responsibility that comes from traveling in areas that appear rugged, but which are actually fragile and easily damaged. Please observe the following rules:

• Most of the Wasatch is a watershed. That means no dogs or horses are permitted in any of the canyons except Mill Creek Canyon. In general, dogs and the outdoors are a bad combination. Dogs chase game, bark and annoy others. Leave your pet at home. If you must bring your pet, keep it on a leash.

• If possible, use the toilet facilities at the trailhead or in picnic areas. If not, bury all human waste at least 6 inches deep and 200 feet from all water sources.

• Don't litter. If you pack it in, pack it out.

• If you're hiking or biking, stay on the trail. Taking shortcuts causes erosion.

• Limit the size of your group, if possible, and respect the serenity of nature during your visit. If you are in a group, be aware of the impact your presence has on others.

• Be prepared. This Boy Scout maxim means many things. It means wearing adequate clothing and boots, taking enough food and water, bringing a first aid kit and knowing where you are going. It also means you should be prepared for sudden and drastic changes in the weather (see the weather Close-up in the Area Overview chapter). Going from Salt Lake City at a 4,300-foot elevation to the mountains at a 10,000-foot elevation is equivalent to traveling to Canada. When it's warm and partly cloudy in the Valley, it might be pouring rain — a cold rain — in the mountains. If you're not used to high elevations, pace yourself. If you're from Kansas, hiking at 10,000 feet will take the wind out of your sails in a hurry. The Wasatch Mountains are steep, and many trails are physically demanding.

If you want a good guide book to the Wasatch mountains, read *Hiking the Wasatch* by John Veranth. This book, as well as maps and guides to the flora and fauna of the mountains, are available at Kirkham's Outdoor Products, 3125 S. State, 486-4161; or Recreational Equipment Inc. (REI), 3285 E. 3300 S., 486-2100. It's also available at local libraries.

Most of the Wasatch range is part of the Wasatch Cache National Forest, which puts it under the rules and regulations of the U.S. Forest Service. For more information and the latest rules, contact one of the following: Wasatch-Cache National Forest Supervisor, 8230 Federal Building, 125 South State Street, 524-5030; or the Salt Lake Ranger District, 6944 S. 3000 E., 943-1794.

Camping and Picnicking

It usually happens around Thursday afternoon. You realize with a shudder that if you have to answer one more phone call someone is going to get hurt bad. There's only one solution: You've got to get the heck out of Dodge. The canyons of the Wasatch offer abundant opportunity to flee

Photo: Utah Travel Council/Frank Jensen

The Albion Basin in the Wasatch National forest is one of many
spectacular mountain wonderlands near Salt Lake City.

civilization's discontents for picnicking and camping. Depending on the weather, the campgrounds in the area are open from May to November.

Big Cottonwood Canyon
7200 S. Wasatch Blvd. (3000 E.), Salt Lake City • (800) 280-2267

Big Cottonwood has six picnic areas and two campgrounds. The first picnic area, Oakridge, is just a mile or so up the canyon, and the farthest picnic area, Jordan Pines, is about 9 miles up the canyon. The same regulations for picnicking apply here as in Mill Creek, except you don't have to pay a fee to exit the canyon. The first campground you'll come to is Spruces, about 10 miles from the canyon's mouth. Spruces is a big campground, with 257 sites, and accommodates trailers and tents. Drinking water, visitor information and restrooms are provided. At 7,360

feet of elevation, the setting is lovely, with a stream, fishing and trails in the area. Try the nice hike up Days Fork. Some sites are first-come, first-served, and some sites can be reserved with a phone call. A single site for eight people or fewer is $11. Fees go up from there, depending on how many people you have in your group. The second Big Cottonwood campground is Redman, about 13.4 miles up the canyon. This smaller campground, at an elevation of 8,300 feet, has 76 sites, some of which you reserve and some of which are first-come, first-served. No group sites are available here, only single sites. You'll pay $10 a night for a campground. Restrooms and water are available.

Mill Creek Canyon
3800 S. Wasatch Blvd. (3000 E.), Salt Lake City • 483-5473

This canyon doesn't allow overnight camping, but you can find plenty of places to picnic. Mill Creek offers 11 places to gobble down your fried chicken or sample your pâté, from the Church Fork Picnic Area 3.2 miles up the canyon to Big Water Picnic Area, about 9 miles up the canyon. Picnicking is free for small groups, but you have to pay $2.25 per vehicle as you leave the canyon. Large group sites (from 50 to a 100 people) must be reserved in advance, and a fee is charged which varies from $50 to $100. Call for reservations.

Little Cottonwood Canyon
9000 S. Wasatch Blvd. (3000 E.), Salt Lake City • (800) 280-2267

Because of its forbidding cliffs and rugged terrain, this narrow canyon has room for little development in the lower part. Two huge ski resorts, Alta and Snowbird, occupy large portions of the canyon, so you won't be able to find a picnic table anywhere, and only two campgrounds — both small — have been built. The first, Tanner's Flat, is 4.4 miles up the canyon at an elevation of 7,100 feet. It has 59 sites, complete with restrooms and running water. You can fish, hike and watch birds in the area, which features tremendous views of the canyon walls. Albion Basin campground is at the end of the Little Cottonwood Canyon Road, about 11.3 miles from the mouth of the canyon. At 9,700 feet, Albion Basin is a special place, with some of the most magnificent displays of wildflowers in the Intermountain West. Albion Basin has restrooms and running water but only 28 spots, so get there early on weekends. A single unit at these two campgrounds costs $9 per night.

Hiking

Big Cottonwood Canyon
7200 S. Wasatch Blvd. (3000 E.), Salt Lake City

Long, lovely and wild, Big Cottonwood Canyon offers majestic scenery, hundreds of miles of great trails and two major ski resorts.

You could hike here for years (as we have) and not travel the same trail twice. The narrow, lower canyon is beautiful to drive through but offers few hiking trails. The upper canyon, scoured out by a glacier, is wider, with many smaller canyons that lead to alpine bowls with great views.

For an easy hike, try the Silver Lake Trail at Brighton, at the end of the Big Cottonwood Canyon Road, 15 miles from Wasatch Boulevard. Park at the Solitude Nordic Center parking lot across the street from the Brighton Store. Silver Lake is right in front of you. This lovely stroll takes you around the lake, through willows, meadows and riparian areas. Just follow the boardwalk around the lake. It's easy to spot trout in the clear streams that feed the lake.

For a bit more adventure, hike up to Twin Lakes. The trail starts at the base of the Millicent ski lift at Brighton and follows a service road from the Evergreen ski lift about 1.4 miles to the lake. The gorgeous trail meanders through limestone outcroppings bordered by fields of wildflowers. The original twin lakes are now one large lake, and the high mountain setting, surrounded by cliffs, is simply soul-stirring. You can continue on past the lakes to Twin Lakes Pass, about another 1.5 miles.

City Creek Canyon
375 North, Canyon Rd., Salt Lake City

For an easy hike on a paved road, try City Creek Canyon, which begins just north of the Utah State Capitol. You can park in one of the visitor parking lots at the Capitol or on Capitol Street, which runs east of the Capitol. Start walking on Bonneville Boulevard, a one-way street with a pedestrian and hiking path. It's a few hundred feet northwest of the Capitol. This street takes you to City Creek Canyon. You can also take Canyon Road (120 E. North Temple) to Memory Grove, then walk through the park to City Creek.

City Creek is a narrow, lush canyon that follows the stream 6 miles to Rotary Park and a large turnaround. You'll see dozens of varieties of native plants along the stream. It's also a prime area for bird watching — more than 100 species of birds have been spotted in the canyon. City Creek receives heavy traffic from joggers and bicyclists, as well as from hikers. Cars are allowed up the canyon on even-number days (with a reservation), and bicyclists are allowed on odd-numbered days only, and not on holidays. Foot traffic is allowed all the time.

To drive up to Rotary Park, call Salt Lake City Public Utilities at 483-6757.

Little Cottonwood Canyon
**9000 S. Wasatch Blvd. (3000 E.),
Salt Lake City**

For tremendous cliffs, rugged granite pinnacles and high peaks, this canyon can't be matched. Cut by a glacier, the U-shaped Big Cottonwood Canyon stretches a spectacular 10 miles from the foothills at 5,000 feet to Albion Basin at 9,000 feet, where it ends. Best-known as the home of world-famous ski resorts Alta and Snowbird, Little Cottonwood Canyon also provides superlative hiking. The best place to start is at Albion Basin, at the end of Little Cottonwood Canyon Road, about 11 miles from Wasatch Boulevard. Albion Basin is one of the best places in the Wasatch to see wildflowers during July and August, so it's very popular.

For a short, easy hike to a beautiful lake below cliffs, take the Secret Lake Trail. The hike starts from the west side of the Albion Basin campground. Park your car in the parking lot. The trail is marked. This is an excellent hike for children. As you walk, notice how the glacier that formed the canyon left scratches in the granite slabs. If you need a more strenuous workout, try Red Pine or White Pine lakes. These are the most popular hikes in the area, so you won't be alone. Both hikes start at the White Pine Trailhead, 5.5 miles up the canyon, and both take you into the Lone Peak Wilderness Area.

Red Pine Lake is a 3-mile hike with a 1,940-foot elevation gain, and White Pine is about 4.5 miles away, with a 2,460-foot elevation gain. The trailhead is paved and has restrooms. A path leads across a stream to a Jeep road. Follow the road for a mile, where the trail diverges to White Pine or Red Pine. Both trails

are wonderful, with panoramic views and scenery worthy of any postcard. If you enjoy looking at the devastation wrought by avalanches, hike up White Pine Canyon. In 1959 a massive avalanche in the canyon knocked down trees 300 years old, some as large as 3 feet in diameter. Remains of the destruction can still be seen.

Mill Creek Canyon
**3800 S. Wasatch Blvd. (3000 E.),
Salt Lake City**

Mill Creek Canyon is a narrow, heavily forested canyon with hikes that vary from steep and strenuous to easy strolls through the woods. Unlike Big and Little Cottonwood canyons, Mill Creek was formed by a stream instead of a glacier. Because of extensive damage to the canyon, overnight camping is forbidden, and every driver exiting the canyon pays a $2.25 fee. A good beginning trail is the Pipeline Trail, which follows an old flume line 5.5 miles up the canyon. You can get on the trail at Rattlesnake Gulch, 1.5 miles up the canyon, at Burch Hollow, 4.2 miles up the canyon or at Elbow Fork, 6.2 miles up the canyon. You can hike as far as you want, then turn around. An intermediate hike that leads you to the Mount Olympus Wilderness Area follows the Bowman Fork Trail. The 4-mile trail begins 4.7 miles up the canyon at the south end of the Terraces picnic area. The first mile of the hike follows Bowman Fork Creek through overhanging branches and past lush patches of elderberry, birch and serviceberry. The trail then leaves the stream and follows switchbacks to White Fir Pass, then passes Yellow Jacket Gulch to Baker Spring at 9,400 feet. You'll find an old stock watering trough here and the remains of a miner's cabin that burned down in the early 1980s. The water is good to drink, and you'll see beautiful displays of wildflowers if you come in July or August. From here, the trail ascends another mile to join Desolation Trail, which connects all the trails that run up Mill Creek and Big Cottonwood Canyons. White Fir Pass is 1.5 miles from the trailhead, with a 1,260-foot elevation gain, and Bakers Spring is 3 miles, with a 2,660-foot elevation gain.

To see the devastating power of avalanches, take a hike up the Porter Fork Trail to the base of Mount Raymond. Over the years a number of avalanches have thundered down from the peaks of Mount Raymond, including one in 1979 that the Forest Service says is the biggest ever in the Wasatch Mountains. You'll see piles of debris and huge trees snapped like toothpicks — a fearsome testimony to nature's fury. This hike begins on the Porter Fork Road, 4.2 miles up the canyon. This is a private road through a cabin area, but the public has a right-of-way for foot traffic. Respect private property and stay on the road. After hiking on the asphalt road for 1.5 miles, you'll walk on a Jeep road for a couple of miles to some mines. The trail continues another mile to the ridge where it joins the Desolation Trail and where you'll see the avalanche path. It's 3.5 miles to the Desolation Trail, with 3,660 feet of elevation gain, which makes it a pretty stiff hike for most people.

Mountain Biking

Excepting the Jordan River Parkway, Salt Lake City proper is utterly devoid of any decent place to bike. You'll find few bike paths, crowded roads, impatient drivers and little respect for bikers. However, the canyons of the Wasatch offer great mountain biking, with terrain that varies from steep, heart-stopping climbs and dangerous descents to mellow rides through sunny glades and deep forests. You can find both single-track and double-track riding in the area. Frequently, mountain bikers and hikers use the same paths. This leads to conflicts, so we recommend you practice courtesy and patience. Because of concerns about safety and erosion, some trails have already been closed to mountain bikes. Mountain bikers must ride responsibly if they want to avoid further restrictions of their sport. In addition to following the rules of etiquette listed under "Wasatch Mountains," mountain bikers must observe the following guidelines when mountain biking in the Wasatch Mountains.

• Yield the right of way to hikers and horseback riders. Slow down, move off the trail and allow hikers and horseback riders to pass. Horseback rides are only allowed in Mill Creek Canyon.

• Slow down around corners and don't skid down trails. This causes erosion. If you're skidding, slow down or get off your bike and walk.

• Like hikers, mountain bikers need to stay on the path. Ride directly over the waterbars on the trail. Stay off muddy areas. Mountain bikes are not allowed in wilderness areas.

• Always wear a helmet.

A superb guide book to mountain biking the Wasatch Mountains is *Mountain Biking Utah's Wasatch & Uinta Mountains* by Gregg Bromka. This comprehensive and artfully written book gives you 356 pages of detailed information on hundreds of trails in the area, along with good stuff about care of the environment, planning your trip and trail access policies. The book is available in bookstores and libraries.

Big Cottonwood Canyon
**7200 S. Wasatch Blvd. (3000 E.),
Salt Lake City**

The lower Solitude Ski Resort, about 12.7 miles up Big Cottonwood Canyon, beckons the intermediate rider with dramatic mountain vistas and challenging riding. Park in the lot by the Moonbeam Center and take the single track up a couple of hundred yards until you see a paved road with a gate. Climb the steep paved road until you come to the Roundhouse Restaurant. You might see chairs here on a patch of grass, so it's a fine place to rest. The views are sublime. When you've caught your breath, follow the main double-track road across the mountain. It's flat through here and easy riding. Keep pedaling until you come to a sign indicating a single track. Turn left and follow the single-track path as it cuts its way through Solitude's ski slopes back to the Moonbeam parking lot.

INSIDERS' TIP

Winters can be cold and snowy in the Salt Lake area, but you can almost always find a dry place to hike on the west-facing foothills around the University of Utah or on trails around the This is the Place Monument, 2601 East Sunnyside Avenue (800 S.).

Beginners looking for a satisfying outing can take the road up Silver Fork Canyon to Honeycomb Canyon. From the Moonbeam Center, pedal west to the Eagle Express Lift and go around it to the paved road. Power up the not-to-steep road through a private home area. The pavement ends at the beginning of Silver Fork Canyon. Follow the double track until it crosses a creek, then take the double track to the left. You'll go up a couple of hills, then come to a single track that goes left. You can take that trail to go back to the Moonbeam parking lot, or you can ride to the end of the road and explore some old mine ruins, then go back the way you came.

City Creek Canyon
375 North, Canyon Rd., Salt Lake City

See the "Hiking" section for a complete description of this canyon and how to get to it. This is a sweet ride and much beloved by Salt Lake cyclists. The trail isn't too steep, the access is easy, and the scenery is terrific. Because of the canyon's popularity, bicyclists are allowed on the road only on odd-numbered days and are prohibited on all holidays. From the mouth of the canyon to the Rotary Park turnaround is about 6 miles. Be courteous of hikers and joggers, and don't descend too fast — the canyon attracts a lot of families, dogs (which are only allowed the first 3 miles) and children.

Little Cottonwood Canyon
9000 S. Wasatch Blvd. (3000 E.), Salt Lake City

Albion Basin is a treasured spot for many Salt Lakers, and what better way to experience the delights of this mountain sanctuary than on a bike? It's easy, too — the Alta Parking lot to Albion Basin is an easy ride up a dirt road. The only kicker is the altitude. You'll start at about 9,000 feet, so if you're a flatlander, you'll start gasping for air as soon as you leave your vehicle. From the Alta ski resort's main parking lot, 8.1 miles up Little Cottonwood Canyon, just head up the Albion Basin dirt road. It's about 3 miles to the campground.

If you're there in July and August, you'll be overwhelmed by the display of wildflowers. Return the way you came, or take the Albion Meadows Trail, which branches off to your left

from the main dirt road as you're headed down the canyon. If you're lungs haven't yet collapsed, try the short but steep 2.5-mile Gad Mountain loop trail. From the main parking lot at Snowbird, pedal up the single-track Dick Bass Highway. You'll immediately plunge into the midst of mountain splendor, with crags, mountains and flowers all around. Bike on until you reach the Gad Valley Trail, near the Big Emma run. Descend to the Creek Road and back to the parking lot.

Mill Creek Canyon
3800 S. Wasatch Blvd. (3000 E.), Salt Lake City

The Big Water Trail will have you whistling "Zippity-do-dah" in no time. It's a glorious, 6.5-mile ride to Dog Lake, a small, alpine lake surrounded by trees. To get to the trailhead, go up Mill Creek Canyon and drive to the end of the road, about 9.6 miles. You'll find a large parking lot and restrooms. The ride to Dog Lake is easy and takes you through verdant forests and along pleasant switchbacks. Once you get to the lake, you can ride the short loop around it and head down the same way, or you can head out on a number of other branching trails. This is the most popular ride in the Wasatch, so be courteous and careful. Many hikers and equestrians use the trail as well.

For a trail with a bit more kick, try the Little Water Trail. It starts just above the head of Big Water Trail and hooks up with the Big Water Trail after about 3 miles, then takes you to Dog Lake. Little Water is much steeper than Big Water. Another great ride that won't tax you too much is the Upper Mill Creek Canyon Trail. Take the Big Water Trail and ride for 1.5 miles, then turn left on the Great Western Trail. After a bit you cross the Little Water Trail. From that point you can continue on for another 6 miles or so. Bikes are allowed on all trails in upper Mill Creek Canyon on odd-numbered days only.

Golf

Although some say it's a perfect way to spoil a nice walk, many Salt Lakers have caught the golf craze in a big way. In a word, they're fanatics. To paraphrase folk singer

John Prine, you can see hordes of folks knocking their Titleists and Maxflis around the old golf course at any time — even in the winter, if a spell of warm weather comes. (In Salt Lake warm in the winter means 45 degrees or more. We told you they're fanatics.) Unfortunately, the number of golf courses in the Salt Lake Valley is inadequate for the population, so trying to reserve a tee time can be frustrating. Salt Lake City has initiated a tee-time reservation service that allows you to reserve a tee time at any golf course operated by Salt Lake City 24 hours a day, seven days a week. Call 485-7730 for more information and to get a subscription form.

The various government entities in the Salt Lake Valley operate 16 public courses in the Valley. Salt Lake County's newest course is the Old Mill Golf Course, just opened in the spring of 1998. All the public courses in the Valley have snack bars, pro shops and equipment rentals. Courses open in the spring as soon as it's warm enough to play and close whenever it's too cold or snowy. Following are descriptions of some of the courses in the Valley (see our Park City chapter for additional courses).

Bonneville
954 S. Connor St. (2140 E.), Salt Lake City • 583-9513

This 18-hole course is nestled in the foothills of the Wasatch and offers splendid views of the Salt Lake Valley to the west and the Wasatch Mountains to the east. Golfers praise the oakbrush-covered hills and dales of Bonneville for their beauty and curse them for their cunning ability to reach out and grab passing golf balls. The first hole is legendary, a par 5 that dips from an elevated tee deep into a swale, then rises 300 yards to a postage stamp-sized green. The diabolical greens are slick, fast and very deceptive. Just remember one thing and you won't go crazy: All putts break toward the Mormon Temple in downtown Salt Lake. Bonneville has a driving range, and greens fees are $20 for 18 holes daily. Cart fees are $20 for 18 holes daily.

Glendale
1630 W. 2100 S., Salt Lake City • 974-2403

If you want a course with broad fairways, short rough and few trees — a place where you can unleash the titanium driver and show your friends what a Tiger Woods drive looks like — come to Glendale. This 18-hole course is long and lean and doesn't penalize the long but errant drive. Three lakes dot the course, which is bisected by the Jordan River. Greens fees are $17 for 18 holes Monday through Thursday and $18 Friday through Sunday and on holidays. You'll pay $20 for a cart for 18 holes. The course has a very nice driving range.

Forest Dale
2375 S. 900 E., Salt Lake City • 483-5420

Forest Dale reigns as the aging but still vital matriarch of Salt Lake City courses. Established in 1904, it's a mature, 9-hole course with big trees, wide fairways and water that comes into play on three holes. It's an excellent course for beginners. Greens fees are $8 Monday through Thursday and $8.50 Friday through Sunday and on holidays. A cart costs $10.

Meadow Brook
4197 S. 1300 W., Murray • 266-0971

Established in 1952, Meadow Brook is an easy 18-hole course that beginners will feel comfortable starting out on. The course

INSIDERS' TIP

Like to ride or watch BMX races? Head out to the county BMX track at the Welby Gravel Pit on the Old Bingham Highway, 9730 S. 5250 W. in West Jordan. You can watch races April through October, schedule practice time and learn about BMX racing. Call 964-6502 for more information.

has a driving range. Greens fees are $17 for 18 holes Monday through Thursday and $18 for 18 holes Friday through Saturday. Cart rentals are $9.50 per person for 18 holes.

Mick Riley
421 E. Vine St. (4700 S.), Murray
• 266-8185

A charming course with mature trees and lots of water, Mick Riley offers fun play for everyone. You'll find two courses here, a 9-hole regular course and a 9-hole par 3 course. A driving range is available. Greens fees for the regular course are $8 Monday through Thursday and $8.50 Friday through Sunday. Rates for the par 3 course are $5 Monday through Thursday and $6 Friday through Sunday and holidays. The course has a driving range.

Mountain Dell Canyon Course and Mountain Dell Lake Course
3287 Cummings Rd., Salt Lake City
• 582-3812

Local golfers acclaim Mountain Dell as the prettiest public course in the area. Located in a lovely mountain valley, it's beautiful anytime, but particularly nice in the spring, when snow covers the surrounding mountain peaks and the dense thickets of black hawthorne bloom with white flowers. Hawks circle overhead, perhaps waiting for an errant drive to stun a rabbit. Mil-

lions of groundhogs live under the fairways, which are pockmarked with holes. Is it time to call Bill Murray? You can choose between an 18-hole mountain course and an 18-hole lake course. On both courses, you'll get your exercise — everything is on a slope, including the undulating greens. Rent a cart if you're not in good shape. Greens fees for both courses are $18 for 18 holes Sunday through Thursday and $20 for 18 holes Friday through Sunday and on holidays. Carts go for $20 for 18 holes every day.

Nibley Park
2730 S. 700 E., Salt Lake City• 483-5418

After Forest Dale, this 9-hole course is the oldest in Salt Lake. Established in 1922, Nibley is short, with no real par 5s, but don't be deceived: This tricky little number will make you understand why golf is called a target game. Stay on the fairway or you'll become intimately acquainted with some of the largest cottonwood trees in the Valley. If the trees don't get you at Nibley, the water will. Two lakes and a stream come into play on seven holes. Even worse, the ducks that inhabit those waters are quite vicious and often refuse to allow lost balls to be retrieved. You must resist the temptation to bonk them on the head with your driver. Nibley has a driving range, and greens fees are $8 Monday through Thursday and $8.50 Friday through Sunday and holidays; carts cost $8.50 daily.

Rose Park
1386 N. Redwood Rd., Salt Lake City
• 596-5030

What other Salt Lake golf courses may lack in sand is more than made up for by Rose Park's Saharan terrain. Maybe the availability of huge quantities of sand at the nearby sand and gravel pits was more temptation than the architect could withstand. Whatever the case, at least 13 holes have sand traps, so bring your wedge. Greens fees are $17 for 18 holes Monday through Thursday and $18 for 18 holes Friday through Sunday and holidays. Carts rent for $20 for 18 holes all the time. A driving range is available.

Riverbend
12765 S. 1100 W., Riverton • 253-3673

Built along the Jordan River, this 18-hole course opened in 1994, which makes it one of the newest golf courses in the state. The front nine is a links-style course with open fairways, few trees, lots of sand and rolling hills. The back nine is more an American style course, with narrow fairways and lots of trees, which of course are still small. It's in excellent shape for a new course. Greens fees for 18 holes are $19 on Monday through Thursday and $20 on Friday through Sunday and holidays. Carts rent for $9.50 per person for 18 holes. You can practice on a nice driving range.

West Ridge
5055 S. West Ridge Blvd. (5600 W.),
West Valley City • 966-4653

This hilly, links-style course offers interesting holes and a superb view of the Salt Lake Valley. As in any links course, the wind can whip up problems, but what's golf without challenges? Located in the foothills of the Oquirrh Mountains, the 18-hole course is home to fox, deer and a variety of birds, in-

cluding the rare burrowing owl. Course pro Mike Richards and superintendent John Brubaker have done a great job in turning this former gravel pit into one of Utah's finest golf courses. Greens fees are $16 Monday through Friday and $18 Saturday, Sunday and holidays. Carts rent for $18 for 18 holes. A driving range is available.

Wingpointe
3602 W. 100 S. • 575-2345

This new 18-hole, links-style course is right by the airport, so expect noise. But if you want to golf like they do in Scotland, this is as close as you'll come in Utah. It's a beautifully designed, tough course — long, with lots of water. Greens fees are $20 for 18 holes daily, and carts rent for $30 for 18 holes daily. A driving range is available.

Rock Climbing

With vertical walls of rock just minutes away from downtown, the Salt Lake area attracts climbers because of its challenging terrain and easy access. Climbers in Salt Lake will find quartzite walls, mainly in Big Cottonwood Canyon, and granite walls, mainly in Little Cottonwood Canyon. Some good guidebooks on rock climbing in the Salt Lake Valley are *Wasatch Climbing — North* by Bret and Stuart Ruckman, *Wasatch Quartzite* by John W. Gottman and *Wasatch Granite* by Dave Smith. *How to Rock Climb* by John Long is a good introduction to the sport.

Techniques and climbing styles differ for quartzite and granite, and you'll find out how to handle both in climbing classes. If you're adventurous and fit, you have a number of options to learn this challenging — and dangerous — sport. We've included information on several of the leading rock-climbing centers.

INSIDERS' TIP

A fabulous place to take a hike in Salt Lake City is along the Jordan River Parkway, which stretches most of the length of the Jordan River. The river flows through the heart of the Salt Lake Valley. You can access the Jordan River Parkway at many points. You'll find solitude, paved paths and picnic tables and see many different kinds of birds. If you're lucky, you might even spot a fox, raccoon or beaver.

Extreme Sports Center
8700 S. Sandy Parkway, Sandy
• 562-1400

This center offers instruction for beginners through advanced. It has a three-story rock-climbing wall for practice with six ropes up the wall offering numerous possible routes and levels of difficulty.

Exum Mountain Adventures
7350 S. Wasatch Blvd. (3000 S.), Salt Lake City • 272-7338

This innovative company will help you realize any of your outdoor dreams, from learning how to rock climb to helping you achieve challenging alpine expeditions. Exum is the only outfitter whose training all takes place outdoors. They're instructors are licensed to teach classes and guide in both Big and Little Cottonwood Canyons. Their skilled guides can teach snowshoeing, alpine and backcountry skiing, as well as rock climbing.

Rockreation Sport Climbing Center
2074 E. 3900 S., Salt Lake City
• 278-7473

The staff here offers a great variety of classes for beginners, intermediate and expert climbers. Expert climbers will teach you to belay, tie knots and lead climb and fill you in on what all that shiny cool gear is used for. More importantly, they'll teach you how to not fall down hundreds of feet to your certain death. Rockreation has a 43-foot-high lead tower with a number of good routes from easy to extremely difficult.

The Wasatch Front Rock Gym
427 W. 9160 S., Sandy • 565-3657

You can choose from a wide variety of classes, including a basics skills class in rope handling, belaying and general safety. They also offer a kid's night on Monday from 6:30 to 8:30 PM where kids 6 to 12 can learn bouldering and basic rock-climbing techniques. The Front Rock Gym has lots of walls to practice on, including a 40-foot lead wall, some bouldering walls, a crack simulator and a "woody" that helps climbers improve their holds.

Gone Fishin'

Utahns are avid fisherfolk. Most Utahns head to the vast hinterlands of the state to angle, but stay-at-homes have a number of places to try their luck. One popular place is the Jordan River, where you can catch carp, catfish and a few trout. Fishing for trout is best toward the south end of the Valley, south of 9000 South. The streams flowing out of Mill Creek Canyon, Big and Little Cottonwood canyons and Emigration Canyon are all planted with pan-size rainbow trout and receive a fair amount of attention from anglers.

Mill Creek has some nice fishable areas, especially towards the top part of the canyon. Park in one of the campgrounds along the road and start walking up or down the creek. A good place to fly fish is about 6 miles up Big Cottonwood Canyon, where the canyon flattens out and some nice marshy areas appear. This is also the case near the Jordan Pines picnic area, about 9 miles up the canyon.

Many people love fishing in Silver Lake and the streams feeding the lake. Silver Lake is at Brighton, at the end of the Big Cottonwood Canyon Road.

If you don't mind a two-hour hike where you gain 2,000 feet of elevation, try Red Pine or White Pine lakes in Big Cottonwood Canyon. Some big fish lurk in the aquamarine depths of these high-altitude lakes. See the "Hiking" section for a description of how to get to those lakes.

Fishing licenses are required for everyone older than 14 who fishes in Utah. A resident fishing license costs $25 and is good for a year. A nonresident can also purchase a one-day license for $5 or a seven-day license for $15. In addition to a license, residents and nonresidents alike must also purchase something called a Wildlife Habitation Authorization, which costs $5. This document is new, and sounds to us like a sneaky way to increase license fees. You can buy a license at any sporting goods store or fishing shop in the area (see the Shopping chapter).

Tennis

Tennis is popular among Salt Lakers, and you'll find courts all over the place. Most of the 21 public high schools in the Valley have courts, which are free to the public and available on a first-come, first-served basis. Look in the white pages of the phone book under "Schools, Public" to find the addresses of these high schools.

Salt Lake County Parks and Recreation administers tennis courts at 20 locations in the Salt Lake Valley. You can call the county at 468-2560 to get the address of the court nearest you. These courts are also free to the public and don't require reservations. The county also gives lessons and offers wheelchair tennis.

Salt Lake City maintains courts at 23 locations, including eight courts at Glendale Park, 1200 W. 1700 S.; eight courts at 11th Avenue Park, 11th Avenue and M Street; 16 courts at Liberty Park (eight of which are lit at night), 1300 S. 600 E.; and eight courts at Dee Smith Park, 1216 S. Wasatch Drive. Call Salt Lake City Parks at 972-7800 for the location of the other tennis courts. Tennis is free at all of the Salt Lake City facilities except at Liberty Park and Dee Smith, both of which have pro shops. Liberty Park charges $3 an hour, and Dee Smith charges $4 an hour.

For those really into the game, the Utah Tennis Association at 5280 S. 320 W., 268-0505, is a good organization to join. The UTA organizes competitive tournaments throughout the state all year. Winter tournaments are played indoors. The group also organizes leagues for players of all ages and every ability level.

Swimming

Casual swimmers, devoted exercise buffs, sunbathers and those who just want to watch the kids splash around in a public swimming pool will find abundant opportunity in Salt Lake Valley. Public indoor pools are available at 11 high schools and junior high schools scattered about the Valley, including the Murray Community Swimming Pool, 5440 South State, 264-7412; the Granite High Swimming Pool, 3505 S. 500 E., 481-7159; and the Mount Jordan Middle School, 9360 S. 300 E., 412-2070. Swimming hours vary at every location, since the rules and regulations are set by different school districts, but in general open plunge hours in the winter

are from 7 to 9 PM on weekdays and from 11 AM to 6 PM on Saturday. Open plunge hours in the summer, when school isn't in session, are roughly 1 to 5 PM and 7 to 9 PM on weekdays and 11 AM to 6 PM on Saturday. None of these pools is open on Sunday. You won't pay much to swim — usually just a couple of bucks for an adult and 50¢ to $1 for children — but fees vary at each pool. These pools all have shallow areas for children, with lifeguards always on duty. No concessions are available, except for vending machines. Lessons are available at all of these pools, as is lap swimming and water aerobics. Lap swimming is usually from 5 to 6 PM both summer and winter with additional hours in the morning during the summer. Aerobic swimming hours vary at each location.

In addition, Salt Lake County Parks and Recreation maintains 18 public pools throughout the Valley. Some of the pools are indoor and some outdoor. All county pools offer swimming lessons, lap swimming, water aerobics and therapeutic water exercise. Therapeutic exercise programs are designed to increase flexibility and range of motion for people suffering from various ills such as arthritis, knee and back problems and amputations. All instructors at all Salt Lake County pools are certified by the American Red Cross. All Salt Lake County outdoor pools are open daily from Memorial Day through Labor Day. Indoor pools are open year around. Call 468-2560 for programs, hours and locations of these 18 facilities.

One of the nicest of the county facilities is the Cottonwood Heights Recreation Center, 7500 S. 2700 W., 943-3190. You can take beginning scuba classes and participate in synchronized swimming. It has a 50-meter outdoor pool, two 25-meter indoor pools and two diving pools with 10-meter diving towers. All of these pools except the diving pools have areas for children, and all have both low and high diving boards. One of the indoor pools was specially designed for therapeutic swimming, and the water temperature is a jacked up a bit for that purpose. The open plunge hours for the two indoor pools are noon to 1 PM on Monday, Wednesday and Friday; 2 to 4 PM on

Wednesday and Friday, 7 to 9 PM Monday through Thursday, noon to 9:30 PM on Saturday and noon to 4 PM on Sunday. The outdoor pool is open from noon to 8 PM Monday through Saturday and noon to 5 PM on Sunday. The outdoor pool has sunbathing areas. A snack bar is open in the summer, and vending machines are available year round. The admission fee is $4 for adults and $2.75 for seniors and youth. Special group rates are available for groups seven and larger.

You'll also enjoy the Steiner Aquatic Center, 645 South Guardsman Way (1600 E.), 583-9713, just south of the University of Utah. The facilities include one 50-meter outdoor pool and one 25-yard indoor pool. Each pool has both low and high diving boards and children's areas. Open plunge for the indoor pool is 7 to 9 PM Monday through Friday, 1 to 3 PM on Friday, noon to 6 PM on Saturday and noon to 4 PM on Sunday. Open plunge for the outdoor pool is 5:30 AM to 8 PM. Sunbathing areas area available. An outdoor concession stand is open during the summer, and snacks such as candy bars, soft drinks and potato chips are available year round in vending machines. Admission is $3 for adults, $1.75 for children and $2 for seniors.

Horseback Riding

Lots of people have horses in Salt Lake Valley, even though it's hard to find a place close by to ride a horse. Most of the Wasatch Mountains east of Salt Lake are watershed areas and don't allow horses or dogs. Dimple Dell Regional Park in Sandy offers some horseback riding, as does Butterfield Canyon in the far southwestern corner of the Salt Lake Valley and various portions of the Jordan River Parkway.

Salt Lake County Parks and Recreation maintains an equestrian park at 10800 South, South Jordan, 254-0106, which serves as a hub for horse fanciers in the Salt Lake Valley (see the "Get Wild" section of our Kidstuff chapter). Included among the facilities and services are stall and walker rentals, arena rentals with stock set up, a three-quarter-mile, year-round race track, grandstand, grounds rentals and a sewer dump. You can watch flat track, barrel and chariot racing.

To rent a horse, go to Valley View Riding Stables, 17000 S. 1300 W., Bluffdale, 253-9088, or Scamper Stables, 3059 W. 14750 S., Bluffdale, 254-6008. These private companies will give you lessons and take you for tours in areas in the southwestern part of the Salt Lake Valley, including some beautiful parts of the Jordan River Parkway and Butterfield Canyon.

No matter what amazing stories you've heard about Utah's incredibly light, powder snow, you've simply got to plunge down the mountain to understand why skiing in the Wasatch Mountains is so unique.

Skiing and Winter Sports

Utah's Wasatch Mountains are renowned for great skiing terrain, sunny skies, easy access and — most of all — powder snow. You can even read it on our license plates: The Greatest Snow on Earth. But these words don't mean a thing until you've experienced the ecstasy of floating down a hill on thigh-deep powder or carved turns so effortlessly you think you're falling through air. No matter what amazing stories you've heard about Utah's incredibly light, powder snow, you've simply got to plunge down the mountain to understand why skiing in the Wasatch Mountains is so unique.

What makes Utah's snow so special? As in real estate, it's location, location, location. The mountains are right where they need to be to reap the abundant snows that come every year. Each winter, storms rise from the warm waters of the Pacific Ocean, and the prevailing westerly winds push these storms eastward toward Utah. The Sierra Nevada Mountains take their share of the snow, then the clouds pass across the arid Great Basin. There, the hot sun and dry air claim more moisture. When the clouds crash into the steep slopes of the Wasatch, the remaining moisture cools rapidly as the clouds rise, and the mountains harvest a bounty of fluffy snow — up to 500 inches a year.

You can ski at seven downhill resorts in the Salt Lake and Park City area, all within 40 miles of the Salt Lake International Airport. Snowbird and Alta are located in Little Cottonwood Canyon, while Brighton and Solitude are in the next canyon to the north, called Big Cottonwood Canyon. These canyons are just east of Salt Lake City. Deer Valley, The Canyons (formerly Wolf Mountain) and the Park City Mountain Resort all are in the Park City area, which is some 32 miles east of Salt Lake. See the Getting Here, Getting Around chapter for information on how to navigate Salt Lake City streets and how to get to Park City. That chapter also tells you about the types of transportation, such as shuttles and private buses, that can take you to the resorts from the Salt Lake International Airport.

In addition to downhill skiing and snowboarding , you can find dozens of places in the nearby mountains to snowshoe or cross-country ski. This chapter will explore all of these possibilities and give you information you need to pick the type of winter recreation best suited to your abilities, interests and financial situation.

For information about lodging, restaurants, child care and so on, see the appropriate chapters for Salt Lake City facilities; if you're interested in Park City, see the chapter devoted to all aspects of that area. Our Mountain Resorts chapter has additional information on the resorts described in this chapter.

Children's ski schools and other skiing adventures for children, including information on the Utah Winter Sports Park, are covered in the Kidstuff chapter.

All seven of the resorts listed in this chapter rent skis and snowboards, assuming snowboarding is allowed, which isn't always the case. Prices range from around $18 for a basic package of skis, boots and poles to $35 for high-performance skis, boots and poles. If you're a beginner to intermediate skier, the basic package will suit you fine. A basic ski package for a child rents for around $12. Renting a snowboard and boots will set you back around $25 to $30. If you're coming in from out of state and you plan on renting equipment, you don't need to call ahead — the resorts have plenty of equipment to meet everyone's rental needs.

If you have your own ski equipment, all the resorts can tune-up and repair your skis and snowboards. None of the resorts rent ski clothes, such as parkas or gloves, so you'll have to bring your own or rent some from one of the ski shops in Salt Lake or Park City. Among the shops that rent ski clothing in Salt Lake and Park City are Utah Ski and Golf, 134. W. 600 S., 355-9088; and Ski Rentals, 102 W. 500 S., 595-0407. The Park City address and phone number for Utah Ski and Golf is 1255 Empire Avenue, (435) 655-8367; for Ski Rentals the address and phone number are Park City Mountain Resort, (435) 649-9690.

FYI

Unless otherwise noted, the area code for all phone numbers listed in this guide is 801.

Downhill Skiing and Snowboarding

Cottonwood Canyon Resorts

Alta
Little Cottonwood Canyon • 742-3333, lodging 942-0404

This legendary resort opened in 1938 and offers some of the most challenging skiing terrain in the world. A former mining town, Alta is blanketed by the most consistent snow in the world, receiving some 500 inches of powder every winter. Expert ski runs such as Devil's Castle and Greeley Bowl draw thousands of hotshot skiers from all over the world to race down the steep slopes. But be advised: These runs are for topnotch skiers only. If you fall, you won't stop for a long time. However, Alta isn't for experts only — beginners and intermediate skiers can all find terrain suitable for their level of expertise.

Alta has resisted development over the years and has remained relatively unchanged, much to the pleasure of local skiers. It's the least expensive resort in the Cottonwood canyons. Alta classifies its terrain as 25 percent beginner, 40 percent intermediate and 35 percent advanced. Snowboards are not allowed.

Location and Transportation: Alta is at the end of State Highway 210, at the top of Little Cottonwood Canyon. It's about 33 miles southeast of the Salt Lake International Airport.

Lifts, Schedule and Prices: Alta is open from mid-November to mid-April. The resort has six double lifts, two triples and four surface tows, all of which are open daily from 9:15 AM to 4:30 PM. An all-day lift ticket is $28; a half-day ticket is $21 for morning (9:15 AM to 1 PM) or afternoon (1 to 4:30 PM). Seniors 80 and older ski for free. For a snow report, call 572-3939.

Ski School and Rentals: Skiing pioneer Alf Engen founded the Alf Engen Ski School in 1948 (see our Kidstuff chapter). This school was recently rated one of the best in the country by *Travel and Leisure Magazine*. The school offers daily morning and afternoon lessons for adults and teens. Reservations for private lessons are recommended. Alta offers four ski shops (Alta Sports, Deep Powder House, Goldminer's Daughter and the Alta Peruvian Lodge) where you can rent whatever ski equipment you need. Call the ski school at 742-2600.

INSIDERS' TIP

For a special treat, cross-country skiers or snowshoers at Solitude can follow a guide to a Mongolian yurt and enjoy a gourmet dinner. For reservations and information, call (801) 536-5709.

Brighton
Big Cottonwood Canyon Hwy.
• **(800) 873-5512, ski school**
(800) 873-5512, Ext. 234

Like Alta, Brighton is a former mining town. Nestled in a valley and surrounded by mountain crags, Brighton is relatively undeveloped and still retains a low-key ambiance. Funky log cabins and small hotels are scattered around the small valley, and hiking trails take off in every direction. In the summer, small lakes, marshy wetlands and flower-filled meadows complete the tranquil scene. During the winter, a thick mantle of snow blankets Brighton, creating a fairyland scene right out of *Heidi*.

Skiing began in the area around 1936. Along with Alta, Brighton is the favorite resort for locals and the place many Utahns first learn to ski. With an average annual snowfall of 500 inches, Brighton offers all types of skiing terrain. The resort classifies its ski runs as 21 percent beginner, 40 percent intermediate and 39 percent advanced. Snowboarding is encouraged.

Location and Transportation: Brighton is at the top of Big Cottonwood Canyon, about 35 miles southeast of the Salt Lake International Airport.

Lifts, Schedule and Prices: Brighton is open from early November through late April. The resort offers two high-speed quad lifts, two triple chairlifts and three double chairlifts. The lifts are open from 9 AM to 4 PM daily. An all-day lift pass costs $29; no half-day passes are available. Children 10 and younger ski free if accompanied by a paying adult. If you're older than 70, you can also ski for free. Night skiing and snowboarding are available from mid-December through early April from 4 to 9 PM. The lift pass for night skiing is $20. Discounts are offered for groups of 25 or more skiers.

Ski School and Rentals: Brighton offers a number of programs for skiers of all ability levels, ranging from private lessons to group lessons and clinics. You can rent anything you need, including a snowboard and accessories, from Brighton Mountain Sports.

Snowbird
Little Cottonwood Canyon
• **(800) 385-2002**

Snowbird is the biggest and most developed ski resort in the Cottonwood canyons, with a number of condominiums, lodges and restaurants, as well as the first aerial tramway in Utah. After years of protest by environmentalists who feared the destruction of Little Cottonwood Canyon, Snowbird opened for business in the early 1970s. Like Alta, Snowbird is a shrine for hardcore powder buffs. Double-black-diamond runs such as Silver Fox, Great Scot and Gad Chutes challenge the most athletic and experienced skier and should only be tried by true experts. With 3,240 feet of vertical drop, Snowbird boasts the longest ski hills serviced by lifts in Utah. Forty-five percent of Snowbird's runs are rated advanced, with 30 percent intermediate and 25 percent beginner. Five hundred inches of powder snow fall annually at the resort.

Snowboarding is encouraged at the snowboard park near the Little Cloud run.

Location and Transportation: Snowbird is near the top of Little Cottonwood Canyon, about a mile below Alta and 31 miles from the Salt Lake International Airport. The reservations office for this resort is at 7350 S. Wasatch Boulevard, Salt Lake City. The reservations number is listed above.

Lifts, Schedules and Prices: In a normal snow year Snowbird is open from November to June. Skiers are transported up the mountain by one quad lift, seven double-chairlifts and one tram that has a capacity of 125 people. The lifts run daily from 9 AM to 4 PM. An adult all-day pass, including the tram, costs $47. An adult all-day pass for lifts only costs $39. An adult half-day pass, including the tram, costs $32; for lifts only the half-day price is $32. Children 12 and younger ski free, and seniors receive a discounted price of $27 for chairlifts only and $34 for chairlifts and tram. The snowline for slope conditions is 742-2222, Ext. 4285.

Ski Schools and Rentals: Snowbird has a staff of 200 certified instructors who offer group and private lessons to skiers of all ability levels, including first timers, women, seniors, snowboarders and skiers with special physical needs. A complete ski and snowboard rental service is available.

Solitude
1200 Big Cottonwood Canyon, Solitude
• **(800) 748-4754**

As was the case in most parts of the Wasatch Mountains, the Solitude area was the scene of intense mining for gold and silver, although no town was every developed in this part of Big Cottonwood Canyon. The resort, which opened its first lift in 1959, stretches for a couple of miles along the edge of the Big Cottonwood Canyon highway. In the last few years Solitude has changed ownership, and a number of new condominiums and restaurants have been built here. With 450 inches of annual snowfall, skiers can find varied terrain that ranges from gentle beginner slopes to expert powder bowls. Solitude's ski runs are rated as 20 percent beginner, 50 percent intermediate and 30 percent advanced. Snowboarding is permitted.

Location and Transportation: Solitude is near the top of Big Cottonwood Canyon, about 33 miles southeast of the Salt Lake International Airport. It's just a couple of miles down the canyon from Brighton.

Lifts, Schedule and Prices: Snow conditions permitting, Solitude opens in early November and closes in late April. Lifts run daily from 9 AM to 4 PM. The resort offers skiers one high-speed quad, two triple chairlifts and four double chairlifts. An all-day pass costs $36, and a half-day pass (12:30 to 4 PM) costs $30. Children 10 and younger and adults 70 and older ski for free. To get a snow report, call 536-5777.

Ski School and Rentals: The celebrated Norwegian ski instructor Leif Grevle has created a variety of ski school programs for skiers and snowboarders that are available for all ages and abilities. You can rent ski gear and snowboard equipment at two rental shops. Call the ski school at 536-5730.

Park City Resorts

The Canyons
4000 Park West Dr., Park City
• (800) 754-1636

The Canyons, formerly know as Wolf Mountain (and Park West before that), is Utah's newest resort and the site of six new lifts, a new lodge and even a gondola. The new owners, American Skiing Company of Bethel, Maine, recently completed $18.2 million in improvements. The new construction includes three high-speed detachable quad lifts, two fixed-grip quad lifts and an eight-passenger gondola. The resort also increased snowmaking capacity. The Canyons offers skiing for all ability levels, with superb expert terrain and excellent beginner and intermediate runs. The resort leads Utah in snowboarding and has constructed a number of snowboarding terrain parks (one of which is lighted at night), that feature jumps, moguls and log and rail slides. This resort receives 300 inches of snow and rates its terrain as 16 percent beginner, 38 percent intermediate and 46 percent advanced.

Location and Transportation: The Canyons is just west of Park City, about 28 miles from the Salt Lake International Airport.

Lifts, Schedule and Prices: During a normal snow year, The Canyons is open from mid-December to mid-April. Skiers are transported by one gondola, three high-speed detachable quad chairlifts, three fixed-grip quad chairlifts and two double chairlifts. The lifts are open daily from 9 AM to 4 PM. A full-day lift pass for adults costs $47, and a half-day pass (12:30 to 4 PM) costs $36. An all-day lift pass for a child (12 and younger) costs $23; and a child's half-day pass costs $18. If you're 65 or older, you can ski all day for $23.

Ski School and Rentals: The Canyons is home to the "Perfect TurnT" program, which aims to ensure all skiers enjoy the sport more and make their best better. Ski and snowboard gear is available at the lodge.

Deer Valley
Park City • (435) 649-1000, reservations (800) 424-3337

Deer Valley is the poshest — and most expensive — resort in Utah. If you like to be pampered, Deer Valley is for you. The excellent service begins as soon as you arrive. A helpful Deer Valley employee will park your car, unload your skis and transport you to the

Avalanches and Winter Safety

The Wasatch Mountains east of Salt Lake City offer unsurpassed beauty and endless possibilities for winter fun, but you must respect their power. Behind the smile of a sunny winter day waits a bite that can be fatal. Storms can blow in quickly, bringing violent winds and blizzard conditions that can lay down 5 feet of snow in a day. If you're not prepared, a trip that starts out fun and frolicsome can suddenly turn miserable — or worse.

Avalanches are an ever-present threat for the backcountry traveler. Hundreds of snow slides cascade down the steep ridges and snow-packed glacial cirques of the

Wasatch every winter. Their power is awesome. They travel at hundreds of miles an hour, snapping off huge trees, moving boulders as big as houses and laying waste to whatever is in their paths. Unfortunately, every season a few unlucky cross-country skiers and snowshoers are caught in the terrifying flood of snow, rocks and trees. Statistics show that fewer than 5 percent of victims caught in an avalanche survive.

— continued on next page

Photo: Bryan Larsen

An avalanche devastated this Utah mountainside in a
furious cascade of snow, rock and other debris.

When you venture into backcountry, you must be ready to encounter bad weather and to survive an avalanche. Following a few simple rules will help you enjoy the magic of the winter woods and return home safely.

• Dress properly and carry safety equipment. You should dress in layers of wool or polypropylene clothing and have a good weatherproof jacket and pants. A warm cap and gloves are mandatory. In addition, you should take along waterproof matches, a candle, fire-starter, a knife, a signal mirror, a space blanket (a lightweight Nylon survival blanket), a map and a compass. A first-aid kit must also be part of your baggage, as well as a small snow shovel and an avalanche transceiver. A transceiver will allow you to be found quicker, should you be buried by an avalanche.

• Take enough to eat and drink. Cross-country skiing and snowshoeing burn a lot of calories. You need a lot of high-energy foods and water to keep you going. Take extra in case you're stranded for a night. You'll need from 2 to 4 quarts of water or other liquid a day. A backpacking stove is handy to melt snow for water so you don't have to carry as much.

• Understand the effects of high altitude. If you're not used to the high elevation (10,000 feet and higher) and thin air of Utah's ski county, you should be cautious about taking long trips. At 10,000 feet, the air's oxygen level is only two-thirds that of air at sea level. The symptoms of altitude sickness are fatigue and weakness, loss of appetite, nausea and drowsiness. If you experience these symptoms, stop and rest, drink fruit juice or eat a candy bar. Then, make your way down the mountain.

• Be aware of hypothermia. Hypothermia is the scientific name for a drop in body temperature. It usually occurs in windy and rainy weather. Although hypothermia affects more people in the summer than winter (most hypothermia occurs between 55 and 60 degrees), it's still a major concern for the skiers and snowshoers. The symptoms of hypothermia progress from shivering to slurred speech and apathy, followed by frequent stumbling, unconsciousness and then death. If you notice anyone in your party suffering from these symptoms, you must act quickly. If possible, get the victim out of the wind and rain, strip him of all wet clothes and administer warm liquids. Then get him into warm clothes and a warm sleeping bag. If the victim is semiconscious, try to keep him awake. To avoid hypothermia, you must stay dry, get out of the wind and build a fire if you feel cold. If you wear the right kind of clothes, don't exhaust yourself and eat and drink enough, you can usually avoid hypothermia, even in foul conditions.

• Never forget about the danger of avalanches! Avalanches are complex natural phenomena and hard to predict. It takes much study and effort to understand them. The best way to avoid becoming a victim is to let an expert make the call. The U.S. Forest Service provides information about snow conditions in the Wasatch Mountains. If they forecast high avalanche conditions, don't venture into backcountry! Most avalanche victims are experienced at their outdoor sport but make errors in judgment. More than 95 percent of avalanches are triggered by the victim, and 95 percent occur in the backcountry. Most avalanches occur during or after a big storm. If you must go skiing during high avalanche conditions, go to a resort, where the staff control avalanches with explosives. You can find out about current avalanche conditions in the Wasatch Mountains by calling 364-1581 or 524-5304.

• Treat the backcountry with respect. Although the mountains are fierce, they are also fragile. "Leave no trace" should be your mantra as you travel the backcountry. Don't litter — trash and discarded food can last for decades. Pack out what you pack in, and don't leave human waste near streams and rivers.

Snowbird Ski Resort averages more than 42 feet of snow and offers one of the longest ski seasons in North America.

base lodge in a comfortable truck-pulled trailer. Once you're on the slopes, snow groomed like a golf green makes skiing a bump-free experience. When you stop for lunch, you'll eat it off china, not a paper plate. Deer Valley receives about 300 inches of snow a year and rates its skiing as 15 percent beginner, 50 percent intermediate and 35 percent advanced. Snowboards are not allowed.

Deer Valley will host the slalom, aerial freestyle and mogul events during the 2002 Winter Olympic Games.

Location and Transportation: Deer Valley is at Park City, about 45 minutes southeast of the Salt Lake International Airport.

Lifts, Schedule and Prices: Deer Valley is open from the first of December to the first of April. You'll find 14 lifts, including two high-speed detachable quads, nine triple-chair and three double-chair lifts, all open daily. An adult all-day lift pass costs $54,

and an adult half-day (1 PM to 4 PM) lift pass is $38. An all-day lift pass for children 12 and younger costs $29. If you're 65 or older, you pay $38 for a lift pass. Discounts for groups of 20 or more are offered, as are a number of multiday lift pass rates. Call for information on these deals. For a snow report, call (435) 649-2000.

Ski School and Rentals: Deer Valley offers an extensive array of group and private lessons for various ages and abilities. The Deer Valley Rental Shop offers a number of different ski rental packages, depending on the type of skis you need and your ability level.

Park City Mountain Resort
Park City • (435) 649-8111, reservations (800) 222-7275

Park City Mountain Resort, which opened in 1963 and is the oldest in Park City, rises to the west of the town and dominates the landscape. It's the largest resort in Utah in the amount of skiable terrain and lift capacity — it has more runs than any resort in the state — and was the first resort in Utah to feature a gondola. The gondola was replaced in 1997 with two new high-speed, six-passenger chairlifts. Even though Park City Mountain Resort receives less snow (350 inches) than the Cottonwood Canyon resorts, $10 million worth of snow-making equipment guarantees good conditions throughout the skiing season. The terrain is classified as 16 percent beginner, 45 percent intermediate and 39 percent expert. The resort is the home of the U.S. Ski Team and the site of the slalom and snowboard events during the 2002 Olympic Winter Games.

Location and Transportation: The Park City Mountain Resort is in downtown Park City, about 32 miles from the Salt Lake International Airport.

Lifts, Schedule and Prices: The resort is open from the middle of November to the middle of April. The mountain is serviced by three six-passenger, high-speed chairlifts, two quads, five triples and four doubles. The lifts are open from 9 AM to 9 PM every day. A full-day lift pass for adults costs $52, and a half-day (1 to 4 PM) lift pass costs $37. A child's (12 and younger) lift pass costs $23, and skiers age 64 to 69 ski all day for $25. Skiers 70 and older ski for free. Night skiing is available from 4 to 9 PM and costs $18 for adults and $8 for kids. For a snow report, call (435) 647-5449 .

Ski School and Rentals: The Park City Ski School offers a complete schedule of classes for skiers and snowboarders of various abilities. They also offer an "Elan Parabolic" course to help skiers learn how to better carve turns. The resort has a number of ski rental shops offering a wide variety of equipment. For ski and snowboard lesson reservations, call (800) 227-7275.

Cross-country Skiing and Snowshoeing

If you hate lift lines and recoil at paying big bucks to ski at a resort, you should consider cross-country skiing or snowshoeing. You get brisk exercise, the freedom of the mountains and the chance to see nature wrapped in her winter mantle. Another plus is that your pocketbook only takes a minor hit. For these reasons, these two winter sports are becoming increasingly popular. The self-propelled skier or snowshoer will find extraordinary variety in the Salt Lake area. If you're experienced and in good physical shape, you can take daylong tours through the backcountry of the Cottonwood Canyons of the Wasatch. Beginners can also find many suitable cross-country and snowshoe tours in the canyons.

Skiers and snowshoers should always check weather and avalanches conditions before setting out. Weather conditions can change dramatically in a short time. See the "Avalanches and Winter Safety" Close-up in this chapter.

If you prefer a resort atmosphere and groomed trails to the backcounty, you can find a number of excellent cross-country runs, many of which are described in the following entries.

Mountain Dell Golf Course
I-80, Parleys Canyon • (801) 582-3812
Mountain Dell Golf Course becomes a winter playground when the snow falls. You'll find this favorite winter haunt of Salt Lake on Interstate 80 about 15 miles east of Salt Lake. Between 5 and 10 kilometers of groomed track is available for cross-country skiers. The course is maintained by the Utah Nordic Alliance, which relies on donations to fund the project. You can't snowshoe on the groomed track, but you can find plenty of other places on the golf course to trek around. You'll also find

some nice, easy trails in the surrounding hills to snowshoe and cross-country on, and they are accessible from the golf course.

Solitude Nordic Area
1200 Big Cottonwood Canyon, Solitude • (801) 536-5774

The Solitude Nordic Area is between Solitude and Brighton ski resorts in Big Cottonwood Canyon and is the oldest groomed cross-country area in Utah. The center provides 20 kilometers of maintained trails for cross-country skiing and snowshoeing. The trails meander through scenic stands of spruce, fir and aspen and provide stunning views of the winter majesty of Big Cottonwood Canyon. Ski accessories, rentals, lessons and snacks are available at the Nordic Center's Silver Lake Lodge. The terrain is rated as 30 percent beginner, 60 percent intermediate and 10 percent advanced. An adult all-day trail pass costs $9, and an adult half-day pass costs $7. Kids 10 and younger ski free.

White Pine Touring Center
1541 Thaynes Canyon Dr., Park City • (435) 649-8701

Located on the Park City golf course in the middle of town, this center offers 18 kilometers of groomed track. If you like to view boutiques, expensive homes and shops while you ski, this course is for you, since much of the course meanders right through Park City. With both flat and rolling terrain, White Pine is suitable for all abilities. Ski rentals and lessons are available. White Pine classifies its terrain as 60 percent beginner, 20 percent intermediate and 20 percent expert. An adult all-day pass costs $6, a half-day pass costs $3, and children and seniors 65 and older ski free.

No fewer than seven professional teams beckon the eager fan to buy tickets and memorabilia, load up on hot dogs and in general spend money and have fun.

Spectator Sports

When Utahns aren't cavorting outside in the mountains, parks or playgrounds, many of them are cheering on one of the region's professional or amateur athletic teams. Utahns are great fans, loyal and knowledgeable. Basketball is especially popular here, and leagues all the way from preteens to the pros — the Utah Jazz and Starzz — receive strong support. In the last few years Salt Lake City has witnessed a boom in spectator sports. Ten years ago Salt Lakers could watch the University of Utah athletic teams, the Utah Jazz and a professional hockey team — and that was about it. Now, no fewer than seven professional teams beckon the eager fan to buy tickets and memorabilia, load up on hot dogs and in general spend money and have fun. So far, fan support for all these additional professional teams has been vigorous, and support for amateur teams hasn't waned.

Following is the lowdown on all the teams, including ticket prices and schedule information.

Basketball

Professional

Utah Jazz
Delta Center, 301 W. South Temple,
Salt Lake City • 325-2500

We took Chicago to six in 1997, and if it hadn't been for those annoying last-second shots by the one they call Michael, Salt Lakers could have been strutting around as world champions of the NBA. Jazz mania ran ram-

pant that year, and after The Steal, The Pass and The Shot by John Stockton in game four, the streets were flooded with jubilant (but law-abiding) fans blowing their horns, blocking traffic, hooting and hollering and otherwise celebrating in a way Salt Lake hasn't seen since Baskin and Robbins announced 10 new flavors at once.

With everyone returning for the 1997-98 season, Jazz fans think this will be their year. Although superstars John Stockton and Karl Malone have both been in the NBA for more than a decade, which is a long time, both are playing with the kind of fire, confidence and leadership that brings home championships. Both players are still in excellent physical condition, and with Stockton back from his knee injury, the Jazz could be a contender for the title. The team is looking for great things from 7-2 center Greg Ostertag, whose apprenticeship has come to an end.

The Jazz play in the Midwest Division of the Western Conference, along with the Portland Trailblazers, the Houston Rockets, the San Antonio Spurs, the Denver Nuggets, the Dallas Mavericks, the Minnesota Timberwolves and the Vancouver Grizzlies. The games are played in the Delta Center, in the heart of downtown Salt Lake City and only 10 minutes from the Salt Lake Airport. The Delta Center opened in 1991 and holds 19,911. The building contains 56 luxury suites, four sky suites and a number of hospitality rooms. Single ticket prices range from $10 to $68 for regular-season games, and season-ticket prices in the upper bowl range from $387 to $1,032. There's a five-year wait for season tickets in the lower bowl — so don't worry about getting any. The regular season starts in early November and lasts until mid-April. Selected games are televised live on KJZZ Channel 14, and all games are aired on the radio station 1320 KFAN (AM).

Utah Starzz
Delta Center, 301 W. South Temple, Salt Lake City • 325-2000

Hey, if the men can do it, why not the women? They said "they got next," and they were right — in 1997 the Women's National Basketball Association made its debut. The league started with eight teams and two conferences, Western and Eastern. Salt Lake was one of the lucky cities selected to have a team. The Starzz played in the Western Conference along with the Phoenix Mercury, the Los Angeles Sparks and the Sacramento Monarchs. Although the Starzz didn't fare too well, finishing last in the Western Conference, attendance was strong, and Starzz forward Wendy Palmer was selected to the All-WNBA second team. The league experienced great success in its pioneering first year, averaging an impressive 9,500 fans per game and earning strong television ratings. The Starzz play in the Delta Center. Ticket prices for 1997 were $5 to $30, and season tickets were $63 to 378 for a 28-game schedule.

> **FYI**
>
> Unless otherwise noted, the area code for all phone numbers listed in this guide is 801.

College

University of Utah Running Utes
Huntsman Center, University of Utah, University and 200 S., Salt Lake City • 581-8314

Led by first-team all-American Keith Van Horn, the Running Utes of the University of Utah finished the 1996-97 season ranked as one of the top-five teams in the country. The Associated Press basketball poll ranked the Utes second in the county. This is the highest a Western Athletic Conference (WAC) team has ever finished in the polls. Van Horn was drafted second by the Philadelphia '76ers, the highest NBA draft pick ever in U of U history. Under dynamic head coach Rick Majerus, the Utes have become a dominant force in college basketball. During Majerus's tenure, the Utes have averaged 22 wins a year and advanced three times to the coveted sweet-16 spot during the March Madness NCAA tournament. They've won three consecutive WAC crowns and thoroughly dominated archrival BYU. Majerus is a consummate tactician and motivator with an unrivaled knowledge of the game. Although the Utes lost Van Horn, they return with a seasoned and talented group of veterans. In the '98 season, the team is led by 6-11 center Michael Doleac, a first-team all-WAC performer in 1996-97. Doleac combines brute force with poise and intelligence. Athletic point guard Andre Miller is also expected to continue his improvement.

The Utes play in the Mountain Division of the Western Athletic Conference, along with Brigham Young, New Mexico, Rice, SMU, TCU and UTEP. Individual-ticket prices range from $9 to $16, and season-ticket prices range from $75 to $150 in the upper bowl. Season tickets for the lower bowl are difficult to come by. The regular season opens the first of December and ends the first of March. Selected games are televised live on KJZZ Channel 14, and all games are broadcast live on KALL 910 (AM).

Football

University of Utah Utes
Rice Stadium, University of Utah, University and 200 S., Salt Lake City • 581-8314

In his eight-year tenure Coach Ron McBride has turned around a struggling Uni-

---

INSIDERS' TIP

Odd But Probably Meaningless Sports Trivia: The names of three out of the seven professional teams in Salt Lake (Jazz, Starzz and Buzz) end in zz. Curious, isn't it?

Everyone is a Jazz fan in Salt Lake City.

versity of Utah football program. Before McBride came to the helm in 1990, the Utes had not won a WAC championship since 1964 and had only 12 winning seasons in the previous 30 years. McBride ended this legacy of futility in no time. The 1994 Utes were ranked 10th in the country, and Utah tied for the WAC crown in 1995, its first WAC championship in 31 years. In 1996-97 the Utes finished 8-4 and played in the Copper Bowl. Most important, McBride defeated hated rival BYU three consecutive times between 1993-95, something that hadn't been done since the late 1960s. McBride is already the second-winningest coach in Utah's 103 years of playing football. McBride's enthusiasm, honesty and concern for his players inspires them to play as hard as they can and have fun. Led by bruising 6-foot, 280-pound fullback Chris Fuamatu-Ma'afala and a talented crop of skill players, the Utes expect great success in the coming years.

The Utes play in the Mountain Division of the Western Athletic Conference, along with Brigham Young, New Mexico, Rice, SMU, TCU and UTEP. Single-ticket prices range from $9 to $16, with season tickets going for $35 to $95. The season opens the last of August and ends the first of December. Selected games are televised live on KUTV Channel 2 and KJZZ Channel 14, and all games are broadcast live on KALL 910 (AM).

Professional Ice Hockey

Utah Grizzlies
E Center, 3200 S. Decker Lake Dr. (2200 W.), West Valley City • 988-8888

You've probably heard the old joke where a guy said he went to the fights and a hockey game broke out. Well, you won't see a bunch of plug-uglies duking it out at a Grizzlies game — at least not all the time. Yeah, the guys will

mix it up when necessary, and they have not one, but two, team dentists, but hockey's the game in the International Hockey League, not street fighting. The Grizzlies play hard and fast, and they skate, defend and score goals with consummate skill — enough to win two consecutive Turner Cups, the IHC mark of eminence.

The Grizzlies play in the Southwest Division of the IHC, along with the Houston Aeros, the Las Vegas Thunder, the Long Beach Ice Dogs and the Phoenix Roadrunners. In 1997 the Grizzlies moved into the E Center, West Valley City's fabulous new hockey arena and events center. Led by the aggressive leadership of city manager John Patterson and the city council, West Valley City has created an elegant, world-class venue for hockey, music and other entertainment. The E Center features seating for more than 10,500 hockey fans and music lovers. This facility is a boon for the Salt Lake Valley and a feather in the cap for West Valley City leaders and citizens.

The Grizzlies play a 41-game season that starts the first of October and ends in the middle of April. Single-ticket prices range from $5 to $35, and season-ticket prices range from $56 to $1,312. You can listen to the Grizzlies on KTKK 630 (AM) and KFAN 1320 (AM) and watch selected games on KSL Channel 5.

Professional Baseball

Salt Lake Buzz
Franklin Quest Field, 77 W. 1300 S., Salt Lake City • 485-3800

After reaching the playoffs four years in a row, 1997 saw the Buzz falter slightly to finish 72-71, good for third in the AAA Pacific Coast League Northern Division. The Buzz are affiliated with the Minnesota Twins of the American League. They play a 144-game schedule that

www.insiders.com

See this and many other **Insiders' Guide®** destinations online — in their entirety.

Visit us today!

Karl Malone

Utah Jazz forward Karl Malone likes trucks. Mack trucks and Peterbilts — anything big, loud and powerful. This is appropriate, because when Malone is headed down the lane for a hammer dunk and catapults his massive 6-foot, 9-inch body toward the basket, all you can think of is a runaway truck. You pity any opponent courageous or foolish enough to stand his ground and be turned into the NBA version of road kill. But it doesn't happen often: Most players defend Malone's kamikaze attacks on the basket by diving for cover.

Close-up

Now in his 13th year, Malone keeps on rolling, amassing record after record and earning accolades as the greatest power forward to ever play in the National Basketball Association. Rugged and relentless, Malone's boxer physique, quick feet and in-your-face competitive spirit have brought him many awards, foremost among them the NBA's Most Valuable Player award during the 1996-97 season. To top it off, the NBA honored Malone (along with team-mate John Stockton) as one of the 50 greatest players in history.

Photo: Utah Jazz

Since his rookie season in 1985-1986, Malone has tallied some amazing career statistics. He's scored more than 25,000 points (ninth on the all-time list), and he holds the NBA career record for most consecutive seasons with 2,000 or more points. He's pulled down more than 10,000 rebounds and hasn't averaged less than 20 points or 9.6 rebounds a game since his rookie season.

No less amazing is Malone's durability. He played in all 82 games for the fifth straight season in 1996-97 and for the ninth time in the past 12 seasons. Despite enduring the ceaseless hacks, fouls and pounding that a power forward is heir to, Malone has only missed four games in his entire career. During that time he's been named to the NBA All-Star Team for eight straight years.

Karl Malone

Unlike other NBA superstars, Malone doesn't dazzle you with acrobatic moves. His leaping ability is average, he doesn't spin like an out-of-control Maytag, and he won't make you jump out of your shoes with a pump fake. Malone doesn't need that kind of superficial embellishment. Like a gladiator, Malone bulls you into submission with brute force. His size and strength make him impossible to stop around the basket, and his speed filling the land on the fast break is astonishing for such a big man. Top it off with a deadly medium-range jumper, and you have all the ingredients to cook up an NBA legend.

Leaving Louisiana Tech in 1985, Malone was drafted by the Jazz as the 13th pick — an incredibly low number for a player of his talents and a historic coup by the Jazz coaching staff. Malone quickly fulfilled their expectations, averaging 15 points and nine

— continued on next page

rebounds a game in his rookie season. Malone's modesty, down-home demeanor and solid family values immediately endeared him to Salt Lakers. His consistency and dependability mirror the beliefs of his adopted town, where flash and dazzle are viewed with suspicion and where people believe in showing up for work — every day.

After 13 years, Malone is Salt Lake's favorite son and most admired citizen. After 1997's disappointment, with the ultimate goal so tantalizingly close, after seeing and feeling the outpouring of support by Salt Lake's frenzied fans, Malone has only one goal: to bring home an NBA championship. Salt Lakers know that Malone will never give up, but no matter what the outcome, the city will always admire him for his grit and determination, his class in losing and his grace in winning.

begins the first of April and ends the end of August. Fan support is great — the Buzz average 9,500 fans a game, which leads the PCL. In 1994 the Buzz broke the all-time PCL attendance record set in 1946 by the San Francisco Seals. The teams plays in the magnificent Franklin Quest Field, widely regarded one of the finest minor league stadiums in the country. The mellifluous-voiced Steve Klauke does the play-by-play on KFAN 1320 (AM). Selected games appear on KTVX Channel 4. Individual-ticket prices range from $3 to $7, and season ticket prices range from $300 to $450 for 72 home games.

Professional Women's Volleyball

Utah Golden Spikers
Salt Lake Community College South City Campus, 1575 S. State, Salt Lake City • 577-4537

Women's professional volleyball has a strong presence in Salt Lake City, with two teams belonging to the National Volleyball Association. The Golden Spikers play their games in the Salt Lake Community College South City Campus. Deitre Collins, a 1988 Olympian, is on the team, as is former all-American Julie Brenner. The season begins in February and ends in April, with the playoffs in May. Single

tickets cost $5, and season tickets are $20 for a 12-game season.

Utah Predators
Salt Lake Community College Redwood Road Campus, 4600 S. Redwood Rd. (1700 W.), Salt Lake City • 485-9799

Along with the Golden Spikers, the Utah Predators belong to the National Volleyball Association. Other teams are located in Tucson, Arizona; St. Louis, Missouri.; Denver, Colorado; Cedar Falls, Iowa; and Omaha, Nebraska. Olympian Kristin Keefe (wife of Utah Jazz player Adam Keefe) is on the team, as are five former all-Americans and seven players 6 feet or taller. Ticket prices and schedule are the same as the Golden Spikers.

Amateur Gymnastics

University of Utah Gymnastic Team
Jon M. Huntsman Center, University of Utah, University and 200 S., Salt Lake City • 581-8314

Coach Greg Marsden has lead the University of Utah women's gymnastics to unprecedented success. His teams had won 10 national titles, and every Utah gymnastics team has finished in the NCAA top 10. University of Utah gymnasts have garnered 18 individual championships and 170 all-American awards.

INSIDERS' TIP

University of Utah basketball coach Rick Majerus emphasizes academics as much as basketball. During his tenure at Utah, 45 players have made the honor roll. The 1996-97 team compiled a glossy 3.03 cumulative GPA during the winter quarter.

This success has been rewarded with tremendous fan support: In 1993 the gymnastics team averaged 13,164 fans, a national record. This makes the University of Utah gymnastics team the biggest-drawing women's athletic team in NCAA history. Tickets are $4 for general admission and $8 for reserved seats.

Professional Auto Racing

Rocky Mountain Raceways
6555 W. 2100 S., West Valley City
• 252-9557

And they're off — 10,000 banshees howling in purgatory can't equal the turbocharged whine let loose when the light turns green at the brand-new, 72-acre Rocky Mountain Raceways. Want pedal-to-the-metal speed? How about sprint cars, super stocks, street stocks, modifieds and some kickin' ministocks? Let's just say that speed freaks feel right at home here. Rocky Mountain Raceways features a three-eighths-mile oval with a dragstrip and a figure eight. All tracks meet specifications set by the National Hot Rod Association.

Action occurs through the summer months, with ticket prices varying from $3 to $10 dollars. Family passes are available for $20 and $30. Family entertainment is emphasized, with special seating set aside where smoking and drinking aren't allowed. The season runs from April through October, with races Thursday through Saturday.

None of these jaunts is more than an hour away, so you can easily get out, see everything and be back in the comforting confines of the Salt Lake Valley in one day.

Daytrips

We've devoted much of our life to exploring Utah, yet there's so much to contemplate in this massive and scenic state that huge portions remain to us just a blank spot on the map. In a place with national monuments bigger than Delaware, seeing everything is the quest of a lifetime.

Whether you're drawn to nature and the outdoors or to museums and gift shops, you'll find innumerable places to indulge your tastes. We've selected a variety of daytrips, so nature buffs and shopaholics will be satisfied. If you're thrilled by nature at her most scenic, savage and unspoiled, the Salt Flats and Antelope Island in the Great Salt Lake will rivet your attention. Lovers of civilization will find much to do in Ogden and Provo. Robert Redford's Sundance Resort and Huntsville in Ogden Canyon offer a bit of both. None of these jaunts is more than an hour away, so you can easily get out, see everything and be back in the comforting confines of the Salt Lake Valley in one day.

Antelope Island State Park

Teeming with wildlife and rich in unspoiled natural beauty, **Antelope Island** in the Great Salt Lake is a fabulous place to spend the day hiking, biking, watching wildlife or simply communing with nature. If you've never seen the Great Salt Lake, Antelope Island is a splendid vantage point, with great views and sandy beaches. The island is largely undeveloped, offering visitors the kind of lonesome vistas, windswept prairies and empty spaces rarely found in today's crowded world. Some visitors say the island, with muted colors and vast grasslands, has the exotic look of the African veldt.

To get there, take Interstate 15 north about 17 miles to Exit 355, then turn west to the causeway. Drive 7 miles until you get to the island. The entrance fee is $6 per vehicle or $2.50 if you ride your bike along the causeway. Call the park staff at 595-4030 or 625-1630 if you require more information.

The visitors center, 721-9569, is on the north end of the island, overlooking Bridger Bay. Here you can view exhibits on the ecology and natural history of Antelope Island and the Great Salt Lake. A small store sells books, maps and other material relating to the island. You can also tour a small art gallery showing works by local artists. Some of the art, all of which is concerned in some way with natural history, is for sale. A short trail leads from the visitor center to an overlook.

History

The largest island in the Great Salt Lake, Antelope Island is a prominent landmark that measures 15 miles long and 5 miles wide, with more than 44 miles of shoreline. Rocky summits rise more than 2,000 feet above the water. For thousands of years Fremont Indians used the island for hunting and gathering. In 1845 legendary explorers Kit Carson and John C. Fremont became the first non-Indians to explore the island, where they glimpsed herds of antelope and gave the island its name. Taking advantage of several springs of fresh water, Mormon settlers began grazing animals on the island in 1848, when it became known as Church Island.

In that same year, Fielding Garr and his family moved to Antelope Island. A skilled mason, Garr built an adobe ranch house for his family. This house, which still stands, is the oldest continually inhabited home in Utah built by non-Indians. Visitors can tour the house on selected days. For more than 100 years the island was used mainly as a pasture of sheep, horses, bison and cows. The state of Utah began acquiring the island in 1960s, and in 1981 the entire island became a state park.

Wildlife

A major attraction of Antelope Island is the abundance and diversity of wildlife. The American bison are perhaps the best-known residents. Before the Indian Wars of 1860 to 1880, during which the U.S. Army starved the Native Americans into submission by slaughtering the buffalo, the herd in America numbered from 50 million to 60 million animals.

By the 1880s only a few hundred bison remained, and the threat of extinction loomed large. Two Utahns, William Glassman and John Dooly, took steps to save the bison by bringing 12 animals to Antelope Island in 1893. Today the herd numbers between 550 and 700 animals, making it one of the largest herds in the United States. The bison are rounded up each October and driven into corrals in the north end of the island. Helicopters and horseback riders are used to drive the herd. The public can view this roundup, which has become one of the wildest and woolliest spectacles in Utah. See the Festivals and Annual Events chapter for a complete description of this roundup.

The island is also home to antelope, mule deer, coyotes, bobcat and perhaps an occasional mountain lion. Because of the rich wetlands and salt marshes that surround the Great Salt Lake, Antelope Island is a birdwatcher's paradise. Avocets, black-necked stilts, plovers and other shorebirds frequent the area. The grasslands of the interior provide prime habitat for birds that eat insects and seeds, such as chukars, meadow larks, horned larks and mourning doves. Various species of owls and raptors are permanent residents. In the Great Salt Lake, huge populations of eared grebes, ducks and phalaropes can be seen gorging themselves on the brine flies and brine shrimp that inhabit the lake. Whatever you do, bring binoculars.

Trails

Hikers, horseback riders and mountain bikers have access to a number of trails. These double-track backcountry trails offer visitors a great chance to view wildlife and enjoy the rugged geography of the island. For those who like a challenge, the 9.2-mile White Rock Bay loop trail is very popular. One spur of this trail takes you along White Rock Bay and up to Beacon Knob, where you'll be treated to fantastic views of the Great Salt Lake. Another spur is to Split Rocky Bay, which takes you on an exciting descent to an untouched beach of white sand. The Elephant Head spur leads to an overlook commanding dramatic views in all directions.

If you want a shorter hike, three trails on the north side of the island are perfect. The 3-mile Lakeside Trail meanders along the lake and around Buffalo Point to Bridger Bay. Probably the most popular hike on Antelope Island is the Buffalo Point Trail, a half-mile trail to an overlook with an incredible view in all directions. The Ladyfinger Point trail is a short hike to Egg Island Overlook.

To protect these trails, please observe the following regulations:

• You must have a permit to use the trail. Permits are available at Park Headquarters.

• Remain on designated trails.

• Pets are allowed, but they must be leashed.

• Pack out all trash.

• No campfires.

• All plants, wildlife and minerals are protected.

• All trail users must be off the trail by 8 PM.

Camping, Concessions and the Marina

You can launch a boat from the marina on the north side of the island. For a sightseeing cruise of the Great Salt Lake on a 63-foot cruise liner, call 583-4400. Prices for a one-hour cruise are $11 for adults, $7.50 for children younger than 12 and $9 for seniors. The family rate is $28. A lunch cruise costs $18 a ticket. The boat sails at 1 and 3 PM Wednesday through Friday and 11:30 AM and 1 and 3 PM on Saturday and Sunday.

Overnight boat docking is $6 plus the entrance fee ($9 for overnight docking and camp-

FYI

Unless otherwise noted, the area code for all phone numbers listed in this guide is 801.

Photo: Utah Travel Council/Frank Jensen

The Bonneville Salt Flats is home to numerous land speed records.

ing on your boat). Boat docks are also available to rent on a monthly basis. Call 560-6622 for more information and prices.

Primitive overnight camping is available at Bridger Bay, White Rock Bay and Bridger Bay Beach. The cost is $8 per vehicle. For group rates and reservations call 773-2941. Reservations are recommended.

You can grab a buffalo burger and other goodies at the **Buffalo Point Restaurant.** Wagon rides and horse rentals are available at the **Fielding Garr Ranch House**, 782-4946. A wagon ride costs $6 for adults, $5 for children younger than 12, and $25 for a family. Horse rental is $22 per person.

Bonneville Salt Flats

One of the strangest places on earth, the Bonneville Salt Flats stretchs into the distance like an immense lake of dazzling ice, hypnotically beckoning visitors to walk out on the firmly packed salt to make sure the otherworldly scene before them is not a trick of light or a heat-induced apparition. Containing more than 30,000 acres, the Salt Flats are utterly devoid of life and so flat you can see the curvature of the earth. The scene is one of utter desolation, as if you'd stumbled on a place where creation was just beginning — or just ended. Visitors come to the Salt Flats to enjoy the stark beauty, to try and understand a geological marvel or to be part of auto racing history.

To get to the Salt Flats, take Interstate 80 west out of Salt Lake City about 80 miles to a marked turnoff. Take the turnoff and drive north a few miles.

Natural and Human History

The Bonneville Salt Flats were formed by the evaporation of Lake Bonneville, a huge freshwater lake that once covered most of Utah. See the History chapter for more information on Lake Bonneville and the Great Salt Lake, the last remnant of Lake Bonneville. The salt flats are flooded each winter with a shallow layer of water. During the summer the water evaporates, and the wind pushes the brine back and forth, sculpting the area into a perfectly flat, smooth expanse of salt, which varies in thickness from 1 inch to 6 feet.

The potential of this natural straightaway for racing was quickly recognized. In 1914 nationally known race driver Teddy Tetzleff came to the flats to attempt a national speed record. He drove a Blitzen Benz at the then astounding speed of 141 mph to set the world land speed record. In the 1930s Utahn Abe Jenkins and British racer Sir Malcolm Campbell competed for speed records. In 1938 Campbell became the first person to reach the speed of 300 mph in an automobile. In the next two decades the speed barriers of 400 mph and 500 mph were eventually broken. In the 1960s and 1970s, jet-powered vehicles came to the flats and caught the attention of the racing world by attaining nearly supersonic speeds. Art Arfons hit 576 mph, Craig Breedlove topped that by reaching 600 mph (the first man to do so) and in 1979 Stan Barret rocketed to 639 mph.

Decline and Fall

Sadly, you won't see the fastest cars in the world today at Bonneville. World-class speed merchants like Breedlove, Richard Noble and Andy Green now head to the Black Rock Desert to race, where a record speed of 714 mph was just reached. Due to decades of extracting potash, magnesium and common table salt from the flats by Kaiser Chemical (now Reilly Industries), Bonneville's blanket of salt has been reduced and thinned. In 1926 the salt flats covered 96,000 acres. Now, industrial activities have reduced that area to around 25,000 acres. The Salt Flats are now too dangerous for extremely high speeds. However, in 1995 a group called Save the Salt set out to rescue this imperiled natural treasure. The group, comprised of race car drivers, the Bureau of Land Management and Reilly Industries (which inherited the problem from Kaiser) devised a plan to restore 1 million tons of salt annually to the flats. The plan called for pumping saline waste water from abandoned evaporation ponds onto the flats. Theoretically, the water will evaporate and leave behind a layer of salt. It will take about five years to see if the plan is working.

Safety Precautions

The Bonneville Salt Flats are administered by the Bureau of Land Management. Because of its fragile ecology, history and unique geology, the area was designated an Area of Critical Environmental Concern in 1985. The following regulations must be observed:

• Stay on existing roads. The salt flats may appear solid, but most of the area is a thin crust of salt over gooey mud. Vehicles can permanently damage the surface.

• Temperatures in the area can hit 100 in the summer and zero in the winter. Be prepared for wilderness conditions.

• Take extra gas and water. You won't find any facilities or services on the salt flats.

• Overnight stays are prohibited. You can find camping on surrounding public land or lodgings in Wendover, about 10 miles west. Call the Wendover U.S.A. Visitor and Convention Bureau at (800) 426-6862.

Sundance Resort

Perched beneath the alpine grandeur of

---

www.insiders.com

See this and many other
Insiders' Guide® destinations
online — in their entirety.

Visit us today!

INSIDERS' TIP

Utah County is the gateway to the southern part of the state. If you're planning a trip to the Canyonlands in southwestern Utah, pick up a copy of *Insiders' Guide® to Southwestern Utah*. It's chock-full of great Insider information on the area.

12,000 foot Mount Timpanogos, Sundance Resort is an all-season recreational wonderland where you can play, summer or winter, to your heart's desire. Whether it's skiing, hiking, biking, summer theater or fine dining, you'll find plenty of it at Sundance. Not only that, but you might actually get to catch a glimpse of cinema superstar Robert Redford, who owns the place.

Sundance is about an hour's drive south of Salt Lake. To get there, take Interstate 15 south of Salt Lake City to Exit 275 (8th North). Go east on 8th North about 3 miles until you come to the mouth of Provo Canyon. Stay in the left lane and take U.S. Highway 189 up Provo Canyon about 7 miles until you see the Sundance exit (Utah 92), then turn left and continue for about 2 miles. The resort's phone number is (801) 225-4107.

Winter Activities

With bounteous quantities of Utah's famed powder snow, Sundance is a thrilling experience for skiers of every ability levels. Four chair lifts service 450 acres of mountain, so downhill skiers can choose from a variety of terrain, from long beginner runs to steep powder bowls. An all-day lift ticket pass for an adult costs $35, and a half-day pass is $27. For children 12 and younger, an all-day pass costs $22, and a half-day pass costs $16. Group rates are available for parties of 15 or more. Rentals, ski instruction and other programs are available for all ages and ability levels.

Cross-country skiers aren't left out of the fun. The Sundance Nordic Center offers 15 kilometers of groomed trails through pristine pine forests and untouched wilderness. The trails are open Wednesday though Saturday for twilight skiing until 9 PM. Instruction and rentals are available. An all-day pass for the Nordic Center trails costs $8. Skiers younger than 12 and older than 65 ski free. For the same price, snowshoers can use trails built especially for them.

Summer Activities

Hiking and mountain biking top the bill for summer outdoor fun. You'll find trails all over the place, from gentle strolls through mountain meadows to 12-mile hikes to the top of Mount Timpanogos. For $12 a day, or $5 for a single ride, bikers and hikers can take Ray's Lift to the top of the mountain, where they can stretch their muscles on miles of newly constructed single-track trails and roads. You can either hike down to Sundance or take the lift. Mountain bike rentals are available, and helmets (included in the rental price) are required for mountain bikers. Other summer activities available at Sundance or in the area include golf, fly-fishing and horseback riding. For other activities close by, read the "Provo" section of this chapter.

Theatergoers will love Sundance. The highly acclaimed summer theater features popular musicals such as *The Music Man* every Monday through Saturday at 8 PM. A natural amphitheater surrounded by a green curtain of fir trees, this theater has one of the most spectacular natural settings imaginable. The younger set will be mesmerized by **The Children's Theatre**, which performs the *Enchanted Pig* every Thursday, Friday and Saturday at 11 AM and 2 PM. Tickets are $7 per person.

Lodging and Restaurants

If you want to stay the night, you'll find elegant accommodations and gourmet dining. In the **Tree Room** you can dine on classic American cuisine, with entrees such as trout, pepper steak, salmon and fresh seafood and other goodies. Prices tend to be expensive, with the average entree around $20. For more informal and less expensive dining, try **The Foundry Grill**, which offers tasty burgers, pizza and pasta.

The Sundance Cottages range from one to three bedrooms and are furnished with Native American rugs, pots and baskets and other handmade furnishings. Rates range from $150 to $425 a night, depending on the season and size of the cottage. You can also rent secluded luxury homes, ranging from two to five bedrooms. Prices vary with the season, but they're always pretty pricey. You'll want to make reservations well in advance for rooms during peak times in the ski season such as the week between Christmas and New Year's Day. Rooms are usually available the rest of the ski season and through the summer. For reservations and information on lodging, call (800) 892-1699.

Provo, Utah

Provo is 44 miles south of Salt Lake City on Interstate 15, just 45 minutes from the Salt Lake Valley. The city, which is the focal point for the area known as the Utah Valley in Utah County, is predominantly Mormon, and the influence of the culture is very pronounced. Provo is home to Mormon Church-owned **Brigham Young University** where the school's strict code of behavior sets the tone for much of the community's deportment. Students, staff and faculty at BYU agree to comply with the school's honor code, which includes living a chaste and virtuous life, obeying the law, using clean language, respecting others and abstaining from alcoholic beverages, tobacco, coffee, tea and substance abuse.

Fewer than 25 percent of the city's restaurants serve alcoholic beverages, including beer, and you can't buy beer in any grocery or convenience store in Utah County on Sunday. In addition, those who attend BYU commit to dress and grooming standards. The code includes wearing modest clothing styles with hemlines on dresses and skirts knee-length or longer. Though Provo is definitely not a party town, there's plenty to do, and we've included some hot spots to make your daytrip here a pleasant one.

Recreation

Utah County offers a wealth of outdoor adventure. Here's a sampler to get you started.
Utah Lake State Park, 4400 W. Center Street, 375-0731, has four boat ramps, a 30-acre sheltered marina, 78 seasonal and transient boat slips (day use is $4), which is perfect for water skiing, boating and fishing. If fishing is your thrill, you can hook some whoppers on the Provo River or in other local waters. **Great Basin Fly & Outfitters, L.C.**, 120 W. Center Street, 375-2424, (888) 323-2424, can set you up with gear and the fishing trip of your dreams. Golfers have several courses to choose from in Provo, and they're open seven days a week unless otherwise noted. **East Bay Golf Course**, 1860 S. East Bay Boulevard, 373-6262, has 18-holes with plenty of lakes and great views. **Seven Peaks Golf Course**, 1330 E. 300 N., 375-5155, has 18-holes with elevated tees, lush fairways and challenging greens. The nearby golf course at **Thanksgiving Point**, 2095 N. West Frontage Road, Lehi, 768-7400, has a new, 18-hole championship Johnny Miller signature course. Thanksgiving Point is closed Sunday. All courses are open daylight to dusk.

Eateries

Provo boasts more than 70 restaurants offering everything from fast food and deli to full-tilt gourmet fare. We've included a few standouts that are open for lunch and dinner.

Mullboons, 3301 N. University Avenue, 373-1161, is a great place for dinner. It serves beer and cocktails and fine American cuisine, and while waiting for your entree you can nibble from a large bowl of shrimp on ice that finds its way to the center of every table. Entrees begin at approximately $15.

Joe Vera's Restaurant has two locations in Provo: 250 W. Center Street, 375-6714, and 1292 S. University Avenue, 377-5044. We would drive the 45 minutes from Salt Lake for their great Mexican food. The price is right, too. The average entree is $5 to $10. Add extra for beer and cocktails.

The Good Earth Natural Foods Cafe and Bakery, 384 W. Center Street, 377-7447, offers a variety of healthy food including soups, sandwiches and pasta dishes starting at around $5.

INSIDERS' TIP

Provo has lots of historic sights. For a brochure detailing the historic buildings on a self-guided tour, stop by the Utah County Visitor Center at 51 S. University Avenue. It's open Monday through Friday from 8 AM to 5 PM and on weekends from 9 AM to 5 PM. Give them a jingle at 370-8393.

Magleby's, 1675 N. 200 W., 374-6249, has great pasta, seafood and steaks. Plan to spend $10 to $15 on an entree.

Los Hermanos, 16 W. Center Street, 375-5732, serves a good south-of-the-border meal for less than $10.

Thrills and Chills

You can splash to your heart's content, work those leg muscles and have a dandy time in Provo at several exciting recreational spots

Seven Peaks Resort, 1330 E. 300 N., 373-8777, is a giant water park with more than 25 heated water attractions. The park is open from Memorial Day to Labor Day, weather permitting, from 10 AM to 7 PM. Admission is $14.50 for adults and $11.50 for children ages 3 to 12. Kids younger than 3 and seniors 63 and older get in free.

If you love to ice skate, you'll have a great time at **Utah Lake Ice Skating**, 4400 W. Center Street, 375-0731. Open during the winter only, skate times are every two hours beginning at noon on weekdays, 2 PM on Saturdays and 1 PM on Sundays. Closing times vary. Admission is $3 for adults and $2 for children ages 6 to 12. Skate rental is $1.

The **Rock Garden Indoor Climbing Gym**, 22 S. Freedom Boulevard, 375-2388, is a good place to experience rock climbing indoors. Hours are noon to 10 PM Monday through Thursday and until midnight on Friday and Saturday. A pass is $5 for the day. Harness and shoe rentals are $2 each.

Museums

Brigham Young University, 450 E. Campus Drive, 378-4678, has a wealth of museums on campus. You might want to start with a free campus tour beginning at 11 AM and 2 PM Monday through Friday or on the hour by appointment. You'll get a look at the campus plus a history of the school and information about its philosophy.

Following the tour, check out the **Monte L. Bean Life Science Museum**, 1430 N. 500 E., east of the Marriott Center, 378-5051. You'll find an extensive collection of insects, plants, reptiles, fish, shells, mammals, birds and eggs for research exhibits. Hours are Monday through Friday, 10 AM to 9 PM, and Saturday, 10 AM to 4 PM. Admission is free.

The **BYU Earth Science Museum**, 1683 N. Canyon Road, 378-3680, has one of the country's most extensive fossil collections including Ice Age mammals and ancient forms of sea life. The museum is open from 9 AM to 5 PM Monday through Friday. Saturday hours are noon to 4 PM. Admission is free, but a $1 donation is appreciated.

The **B.F. Larson Gallery** and **Gallery 303** in the Harris Fine Arts Center, 1679 N. Campus Drive, 378-2881, feature temporary exhibits by contemporary artists. Hours are 9 AM to 5 PM, and admission is free.

The **Museum of Art**, 1681 N. Campus Drive, 378-2787, is one of the largest art museums in the west. Hours are Monday through Friday 10 AM to 4 PM, except Thursday when the museum is open until 9 PM. Saturday hours are noon to 5 PM. Admission is free.

The **BYU Museum of Peoples and Cultures**, 700 N. 100 E., 378-6112, features anthropological artifacts from various cultures throughout the world. Hours are Monday through Friday 9 AM to 5 PM. Admission is free.

Off the campus of BYU you'll find several other museums worth noting. The **McCurdy Historical Doll Museum**, 246 N. 100 E., 377-9935, is an award-winning museum in a restored carriage house with more than 4,000 dolls in various costumes in historic settings. Hours are Tuesday through Saturday 1 to 5 PM. Admission is $2 for adults and $1 for children younger than 12.

The **Hall of Fame Museum of National Awards Vehicles**, 407 W. 100 S., 373-3040, has four one-of-a-kind vehicles that have been winners of eight Grand National Awards along with oodles of other nifty award-winning modes of transportation. Hours are Monday through Wednesday 10 AM to 5 PM and Thursday through Saturday until 8 PM. The museum opens at 2 PM on Saturday. The cost is $6 for adults and $3 for children ages 5 to 11. Kids younger than 5 get in free, but all children must be accompanied by an adult.

Shopping

You can shop 'til you drop near Provo in more than 195 stores at Utah's largest shopping mall, **University Mall**, 1300 S. State Street, Orem, 224-0694. The center offers a variety of wares from national chains to locally owned and operated shops. You'll also find some fun places to spend money in downtown Provo in the historic Provo Town Square as well as on Center Street.

Red Coyote Outfitters, 45 East Center Street, 373-3338, is a fun, family-owned contemporary Southwestern shop worth the trip south. It sells upscale clothing for women and men, including a line of 1800s retro men's wear right out of the movie *Tombstone*. You'll also find beautiful Austrian boiled wool coats and jackets as well as some fine leather wraps. In addition, the home furnishings department specializes in the log-cabin look with cozy sheets and blankets, furniture and accessories. Everything here is woodsy yet modern and definitely not just for cowpokes. Red Coyote is open Monday through Saturday, 10 AM to 6 PM.

One of the best ways to remember your visit to Utah is with a custom-framed limited edition print of our most spectacular natural wonders by one of Utah's nationally known artists. At the **Window Box**, 62 West Center Street, 377-4367, you'll find an excellent selection of quality art work representative of the area. You can take it with you or have the shop ship to your home. The Window Box is open Monday through Saturday, 10 AM to 5:30 PM.

Ogden, Utah

If you want to head north for the day, Ogden, in Weber County, is a good choice for a daytrip. Just 35 miles from the heart of Salt Lake City on I-15, the city and its surrounding countryside offer plenty to see in summer and

winter. Ogden's beauty is worth the trip. Besides the sights in the city, the scenic drive through nearby canyons will give you a first-hand look at the beauty of this northern Utah spot. The maps in the front of the book will help you find your way.

While you're visiting the Ogden area, you can commune with the outdoor and enjoy a variety of recreational activities. In this section, we've included some good bets. Can't resist the urge to shop? We've included the places Insiders enjoy most.

If you get the hungries, check out **Utah Noodle Parlor**, 319 Washington Boulevard, 394-6002. Insiders enjoy this Chinese restaurant, and you can get out the door with a full tummy for less than $10 per person. **The Timbermine Restaurant**, 1701 Park Boulevard, 393-2155, is only open for dinner, but if you want a tasty steak or seafood dinner before heading back to the Salt Lake Valley, the Timbermine's the place. Entrees range from $12 to $16. We've mentioned a few other dining possibilities throughout this section.

FYI

Unless otherwise noted, the area code for all phone numbers listed in this guide is 801.

Scenic Excursions

Ogden Canyon is known for its spectacular views. From the top you can see the town of Huntsville and the spectacular Pine View Dam. At the mouth of the canyon, you'll marvel at the 150-foot-high cascading waterfall that drops to the river below. To get to Ogden Canyon, drive east on 12th Street. The topography changes from city to a mountain canyon in a matter of minutes.

Ooh-Aaah Falls, which we described above, is an awesome spectacle. Witness nature's own rock show here with a stunning geological history of northern Utah in the canyon walls. While you're in the area, stop at **Rainbow Gardens**. Many years ago this was a hot-springs resort with a hotel, cafe, spectacular buffet, swimming

---

INSIDERS' TIP

You can cycle on city roads and mountain trails all over Ogden and the surrounding areas. For the location of mountain bike trails and trail maps, call Golden Spike Empire, 627-8288.

pool, Turkish bath and massage services. The 140-degree waters, which smell like sulphur, are believed to have medicinal qualities. Today Rainbow Gardens is transformed, but it's still a unique place. It has a bowling alley, the **Greenery Restaurant** — a good place for a light lunch — and a wonderful gift shop with many unusual items. It's fun to browse here, whether you spend a little or a lot.

At the top of the canyon, follow the signs and drive toward **Huntsville**. You won't want to miss this charmer of a town. Here you'll find the **Shooting Star Saloon**, 7345 E. 200 S., 745-2002, is a favorite of Insiders from Salt Lake City and Ogden. The food is good — try the world-famous Star Burger — but the ambiance is the real attraction. This is the oldest continuously operating saloon in Utah. The Shooting Star was built in 1879. The oak bar, which is a real conversation piece, was added in 1895. There's a stuffed Saint Bernard's head hanging on the wall.

The **Abbey of Our Lady of the Holy Trinity Monastery**, 1250 S. 9500 E., 745-3784, is also a must-do in Huntsville. This is a community of Catholic monks belonging to the Order of the Cistercians of the Strict Observance, often called Trappists. The monks came to this area in 1947 and established a monastic community dedicated to an austere and simple life of prayer and inspired manual labor. The sale of honey and bread made on this working farm helps support the monastery, and these delicious treats are worth the drive to Huntsville from just about anywhere.

From Huntsville, head for **Mountain Green** on Utah Highway 67. This is **Trappers Loop**, a 10-mile drive with plenty of rolling hills covered in aspen and oak and great views of **Mt. Ogden** and **Snow Basin Ski Resort**.

Leaving Mountain Green, head west on Interstate 80 to **Weber Canyon** where you'll follow the route of the transcontinental railroad through pine-covered mountains inhabited by a variety of wildlife. To get back to Ogden, take I-15 and follow the signs.

Recreation

If you're a skier, you might get a thrill on the slopes near Ogden.

Snow Basin Ski Resort in Huntsville, 399-0198, offers 1,800 acres of magnificent trails, bowls, glades and chutes. The resort has 39 designated runs for skiers and snowboarders and a 2,400 vertical drop.

Powder Mountain in Eden, 745-3771, 19 miles northeast of Ogden, has 30 designated runs for some fantastic skiing, snowboarding and night skiing. With an average snowfall of more than 500 inches, delicious deep powder and a vertical drop of 1,980, Powder Mountain offers a great skiing experience.

Nordic Valley Ski Mountain in Eden, 3567 Nordic Valley Way, 745-3511, provides an economical day or night of skiing on beautiful groomed slopes, just right for all levels of skiers. The area has two lifts and 18 trails with a vertical drop of 1,000 feet. The average snow fall is 300 inches.

Cross-country skiers can get the scoop on trails and tours from the **U.S. Forest Service**, 625-5306. To find out about snowmobile areas in Ogden, call the U.S. Forest Service or **Utah State Parks and Recreation**, 538-7220.

Flatlanders might feel a little more comfortable on the ice rather than on Ogden area snowy slopes. **The Ice Sheet**, 4390 Harrison Boulevard, 399-8750, has an Olympic-size arena open to the public seven days a week, noon to 9 PM, but it's advisable to call ahead and verify. Admission is $3.25 for adults, $2.75 for senior citizens and children age 3 through high school. Skate rental is $1.25 per person.

If golf is your favorite pastime, you can play on several courses in Ogden. The **El Monte Golf Course** is a public nine-hole course with rolling hills and old-style greens situated at the mouth of Ogden Canyon at 1300 Valley Drive, 629-8333. For a challenging game with difficult greens and stunning views, try **Mount Ogden Golf Course**, 3000 Taylor Avenue, 629-8700.

For miniature-golf fun check out the **Golf City Family Fun Center**, 1400 E. 5600 S., South Ogden, 479-3410. You'll find batting cages, a par 3 course and a lighted driving range. **Mulligan's**, 1690 W. 400 N., 392-4653, offers a 36-hole miniature golf course and a lighted driving range.

Sightseeing and Attractions

A daytrip to Ogden wouldn't be complete without seeing the historic sites of the area. Ogden has many museums and attractions that revel in the past.

The **Daughters of the Utah Pioneers Museum** and **Miles Goodyear Cabin**, 2148 Grant Avenue, 393-4460, are on the grounds of the Ogden LDS Temple and Tabernacle. The cabin, constructed in 1845 was the first permanent pioneer home in Utah, built by trapper Miles Goodyear. The museum houses a collection of artifacts, photographs and memorabilia from the pioneer era. Hours are 9 AM to 5 PM Monday through Saturday. Admission is free.

George S. Eccles Dinosaur Park, 1544 E. Park Boulevard, 393-DINO, provides a step far back in time with scientifically accurate replicas of prehistoric creatures. These reproductions range from full-size to half-life-size. The exhibit depicts crawlers, dinosaurs, marine creatures and flying reptiles dating from the late Triassic area through the Jurassic and Cretaceous eras, 230 million to 65 million years ago. Hours are Monday through Saturday 10 AM to 6 PM and Sunday noon to 6 PM. Admission is $3.50 for adults, $1.50 for children ages 3 to 17 and $2.50 for seniors. The Park is closed between October 31 and April 1.

The **Eccles Community Art Center/Carriage House Gallery**, 2580 Jefferson Avenue, 392-6935, features a permanent art collection as well as special exhibitions throughout the year. The art center is housed in a Victorian mansion. The Carriage House Gallery sells specialty gift items created by local artists. Hours are Monday through Friday 9 AM to 5 PM and 10 AM to 4 PM on Saturday. Admission is free.

Ogden Nature Center, 966 W. 12th Street, Ogden, 621-7595, is a wildlife sanctuary where you can see birds, snakes, raccoons and other animals living in an urban setting with nature trails, self-guided observation stations, shaded picnic areas and a museum. Hours are Monday through Saturday 10 AM to 4 PM. Admission is $1.

Union Station Museums, 2501 Wall Avenue, 629-8444, house several collections of interest to early Western Americana buffs. The **Utah State Railroad Museum** celebrates Ogden's history as a rail center in the West since 1869. The depot is still active today as a center for Western freight operations. The **Browning Firearms Museum** displays both original and production models of world-famous Browning arms. Historical photographs and artifacts of John M. Browning are included in the exhibits. The **Browning-Kimball Car Collection** holds classic and antique automobiles from the early 1900s along with a history of each car. The **Natural History Museum** displays remnants of the area's geologic past. The **Spencer S. and Hope F. Eccles Railroad Center** presents the largest and most historic railroad rolling stock in the world in an outdoor pavilion. The **Wattis-Dumke Model Railroad Museum** features an HO-scale model railroad with a dozen trains running on eight different layouts. The railroad depicts the construction and geography of the 1,776-mile transcontinental route. The **Myra Powell Gallery** exhibits diversified artwork through invitational and competitive shows. Museums in Union Station (except the Myra Powell Gallery, which is open Monday through Friday from 10 AM until 5 PM and has free admission) are open Monday through Saturday from 10 AM to 6 PM. During the summer, the museums are also open on Sunday from noon to 5 PM. Admission is $3 for adults, $2.50 for senior citizens and $1 for children ages 1 to 12. One ticket gets you into all the museums. Add 6 percent sales tax to the ticket price.

You'll also find a restaurant, gift shops and a train shop in Union Station. The building is listed on the National Register of Historic Places.

INSIDERS' TIP

For information on off-highway vehicle trails and trail maps, contact the Utah Parks Department, 538-7220, or the U.S. Forest Service, 625-5306.

Shopping

Ogden has two malls: **Newgate Mall**, 36th and Wall Avenue, 621-1161, and **Ogden City Mall**, 24th and Washington Boulevard, 399 - 1314. In addition to the malls, you'll find many small specialty shops scattered here and there in Ogden, many selling handcrafted items. It's fun to "discover" these stores as you meander through town.

Historic 25th Street, between Wall and Grant avenues, has a number of good antique stores and unique little shops. The **Needlepoint Joint**, 241 Historic 25th Street, 394-4355, has everything to delight the heart of fine stitchery buffs, including tools and supplies for knitting, crocheting, needlepoint, spinning and weaving. The shop has a bazillion tools including a vast selection knitting needles from nearly a dozen manufacturers and many hard-to-find items. It also carries yarns and threads galore. Salt Laker's are very fond of this great store and don't mind the 45-minute drive to get the best. It's open Monday through Saturday, 10 AM to 5:30 PM.

Pan Handlers, 260 Historic 25th Street, 392-6510, is a must-do gourmet kitchen store with absolutely everything for the cook including full kitchen accessories, gourmet food items and gift baskets. Pan Handler's also has a cooking school. While you're there, ask the owner to give you the low-down on this historic block. He's very well-informed. The shop is open Monday through Saturday, 10 AM to 6 PM.

Historic 25th Street is loads of fun, and you can drop in for lunch at one of the restaurants on this street. **The Daily Grind**, 252 Historic 25th Street, 629-0909, serves a variety of great coffees as well as soups and sandwiches.

Approximately five blocks south of the historic district you'll find **Burton Furniture Arts**, 3160 Grant Avenue, 394-5435. If you love interesting custom-made furniture, you won't want to miss Burton's. This delightful place — a spacious workshop rather than a showroom — is filled with unique and interesting furniture in various stages of completion. Co-owner Christopher Burton will personally show you around while explaining the various techniques he uses to create the individualized pieces that are Burton's trademark. Ask him to show you the tools used to make the furniture — you'll be amazed. The company custom builds furniture, refinishes, restores, paints and adds moldings and metal plating to old and new furniture. Their hand-detailed screens are exquisite. Don't be shy about stopping by if you're from out of town. Burton's has clients all over the country. The shop is open Monday through Friday 10 AM to 5 PM.

Whether new or previously owned, homes here are a good value. Since home and family are at the core of life in the Salt Lake Valley, we take pride in our homes and neighborhoods.

Neighborhoods and Real Estate

Although Salt Lake residents have seen home prices soar over the past several years, the real-estate market here is stabilizing. The average home in the Salt Lake Valley sells for $150,217, and one out of three Salt Lakers is a homeowner. The cost of living in the Salt Lake Valley, according to the American Chamber of Commerce Research Association, is 3 percent below the national average. Home building has slowed after several years of brisk construction, but builders still are breaking ground for new homes and developments with a steady pace. Whether new or previously owned, homes here are a good value. Since home and family are at the core of life in the Salt Lake Valley, we take pride in our homes and neighborhoods.

Overall, the quality of homes available here is very good. The Salt Lake Valley's economy is strong, and Utah's fiscal growth rate is approximately three times the national average. We have plenty of jobs and consistently maintain one of the lowest unemployment rates in the nation. Together, these indicators make the Salt Lake Valley an attractive location for home buyers. Those are the facts. What's the real reason families remain here generation after generation and new residents continue to make this their home? Aside from being one of the most beautiful places on earth, it's probably the people. As Salt Lake continues to grow and take its place among the prominent communities across the nation, it endures as a pleasant city with strong neighborhoods and wholesome values.

Before you spin your wheels looking for your dream home, we'd like to give you some insight into the Salt Lake real-estate market.

When we speak of Salt Lake, we mean the Salt Lake Valley, which includes both Salt Lake City and Salt Lake County. (Our Getting Here, Getting Around chapter provides an explanation of the geographic area.) Although nearly a million people live in the Salt Lake Valley, it still has a small town feeling. Many of our neighborhoods have become so large they have been incorporated into towns and cities like Murray, Sandy and West Valley City. To locals, they're still neighborhoods. Whether the coordinates call it Riverton, Cottonwood or Rose Park, we say "Salt Lake" because it's all part of the Salt Lake Valley. In this listing we have used the words city, town and neighborhood interchangeably, since to us they are all the same.

The neighborhoods in Salt Lake began in what is now the downtown and Capitol Hill area and spread east, south and west as the population increased. Eastside neighborhoods were always considered more elite locations than westside properties. To some extent, that is still the case today. As the need arose to spread outward from the city, many developments sprang up in the Wasatch foothills on the eastside and moved south at the base of the mountains as far up as it was feasible to build. These neighborhoods took their place on the roster of better locations. Today, the middle, south and southwest areas of the Valley are well developed, and you'll find luxury homes here on a par with those on the eastside. Unfortunately, old sentiments are hard to put aside. Though living on the west side of town — that is, west of State Street — won't brand you as coming from the wrong side of the tracks, an eastside address carries more prestige (and generally costs more.) One exception is the new Soho-style development blossoming west of State Street in the downtown area. To get a feel for this neighborhood, see to the introduction to the Arts chapter.

Local entities such as school districts, counties, towns and special taxing districts set the rate of property tax, so where you live in the Valley will determine how little or how much property tax you will pay. City and county services vary, too.

To understand Salt Lakers you have to visit their neighborhoods, look at the homes, feel the ambiance and see the people. Each neighborhood across the Salt Lake Valley has a distinct personality — a culmination of its architectural styles, history and residents. In the "Neighborhoods" section that follows, we have provided an Insider's tour of many locations and information on the types of homes that dominate that area, their inhabitants and a guideline for pricing. A quick study of the maps at the front of the book will familiarize you with the locations in no time. The north, south, east or west coordinates in the neighborhood's listing will tell you where the area is in relation to the city's center.

If you have fallen in love with our mountains and want to make your home there, you might enjoy reading the real-estate section of our chapter on Park City.

Neighborhoods

Arlington Hills

If you are looking for quiet elegance, Arlington Hills is one of Salt Lake's older, more elite neighborhoods. Close to downtown, this eastside neighborhood has been the address of generations of prominent business and so-

FYI

Unless otherwise noted, the area code for all phone numbers listed in this guide is 801.

cial figures. Mature landscaping and the many classic homes here create a feeling of dignity and privacy. Ensign Elementary, Bryant Intermediate and West High are considered three of the most desirable public schools in the Valley, and Arlington Hills falls within their district. Home prices range from $200,000 to upward of $1 million.

The Avenues

The Avenues is a highly desirable in-town address. This is the only area in the city not on the grid. The Avenues' blocks are about half the length of a city block. The streets run west to east, A through U, followed by Virginia Street (1350 E.), and from South Temple north from 1st through 18th Avenue. The narrow streets can get quite steep in some parts of the Avenues. I and E streets are well-plowed in winter to get you up to the higher Avenues or down the hill to South Temple.

South Temple to 9th Avenue is considered the lower Avenues. The quaint architecture runs from Victorian to high-rise modern condominiums. The eclectic mix of residents include educators, artists, business executives, doctors and lawyers. The historic merits of some properties continue to draw people to this neighborhood. Much of the property is still a handiperson's dream. Restoration has been ongoing for about 20 years, and some homes are truly showplaces. The Avenues' residents are outspoken about the preservation of historic properties and zealously work to protect the older homes in this area. Prices for lower-Avenue properties range from the mid-$100,000s to the low-$400,000s.

The upper Avenues, from 10th to 18th Avenue and above to Edgehill Drive, offer a spectacular view of the city. These homes began to creep up the hill during the '50s and '60s

---

INSIDERS' TIP

The annual Greater Salt Lake Parade of Homes, which has been showcasing new-home developments since 1946, is the perfect way to preview the latest in style and location in the Salt Lake Valley. Look for information in the real-estate section of the *The Salt Lake Tribune's* Sunday edition during August.

and become more modern in design as you go higher. Upper Avenues home prices average $350,000. You can find million-dollar homes, but a real bargain does present itself occasionally.

Elementary school children on the lower Avenues attend Lowell, and upper Avenues' kids go to Ensign. Both schools matriculate to Bryant Intermediate and West High School.

Canyon Rim

Houses in the eastside Canyon Rim neighborhood are modest and cozy. Many were built as basement homes after World War II, when returning G.I.s could only afford to build the basements. The main story was added years later as the family's income improved.

Driving down the tree-lined streets, you can almost taste fresh-baked pies. The area, which has a median age of 31.4, is very family-friendly. Three elementary schools, two middle schools and two high schools, all in the Granite School District, educate the neighborhood children. Most of the nearly 8,000 people who reside in the Canyon Rim take pride in their houses and yards. Home prices are between $150,000 and $190,000. The area is close to shopping and convenient to any part of the Valley.

Capitol Hill

This neighborhood is a very special place with blocks and blocks of charm punctuated by narrow and often steep streets. This lovely little area is the oldest-surviving neighborhood in Salt Lake City. Capitol Hill combines a variety of architectural styles including Greek Revival, Federal, Queen Anne, Beaux-Arts and Victorian classic. Building in this district began in the 1850s and continued until the 1930s. Many of these beautiful homes fell into disrepair after World War II. The neighborhood has regained its dignity, and many of the older homes have been restored. Quite a few structures are on the National Register of Historic Places. The community has four sub-neighborhoods: City Creek in the canyons east of the Capitol building, the Marmalade district to the west, Wasatch Springs to the north and Heber's Bench just below the Capitol to the south. Watching the sunset is a great pastime here.

The average price of a home in the Capitol Hill district is $205,000. Homes have recently sold for as much as $2 million and as little as $130,000. The district attracts many single professionals or couples with no children, although this is a desirable location for families.

Cottonwood Heights

Located between 6600 and 9000 S. and 1300 and 3000 E., Cottonwood Heights began to boom during the post-World War II years of 1950 to 1980. More than 30,000 people, median age of 25.3, live in this beautiful community today. Thick with mature trees, the area has a rural feeling yet is close to everything in the Valley. The residents of the area are active in community affairs and have protected the neighborhood from too-rapid growth and inappropriate development.

The average cost of a home in this well established neighborhood is $221,557. Elementary and middle school children matriculate to Brighton High School.

Draper

Kids, horses and a country feeling are the main events in Draper. The area has preserved much of its rural flavor, although large new homes have begun to pop up en masse over the past two decades. Located 18 miles from downtown, Draper's 13,000 residents enjoy the country life without being cut off from the mainstream.

This neighborhood reaches from 11900 to 15900 S. and 1100 W. to 2500 E.. New homes average $225,000 while smaller, older homes are selling for between $110,000 and $140,000. The Jordan School District educates Draper's children. With so much development in the south end of the Valley and breathtaking mountain views, Draper is a very happening place.

Emigration Canyon

Have you always dreamed of living in a mountain cabin? You can build your cabin in Emigration Canyon, though million-dollar estates on large lots are becoming more common in this beautiful area situated just east of Hogle Zoo on Sunnyside Avenue (800 S.) Newer developments with their breathtaking views seem far removed from the hustle and bustle of city life, but this neighborhood is actually very close to the city center.

The average price of a home in Emigration Canyon is $440,000, but homes range from $125,000 to $1.25 million. Residents represent a mix of singles, couples and families.

Ensign Downs

Set in the foothills behind the capital, this area offers some pretty remarkable views. Development began around 1960 and was slow going until 1990 when it picked up at a rapid clip. This neighborhood is very appealing for professionals with families. Ensign Downs is only five minutes from downtown and 10 minutes from the University of Utah Research Park area.

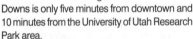

www.insiders.com

See this and many other **Insiders' Guide®** destinations online — in their entirety.

Visit us today!

While the average home sells for around $520,000, you can sometimes find a bargain for as little as $190,000. Prices do go as high as $700,000. This area has the city's only gated community.

Federal Heights

Driving through Federal Heights, east of Virginia Street (1350 E.) between South Temple and 11th Avenue, caught up in the moment, one might believe that all is well with the world. The beautiful tree-lined streets and sturdy, striking homes give Federal Heights a very solid feel. This exclusive older neighborhood is architecturally mixed, and many homes are listed on the National Register of Historic Places. Newer homes are spread out and more contemporary in design.

The average selling price is around $347,000. New listings are upward of $515,000. The area is a good family neighborhood, close to the University of Utah and downtown.

Harvard-Yale

There are more than two streets in this east-bench neighborhood, but if you mention Harvard or Yale, people will know the address and regard it highly. This well-established community encompasses 800 S. to 1300 S. and 1300 E. to Foothill Boulevard. Harvard-Yale is, in a word, quaint. Large trees form a crystal canopy over many of the streets in winter and a lush green arbor in summer. The unique architecture ranges from small, charming single-level bungalows to stupendous English Tudors. There are so many interesting homes it's hard to decide which to admire the most. The area's public school district, which includes Bonneville Elementary, Clayton Middle School and East High, is highly sought after.

Prices range from $130,500 to $375,000, with the average listing price in the Harvard-Yale area around $209,000.

Holladay

Holladay begins at 4500 S. and about 1300 E. and runs south to 6800 S. and east to Interstate 215. Sections of the neighborhood are quite old. Early pioneers settled along the creek that runs through the area in 1847. There are some lovely older homes here, some with deep frontage that was once used for livestock. Holladay has the oldest median age in Salt Lake County, although its schools are some of the best in the Granite District. Olympus High School, Olympus Middle School and Cottonwood Elementary all have outstanding academic records.

Home prices range from $120,000 to $6.8 million. Average and median prices are $465,000 and $310,000, respectively. The area has a well-established, friendly feel and a blend

---

INSIDERS' TIP

To help revitalize neighborhoods in the Salt Lake Valley, Neighborhood Housing Services Inc. has purchased homes in disrepair, refurbished them and put them back on the market. In addition, they have helped neighbors secure low-cost loans to upgrade their properties and enhance the community. To find out more about Neighborhood Housing Services Inc. call 539-1590.

Photo: Salt Lake Convention and Visitors Bureau

Wide-open spaces and breathtaking views are
just a short commute away from the city.

of architecture that includes many large, comfortable homes built from the 1950s to present. The area offers plenty of shopping, entertainment and recreation nearby. Residents consider this 7-square-mile area a slice of heaven.

Kearns

A middle-aged community that got its start after being an adjunct Army Air Force training center known as Camp Kearns during World War II, Kearns now has about 30,000 residents. Noted for its community involvement, impressive youth recreational programs and generosity, Kearns is an affordable neighborhood popular with young families in the Salt Lake Valley. Speed skaters from all over the world will gather in Kearns during the 2002 Winter Olympics to compete on the newly completed outdoor speed-skating oval (see our Parks and Recreation chapter). Home prices range from the high $80s to low $100s.

Magna

The Salt Lake Valley has several Mayberry R.F.D.–type communities, and Magna is certainly one of them. This close-knit, friendly town was founded in 1891 and soon became renowned for its copper mills in nearby Bingham Canyon. When the Utah Copper Company (later known as the Kennecott Copper Corporation) was founded in the early 1900s, workers moved to Magna to be close to their jobs. Although the town is growing and many new homes now dot the town's landscape, Main Street looks much the same as it did nearly 100 years ago.

Magna begins at the Salt Lake City limits on 2100 S. and runs to 4100 S. and from 7200 W. to the Oquirrh Mountains, and covers about 4,200 acres. About 23,000 people call Magna home today. Although the most expensive home in Magna recently listed for $248,500, houses are being offered for as little as

$49,000. The average and median prices in the area are $94,281 and $87,900, respectively.

Midvale

Another charming small town, Midvale, which sits between 7000 S. and 9000 S., may be losing its "quaint" status to become a large development, one that includes a hotel and convention center, hiking and horseback riding trails, a mining museum and business park in an area called the Mill-at-Midvale. An 18-hole championship golf course will be the icing on the cake.

Current home prices in Midvale range from $94,900 to $164,900, but Realtors expect the real-estate market to go through the roof once 50 affordably priced new homes are completed in conjunction with the Mill-at-Midvale development, which is scheduled for completion in late 1998. Residents generally are pleased with the plans, and while progress may inch property values upward, Midvale is still a delightful family community.

Murray

Low property taxes, due to a strong sales-tax base generated by more than 3,600 licensed businesses operating within the city limits, make this attractive city even more appealing to home buyers. An excellent school system, plenty of recreation and affordable homes put Murray on the map as a desirable neighborhood.

Situated between 4500 S. and 7000 S. in the mid-Valley, Murray boasts six public parks, an ice-skating rink, two swimming pools, two public libraries, two public golf courses, eight covered picnic areas, six tennis courts and six baseball diamonds. Not a bad place for kids! The area is about 30 minutes from the major ski resorts.

Average and median home prices are $118,000 and $124,000. Murray is a fully developed 'burb with shopping strips and subdivisions that have popped up over the past several years. The occasional estate adds to the housing mix, too. The older properties that give Murray the small-town look are delightful. These comfortable, modest family homes are wonderful places to raise children and are priced lower than homes in the newer housing developments.

Olympus Cove

Located above Wasatch Boulevard between 3700 S. and 4800 S., on the southeast bench, Olympus Cove perches over the city at the foot of Mount Olympus like a trusted sentry. The area began to develop during the late 1940s and early '50s, hitting its stride in 1958 with the development of a 100-lot subdivision. Surrounded by three mountains, Olympus Cove ("the Cove," to locals) is one of the city's best neighborhoods. The architecture in the Cove generally maximizes the extraordinary view of the city and sunsets on the Great Salt Lake. Schools serving the the area are top-rated and include Oakridge Elementary, Wasatch Middle School and Skyline High School. The average price of a home in Olympus Cove is $370,000.

Riverton

There was a time when the Riverton's doctor made house calls and took his fee in chickens and fresh vegetables — or took no fee at all if the family didn't have anything to spare. Times have changed a little, but not that much. Riverton residents are still very community-minded and think nothing of giving a little of their own to help a neighbor.

Located between 11800 S. and 13800 S. and 900 W. and 3600 W. in the south end of the Salt Lake Valley, Riverton is a popular place to raise a family. The quiet country setting is enhanced by two 10-acre community parks, an 18-hole golf course, the strength of the Jordan school district and spectacular mountain views. Property values in Riverton, which

INSIDERS' TIP

The Salt Lake Board of Realtors can tell you if the real-estate company you choose is a board member, or refer you to the correct board office in the neighborhood where you're shopping for property. Their number is 486-4465.

was established in 1865, have jumped rapidly in the past five years in keeping with the trend throughout the rest of the Valley. The average price of a home today is $185,695, up considerably from $71,500 in 1991. Some families in Riverton have developed deep roots here, some four generations strong.

Rose Park

The streets in Rose Park have lovely names like Nocturne, American Beauty and Capistrano. Many houses in the area have manicured lawns and flower beds that would make any garden club proud. Between 600 and 1700 N. and 900 W. and Redwood Road (1700 W.), this area has been both heaven-on-earth and a heartache to local residents.

When high crime began to encroach on sections of the neighborhood several years ago, this tight-knit community fought back with one of the most active Mobile Watch units in the state. Local volunteers took control of their turf and, according to the Salt Lake police department, they are doing very well. Many of Rose Park's residents have lived in the area for 30 and 40 years and quite a few are retired.

Established as a community after World War II, the modest houses on tree-shaded streets are currently priced in the $80s.

Sandy

Once considered a bedroom community to Salt Lake City, Sandy is now the fourth-largest city in Utah with more than 90,000 residents. Nineteen elementary schools, six middle school and four high schools, all in the Jordan school district, educate Sandy's young people. There are a lot of young people in Sandy. This is a real family-oriented community. The median age in Sandy is 41.3.

Some of the first subdivision homes in Sandy were modest look-alikes that got people out of the bustling city but not so far south that they couldn't commute. Today, the area, which is 13 miles from the city's center and situated between 7800 S. and 121000 S. and the Jordan River and 1300 E., still has its share of small homes, many of them fixer-uppers, but medium-size homes and large luxury homes are just as common.

The average price of a home in Sandy is $259,265. The mountain views are really spectacular, and Sandy is close to shopping, businesses and entertainment in the south Valley. Area ski resorts are about 20 minutes away.

South Jordan

Located primarily between 300 and 7200 W. and 9200 and 11800 S., South Jordan was incorporated in 1935 and is now home to more than 23,850 residents. The area, which has an extraordinary view of the Oquirrh Mountains to the west, has experienced unparalleled growth and construction during the past five years. Large homes, purchased for less money than in other neighborhoods in the city, will hopefully appreciate rapidly as the area develops. This is what new residents are banking on in South Jordan. The rural setting is a real enticement to city dwellers tired of the hustle and bustle. Besides homes, which average around $181,820, there's a lot of development, including multiple-family dwellings, shopping centers and entertainment complexes, to support the influx of people.

St. Mary's

St. Mary's of the Wasatch Academy, a Catholic girls school that had operated since 1926, sold this small section of land to a developer in 1957. The original neighborhood was built on 135 acres. When the school closed in 1970, the rest of the Wasatch Academy land was sold for development. This quiet hideaway between 1300 and 1600 S. and Wasatch Drive to the foothills on the city's east bench, is one of the loveliest and most desirable locations in Salt Lake City. Most of the homes are large and speak for themselves. Property values were high at the outset and have continued to increase. The most expensive home in the neighborhood was listed at $1.8 million. The average home price is about $350,000. Many prominent locals call this neighborhood home.

Sugarhouse

The tree-lined streets and older homes in the Sugarhouse area, many of which are listed on the State and National Register of Historic Places, make it a treasured location for residents who appreciate the past. Restoration continues to be an important aspect of this neighborhood. Many smaller homes have been spruced up in recent years. Some of the smaller, older homes are charming and neat as a pin.

Situated between 1300 and 3300 S. and 500 and 2300 E., approximately 10 minutes from the city's center, Sugarhouse is home to Westminster College, founded in 1897, Utah's oldest four-year liberal arts college. Two of the city's oldest public golf courses — Forest Dale and Nibley Park — are in Sugarhouse (see our Parks and Recreation chapter).

Sugarhouse Park is a great place for families to enjoy a picnic. Joggers can run along the rolling hills of the park's 2.3-mile perimeter. The population of Sugarhouse is about 58,000 and includes an eclectic mix of professionals, retired individuals, students and families. The median age is 44. Property in the area sells for $129,030 to $212,000.

West Jordan

Located between 900 and 8600 W. and 6200 and 10200 S., West Jordan is currently the seventh-largest city in the state. Twenty-five percent of the buildable land in Salt Lake County is found in West Jordan, and 895 national and international companies do business here. For the local work force, that means more than 11,000 jobs. Careful planning is the key to West Jordan's future. West Jordan has one of the Valley's youngest populations, with a median age of 20.6 and 46 percent of the population younger than 18. The average listed price for a home is $170,330.

West Valley City

West Valley City incorporated the communities of Granger, Hunter and Redwood into one large city in 1980. Located between 2100 and 4700 S. and 1200 and 7200 W., it is the second-largest city in the state with a population of nearly 100,000. The area has attracted several large international businesses and built a new industrial park, a 27-hole golf course and an impressive recreation center. Crime in "West Valley," as it's called by locals, has climbed during the past two decades, but law enforcement officials say that while it is not on the decline, the rate of increase has dropped off considerably. The average asking price for a home in West Valley is about $121,000. The median age is 38.5. The area's children are educated at Valley Crest Elementary, Valley Junior High and Granger High School.

Real-estate Companies

The Salt Lake Valley has scores of good real-estate companies to assist you in finding the perfect home for your lifestyle. We've included a representative list of qualified companies ranging from large national franchises to midsize, locally established firms. In addition to telling you a little about the kind of companies they are, we've provided an overview of the types of properties they generally sell and the locations where they most often do business. Any one of the companies we have included can help you find your dream home anywhere in the Salt Lake Valley.

Chapman, Richards and Associates

1414 E. Murray-Holladay Rd. • 278-4414, (800) 456-5192

This company's philosophy is "Give the best service all the time." Scott Chapman and George Richards established this real-estate company in 1978, combining their knowledge of the real-estate profession into one company. They specializes in residential real estate with an emphasis on new construction. The company also has commercial and relocation departments and is the representative for RELO, one of the largest relocation companies in the country.

Chapman Richards has 80 full-time

agents, 31 of whom have received the Salt Lake Board of Realtors Superior Achievement Award. Both Chapman and Richards have been supportive of many community and charitable organizations including the initial fund raising for the Ronald McDonald House. Richards served as federal district coordinator, representing the needs and concerns of real-estate professionals in Utah, to two U.S. legislators and has been a trustee for the Strategic Action and Realtor's Action Committee.

Coldwell Banker Premiere Realty

220 Morris Ave., Ste. 440, Salt Lake City • 484-1500, (800) 451-3850
7351 Union Park Ave., Midvale • 568-9000
2180 S. 1300 E., Ste. 140, Salt Lake City • 486-3175
7884 S. Redwood Rd. (1700 W.), Salt Lake City • 566-7866

An affiliate of the large national company, Coldwell Banker Premiere has local roots. Steve Webber started Webber Real Estate in 1983 but sold the company to Coldwell Banker in 1995. Sears, which owned the national company in 1989, began selling some of its companies and, re-enter Scott Webber. He and his brother, Steve, and father, Richard, bought back the original company and continued their affiliation.

The company has 160 agents in three offices serving the Salt Lake Valley who sell residential real estate in all neighborhoods. Their Previews Exceptional Properties Division handles luxury home sales. The company has a strong relocation department and is affiliated with HFS, one of the largest relocation firms in the country. All agents are full time, and many have received top awards. Joan Pate, an agent with Coldwell Banker Premiere in Salt Lake, recently earned the No. 7 position out of 56,000 agents in the national company.

Scott has been involved with fund-raising for Ballet West, and the company has been a strong supporter of a local shelter for battered women and children. Overall, the Salt Lake company is second in production within the national organization, and the Salt Lake offices produce at a rate three times higher than the national average.

Lewis, Wolcott & Dornbush Real Estate

2348 S. Foothill Dr. • 467-2100, (800) 382-7183

Many of the 26 seasoned agents who make up the Lewis, Wolcott & Dornbush team are award winners, with 62 percent of them holding the LWD Superior Achievement Award. Jim Lewis, president of the company, was the originator of the Lewis, Wolcott & Dornbush concept. He has been active in real-estate sales and development in the Salt Lake Valley and Park City for many years. Robert Dornbush came from Atlanta where he was head of the Dornbush Group and president and CEO of Chicago-based Itel Distribution. He has been instrumental in guiding LWD into a position of dominance in the sales and marketing of Salt Lake's westside residential areas. Linda Wolcott, principal broker for the Salt Lake office, has 20 years experience in top residential sales. She is a former president of the Salt Lake Board of Realtors and a lifetime member of the board's Million Dollar Club.

Lewis, Wolcott & Dornbush is a member of the nationally recognized Genesis Relocation Network and the sole Utah affiliate of Sotheby's International Realty and the Estates Club, both distinguished international real-estate marketing organizations.

The company represents many exclusive properties, and it also sells numerous starter homes in such neighborhoods as Rose Park and West Valley.

Mansell & Associates

6995 S. Union Park Ctr., Midvale • 567-4000, (800) 950-3945
12288 S. 900 E., Salt Lake City • 571-7878
2319 S. Foothill Blvd., Salt Lake City • 467-9000
9046 S. 1510 W., Salt Lake City • 569-8880

Brothers Dave and Al Mansell opened Mansell & Associates in 1975. Today they have 460 agents in 15 offices from Logan, Utah, to Las Vegas. As members of Home Franchise Services (HFS), the largest relocation company in the country, they can network with 450 independent brokers and 53,000 independent agents nationwide. Local agents have received top awards in the industry and were recently honored with the Utah State Ethics in

Business Award sponsored by the Better Business Bureau. Partner Russ Booth has served as president of the National Association of Realtors, the only partner in a commercial real-estate company in Utah ever to hold the position.

Ninety percent of Mansell's business is residential, although they the agency does offer commercial real-estate services. Their average sale is higher overall than the average home sale of $150,000 in the Salt Lake Valley. Active with many charitable organizations, Mansell has been highly visible with the historical preservation of older homes in the Salt Lake Valley.

Plumb & Company Real Estate
1001 E. 2100 S., Salt Lake City • 486-7428

Rick Plumb started Plumb & Company about 20 years ago, then decided to get out of the real-estate business eight years later. Brother Bob, along with Greg Gaddie and Bob's good friend from grade school, Jeff Wells, bought the company, and today, the three partners and 11 agents sell much of the property in the downtown, Avenues, Harvard-Yale and Sugarhouse areas. The agents, most of whom have 12 or more years of experience, are award winners and tops in the industry. Don't let their low-key style fool you. They really know the business, and it's hard to find an Insider who hasn't heard of them. They specialize in older homes and are actively involved with the preservation of historic property.

Prudential Prestige Real Estate
716 E. 4500 S. Ste. S-260, Salt Lake City • 288-9800, (888) 671-9800

A phenomenon among Prudential's international companies, the 5-year-old Salt Lake office has risen to the top with meteoric speed. David Weissman, CEO and managing partner, along with five other partners and more than 75 agents have many years experience in the real-estate field; they average seven years per agent. Many agents are consistent award winners, and several have received Prudential's highest national awards, the Pinnacle and Top of the Rock, competing against the 40,000 agents within the company. The local office has broken all national records for performance ratings with Prudential.

Prudential Prestige sells property throughout the Salt Lake Valley, including many luxury homes. Their average sale exceeds the $150,000 average cost of a home in the Valley. Showing a strong community spirit, the local company has lent support to various charitable organizations.

Ramsey Group Real Estate
675 E. 2100 S., Salt Lake City • 467-6688

The six partners and 14 sales agents at the Ramsey Group have made their mark on the real-estate profession in Salt Lake since opening their doors in 1984. Rhoda Ramsey was the first woman to receive the Salt Lake Board of Realtors' Salesman of the Year Award. Georgia Ball, Jodie Bennion and Sue Christensen have since earned the honor. Marcia Peterson has twice been a finalist. Ramsey has also been honored as *Utah Business Magazine*'s Woman of the Year and with the Salt Lake Board of Realtors President's Award. Ball became the first woman in the history of the Salt Lake Board of Realtors to be elected president and has been honored as Realtor of the Year. The National Association of Women Business Owners has also honored Ball, a partner in the firm, as a Business Owner of the Year. She was the 1997 president of the Utah Association of Realtors.

The Ramsey Group is the only real-estate company in the greater Salt Lake area listed in the current *Who's Who in Luxury Real Estate*, a national publication. Bennion is the first woman to serve on the board of directors of the Salt Lake County Club.

The women at the Ramsey Group support the community by participating in a variety of activities including in the national reading initiative called Project 2000 and the Neighborhood Housing and Neighborhood House Child/Senior Day-care Project. They celebrated their 10th anniversary by donating a playground for the children at Traveler's Aid Homeless Shelter.

Wardley Better Homes and Gardens
5296 S. Commerce Dr. (300 W.) Ste. 300, Salt Lake City • 288-8810, (800) 733-1921

From humble beginnings, Lynn Wardley became a member of the Better Homes and

Gardens national franchise system in 1974. The company now has six locations in the Salt Lake Valley and 800 agents. The agency sells property in all neighborhoods throughout the area and is particularly helpful in educating and assisting first-time buyers. Seven full-time agents staff their relocation department and pride themselves on helping families and companies relocate to the Salt Lake area. Many of Wardley's local agents are award winners for top sales in the area. Wardley continues to be politically active and was a delegate to a recent Republican National Convention. The company has the largest real-estate school in the area in addition to its own insurance and mortgage departments.

Rentals

The Salt Lake Valley rental market has the lowest vacancy rate in nation — 2 to 3 percent — so finding a place to rent can be tricky. Rents are not regulated, so landlords can charge whatever they want, despite the condition of the property. As a result, rental property can be costly. If you have some time and a little patience, you might find just the right rental priced within your budget.

Salt Lakers have learned that the best way to find a good rental property in a highly desirable neighborhood is by word of mouth. Get to know the neighbors and ask who might be moving out. We don't want to imply that finding a place to live calls for desperate measures, but some locals, especially those looking for rentals on the Avenues and in other intown locations, have been known to drive around looking for moving trucks. The freebie racks at most grocery stores carry *Apartments for Rent*, a publication that lists apartment rentals in the area.

A few rental agencies also handle homes, duplexes and small complexes (those will fewer than four units), but you'll pay a one-time fee for their services. If you go this route, check out the company before you pay the fee. We recommend you go with a company with a lot of experience in the market or someone who is a longtime resident themselves.

TLC Rentals
7777 S. State St., Midvale • 566-1777

This company meets the our criteria for a good rental agency. They have an excellent reputation, and agents have lived in the community for more than 40 years and know the area well. The one-time fee of $50 will give you new listings every day for up to 90 days. There are no additional or add-on fees. You can call everyday to get new listings by phone. Check their standing in the community, or that of any other rental company you encounter, by calling the Better Business Bureau, 487-4656. TLC's hours are 9 AM to 6 PM Monday through Friday and 10 AM to 3 PM on Saturday.

Higher education continues to be important. More than 24 percent of our adult residents have four-year college degrees or higher.

Education

Education has always been a priority for the residents of the Salt Lake Valley. Jane Dillworth held classes for young pioneer children in a tent within weeks of her arrival in 1847. By 1850 schools were springing up all over the city, and plans were under way to build a schoolhouse in every ward (Mormon congregation). The territorial legislature passed the first public school law in 1851 creating the office of superintendent of schools and providing for one or more schools in each town to be supported by local taxation. Family schools, or home schools as we now call them, were financed by individuals such as Brigham Young, who educated his more than 50 children at home.

Educating the children of Zion, as the Salt Lake Valley was called, was not to be a simple matter, however. Over the next 20 years, disagreements arose about how education should be carried out. The Mormon influence in the public school curriculum had begun to cause problems with non-Mormons and raised questions as to the supervision of the educational system. The Mormons were uncomfortable with the number of non-Mormon schools — many offering free tuition to Mormon children — and the lay influence in education and began to develop a system of church schools.

The matter of education heated up again between Mormon and non-Mormon families in the late 1880s, and Mormon officials called upon every stake (a regional grouping of wards) to establish an academy in its area. In effect, by 1890 public schools weren't serving the needs of either Mormons or non-Mormons, although the legislative assembly provided for the first territory tax-supported schools that same year. It took nearly a decade for the free public school movement to take hold. Today the state oversees 40 public school districts, and education is as important as it was when Jane Dillworth began teaching the three Rs to pioneer kids more than 150 years ago.

Each year the state Office of Education and the Utah legislature look at new and better ways to educate students and keep abreast of changing technology with an eye toward the future. Controversy continues to plague public education. Recently some schools and districts have debated the matter of public prayer as part of the high school commencement program, the alleged emphasis on Christian music sung by school choruses during the holidays and whether or not gay and lesbian student clubs should be allowed as part of school-sanctioned extracurricular activities.

Still, public elementary and secondary schools seem to hold their own in national academic testing. Programs have been expanded to help non-English-speaking students and their families, and the board of education has become more sensitive to the needs of the Valley's growing minority population.

Classes are larger than in many other states this size because of the high birthrate and inordinate number of children of school age, but educators continue to get good results, and overcrowding doesn't appear to impede the educational process in public institutions.

Since Utah schools have fewer dollars per student than any other state in the nation, additional money is always needed to keep up with educational challenges, and many businesses have lent their support to the cause of better education for area children. Several public school districts have created educational foundations that raise monies for their districts. Nearly half the state's annual budget is spent on public education.

Higher education continues to be important. More than 24 percent of our adult residents have four-year college degrees or higher. Outside the area of traditional education, many residents continue training in a variety of trade and technical schools offering both mainstream and nontraditional curricula. In addition, many adults continue the process of education through a legion of workshops and lectures on subject that range from time management to herbal remedies. The *Deseret News* and *The Salt Lake Tribune* provide listings of the vast selection of programs available for nontraditional students. For more information on these resources, check out the Media chapter.

In this chapter we have provided an overview of the public and private elementary and secondary schools in the Salt Lake Valley. We've also included information on our colleges and universities, trade and professional schools and resources for continuing education.

Kids are among our greatest treasures, and the area's many opportunities for early education and child care are evidence of this. You'll find many specialized programs for preschool through kindergarten as well the scoop on child care in the Child Care chapter.

child younger than 7 entering school for the first time in Utah must present documentation from a licensed physician that they have conducted a vision screening to detect the presence of amblyopia and other vision defects.

Children entering kindergarten for the first time must be 5 years old before September 2 of the year in which admission is sought. Any person having control of a minor child between 6 and 18 years of age must send the minor to a public or regularly established private school during the term of the school year of the district in which the child resides. Misdemeanor charges may be filed against individuals who do not comply with the compulsory education requirement.

To find out about home schooling your child, contact the Office of Education at the number listed above.

Free education is provided through the public school system for all disabled individuals between 3 to 22 years of age. To find out about programs for students with disabilities, call the individual school districts or the Office of Education.

Elementary and Secondary Schools

Public Schools

The Salt Lake Valley has four public school districts: Granite, Jordan, Murray and Salt Lake City. To enroll a student in a public school in one of these districts you will need to contact the State Office of Education, 250 E. 500 S., 538-7500, for the name of the school your child will attend based on your address.

All students entering public schools in the Salt Lake Valley must present a birth certificate and a record of current immunizations. A

School Districts

Granite School District
340 E. 3545 S., Salt Lake City • 263-6100

Granite is Utah's largest school district — the nation's 28th-largest — covering 300 square miles of urban and suburban area in the southeast and portions of the midsection of the Valley. The district serves more than 75,000 pupils. Students here score slightly lower than the Utah and national averages overall on SAT tests but achieve 1.5 points higher overall than the nation on ACT scores. Students taking the district's Advanced Place-

---

INSIDERS' TIP

During the early settlement and burgeoning educational years in the Salt Lake Valley, Brigham Young spent $20,000 and more than a decade trying to develop the Deseret Alphabet, which used phonetic symbols to help non-English-speaking immigrants communicate and to further isolate or individualize the Mormons. The alphabet was not a success.

ment (AP) tests score more than 8 percent higher than the national average.

The district operating budget of approximately $326 million provides for nine high schools, 15 junior high schools and 62 elementary schools. Special education programs, including an alternative junior and senior high school, are also available for students with disabilities or special needs. Many of the elementary schools operate on a year-round schedule.

Because of the large number of children in the district, the student-to-teacher ratio is high: 22-to-1 in kindergarten, 25-to-1 in grade 3 and nearly 28-to-1 in grade 6. Still, the district has been recognized nationally for academic excellence and innovative leadership. The district offers Enrollment Option within the district on a space-available basis so that parents can choose the school their child will attend within the district regardless of where they live.

The ethnic background of students in the Granite School District is 85 percent Caucasian, 8 percent Hispanic, 5 percent Asian and Pacific Islander, 1 percent American Indian and 1 percent African American.

Jordan School District
9361 S. 300 E., Sandy • 567-8100

This district serves nearly 73,000 students living in the south and southwest Valley. Jordan's operating budget of more than $360 million annually provides for 47 elementary schools, 15 middle schools and nine high schools in addition to three special schools for youth in custody and children with disabilities. Many elementary schools operate on a year-round basis. The district's ethnic profile is 94.4 percent Caucasian, 3.4 percent Hispanic/Latino, 1.5 percent Asian/Pacific Islander, 0.3 percent Native American and 0.4 percent African American.

The district's gifted and talented program serves students in grades 1 through 9 with concurrent enrollment programs for high school students at Salt Lake Community College, Brigham Young University and the University of Utah. SAT scores for Jordan District 11th grade students are slightly higher than the state and national averages. The student-to-teacher ratio varies with each grade. For example, a kindergarten classroom may have

44 students and one teacher while high school classes may have a 25 students per teacher. Jordan's Choice Program allows families to choose which school within the district their child will attend, if space allows. Not all schools in the district participate in the program.

Murray School District
147 E. 5065 S., Murray • 264-7400

Murray schools are in the midsection of the Valley. The district operates with an annual budget of approximately $32.5 million for 11 schools: seven elementary, three junior high and two high schools. Total enrollment in the district is less than 7,000 students, and less than 1 percent of the enrollment is made up of minority students. Though the pupil-to-teacher ratio is only 20.5-to-1 in the first grade, the ratio increases steadily to nearly 25 students per teacher in the high schools.

Students in the Murray district score nearly one percentage point higher on ACT scores than the national average. Advanced Placement Programs are available in one of the district's high schools. Concurrent enrollment at Salt Lake Community College is also an option for students. Perspectives, the district's gifted and talented program, is available in each elementary school in the district. The Summit Program at Creekside High School offers smaller classes and programs devoted to individual rates of progress to students with difficulty earning credit in a traditional high school setting. The program is also available at Murray High School for 8th-grade students.

Four Murray elementary schools qualify for Title I services, and the district's special education services provide programs for students with physical, emotional and learning disabilities.

Murray is a leader among public schools in the state in the use of technology. The Internet is available in almost every classroom in the district. Filtering software through UtahLINK helps students and teachers use the Internet for appropriate purposes. In addition to a teacher's computer in each classroom, student computer labs are in all school media centers. The Murray Early Childhood Education Center, 73 W. 6100 S., is the only facility of its kind in the state. This center houses all of Murray's district and federal government preschool programs. Nearly 250 children from ages 3 to 5 visit the center each week.

Salt Lake City School District
440 E. 100 S., Salt Lake City • 578-8599

The Salt Lake City School District educates more than 25,000 students at an annual cost of approximately $123 million. The student-to-teacher ratio is approximately 23-to-1. The dropout rate for students in grades 7 through 12 is approximately 9.5 percent. Students in the city's district score approximately 1 percent higher than the national average on ACT tests, and high school seniors who take the CEEB Scholastic Achievement Test, the second major college entrance exam, score slightly higher than the national average.

The Salt Lake City School District serves the highest number of low-income families in the state and the largest number of students in the state who come from households where limited or no English is spoken in the home. The minority population of the city's school children is 34 percent, including 20 percent Hispanic, 4 percent Asian, 3 percent African American, 3 percent Native American and 5 percent Pacific Islands; 66 percent are Caucasian.

The district has 37 campuses including 27 elementary schools, five middle or intermediate schools, three high schools, one alternative high school at four sites and the Matheson Head Start. The district also operates programs at the Guadalupe Center and Travelers Aid homeless shelter. We've provided information about these two exceptional programs at the end of the "Public Schools" section. Five elementary schools operate year-round. Horizonte Instruction and Training Center (the alternative high school) also operates year-round. The Open Classroom program, a parent cooperative, is available at Washington Elementary, and the Curriculum and Assessment Lab, a multi-age program, is offered at Ensign Elementary. Among special programs in the system are the Academy of Finance offered at East High School, Television Production at Highland High and the International Baccalaureate at West High School. The Extended Learning Program (ELP) for gifted students is available in all elementary and middle schools. English as a Second Language (ESL) is offered in one elementary school and one high school in the city.

The Salt Lake City School District was the recent recipient of Annenberg Challenge Grant that was matched in part by the Eccles Foundation in Utah. The district will use the grant to support reform of the school district through advocacy and accountability.

Alternative Education

Salt Lake City schools administer a variety of special programs for students with special needs from behavioral or learning problems to programs for disabled students.

Horizonte Instruction and Training Center
1234 S. Main St., Salt Lake City • 578-8574

This center provides an alternative high school situation to meet graduation requirements. Along with academic courses, students develop career plans and participate in vocational training. Day and evening classes and flexible scheduling accommodate students needs, and a Young Parents Program provides high school services to pregnant and parenting teens. The computerized learning center allows individualization of the curriculum.

The Guadalupe Schools
340 S. Goshen St., Salt Lake City
• 531-6100

For more than 25 years this center has served the educational needs of disadvantaged children and adult immigrants and refugees on Salt Lake's west side. Its programs address the issues surrounding poverty, illiteracy, school dropout and the ensuing social cost. The school's two educational programs — the Early Learning Center (ELC) and the Voluntary Improvement Program (VIP) — are open to students from all ethnic and religious backgrounds. Support is provided by a cross section of civic-minded organizations and individuals in the community. Religious support is ecumenical.

Marilyn Treshaw Elementary School
210 S. Rio Grande St., Salt Lake City
• 531-1507

Established in 1982, soon after the Traveler's Aid Shelter began assisting clients in the Salt Lake area, this school for children of families living in the homeless shelter operates today with assistance from the State Office of Education through the Chapter I program. Education is provided on-site to students in kindergarten through 6th grade. It provides a full curriculum in addition to guidance for students who are in a transitional stage of their lives.

Annually, the school serves approximately 300 students, who stay in the program for up to 12 weeks. Class work is individualized, and older students help younger children. Students also receive the support of part-time teachers and volunteers. This extraordinary program has made a significant difference in the lives of many children in the Valley.

Private Schools

Several of Salt Lake's early parochial schools still operate today alongside more-recently established schools that represent specific denominations. Many students with no religious affiliation attend these schools because of the outstanding academic programs offered. In addition, our area has a host of nondenominational private schools with na-

tionally acclaimed curricula. We have private schools with specific academic focus and schools with a more general focus. In the Salt Lake Valley you'll find nearly 200 campuses with programs from preschool through grade 12.

Tuition to private and parochial schools ranges from less than $1,000 per year to more than $10,000.

Anchor Christian Academy
1880 E. 5600 S., Holladay • 272-9405

This 25-year-old school is affiliated with Anchor Baptist Church, serving children in kindergarten through grade 12. The Christian curriculum is an individualized Accelerated Christian Education program. The school groups students in kindergarten and 1st grade in one classroom and places the remaining students in an open learning center. The school has an enrollment of fewer than 50 students with a student teacher ratio of 25-to-1. A dress code is enforced.

Carden Memorial School
1452 E. 2700 S., Salt Lake City
• 486-4895

A private, independent, nonsectarian Christian school, Carden Memorial was founded in 1949 by the late Mae Carden, who emphasized clear and specific guidelines for behavior and good manners as the foundation for a successful academic endeavor. The Salt Lake school opened in 1969 and presently has nearly 400 students in preschool through grade 8, with a 10-to-1 student-to-teacher ratio. Children receive a broad academic program which includes the arts in addition to classes in English, history, mathematics, geography, Bible study, science, French and Latin, physical education and computer. *The Parents' Guide to Alternatives in Education*, a national directory of alternative schools, featured the Salt Lake City school in a recent edition.

Catholic Church Diocese of Salt Lake City
27 C St., Salt Lake City • 328-8641

The diocese runs 13 schools throughout the Valley including 11 elementary schools and two high schools. In addition, it operates three preschools. Each of the schools has an enrollment of approximately 300 students, with a student-to-teacher ratio of 25-to-1. Operating costs are subsidized by parishes in the Valley, and tuition is less than other private schools. Students do not have to be of the Catholic faith to enroll. Judge Memorial High School has held the reputation as one of the Valley's best schools for more than 75 years.

Challenger School

1325 S. Main, Salt Lake City • 487-9984
4555 S. 2300 E., Salt Lake City
• 278-4797
1260 E. 8600 S., Salt Lake City
• 561-9494
10693 S. 1000 E., Salt Lake City
• 572-6686
2247 W. 8660 S., Salt Lake City
• 565-1058
Corporate office, 571 W. 9320 S., Salt Lake City • 569-2700

Challenger has operated preschool and elementary school programs for children in the Salt Lake area since 1963. This nondenominational school focuses on excellence in education through traditional academic programs with an emphasis on creative teaching techniques. Students typically score in the 90th percentile on standard national tests.

The school's combined enrollment is approximately 6,000 students, with a student-to-teacher ratio of about 14-to-1 in the lower elementary classes and 24-to-1 in the upper elementary grades.

Christ Lutheran School

240 E. 5600 S., Murray • 266-8714

The curriculum at Christ Lutheran is based on guidelines for elementary and middle schools in the state of Utah as well as on the Lutheran Elementary Schools program called Integrating Faith. The school has been educating children in the Salt Lake Valley since 1955. It has 10 large classrooms, a media center, computer and science labs, an athletic field and a gymnasium. It offers before- and after-school child-care facilities. The school enrolls approximately 250 students from kindergarten through grade 8. The student-to-teacher radio is 19-to-1.

Grace Baptist School

4880 W. 4100 S., Salt Lake City
• 968-4843

The classes at Grace Baptist are very small; the student-teacher ratio is about 15-to-1. The school's total enrollment is approximately 60 students in kindergarten through grade 12, and students are instructed using A Beka Christian curriculum. Grace Baptist has been part of the Salt Lake education scene for more than 13 years. In addition to Bible studies the school emphasizes academics, patriotism and discipline.

Grace Lutheran School

1815 E. 9800 S., Salt Lake City
• 572-3793

Grace Lutheran offers education programs for children in preschool (3- and 4-year-olds) and kindergarten through grade 8. The curriculum addresses spiritual, emotional, social, physical and academic goals. Class sizes are limited to between 14 and 25 depending on the grade, with a total enrollment of nearly 200 students. The traditional academic program is enhanced by music study, art, sports and computer programs. The school also offers an extended afterschool program.

Hawthorne Academy

2965 E. 3435 S., Salt Lake City
• 485-1801

This is a college-preparatory school for high school-age students in grades 9 through 12 and is accredited by the National Association of Schools and Colleges. The nondenominational school offers programs in a traditional curriculum, operating on a collegiate schedule of one to two hours of instruction per subject every other day and two to three hours of outside study for each hour of class time. Teachers at Hawthorne stress the individual academic needs of students.

Intermountain Christian School

6515 S. Lion Ln., Salt Lake City
• 942-8811

ICS is a ministry of the Evangelical Free Church of Salt Lake City, founded in 1982. The school has an enrollment of more than 400 students in kindergarten through grade 12 and a half-day preschool program for chil-

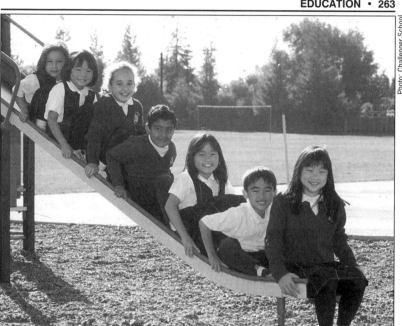

Photo: Challenger School

Kids are one of the most important aspects of our community. A wide variety of educational options are available to area children in public and private schools.

dren 4 years old. The Bible-centered, Christ-honoring program uses traditional approaches to academics in small classes for more individualized attention. The school has a strong fine-arts program and uses Saxon Math in kindergarten through grade 8.

The student-to-teacher class ratio is 15-to-1 in preschool, 18-to-1 in kindergarten and 25-to-1 in elementary. Class size is limited to 30 students per teacher in the middle and high school programs. Teachers in preschool and kindergarten have a classroom assistant.

Jewish Community Center
2425 E. Heritage Way, Salt Lake City
• 485-4507

Classes at the Jewish Community Center Elementary school are small, and the student-to-teacher ratio of 15-to-1 is one of the best in the Valley. The school gets high marks for academics and is well-known for the use of

stimulating, challenging and enriching integrated curriculum and teaching techniques, which help students learn better. The integrated curriculum presents information in context as part of the whole rather than approaching subjects individually. To enroll a child in the JCC's elementary school, you must be a member of the JCC but do not need to be of the Jewish faith. In addition to the yearly tuition, the center charges an additional fee for food service (students receive a kosher lunch). Limited scholarships are available.

Jordan Valley Christian School
9400 S. Redwood Rd., Salt Lake City
• 255-9649

This school offers an assisted home-school program for grades 1 to 12 that brings students into the classroom two days each week for testing. The Christian-based academic program requires parents to oversee the study.

Jordan Valley Christian School uses the Accelerated Christian Education (A.C.E.) program.

Lutheran High School
4020 S. 900 E., Salt Lake City • 266-6676

With an emphasis on academics and Christian education, this school has been teaching children in the Valley since 1984. More than 100 student are enrolled in grades 9 through 12. The curriculum offers traditional courses in addition to advanced placement in literature, chemistry and calculus. At the end of 1997, the school had 20 National Honor Society scholars. Many graduates are awarded scholarships to leading universities. Salt Lake Lutheran High faculty is made up of eight full-time and two part-time teachers, giving it a student-to-teacher ratio of 12-to-1.

Mt. Vernon Academy
184 E. Vine St., Murray • 266-5521

Mt. Vernon Academy, established in 1975, uses Saxon Math in grades kindergarten through 12 and Open Court as a basic reader that is preceded by a step-by-step phonic reading program. Singing is taught in all grades, with instrumental music instruction in grades 3 through 6. Students in grades 7 through 12 can choose core and elective classes including math (through basic calculus), English, journalism, science (biology, chemistry and physics), history, foreign languages (Spanish, French and German), computer literacy and word processing, English as a Second Language and LDS seminary classes.

The school strives to inspire spiritual and academic growth in its students and is fully accredited by the Northwest Association of Schools and Colleges. The school offers individual and family tuition rates. Classes are small, with an average of 12 students per teacher. Total enrollment is approximately 125 students.

Realms of Inquiry
1140 S. 900 E., Salt Lake City • 467-5911

A full-day academic curriculum is offered to students in kindergarten through grade 12 with a half day program for preschoolers. This school, founded in 1972, serves gifted, talented and creative children with a minimum IQ of 120 in upper grades. Lower grade students are more selectively evaluated. In addition to a core curriculum-based academic program which includes foreign language study, the school emphasizes drama, music, art and outdoor activities such as skiing, backpacking, cave exploring, river running, rock climbing and survival trips. The school offers teacher-mentor programs in the area of students interests. Realms has approximately 100 students and an average class size of 15.

Reid School
2965 E. 3435 S., Salt Lake City • 466-4214

Reid is the first private school in the area to be totally dedicated to the use of Exemplary Center for Reading Instruction educational methods. The school, which has an enrollment of approximately 150, was established in 1987. The focuses are on outstanding academic achievement, the development of individual talent and building student's self-esteem. Classes are provided in kindergarten through grade 8, with a student-to-teacher ratio of 20-to-1. Students typically place high in state and national competitions. The school also offers preschool and summer programs for school-age children.

Rowland Hall-St. Mark's School
Lower grades, 205 E. First Ave., Salt Lake City • 355-7485
Upper grades, 843 Lincoln St., Salt Lake City • 355-7494

Since 1880 Rowland Hall-St. Mark's School has been providing quality education based

---

INSIDERS' TIP

Interested in learning the art of primitive basketry? The U. of U. Division of Continuing Education offers a workshop using techniques such as plain weaving, twining and twill weaving. Participants gather their own materials. Call 581-3692 for details and the lowdown on other unique classes.

on the philosophy of excellence in education along with the elements that provide ethical development among students. Classes are small, with a student-to-teacher ratio of 14-to-1 in the lower grades and 20-to-1 in the upper grades.

Lower school programs take its approximately 300 students through a balanced liberal arts curriculum in kindergarten through grade 5 in preparation for continued studies with the school. Students study foreign languages, character education and computer science in addition to traditional programs.

Academic requirements in the upper school, grades 6 through 12, are geared toward future college enrollment, encouraging application to the best institutions in the country. ACT and SAT scores rank well above the state and national averages for the nearly 650 upper-school students.

The school offers a winter sports program in both the upper and lower schools which includes alpine skiing in addition to other sports.

The Waterford School
1480 E. 9400 S., Sandy • 572-1780

Waterford has become a showcase for the application of computers in education, and the U.S. Department of Education has recognized it as one of the top 12 schools in the nation for academic and technological excellence. The low student-to-teacher ratio (an average of 10 students for every teacher and a 3-to-1 student ratio in upper grades) and high SAT scores — more than eight points higher than the national average and one point higher than the state average — have placed Waterford and its computer-based learning on the cutting edge of education. Waterford has produced several National Merit finalists as well as students with national science awards, top prizes in the state language fair and one Rhodes Scholar. With an enrollment of nearly 900 students, the school employs more than 64 faculty members for students in kindergarten through grade 12. Waterford also has a preschool for children 3 and 4 years of age.

Higher Education

Salt Lakers continues their educational

opportunities beyond high school through the University of Utah, a branch campus of Brigham Young University, a four-year college and several two-year colleges. In addition, the region has several centers geared to specific vocational pursuits.

In 1850, the first institution of higher education in Salt Lake City, the University of Deseret, opened its doors. Geared to training teachers, the institution closed two years later for lack of support. Deseret reopened in 1867 as a commercial college with a systematic collegiate curriculum. The 223 students, half of whom were women, were initially enthusiastic, but interest soon waned and the school didn't fair much better the second time around. The college was moved to the Fort Douglas military reservation in 1892 where the third attempt at creating a university for the people of Zion was successful under the name University of Deseret-Utah. The name was changed to the University of Utah in 1902.

Brigham Young University was established in 1889 as the Mormon church's institution of higher learning and the center of church education in Provo, Utah, 40 miles south of Salt Lake City. BYU now operates a small campus in Salt Lake City and offers general education courses toward a degree from BYU in Provo.

The Salt Lake Collegiate Institute College was established by the Presbyterian Church in 1875. The name was later changed to Westminster College. The school became a four-year college in 1944, and in 1975 ownership and executive direction was given to an independent board of trustees.

The schools described in this section offer degree programs from associate to doctorate.

Colleges and Universities

Brigham Young University
1521 E. 3900 S., Salt Lake City
• 273-3434

The Salt Lake campus of Brigham Young University offers classes in general education for college students. Depending on the student's major, up to 61.5 credits of general education may be taken at the Salt Lake campus. The Salt Lake location also offers programs in genealogy certification, dietary managers certification, teacher recertification, urban elementary teacher certification, master of public administration and much more. To find out more about Brigham Young University, see the section on "Provo" in our Daytrips chapter.

LDS Business College
411 E. South Temple, Salt Lake City
• 524-8100

Established in 1886 by the Church of Jesus Christ of Latter-day Saints, this business college offers Associate of Science and Associate of Applied Science degrees in accounting, computer and information systems, business and entrepreneurship, health services, interior design and office administration. Students participate in social activities sponsored by the school including student government, LDS Student Association socials, dances, forums and devotional lectures, service projects, sororities and fraternities. Two on-campus residences provide 125 beds for women, and other off-campus school-sanctioned housing is available for men and women. More than 1,000 students attend the school each year.

Mountain West College
3098 Highland Dr., Salt Lake City
• 485-0221

This school is accredited by the Accrediting Council for Independent Colleges and Schools and awards diplomas and two-year associate degrees to students in business related disciplines. Classes are offered in accounting, business management, computer information systems, paralegal, medical assisting, office administration and travel and tourism. Mountain West is part of Corinthian Colleges Inc., which operates 36 schools nationwide. The Salt Lake school has operated since 1982.

Salt Lake Community College
Main campus, 4600 Redwood Rd., Salt Lake City • 957-4111
1575 S. State St., Salt Lake City
• 957-3000
551 N. 2200 W., Salt Lake City
• 355-2527
1040 W. 700 S., Salt Lake City
• 328-9200
830 E. 9400 S., Salt Lake City • 957-3717
9221 S. Redwood Rd., Salt Lake City
• 566-4105
1521 E. 3900 S., Salt Lake City
• 957-3106

The college offers programs leading to Associate of Applied Science degree, Associate of Arts degree, Associate of Pre-Engineering degree and Associate of Science degree. The school opened in 1948. Approximately 43,000 credit and noncredit students attend classes on the main Redwood Road campus or at one of the satellite campuses each year. The school, which employs 882 full-time and 1,700 part-time personnel, consists of schools of Business and Industry, Continuing and Community Education, Humanities and Science and Technology.

Among the features here are 18 apprenticeship programs and 30 short-term vocational training programs designed to meet the needs of individuals with disabilities or of those who are socially, economically and/or vocationally disadvantaged. The school also provides nearly $2 million in contract training to more than 600 area businesses and industries. Union Pacific Railroad brings workers to SLCC from 22 states for custom training programs.

The University of Utah
210 S. President's Cir., Salt Lake City
• 581-7200

The University of Utah, with an enrollment of more than 26,000 students, encompasses a medical school and is among the top 50 public research universities in the nation. Inventions that have come out of the university's research program include an implantable artificial pancreas, a method of coal liquefaction, a new artificial heart and a system for removing lead from drinking water. The school is known for its technology-transfer program, which moves state-of-the-art research into practical application in the business world.

The campus, which includes the health sciences complex, Research Park and Fort Douglas, encompasses 1,494 acres covered by more than 9,000 trees and shrubs.

Sixty-eight undergraduate degree programs are offered plus more than 50 teaching majors and minors. The College of Law's Wallace Stegner Center for Lands, Resources and the Environment, named after the Pulitzer Prize-winning author, focuses on Western people and issues. The Law School has one of the first masters programs in environmental, natural resources and energy law in the country. The College of Science offers the Intermountain West's only combined bachelor and master of science degree in biology emphasizing molecular biology/genetic engineering. The College of Business is the nation's only joint Center for International Business Education and Research, which is administered with Brigham Young University in Provo. The Architectural School at the U of U offers the Intermountain West's only degree in historic preservation.

Campus life is always bustling. In addition to academic pursuits, students enjoy the Utah Museum of Fine Arts, the Utah Museum of Natural History and Red Butte Gardens and Arboretum, all located on campus. You can read more about the Fine Arts Museum in the Arts chapter, and turn to our Kidstuff and Sightseeing and Attractions chapters to check out the Natural History Museum and Red Butte Gardens.

Student housing is available on campus. Three dormitories house approximately 1,200 students. In addition, married-student apartments for couples and single-student apartments for medical students are available on campus.

The U of U also has Western Athletic Conference (WAC) championship teams in men's and women's basketball, and the Lady Utes

gymnastics, which has won nine national championships in the past decade. Other top teams include the NCAA championship skiers and the Running Utes football team of Freedom Bowl championship fame. University athletes have earned 67 national team and individual championships and 46 conference team championships in the past 15 years. Ten women's teams and nine men's teams compete in the WAC in Division I of the NCAA. See the Spectator Sports chapter for more information.

Westminster College
1840 S. 1300 E., Salt Lake City
• 484-7651

Westminster has the distinction of being the only coeducational, independent, nondenominational liberal arts college in the state. Approximately 2,000 students attend Westminster on a full- or part-time basis annually. The college has two residence halls with co-ed housing by floor and wing. Approximately 175 students live on-campus. Eighty percent of the students are residents of the state; less than 8 percent of the student body is made up of minority students.

Four schools operate within the college: School of Arts and Sciences, Bill and Vieve Gore School of Business, School of Education and St. Mark's-Westminster School of Nursing. The college offers 27 majors and programs and four graduate programs in business administration, education, nursing and professional communication. Westminster employs 93 full-time and 100 part-time faculty members of which 83 percent hold a doctorate or professional terminal degree.

Two intercollegiate teams, men's soccer and women's volleyball, compete in National Association of Intercollegiate Athletics District II. The college has a lively cultural scene filled with community concerts, theater, lectures and musical events throughout the year. *U.S. News and World Report* consistently lists Westminster College among the nation's top 28 public and private colleges and *Peterson's Guide to Competitive Colleges* lists Westminster in the top 10 percent of 3,600 U.S. public and private colleges and universities.

Vocational and Professional Schools

The Center for Travel Education
9489 S. 700 E., Salt Lake City • 572-3454

For anyone interested in a career in the field of travel and tourism, the school offers a comprehensive program covering reservations, geography, computer reservation systems, fares and tickets, leisure travel, sales and customer service and resume writing and interviewing skills. The 11-week program includes 156 hours of classroom instruction. Upon completion of the course students receive a certificate of graduation, and CTE offers placement assistance for up to two months following graduation.

Certified Careers Institute
1455 W. 2200 S., No. 200, Salt Lake City • 973-7008

Certified has been teaching career computer courses since 1983. Classes are offered in programming, network administration, data processing and computer/electronic repair. The school also offers an associate's degree program in computer science. Financial aid is available for qualified students, and the school is approved for veterans. Placement assistance is provided upon completion of courses. Certified is accredited by the Accreditation Commission of Career Schools and Colleges of Technology. Day and evening classes are available.

Intermountain College of Court Reporting
5980 S. Fashion Blvd., Murray • 268-9271

The school teaches the basics in court reporting including an introduction to the course, English, anatomy and medical terminology, legal terminology and deposition classes. In addition, students are drilled for speed and accuracy and complete 40 hours of verified internship before graduation. Classes are offered during the day and evening for a total of 75 hours of instruction over a five-week period. The school offers a free placement assistance program to graduates. Utah law requires the Registered Professional Reporter test, which is given by the National Court Reporters Association twice a year (May and November) in Salt Lake City.

ITT Technical Institute
920 W. Levoy Dr., Salt Lake City • 263-3313, (800) 365-2136

Industry-experienced faculty provide training in employment-focused educational programs including two-year Associate of Applied Science degrees in electronic engineering technology and computer-aided drafting and three-year Bachelor of Applied Science degrees in electronic engineering technology and industrial design. The philosophy is to learn by doing. Financial assistance is available for qualified applicants and placement assistance is provided for graduates.

International Institute of Hair Design
5712 S. Redwood Rd., Salt Lake City • 966-4536
3474 S. 2300 E., Salt Lake City • 278-4656

International uses a step-by-step process beginning with basics and working toward advanced concepts of cosmetology and hair design. Classes are available during the day and evening. The 2,000-hour course can be completed on a full- or part-time basis. Upon graduation, students are required to take a state licensing examination.

Myotherapy College of Utah
3350 S. 2300 E., Salt Lake City • 484-7624

If you're interested in a career in massage therapy, MCU offers a 780-hour certification course with daytime classes Monday through Friday for nine months. Evening classes are also available. Completion of the program qualifies students to sit for the Utah license examination as well as the national certification exam. MCU is accredited by the Accreditation Commission of Career Schools and Colleges of Technology and is a member of Career College Association. The school is internationally certified.

Rocky Mountain Bartending Academy
350 S. 400 E., Ste. G-3, Salt Lake City • 532-7127

For anyone interested in a full-time or part-time bartending career, this school can teach you the fundamentals as well as providing some expanded information in two-hour, three-hour or five-hour per week courses for a total of 24 hours. You will learn how to mix all classic and modern drinks, refine customer relations skills and get hands-on experience. Rocky Mountain is one of the only bartending schools in the country to offer Training and Intervention Procedures (T.I.P.S.) certification, a program sponsored by Anheuser Busch to increase awareness of alcohol abuse. The academy offers a placement assistance service to graduates. The school has been in business since 1933.

Utah Career College
1144 W. 3300 S., Salt Lake City • 975-7000

This school offers training and associate's degrees in the fields of healthcare, business and hospitality, multimedia, office careers, and automotive repair. Classes are small and available during the day or evening. Some college credits may be transferable. The school offers financial assistance to qualified students and a placement assistance program upon completion of courses.

Contractor's License Center
461 E. 200 S., Salt Lake City • 364-9200, (800) 397-9201

This school offers preparatory classes for taking the examination for contractors license for the State of Utah through the Division of Occupational and Professional Licensing. Course work covers business and law, trade courses and workshops for test preparation. Classes are held during the day and evening.

In addition to the classes listed above, the school sponsors lectures on bonding, mechanic's liens and builder's insurance.

Violin Making School of America
308 E. 200 S., Salt Lake City • 364-3651

Established in 1972 by Peter Paul Prier, this school is the first of its kind in the United States. The talented faculty teaches such subjects as woods and tools, construction, playing of stringed instruments, mechanical and artistic drawing, orchestra, history and technical repair. Upon completing the four-year program, graduates receive job-placement assistance from the school. The founder and director is a member of the Entente International des Maitres Luthiers et Archetiers D'Art, the American Federation of Violin and Bow Makers and the German Violin Makers Federation.

Special Education and Resources

State Office of Education
250 E. 500 S., Salt Lake City • 538-7500

The State Office of Education is a clearinghouse of information on programs for students with special needs such as at-risk, disabled and non-English-speaking. It also offers family educational assistance. If you need information about any school in the area, including private nondenominational and parochial schools, the staff at this office can point you in the right direction.

Utah School for the Deaf and Blind
2870 S. Connor St., Salt Lake City • 464-0840

A phone call to the school will put you in touch with the many programs available to students of all ages who are visually and hearing impaired. The staff is well-informed and very cordial.

In Salt Lake City, which has more children than any other city its size in the country, the child-care question is an important one.

Child Care

Who's minding the little ones? In Salt Lake City, which has more children than any other city its size in the country, the child-care question is an important one. And in Utah, which has the highest birthrate the nation, the issue will continue to have an impact as we approach the next millennium.

Many families want child care to be a family affair. It's not unusual for extended family members to care for nieces and nephews or grandchildren while mom and dad are away at work. Mormon families tend to be large here, so aunts, uncles and cousins are in plentiful supply. Besides family members, parents often rely on neighbors with kids of their own to care for their children during the day in a home environment. The down side of this scenario is that some of these day-care providers are not licensed.

Salt Lake City is a close-knit community where a referral from a church acquaintance or family member can carry a lot of weight. Unfortunately, the provider may not be properly insured, the home may not meet safety or sanitation requirements, and the caregiver may not have the proper training. Being a good mom or dad doesn't necessarily guarantee that the individual will be a good care provider for other children. If you are looking for day care in a private home, we recommend you check on the provider's license and credentials. Utah law requires licensing for every family child-care home with a maximum of six children (including the provider's own children), every family group-care home with up to 12 children and two care providers, and every center with 13 to 200 children.

In July 1997, licensing of child-care providers and centers was shifted from the Department of Human Services to the Department of Health, and a thorough assessment of child care in the area was undertaken. Drop-in child-care centers in shopping malls, spas and the like were not required to be licensed before July 1997. Our listing does not include drop-in centers because the licensing process will take time to complete, so we aren't certain who has a license and who doesn't. You will want to check this out before you drop off little ones. Current licensing covers only health and safety certifications and does not assess provider training. Licensing does include a criminal background check.

As Utah moves forward to attain more in-depth licensing procedures, the quality of care should improve. Sad to say, we are a little behind the times in scrutinizing child care.

Throughout the Valley you'll find hundreds of well-known chains and private day-care facilities. As we have indicated, all facilities with six or more children are required to have a license, but it never hurts to check. A license alone does not guarantee adequate child care. If you are considering the day-care center route as a solution to your child-care needs, it's a good idea to visit the facility several times before making a decision. Drop in at different times during the day for a spontaneous look around. Don't be shy about asking for the names of other parents who have entrusted their children to the day-care center. Quality child care, as with quality in any profession, is improved with training. When you investigate child-care facilities, it is wise to ask about the provider's educational background and training as well as checking out the physical facility. The same criterion applies to family child-care home and family group-home providers.

In the next sections, we provide information on places you can call if you are seeking child care in your home or in a center, including the scoop on babysitters, nannies and au pairs.

Resources

In the Salt Lake Valley we have day-care facilities to mind the children, feed them meals and supervise their play. We also have day-care facilities that focus on early childhood development and learning. Many of our parochial and private schools offer preschool and day-care programs with an emphasis on early learning. Some of the best day-care centers have waiting lists. The resources listed below will help you get through the maze of day-care and preschool providers. You will also find a complete list of day-care providers in the Yellow Pages under "Child Care" and preschool listings under "Schools, Academic — Preschool and Kindergarten."

Several organizations sponsor summer programs for kids. Check them out in our Kidstuff chapter under "Campy Kidstuff."

Children's Service Society of Utah
124 S. 400 E., Salt Lake City • 355-7444

This is a gold mine of help for parents with child-care needs and a good place to start your search for good child-care arrangements. The organization connects families with licensed child-care providers — including in-home, group and day-care centers — throughout the community and keeps track of providers in the area. Working as a clearinghouse for families and providers, it educates consumers on what to look for in a day-care situation, what they should know about day care in Utah and how to choose the right place for their needs. Trained counselors discuss parent/child requirements during an initial 30-minute session. Parents receive referrals and monthly updates on providers as part of the service. The Utah State Department

of Child Care funds this nonprofit organization. The service is free to both parents and providers. Call for an appointment.

Consumer Protection Agency
160 E. 300 S., Salt Lake City • 530-6601

You can ask about licensing or license revocation of day-care providers in the Salt Lake Valley through this office of the Commerce Department of the State of Utah.

Better Business Bureau of Utah
1588 S. Main St., Salt Lake City
• 487-4656

This organization can tell you if a complaint has been filed against a day-care provider. Beyond "yes" or "no," they don't provide much information, but you'll know if someone was dissatisfied with the provider's services.

Babysitting

Many families rely on friends and relatives for babysitting while they enjoy an evening out on the town. Young teens in the Salt Lake Valley often subsidize their weekly allowance quite handsomely by babysitting for neighbors. Presently there are no regulations for licensing babysitting companies in the Salt Lake area. In the past, a few babysitting companies have offered services, but we were unable to find enough information on them for inclusion in this listing. If you do stumble onto a babysitting service in the area, check it out thoroughly before you use its services. At the very least, the service should have a business license and carry a bond. Several companies that specialize in long-term nannies do occasionally provide a sitter for the night with adequate notice. Check them out in the next section.

Nannies

Salt Lake City may very well be the biggest nanny and au pair connection outside London. Young LDS girls who help raise brothers and sisters in their own large families are sought as nannies because of their experience with young children and the family values the LDS church instills in its young people. Many eligible home-grown nannies are exported to families in other parts of the country. The classified section of our Sunday newspaper is full of ads from New York, California and parts between requesting the services of nannies from our area.

Application fees range from $15 to $75, and local nannies generally charge between $800 and $875 per month. Out-of-state families will pay between $800 and $1,375 per month for a nanny from the Salt Lake area. Day rates range from $8 to $10 per hour and full- and half-day rates of approximately $100 and $50 respectively can be arranged through some agencies. You may pay an application fee in addition to the hourly or day rate. You can find good nannies for local employment through the following agencies.

Au Pair Program USA and Childcrest
6985 S. Union Park Ave., Ste. 340, Salt Lake City • 255-7722

This company has been supplying nannies and au pairs to Insiders and clients throughout the world for more than 15 years. Nannies and au pairs are put through rigorous screening before they are sent into the home. Au pairs must submit to a credit and criminal check, provide a physician's report, undergo a personal interview with the agency and have at least four child-care references and two personal references. Nannies undergo similar background and personal checks. The agency can hook you up with a well-qualified nanny or au pair while you are in the Salt Lake area or furnish you with this type of child care in another location. The service agency does not have hourly or short-term nanny services.

Helpers West
443 E. Pepperidge Dr., Salt Lake City • 561-8889

This is Utah's oldest nanny agency. The company has been in business since 1984 and is a member of the International Nanny Association. The company supplies live-in nannies locally or out-of-state for a year or more or for a shorter period of time (one to two months). This agency does background checks, but they vary in depth according to circumstances. Nannies are trained with a video and are required to be certified in CPR and first aid. If they will be caring for children in a home with a swimming pool, they must have lifesaving certification. Depending on availability, you can hire a nanny for the day or by the hour through this agency. Advance notice is required. One to three weeks is preferable.

The Nanny Connection
1231 S. 425 W., Bountiful • 295-6496

The agency is in Davis County, just north of Salt Lake City. Although this is a little outside the areas we've covered geographically in this book, this company has an excellent reputation and is a good resource for nanny services inside and outside the area. They do provide short-term services for skiers, vacationers and people who travel with their children on business. The 12-year-old company does a very comprehensive background check on their nanny candidates, including a personality and psychological profile, criminal investigation and references. The nannies receive extensive training in everything from bathing an infant to safety in public places. If you need the services of a nanny while you are in the Salt Lake area, The Nanny Connection can accommodate you for a week to 10 days, several months or, if they have nannies available, for a night while you go out on the town. You will need to give the agency as much notice as possible for short-term services — a week or more if you can. Most of the nannies who provide short-term care live on the east side of the Salt Lake Valley.

Besides a very impressive traditional healthcare community, Salt Lake City offers many opportunities for alternative healthcare.

Healthcare

We sincerely hope that while you're visiting the area you remain the picture of good health, but if you need the services of a hospital or healthcare provider, rest assured, you're in good hands. Besides a very impressive traditional healthcare community, Salt Lake City offers many opportunities for alternative healthcare.

Based on our healthy lifestyle, access to quality healthcare and statistical data on disabilities, disease and mortality, Utah is the healthiest state in the nation, according to the Northwestern Life Insurance Company. The ranking is based on a comparative analysis of the relative health of the population in all 50 states. In addition, the Public Health Report Card, published by the American Public Health Association, ranks Utah in the top 12 states in medical care access, healthful neighborhoods, healthful behaviors and community health service. According to the findings of the Utah Department of Health, we also have the lowest rates of infant mortality and death from vehicle accidents in the nation. Heart disease, obesity, lung cancer, breast cancer, liver cancer, tuberculosis and work-related deaths are consistently lower than the rest of the nation's. Our healthy habits mean that we spend 26 percent less than the national average on healthcare.

Major medical facilities in the Salt Lake Valley provide short-term acute and intensive care, alcohol and chemical dependent and psychiatric care, long-term care, rehabilitation facilities and special centers such as our Intermountain Burn Unit and hospice facilities. Area hospitals have urgent-care facilities either separate from or operating with the hospital on the same property, and all area hospitals have physician-referral services. The University of Utah Medical Center and the University of Utah School of Medicine not only provide patient care but operate as a teaching hospital with extensive involvement in medical research. The area's Intermountain Health Care — a charitable, community-owned nonprofit organization based in Salt Lake City that operates four local hospitals in the Valley — has been the recipient of the National Quality Health Care Award, and its Primary Children's Medical Center has been singled out as one of the top 10 children's hospitals in the nation. Throughout the state we have more than 85 bio-med/medical-related companies that, through a biomedical task force and association, share information with each other as well as with the state's five universities.

The growth of the Salt Lake Valley ensures that we will continue to be a center for research and high-quality healthcare, providing a wide selection of lower-cost care options and a continuing contribution to the future of the nation's healthcare industry.

Wellness is an important part of our daily lives in the Salt Lake Valley, and many Insiders choose an alternative approach to healthcare. Early medical doctors in Utah often relied on natural healing remedies such as herbs and teas in place of more traditional treatments like bleeding patients or performing surgery under unsanitary conditions. Many combined both traditional and naturopathic care and continued to do so even after the community's hospitals and clinics began to develop. Pioneer midwives delivered hundreds of babies in the early days, and midwifery-assisted childbirth is still a preference today among many local women. Insiders continue to embrace alternative treatments in conjunction with or independent of allopathic care.

No matter where you are in the city and no matter what your preference for treatment, healthcare is close at hand. Who knows, maybe our healthy lifestyle will rub off on you, but it's always good to know these facilities are here if you need them.

Hospitals

Alta View Hospital
9660 S. 1300 E., Sandy • 576-2600

This hospital is one of four Intermountain Health Cost (IHC) facilities in the Salt Lake Valley. Alta View began operation in 1982 to serve the healthcare needs of residents in the south Valley. Since that time the 70-bed facility on a 38-acre campus has provided a full spectrum of inpatient and outpatient services and is well-known for the high quality of its key specialties: women's care, medical/surgical services and orthopedics and sports medicine. In 1996 Alta View was named as one of the top 10 hospitals in the country with fewer than 250 beds. This ranking by an independent group of healthcare consultants was based on mortality rates, complication rates, average length of stay and expenses per patient. The hospital was also cited for its high-quality outpatient and women's health programs.

Cottonwood Hospital
5770 S. 300 E., Murray • 262-3461

Cottonwood is another in the group of IHC hospitals serving the community. The hospital began because of efforts by Mormon women in the Relief Society, a women's organization in the LDS church that focuses on charitable works. Cottonwood was originally known as Cottonwood Stake Maternity Home. (For readers who are not familiar with terms used in the Mormon church, a "ward" is a congregation, and a "stake" is a regional grouping of congregations, not unlike a parish.)

The sisters of the Relief Society in the mid-Valley were concerned that the closest hospital was 10 miles away in the city and many women were having babies at home, which often placed their health and the health of their newborn in jeopardy. The women purchased a house in downtown Murray, and in 1924 the maternity hospital opened its doors with 10 beds. Cottonwood served approximately 101 patients in the first 10 months, and 13 additional beds were soon added.

In 1961 ground was broken on a new Cottonwood Hospital at the present location. This 227-bed facility on 15.5 acres has earned national acclaim for sports medicine and spinal and orthopedic care as well as for its women's services. The U.S. Ski Team, based in Park City, uses Cottonwood's 14-bed orthopedic speciality hospital for conditioning, prevention and rehabilitation services. The Intermountain Spine Institute at Cottonwood draws patients from throughout the country. Cottonwood has a 10-bed intensive-care unit, a 16-room emergency department, a 30-bed general medical nursing unit, a 23-bed general surgical nursing unit and a 10-bed oncology unit. With a medical staff of more than 550 members, more than 50 specialities are represented.

Columbia St. Mark's Hospital
1200 E. 3900 S., Salt Lake City
• 268-7111

In 1872 Salt Lake City was a bustling town where mining and the railroad created a regional center for commerce, industry and transportation. Medical care, however, was almost nonexistent. Residents relied primarily on home remedies for the treatment of illness and disease. Hundreds of workers in mines and on the railroad suffered a variety of job-related illnesses and injuries with no opportunity for proper care. Episcopal Bishop Daniel S. Tuttle, concerned over the lack of medical care in the Valley, recruited the support of his local congregation and prominent businessmen to create a hospital to service the community. Housed in an adobe building in downtown Salt Lake, the original St. Mark's Hospital had six beds, one physician who worked without pay and all male nurses. Lead poison-

FYI

Unless otherwise noted, the area code for all phone numbers listed in this guide is 801.

INSIDERS' TIP

Spanish-speaking visitors will find support services in Salt Lake City by calling the National SIDA hotline at (800) 344-7432.

ing, an occupational illness incurred by many miners, was the most commonly treated illness followed by appendicitis and typhoid fever.

By 1879 St. Mark's had doubled its capacity to 12 beds with the purchase of a larger building a block away. But within 15 short years St. Mark's was busting at the seams, and a new building with an operating room, drug closet and 35 beds was opened on the city's near west side. The hospital had its first X-ray machine by 1902, and beginning in 1925, St. Mark's housed what was known as the Shriners Crippled Children's Ward for children who suffered from orthopedic conditions and whose parents could not afford to pay for surgical treatment.

In the spring of 1973 St. Mark's Hospital moved from its west side location to the present address, and in 1988 the Episcopal Diocese of Utah sold the hospital to Hospital Corporation of America which later merged with Columbia. After more than 125 years, St. Mark's is still serving the community. Today the facility has 306 beds and provides women's and children's services, as well as cardiology, orthopedic and oncology services. It also has many specialized centers including rehabilitation, sleep disorders and a senior health center. The hospital uses the most sophisticated technology and equipment available and sponsors communitywide health-education programs.

Jordan Valley Hospital
3580 W. 9000 S., West Jordan
• 561-8888

This hospital belongs to the family of Paracelsus Healthcare facilities in the Salt Lake area. Paracelsus is a Texas-based corporation with three facilities in the Valley in addition to a hospice. Jordan Valley began providing service to the communities in the southwest part of the Valley in 1983. The hospital has a Women's Center with LDRP (labor, delivery, recovery, postpartum) suites and a complete gynecological program. The center prepares a monthly newsletter for women in the community that covers timely topics and women's health concerns. In addition, the hospital offers same-day surgery, cardiac rehabilitation, an intensive-care unit and pediat-

rics. The emergency department is staffed 24 hours a day, seven days a week with certified emergency physicians, nurses and emergency medical technicians.

LDS Hospital
Eighth Ave. and C St., Salt Lake City
• 321-1100

LDS Hospital, built in 1905, is the largest hospital in the Intermountain West and the flagship of IHC's 23-hospital network in the Intermountain West. This 520-bed facility has earned international acclaim for its clinical expertise and research in cardiology, pulmonary, oncology, trauma and organ transplants. The hospital's transplant team replaces hearts, kidneys, pancreases, livers, bone, bone marrow, heart valves, eyes, tendons and skin. The UTAH-Cardiac heart transplant team, including LDS and three other Utah hospitals, offers the highest survival rates of any heart-transplant program in the world.

LDS is the only comprehensive blood bank in the region and the major source of blood and blood products to hospital patients in the state. It's one of two Utah hospitals designated as Level I trauma centers, treating many of the area's most critically ill or injured patients, and is the home base for IHCs Life Flight air-ambulance program. The hospital operates five intensive-care units, including a 16-bed shock/trauma/respiratory ICU, and runs a 22-bed emergency department.

LDS is a teaching hospital where nurses, technologists and, in conjunction with the University of Utah School of Medicine, residents and interns are trained. The hospital also provides continuing medical education for practicing healthcare providers throughout the west. The hospital is a world leader in computerized patient-care systems.

LDS Hospital was one of five hospitals in the area owned by the Mormon Church between 1905 and 1940. On the hospital's dedication, the Mormon church-owned *Deseret News* carried the following editorial on January 6, 1905: "The hospital is to be constructed along the lines of 'Mormon' regulations. These include faith as well as works, temperance, morality, cleanliness, order, and discipline without bondage and without bigotry. The afflicted of all shades of belief will be welcome there.

The skill of the best physicians, surgeons and nurses will be utilized."

The Church of Jesus Christ of Latter-day Saints (LDS) turned the hospital over the Intermountain Health Care in 1975.

Pioneer Valley Hospital
3460 S. Pioneer Parkway, West Valley City • 964-3100

This Paracelsus facility in the midwest part of the Salt Lake Valley was built in 1963. The hospital has 139 beds and treats an average of 42 patients each day. Pioneer Valley's facilities include birthing suites, a spine center, a sleep disorders clinic, a work performance and wellness center and a cardiac catheterization (angiogram) lab. Among its services are industrial medicine and magnetic resonance imaging (MRI). The hospital's physical therapy department includes arthritis aerobics, prenatal aerobics and sports medicine, and Pioneer Valley also operates a headache clinic. The fast-track emergency care operates 24 hours a day with eight full-time emergency medicine specialists treating approximately 100 people each day. This hospital has the busiest ER in the Valley. Outpatient surgery is also available at this hospital.

Primary Children's Medical Center
100 N. Medical Dr., Salt Lake City • 588-2000

The Mormon Church Primary Association, the organization within the church that provides religious instruction to children up to 12 years old, played an important role in initiating Primary Children's Hospital in 1927. The first hospital was established as two three-bed wards — one for boys, another for girls — in what is now called LDS Hospital and was designed to offer medical care to children suffering from physical disabilities. As time went on, the hospital also served as a convalescent center for children, since the nature of childhood illness and medical treatment often required extensive hospital stays. Children recuperated here from rheumatic fever, polio, congenital birth defects and other illness here, and any child up to age 12 was admitted no matter what their race or religion or their ability to pay. Primary Children's soon outgrew the allotted space at LDS Hospital and moved to another location in 1922. Funds were needed to support the increasing demand for pediatric medical care, and the Primary Association began a fund-raising campaign which called for the donation of pennies. Penny boxes were set up at Mormon ward houses, and later the drive went door to door. For generations Mormon and non-Mormon children have given pennies during the annual children-helping-children fund drive.

The hospital grew, expanded its services, and by the late 1940s Primary Children's had evolved into a general pediatric hospital with a new facility on 12th Avenue and D Street. Now known as Primary Children's Medical Center, the hospital has been in its present location since 1990. The 232-bed facility, now part of the IHC family of hospitals, is equipped to treat children with complex illnesses and injuries. Affiliated with the Department of Pediatrics at the University of Utah, it provides care for children throughout the Intermountain West and is one of the foremost pediatric hospitals in the country.

Salt Lake Regional Medical Center
1050 E. South Temple, Salt Lake City • 350-4111

Two sisters of Holy Cross in Indiana traveled to Salt Lake City in 1875 to provide medical care to the miners and settlers in the Salt Lake Valley. They established a 12-bed hospital and recruited doctors to help them in their mission. The original hospital, known as Holy Cross, was in a rented building near the downtown area. In 1881 construction began on a new hospital at 1050 E. South Temple, the present location. In 1994 the sisters of Holy Cross divested their Utah assets, and the name became Salt Lake Regional Medical. Paracelsus Healthcare Corporation acquired the hospital in 1996. Today the 200-bed, full-service facility offers a wide range of treatment from cardiac care to women's service and outpatient to emergency care and major surgery.

Shriners Hospital for Children
Fairfax and Virginia Sts., Salt Lake City • 536-3500

Shriners Hospital for Children in Salt Lake City is a 40-bed orthopedic facility specializing in the care of children with bone, muscle

Photo: University of Utah Health Services Center

The Salt Lake Valley has two hospitals designated as Level 1 trauma centers, equipped to treat victims with multiple or life-threatening injuries. Both provide air ambulance services.

and joint problems. The hospital has been providing care for children in the Intermountain area since 1925, and today, in its newly dedicated $33 million facility, which was completed in 1996, medical services are available to kids from newborn to age 18 who would not otherwise have the opportunity for treatment. Specialties include treatment for cerebral palsy, club foot, hip problems, juvenile arthritis, limb deficiencies and deformities, rickets, scoliosis, spina bifida and other problems. The facility has an in-house orthotics and prosthetics center, a hydrotherapy pool, a movement analysis laboratory, a 3,000-square-foot play area and four apartments for parents and other family members. Besides treatment, the hospital offers a free screening program available to all children in need of orthopedic care. All services are paid for by Shriners philanthropy.

University of Utah Health Services Center/University Hospital
50 N. Medical Dr., Salt Lake City
• 581-2121, (800) 453-0122 outside Utah, (800) 662-0052 in Utah

The University of Utah Health Services/University Hospital has been a leader in research since the 1950s, when cancer research moved

to the head of its many programs and the hospital and medical school joined with four other hospitals in the United States to seek a cure for infantile paralysis. When the hospital moved to the campus of the University of Utah in 1965 — expanding its teaching, research and patient-care programs — the national medical community began to take notice. As the facility moves into the 21st century, more than 400 medical students and 500 medical residents and fellows, along with hundreds of healthcare students in nursing, pharmacy, physical therapy, cytotechnology, and radiologic technology, receive vital clinical training at this facility.

Some 700 faculty members in the school of medicine are involved in more than 500 research projects. Among the special research centers are the Institute of Human Genetics that houses a world-renowned genetics research program; a multidisciplinary cancer institute; the Center for Toxicology; the Cardiovascular Research and Training Institute; the Institute of Biomedical Engineering/Division of Artificial Organs; and the Center for Diagnostic Imaging Research. Today this 395-bed, primary referral facility offers the most up-do-date treatments and consultation services to Utahns and residents of the five surrounding states. University Hospital and its clinics — including the University of Utah Neuropsychiatric Institute and various satellite clinics — is a component of the University of Utah Health Services Center serving the clinical arm of the medical school and the colleges of pharmacy, nursing and health.

The hospital has many specialty programs including burn and trauma, heart, kidney and bone marrow transplants, newborn intensive care, lithotripsy and cancer care. The Intermountain Regional Burn and Trauma Center has 13-beds, its own operating room, hydrotherapy facilities, physical therapy and burn clinic. The hospital's transplant facility has performed more than 1,000 kidney transplants since it opened in 1965. Patients have received cochlear implants since the program for the profoundly deaf began in 1984, and more than 5,000 patients have received intraocular lens transplants since 1978. University Hospital is a designated Level I trauma center, equipped to treat accident victims with multiple or life-threatening injuries. The hospital's AirMed provides air-ambulance services to many of these victims and other seriously ill patients who require specialized services in Utah and the Intermountain area.

Veterans Administration Hospital
500 Foothill Blvd., Salt Lake City
• 582-1565

The Veterans Administration Hospital is a 180-bed tertiary referral center serving veterans in the Intermountain West including Utah and parts of Wyoming, Idaho and Nevada. The hospital also provides services on referral to patients from secondary-level VA medical clinics in the Rocky Mountain area.

Alternative Healthcare

Salt Lake Valley has a variety of alternative healthcare options. In the Salt Lake area you'll find practitioners who specialize in everything from acupuncture to transpersonal therapy. We have many naturopaths, homeopaths and midwives and practitioners whose methods include healing touch, holotropic breathwork and other unique practices.

For many years, finding a recommended practitioner in a specific field was difficult for Salt Lakers because we were limited to specific listings in the Yellow Pages or weren't certain what approach would be most appropriate. Help has arrived in the form of a comprehensive book titled *Utah Guide to Healthy Healing*, published by S.L.C. Publications, a local company. The contents cover a spectrum of 72 skills and numerous practitioners — more than 200 — throughout the state. You can get the book at Barnes and Noble Booksellers and Media Play or directly from S.L.C. Publishing, 1415 E. 2100 S., Salt Lake City, UT 84105, 483-2911.

To find out about lectures, seminars, holistic health fairs and other such happenings in the Salt Lake Valley, the *Catalyst*, a free periodical, is an excellent resource (see our Media chapter).

Health Resources
AIDS/HIV/STD Referral Services

AIDS information and referral service, 487-2100 HIV/STD

Testing Center, 534-2666

National STD Hotline, (800) 227-8922

National AIDS Hotline, (800) 342-2437

People with AIDS Coalition, 484-2205

Planned Parenthood, 322-5571

Project Inform (HIV/AIDS treatments), (800) 822-7422

University of Utah HIV/AIDS clinic, 585-2031

Utah AIDS Foundation, 487-2323

Utah AIDS Foundation hotline, (800) 366-2437

Substance Abuse Resources

Alcohol/Drug Help line, 581-8228

Alcoholics Anonymous, 484-7871

Cocaine Anonymous, 264-5658

Narcotics Anonymous, 296-4044

Emergency Support Services

24-hour crisis line, 483-5444

American Red Cross, 467-7339

Catholic Community Services, 977-9119

Rescue Mission, 322-1302

Travelers Aid, 328-8996

Community Resources

We've included several community resources to help you find out where to go and how to get healthcare and related services in the Salt Lake Valley. A good place to begin is the Salt Lake City/County Board of Health, 2001 S. State Street, 468-2750.

The Indian Health Care Clinic, 610 S. 200 E., 534-4555, provides healthcare services to Native American people in the Salt Lake Valley.

You can also get information and help from the divisions of the Board of Health listed below:

Environmental Health Division
1954 E. Fort Union Blvd., Salt Lake City
• 944-6600

This arm of the Board of Health provides information and education on environmental health issues that affect the community. To find out about Environmental Risk Reduction including injury prevention, radon education and air quality education, call 944-6600. To report a vehicle air polluter, call 944-SMOG.

For environmental sanitation and safety complaints including abandoned vehicles, animal-bite monitoring, cosmetology, massage, tattoo and tanning, housing complaints, noise and nuisance control, solid and infectious waste, Utah Indoor Clean Air Act monitoring and control of zoonosis (diseases transferred from animal to humans), call 944-6641. For information or to report a violation regarding the handling of food, including day-care and nursing-home food programs, call 944-6620.

Questions about water quality and hazardous waste including asbestos, hazardous water disposal, septic-tank drain fields and surface- and storm-water regulation can be directed to 944-6700. Hazardous Waste recycling questions about paint, pesticide, antifreeze, oil and other hazardous materials can be directed to 944-6697.

Family Health Services Division
2001 S. State St., Salt Lake City
• 468-2720

This city/county health service division provides a variety of health services at the main location on State Street. In addition, health centers in other areas of the Salt Lake Valley provide a range of care options. Call the number listed above for addresses and phone numbers of these satellite sites.

The Medical Assessment Center at this location can provide info on occupational and industrial health clinics and breast and cervical cancer screening; call 468-2800 for details. To find out about mammography and prevention education, call 468-2838. The immunization information line is 534-4693. For information about public health nurses in schools, infant and development programs and teen pregnancy prevention, call 468-2732. Information on prevention and education for cardiovascular and communicable disease, hygiene education, tobacco use prevention and work-site wellness programs can be obtained by calling 468-2738.

Urgent Care

In addition to the urgent-care centers described below, you'll find walk-in clinics in the emergency departments of all area hospitals.

Intermountain Health Care InstaCare Centers
3934 S. 2300 E., Salt Lake City
• 321-1980
3845 W. 4700 S., Salt Lake City
• 964-4010
55 N. Redwood Rd. , Salt Lake City
• 321-2490
620 E. 2100 S., Salt Lake City • 321-2485
2530 W. 4700 S., Salt Lake City
• 967-7667

These centers provide physician services for urgent-care medical problems between 8 AM and 10 PM at various locations away from their hospital facilities.

Salt Lake is the 35th-biggest market in the country for radio and television.

Media

Salt Lake City has a spirited media scene, with two daily newspapers, a host of alternative publications, numerous radio stations and TV affiliates including Fox, NBC, CBS and ABC. TCI provides cable service. The various neighborhood communities in the Salt Lake Valley, such as Murray, Sandy and Midvale, all have weekly papers. Competition among the media is intense, especially among the evening local television news programs and the two daily newspapers, one liberal and morning (*The Salt Lake Tribune*) and one conservative and evening (*Deseret News*). The rivalry between the newspapers mirrors the Mormon, non-Mormon divisions that have been an animating force in Utah politics and culture.

Salt Lake is the 35th-biggest market in the country for radio and television. For years Channel 5, the NBC affiliate, has consistently drawn the highest viewer ratings in the critical evening newscasts, with broadcaster Dick Nourse and eccentric but likeable weatherman Mark Eubank proving perennially popular. Nourse has been on the air for more than three decades, one of the longest stints in America. Channel 4, the CBS affiliate, is currently number two in news rating, but ABC affiliate Channel 2 has taken aggressive measures to catch up.

Salt Lakers are community minded, so they use all the media to stay informed and discuss issues of the day. The letters to the editor sections in both daily newspapers are avidly followed by community leaders and the general populace alike, and talk radio acts as a community forum where grievances are aired and controversies, such as the coming 2002 Winter Olympics, are debated.

Daily Newspapers

Deseret News
30 E. 100 S., Salt Lake City • 237-2900

The oldest daily newspaper in Utah, the *Deseret News* was started in 1850 by the Mormon church and is still owned by that organization. Circulation stands at 62,300 daily and 67,500 on Sundays. Circulation has declined steadily in the past decades and continues to go down. Area media critics attribute these problems to the fact that the *Deseret News* is an afternoon paper (afternoon papers are in difficulty all over the country), and because many Salt Lakers believe that its ownership doesn't allow for unbiased news coverage of local controversies.

The *Deseret News* recently moved into a new building and hired John Hughes as editor. Hughes is a Pulitzer-Prize-winning journalist and the former editor of the *Christian Science Monitor*. He is also the first non-Mormon to be named editor. Hughes has expanded the paper's coverage of science, technology, religion and other subjects less tied to breaking news. You'll find local and international news, politics and sports in each edition. Special sections include food on Tuesday, science and technology on Wednesday, leisure and the outdoors reporting on Thursday and automobiles and entertainment on Friday. On Saturday the paper publishes a pull-out section on Mormon church news. Other religions are also covered on Saturday, but not in the stand-alone section. Sunday's edition covers business, travel, home real estate and arts. Since 1952, the *Tribune* and *Deseret News* have jointly operated in the areas of advertising, circulation and production. Even though *The Tribune* circulation is double that of the *Deseret News*, profits are split 58 percent for the *Tribune* and 42 percent for the *Deseret News*.

The Salt Lake Tribune
143 S. Main St., Salt Lake City • 237-2900

Founded in 1871 by ex-communicated Mormons, *The Salt Lake Tribune* was created to counteract the political and cultural power of the Mormon church in Utah. Since then, it's been the moderately liberal, non-Mormon, voice of Salt Lake City and Utah. For many years *The Tribune* was owned by the Kearns family, whose wealth came from patriarch Thomas Kearns, an Irish immigrant who made a fortune in the Park City, Utah, mines. He was elected to the U.S. Senate and bought *The Tribune* in 1901. Recently, cable giant TCI purchased the *Tribune*. *The Tribune*'s circulation is 129,000 daily and 162,000 on Sunday. Circulation is growing, and the paper is enjoying record success.

Editor James E. Shelledy has revamped the paper in the last several years with expanded coverage of religion, business, high school sports, the environment and science. Shelledy has also emphasized the importance of appealing to women and minorities and has beefed up *The Tribune*'s statewide coverage. Besides the usual coverage of local and international news, sports and politics, *The Tribune* publishes daily special sections. The special sections include a technology section on Monday, an environmental section on Tuesday, a home and garden section on Wednesday, along with a special section called "Citizens," where readers can write lengthy articles on whatever subjects they choose. The Thursday edition highlights health and science, and on Friday you can find a compete calendar of events and a section on home and family. Saturday's issue covers religion in-depth, and Sunday's paper reports on business, travel, real estate and arts. In the past few years the paper has published remarkably in-depth special reports on the Great Salt Lake and the nearby canyons of the Wasatch Mountains. Columnists Rolly & Wells and longtime environmental columnist Tom Wharton are popular writers, as is humor columnist Robert Kirby.

Weekly and Monthly Newspapers and Magazines

Catalyst
362 E. Broadway (300 S.), Salt Lake City
• 363-1505

Salt Lake's New Age community has been well served for 16 years by this intelligent,

thoughtful and gentle monthly publication. You'll find thorough coverage of the environment, health, arts and politics, all delivered with a holistic twist. Publisher Greta Belanger deJong focuses on publishing positive articles that highlight local personalities and their contributions to the community. Columnist John deJong writes entertaining columns decrying the deteriorating state of the world, the increasing gap between the rich and poor and so on.

Catalyst provides an excellent alternative community-resource directory on categories such as housing, arts and crafts, gardening, books, herbs, yoga, religion and the like. You'll also find a thorough calendar of events and a letters to the editor section. *Catalyst* distributes 23,000 free copies at 450 locations along the Wasatch Front, in libraries, coffee shops and brewpubs.

Cycling Utah
P.O. Box 57980, Murray UT 84157
• 268-2652

Area bicyclists go to this free monthly magazine for information about Salt Lake race results, bicycling clubs and other issues that affect two-wheeled travel. The magazine also provides good information about trails and a calendar of events. Look for it in bicycling shops, sporting goods stores and coffee shops.

The Enterprise
136 S. Main St., Kearns Bldg. No. 721, Salt Lake City • 533-0556

You can read all about doing business along the Wasatch Front in this weekly newspaper. Along with news, the paper publishes a few columns, mainly by local business people and patriotic folks such as Thomas Sowell and Patrick J. Buchanan extolling the virtues of free enterprise. *The Enterprise* is published weekly; a subscription costs $48 per year.

Event Newspaper
1800 S. West Temple, Ste. 205, Salt Lake City • 487-4556

Intelligently edited and elegantly written, the *Event Newspaper* focuses on news, arts and the environment. First published in 1981, it's the original alternative newspaper in the Salt Lake area. Editor Paul Swenson and publisher James Major have assembled a talented staff of contributors whose well-researched investigative articles shed light on local controversies often left untouched by the *Tribune* and *Deseret News*. Swenson writes with a deft, poetic touch and has a thorough knowledge of the Salt Lake scene. His knowledgeable and wide-ranging film criticism is not to be missed. Carol Von Schmidt writes an informative column on wine, and the paper offers other fine columns on beer, dining and theater. A complete calendar of events published every issue rounds out this publication. The *Event* publishes 36,000 copies of the newspaper every Thursday, which are available free at 900 locations, including libraries, coffee shops, bookstores and brewpubs.

Mountain Times
60 W. 400 S., Salt Lake City • 575-6101

The *Mountain Times* covers much of the same territory as the *Sports Guide*, but with more of an emphasis on environmental news and the Park City scene. Editor Chrisopher Smart's editorial is always well-written and thoroughly researched. Columnist Jim Stiles, editor of the *Canyon Country Zephyr* in Moab, provides wry commentary on the modern West from the Ed Abbey school of outdoor writing. It's published monthly, and 30,000 copies are distributed free at coffee shops sporting goods stores along the Wasatch Front.

Salt Lake City Magazine
1270 W. 2320 S., Ste. A, Salt Lake City • 975-1927

Salt Lake City Magazine is Salt Lake's nicest looking periodical, with glossy paper and slick advertisements of gracious living. Editor Barry Scholl, a longtime Salt Lake journalist, has put together an intriguing mixture of professionally written feature articles and departments covering entertainment, politics and people along the Wasatch Front. Scholl frequently writes about the environment, and he's moving the publication more in that direction. Nice design and artwork have won *Salt Lake City Magazine* a number of awards, such as the 1995 Ozzie Gold Award for best cover. It's published bimonthly and costs $15 a year. You can buy it in any area

bookstore for $3.50. Circulation stands at around 17,500.

Salt Lake City Weekly
60 W. 400 S., Salt Lake City • 575-7003

Salt Lake City Weekly publishes 50,000 copies each Thursday, which can be picked up at no charge at 1,100 locations in the Salt Lake Valley, including libraries and coffee shops. The SLCW covers pretty much the same ground as the *Event*, but its tone is more sensational — articles on topless dancers, phone sex and the like are often published. *SLCW* takes frequent potshots at other Salt Lake media, including the *Event* and *The Salt Lake Tribune*. While the editorial quality may not be as high as other publications, the relentless, aggressive stance of the investigative articles and publisher John Saltas's fearless pursuit of corruption in high places have brought new energy to a sometimes sleepy media scene in Salt Lake City. Columnist John Harrington keeps things stirred up with take-no-prisoner columns attacking the privileged and defending the disenfranchised. Food columnist Ted Scheffler writes about food with holy reverence and no snobbery — he likes all food, as long as it's well-prepared. Other columnists cover sports, movies and drama.

Sports Guide
772 E. 3300 S., Salt Lake City • 467-9516

This free monthly magazine describes itself as an outdoor recreation, fitness and travel guide for the West. You'll find a bracing mixture of articles on skiing, mountain biking, hiking, outdoor fitness and nutrition, illustrated with black-and-white photos and art. Editor Drew Ross has created a brash and fun-loving publication that's informative and easy to read. Contributing editor Jerry Spangler writes insightful and amusing articles on local environmental controversies, often skewering the anti-environment leanings of the Utah State Legislature. Articles on birdwatching, butterflies and other regional flora and fauna, some written by *Insiders' Guide*® coauthor Bryan Larsen, occasionally season the fare. Departments include a calendar of events for outdoor sporting and an adventure directory for outdoor outfitters, clubs and instructors. The *Sports Guide* can be picked up at hundreds of Wasatch Front locations, including coffee shops, libraries, brewpubs and sporting goods stores.

The Utah Runner and Cyclist
P.O. Box 58344, Salt Lake City UT 84158
• 467-4203

Writer and athlete Richard Barnum-Reece has published this free magazine on the Utah running and cycling scene for more than a decade. If you read nothing else while in Utah, make sure you read the entry form for the Crazy Bob's Bair Gutsman mountain race. Lines like "snake kits, water bottles and last rites are mandatory," make you realize that this is a foot race like no other. The magazine is published quarterly, and the Crazy Bob's Bair Gutsman entry form is published in the summer edition. You'll find it in all the important places — coffee shops, brewpubs and libraries.

Television

Clicking on Salt Lake television stations summons a wide variety of offerings. The best station around is PBS affiliate KUER Channel 7, where producer Ken Verdoia presents some outstanding documentaries on subjects of local interest, such as Utah history and environmental controversies. Channel 5 produces a popular outdoor show, called "Outdoors with Doug Miller," that airs Saturday night at 11 PM. TCI gives TV viewers access to 19 standard channels and seven premium channels, including Disney, Encore, HBO, Starz! and The Movie Channel.

If you're a fan of Brigham Young University football, KBYU Channel 11 often plays reruns of old games on Saturday night. Channel 11 also runs a lot of the Mormon church's religious programming. Here's a list of Salt Lake television stations:

KUTV Channel 2 (ABC)
KTVX Channel 4 (CBS)
KSL Channel 5 (NBC)
KUED Channel 7 (PBS, Community)
KBYU Channel 11 (PBS, Religious)
KSTU 13 (Fox)
KJZZ 14 (Independent, Jazz basketball)

Cable Television

TCI is the only cable provider in the Salt Lake area. You can contact them at the following locations: Salt Lake, 1350 E. Miller Ave. (3130 S.), 485-0500; West Valley, 1649 W. 4200 S., 261-2662; and Sandy, 12222 S. 1000 E., 572-4000.

Radio

You can find just about any kind of music, news or talk you want on Salt Lake's radio stations. KUER-FM, the PBS affiliate, produces an intelligent half-hour news show on local issues that comes on every Friday at 4 PM. KRCL-FM, Utah's only nonprofit, community-oriented radio station, plays an eclectic mix of blues, folk, bluegrass, reggae and a host of other genres. Its community affairs programs are superb.

Longtime DJ Tom Barberi is the most widely recognized radio personality in the area. For 27 years he has been the liberal "voice of reason" at KALL radio (910 AM), where his amusing and caustic commentary on the vagaries of Salt Lake culture attracts huge numbers of listeners. Vowing to "legalize adulthood in Utah," Barberi doesn't hesitate to take on the Mormon church, conservative legislators or whatever tomfoolery he deems worthy of attack. Another popular radio station is KSL radio (1160 AM), owned by the Mormon church. KSL mixes news, traffic reports and talk in a fast-paced format. KSL disk jockey

INSIDERS' TIP

NBA basketball fans will want to tune into Channel 14 for Utah Jazz basketball. Hot Rod Hundley and Ron Boone provide play-by-play.

Doug Wright hosts four hours of talk radio in the day that generally follow conservative lines of thought. Wright's genial personality, pleasing bass voice and fair treatment of all points of view wear well with Salt Lake listeners. He's been on the air at KSL since 1985.

Talk radio addicts can also tune in to KTKK-AM, the only station in Utah devoted solely to talk radio. KTKK has a changing lineup of conservative and liberal hosts. As befitting a city that was once a theocracy, you can find all kinds of religious programming. Jazz music aficionados can listen to Wes Bowen on KUER every night from 7 PM to 9 PM. If you yearn for Mozart, KUER and KBYU will fill the bill. For country, try KKAT or KSOP.

Disk jockeys Kerry Jackson, Gina Barberi and Bill Allred on X-96 FM (KXRK 96.3 FM) host a popular morning program where they poke fun at Utah's ruling class and satirize local and national issues. For the popular "boner of the day," they select three examples of human folly from local and national news, then allow listeners to vote on which one deserves the honor.

The following is a list of radio stations in the Salt Lake area:

Adult Contemporary
KBEE 98.7 FM
KFAM 700 AM
KISN 97.1 FM
KRKR 107.9 FM
KSFI 100.3 FM
KTKL 92.1 FM
KUMT 105.7 FM

Children
KCNR 860 AM
KKDS 1060 AM

Classical
KUER 90.1 FM
KBYU 89.1 FM
KCPW 105.1 FM

Community
KRCL 90.9 FM

Country
KSOP 1370 AM/104.3 FM
KUBL 93.3 FM

KKAT 101.9 FM
KBKX 106.5 FM

Jazz
KBZN 97.9 FM

News/Talk
KTKK 630 AM
KALL 910 AM
KTUR 1010 AM
KSL 1160 AM

Oldies
KSOS 800 AM
KDYL 1280 AM
KLO 1430 AM
KODJ 94.1 FM
KLZX 103.1 FM
KRSP 103.5 FM
KLZX 106.9 FM

Religious
KANN 1120 AM (Evangelical Christian)
KSRR 1400 AM (LDS contemporary music)
KEYY 1450 AM (Christian)
KHQN 1480 AM (Hare Krishna)
KYFO 1490 AM/92.7 FM (conservative Christian music)
KLLB 1510 AM (black gospel/Christian)

Rock
KTCE 92.3 FM
KURR 99.5 FM
KBER 101.1 FM
KENZ 107.5 FM

Spanish
KSVN 730 AM
KMGR 1230 AM
KCPX 1600 AM

Sports
KISN 570 AM
KFNZ 1320 AM

Top 40
KQMB 102.7 FM
KWCR 88.1 FM
KXRK 96.3 FM
KZHT 94.9 FM
KZHT 97.5 FM

Every major and many smaller denominations are represented along the Wasatch Front. Nondenominational groups and a growing number of metaphysical faiths have a presence here today.

Religion

Salt Lake City, unlike any other major city in the United States, was established as a religious community. In the city's first decade, approximately 98 percent of the residents were members of the Church of Jesus Christ of Latter-day Saints (Mormons) whose political, educational and social life blended into one principle under which their communities functioned. The exclusivity of their theocratic world did not endure, however. In fewer than 15 years people of non-Mormon persuasion migrated to the area, and, though conflicts arose, the various other faiths dug in, and the culture broadened its spiritual offerings. Four decades after the Mormons arrived in the Salt Lake Valley the religious population in the state included 50 Baptists, 350 Presbyterians, 400 members of the Congregational and United Church of Christ, 450 Methodists, 600 Episcopalians, 1,700 Roman Catholics and 106,000 Mormons, who then represented only 63 percent of the population.

Statewide, the percentage of Mormons has remained very high — now estimated at more than 70 percent — while the percentage of Latter-day Saints in Salt Lake City has declined. Today, Salt Lake City remains the worldwide headquarters for the Mormon church with more than 500,000 members in the Salt Lake Valley — 64 percent of the population — but the city continues to offer a wide range of spiritual opportunities. Every major and many smaller denominations are represented along the Wasatch Front. Nondenominational groups and a growing number of metaphysical faiths have a presence here today.

When Mormon pioneers arrived in the Salt Lake Valley in 1847, they immediately set up houses of worship throughout the community. The Mormon Temple was built between 1853 and 1893 and plays an important role in the life of Latter-day Saints. Here, faithful members who live according to the teachings of their church participate in sacred ordinances such as baptism and marriage. Mormon Church Headquarters, 50 E. North Temple, 240-1000, can provide information on services at more than 1,000 LDS congregations here. You can read more about the LDS Temple and Temple Square in the Sightseeing and Attractions chapter. The History chapter at the beginning of the book includes more information about the Mormon Church.

Bishop Daniel S. Tuttle came to Salt Lake in 1867 to organize Episcopal religious activities in the area. Cathedral Church of St. Mark's was completed four years later in 1871 at 231 E. 100 S. and remains a landmark building today. The chancel was added in 1901, and the front vestibule was added in 1958. The church underwent a major renovation in the late 1980s. In addition to providing religious services to the community, the Episcopal Church built a hospital in Salt Lake City and opened two schools, Rowland Hall and St. Mark's Episcopal School, which now operate as a single school. St. Mark's Hospital is no longer owned by the Episcopal Diocese and functions under the name Columbia St. Mark's (see our Healthcare chapter). The school offers exemplary education to area children (see our Education chapter). For information on Episcopal services in the Valley, contact the Episcopal Diocese of Utah, 80 S. 300 E., 322-4131.

INSIDERS' TIP

Several area churches are listed on the National Register of Historic Places. To find out about tours of these historic houses of worship contact The Heritage Foundation, 485 N. Canyon Road, 533-0858.

The first consecrated Catholic church in the area was St. Mary Magdalene which began offering mass in 1871. Cathedral of St. Mary Magdalene, later changed to Madeleine, 331 E. South Temple, 328-8941, was dedicated in 1909. The magnificent stained-glass windows were made in Munich, Germany. A recent $10 million renovation restored the frescos, painted columns and vaulted ceiling in this beautiful cathedral which is listed on the National Register of Historic Places. In addition to establishing churches throughout the Valley, the Catholics opened a hospital in 1875 with assistance from the Holy Cross Sisters. The original facility was in a rented building on 500 East. In 1881 construction began on a new hospital at 1050 E. South Temple. The facility is still in operation today under the name Salt Lake Regional Medical Center (see our Healthcare chapter).

Catholics also built schools in the , including St. Mary's Academy, which opened its doors as a school for girls in 1875 at 200 West. St. Joseph's School for Small Boys was opened the following year in an adjacent building. The schools operated until 1926 when St. Mary of the Wasatch College and Academy was completed on the city's east bench. St. Mary's closed in 1975. St. Ann's Orphanage was opened in 1900 with the help of the Thomas Kearns family. The orphanage served many children including those who were orphaned because of mining disasters. Today the Kearns-St. Ann's School serves the needs of area children as a parochial school (see our Education chapter). For information on worship services and schools, contact the Catholic Church Diocese of Salt Lake City, 27 C Street, 328-8641.

The First Presbyterian Church was dedicated in 1874 and moved to it's present location at 12 C Street in 1905. The architecture is English-Scottish Gothic Revival copied from the Carlisle Cathedral in England, complete with crenelated bastions. The exterior was constructed of local red sandstone. The church has exquisite stained-glass windows and a prominent rectangular tower. You can call 363-3889 for the times and locations of Catholic church services in the Valley.

FYI

Unless otherwise noted, the area code for all phone numbers listed in this guide is 801.

The original Methodist church in Salt Lake City was built in 1875. In 1905 the church bought property at 203 S. 200 E., and the First Methodist Episcopal Church offered services in its newly constructed building that same year. Episcopal was dropped from the name in 1939. In 1960 the sanctuary and chancel beautification project was completed. Dark mahogany wood on the chancel and choir loft was replaced with light birch and alder. The beautiful paneled mosaic on the wall of the sanctuary, called "The Incarnation," shows the nativity, the shepherds and the wise men. The church has an elevator to accommodate members with disabilities. You can call 328-8726 for information and the locations of other Methodist churches in the area.

The Swedish Lutheran Church was established in Salt Lake City in 1882 when five people, including the pastor and his wife, met in St. Mark's Episcopal School House. They were officially called Zion Swedish Lutheran Church of Salt Lake City. Holy Trinity Lutheran Church was established in 1890 with 36 members in the English-speaking congregation. Mt. Tabor Evangelical Lutheran Church was established in 1907. In 1980 the Utah Lutheran Ministry Council linked all major Lutheran churches in the state. Zion Lutheran Church, 1070 Foothill Boulevard, 581-2321, will provide information on Lutheran services in the area.

A congregation of 16 people built the First Baptist Church in Salt Lake in 1884. Eight years later the East Side Baptist Church was constructed although the building was later sold to Calvary Baptist. Calvary has been serving the spiritual needs of Salt Lake's African-American citizens since the late 1800s. Baptists adhering to the practices of all four groups of Baptist churches conduct services throughout the Valley. The Salt Lake Baptist Association, 334 S. 1300 E., 581-1624, can provide more information.

The cornerstone of the B'nai Israel Synagogue at 249 S. 400 E. was laid on the northeast corner of the building in 1890. This was

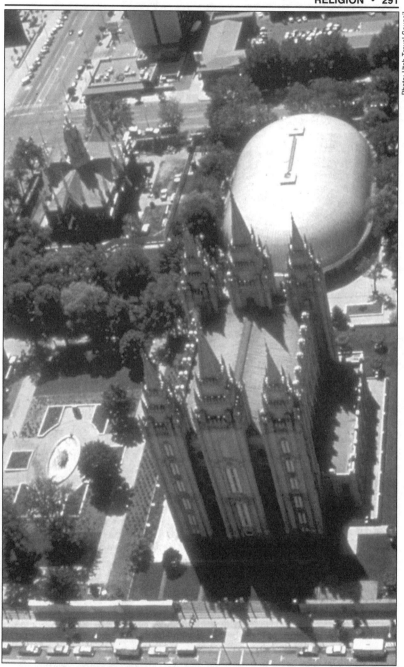

Temple Square seen from the air gives a good perspective on the size of the complex where Mormons visit their temple and do missionary work.

the home of the first Jewish congregation in the Valley. The congregation was split by internal differences in 1899, and the splintered group formed Congregation Mortefiore. The two congregations were joined in the United Jewish Council in 1930. They established a Jewish Community Center and in 1972 joined to create Congregation Kol Ami. For information on Sabbat, education and other services provided for the Jewish community, contact the Jewish Community Center, 2416 E. 1700 S., 581-0098, or call Congregation Kol Ami, 2425 E. 2760 S., 484-1501.

Holy Trinity Greek Orthodox Cathedral was constructed in 1924 at 279 S. 300 W. This handsome building, which is on the National Register of Historic Places, reflects true Byzantine tradition and forms the shape of a cross. The altar faces east toward the rising sun, the source of light and the symbol of Christ. A cross embellishes the central and belfry domes. Holy Trinity was the second Greek church built in Salt Lake City. The first, completed in 1905, quickly grew too small for the growing population. The Greek community in Salt Lake City today is the largest between Chicago and San Francisco. Call 328-9681 for information and locations for worship services.

The Unitarian Society established a presence in the Valley in 1891. Early services were held in the parlor of a local hotel. Today's services are held in the First Unitarian Church at 569 S. 1300 E., a comfortable American Colonial-style building. The interior has high ceilings, three stairs rising from the main floor to the chancel and large windows that let in plenty of sunlight. Following worship services, which occasionally include instrumental and organ music — sometimes jazz — gatherers join together in Eliot Hall, the church's social center, for refreshments. For information about ser-

vices at the Unitarian churches in the area call 582-8687.

The First Church of Christ Scientist is at 352 E. 300 S. in Salt Lake City. Built in 1897, this Richardsonian-Romanesque structure constructed of local red brick and sandstone has stunning windows. The beautiful east window is Tiffany glass imported from Italy and leaded in Chicago. It is a partial replica of a painting by 19th-century German artist B. Plockhorst. The cross and crown are prominent in the south and north windows, and the art glass in the west and north windows feature lily medallions in natural and pastel colors. The handcarved pews and woodwork in the foyer and on the balcony stairway are impressive. The church's organ, installed in 1901 and rebuilt in 1934, has 1,034 pipes. For information on services at this church, call 363-7127.

Many young Japanese men came to the area to work on the railroad in the late 1800s. By 1920 nearly 3,000 Japanese lived in the area. To meet their spiritual needs, places of worship were established in the Valley. The Japanese Church of Christ of Salt Lake was established in 1918 after more than 15 years of missionary effort by the Congregational Churches of the Pacific Coast and the Presbyterian Church. Today, the Japanese Church of Christ at 268 W. 100 S., 363-3251, ministers to approximately one-fourth of the Japanese population in Salt Lake City. The exterior of the sanctuary building has a decidedly Protestant-Christian design, but the education/social building and office building are Japanese in design with a lovely Japanese landscaped garden. Services are held in English and Japanese.

Although services had been held sporadically in various locations around the city beginning around 1918, the first Buddhist

---

INSIDERS' TIP

Midnight mass on Christmas Eve at the Cathedral of the Madeleine, 331 E. South Temple, is attended by people of all faiths in the community. If you want to attend, call for tickets well in advance. The number is 328-8941.

temple was constructed at 247 W. 100 S. in 1920, and the Intermountain Buddhist Church was incorporated in 1926. In 1962 the temple was demolished, and the congregation moved to a new temple designed in a traditional Buddhist architectural style at 211 W. 100 S. Call 363-4742 to inquire about services.

The Kanzeon Zen Center of Utah is at 1274 E. South Temple. Call 328-8414 for information on the meditation training center for Zen Buddhism.

The various faiths in the Salt Lake Valley coexist in a healthy spiritual environment. It would be impossible to give listings for every denominational and nondenominational congregation and group but we've listed quite a few for general reference. Call the Salt Lake Christian Center, 4300 S. 700 E., 268-2178, for information on Assemblies of God services. The Church of Christ, 662 E. 1300 S., 467-0974, will provide information on its services. The Evangelical Free congregation meets at 6515 S. Lion Lane. Call them at 943-0091, for details. The Interdenominational Salt Lake City Foursquare Church meets at 1086 S. Jefferson Street (465 East). Call 363-3113 for information. You can get information about the Islamic Society of Salt Lake, 740 S. 700 E., by calling 363-7822. You'll find the Jehovah's Wit-

ness congregation at 2240 S. 600 E., 487-9456. To get information on Nazarene congregations contact First Church of the Nazarene, 2018 E. 2100 S., 486-0522. Pentecostal services are held at Faith Temple, 1510 Richards Street (40 West), 486-5970, and Quaker Meetings are held at Realms of Inquiry School, 1140 S. 900 E., 359-1506. The Salt Lake Christian Fellowship meets at 615 E. 9800 S., 572-0211, and the Central Seventh-day Adventist Church at 460 S. 800 E., 364-1603, can give you information about its worship services. United Church of Christ holds services in Holladay at 2631 E. Murray-Holladay Road; call 277-2631 for times and other locations. Unity services are held at Unity of Salt Lake, 141 E. 5600 S., Murray, 281-2400. You can get information about the Church of Scientology, 1831 S. 1100 E., by calling 485-9992.

Many other nondenominational and metaphysical groups hold worship services throughout the Valley. *The Catalyst*, the *Deseret News* and *The Salt Lake Tribune* are excellent resources for finding these organizations (see our Media chapter). You'll also find listings under "Churches," "Mosques," and "Synagogues" in the Yellow Pages.

If you are interested in schools operated by religious organizations in the area, look in the Education chapter under "Private Schools."

Residents of Park City need only walk out their doors to find a splendid smorgasbord offering skiing, fishing, mountain biking, boating and hiking. In addition, fine dining, shopping and other big city amenities beckon from every corner.

Park City

Nestled in a high mountain valley 32 miles east of Salt Lake Valley, Park City is a recreational boomtown with a phenomenal growth that continues both to delight and dismay residents. A few decades ago Park City was an impoverished, run-down town of 1,366 people, most of whom were unemployed or retired miners. Today, 6,900 people call Park City home, and the growth shows no signs of slowing — some estimates show Park City's population swelling to 70,000 in 20 years.

The per capita income of Park City and surrounding Summit County is around $29,000 — the highest in Utah. The reason the rich come to live in Park City is obvious. The stunning peaks of the Wasatch Mountains dominate the city. There is no escaping their serene and calming beauty. Thousands of square miles of forests, fields and wild land lie within an hour's drive. Residents need only walk out their doors to find a splendid smorgasbord offering skiing, fishing, mountain biking, boating and hiking. Park City boasts a thriving art scene, and fine dining, shopping and other big-city amenities beckon from every corner.

Although growth has utterly transformed the surrounding area, Historic Main Street still retains its romantic ambiance and the flavor of the Old West.

History and Overview

Boom

Like other boomtowns, Park City has many histories. Before snow and scenery brought wealthy suburbanites flocking to the high country, miners dug silver out of the rocky crests of the mountains. Before them, the lust for beaver pelts led rugged mountain men to the Wasatch Mountains. Earliest of all, Native Americans wandered the meadows in the summertime gathering bulbs, crickets and berries for winter feasting, repeating a pattern their ancestors had followed for thousands of years.

The true history of Park City depends on your perspective. But mining was the engine that brought men and machinery to the area and forever changed this mountain retreat. The gold and silver extracted from these slopes created one of the richest mining camps in the West — a place whose mines created a couple of dozen millionaires and gave up ore worth more than $400 million. One of these was financier and mining magnate George Hearst, the father of famous newspaper publisher William Randolph Hearst.

The mining boom started in 1868, when three soldiers from Col. Patrick E. Conner's company discovered a rich outcrop of quartz south of the city, then called Parleys Park. The ore sample assayed at 96 ounces of silver per ton, with profitable portions of gold and lead. A few years later the mine, named the Flagstaff, began operation.

As the news got out, the narrow canyon became the scene of a full-fledged gold rush. Thousands of miners flooded in, living in tents and tumbled-down shanties. Eager entrepreneurs opened a boarding house, general store and other businesses. Gambling, prostitution and a river of whiskey soon elbowed their way in and joined the party. Wild and woolly, Park City sprung up overnight.

The biggest strike of all came in 1872, when a prospector named Rector Steen found an outcropping of promising ore in Ontario Canyon. The ore assayed at 400 ounces of silver per ton — a true mother lode. The news spread fast, and Hearst bought the Ontario for $27,000. Hearst made out like a bandit — the Ontario produced $50 million worth of ore and paid dividends of $15 million. Within 20 years the Park City area was honeycombed with mines.

Colorful Characters

Mining drew a colorful cast of rough-and-tumble characters whose exploits are still talked about among native Park City residents. "Paddy the Pig" could put away a whole roast beef at one sitting, and "John the Baptist," an emaciated man of God, preached the end of the world while digging in the dirt.

Professional gamblers, prostitutes and dozens of saloons made the town distinctly different from the tranquil Mormon communities surrounding it. Because Brigham Young discouraged mining, few Mormons lived in Park City, and those who did kept their beliefs quiet. Workers of all nationalities left unpromising conditions at home and came to work in the dirty and dangerous mines. Cornish men, called "Cousin Jacks" by the other miners, were sought for their mining skills. Their colorful lingo enlivened the daily conversations, and they coined the terms "hard-boiled hats," and "Tommy Knockers" (evil little creatures whose strange noises in the mine shafts terrified the workers).

Hundreds of Irishmen fleeing the potato famine of 1847-54 ended up in Park City. One of these Irishmen was Thomas Kearns, who came to town as a pauper and left a millionaire. Kearns was elected a U.S. senator in 1900 and later bought *The Salt Lake Tribune* newspaper, which was controlled for many years by the Kearns family.

Bust

By 1880 Park City was a fair-sized town with a population of 3,500 and a promising future. Schools and churches had been established, as well as a newspaper called the *Park Record*. But trouble haunted Park City in the 1890s. Silver prices plummeted, and a se-

FYI

Unless otherwise noted, the area code for all phone numbers listed in this chapter is 435.

ries of fires almost completely destroyed the town. The Great Fire of 1898 incinerated more than 200 houses and businesses and left 500 people homeless. Gradually, the silver in the mountain played out, and Park City declined.

The coming of Prohibition brought new woes. As the wettest spot in Utah, federal officials gave it special attention. The harassment caused many residents to move away. The Depression of the '30s dealt the city a further blow. Mines closed, miners left for richer areas, and Park City turned into a boarded-up, ramshackle place of only a few thousand residents.

Renewal and Growth

Another kind of boom — skiing — saved Park City. After World War II, the growing wealth of the middle class and the increasing interest in winter recreation led to the rebirth of Park City.

Snow Park, the first ski resort in Park City, opened in 1946. In 1963 the Treasure Mountain Resort (now called the Park City Mountain Resort) opened for business, and Park City's luck changed. The main attraction of the resort was a 2.5-mile-long gondola, at the time the longest in North America. People began moving back to Park City, and the real-estate market skyrocketed. As interest in skiing gathered momentum, two more resorts opened. The Canyons (formerly known as Park West, then Wolf Mountain) was built in 1968, and Deer Valley Resort opened in 1981. Together, these three resorts offer 4,200 acres of skiing, with hundreds of trails, dozens of ski lifts and terrain suitable for beginners and daredevils alike.

The newest attraction in town is the Utah Winter Sports Park, built as a site for the 2002 Olympic Winter Games. The $45 million facility has areas for both freestyle and Nordic ski

INSIDERS' TIP

Park City is less than an hour away from the Salt Lake International Airport. Just hop on six-lane Interstate 80 and drive east — you can't miss it! Once in town, use the Main Street Trolley and free citywide bus service to get around.

Oral History: The Path of a Country Boy, Francis G. Tate

Francis Tate grew up near Heber and in the mountains above Salt Lake City. Here, in his own words, he shares his earliest recollections, beginning in 1923 at age 4, of youth, the mining industry and the evolution of Utah's ski industry, as well as reflections on the changing times from his perspective in 1997 at the age of 78.

I was born in 1919 on a farm in Midway, Utah. My father farmed and raised cattle, and he raised horses for the mines. Then the mines got electricity, so that took care of that, and he went into dairy farming and beef cattle. Dad started working for Utah Power and Light and rode his horse across the mountains to do swing-shift work for the power company when people went on vacations or took a few days off. He'd ride over and work at the hydro station in Millcreek Canyon, then he'd ride his horse back over the tops of the mountains to the other side, back to the farm.

Close-up

In 1923, when I was about 4 years old, we moved to a hydroelectric plant, and Dad started working for Utah Power and Light full time. The power plant was at Murdock, near Hailstone, on the Provo river about 8 miles north of Heber City. I started school there and mostly grew up there, too. Sometimes we had to walk down to the road to catch the school bus, but in the winter we got them to come up the road. There were people from Midway, Charleston and Heber that all went to the same school. It was cold during the winter. We would put our clothes in bed with us to warm them up, then lay them out and jump into them and run into the front room to get warm by the stove.

My grandfather and step-grandmother, May, stayed on in Midway in the farmhouse. They continued farming then sold some of the land to the sheep men. We kept the house and the land after they died, and later it was our summer home.

There wasn't much to do in those days [mid-1920s]. We did a lot of church activities. We had to go to Heber to church, but everyone was a Mormon, and we did church activities together. We had this old Essex touring car, and you had to put the flaps down to keep the snow out in the winter. One day the flaps were blowing, and cold air was coming in, and Dad reached around in the back seat to close the flaps and ran off the road. No one was hurt, but we were stuck there because the snow was so deep.

In the summer we hiked around in the hills, and we learned to swim in the Provo River. We piled up rocks, and it made a pool. Fishing was excellent. One time we had these bamboo poles, and we put a cork on the line and a grasshopper then threw it down through the rapids. I got so many fish! They were almost 2 feet long. Beginning in 1929, I brought my horse up to Murdock from the farm in the summer for a couple of years, and I'd ride down to get the milk in the early morning then I'd go off fishing. I rode up into the hills into the old mining places.

I got into the Boy Scouts and was the youngest Eagle Scout in the council. Our dads helped us build a log cabin when we were about 12 or 13. We got our lifesaving badges at Luke's hot pots.

In the winter there wasn't much to do either, and then when I was about 10 [1929] we started skiing. We'd been reading a lot about skiing being quite popular. We got skis for Christmas, and we started to ski near the power plant. We had very little control, and we didn't really know what we were doing or how to stop. There were no instructors, and

— continued on next page

no one taught us how to ski. We just had to figure it out. We read the magazines and some books on skiing then went out and tried what we saw in the pictures. The first skis were mostly pine, but mine were made out of ash so they were stronger and the tips didn't break off. The Hansen boy's pine skis broke the tips when they hit the fence, but mine didn't. We made some of our skis in school. We cut them with green timber and left them in a press the whole school year, then at the end of year we shaped them. They were pine. A teacher at school — the commercial arts teacher — built a jump with a little run on it, and we skied there. The skis had a leather toe piece that fit around your toe, and we just wore boots that we kept oiled with mutton tallow that we heated. It would seep into the leather and keep them waterproof. We got pretty good, but the toe kept slipping off, and our foot went into the snow. So we got an inner tube, and we cut it cross ways and cut big elastic bands out of it, and we put those around our ankle and then when we put our toe through the toe strap we pulled it out and put it under our toe to keep us in the ski. It worked pretty good.

At Murdock they had a pipeline for about 2 miles coming from the water farther back up the hill down to the power plant that ran the turbine that ran the generators that produced electricity. The power plant was farther up the canyon, and it was flushed back into the Provo River. We built a little jump because there wasn't anything else to do but jump, and we'd jump a little ways — it wasn't too steep — and sometimes we'd make it and sometimes not. There was a big pipe about 6 feet in diameter that fed the water into the turbine generator, and it came through a swell and up over another hill and down under the powerhouse. We'd go up there and come down off the pipe that was our jump. You should have a steep landing place, but we were novices and didn't know much about it so we'd go up the hill and come down and jump off that pipeline and land on the flat. If you couldn't steer your skis very well then you might run into the barn, which we did some of the time.

My leg had problems and I had quite a few operations when I was about 11 years old or so. The bone was bruised and got infected. Penicillin would have taken care of it if we'd had it. The last time they did the operation the doctors left it open to drain. They said if it didn't work they were going to put maggots in it, but it worked. We had to go to Salt Lake for the operations. The road was pretty rough between Heber and Salt Lake. When we got there, we stayed with some friends in Sugarhouse and took the streetcar to the hospital. I had a heavy cast, and I don't think I skied then, but a few months later when I got a smaller cast I skied. But the cast got wet and deteriorated around the toes. Mother and I got a piece of inner tube and cut it and sewed it so I could slip it over my toes to keep the water out. I put some thick socks on and the inner tube and skied with the cast, first with one ski, and then I got the cast in the toe strap and skied normally. After the leg healed I had to protect it, so Dad and I made a brace after the surgery to keep me from hitting the bone. We took pieces of rawhide from the tops of snowshoes and took the varnish off one side then wet it and curved it around to dry and put sheep skin inside. I used to hit on it with my ski pole and tell people it was a wooden leg.

When we skied around the power plant, we hiked into places we hadn't been before in the winter. It was beautiful. Just snow and trees. No one went in there, in the canyon by the power plant, except us to ski. The snow was heavy on the pine trees and pretty deep on the ground. It was snow and trees and quiet. We fooled around like that for quite a while, then Dad moved down to a power plant in Salt Lake at the mouth of Big Cottonwood Canyon when I was about 15. Skiing was a little different because they didn't ever clear the roads going up the canyon but we could walk up the road and ski down. We could sleigh ride from the upper powerhouse about 3 miles down the road. When cars came we could go faster than they did.

— continued on next page

Photo: Unknown

Francis G. Tate, taken around 1940.

Then Alf Engen came to town. He was a skier from Norway. He got the CCC — the Civilian Conservation Corps — to build a ski jump about 3 miles down canyon from Brighton. The CCC camp was just up the hill for the power plant in Big Cottonwood Canyon. During the Depression, the government set up the CCC to get boys from the East to come out and work for money to send home to their families. They did all the picnic areas in Big Cottonwood Canyon — built and maintained them and built bridges across the creek in Big and Little Cottonwood canyons. We had to get more serious about jumping so we needed new skis with three grooves in the bottom instead of one and the ski was a little longer. We started getting real bindings on the skis, and the Army bought some of these good ski boots for the CCC boys, and we got some, too. The toe went in a frame with a toe strap and around the heel and tightened up. In jumping skis, the heel should hold tight but come off the ski a little so you can land on a downhill slope. We used these on alpine and Nordic skis. We had a contest. A whole lot of boys, all friends, jumped at the same time, and I came in fourth, and I was happy about that. The wind was up and they strained themselves, and when they landed they fell. But I just took my time and kept my arms to my sides like they do now.

They opened up Brighton first and put a T-bar in on the hill, a rope on a cable that you

— continued on next page

put between your legs. Then they put the Alta ski lift in, and it got better and the shoes got better. Then we started using poles. They opened Ecker Hill and held national jumping contests, and Engen usually won, although we had some of the best skiers from all over because it was one of the best ski hills at the time. Then we got into more elaborate skis and equipment. The bindings got better, and for years we used a cable binding, and if you were going to jump you could run the cable through one bracket to loosen or tighten for jumping. They got quick release so you didn't break your leg. It got better and better.

We kind of settled on skiing at Alta because it was the steepest and quite a bit better than the other places. Alta used to be a mining town, but they weren't mining when the skiing started to be a big deal. But some of the old buildings were used for skiers, and some were covered with snow, and we skied over the tops of them. The tailing piles made good jumps. One or two winters we went up there during the Christmas holidays and stayed in cabins, but we had to hike in for a couple of miles. We'd build jumps and come down through the trees and circuitous slalom and then hike back up. And when we built the jump we'd have to tromp the hill down, and we'd all get together and go sideways up the hill to pack it down so we had a smooth place to land. Some of the boys started hot-dog skiing which they now call aerials with flips.

The resorts started to develop, and first we had a chair, then two chairs, then quads and now they can accommodate hundreds of skiers an hour. In the '30s Brighton had summer homes, and a lot of rich and famous people from Salt Lake stayed there all summer. Some of the children they took up were what we called retarded. We played and hiked up there in the summer. They built the Alpine Rose Lodge, and it was a place to stay all night. It was very beautiful. Miners were the only ones who lived in Alta then. Just one miner, I think. He was the mayor, and he watched over he mines. The first lodge was built in Alta by the Union Pacific Railroad in the very early '40s. Most of the people who skied were locals. Some people started coming in by train, but skiing was just our local sport. Someone must have figured that it was going to be a pretty big industry here, but we just skied because it was fun and something to do.

In the summer I spent time minding the cows in Midway after we moved to Salt Lake. We stayed in the farmhouse, which never had plumbing, and we pumped water from the well. We had a wood stove in the kitchen for cooking and a stove in the main room to heat the house. We went to see friends who were farmers over in Snyderville and hunted squirrels and hiked around. They had an ice house, and in the winter they cut ice out of the lake and covered it with straw and it lasted until September. My friend, Fat Green, got a Star automobile from someone at the power plant. We were in high school then. In the summer he was working in the pea vinery where they took all the peas and all the green stuff and smashed it up and put in the silo to feed the cows. He had money. On weekends we took that car and roamed around the countryside, and it would break down, and we'd get it running and we'd go again. We went to the Homestead in the summer, and the water was hot. We'd swim all day.

A lot of my friends fathers worked in the mines in Park City when I was still in school. They paid pretty good money in those days. We used to go to Scouting events in Park City. We were all pretty close. Three or four of us played football, and in the summer we had a squirrel-tail contest. At the end of the summer whoever had the most squirrel tails got taken to dinner. You could get a steak dinner with everything for 75¢ in those days. Not too much skiing went on during the war. The boys who were healthy enough to ski were in the service. I didn't go in the service because of my leg.

I went on a mission for the Mormon church. I sloughed school one day and went to Salt Lake. The man who drove us had been the mission president in South Africa and he was talking about South Africa. That's when I decided to go on a mission to South Africa for the

— continued on next page

church. I left in January of 1940. We went from Salt Lake to New York by way of Omaha and Chicago. We had a good time — a bunch of boys who had never been away from home. Before we sailed for South Africa we went to all the clubs in New York and saw all the big stars of the time. This wasn't part of the missionary program. We sailed on the Moore-McCormack Lines S.S. *Brazil* out of New York, and we knew we were a long way from the farm by then. We stayed in Capetown, Port Elizabeth and East London until November of that year, but the war was heating up, and the church was told to get the missionaries out so we sailed at night on a British ship from Port Elizabeth to Cape Town then out into the Atlantic on the S.S. *President Polk*, an American cruise ship that went to Trinidad for refueling and then to New York. Most of the boys were scattered around the states then to finish out their mission.

After I got back, I finished at the University and got a degree in engineering. I taught skiing to the Boy Scouts, and I loaded ammunition in my spare time. After the war when the boys came back from Germany they brought back a lot of 9 mm German rifles, and we didn't have much of that kind of rifle around here so they sold them in a gun shop. I loaded the shells. I loaded 100,000 rounds of ammunition in one year for deer hunters.

We've all evolved. We just grew up — the people and the towns and the way of our life. First we had horses, and then we had cars. We grew up in the ski industry, too. Our first equipment was quite primitive. Then it got better, and there was more. It was safer. Skiing used to be hard work, hiking up the hill to ski down. You didn't get as many runs, and at the end of the day you were about to drop over from being so tired. Now I think it's good to have Olympics here. It will give us exposure to the world. The missionaries do that too, you know, but people don't understand the Mormons, and this is a good opportunity to see what we're like — that we're like other people.

---

jumping and a track for bobsled, luge and sled runs. In the winter visitors can ride five different kinds of sleds on the track; summer riding is done on wheeled sleds on the track's concrete surface. (See our "Sightseeing and Attractions" section of this chapter for more information on this attraction, as well as information on Park City's Silver Mine Adventure.)

In the past 20 years the Park City area has been among the most economically vital areas in the United States. The city throbs with prosperity. But affluence doesn't come without a price. Park City is experiencing the same problems that have beset other western resort towns, such as Aspen, Colorado, and Jackson Hole, Wyoming. Residents are watching with dismay as urban sprawl replaces bucolic farmland and empty hillsides.

Luxury homes sell for as much as $2 million in Park City and surrounding Summit County, but more modestly priced homes are also available (see the "Real Estate" section of this chapter). In 1992, after three years of heated discussion, a new zoning plan was adopted by the Summit County Commission. The heart of the plan calls for growth to be controlled and di-

rected into areas most suitable for development. Rural lands and environmentally sensitive areas would be left in their natural state. Density requirements were put into place to control the number of structures allowed per acre, and provisions were made for desperately needed affordable housing. The plan has had mixed success — developers have filed a number of lawsuits contesting the legality of the ordinance. The zoning plan has done nothing to halt the pace of development. Plans are afoot in the Park City area for hundreds of new houses, dozens of hotels and condominiums as well as a variety of golf courses and other development. Some welcome the growth, which they insist is a sign of economic vitality. Others regret losing the charming small town of yore.

Historic Main Street

Through constant change, Park City's mining heritage and authentic western architecture have been preserved in the Historic Main Street district. Main Street is a narrow artery at the mouth of a canyon, paralleled by a few other streets higher up the mountain side. Most of the Main Street structures date from the Great Fire of 1898. Charming and picturesque, Main Street and the surrounding structures display a fascinating variety of building styles and materials, all of which convey the rough-and-ready ambiance of frontier America.

Historic Main Street is now the center of Park City's vital downtown district, with art galleries, clothing boutiques, home furnishing shops and other stylish emporiums. See the "Shopping" section of this chapter for a description of what's available. You can also find dozens of restaurants and clubs along Main Street, as well as inns, hotels and bed and breakfasts. Read the "Accommodations" and "Restaurants" sections to discover the abundant choices you have in these areas.

www.insiders.com

See this and many other **Insiders' Guide®** destinations online — in their entirety.

Visit us today!

With the best-preserved mining business in Utah, Main Street is listed on the National Register of Historic Places as a Historic Commercial District, and most of the buildings in the area are listed in the National Historic Register.

The Vital Present

Fluffy powder snow is the economic engine that drives Park City, and the town revolves around winter sports. But Park City is also the site of many summer activities and has become a popular year-round resort. Mountain bikers can tour the region's hidden wild country on more than 50 miles of marked trails, at all skill levels. Golfers can tee off from six nearby golf courses. More than 40 unique boutiques, markets and emporiums tempt shoppers. Many special events and festivals, such as the world-famous Sundance Film Festival and the Park City Arts Festival, bring revelers to the city during summer and winter. To learn more about Park City's arts and annual events, see the section devoted to those subjects in this chapter.

Whatever you choose to do, Park City will jump-start your senses like nowhere else. The town hums with life, and before you know it you're wide awake, aware of everything and taking pleasure in whatever you're doing, whether it's skiing, golfing, shopping or savoring the harmonies of a string quartet. A simple thing like smelling the piney air or lingering on a mountain vista suddenly becomes the most significant thing you've ever done. Here, the moment is what counts, and you want to grab it with both hands. Visitors and residents alike agree on one thing: Park City casts a spell. Don't try to resist it — you can't. Just sit back and enjoy the plentiful delights of this very special place.

Getting Here, Getting Around

Park City is in Summit County, 36 miles east of the Salt Lake International Airport and a scenic 30-minute drive up Parleys Canyon from the heart of Salt Lake City. Six-lane Interstate 80 delivers you to the doorstep of Park City's winter wonderland and summer playground and other Summit County sites. U.S. Highway 40 paves the way to and from nearby Heber and Midway. Utah highways 35, 65, 150, 224, 248 and 32 get you off the beaten path in Summit and nearby Wasatch County.

Once in town, you will note that unlike Salt Lake City, Park City wasn't laid out on a grid. Streets were arranged willy-nilly, hugging the bends and turns of the mountain topography. Main was the town's first street, a ragtag dirt road that led to the mines in nearby canyons. Boarding houses were built on upper Main in what we now call Old Town, and merchants set up shops farther down the hill on what is now Historic Main.

Over the next century development slowly spread up the mountain. Streets took their names and direction from the particular enterprise the road was to serve. In the 1960s and 1970s, when the ski industry took hold, the tiny mining town spread in all directions, creating new roads with a variety of names, such as Prospector, Bonanza and Silver King, reflecting back on the early mining days.

Don't expect to find 350 Main Street and 351 Main Street across from each other. Changes in the cross-streets over the years have made the numbering less than uniform.

In spite of the boom, Park City isn't very large, so it's easy to get around (see the map at the front of the book). Folks here are pretty considerate when it comes to driving, and locals expect even the quickest-paced New Yorker to fall in line with the more leisurely tempo right from the start. Might as well, you'll just get frustrated if you think you can move at warp speed here.

Once you pull off the interstate, you'll instantly be aware that Park City is a hamlet, with farms and quaint older homes lining the road into the center of town. Ahead and to either side are mountains and more mountains — snow-capped in winter, lush green in summer and a veritable artist's palette of crimson and ocher in the fall. Main Street (U.S. Highway 224), Park Avenue and Swede Alley are the three primary streets running parallel to each other through the center of town. Traffic can be slow-moving as skiers come and go, especially during midmorning and late afternoon. Summer traffic is lighter. Relax, check out the scenery and go with the flow.

Most people, once they get into the center of things, prefer to get around on foot. The sidewalks on the three major streets are quite narrow, and you'll be sharing them with lots of other pedestrians. If you like to amble along at a slow pace, it's a good idea to move to your right so others can pass. Bumping shoulders can be fun, though, and sometimes you can strike up a conversation with the most interesting people.

In addition to the town proper, which includes Prospector Square (one of the oldest developments in Park City and the location of many condominium hotels and restaurants), Historic Main Street and Old Town, the area has three ski resorts. These sit at the town's entrance, in it's center and at the far end. A word or two to clarify "resort": We use resort to mean a specific mountain area designated for skiing or summer adventures such as hiking and biking, not a resort hotel.

As you enter Park City off Interstate 80, The Canyons Resort is on your right, approximately 4 miles past the exit. The Canyons was originally called Park West and, until recently, Wolf Mountain. Lower Town and Park City Mountain Resort are a few miles farther up the road. Ahead, on the far end of town, sits Deer Valley Resort. You can go from the Park City Exit off I-80 to the Deer Valley Resort in about 15 minutes on the busiest of days. A quick look at the map in the front of the book will get you acquainted with the area in no time.

Park City offers some excellent public transportation, all free, to get you around town. We've included the details in the section that follows. If you choose to get around by car, be ever mindful of foot traffic — there's a lot of it. You'll want to park your car at some point during your visit, so we've included some pointers about that, too. Whether on foot, aboard the Main Street Trolley, the city bus or your own automobile, you'll get around just fine.

One big advantage to this charming mountain town is that it's almost impossible to get lost in. Besides giving you information on how to get here and get around, we've filled this chapter with lots of detail on where to go, where to stay and what to do. Check it out on the following pages.

Parking

You'll find ample free parking at all ski resorts in Park City; hotels provide free parking for their guests. The best way to see the historic aspects of the town is on foot, but you may need to drive to the area first and then to take your stroll along Main Street. Metered parking is available at the curb on Main Street or behind Main Street on Swede Alley. You'll need nickels, dimes and quarters for the meter, and $2 gets you two hours of parking.

Transportation

Getting around in Park City is easy. You can ride free on the citywide bus from 7:37 AM to 1:10 AM during the winter and from 7:40 AM to 10:30 PM during the summer. The free Main Street Trolley runs guests up and down Historic Main Street every 20 minutes, seven days a week, from 1 until 5 PM in both summer and winter.

The ski lift at Deer Valley operates in the summer to take bikers and hikers up the mountain to a variety of trails. Several companies provide private and regularly scheduled transportation to and from Salt Lake International Airport and Park City. As a general guideline, the cost of transportation to and from Park City and the airport is $20 each way, generally by van, for one person. The cost is also $20 each way from Park City to the ski resorts at Alta, Brighton and Solitude.

Of course, the mode of transportation affects the price greatly. Limousine service to and from the airport to Park City can run as high as several hundred dollars. Some companies have a two- to four-person minimum, and some offer only limited service during the summer. Many shuttle services also offer local taxi service. Rates vary by season and your itinerary. Some transportation companies offer expanded services (see the following listings) such as sightseeing tours and shuttles to and from downtown Salt Lake and the area's other ski resort.

All Resort Express
1221 Sidewinder Dr., Park City • 649-3999, (800) 457-9457

This company offers scheduled and private service to and from the airport and Park City. Tours, charters, sightseeing and limousine service are also available.

Day Trips Transportation
1950 Woodbine Way, Park City • 649-8294, (800) 649-8294

Year-round daily taxi service to and from the airport and Park City is available from 6 AM to 2 AM. There's a three-passenger minimum for private transport. The company provides sightseeing tours and limousines are also available.

DLS/Gus Transportation
3939 S. Wasatch Blvd., Holladay • 649-2077, (801) 277-1214, (800) 837-6490

Top of the line limousines and luxury sedans, 4x4s, Suburban and 15-passenger vans are available for passenger transfer to and from the airport and Park City. The company can arrange airport meet-and-greet or private service.

Le Bus
542 S. 2165 W., Salt Lake City • (801) 975-0202, (800) 366-0288

This company provides private group transfers or charters to Park City and other locations throughout the state.

Lewis Bros. Stages
1700 Park Ave., Park City • 649-2256, (800) 826-5844

Year-round door-to-door scheduled airport transports are available from Lewis Bros. The company will also arrange sightseeing tours and special charters for groups.

Ol' Miners Taxi and Tours
187 Daly Ave., Park City • 649-4185

This company specializes in personalized tours of Old Town, Deer Valley, the mining areas and other places of interest in and around Park City.

Park City Express
2627 W. Kilby Rd., Park City • 645-7250, (800) 7-AIRPORT

Park City Express provides year-round taxi service, airport-shuttle service, tours, charters, sightseeing and limousines.

INSIDERS' TIP

Park City's altitude literally can be a breathtaking experience to folks who come from a sea-level location. Take your time, and if you get lightheaded, sit for a few minutes and rest.

Whether you visit Park City in the summer or winter, you're bound to fall in love with this spectacular mountain resort.

Park City Transportation Services
1555 Lower Iron Horse Loop Rd., Park City • 649-8567, (800) 637-3803

Service is provided to and from the airport and Park City from 5 AM to midnight daily, every 20 minutes during the winter and once an hour during the summer. The company also provides shuttle service to the downtown Salt Lake City area.

Powder for the People
1776 Park Ave., Ste. 4, Park City • 649-6648, (888) 482-7547

Charter and sightseeing tours are available from this company along with regular transfer to and from the airport and Park City. Shuttle service to other ski resorts is also available. Service is limited during the summer but regularly scheduled shuttle service is available during the winter.

Rocky Mountain Super Express
60 S. Redwood Rd., Salt Lake City • (801) 485-4100, (800) 397-0773

This company has a two-person minimum on airport to Park City transportation. Hours of operation are 5 AM to midnight daily.

Summit Transportation
775 Parkview Dr., Park City • 649-3292, (800) 388-5289

Summit will arrange personalized meet-and-greet pickup at the airport gate as well as private vehicles for transfer to Park City by appointment. There's a four-person minimum for this service. Limousine service and sightseeing tours are available. The company operates during the winter only.

Real Estate

It was love at first sight. You're smitten with the mountains, the friendly people and all the great adventure available year round in Park City. What about buying your own piece of Park City? We have provided an overview of the real-estate market in Park City for those who may want to purchase a home or condominium for seasonal or year-round living or as an investment. The Park City real-estate market has recently calmed down and is showing less dramatic, more realistic increases than it did in 1995, when prices skyrocketed.

In the mid '70s a little old shack of a house in Old Town could be snatched up for less than $20,000. Today, that same house would sell for approximately $200,000. Many locals just shake their heads when the subject of Park City real estate comes up. It's that old refrain, "I shoulda bought Park City when I had the chance." Some did, and now they are happily sitting on their personal gold mine.

For many years the tourism industry has driven Park City real estate. The market for condominiums in particular is steered by rental units and the rate of return on investment. Current sales are beginning to shift from condominium properties to single-family homes. The shift has occurred because people coming from out-of-state and workers in Salt Lake City have begun to realize they can live in the mountains or Salt Lake's mid- and south Valley and be at work in downtown Salt Lake in about the same drive time.

Park City housing ranges from new, multi-level luxury condominiums to pleasant older condos built nearly 30 years ago, and from enormous log and stone estates with four or more bedrooms to the smallest wood-frame homes with historic character. Some have gingerbread trim and ooze charm while others have no frills at all, sadly resembling roughly built, pricy shacks. Although most of the older property has already received a face-lift, grants are available to renovate historic property.

The areas in the county with the most real-estate activity in or near Park City include Deer Valley, Thaynes Canyon, Old Town, Park Meadows and the Snyderville Basin. Dennis Gray of Flinders Realty and Exchange, the statistics spokesperson for Park City Board of Realtors, provided the following statistics on property sales in the area for the first six months of 1997. The average cost of a single-family home in Summit County was $399,000. Deer Valley homes averaged $1,656,000, while

FYI

Unless otherwise noted, the area code for all phone numbers listed in this chapter is 435.

properties in Park Meadows averaged $538,000. Thaynes Canyon homes averaged $823,000, and the average home sale in the Snyderville Basin was $341,000. Old Town properties averaged $281,000. Total sales of single-family homes for the first six months of 1997 were approximately $90 million, a 12-percent increase over the previous year.

Condominium sales in the area averaged $303,000. Most condominium sales occurred within the city limits. Deer Valley condos sold for an average of $614,000, Park Meadows at an average of $391,000. Condominiums near the ski areas, exclusive of Deer Valley, sold for an average of $213,000. Old Town condominiums averaged $285,000. Condos range from studios to very large five- and six-bedroom units and represent a variety of types — from older remodeled properties to new luxury styles. Total condominium sales for the first six months of 1997 were $60 million, 20 percent less than the previous year.

Long-term Rentals

If you plan to work in Park City — or be a ski and summer-trail bum — and don't plan to buy property, you will probably want to arrange a long-term rental. Long-term rentals in the immediate vicinity are broken down into three categories: affordable housing, in which income determines the rental rate; low-income housing, which is rented to families who receive public assistance or minimum wage; and regular unregulated housing.

The Park City rental market mirrors Salt Lake City's low vacancy rate, and affordable long-term rentals in the immediate area can be difficult to come by. Many people who work in Park City live near the resort area in the

---

INSIDERS' TIP

Park City's temperature in summer is a cool 10 degrees lower than in the Salt Lake Valley. In winter, Jack Frost is ever-present to bite your fingers and toes if you don't dress warmly. The air in the mountains is arid, just like it is the in valley. You'll want to bring plenty of lip balm, hand cream and moisturizer when you visit the area.

smaller towns area such as Heber, Midway, Coalville, Kamas, Francis and Marion where, although rentals are also limited, the cost is more manageable.

The classified section of *The Park Record*, the local newspaper distributed every Wednesday and Saturday, is a good source for rental properties. Real Estate agents generally don't handle long-term rentals. The average monthly prices for Park City rental units are as follows: Studios, $500 and $625; one-bedroom apartments, $600 and $750; two-bedroom apartments, $800 and $1,000; two-bedrooms plus a loft, $1,200; and three-bedroom units, $1,200 to $1,500.

If you're looking for a short-term rental or a skiing or summer vacation place, see our "Vacation Rentals" section of this chapter.

Accommodations

Park City and the nearby areas offer every imaginable accommodation: hotels, luxury resort-condominium hotels, private homes, bed and breakfasts and rustic country inns. In addition, several companies will make reservations for you at any hospitality site in Park City or plan your entire vacation from start to finish. This section includes many selections from the hotels available in Park City. Also see our "Bed and Breakfast" section.

You can check out the campgrounds in and near Park City in the Parks and Recreation chapter of the book.

See the "Vacation Rentals" section of this chapter for information on property management companies that handle reservations for a variety of condo and private-home properties. That section also lists privately owned condominiums and home rentals, reservationists and destination planners.

Unless otherwise indicated, hotels and condominium hotels in Park City have wheelchair-accessible rooms. Individuals with special needs should inquire when making reservations. Smoking and nonsmoking rooms are available in most hotels and condominium hotels. The exceptions have been noted in the individual listing.

Many hotels have restaurants and non-exclusive private clubs on the premises. If you have never visited Utah before, you probably don't know what we mean by a private club. If you're planning to enjoy a cocktail anytime during your stay, you better brush up on the liquor laws (see our Nightlife chapter).

Park City has plenty of great guest rooms available throughout the year. Naturally, with some of the finest skiing on earth, winter availablity is not as plentiful as summer. Always make reservations well in advance for any season. Book accommodations in early November for a December through March ski trip. If you wait until the last minute, you'll probably still find a room, but you won't have as many options.

Price Code

The hotel listings include a dollar symbol showing a price range for a one-night stay, midweek, double occupancy. Pricing information is provided as a general guideline. Unless otherwise indicated, hotels and condominium hotels accept major credit cards.

Rates vary according to the season. They are highest during the ski season, which varies each year according to snow conditions but runs more or less from Thanksgiving to mid-April. Within that period, rates are about 10 percent higher during the peak holiday times of December 20 to January 1 and President's Day weekend in February.

Rates are 30 percent lower during the summer season, Memorial Day to late September, and 40 percent lower during the shoulder seasons, mid-April to mid-May and mid-September to mid-November.

However, availability is another matter. Although there is a big rush for rooms for the holiday season, March is the busiest month of the year in the ski industry.

In short, you'll pay more for a room in peak season, but you won't find as many rooms in March. Plan ahead.

$	Less than $125
$$	$126 to $185
$$$	$186 to $250
$$$$	$251 to $350
$$$$$	$351 to $450

Hotels

Best Western Landmark Inn
$ • 6560 N. Landmark Dr. • 649-7300, (800) 548-8824

The 106 rooms here are pretty basic but nice and clean, and the price is right. Unless you feel you must slather yourself in true resort luxury, your stay at the Landmark can be enjoyable. Situated at the junction of Utah Highway 224, the hotel is near the center of Park City and offers a free shuttle to and from Historic Main Street and the ski areas. Inexpensive breakfast, lunch and dinners are available at Denny's on the property, or you can shuttle to town for upscale victuals. The hotel features an indoor pool, hydro-spa and exercise area. A sun deck exposes you to the rays as well as the view. You can buy hooch in the state-owned liquor store in the hotel. The lobby is spacious with a fireplace and plenty of seating for casual conversation and people watching.

Chateau Apres Lodge
$ • 1299 Norfolk Ave. • 649-9372, (800) 357-3556

This family-owned and operated ski lodge provides clean down-to-business accommodations for skiers. Located 150 yards from ski lifts, the chalet-style lodge has 32 private and dormitory rooms. Guests receive a free continental breakfast before hitting the slopes and hot cider after skiing. The large fireplace in the lobby is a great place to unwind and enjoy conversation. It's open during the winter for individuals and groups and during the summer for groups only.

Olympia Park Hotel and Conference Center
$ • 1895 Sidewinder Dr. • 649-2900, (800) 754-3279

The Olympia's 203 newly remodeled guest rooms, including 10 luxury specialty suites, are roomy and well-appointed. The hotel also offers 110 studio, one- and two-bedroom units with various amenities including fully equipped kitchens, fireplaces, balconies, cable TV and some spectacular views.

This all-in-one hotel features ski rental and storage, a video-game room, indoor pool, hot tub and sauna, plus business amenities and conference rooms. The Pantry Restaurant serves breakfast, lunch and dinner. The Pub, a private club adjacent to the restaurant, offers libations, a big-screen television, darts and a great place for visiting with friends.

Radisson Inn Park City
$$ • 2121 Park Ave. • 649-5000, (800) 333-3333

Comfy rooms, 131 of them, nicely appointed suites, six in all, plus pay-per-view movies make this hotel a great hangout for golfers, skiers and biking and hiking enthusiasts. The large indoor/outdoor pool has great mountain views. Skiing is just down the road, and the Park City Municipal Golf Course is across the street. Radigan's Restaurant on the property is open for breakfast, lunch and dinner.

Stein Eriksen Lodge
$$$$ • 7700 Royal St. • 649-3700, (800) 453-1302

Warning! Allow a few moments to get a grip when you first embrace the drama of this spectacular lodge. Situated at 8,200 feet midmountain in the Silver Lake area at Deer Valley resort, the lodge is named for Olympic Gold Medalist Stein Eriksen and emanates an aura of European luxury with all the modern conveniences you'd expect in a world-class resort.

Each room and suite is decorated with imported fabrics, heavy brushed pine from Spain, hand-crafted Portuguese tiles and hand-painted

---

INSIDERS' TIP

There's nothing more glorious than a brisk run down the slopes on a sunny winter day. Park City has lots of bright ski days but be sure to use a good sun block on your face and other exposed areas. The sun reflecting on the white snow can burn fair skin quickly. Don't forget to protect your eyes from the intense rays.

Italian chandeliers — a veritable United Nations of opulence. More than 145 fireplaces lend warmth and comfort to the lobby and to many of the 130 rooms and suites. Guest rooms are all decorated in Scandinavian color schemes with oversize bathrooms featuring jetted whirlpool baths. Every bed has a down comforter to snuggle under. Guest rooms have fully stocked sundry bars with all the important things you might've left at home: lip balm, disposable cameras, film, suntan lotion, headache remedies plus nibbles and soft drinks. The rooms have humidifiers and safes as well as other extras you just can't live without. The lodge also has a year-round outdoor heated pool, hot tub, sauna, fitness room and massage therapy in the spa facility. The underground garage is heated and valet parking, heated sidewalks, boot warming and equipment storage are provided.

There's more! For skiers, this ski-in/ski-out lodge has a ski rental and repair shop with overnight tuning and attendants to facilitate the handling of all sports equipment. The lodge has truly gone to the outer limits to provide comfort and courtesy, attending to travelers' needs with utmost care.

The food at the Stein Eriksen Lodge is spectacular, too. See the Glitretind in the "Restaurants" section of this chapter for mouthwatering details on the superior fare and award-winning wine list. The Birkebeiner's offers lunch and dinner in a more casual atmosphere with lighter bistro-style dishes and a very well-thought-out children's menu. It goes without saying that the views are magnificent.

The service is professional and friendly. The concierge is well-informed and ready to answer questions or make a multitude of important arrangements. Were that not enough, Stein Eriksen Lodge has been given an array of impressive awards including *Wine Spectator*'s Award of Excellence and the *Condé Nast Traveler* Readers' Choice Award for "Best Mainland Resort." If you don't feel pampered after a visit to Stein Eriksen's, you just weren't trying.

Yarrow Resort Hotel and Conference Center
$$ • 1800 Park Ave. • 649-7000, (800) 927-7694

The year-round outdoor pool, hot tub and fitness room are a nice complement to the 181

guest rooms and suites offered by the Yarrow. Cozying-in isn't hard to do here. The rooms are nicely appointed with a warm inviting ambiance and include many extras such as hair dryers, iron and board, cable TV, radio and movies. You can get a hearty breakfast, quick lunch or full-course dinner in the 1800 Park Avenue Cafe located on the property or enjoy a beverage in the Pub. Studio and one-bedroom condominiums are also available. You can shop or catch a flick at the Holiday Village Mall next to the Yarrow or shuttle to Main Street and the ski areas.

Hotels near Park City

Homestead Resort
$$ • 700 N. Homestead Dr., Midway • 654-1102, (800) 327-7220

This is off the beaten path but no accommodations listing would be complete without the century-old Homestead (see the Close-up in this chapter). The resort has more than 100 sleeping rooms including standard guest rooms and luxury suites and 18 new luxury executive cottages designed to accommodate business travelers. In addition, the Homestead has family rooms that include bunks and queen-size beds. The various buildings scattered about the property are connected by a scenic walkway. The decor throughout the property ranges from New England to Southwestern to classic traditional. Most units have a private entrance and verandas. Amenities vary according to your choice of room. The gathering room in the main building has a fireplace.

Regardless of the accommodation you chose, all guests have access to the swimming pool, stables, lawn games, golf, restaurants and other amenities offered by the Homestead. For a more intimate setting, see the listing under "Bed and Breakfasts and Inns" section in this chapter. Homestead restaurants are listed in the "Restaurant" section of this chapter, and summer and winter sport activities are included in the "Sightseeing and Attractions" section.

Hylander Motel
$ • 425 S. Main, Heber • 654-2150, (800) 932-0355

This is a a pleasant, clean, friendly 22-room motel just 15 miles from Park City. The beds are big, the rooms have refrigerators and microwaves and the price is right. Is it the '70s in Heber? The hotel also has a heated outdoor pool. Insiders have been eating breakfast, lunch and dinner at the nearby Hub Cafe, well, forever. Chick's Cafe has been serving up food for a long time, too. Granny's Drive-in has award-winning milkshakes and the Wagon Wheel Cafe next to the Wagon Wheel Gas and Convenience is a good bet. Not much is open in Heber after 10 PM.

Condominium Hotels

The properties listed below are called condominium hotels because the accommodations offered include hotel rooms, studios and two-, three-, four- and five-bedroom condo units with some traditional hotel amenities. Unlike hotel properties that have an average rate based on the season and day of the week, condominium hotels vary in price based on the size and extent of amenities provided in the unit. Prices range from $200 per night for a single hotel-style room to $225 for a one bedroom condo, $250 for a two-bedroom condo, $300 for a three-bedroom condo, $375 for a four-bedroom condo and from $450 to $685 for a five-bedroom condo. During the peak holiday period, rates can increase by 10 percent, and in the summer and shoulder season, rates are 30 to 40 percent less than the average rates we've listed. The prices listed in this section represent an average for a one-night stay, midweek, double occupancy.

All Seasons Condominiums
$$$$ • 1585 Empire Ave., Park City
• 649-5500, (800) 331-8652
All Seasons specializes in deluxe two- and three-bedroom condominiums by the 8th fairway of Park City Municipal golf course. Amenities include laundry facilities, daily maid service, hot tub, cable TV pool and fireplaces.

Copperbottom Inn
$$$ • 1637 Shortline Dr., Park City
• 649-5111, (800) SKI-2002
In the center of Park City, these cozy one- and two-bedroom condominiums have fireplaces, indoor sauna and whirlpool. Chez

Betty, a popular Park City eatery, is located on the property.

Inn at Prospector Square
$$$ • 2200 Sidewinder Dr., Park City
• 649-7100, (800) 453-3812
This complete 206-room condominium hotel has a full-service athletic club with lap pool, laundry facilities, cable TV with VCR and daily maid service. Concierge services are available and conference facilities may be booked by guests. Some units have fireplaces; nonsmoking rooms are available. The Grub Steak Restaurant is on the property.

The Gables
$$$ • 1335 Lowell Ave., Park City
• 649-0800, (800) 443-1045
The Gables offers 20 one-bedroom condominiums and penthouses with fireplaces and daily maid service. Guests can enjoy the hot tub, pool and sauna, cable TV and VCR. Laundry facilities are provided. Concierge and conference services are also available. Located at the base of the Park City Mountain Resort, this property is close to shops and restaurants.

The Lodge at the Resort Center
$$$ • 1415 Lowell Ave., Park City
• 649-0800, (800) 453-3812
This lodge is a ski-in, ski-out property at Park City Mountain Resort. It boasts 168 rooms, including deluxe hotel units and studios to four-bedroom condominiums with cable TV and VCR. An outdoor heated pool with indoor/outdoor whirlpool, indoor sauna and steam room are available to guests. Laundry facilities and daily maid service are also provided. The lodge has meeting and conference rooms and concierge service. The complex has a restaurant on the property.

Marriott's Summit Watch Resort
$$$ • 378 Main St., Park City • 647-4100,
(800) 223-8245
This property may be a lot different from what you are accustomed to with the chain. The 82 studio and two-bedroom units offer luxury appointments. The master suites have fully equipped kitchens, living rooms and dining rooms. The baths have stretch and soak-jetted tubs. The property features a pool and

hot tub plus a fitness facility. All units have cable TV with VCR. Daily maid service is available, and some units have laundry facilities. Concierge service is available, and a restaurant is on the property.

Park Plaza Resort
$$ • 2060 Sidewinder Dr., Park City
• 649-0870, (800) 438-6494

The one- and two-bedroom condos are complete with cable TV and VCR, fireplaces, laundry facilities and daily maid service. Park Plaza also has a pool and hot tub.

Park Regency Resort
$$ • 1700 Prospector Ave., Park City
• 645-7531, (800) 438-6494

These one- and two-bedroom condominiums in Prospector Square feature professionally decorated rooms with cable TV and VCR, laundry facilities, hot tub and pool. Daily maid service is available.

Park Station Condominium Hotel
$$$$ • 950 Park Ave., Park City • 649-7062, (800) 367-1506

This 50-room condominium hotel has three-bedroom units with fireplaces and cable TV. A pool, sauna and hot tub, laundry and daily maid service are provided. Conference facilities are available to guests of Park Station.

Parkwest Village Condominiums
$$$$ • 3819 N. Village Round Dr., Park City
• 645-8983, (800) 421-5056

This property has hotel and one- to five-bedroom condominiums with unobstructed views of the mountains, meadows and evergreen trees. The condos feature fireplaces and cable TV and VCR. A pool, sauna and hot tub are available in some units.

Powderwood Resort
$$$ • 6975 N. 2200 W., Park City
• 649-2032, (800) 223-7829

Outdoor barbecue and picnic areas are available for these four one- to three-bedroom condominiums. The property also has a pool, hot tub and sauna. Some units have laundry facilities, cable TV/VCR and daily maid service.

Shadow Ridge Hotel and Conference Center
$$$$ • 50 Shadow Ridge, Park City
• 649-4300, (800) 451-3031

The 150 condos in this condominium hotel at the base of the Park City Mountain Resort offer deluxe studio to three-bedroom accommodations. Amenities include pool, hot tub and sauna, fitness facility, daily maid service, laundry facilities and cable TV with VCR. Some rooms have fireplaces. Concierge services and conference facilities are available to guests, and a restaurant is on the premises.

Silver Cliff Village
$$$$ • 1485 Empire Ave., Park City
• 649-5500, (800) 331-8652

Silver Cliff Village is a 12-unit condominium offering two-bedroom units with two baths and two fireplaces, cable TV and daily maid service. Guests can enjoy the condo's hot tub and are within walking distance of Park City restaurants and shopping.

Silver King Hotel
$$$ • 1485 Empire Ave., Park City
• 649-5500, (800) 331-8652

The Silver King offers 63 deluxe full-kitchen studio to two-bedroom condominiums, many with fireplaces, and all featuring comfy decor. Baths have jetted tubs, and laundry facilities are in each condo suite. The property has full-service meeting and conference facilities and a year-round indoor-outdoor pool, hot tub and sauna. Cable TV with VCR are provided in each unit. Daily maid service is available.

Silver Queen Hotel
$$$ • 632 Main St., Park City • 649-5986, (800) 447-NICE

An all-condominium hotel with 12 one- and two-bedroom suites, this property offers cable TV in each room, fireplaces, laundry facilities and daily maid service. The outer facade was designed to look like the Park City Bank's that went under in 1893. Before the Great Fire of 1898, this site was home to the Parlor Restaurant, which the *Park Record* called the Delmonico of Park City. Later it was the Jim Lee Cafe. It has also been the First and Last Chance Saloon.

Snow Flower Condominiums and Reservations

$$$$ • 400 Silver King Dr., Park City • 649-6400, (800) 852-3101

These studio to five-bedroom condominiums with outdoor barbecue areas, tennis courts and underground parking have an on-site 24-hour manager. Laundry facilities, cable TV and VCR are provided.

Treasure Mountain Inn

$$$ • 255 Main St., Park City • 655-4500, (800) 344-2460

Standing on the former site of Welch, Driscoll and Buck's General Store incorporated in 1898, Treasure Mountain was Park City's first condominium hotel and the first of its type in the United States. The 39 studio to two-bedroom condos offer a pool, hot tub, laundry facilities, cable TV/VCR and daily maid and concierge service. Nonsmoking rooms are available. The complex also has a restaurant on the property.

Bed and Breakfasts & Inns

The bed and breakfast and inn experience in and near Park City offers historic charm as well as picturesque country retreats. You'll find some properties decked out on a grand scale, while others are simple and cozy.

Smoking is not permitted in any bed and breakfast or inn in the area, but some proprietors will allow smoking on the grounds. Ask about the smoking policy when you make reservations. Pets are not welcome in these properties, and many accommodations aren't suitable for children. Most of the older properties are not wheelchair-accessible. If you have special requirements please check with the innkeeper when you make reservations. See our Bed and Breakfasts and Inns chapter at the beginning of the book for a description of the differences between inns and bed and breakfasts.

Bed and Breakfasts and Inns Price Code

Each listing includes a dollar symbol showing a price range for a one-night stay, midweek, double occupancy. Pricing information is provided as a general guideline. Unless otherwise noted, the bed and breakfasts and inns listed here accept major credit cards. Rates vary according to the season. High season, which peaks from approximately December 20 to January 1 (and President's Day weekend in February), is the ski season. This varies each year according to snow conditions, beginning when the lifts open around Thanksgiving and ending when the lifts close in mid-April. Rates are slightly lower during the summer season, Memorial Day to late September, and lowest during the shoulder seasons of mid-April to mid-May and mid-September to mid-November.

$	Less than $65
$$	$66 to $125
$$$	$126 to $185
$$$$	More than $185

1904 Imperial Hotel and Bed and Breakfast

$$ • 221 Main St. • 649-1904, (800) 669-8824

One of only four turn-of-the-century boarding houses still standing in Park City, this charming, nicely restored bed and breakfast has served as a boarding house, hospital and house of ill-repute since its construction in 1904. All 10 rooms feature period decor and furnishings. The Glen Allen room overlooks Main Street and has two single beds and a Roman tub. Little Belle also has a Roman tub and a queen-size bed. The Quincy is the largest room on the second floor with a king-size bed, sitting area and Roman tub. The original claw-foot tub in the Mayflower room on the third floor is a real treat. The Anchor room, also on the third floor, has a spiral staircase and loft, a king-size and two single beds and a Roman tub.

Guests are treated to a delicious breakfast each morning and can relax away the evening in the parlor by the fireplace. The establishment has an indoor hot tub. The innkeeper is always on hand to answer questions about the area and provide historical insights into the old hotel.

Angel House Bed and Breakfast

$$ • 713 Norfolk Ave. • 647-0338, (800) ANGEL-01

You might be touched by an angel in this lovely 1889 Victorian bed and breakfast. The nine guest rooms, each with grandly romantic appointments, are named for angels who embody romance and pleasure in the natural world. Michael and Faith, angels of protection, offer a lovely room with a fireplace, crystal chandelier, antique queen-size bed and fainting couch. Chamael and Amora, angels of love, have a king-size canopy bed, clawfoot tub and seated vanity. A queen-size antique Egyptian brass canopy bed, antique dresser and claw-foot tub belong to Christine, the angel of understanding. Peace angels Uriel and Aurora offer a four-poster bed with antique armoire and dresser, and Zadkiel, angel of freedom, offers a beautiful bay window along with antique furnishings. Victoria, also an angel of freedom, offers guests an antique French bed and a stunning view of the morning sunrise. Mary, angel of mercy and Jophiel, angel of wisdom, each offer a unique and elegant room with many special touches.

All rooms have a full private bath and each room has a down comforter and fine linens. Guests receive a heavenly gourmet breakfast and afternoon hors d'oeuvres and use of the parlor with its fireplace, library, TV/VCR and stereo. Massage service is also available. The Angel House is a ski-in/ski-out facility next to 2,000 wooded acres for hiking and mountain biking.

Goldener Hirsch Inn

$$$ • 7570 Royal St. E. • 649-7770, (800) 252-3373

Ski Magazine, *Town & Country* and *Condé Nast Traveler* have all had something impressive to say about this 20-room inn located just steps away from the Sterling chairlift at Deer Valley. Inspired by Countess Harriet Walderdorff, founder of the world-famous Hotel Goldener Hirsch in Salzburg, Austria, the accommodations are decorated in authentic European style with alpine architecture, select Austrian antiques and imported fabrics. Austrian craftspeople created the stenciling and woodwork. Each room has a king-size bed with down comforter, refrigerator and minibar. Many rooms have wood-burning fireplaces and all the bedrooms have ambiance galore.

Could there be any reason to leave these comfortable, elegant rooms? Skiing and outdoor recreation might get you moving. The other reason might be repast. As it happens, the Goldener Hirsch has a restaurant on the property. If you thought you were in the lap of luxury in your quarters, lost in a moment of indecision about which continent you were on, wait until the meal is served. The continental breakfast is on the house. For the rest of the menu, you're on your own. The restaurant offers seasonal menus that include continental and wild game specialties and traditional Austrian dishes. The wine selection was given the Award of Excellence nod by *Wine Spectator* magazine. The wine listing is six pages long. Need we say more? To find out more about the Goldener Hirsch Restaurant, see the "Restaurant" section in this chapter. If you are looking for excellence, you probably won't be disappointed.

Graystone Lodge Bed and Breakfast

$$ • 40 W. Boulderville Rd., Oakley • 783-5744, (800) 675-8397, ext. 5744

Oh, this is so lovely and rustic! In the foothills of the Uinta Mountains, this quiet little bed and breakfast has guest rooms in the lodge and in a separate guest house. Each lodge room has a private bath and private entrance. The outdoor hot tub is just a few steps away. The double-size bunks are charming, enclosed with wooden boards to the ceiling on three sides with a draw curtain at the opening. The owners serve early morning coffee, tea and juice in the common area and a full country breakfast in the great room. The guest house offers a studio and one-bedroom apartment with kitchen, shared washer and dryer and private baths; each unit sleeps up to four guests. Oakley is 15 miles east of Park City. From Salt Lake City stay on I-80 past the Park City and Heber exits to the Wanship exit.

Homestead Resort
$$ • 700 N. Homestead Dr., Midway • 654-1102, (800) 327-7220

The bed and breakfast at the Homestead is in the historic Virginia House. Each of the eight rooms is nicely appointed with antiques, and the wallpaper, upholstery and linens all keep with the character of the home. The rooms are distinctive, each with a queen-size bed and private bath with a shower. The large solarium at the back of the building served as a dining room when the original owners began to provide hospitality to visitors in 1886. Here guests can watch TV or share conversation. Just outside the solarium is a hot tub especially for bed and breakfast guests.

The Homestead has begun to add TVs to each room, and the Virginia House is now air conditioned. Guests receive a voucher for a buffet breakfast served each morning between 7:30 and 11:30 AM at Fanny's. The buffet features pancakes, scrambled eggs, fruits, pastries, juice, coffee, tea or hot chocolate and is a scaled-down version of the Homestead's popular Sunday brunch. Guests at the bed and breakfast have access to the swimming pool, stables, lawn games, tennis and golf, restaurants and other amenities offered by the Homestead.

Knowing where to begin when describing this wonderful property is difficult. For additional information about the Homestead Resort, please refer to the "Hotel" section in this chapter. Also see the Close-up on the Homestead. Don't miss all the recreational opportunities available at the resort. We've listed them in the "Sightseeing and Attractions" section of this chapter on Park City.

Inn on the Creek
$$ • 375 Rainbow Ln., Midway • 654-0892, (800) 654-0892

This romantic little bed and breakfast has eight spacious sleeping rooms, all with their own gas-log fireplace, in-room TV/VCR, private bath with shower and jetted tub. A complimentary breakfast is served daily. Besides the bed and breakfast, the Inn on the Creek chalets offers family and group accommodations with private rooms from studio — with a Murphy bed in the living area — to a five-bedroom chalet with a gas-log fireplace in each

bedroom. The larger units have kitchens and smaller units have kitchenettes. All chalet rooms have TV/VCR and showers and jetted tubs.

Old Miners' Lodge — A Bed and Breakfast Inn
$$ • 615 Woodside Ave. • 645-8068, (800) 648-8068

History abounds in this old miner's lodge built around 1889 to provide sleeping quarters for single men who worked the Woodside mine in Park City. The two-story building with a balloon-style frame, called "generic Victorian with western flavor," was constructed out of used lumber salvaged from the surrounding mines. The original building had dorm rooms and a kitchen shanty. An addition was made to the building in 1898. Electricity was added in 1912, and indoor plumbing made the lodge modern in 1919. In the early '20s the lodge converted to small apartments and rented to married miners. In the 1960s a third section was added, and it became a motel. Until then, the lodge had always housed miners. In 1983 Hugh Daniels and his partners purchased the property and a full-scale restoration project began.

The 10 charming rooms, richly decorated with antique and country furnishings, are named for historic Park City personalities such as Black Jack Murphy, Parley P. Pratt or Jedidiah Grant. Each room has its own personality — one room has oak wainscoting, others have a claw-foot bathtub/shower combination, and yet another's entryway looks like a mine tunnel. The rock walls and 20 stone steps leading to the expansive front porch have recently been restored. Some rooms offer a view of the porch while others look out on spectacular hills or Old Town. Down-filled pillows and comforters and terry-cloth robes cozy guests in for the night. Extra-large towels are available for the guest's shared hot tub. The large fireplace in the gathering area is great for conversation.

Complimentary refreshments are served in the evening by the fire. A hearty, complimentary breakfast is served every day along with fresh coffee, tea and nectars. To get to the Old Miner's Lodge, take Park Avenue to 8th Street. Turn right and drive one block to

Woodside Avenue. Turn left on Woodside and proceed 150 yards. The lodge is on the right.

Old Town Guest House
$$ • 1011 Empire Ave. • 649-2642, (800) 290-6423 ext. 3710

If you're interested in the outdoors, like to hike, bike, ski and generally become one with nature on an interactive level, you have a lot in common with the owner of this historic bed and breakfast. Each of the four comfortable rooms has lodgepole pine furniture, and all offer a different choice of accommodations including a suite with queen and bunk beds. Some have full private baths with jetted tubs, others have showers. Guests can enjoy the hot tub under the stars at the end of the day, snuggle up in a flannel robe, visit around the fireplace in the common area, or borrow a movie from the movie library.

A hearty breakfast is provided in the morning, and afternoon snacks are available. If you're the kind of guest who wants to breakfast in bed and linger about all day, you might feel left out here. Most guests, like the owner, are active and enjoy the mountains with an intense passion. The owner will book backcountry ski trips, mountain biking tours and fishing trips for guests. Let her know you want to participate in these activities when you call to book the room.

Owl's Roost Country Inn
$$ • 2326 Comstock Dr. • 649-6938

This country inn offers four pleasant one- and two-bedroom suites with contemporary furnishings, private baths, family room with stereo, TV and VCR and a fireplace. The guest rooms also have a TV. No fussy antiques here, and this isn't the kind of bed and breakfast you would choose for a romantic getaway. If you are looking for comfortable accommodations in a newer home with few frills, you might enjoy the Owl's Roost. One guest remarked that it was like going home to your mother's without the nagging. The property has an enclosed wooden deck (heated in winter) and a patio barbeque.

The owner serves a hearty country breakfast each morning that includes peaches-and-cream French toast or orange yogurt waffles, baked breakfast casseroles, fruit and home-made muffins, coffee, tea and juices. Light refreshments are served in the afternoon. If you just want a simple, clean place to stay with a friendly innkeeper who won't boss you around like your mom, this place could do it for you.

Patricia's Country Manor
$$ • 80 W. 100 N., Kamas • 783-2910, (800) 658-0643

Patricia and her husband, John, were high school sweethearts who went their separate ways, rekindling the flame after 28 years when they met again at a class reunion. They've put their heart and soul, and the knowledge they gained living in Europe for several years, into this lovely bed and breakfast just 13 miles east of Park City. Patricia, who comes from a family of professional bakers, is up every morning at 4 AM to set the pecan sticky buns that are served daily at breakfast. Refreshments are served in the afternoon.

The five guest rooms are decorated with lovely antiques. The great room has a fireplace and a doll collection from around the world. The garden yard is inviting and the covered patio has a barbecue for guests to enjoy in warm weather. The outdoor hot tub provides wonderful relaxation in a country setting. As an extension of their gracious hospitality, the owners will make you a box lunch to go as you explore the wealth of recreational opportunities in Kamas and nearby Park City.

To get to Patricia's take the Denver/Heber Exit 148 of Interstate 80. Turn onto U.S. Highway 40 East and go approximately 2 miles to Exit 4 for Park City and Kamas. Follow the signs to Kamas then make a left turn at the Kamas Food Town Supermarket and drive three blocks. Patricia's is on the northeast corner of 1st North.

Snowed Inn
**$ • 3770 N. Utah Hwy. 224
• 649-5713, (800) 545-7669**

At the entrance to Park City, this charming inn is housed in an elegant Victorian-style home designed to replicate a Midwestern family mansion. Built with luxurious mahogany woodwork and appointed with unique period antiques, the 10 rooms offer private baths with soaking tub, beds that look so comfy you could stay in them all day, down-feather comforters and extraordinary views of Park City, The Canyons and the Snyderville Basin. Complimentary continental breakfast is served daily at the Snowed Inn Restaurant, which is also open for dinner. For more information on its extraordinary cuisine, see its write-up in the "Restaurant" section.

Washington School Inn
$$ • 543 Park Ave. • 649-3800,
(800) 824-1672

This old four-story schoolhouse was built in 1889 of limestone brought from nearby Peoa and managed to escape the Great Fire of 1898. Home of the three Rs for Park City children until 1931, the school had three large classrooms that were 30-by-30 feet with 16-foot ceilings and a foyer that ascended three stories to the belfry. The exterior bell tower was beautifully carved and topped with a "witch hat" dome.

The schoolhouse cost approximately $13,000 to build plus an additional $698 to furnish. In 1936 the school was sold to the Veterans of Foreign Wars for $200 and served as a social hall until the '50s. Restoration of the exterior began about 20 years later. Eventually the interior was restored at a cost of $1,250,000, and in 1985 the Washington School reopened as a 15-room inn featuring 12 guest rooms and three deluxe suites.

The intimate guest rooms are uniquely decorated with a bent toward comfortable luxury. The beautiful wall coverings and upholstered pieces add the festive ribbon to the package. Guests can enjoy the Jacuzzi or sauna and exercise equipment available at the inn. The delicious breakfast is complimentary and so is afternoon tea. The mezzanine area includes a library, TV/VCR and games. The Washington School is family owned and operated.

Vacation Rentals

The listings in the first section of "Vacation Properties" are property management companies who manage properties for condominium and home owners in the Park City area. In addition, they act as booking agents, not unlike a travel agent, for hotels and resorts in the area. The companies find the type of property you wish to rent for the length of your stay within your price range. During the winter months, some companies require a minimum stay, which varies from company to company, for condominium and private home rental. Rates vary from $30 in the summer and $65 in the winter to $1,500 per night in summer and winter. Besides the rental fee, some companies charge a cleaning fee.

Children are welcome in most properties but pets are not always considered ideal guests. Some companies allow smoking while others do not. When contacting these companies to make a reservation, please be specific about your requirements and special needs.

The second section in "Vacation Properties" lists homes and condominiums managed by the owners. These properties are not generally the owner's personal residence although some owners use their homes and condos occasionally during the year. Rentals like these are primarily investment properties and, although they are fully furnished, you aren't likely to find aunt Ida's handmade quilt on the bed or a fancy Cuisinart in the kitchen.

The owner's have individual policies regarding children, pets and smoking. Please ask about policies and the rules of the house when you make reservations.

Wheelchair accessibility varies with each property so be specific about special needs.

The rates for owner-managed properties range from $75 to $500 per night during the summer and from $100 to $850 per night during the winter.

Once you've booked your vacation property you'll need to know how to get around in Park City. Check out the section called "Getting Here, Getting Around" in this chapter to learn about the areas and neighborhoods in Park City. Information on free shuttle services is listed there, too.

No need to arrive at your Park City rental and find the cupboards bare. The Shelf Stockers is a pre-arrival grocery service that will stock the refrigerator and cupboards of your rental home or condo before you arrive. You can reach them at 645-9931.

Property-management Companies

Acclaimed Lodging
375 Saddle View Way, Park City
• 649-3736, (800) 552-9696

This company books hotel rooms and studio to four-bedroom condominiums and private homes. Many properties are on the golf courses. Amenities include pools, hot tubs and saunas, daily maid service, cable TV/VCR and fireplaces. Nightly, weekly and monthly rates are available.

Accommodations Unlimited
1351 E. Kearns Blvd., Park City • 649-1128, (800) 321-4754

Condominiums and private homes on or near golf courses in Park City are the specialty of this company. Amenities include pools, hot tubs and saunas and cable TV.

Blooming Enterprises Lodging
1647 Short Line Rd., Park City • 649-6583, (800) 635-4719

A minimum four-night stay is required in the luxury studio to five-bedroom condominiums and private homes managed by this company. The amenities vary in each unit but generally include concierge services, hot tubs, laundry facilities, nonsmoking units, saunas and cable TV/VCR.

Budget Lodging & Reservations
1790 Bonanza Dr., Park City • 649-2526, (800) 522-7669

Budget handles pleasant studio to three-bedroom condominiums with cable TV, pools and hot tubs.

Central Reservations of Park City
750 Kearns Ave., Park City • 649-6606, (800) 243-2932

This is a full-service company managing more than 300 studio to six-bedroom homes and condominiums in Deer Valley, Park City and The Canyons. Summer packages and full ski and air packages are available. Amenities vary with each property but generally include concierge services, cable TV/VCR, daily maid service, fitness facilities, pools, hot tubs and saunas, laundry facilities, fireplaces, tennis and a restaurant on property.

Condominium Rentals of Park City/ Intermountain Lodging
1776 Park Ave., Park City • 649-2687, (800) 221-0933

Park City lodging for all budgets is the focus of this company, which offers studios to three-bedroom condominiums with nightly, weekly and monthly packages. Amenities vary with accommodations but generally include pools, hot tubs and saunas, fitness facilities, tennis, laundry facilities, cable TV, concierge services, conference rooms and nonsmoking units. Some accommodations have a restaurant on the property.

Country Vacations
• 336-2451

You can book daily, weekly and monthly accommodations in hotel and two-bedroom condominiums through Country Vacations. Amenities vary but generally include pools, hot tubs, laundry facilities, daily maid service, cable TV, conference facilities and nonsmoking rooms. Some accommodations have restaurants on the properties.

Deer Valley Lodging
1375 Deer Valley Dr. S., Park City
• 649-4040, (800) 453-3833

The company represents 250 well-appointed, fully equipped one to four-bedroom private homes and condominiums in Deer Valley. Amenities include pools in many locations, hot tubs, saunas, laundry facilities, cable TV/VCR, conference facilities, fireplaces and nonsmoking units.

Edelweiss Haus
1482 Empire Ave., Park City • 649-9342, (800) 438-3855

Edelweiss House is a small company with centrally located hotel and one- and two-bedroom condominium properties. Amenities include cable TV/VCR, pools, saunas, hot tubs, laundry facilities, conference rooms and fitness facilities. Some units have fireplaces and daily maid service. Smoking and nonsmoking properties are available.

High Mountain Properties
875 Iron Horse Dr., Park City • 655-8363, (800) 239-6144

A small, friendly company with studio to six-bedroom condominiums and private homes, High Mountain Properties offers such amenities as conference facilities, cable TV/VCR, fireplaces, pools, saunas and hot tubs, daily maid service, tennis, laundry facilities, and nonsmoking accommodations. Some properties offer concierge services.

Identity Properties
375 Saddle View Way, Park City • 649-5100, (800) 245-6417

Identity offers choice properties on the Park City golf course in nearly 200 hotel and four-bedroom condominiums. Amenities include pools, hot tubs and saunas, laundry facilities and cable TV. Some properties offer tennis, conference facilities, daily maid service and a restaurant on the property. Nonsmoking units are available.

Mine Camp Inn
245 Park Ave., Park City • 649-2577, (800) 543-7113

A small company, Mine Camp Inn offers cozy one- to three-bedroom condominiums one block above Old Town. Amenities include hot tubs and saunas, cable TV and nonsmoking accommodations.

MTA Resorts
• 531-1666

MTA offers homey studio to three-bedroom condominiums at the base of the Park City Mountain Resort. Amenities include pools, saunas and hot tubs, cable TV/VCR, fireplaces and fitness facilities. Some units have laundry facilities.

New Claim Condominium Suites
750 Kearns Ave., Park City • 649-7100, (800) 453-3812

This company offers nicely appointed one- and two-bedroom condominium suites with access to Prospector Athletic Club and conference center. Other amenities include laun-dry facilities, cable TV, tennis, fireplaces, daily maid service, nonsmoking accommodations, concierge services and a restaurant on the property.

Owners Resort and Exchange
• 269-1666, (800) 748-4666

ORE provides refurbished studio to three-bedroom condominiums within walking distance of ski areas and attractions. Amenities include pools, hot tubs and saunas, laundry facilities, cable TV/VCR, fireplaces and conference rooms.

Park City Reservations
1700 Park Ave., Park City • 649-9598, (800) 453-5789

Park City's oldest local company offers more than 300 hotel to five-bedroom condominiums and private homes throughout Park City, Deer Valley and The Canyons. Amenities vary according to the property but generally include pools, hot tubs and saunas, cable TV and laundry facilities. Nonsmoking accommodations are available and a restaurant on the property.

Park City Resort Lodging
1375 Deer Valley Dr. S., Park City • 645-8200, (800) 545-7669

This company represents high-quality condominium and inn properties in hotel and one- to three-bedroom units. Amenities include cable TV/VCR, hot tubs, fireplaces, laundry facilities, conference rooms, nonsmoking accommodations, concierge services and restaurants on some properties. Many units have pools.

Park City Travel and Lodging
50 Shadow Ridge Dr., Park City • 645-8200, (800) 421-9741

This small company offers full-service vacation packages that include discounted airline tickets. Accommodations include hotel to six-bedroom condominiums and private homes with amenities that include pools in some locations, hot tubs and saunas, fitness facilities, fireplaces, laundry facilities, cable TV/VCR, daily maid service, conference facilities, concierge services and nonsmoking accommodations.

R & R Properties
2064 Prospector Ave., Park City
• 649-6175, (800) 348-6759

R & R is a full-service management company that offers studio to three-bedroom condominiums, private homes and bed and breakfasts with monthly and short-term rates. Amenities include fireplaces, laundry facilities, pools, hot tubs and saunas and tennis. Cable TV and VCR are available in some units. Nonsmoking accommodations are also available.

Resortex — Park Avenue Condos
• 649-4500

The studio and one-bedroom condominiums are next to the Park City Golf Course on the free shuttle-bus route. Amenities include pools, hot tubs and saunas, tennis, cable TV/VCR, fireplaces, laundry facilities and nonsmoking accommodations.

Silvertown Lodging Inc.
1505 Park Ave., Park City • 649-9022,
(800) 666-9022

These centrally located hotel and one- to three-bedroom condominiums have on-site management. Amenities include conference facilities, cable TV/VCR, hot tubs, tennis, laundry facilities and nonsmoking accommodations.

Snow Park Accommodations
1375 Deer Valley Dr. S., Park City
• 649-0644, (800) 452-1384

These luxury one- to six-bedroom condominiums and private homes in lower Deer Valley require a minimum three-night stay. Amenities include weekly maid service, TV/VCR, pools in some units, hot tubs and saunas. Some units offer tennis, daily maid service, laundry facilities and nonsmoking accommodations.

Owner-managed Properties

The 1894 Miner's House
• 655-0644, (800) 799-8329

Near the base of Main Street and the Town Lift, this property offers a studio and one-bedroom condominium in a restored miner's home. Laundry facilities and cable TV/VCR are included. This is a nonsmoking property.

A/G Resort Condos
• (801) 364-2275, (800) 484-1062

This three-bedroom condominium in lower Deer Valley offers cable TV/VCR, laundry facility and a hot tub. This is a nonsmoking property.

Access Properties
• (800) 748-4629

This owner has three units including studio and one-bedroom condominiums with fully equipped kitchens. They are on the free shuttle bus route in the Prospector Square area. Amenities include cable TV/VCR, daily maid service, pools and hot tubs. Some units have laundry and fitness facilities. These are a nonsmoking units.

Alpenglow Vacation Properties
• 647-5660, (800) 754-0563

These owners have three new three-bedroom homes near Main Street. Each home is beautifully furnished and comes with a fireplace, hot tub, laundry facilities and deluxe pillow-top mattresses. These are nonsmoking properties.

Alpenhof Condominiums
• (801) 277-4388

On-site management watches over this owner's nine condominiums with one to three bedrooms, near the park and golf course. Amenities include laundry facilities, fireplaces, and TV/VCR. These are nonsmoking properties.

Alpine Lodgings
• 649-2880, (800) 649-2880

The owner's three-bedroom condo is in Old Town, and the four-bedroom home is in a quiet neighborhood. Weekly and monthly rates are available. Amenities include cable TV and hot tubs, plus a sauna at one of the locations. These are nonsmoking accommodations.

Anchorstone L L C
• (801) 277-4371

This owner offers a condo with up to three bedrooms, close to the golf course.

Amenities include a pool, hot tub, laundry facility and cable TV/VCR. This is a nonsmoking unit.

Anderson Apartments
• 649-9224

Three comfortable apartments include a studio to two bedrooms on 5th and Main streets. Laundry facilities and private parking are available.

Aspen Hideaway
• 649-7586, (888) 332-0355

This three-bedroom home with two baths is nestled on a mountainside on 10 secluded acres covered with aspen trees next to The Canyons ski area. Amenities include TV/VCR, hot tub, laundry facilities and a fireplace. This is a nonsmoking property

Blue Victorian Guest House
• 649-6039

You'll find an elegantly restored Victorian home in Old Town with two- to three-bedroom that sleeps six. Amenities include cable TV, laundry facilities and a hot tub.

Brookridge Condominiums
• 467-6768

This owner has one- and two-bedroom condominiums in Old Town with a custodian on the premises. Amenities include fireplaces, fitness facilities, hot tubs and saunas, laundry facilities and cable TV.

Carriage House Condo
• 649-0818

This nice little one-bedroom condominium is on the free bus route. Amenities include a pool, hot tub, fireplace, laundry facilities, cable TV and VCR.

Celeste's Condo
• 532-3812

Celeste's is a nonsmoking unit with two

FYI

Unless otherwise noted, the area code for all phone numbers listed in this chapter is 435.

bedrooms that sleeps six. Amenities include a fireplace, pool, hot tub, laundry facilities, and cable TV/VCR.

Deer Haven
• 942-0447

A deluxe four-bedroom condominium with a minimum four-night minimum stay offers a pool table, cable TV/VCR, hot tub and laundry facility. This is a nonsmoking unit.

Deer Run House
• (312) 829-8720

This five-bedroom, four-bath, custom-built home has a great view. Amenities include a hot tub, pool, laundry facility, cable TV and VCR. Deer Run House is a nonsmoking property.

Eagle's Nest
• (800) 524-8824

Stylishly decorated, these one- to three-bedroom condominiums are close to Old Town and the ski areas. Extended-stay rates are available. Amenities include pools, hot tubs and saunas, fireplaces, TV/VCR and laundry facilities. All four condominiums are nonsmoking.

Flynt Ridge
• (800) 262-1141

This spacious four-bedroom duplex on Rossi Hill between Park City and Deer Valley sleeps up to 10 people. Amenities include laundry facilities, hot tub, fireplace, cable TV and VCR.

Gary Group
• (310) 842-8400, (800) 472-9472

Southwest decor dominates these two close-in, three-bedroom luxury condominiums offered by this owner. Amenities include hot tubs and cable TV. These are nonsmoking units.

INSIDERS' TIP

Baby Gear by Guardian Angel rents baby furniture, back packs, strollers, sleds, humidifiers, monitors and car seats. Call them at 645-6043.

Guinness Chalet
• 649-0597, (310) 598-1371

This two-bedroom condominium overlooking the golf course is near the ski areas. Amenities include a pool, cable TV and VCR. This is a nonsmoking property.

Jack's Shacks
• (801) 278-3241

Jack's four "shacks" — actually, condos with great views — are close to town. The two-bedroom units have full kitchens and fireplaces plus laundry facilities, hot tubs and saunas.

Joyce's Condo
• 484-0489, (800) 594-8920

This two-bedroom condominium, decorated with a Southwestern flair, is 100 yards from the Park City Mountain Resort. Amenities include a pool, sauna and hot tub, fireplace, laundry facility and cable TV/VCR. Joyce's is a nonsmoking condo.

Lowell Avenue Duplex
• 649-1538, (800) 484-9667, Ext. 8824

These two log homes near Old Town have three bedrooms and offer fireplaces, hot tubs, laundry facilities, and cable TV/VCR. There's no smoking allowed in these properties.

Marinangel Lodging
• (815) 385-1301, (800) 637-1218

You'll have to stay a minimum of four nights at this 3,000-square-foot, four-bedroom mountain condominium. Amenities include a trout pond, garage, laundry facility, fireplace, hot tub and sauna and cable TV with VCR.

Mary E. Sullivan Historic Home
• 485-0526, (800) 803-9589

This unique, fully restored 1892 Victorian home has three bedrooms with three baths and sleeps from two to eight people. Amenities include a hot tub, laundry facility and cable TV with VCR. You can catch the Main Street Trolley at the front door. This is a nonsmoking accommodation.

Miner's Keep
• 649-2072, (800) 272-1302

Nightly or weekly rates are available in these four condominiums, each with two bedrooms. They feature hot tubs, laundry facility and cable TV/VCR. These are nonsmoking units.

Peoa Vacation Cottage
• 783-5339

Located on 4 acres of private land in Peoa, Utah, 15 minutes from Park City, this two-bedroom cottage offers daily maid service and laundry facility.

Pinnacle Peak Condo
• (912) 477-3784

This four- to five-bedroom condominium is a quarter-mile from Deer Valley. Features include a hot tub and sauna, laundry facility, fireplace and cable TV/VCR. Daily maid service can be arranged. A minimum four-night stay is required.

Resortside Homes
• 649-3807, (800) 225-6163

Nine deluxe three- to five-bedroom homes at the base of Park City Mountain Resort are available with fully equipped kitchens, laundry facilities, hot tubs and cable TV with VCR.

Saddle Condo
• (800) 862-9342

This five-bedroom home in Park City has many extras including a billiard room, trout pond, two hot tubs and two master suites. A laundry facility, cable TV and sauna are also available. This is a nonsmoking property.

Silvermine West
• 645-9876

One property is on the golf course and the other is in Park City. The three-bedroom condos offer cable TV/VCR and laundry facilities. One property features a pool, hot tub and tennis.

Windmarq L.C. Homes
• 645-3995, (888) 635-3995

This private home with great views features a hot tub and sauna, fireplace, laundry facility, cable TV and VCR.

Winn Property Management
• 649-2643

A fully equipped, four-bedroom custom

home in the Prospector Square area, this unit has a hot tub, laundry facility and cable TV/VCR. It's near biking, fishing and hiking.

Woodruff Family Condo
• (713) 984-2635, (800) 382-8035

This three-bedroom, three-bath condominium on the Park City Golf Course has lots of extras including laundry facilities, a fireplace, TV/VCR plus pool, hot tub and sauna access.

Reservation Services

ABC Reservations Central
514 Main St., Park City • 649-ABCD, (800) 820-ABCD

This company books lodging and all the extras for vacations. Accommodations include two to six bedrooms in condominiums and private homes. ABC can put your ski or golf packages together, arrange transportation and put all the details in place.

Avenir Travel and Adventure
2929 Sidewinder, Park City • 649-2495, (800) 367-3230

Avenir is a full-service travel agency offering flight reservations and accommodations in hotel and two to six-bedroom condominiums and private homes.

Condo Destinations
3263 E. 3300 S., Salt Lake City
• (801) 466-1101, (800) 444-9104

This full-service travel agency arranges weekend getaways, reunions, golf vacations and more. Accommodations can be booked in hotels and two to five-bedroom condominiums and private homes.

Delta Dream Vacations
• (954)-522-1440, (800) 872-7786

Delta books hotels and one- and two-bed-

room condominiums plus vacation packages that include airline reservations.

Deer Valley Central Reservations
1351 Deer Valley Dr. S., Park City
• 649-1000, (800) 424-3337

Owned and operated by Deer Valley Resort, the company books hotels and two- to four-bedroom condominiums and private homes. It also plans custom vacations. Discount lift tickets are available with your lodging rental.

Morris Vacations
240 E. Morris Ave., Salt Lake City
• (801) 483-6107, (800) 695-4000

This is a full-service tour operator/travel agency. It books hotels and studio to four-bedroom condominiums and ski packages.

Park City Custom Vacations
2001 Cooke Dr., Park City • 645-7902, (800) 646-7333

A wholesaler for golf and activity-inclusive packages including ski vacations, this company books studio to four-bedroom condominiums and private homes and air and ground transportation.

Park City Express Reservations
2627 W. Kilby Rd., Park City • 645-7250, (888) 4-PARKCITY

Activity packages and hotel and two- to six-bedroom homes and condominiums plus bed and breakfasts are available through this company.

Park City Ski Holidays
1310 Lowell Ave., Park City • 649-0493, (800) 222-7225

This company offers a wide variety of lodging in the Park City area from hotels to five-bedroom condominiums and private homes. Packages can be arranged for a complete vacation.

INSIDERS' TIP

Some people in Park City think man's best friend deserves the best. Happy Hounds is a dogs-only resort that treats pets like royalty. His/Her poochness will be fed, exercised, lodged and loved just like they are at home. Happy Hounds' nightly rate is approximately $30. For more information call 647-0122.

Park City Travel and Lodging
50 Shadow Ridge Dr., Park City
• 645-8200, (800) 421-9741

This full-service travel agency offers complete vacation packages. Accommodations are available in hotels and up to six-bedroom condominiums and private homes.

Snow Valley Connection
1800 Park Ave., Park City • 645-7700,
(800) 458-8612

Snow Valley Connection is a full-service travel agency booking rentals in hotels, large condominiums, private homes and bed and breakfasts. It also arranges air and ground transportation and vacation packages.

Destination-management Companies

Utah Escapades
2690 Sidewinder Dr., Park City • 649-9949,
(800) 268-UTAH

If you don't want to bother with the details, this company will plan your entire vacation: transportation, accommodations, activities, tours and events — the works.

Western Destination
• (801) 566-4626, (800) 330-7244

Another all-in-one company, Western will put a complete vacation package together and arrange all the details of your visit.

Restaurants

You've spent the day hiking, biking or skiing on the most incredible snow in the world, and now you're hungry. Park City's got your appetite covered, but a warning is only fair: Park City diners are very discriminating. True, you can get a burger on the run at a typical fast-food joint, but even for a quick bite, fresh natural ingredients thoughtfully prepared with an artistic touch are the hands-down choice here.

Park City may be small, but it has an abundance of great restaurants offering a selection of world-class fare served in many unique settings. For those who want the basics, homemade and whole-grain items appear with frequency on menus throughout the area.

The international cuisine in Park City is comparable to that of New York or San Francisco. Local chefs have a flair for regional cooking, including wild game and trout, prepared as you have never imagined. Desserts are often beyond amazing. Some restaurants' sweet offerings are so delicious you're going to want to go out and build a shrine to these goodies. Menus in Park City restaurants vary from summer to winter, but whatever the season, the food is spectacular.

We're quite spirited here, too. Most Park City restaurants offer a complete selection of alcoholic beverages. Our brewpubs offer Park City inspired ales and lagers. Both distilled liquors and fine wines are available in most restaurants. Two of our restaurants — the Glitretind and the Riverhorse Cafe — have been recognized by *Wine Spectator* for their impressive selections from the world's most renowned vineyards. (See our Nightlife chapter for the lowdown on buying and consuming alcohol in Utah.)

Smoking is not allowed inside or in the patio area of any Park City restaurant. You can smoke in the nonexclusive private clubs.

A word is in order about restaurant hours in Park City. To say that hours vary is an understatement. During the winter months restaurants generally open for dinner an hour earlier than they do in the summer and close an hour later, but some eating establishments think a half-hour on either end of their schedule is sufficient. Others have a specified opening time, but the closing time is sort of open-ended. If it's busy, they will stay open later than 10 PM. If it's a slow night, they may close at 9 PM. Some restaurants are only open in the winter. We've noted the few that do not have summer hours. It's wise to call ahead for hours and ask about reservations. Some restaurants accept them sometimes, and others don't accept them at all. A few restaurants require reservations, and we've noted that information in the listing.

In most Park City eating establishments casual attire is acceptable.

The following is a brief representation of more than 90 restaurants serving gourmet

European, Southwestern barbecue, nouveau cuisine, Mediterranean, American bistro, Thai and Italian creations certain to seduce your taste buds. So settle back, enjoy the spectacular views, and be prepared to be delighted. From the bottom of our discerning hearts we wish you bon appetit!

Price Code

The price code listed for each restaurant represents the cost of a meal for two, exclusive of cocktails, tax and gratuity. Unless otherwise noted, restaurants in Park City accept major credit cards. Some cards are not as popular as others, so before you leave for the restaurant or pop in on the spur of the moment, check with the maitre d' or host. Nothing will take the wind out of your spontaneous sail like a rejected form of payment.

$	Less than $20
$$	$21 to $40
$$$	$41 to $60
$$$$	$61 to $100
$$$$$	$101 and more

350 Main Seafood and Oyster Co.
$$$ • 350 Main St., Park City • 649-3140

This is Park City's only oyster bar. Yes, here we are in the desert with fresh-off-the-boat fish. Surprised? Fresh fish and seafood are flown into Salt Lake International Airport each day so Park City diners get the same excellent fare they would on the coast. You'll have to pretend to smell the sea while you wait, but once you put morsel to mouth you'll swear you're on the wharf.

Skiers, celebs and locals hang out here, and many enjoy the cornmeal-crusted sea bass, calamari and crab won tons. Anything the pastry chef does with chocolate for dessert is worth ordering. The setting is beautifully historic, the atmosphere is fun, and the food is impeccably fresh. Mr. J.C. Penney used to own this building, which was home to his subsidiary department store, The Golden Rule,

in 1909. Penney believed in the principles of providing a quality product for the money. Apparently, so do the owners of the 350 Main Seafood and Oyster Co. It's open daily for dinner only.

Acme Late Night Diner
$ • 268 Main St., Park City • 655-8636

This is a funky, feel-good, late-night diner that looks like a combination Bohemian coffeehouse and truck stop. The food is old-fashioned diner style, sans the grease. Late-night dishes include ground turkey and vegetable meat loaf with whipped potatoes or homemade shepherd's pie. The diner also features a tasty Waldorf and tabouli salad as well as garden burgers or a rib-sticking Portobello mushroom sandwich.

Specialty drinks include toffee coffee and a really good Creamsicle. The gourmet coffee is always on. The owners call their fare "eclectic food for healthy people." The big-covered porch out front is inviting. Once inside, if you can get past the people watching, you will notice several intriguing ceiling fans which operate from a pulley above the front door. The Acme Diner is open daily except Tuesday for dinner. The diner is inside the Morning Ray Cafe and Bakery. Take-out items are available.

Adolph's
$$$ • 1500 Kearns Blvd., Park City • 649-7177

A highbrow Park City eatery for more than 20 years, Adolph's offers traditional continental and European cuisine. Sumptuous entrees include fillet of beef Oscar, saddle of venison, rack of lamb, Châteaubriand and a delightful Swiss fondue.

Adolph's is open for dinner seven nights a week. Reservations are recommended.

Alex's Bistro
$$ • 442 Main St., Park City • 649-5252

This wonderful little bistro is in the basement of the old Andrew Furniture and Hardware building which was rebuilt after the Great Fire of 1898. Alex's presents a selection of authentic French entrees including frog's legs, breast of duck, lamb shanks, fresh Utah trout in season and sautéed veal. The after-hours menu, which goes until the wee hours, includes soups, salads and lighter fare. Jazz and blues are featured on weekends beginning at 8:30 PM. Dinner is served Tuesday through Sunday.

Baja Cantina
$$ • 1284 Empire Ave., Park City Resort Center • 649-BAJA

For fine chow and fire sauce, the Baja Cantina is a good choice. You'll find Insiders elbow-to-elbow in the dining room of this pleasant little restaurant serving good Mexican and Southwestern fare. The Baja Fiesta — The Whole Kitchen features a beef taco, cheese enchilada, chili relleno, tamale, rice, beans and a large doggy bag. Lighter meals feature ensaladas that include a Toucan taco salad, fajita or curnavaca chicken salad with cilantro vinaigrette. Several items are low in fat, which they indicate on the menu. The restaurant offers a children's menu for niños younger than 10; Mexican dishes or a burger and fries are all $3.99.

Baja Cantina is open Monday through Saturday for breakfast, lunch and dinner and Sunday for brunch, which is a good bet if you're off to a slow start or just want to relax and enjoy the day at a low-key pace.

Bangkok Thai on Main
$$ • 605 Main St., Park City • 649-8424

This sister establishment to the popular Salt Lake restaurant was well received when it opened in 1992 in the Park Hotel. The impressive menu features homemade curries, wok dishes, Thai barbecue and several house specialties including Bangkok Thai on Main, a delicious red curry saute with seasonal fresh vegetables. You can't go wrong with the rice and noodle dishes here. Pad Thai, a rice and noodle stir-fry with shrimp, chicken, green onions, egg and the restaurant's own Pad Thai sauce is especially good.

It's open seven days a week year round for dinner; lunch is also served during the ski season.

Chimayo Restaurant
$$$ • 368 Main St., Park City • 649-6222

In the 1880s this building, set on the edge of the old Chinatown, was Park City's library. Julius Frankel, an Orthodox Jew, moved his clothing store to this location in 1907 and confused his customers by closing on Saturdays and Jewish holidays. There's no confusion at Chimayo. The restaurant is open on Saturday (Wednesday through Friday, too), and the intent is unmistakable: to serve authentic Mexican and Southwestern cuisine in an extraordinary atmosphere.

Given the owners' enormously successful history with cuisine in Park City — they also own Grappa Restaurant up the street — it isn't surprising that locals have embraced Chimayo. If you have enjoyed fine dining in a pleasant atmosphere in Mexico or just had vivid fantasies about it, you might have to pinch yourself as a reminder that you are so far north of the border.

The decor immediately takes you in and sets the mood. The tile work is subtle and exquisite. The fountain sculpture in the center of the main dining room rises to a series of bird cages hanging from the ceiling. The little birds chirp away the evening with all their might. Subtle lighting creates a beautiful mood. Sturdy tables are set with festive tableware, and the floral arrangements are simple though uncommon. Large round glass vases hold small yellow wildflowers while whole lemons float about the stems.

Now that the mood is clearly set, the food must do its part to enhance the experience and it does so to a fair-thee-well. The appetizers are unusual. Try the barbecued duck enchilada with roasted green chili sauce or one of the lovely soups, such as the sage-roasted chicken and grilled vegetables with a cheddar jalapeño roasted-corn dumpling. You can make a meal of soup and one of the spectacular salads like a mixed affair with prairie greens and wildflowers tossed with Queso Fresco and cilantro jalapeño vinaigrette or the Oaxacan seared scallop salad with grilled wild mushrooms. Chimayo's entrees are equally innovative. The elk and grilled vegetable burrito wrapped in a whole-wheat tortilla with green chili and roasted garlic, demi-glace seasoned with Mexican oregano is unusual and very good. Chimayo treats the free-range chicken, salmon, spareribs and Texas strip steak with equal flair.

Chimayo serves lunch and dinner; it's closed Monday and Tuesday.

Burgie's
$ • 570 Main St., Park City • 649-0011

This is the place for burgers, and it's a favorite with local kids. The decor is unremarkable but comfortable, and the service is friendly. Burgers come in quarter- and half-pound sizes. Choices include the Burgie, a plain hamburger on a bun with lettuce, tomato, onion and pickle; a Black Jack burger with Jack cheese and Cajun spices; Phil's burger topped with fried egg and bacon; the Black & White burger with garlic and cracked pepper; and freshly ground turkey, lamb, buffalo or veggie and Mexi-veggie burgers.

For nonburger eaters Burgie's serves basic sandwiches such as tuna melts, grilled chicken, strip steak and a Burgie's Chili dog. The kid's burger is garnish-optional. Grilled cheese, hot dogs and chicken fingers are also available for little ones, and all kid meals come with waffle fries, a speciality of the house. The old-fashioned milk shakes are smooth and delicious.

Burgies is open daily for lunch and dinner.

Cafe Terigo
$$$ • 424 Main St., Park City • 645-9555

Celeb watch! This restaurant is a favorite Sundance Film Festival hangout. The interior is light and airy with an informal LA feel. The food is called "new American eclectic." Terigo's salads and appetizers are unique. A caramelized onion, wild mushroom and rosemary pizzette with garlic-infused olive oil and mozzarella cheese is a favorite. So is the delicious salad with grilled prosciutto wrapped around goat cheese filled with radicchio leaves served on mixed greens with olive oil and balsamic vinegar. The chef does a nice job with rainbow trout, roasted lemon-garlic chicken and pan-seared duck breast. Grilled fish-of-the-day is usually available. Save room for dessert. Terigo's bread pudding is famous among loyal diners here.

Terigo is closed on Sunday and Tuesday and serves lunch and dinner the rest of the week.

Cisero's
$$ • 306 Main St., Park City • 649-5044

Cisero's home has an illustrious history. The Great Fire of 1898 is believed to have started in this building in what was then the American Hotel (see the "History and Overview" section for more about the Great Fire). Following the fire, the McPolin brothers of South Dakota purchased the land and the remains of the building and opened McPolin Bottle Works. Several businesses occupied the corner of the building including the Vienna Pool Room which closed in 1920. The front of the restaurant is intimate with an upscale mining-town ambiance. The newly remodeled back room is bright and airy but carries the charm of the front end well.

Cisero's caters to local tastes with a dinner menu featuring Italian and seafood specialties during the summer and serves lunch and dinner during the winter months. The cioppino, or seafood stew, is very good, as is the vegetarian casserole. Sunday brunch throughout the year includes a hearty fare as well as tempting pastries which you can smell when you walk in the door.

During the summer the restaurant features a Monday-night spaghetti special. Wednesday is kid's night: Children ages 7 to 10 dine for 99¢ ($1.99 for children ages 11 and 12). Cisero's is open for dinner daily. In the winter the restaurant opens 30 minutes earlier and also serves lunch.

Eating Establishment
$$ • 317 Main St., Park City • 649-8284

The Eating Establishment has been serving Park City good food at breakfast, lunch and dinner for more than a quarter-century. The decor doesn't have a strong theme compared to some eateries on Main Street, but the menu is an attention-getter. The house specialties include Western cuisine such as Kansas City strip steak and mountain trout. The barbecue is tasty here and features beef brisket, pork, chicken and baby-back ribs. You can really pig out on barbecue on Sunday nights with an all-you-can-eat barbecue special. Appetizers here put a spin on the traditional. Try the jalapeño poppers if you're brave. The Eating Establishment also serves pasta dishes, burgers and sandwiches, salads and desserts. It's open for breakfast, lunch and dinner daily.

Gamekeepers Grille

$$$ • 508 Main St., Park City • 647-0327

The casual hunting-lodge decor goes well with the sustenance in this charming restaurant. The menu is Western to be sure, and everything is fresh and tasty. Blue-corn flatbread with spit-roasted chicken, Jack cheese, red onions and peppers or the warm sweet potato chips with sauce are just a sampling of the tasty appetizers. Many regional specialties including bison stew, medallions of venison in black currant mushroom sauce, roast pheasant and wild-mushroom pie with an onion biscuit. Maple pecan-crusted trout with roast vegetables and chili polenta is also worth the price. The restaurant serves a variety of outrageous desserts and a few simpler selections including an apple-pear cobbler served warm with toasted-almond ice cream. The restaurant is open Monday through Saturday for dinner only.

Glitretind Restaurant

$$$$ • 7700 Stein Way, Silver Lake Village, Deer Valley • 649-3700

This premier restaurant is found midmountain in the Stein Eriksen Resort at Deer Valley. The decor is warm and bright, integrating the elegance established throughout the resort. An award-winning wine list offers 225 wines, and special wine orders are available.

The dinner menu is simply exquisite. For your appetizer you may choose from braised venison osso bucco, smoked salmon and leek terrine or carpaccio of buffalo. The signature appetizer at the Glitretind is crisp potato lasagne. Tempting salads include arugula and watercress with baked pear and Roquefort tart or spinach and braised duck. Entrees include marinated Russian wild boar accompanied by savory crab-apple pie and wild broccoli, mushroom-dusted halibut complemented with a shellfish and shiitake ragout. Other specialties include mustard-crusted rack of lamb with lentil arugula strudel and a wild-game mixed grill served with truffle potato puree, game jus and huckleberry chutney.

Glitretind serves breakfast, lunch and dinner Monday through Saturday year round; a skier's buffet is available at lunchtime during the winter months. Live jazz is featured during the astonishing Sunday brunch. Did we mention the views? Awesome!

Goldener Hirsch Restaurant

$$$$ • 7700 Stein Way, Silver Lake Village, Deer Valley • 649-7770

Of course you will find Weiner schnitzel on the menu at this elegant Austrian restaurant in the Goldener Hirsch Hotel. Provimi veal cutlet served with spaetzle, red cabbage and julienne vegetables is also available for lunch or dinner. For dinner, the horseradish-crusted tournedos of salmon served on watercress with blue potato, carrot and celery root batonettes make a good choice. Also try the smoked trout and cromini mushroom with crème fraîche, an excellent soup to begin the meal, or the tasty five-onion soup with Gruyère and Emmenthaler.

For lunch the restaurant puts a twist on the traditional Reuben with smoked salmon on rye and sauerkraut. Sunday brunch can be quite exciting. The hazelnut-crusted Utah trout with eggs and house potatoes is a regional specialty. For a delicious twist on a classic dish, choose smoked salmon Benedict with tomato-and-chive hollandaise.

Lunch is served Friday and Saturday, and dinner, Wednesday through Sunday.

Grappa Italian Cafe

$$$ • 151 Main St., Park City • 645-0636

Impeccable service, excellent food and rich ambiance are the keys to this A-list restaurant's success. Grappa resides at the top of Main Street in the old Royal Boarding House built in 1898. The building survived the Great Fire and changed hands several times. In 1940 the American Building and Loan Company repossessed the building for the owner's failure to satisfy a construction and repair lien. The building's stunning rock wall is original.

The northern Italian cuisine at Grappa is superb. The osso bucco Milanese is outstanding — slowly braised in a rich veal stock fortified with red wine and tomatoes then served over a generous helping of homemade herb spaetzel with assorted vegetables. The herb-grilled lamb chops with asparagus charlotte are also sensational. The asparagus charlotte is made with roasted-garlic mashed potatoes wrapped in tender asparagus shoots. Everyone has a favorite at Grappa. Some just go for a pasta specialty like the cappellini à la Checca calamari. More traditional tastes lean toward spaghetti with Italian sausage and roasted peppers or the linguine with seafood and garlic-and-basil broth.

The appetizers are just plain thrilling, and the soups and salads are unique. The grilled sea scallops served on blinis made with chopped pine nuts in the batter garnished with light basil sour cream and Osetra caviar gets a standing ovation. The yellow tomato soup with pesto and sweet red peppers is, ah, bellissima.

Sunday brunch, served during the summer only, is leisurely and delicious on one of the patios that wrap around the front and side of the building on three levels. The views are wonderful. It looks like Park City but feels like northern Italy. Grappa's serves dinner Wednesday through Saturday. Reservations are a must!

The Grub Steak
$$$ • 2200 Sidewinder Dr., Park City • 649-8060

For more than two decades The Grub Steak has been serving up great grilled steak to a hungry Park City crowd. The restaurant serves good seafood and fish, buffalo cooked a variety of ways, chicken plain to teriyaki, ribs, kebobs and other specialties. But a good, juicy steak is the best reason to visit The Grub Steak.

They just don't mess around when it comes to their namesake. Steak is served the way you like it for size, trim and doneness. Choose from 8 to 12 ounces, Black Angus, New York to top sirloin. The prime rib feels like it's going to melt in your mouth, and The Grub Steak cut, 20 ounces on the bone, will curb the biggest appetite. The salad bar features 35 items, and the desserts are homemade, gooey and good. The restaurant offers a children's menu.

The Grub Steak features live entertainment on Friday and Saturday nights, and diners can enjoy their meal outdoors during the summer. Lunch and dinner are served Monday through Saturday.

Ichiban Sushi and Japanese Cuisine
$$ • 586 Main St., Park City • 649-2865

When we cautiously add "best" to a restaurant listing, there has to be a good reason. It's not surprising that Ichiban owner and sushi chef Peggi Whiting's artful creations have earned the title "best sushi in the Wasatch Mountains" by locals. She studied the art of sushi preparation in Japan apprenticing under Sushi Master Inou in Tokyo. (Master Inou is registered with the Japanese government as a national treasure. No kidding.)

Chef's special rolls, good for the uninitiated sushi palate, include Charlie, made with yellowtail tuna, scallops and shrimp tempura fried and covered in sweet eel sauce. Another good choice is Mickey's Mega Roll, made of soft-shell crab, shrimp tempura, flying-fish eggs, green onions and pickled ginger and cucumber.

If you're more familiar with these delicacies, the fresh salmon, octopus or soft-shell crab might suit your palate. For the very experienced, Ichiban offers squid, sweet shrimp and mackerel along with many other choices. The Maki Sushi selections are very good, as is the Sashmi combination with yellowtail, octopus, salmon and squid. Ichiban serves a variety of tasty teriyaki dishes, tempuras, sukiyaki and other Japanese specialties.

Dinner is served daily, and outdoor dining is available during the summer.

Irish Camel Ltd.
$$ • 434 Main St., Park City • 649-6645

The Irish Camel Ltd. serves Mexican food. Go figure. The owners are part Irish, and they have a thing for camels. The building once belonged to the Rocky Mountain Bell Telephone Company, the first tenant in 1898. The lower floor of the building held offices and private talking booths. Employees lived in the apartments upstairs. The restaurant's kitchen is in the basement, but the food is served at the right temperature despite the distance.

The decor is funky, and the most popular menu items include the giant folded burrito, chicken entrees and anything with blue corn. Friday is fish taco night. There's no live entertainment unless you count the waitstaff, who have been known to spontaneously break into dance. Irish Camel is open daily for lunch and dinner.

Juniper at the Snowed Inn
$$$ • 3770 N. Utah Hwy. 224, Park City • 647-3311

The seasonally influenced menu at this wonderful restaurant changes frequently because the owners use locally grown fresh fruits and vegetables in abundance during the summer and fresh produce is flown in during the winter. The plum-and-sesame-glazed bluefin tuna served with potato and leek cakes and accompanied by a cantaloupe salsa is a fine example of the use of local produce. Seafood dishes are also a specialty. Seafood is fresh from the boat to the airport to the Juniper's kitchen. The lobster ravioli with vanilla sauce or the malted blue-corn cake with smoked seafood sausage served with red pepper marmalade are unusual and delicious beginnings.

Dinners include a grilled buffalo ribeye with horseradish smashies and fried leeks with wild mushroom sauce, or perhaps you would fancy something more traditional such as grilled pork chops on potato and peanut pancakes. If you can't decide, order the chef's choice: three courses prepared especially for your table.

You can choose from several desserts, but think seriously about the Black Dragon. The semisweet, milk chocolate and hazelnut custard in this elegant treat is wrapped in milk chocolate and topped with a fresh raspberry sauce. Oh, my!

The restaurant is in a charming Victorian bed and breakfast inn just as you enter Park City (see the "Bed and Breakfasts and Inns" section). The beautiful patio and front porch are wonderful places for summer dining. Juniper is open for dinner daily except Wednesday.

Main Street Pizza and Noodle
$$ • 530 Main St., Park City • 645-8878

The aroma is going to grab you when you walk in the door, and then you won't know what to order. It's so Italian and so mouth-watering. This is très casual, and the service is so pleasant you'll be glad you stopped by. We'll start with the pizza: The dough is made on the premises, and you can choose your own toppings from a wide selection including artichoke hearts, asiago cheese, sun-dried tomatoes, smoked Gouda and a host of regular toppings.

Then we have the specialty pizzas which include barbecued chicken, hot and spicy Southwestern burrito, focaccia, the cholesterol hiker, the Maui mamma, Santa Fe chicken, mountain garden and five-cheese — a blend of smoked Gouda, Parmesan, feta, mozzarella and asiago. Main Street also serves pasta, calzone and stromboli and some not-so-Italian items such as stir-fry, chicken Oriental pasta salad and fresh-cut french fries with homemade fry sauce. Soft drinks, beer, granitas, milk shakes and a variety of coffee beverages are also available. The restaurant is open daily for lunch and dinner.

Mercato Mediterraneo Di Nonna Mario
$$$ • 628 Park Ave., Park City • 647-0030

The building is solid concrete, which allowed it to halt the Great Fire's spread down Main in 1898. And you won't find ladies of the evening in the Mercato today, but from 1940 until she was closed down, Maureen "Ma" Foster ran a hotel here, one of Park City's last such "houses." Mercato features a full European food bazaar with a restaurant, bakery, specialty food market and deli. Thin-crust pizza is baked in a wood-fired brick oven and offers a few unusual toppings including Brie and capers.

Mercato serves a variety of appetizers, soups and salads including a traditional gazpacho and a Tuscan summer salad made with bread, tomato, red pepper, cucumber, fennel, sweet onion and basil. Sandwiches are anything but run-of-the-mill. They include a delicious trota affumicato (baked smoked trout with sun-dried tomato relish, arugula and fontina served on house focaccia) and an intriguing combination of artichoke and olive spreads with oven-roasted tomatoes, red peppers and hazelnuts with Gruy˜ère served on house focaccia baked in the wood-fired oven. Main courses run from light to hearty.

The atmosphere is pleasant and makes you feel like hanging around to savor the flavor of the Mediterranean ambiance. Lunch and dinner are served daily. Outdoor dining is available during the summer.

Mileti's Restaurant
$$ • 412 Main St., Park City • 649-8211

Poor August Fuelling. He fell from grace by marrying a circus performer. What was the demoted Bavarian general to do but open a bakery in Park City on this site? That was in the 1880s. The building was destroyed in the Great Fire of 1898 but rebuilt and today is home to Mileti's, a popular eatery in the historic part of town.

The restaurant serves a variety of delicious pasta dishes and mouth-watering main courses including a premier port picata and a truly delectable chicken Giovanni. The sauteed chicken in this dish is topped with artichoke hearts, kalamata olives, pine nuts and mushrooms in a light cream sauce. The atmosphere is inviting, and Mileti's, which is open daily for dinner, draws a regular crowd of locals.

Morning Ray Cafe and Bakery
$ • 268 Main St., Park City • 649-5686

"The Ray," as locals call this place, is open daily for a hearty breakfast and lunch. The fine homemade French and Danish pastry, gourmet baked goods, custom cakes and fresh breads are extraordinary. From cheesecakes to pie and tarts, you're going to be in love with every single mouthful of the extraordinary baked goodies. Cakes, such as fresh lemon and banana layer varieties, which serve 16 people, cost $22. The bourbon pie with semisweet chocolate, walnuts, butter and bourbon serves 12 to 16 people and costs $16. The spinach brioche, assorted Danish pastries and butter, almond or Jarlsberg croissants are $16 a dozen.

You can sip a cup of coffee and munch on a pastry at the quaint little counter or take the sweets home. The atmosphere is intimate, and

the staff is laid back and extremely nice. The building has had several reincarnations: It was converted into a dance hall in 1913 by James Rasband, Park City's first Mormon bishop. Later, it served as the home of the now-defunct Mrs. Fields candy factory and cookie-college dormitory.

The Acme Late Night Diner (see its separate listing) is inside the Morning Ray. The cafe is open during breakfast and lunch hours daily.

Mt. Air Cafe
$ • 1900 Park Ave., Park City • 649-9868

This is a legendary Park City restaurant. The food isn't sophisticated, and the people don't put on airs, but you can get a fine breakfast of eggs, sausage, potatoes and plain old coffee, all listed on the menu by their commonly known names. Lunch doesn't come with much besides a typical sandwich — patty melts, cold turkey and Swiss or a club — but the fries are homemade. Dinner isn't fancy either: fish and chips, country-fried steak, breaded veal with brown or country gravy. Families always feel welcome here, the servers are pleasant, and you can pronounce everything on the menu. It's open for breakfast, lunch and dinner daily.

Nacho Mama's Cafe
$$ • 1821 Sidewinder Dr., Park City • 645-8226

This lively Mexican/Southwestern restaurant offers more than 40 items on its menu from appetizers to combination plates. The burritos are tasty, and the enchiladas are prepared just right. Mama's combos include several mix-and-match enchilada, taco and burrito selections. The restaurant prepares beef Southwestern-style and offers several specials including black bean or pecan chicken, Mama's spicy vegetables and pork with three different chiles. Many items on Mama's menu are totally vegetarian. The restaurant is open daily for dinner.

Park City Pizza Company
$$ • 430 Main St., Park City • 649-1591

When Joseph E. "Pop" Jenks Jr. died in 1971, businesses closed their doors for the memorial service. He was one of the most loved and respected figures in Park City. Pop traveled through Colorado and Utah selling photographic services, arriving in Park City with empty pockets. Some say the only reason he stayed was because he was too poor to leave. He plied his photographer's trade at this address and finally bought the building in 1919. Known as "Mr. Park City," Pop opened a confectionery here to supplement his photography income and eventually opened Lower Pop Jenks' Cafe on Park Avenue.

The spirit of Pop Jenks must be looking out for the folks at Park City Pizza who now occupy the building because they have made quite an impression on locals with their hand-formed and tossed wheat- or white-crust pizza with either traditional tomato or pesto sauce. The Park City version has sausage, mushrooms, olives and red onions, and the Lumberjack has pepperoni, sausage, Canadian bacon and ground beef. If you aren't a meat eater, try the Weed Eater with mushrooms, olives, red onion and green pepper. The So. Cal — shorthand for Southern California — comes with avocado, mushrooms, pineapple and Roma tomatoes. And the Moab, named for a city in southern Utah, is loaded with zucchini, red bell peppers, roasted garlic and mushrooms.

Pasta dishes include standards such as spaghetti with freshly made sauce (with or without meatballs), ravioli Florentine, tricolor tortellini and cheese or beef ravioli. You can order a simple garden salad or antipasto or make your own at the salad bar. Sides of garlic bread, cheese bread, French bread pizza, bread sticks and sauce and homemade soups are also available. You can have lunch and dinner here daily. Park City Pizza Company also delivers.

The Riverhorse Cafe
$$$ • 540 Main St., Park City • 649-3536

A trendy restaurant serving a variety of excellent food including creative pasta dishes, the Riverhorse is in the upstairs of the historic Masonic Hall built in 1908 by Ellsworth J. Beggs for $6,000. The center window of the two-story building features depictions of the Mason's two predominant symbols, the compass and the square, merged into a diamond shape. The Masonic Hall was an important

part of the social structure in the early 1900s since non-Mormons were excluded from the state's largest social organization. Masons from Salt Lake City came here by special train for meetings and social activities.

Riverhorse has become an important part of the social scene in Park City as well. The award-winning restaurant is widely recognized for its cuisine and its acclaimed wine selection. Diners can linger over coffee and dessert in the main hall, enjoy their meal in the atrium (where Utah's finest jazz and pop musicians perform Friday and Saturday evenings) or be served on the balcony overlooking Main Street in summer. Entrees include 21-day dry-aged steaks, Norwegian salmon, seared ahi tuna and a wide selection of skillfully prepared nightly specials. The desserts at the Riverhorse are fab-u-lous!

The restaurant is the first in Utah to receive the prestigious Distinguished Restaurants of North America (DiRoNA) Award. The restaurant is open dinner nightly.

Seafood Buffet
$$$$ • 2250 Deer Valley Dr. S., Snow Park Lodge, Deer Valley • 649-1000

You need a plump wallet for this lavish seafood experience, but it's worth every penny. The buffet is served during the winter only, but locals dream about it all year long. The buffet includes hot appetizers, choices from the carvery, hot entrees and desserts. Selections vary, but you might begin with grilled quail won tons, Cajun crab cakes, smoked shrimp quesadilla, steamed clams, Dungeness crab legs, tiger shrimp, Tekkamaki, California sushi rolls and herring in cream sauce. Complement these sumptuous starters with the seafood bisque with crawfish tails and Caesar or spinach salad.

Now, clear your palate with a sip of wine from the excellent wine list or cold mountain water and begin again. The yellowfin tuna with green-olive pesto is lovely, as is the honey-soy glazed Chilean sea bass with ginger butter for which the buffet is famous. So many choices, so little time. The carvery and hot entree tables make choosing difficult, but the prime rib is a nice departure from the seafood extravaganza. If you have room, the desserts are memorable, and the selection is, again, overwhelming. The chocolate bread pudding with hot caramel sauce is worth its weight in calories.

The buffet is served Monday through Saturday evenings. The restaurant begins taking reservations for the winter season in November.

The Stew Pot
$ • 1375 Deer Valley Dr., Park City • 645-7839

Up the hill from Main Street in the Deer Valley Plaza, The Stew Pot is a great place to enjoy the clean air and cool views afforded in the mountain setting. The food is appetizing, and portions are generous. From salads, soups and stews to sandwiches you can't go wrong with this American fare. The curried chicken sandwich is excellent, and it works well as a salad, too, with lots of greens. Grilled specialties include the mountain, bird or deep-sea burger. Dinner features a catch-of-the-day, jambalaya and several delightful chicken entrees. Outdoor dining is available during the summer. The Stew Pot is open Monday through Friday for lunch and dinner and Saturday and Sunday for breakfast (served through lunchtime), lunch and dinner.

Szechwan Chinese Restaurant
$$ • 438 Main St., Park City • 649-0957

The beautiful pressed-metal facade on the front of this building came from a mail-order catalog in 1899. When fire destroyed the building, the facade was all that survived. The Szechwan Chinese Restaurant is a good place to get to know Park City Insiders. The establishment serves a complete Mandarin and Szechwan menu including more than 100 items ranging from appetizers to house specialties. Choices include a good selection of seafood, poultry, pork and beef dishes, lomein, fried rice and vegetable dishes. All the selections are MSG-free. Lunch and dinner are served daily.

Taste of Saigon
$$ • Galleria Mall, 580 Main St., Park City • 647-0688

If you enjoy Vietnamese food, you won't be disappointed at this wonderful restaurant. The cuisine is authentic, and the menu is enormous. Everyone has a favorite, but you might be delighted by one of several pan-fried noodle dishes or the savory pork in a clay pot. The restaurant serves homemade desserts. Taste of Saigon is open daily for lunch and dinner, with a sunset special from 5:30 to 7 PM that features an appetizer and an entree with steamed rice for $9.99.

Texas Red's Pit Barbecue and Chili Parlor
$$ • 440 Main St., Park City • 649-7337

This Victorian frame building constructed in 1900 was once home to Park City Variety, a confection and sporting goods store with a thousand and one selections. Its present occupant seems to have just as many. How many ways can you serve barbecue? Texas Red's has sausage, beef, pork, chicken, turkey, and ribs plus combos and a Luckenbach special served with sauerkraut instead of cole slaw. Now, let's talk chili. How about chili nachos, grilled sausage with chili, a bowl of chili verde, chili verde burrito plate, chili with beans, real two-alarm chili, a chili burger and a baked potato stuffed with chili.

Meats are slow-cooked over applewood, and the restaurant boasts the most downhome menu north of Fort Worth. If your palate isn't anxious for a searing, another Texas favorite such as chicken-fried steak, catfish or the T-bone steak might be a better choice. A tame yet savory vegetarian lasagne is available for folks who don't eat meat. The Little Shaver's menu for children younger than 12 features the Sloppy Red sandwich, barbecue plate, junior burger, chicken-fried steak or fish and chips, each $3.95. Lunch and dinner are served daily.

Wasatch Brew Pub & Tavern
$$ • 250 Main St., Park City • 649-0900

Oh where, oh where does one begin. The beers are varied and extraordinary (see our "Nightlife" section for details), and if you drop in at dinner time, you'll be delighted with the variety of dishes on the menu, all served with the chef's choice of starch and Wasatch Beer bread. If it's in season, the fresh Utah trout sauteed and served with roasted-garlic herb butter is excellent. Other Brew Pub specialties include the Pub burger, Milwaukee bratwurst,

English fish and chips, grilled chicken pesto, Park City cheese steak and coconut beer-batter shrimp, all served with a side of Pub fries and cole slaw.

You can enjoy the action on Main Street from the patio in summer or sit indoors and ogle the vats and vats of beer brewing before your eyes. The Brew Pub is open daily for lunch, dinner and late-night noshing.

Zoom Roadhouse Grill
$$ • 660 Main St., Park City • 649-9108

Zoom has an Old West feeling enhanced by the original flooring from the old railroad depot. The open grill and bar in the back room provides a pleasant, busy atmosphere, and the front dining room is open and airy. For lunch Zoom serves a great salad. Grilled chicken and pear is an interesting combination. The sandwiches are anything but boring. The eggplant muffaletta or a grilled Black Angus burger are classic. Pizza and pasta dishes are tasty, and the Zoom peanut-butter brownie is a sure thing. Homemade ice cream is also a specialty.

Dinners get a little more serious. For starters, the potato flapjack with smoked red trout is a crowd pleaser. Main plates include a variety of basic and not-so-basic entrees. If you're longing for some Southern cooking, the pan-fried catfish with black-eyed peas and collard greens will make you happy. If that's not your style, go for the 10-spice salmon with Chinatown stir-fry or the more traditional grilled pork chops with garlic mashed potatoes and heirloom succotash. Vegetarians might savor the grilled vegetable skewer with pan-seared tofu cakes. If you haven't had your daily fix of chocolate, order the bittersweet chocolate cheesecake for a rush. Zoom is open for lunch and dinner daily.

Nightlife

With mountains to ski and hike, trails to bike, streams to fish and reservoirs to boat, you'd think these Park City folks would be too tired for evening merrymaking. But the energy never stops flowing in this festive mountain town. For a place with only 7,000 people, Park City booms at night, especially in the winter,

when thousands of skiers flock to town. Park City's Historic Main Street is where the action is. Eight private clubs line the street, all within a quarter-mile or so of each other, and throngs of tourists and locals alike can make the street echo with the sounds of people having fun. It's probably the rockingest stretch of street in Utah.

Before you set out on your evening on the town, review Utah's liquor laws in the main Nightlife chapter.

Park City has two liquor stores. The larger one is at 1901 Sidewinder Drive, 649-7254, in Prospector Square. The store is open from 10 AM to 8 PM and has a great wine selection. The second is at 524 Main Street, 649-3293. It's open from 11 AM to 10 PM. Utah State liquor stores accept payment by credit card, cash or check and are closed holidays and Sundays. You must be 21 to purchase liquor.

Smoking is not permitted in any restaurant or public building in Park City. The only place you can smoke is in a private club, and not all private clubs allow smoking.

Pubs and Taverns

Mulligan's Irish Pub and Restaurant
Across from the Town Lift at the bottom of Main St., Park City • 658-0717

With Guinness on tap and real cottage pie, you'll think you're in downtown Dublin in this mellow establishment. If those pleasures aren't enough to transport you back to the old country, the hearth fireplace, Irish pottery and other memorabilia will. You won't find a youthful, raucous crowd here — just a great place for the timeless traditions of Ireland, be it live music, food or drink. Remember: "Cead Mile Failte."

Wasatch Brew Pub
250 Main St., Park City • 645-9500

Wasatch Brew Pub began the brewpub revolution in Utah and has won awards for its honey lager and creamy stout. They describe their mission like this: "We drink our share and sell the rest." Judging from the satisfied crowds, their products must be pretty darn good. Patrons prefer the raspberry wheat beer, but you can get lagers, ales, stouts, porters and other specialty beers, such as Belgian beer.

The Wasatch Brew Pub is a comfortable place with open wood beams, a great patio and a full lunch and dinner menu of sandwiches, salads and pasta dishes. From the bar you can contemplate the gleaming steel storage tanks and satisfyingly arcane brewmaking equipment. See the section on Park City restaurants for more about dining here.

Broken Thumb
690 Park Ave., Park City • 647-3932

The Broken Thumb is Park City's closest thing to a neighborhood bar. Small and intimate, it's a great place to grab a garlic burger, eat some Thumb's Kickin' Chicken Wings, drink one of Park City's local brewpub offerings and watch sports on TV. Great service and reasonable prices make this a favorite hangout for locals.

Private Clubs

Adolph's
1500 Kearns Blvd., Park City • 649-7177

Park City's upper crust meets at this elegant establishment to chart out the next big real-estate deal. Definitely upscale, Adolph's caters to a dressed-up crowd with plenty of money. But that doesn't mean the place doesn't rock from time to time — even the well-heeled are known to occasionally kick up their heels. Adolph's seats 40, and you can sip your libation on tall bar stools at round cocktail tables or in booths. Lovely subdued lighting lends the place an air of mellow intimacy. You'll be riveted by the beautiful tempered-glass wall that separates the private club from the restaurant (see the "Restaurants" section).

The Alamo Saloon
447 Main St., Park City • 649-2380

Locals love this longtime Park City estab-

lishment. No ferns are to be found here, but you might find some stuffed animal heads, and you'll definitely find some great pub grub like Philly cheese steaks and burgers. With two pool tables, darts and live music almost every night, you can always find something here to elevate your spirits and banish the blues. Alamo is home base for the Park City Rugby Club as well as various other athletic teams. When one of these teams celebrates a victory, the spirit is festively raucous and the din considerable.

Cisero's
306 Main St., Park City • 649-6800

Rustic meets wild in this casual private club located in a historic, 100-year-old building. Live music from Wednesday to Saturday can get the crowd revved up and dancing 'til dawn — or at least 1 AM, when private clubs in Utah must close. You'll find plenty of good pub grub, a pool table, a big-screen TV and two bars. Upstairs, you dine in fine style (see the "Restaurants" section).

The Club
449 Main St., Park City • 649-6693

The Club is the oldest bar in Park City, with a pedigree that goes back to the late 1800s. If you want real Western flavor and raw-boned decor, this is the place to go. It has mounted animal heads and a long, wooden bar upstairs, just like the kind Kitty and Marshall Dillon used to lean against. In the summer eat your burgers on the pleasant, shaded deck. To keep your feet happy, you can dance to a DJ rock 'n' roll on the weekends, when the place really rocks.

Cooters
2121 Park Ave., Park City • 649-5000

At Cooters you can see for miles and miles — the place should probably be renamed "Windows." This second-story bar simply has the best views in Park City. If you like to savor

---

INSIDERS' TIP

The hard-bitten Park City miners all but ignored Prohibition and weren't about to let the feds in far off Washington ruin their fun. In 1921 Park City boasted 21 bars, and all but one of them served liquor.

a drink while lost in the blue mists of the mountainous horizon, you'll love every minute of it here. When evening closes in on the view, a big-screen TV, live music, a pool table and other amusements will pick up the slack. The food is great, especially the chicken dishes. Cooters is in the Radisson Inn on the Park City Golf Course.

The Cozy
438 Main St., Park City • 649-6038

You can get anything you want at The Cozy. Want to dance, play video games or pool, watch sports? No problem — The Cozy has it covered. The Cozy attracts a younger crowd that likes to get wild on the weekends, when live music is available. The walls are covered with photos of Park City's mining history and former days as a wild-and-woolly Western town.

The Jammin' Salmon
Z Place on Main St., Park City • 658-3474

Outfitted with gleaming, seasoned lodgepole pine cut in Montana, the Jammin' Salmon is one of Park City's newest and most attractive private clubs. The owners love to fish, and snapshots and woodcuts of fish provide the decorating motif. This rocking roadhouse serves great food, including celebrated hot wings and salmon eggs. With Park City's smallest dance floor, everybody gets intimate when the live music brings people to their feet. The music ranges from jazz and blues to bluegrass and rock. NBA superstar Karl Malone was seen on TV wearing a Jammin Salmon hat.

Lakota Restaurant and Bar
751 Main St., Park City • 658-3400

For a quiet conversation and upscale surroundings, try the Lakota. This elegant bar and restaurant boasts the best sound system in Park City. You can order anything from beer to Martel brandy, and the place is also cigar-friendly. Whatever you choose, you'll enjoy it surrounded by sophisticated elegance. You'll also have a great view of Park City's Town Lift ferrying skiers up the mountain. The food is justly celebrated as some of the best in the state. The wild rice soup draws raves, and locals love the roasted-garlic chicken with a side of mashed potatoes.

Mileti's
412 Main St., above Mileti's Restaurant, Park City • 649-8230

Mileti's is the oldest private club on Main Street. Quiet and dark, it's a favorite with locals, who love the cozy intimacy and comfortable sense of privacy. If you want to have a tête-à tête with your adult friends, there's no better place. The food is superb, especially the daily seafood specials and the Italian dishes. Imported beers and beer on tap give you a number of choices for evening libation.

O'Shucks
Z Place on Main St., Park City • 645-3999

O'Shucks was a tavern for years but recently changed to a private club. Located in the same building as the Jammin Salmon and just across the hall, O'Shucks appeals to the same crowd and offers a similar ambiance. With 20 beers on tap, this is a must stop for brew lovers. While you're here, try the garlic burger — it's perfect with any beer.

Saddle and Spur
The Canyons Resort • 649-2086

This is the only country-and-western place in Park City. On the weekends the downstairs dance floor hops with country-and-western dancing and general whoopin' and hollerin'. Upstairs, you can shoot some pool, get a drink at the Western-style bar and talk away the night. If you feel your Western swing needs some fine tuning, lessons are available on-site by swivel-hipped and experienced teachers.

Coffee Shops

Bad Ass Coffee Company
651 Park Ave., Park City • 655-9811

If you have a yen for pure Kona coffee, this unusually named place can give you a fix. They sell espresso, whole beans and all roasts and flavors. It's laid-back and comfy, with plenty of spots to sip your high-priced Hawaiian coffee. To go with your coffee, try a bagel, fresh dessert or macadamia nuts. Apparently, the name comes from the disposition of the donkeys formerly used to transport the beans down from the Hawaiian hills.

Starbucks
402 Main St., Park City • 658-1832

If a cappuccino or mocha java sounds better than a gin and tonic, this national chain will provide the caffeine break you need. They provide all manner of coffee drinks, cakes and tortes, gifts, caps, clothes and so on. You can also stock up on fresh coffee beans, ground or whole-bean. On the weekend, Starbucks is open until 10 at night; weekdays they're open until 9 PM. This is a nice place to watch the crowds, read about Park City or plan the rest of your vacation.

Movie Theaters

Holiday Village Cinemas 3
1776 Park Ave., Park City • 649-6541

Park City has only one movie house, but it's a doozy, with three screens and seating capacity of 600. Owned by Cinemark Theatres, the Holiday Village Cinemas 3 have been entertaining Parkites since 1985. These folks make it easy for you to hunker down in the super-comfortable bucket seats and watch top-flight, first-run movies. There's no shortage of tasty treats in the lobby, either, with buttered popcorn, a variety of soft drinks in all sizes and the usual tried-and-true movie-house favorites.

The movie house opens at 3:45 PM, and the first show starts at 4 PM. Admission for adults is $3.50 before 6 PM and $5.75 after. Children and seniors cost $3.50 at all times.

Shopping

You've come for the grand mountain vistas, the pine-scented air, the variety of outdoor recreation and fine dining, but what will really grab you in Park City is the shopping. You'll be knocked out by the variety, the quality and the sheer fun of checking out the great boutiques and fun shops in this resort town. You'll find everything from traditional souvenirs to high fashion, outdoor gear, children's clothes, jewelry, books, shoes and gewgaws and knickknacks galore. Park City has a particularly wide vari-

ety of furniture stores that carry rustic, Western-style, pine-log furnishings.

It's an affluent town, and merchants carry mostly high-end goods and cater to its well-heeled shoppers. Be prepared to pay top dollar for most of what you buy. Shops are concentrated on Historic Main Street in the heart of downtown Park City and in the Factory Stores at Park City, a merchant-direct outlet at Kimball Junction, across from Exit 145 off Interstate 80, a few miles from downtown. Following is a list of the classiest emporiums and best-buy shops arranged by category of merchandise. Also see the "Arts and Annual Events" section of this chapter if you are in the market for fine art.

Apparel

Family Apparel

Dugins West
425 Main St., Park City • 649-5817

Here's one store everybody will flock to. Dugins West offers a huge selection of printed sportswear from infant to adult. Everything is silk-screened or embroidered, and you can find clothing that carries homespun remarks, pithy aphorisms, simple sayings and flippant witticisms. You'll find sweatshirts, T-shirts, golf shirts, hats, eyewear and ski pins. Dugins also offers gift certificates and a large selection of 2002 Winter Olympic memorabilia.

Guess?
6999 N. Landmark Dr., Factory Stores at Park City • 645-9550

If it's contemporary fashion, you'll find it in this store, which carries the famous Guess? style and quality in apparel for men, women and juniors. The selection is huge, the service is tip-top, and the feeling is fun and friendly. Merchandise is direct from the factory, which means you can save substantial amounts of money

Hilda
335 Main St., Park City • 649-7321

Pure luxury awaits you at Hilda's, where casual elegance is a way of life. Your mood will elevate just looking at the stunning fashions and great upscale brands, such as Paul

& Shark, Paula Lishman and Cole Hahn. This is a very good shop if you dig the Norwegian keep-warm look.

Park City Pendleton
333 Main St., Park City • 649-0555

You'll delight at the full array of world-famous Pendleton products. In addition to clothing, the store carries the collectible line of Pendleton blankets and accessories. If you've never seen the beauty and rugged variety of Pendleton's Legendary line of blankets, all based on Native American motifs and designs, take some time to drop in and view these gorgeous works of art. This shop is also the only local distributor of the Utah Centennial Blanket, which celebrates Utah's 100 years of statehood. Other famous names here are Geiger, Susan Bristol, Filson and Tundra in an extensive selection for both men and women.

Rugged Elegance
608 Main St., Park City • 645-7600

You'll enjoy your shopping experience at Rugged Elegance, one of the oldest clothing stores in Park City. Established in 1983, it sells men's and women's clothing and shoes, including an extensive line of NAOT, Sunami and True Grit. You can also find unique activewear, original silkscreen tees, sweats, jewelry and accessories.

Men's Apparel

Brook Brothers Factory Store
6699 N. Landmark Dr., Factory Stores at Park City • 649-9001

F. Scott Fitzgerald wore Brooks Brothers suits, and Hemingway didn't. What does that mean? Just this: Not only was Fitzgerald a better writer, he was also a better dresser. Since 1928 classy dressers have coveted the traditional lines of Brook Brothers, which de-fine American style. You may not be able to write like Fitzgerald, but at least you can look like him. Even better, you can buy these clothes at great values at this factory outlet.

Van Heusen
6699 N. Landmark Dr., Factory Stores at Park City • 649-1713

One of the oldest and most-trusted names in men's apparel, Van Heusen has been clothing American males for decades. The dress shirts are classic for the boardroom, the theater or a fine restaurant, and you can also shop here for accessories and other sportswear such as sweaters, jeans, ties and belts.

Wemco Factory Store
6699 N. Landmark Dr., Factory Stores at Park City • 645-7610

You'll be tongue-tied, if not fit to be tied, when you enter Wemco's and contemplate walls, racks and bins of ties — more than 10,000 at last count. Wemco's, the world's largest tie manufacturer, offers such famous names as Tabasco, Endangered Species and Oscar de la Renta. These ties, most of which are silk, are available in every design and style imaginable.

Women's Apparel

Cotton Jenny
333 Main St., Park City • 647-3002

Finally, here's a place that sells women's and girls' clothing you can live in. What a relief! Cotton Jenny carries basic affordable items such as jeans, dresses and skirts all made from comfortable cotton. Short of silk, nothing feels so smooth, cool and sensuous against your skin as high-quality cotton. You'll shop in confidence here surrounded by brands such as City Lights, PA Company, Basic Threads, Ivy Brown Jeans and Sara Arizona.

INSIDERS' TIP

Why not start at the base of Historic Main Street and shop in an uphill direction? Main Street is at the heart of Park City's commercial district, and when you get hungry, you can find numerous great places to eat and drink.

Gazelle
Silver Lake Village, Deer Valley • 649-4711

What's gorgeous enough to put on your wall, but doubles as clothing? Call it wearable art and come to Gazelle to see it. The fabrics are luxurious, and the designs are stunning. They also have fabulous lamps, exotic craft items, jewelry and a wide variety of furniture and accessories.

Great Garb
540 S. Main St., Park City • 649-2422

For the best in city-bred fashions for ski-country living, take a stroll through Great Garb. With a crystal chandelier, antique armoires and gold mirrors, you'll feel pampered as soon as you step through the door. Owner Bob Haedt hand-picks his extensive stock of women's clothes from select names in the fashion industry, including Velda, Harari, Votre Nom and Bisou-Bisou. You'll find sweaters, pants, evening wear and a variety of other classy clothing.

Hay Charlie
541 Main St., Park City • 649-7767

The sparkle of silver and rich sheen of finely worked leather will rivet your attention at this elegant Western emporium where everything is handmade. You won't find the likes of this gear anywhere else in Utah. Go ahead, run your fingers along the fine handcrafted boots, made from ostrich, alligator or just about any other leather you can imagine. The sensation is unmistakable: It's the feel of the best materials and fine craftsmanship. Hay Charlie offers belts, sterling silver buckles, coats, jackets and Stubbs shirts.

Nativo
312 Main St., Park City • 645-8088

This sophisticated boutique has it all, from top-of-the-line clothing like Eileen Fisher, Margaret O Leary and Ballinger Golds to sexy lingerie from the appropriately named Hanky Panky line. You'll find both exquisite casual and evening wear as well as unique jewelry from top designers like Wendy Rigodi and John Hardy. Nativo also sells interesting pottery and furniture.

Children's Apparel

Carter's Childrenswear
6699 N. Landmark Dr., Factory Stores at Park City • 649-4402

Nobody has done it better for longer. For 130 years this venerable institution has manufactured quality baby and children's clothing. The selection is vast, and you can choose from layette, newborn, infant and toddler sizes in sleepwear and underwear as well as boy's and girl's fashions.

Chicken Lipps
333 Main St., Park City • 655-9666

The name may make you think of a tragically unfortunate idea for fast food, but the great kidstuff this store stocks makes up for it. Chicken Lipps is a one-stop children's shop. The bottom line: They have what you need in infants' and children's clothing from sizes 0-14. They also have Park City souvenirs, T-shirts, educational toys and accessories.

Books

A Woman's Place
Park City Plaza, 1890 Bonanza Dr., Park City • 649-2722

If you're a man and you've pondered that age-old question, "What do women really want?" here's a good place to try and find out. If you're a woman and you already know, you'll still want to come here. A Woman's Place lives up to its name: The store stocks copious quantities of books by, about and for women. This popular bookstore stocks fiction, nonfiction and children's books, as well as stationery, invitations, cards, gift-wrapping supplies, gifts and original artwork. It also sponsors periodic readings by local and national authors.

Dolly's
510 Main St., Park City • 649-8062

If your mind is active and your imagination runs free, Dolly's eclectic assortment of books will exert a magnetic force. You'll be pulled from poetry to history, biography to

Photo: Park City Chamber/Bureau

Shopping in Park City is a great pastime in the
area's quaint boutiques along Main Street.

natural science, psychology to cooking. At
Dolly's there's no true north, and an adventure beckons down every aisle. Along with
books, Dolly's sells CDs, cards, journals,
maps, puzzles and various Park City memorabilia.

Summit Books and Coffeebar
780 Main St., Park City • 655-9446

This independent, full-service, general
bookstore is a delicious place to spend the
afternoon browsing aimlessly among the
stacks of books, gaping at nothing, your
mind awhirl with random thoughts, drifting
from subject to subject, time an alien concept. When you've found what you want (as
you undoubtedly will, because the selection
is huge) you can read it at the coffeebar
while listening to great music. The shop also
has a newsstand and sells stationery and
periodicals; the staff can also accommodate

special orders and will gift wrap and ship
orders anywhere.

Furniture

Mountain Comfort Furnishings
**2756 W. Rasmussen Rd., Park City
• 647-5880**

Mountain Furnishings buys direct from the
vendors, so you'll save a bundle when you shop
in this warehouse stuffed to the rafters with rustic home furnishings. They carry sofas by Rowe,
with washable slip covers. If there's a place in
your home or heart for a chandelier made from
deer or elk antlers, Mountain Comfort carries a
number of such items from a company called
the Antler Shed. Another company, a husband-
and-wife team called Colorado and Dallas,
makes rustic, wrought-iron home accessories
ranging from lamps to toilet paper holders.

Natural Instincts
632 Main St., Park City • 655-3401

Rustic and comfortable describes this high-end furniture store. The staff here will design your home for you, or you can come in and choose from among the selection of handmade sofas, lamps, beds and every other variety of furniture. Many pieces come from Park City artisans.

San Francisco Design
1890 Bonanza Dr., Park City • 645-7072

Just the name conjures up a feeling of style. Breezy, hip, always creating a new look and feel, this great store delivers contemporary and rustic elegance in furniture, unique leather, marble, wood, lighting, bedding and accessories. For a contemporary style, try products from Thayer & Coggins. If the woodsy look is more your thing, San Francisco Design stocks a fine selection of Lorts, Leathertec and Lee products.

Sweetwater Ranch
333 Main St., Park City • 655-8875

It's a cliche, and a hoary one, and we wish we could find something more original, but, frankly, we're stumped, so here goes: Sweetwater Ranch will make your dreams come true. The authentic, often one-of-a-kind Western furniture designs of Sweetwater Ranch will make your dream home a reality. These creations are very posh and upscale, yet remain relaxed and comfortable, allowing you to enjoy the comfort, the romance and the relaxed lifestyle of the great American West today. Sweetwater Ranch sells the only authentic Molesworth furniture reproductions in the country.

Gifts and Home Accessories

It Makes Sense
333 Main St., Park City • 645-7184

Aromatherapy has been used for centuries to cast a sensual spell and create the mood you want, from whimsical to passionate. For romance, try the fragrance of sandalwood and the lingering scent of chamomile. To soothe irritated nerves, try a lavender-scented bath. It Makes Sense offers both distillers and fragrances for bath and home. You can look through a large selection of essential oils, massage oils, bath gels, environmental sprays and candles.

Mikasa
6699 N. Landmark Dr., Factory Stores at Park City • 645-9750

Pamper your eyes with the magic of glimmering glassware. Watch light dance through crystal, turning goblets into enchanting liquid jewels. Mikasa is a fairyland of changing colors and perfectly curving lines. Your view of gracious dining and elegant entertaining will never be the same. The store stocks dinner ware, stemware, flatware, wedding gifts and decorative accessories.

Mountain Retreat
333 Main St., Park City • 647-3023

Mountain Retreat carries beautiful, affordable accessories for the home and many great gift items. Their eclectic collection of European-style accessories includes candles, crystal, bronze castings, silver-sterling decorations and needlepoint items. This is the kind of fragrant, homey place where you can poke around for hours, imagining how this or that might look perched on that shelf or sitting on that table. Mountain Retreat will also create unique custom floral arrangements for you. Interior design services are also available.

Park City Jewelers
580 Main St., Park City • 649-6550

Rare colored gems from around the world surround you in this upscale boutique. Lovely rings, artistic brooches, uniquely attractive bracelets — if you love truly original jewelry, gemstones and rock carvings, Park City Jewelers will provide hours of browsing and shopping pleasure.

Southwest Expressions
333 Main St., Park City • 649-1612

The Raul Zea furniture designs rivet your attention the minute you walk into Southwestern Expressions. Regal and classic, these pieces take you back to the geometric purity of American Indian culture. At Southwest Expressions you'll also find Pena timepieces and jewelry designed by famed designer Ray Tracy and beautiful Southwestern jewelry including Hopi overlay, Zuni inlay and Navajo silver. In addition you can shop for unique Southwestern home furnishings and accessories, rugs and pillows.

U.S. Olympic Spirit Store
Caledonia Building, 751 Main St., Park City • 655-7597

Caught the 2002 Winter Games fever yet? Well, if you haven't, you will. Get the latest gear in genuine U.S. Olympic merchandise at this store, where every purchase goes directly to support America's Olympic athletes. Among the collectibles available here are T-shirts, sweatshirts, hats, flags and jackets.

Outdoors Stuff

ColeSport
1615 Park Ave., Park City • 649-4806

Park City is a paradise for mountain bikers, with trails snaking up and down every mountain for riders of every level and ability. ColeSport should be your first stop to gear up. They'll put you on the right bike with the right clothes so you can zoom down steep descents or chug along on nice, comfortable paths — whatever fits your style. The sales staff knows everything about biking in the Park City area, so they can direct you to trails that best suit your abilities. ColeSport also has a nice selection of tennis gear and in-line skates.

Destination Ski and Sports
738 Main St., Park City • 645-5336

When you want to look good in that classic Western way, head down to Destination Ski and Sports. The shop carries a mighty fine selection of resort Western wear from trusted names like Woolrich, Pendleton, Dan Post and Dingo. If you've never swaggered around town in a 10-gallon beaver-felt hat wearing genuine lizard-skin cowboy boots and a thick wool buffalo-plaid shirt, mister, you ain't done nothin'. They also carry ski equipment and clothing from makers such as Helly-Hansen, Columbia, Serac, Authier, Pre and Volkl.

Eddie Bauer
Factory Stores at Park City, 669 N. Landmark Dr. • 647-0669

Eddie Bauer is one of the most respected names in outdoor gear, and it seems like everybody loves their products for stylish innovation, quality and dependability. You can save big bucks at this store on genuine Eddie Bauer overstocks and discontinued items. You'll find a comprehensive inventory of outdoor clothing, accessories and gear.

Great Outdoor Clothing Company
6699 N. Landmark Dr., Factory Stores at Park City • 645-7979

You won't believe the super deals you'll find here on outdoor equipment for the whole family. You can save big — up to 60 percent — on skiwear, sporting goods, backpacks and outdoor clothes. And this isn't third-rate stuff from some company you've never heard of. You'll find top-of-the-line products from companies such as Columbia, Cannondale, Eagle Creek, Hi-Tec, Black Ice and Gramicci. For an outdoor sports buff, it's almost too much excitement.

Jans Mountain Outfitters
1600 Park Ave., Park City • 649-4949

Whether it's skiing, fly-fishing, mountain biking, golf or backpacking, Jans has what you need for the maximum amount of summer and winter fun. The store stocks an amazingly wide selection of outdoor toys, clothes and accessories. The sales staff at Jans is experienced in outdoor sports and knows about the equipment they're selling. This means they can match the equipment they sell you with your ability level — which is vitally important. When it comes to skiing, Jans is especially helpful. Want some killer moguls and extreme descents, or do you prefer long and gentle runs groomed like a carpet? No problem. Jans Mountain can help you find the right place to ski. Jans also offers a variety of clinics, guided trips, equipment rentals and other services.

Rocky Mountain Wild Bird Station
875 Iron Horse Dr., Park City • 647-5990

Bird watching is the fastest-growing outdoor sport in the country. This fabulous pastime combines physical exercise, the thrill of the chase and the chance to become part of timeless rhythms of nature. Rocky Mountain Wild Bird Station can give you the advice, guidebooks and other paraphernalia you need to observe birds in the Park City area. The shop also has a wide selection of bird seed, bird houses, hummingbird feeders and avian art.

White Pine Touring
201 Heber Ave., Park City • 649-8710

Here's another great place where you can get anything you want for outdoor fun. You can find all types of skis from downhill to telemark, as well as snowshoes. And that's just the beginning. Bikes, camping gear, clothes, guided tours, rentals — it's all here for your delectation.

Sightseeing and Attractions

Not too many places offer remote wilderness and sophisticated summer and winter resort activities in the same location. We do! Our three ski areas are world renowned, and there's a lot to do besides ski once Jack Frost makes his annual visit. Summer is a great time in Park City, too. The mountains are alive with hiking and biking trails, and the resort areas provide a wealth of fun things to do.

We've named this chapter "Sightseeing and Attractions" but perhaps would be more aptly called "Stuff to do in Park City." You won't find turnstiles and theme parks here, and we don't have a lot of typical attractions that are the meat and potatoes of other vacation spots. When we visit Park City, we go for the whole package — the scenery, the fresh air, the sports, the food and the fascinating people. The area's restaurants offer delicious regional cuisine, and sometimes lunch or dinner in one of our more than 90 eateries followed by a leisurely stroll down Historic Main Street browsing in the antique shops and eclectic boutiques can take up an entire day.

The history of Park City is well-preserved on Main Street so, for those who enjoy a look into the past, this might qualify as a sightseeing and attraction activity. For others, a day of golf or tennis or swishing down the Alpine Slide can be pretty satisfying. Park City's annual festivals are worth a few days in the mountains. The arts have a lot to offer, too. Of course, if it's winter, skiing is probably on your mind.

Finding your way around Park City isn't difficult at all. The town is small — you can see from one end to the other from the center of Park City — and the folks here are quite helpful. Park City people are pretty low-key so don't be surprised if you arrive at a location at the time specified for opening and no one's there. Go to Bad Ass Coffee or Starbucks and grab a cup. They'll be along shortly. Life moves at its own pace in Park City, and we like it that way.

We've divided this section into "Attractions" and "Adventures" to make it easier to plan your time in Park City. And at the end of the chapter you'll find several places especially fun for children.

Attractions

Alpine Slide
1310 Lowell Ave., Park City • 647-5333

Great summer adventure awaits the whole family on the Alpine Slide at Park City Mountain Resort. Ride up the payday ski lift to the top of the slide, grab a sled and head for the starting gate. On the way down the mountain you can reach speeds of up to 25 mph. Don't worry, riders can control their speed with a hand-held braking system. The half-mile concrete side-by-side track is perfect for the competitors in the family. This exhilarating rush costs a mere $6.25 for adults and $1.75 for children ages 2 to 6 who ride with an adult 18 or older. A five-ticket adult pass is available for

$26.25 (that's five rides for the price of four.) Hours are noon to 10 PM on weekdays and 10 AM to 10 PM on weekends and holidays.

The Heber Valley Historic Railroad
450 S. 600 W., Heber • 654-5601, 581-9980

Locals call this train "The Heber Creeper" because that's what it was for many years. You'll find information on the old 1907 steam locomotive, Engine 618, under its new, official name, Heber Valley Railroad. The historic train boasts authentically restored vintage coaches and offers visitors the romance of the rails on pleasant three-hour countryside rides into the past. The train travels through the Heber Valley — passing farms, fields, livestock, rivers and streams — around Deer Creek Reservoir, a popular fishing spot (in summer if the lake is calm you can see hundreds of monster carp sunning in the shallows) and into the mountains where it descends into Provo Canyon.

You'll hear the sounds of the whistle bouncing off the cliffs. Slowing through the canyon so you can enjoy the splendor of the mountain, the train makes a stop at Vivian Park where you can spend the 30-minute layover wandering through the grounds. All aboard for the trip back to Heber. Climbing out of Provo Canyon the engine chugs, steams and smokes with all her might. By the end of the trip the firemen will have shoveled more than two tons of coal.

The railroad operates on a year-round schedule. During the summer, the Blue Grass Express offers an evening ride with live bluegrass music. Winter rides in the cold crisp are an awesome experience. The air is cold and still. Everything seems to be in slumber except the engine with her billows of smoke as she huffs and puffs along the track. Intrepid riders can enjoy the open-air car for a one-on-one experience with nature. The not-so-hearty will ride in comfort inside the car heated by a potbellied stove. The three-hour excursion leaves at 1:30 PM daily. The cost for adults is $17, and children younger than 12 ride for $10.

A shorter excursion is available for children ages 3 through 12 accompanied by an adult. The Charleston Chalet Excursion chugs through the farm lands of Heber to the base of the Wasatch Mountains and back in an hour.

The cost for this short run is $8 for adults and $5 for children. The train leaves at 10 and 11:30 AM daily.

The vintage cars have standard restroom facilities, open-air observation cars and a full-service refreshment car where you can purchase snacks and drinks. Open-air cars have been modified to provide limited wheelchair access. Wheelchair-accessible restrooms are available in the terminal but not on the train. Infant and car seats are not compatible with or safe to use on historic railroad equipment. Storage for infant and car seats and strollers is not available on the train.

Park City Museum and Visitor Information Center
528 Main St., Park City • 649-6100, (800) 453-1360

Park City's history is well-preserved in the visitor center museum. Inside you'll find a well-informed staff and many informational brochures on the history of Park City. The interactive displays show the mining and ski industries in their early stages and how these two phases in the development of Park City overlapped at one point. A short mine tunnel lets visitors see firsthand what mining was all about. A history of ski jumping in Park City is thoroughly depicted and, down in the depths of the basement of the museum, visitors can walk into the small dark concrete cells of the Utah Territorial Jail for a real eye-opener. The museum has plenty of artifacts and information to hold your interest. Hours are 8 AM to 5 PM Monday through Friday.

Silver Mine Adventure
Utah Hwy. 224 • 655-7444, (800) 467-3228

A journey into the Ontario Mine shaft 1,500 feet below the surface and 3,200 feet into the mine tunnel is a rare adventure. Guides provide information on the mine's operation at the turn of the century. During the 1800s the mines in Park City produced $400 million in revenue, and, although they have been idle since 1982, Park City's mines still hold silver. Displays include touch-screen interactive computers, historic dioramas, a geological wall and the Mine Mythology display. Kids can dig for pyrite and silver ore in a designated area.

The mine, which is 1½ miles south of Park

City, is open year round seven days a week. Summer hours are 10 AM to 8 PM. Winter hours are noon to 6 PM. Admission is $14 for adults and $6.50 for children ages 4 to 12 and senior citizens. Mine drifts are 50 to 55 degrees in some areas so dress warmly. Jackets and durable shoes are suggested. You can enjoy a miner's lunch at the Lunch Bucket Cafe at the mine.

Utah Winter Sports Park
3000 Bear Hollow Rd., Kimball Junction
• 658-4200

Built as a site for the 2002 Winter Olympic Games, this $45 million facility has a Nordic ski jump area, freestyle aerial hill and a 1,335-meter-long track for bobsled, luge and skeleton-sled runs that are open winter and summer to amateurs and professionals. The park offers five different ice-track sledding opportunities in winter. The bobsleds reach speeds of up to 70 mph, giving passengers a great rush along the narrow track. Feeling the five Gs of centrifugal force is an awesome experience.

During the summer visitors can ride in one-passenger sleds on the same track. The pace is a little slower, but you still get a rush. The rides are $27 each.

Observers or professional Nordic ski jumpers can experience the thrill of "getting air" off a 90K jump that propels skiers up to 250 feet through the air. Freestyle aerialists also use the park in warmer months for training at maximum elevation. From the ramp aerialists can achieve heights of 55 feet with plenty of time to twist, flip and kick before landing in a 750,000-gallon pool. Spectators can experience the excitement vicariously each Saturday between 11 AM and 3 PM from mid-July to October.

The cost of admission on event days is $5 per person. On nonevent days the cost is $5 per car. The park is open Tuesday through Sunday from 9 AM to 5 PM.

Adventures

Ballooning

One of the best ways to see Park City is aloft in a hot air balloon. Drifting above the valley across open spaces and mountains, you'll get a bird's-eye view of the snow-capped peaks, ski resorts and the city below. An exhilarating morning ride provides a new and heightened perspective on the extraordinary scenery afforded by the Park City area. Mornings are the safest and most beautiful time of the day to float along in a balloon so you won't want to miss this wonderful sunrise opportunity. The price of this lofty adventure ranges from approximately $69 to $150 depending on the length of the flight and package.

Sunrise Fantasy, 649-1217, (800) 287-9401, is your source for cloud-nine adventures. In the fall of 1997, this 15-year-old company purchased nine other long-established ballooning companies in Park City, so you can get the hot-air balloon ride of your life year-round without too much shopping around. Skyward adventurers can enjoy a traditional champagne toast (nonalcoholic champagne is available) on this company's sunrise fantasy balloon voyages or book the works including a continental breakfast with the flight. All pilots are FAA certified.

Fishing

Fishing in the local area is one of the most enjoyable sports imaginable. The wa-

FYI

Unless otherwise noted, the area code for all phone numbers listed in this chapter is 435.

INSIDERS' TIP

Park City has many ways to burn calories and get your heart pumping outdoors, but if you want to play tennis, swim or work up a sweat with aerobics or fitness equipment, you have two choices: Park City Racquet Club at 1200 Little Kate Road, 645-5100, and Prospector Athletic Club at 2080 Gold Dust Lane, 649-6670. Fees vary according to your activity.

Photo: Park City Chamber/Bureau

Some of the best views of Park City and the
surrounding areas are the bird's-eye view.

ters are clear and beautiful, and the mountain setting can take your breath away. It doesn't matter if you've never fished before. The companies we've listed offer guides and instruction for beginners and seasoned anglers. Most companies are exclusively catch and release.

Jans Mountain Outfitters
1600 Park Ave. • 649-4949, (800) 745-1020

This company can put you together with the gear you need and take you to their favorite local spot for guided half- and full-day outings. Jans' offers private three-hour fly-fishing lessons at $75 per hour. The cost of a half-day guided fishing trip is $200 for one person. The full-day trip for two people is $275.

Local Waters Fly Fishing
• (800) 748-5329

This company offers guided fishing trips on local waters as well as at other locations throughout the state. The seasoned instructors and guides can take you to their special out-of-the-way places where the fish are big and plentiful but where you won't be elbow-to-elbow with other fly fishermen. The fishing season is long here, and Local Waters can take you to elevations of up to 10,000 feet where the air is clean, the snow may still be on the ground, and the fish are ready and willing to put up a good fight. Although the company doesn't have a rental shop, it can get you into the gear you need for your outing. Only high-end performance equipment is used. Since the adventure is walk-and-wade and the waters are often chilly, you'll want to bring along waders or wading booties and quick-drying shorts depending on the lateness of the summer. Local Waters has waders for rent if you left yours behind, and they are carefully selected for Western stream fishing.

Tasty streamside lunches are provided for all-day trips, and half-day outings come with ample snacks. Instruction or tips on casting and knots, Bugs 101, local stream lore, "fish psychology" and suggestions for lure selection are always available. The company has seven guides specializing in fishing for first timers.

The cost of an all-day walk-and-wade for one or two people, including lunch, is $210. The half-day price is $150. For an additional fee of $80 per person you can add more people to your group. The half-day add-on price is $55 per person. Equipment rental is very inexpensive: A Sage rod, reel and line is $20; waders and booties are $15.

Park City Fly Shop
2065 Sidewinder Dr., Park City • 292-3951, 645-8382, (800) 324-6778

This company specializes in fly fishing on the Provo River, ranked one of the top-10 wild-trout fisheries in the country. Whether you want instruction or "just the fishing," their guides are ready to accommodate your fishing adventure. Full- and half-day fishing trips are available. Prices range from $160 for a one-person, half-day trip to $325 for a three-person, full-day trip. The most popular fishing trip is a two-person, half-day outing at $185; the two-person, full-day trip is $260. Lunch is included on full-day trips, and equipment rental is available. Beginners and advanced fishermen are welcome.

Hiking

Hiking and biking are two of the most extraordinary summer outdoor endeavors available, courtesy of Mother Nature, in Park City and the surrounding areas. The area has miles and miles of unbelievable hiking trails, and many are close to the center of town. Rather than repeat ourselves here, you might want to look at the Mountain Biking listing below. Here you'll find details about riding the ski lift to the trails and a number to call to order a great book that lists every trail in the area. Instruction on climbing and hiking plus guided tours is available from several companies in the Park City area. We've listed a few in case you don't want to explore on your own.

Norwegian School of Nature
1912 Sidewinder Dr., Park City • 649-5322, (800) 649-5322

You can experience the wild side of the area around Park City or in the Wasatch-Cache National Forest with guided trail hikes based on *frilufts liv*, Norwegian for open-air life or the nature-life approach to living that de-emphasizes stress and competition. The school's philosophy is slow down and enjoy the journey through life and look at alternatives to the way we consume nature. Daily and weeklong programs are available to individuals and groups, and special children and family programs are also offered. Nature buffs can explore the area's plant and animal life and discover the geography and geology of the Wasatch Mountains on mentor-guided hiking excursions. The cost is $35 per hour per person for one hour, $22 per person for two hours and $17 per person for three hours or longer. Lunch is available for $12 per person. Basic equipment is available at no cost.

Winter programs, which include cross-country skiing, treks and snow cave sleep-overs, teach visitors how to travel or move in nature

---

INSIDERS' TIP

The National Ability Center offers year-round sports and recreational opportunities for children and adults with disabilities including summer horseback riding, swimming and water-skiing. A winter ski program is at the Park City Mountain Resort. Activities are geared to the entire family. To find out more call 649-3991.

rather than survive nature. Winter fees are the same as summer. Equipment is not available, but the school will direct you to the best places to rent gear. The school is a nonprofit outdoor educational organization, established in 1980. Corporate programs are also available.

White Pine Touring
201 Heber Ave., Park City • 649-8710
Hang Time
201 Heber Ave., Park City • 649-8709

This company offers hiking and mountain climbing adventures for the whole family. The introduction to rock climbing includes basic instruction, equipment rental and a day pass for $25. The kid's day camp program focuses on safe instruction in hiking, climbing and biking with an emphasis on taking responsibility for your enjoyment of the outdoors and wilderness etiquette. The program runs during the summer and costs $135 per child. Participants must be 13 and older. A children's climbing program is also available at $30 per child for two hours of instruction. Full- and half-day tours are available with a two-person minimum. The cost is $75 for a full day and $50 for a half-day. This includes equipment rental and transportation.

Hang Time, White Pine's new indoor climbing facility, offers instruction as well as birthday parties for kids.

Horseback Riding

Guided horseback rides are available from several stables in Park City and nearby areas. One-hour rides are available, and some companies offer ride-and-dine and special rides for children.

Country Trails
• 336-2451, (800) 371-2451

Horseback riding with a variety of extras is available through this company. Country Trails can arrange group and individual one- and two-hour rides and breakfast and Dutch-oven dinner rides. This is a real adventure and a lot of fun for all ages.

The Homestead
700 N. Homestead Dr., Midway • 654-1102, (800) 327-7220

One-hour rides on the resort property are available for $20 per person on weekdays and $25 on Saturdays and holidays. Two-hour rides are $35 per person. The Homestead offers a two-hour horseback ride and lunch for $40. Children must be 6 or older to ride (8 or older for the two-hour ride). A 30-minute barnyard ride is available for kids younger than 6 for $5.

Red Pine Adventures
• 649-9445, (800) 417-7669

Red Pine provides lunch and dinner tours on horseback on 10,000 acres of privately owned land. The full- and half-day tours take you through the glorious countryside around Park City where you might see deer, moose and elk (it's unlikely you will spot mountain lions and bobcats) in both summer and winter. Dutch-oven lunches and dinners are provided during the summer, and meals are served at The Canyons resort area in winter. The price is $50 for the ride and lunch and $70 for the ride and dinner. Reservations are required.

Rocky Mountain Recreation
• 645-7256

One- and two-hour horseback rides are available from Rocky Mountain plus a four-hour breakfast or dinner ride. You'll find them at the Deer Valley Resort and the Park City Mountain Resort. Prices are $24 for adults for one hour and $22 for children younger than 12. Two-hour rides are $36 for adults and $34 for kids. Breakfast and dinner rides are $76 for adults and $74 for children.

Golf

At 7,000 feet, golf becomes a curious sport. The phenomenon of high-altitude golfing is called ego-golfing. When players tee off, they notice the ball soaring farther than they may be accustomed to at sea level or lower altitudes. Because the air is thinner at high altitudes, there's less gravity to bring the ball to earth. You can expect to play a better game, which is always an ego booster. Golfers can leave their long drivers at home or bring them and try to reach the short par 4s in one!

Our golf courses boast abundant lakes and trees, and the spectacular mountain views are breathtaking.

The Homestead Resort

Nestled beneath cottonwood trees at the end of a quiet country lane in Midway, just 15 minutes from Park City, the Homestead Resort has been a favorite spot for families for many generations. This idyllic retreat is the local equivalent of the once popular Berkshire and Pocono resorts in the East. The Homestead has seen many young people grow a foot since the previous summer. It has marked significant passages in the lives of those who have shared summer vacations and winter retreats on the sprawling grounds amid willow and aspen perfumed with the aroma of fresh earth, alfalfa and grass and seasonally blanketed by snow.

Winter sleigh rides are etched on the tablets of our mind like a Currier and Ives scene — horses tromping stout-footed through the deep white powder of the day's new snowfall and children bundled in thick woolen clothing, hearts beating to the jingle rhythm of the silver bells. Memory still holds the blush of a first kiss on summer hay rides as the wagon bounced along roads rutted by early August rain under the watchful eye of the moon. The long drive up a tedious road to the mountains was easily endured by the thought of Sunday brunch waiting at the other end. Family members have been celebrated here, welcomed home and bid farewell. Promises have been made and many faded romances have been rekindled at the Homestead.

The resort began as a family homestead in the late 1800s when Swiss-born Simon Schneitter began farming the land where the Homestead now stands. For his efforts he cultivated an abundance of pot rock — a soft porous lava-like rock formed from the mineral debris of warms springs — and a premier spring began spewing warm water and minerals from the depths of the ground. The Homestead is situated on a geologically active site where underground water, rich in minerals and heated by the earth's interior, bubbles up through cracks in the surface.

Centuries of buildup have created a dome, locally known as a hot pot, which sits to the north of the present-day resort's main building. The hot pot is 55 feet high and 400 feet in diameter. The water's surface rests about 45 feet below the top of the dome. Warm liquid runs down to a depth of about 65 feet, maintaining a temperature of around 90 degrees.

Soon after the discovery of Schneitter's warm spring neighbors began to drop by, a few at a time, to swim in the soothing mineral bath. By the time they started arriving by the buggy-load, Schneitter had figured a way to capture the essence of his spring and turn it into a profitable enterprise. He piped water from the hot pot into a newly built, wooden enclosed pool and by 1886 opened the area's first resort, called Schneitter's Hot Pots.

As visitors finished bathing, many had developed an appetite. No stranger to the ways of European resorts, Schneitter knew his guests would relish a well-prepared meal. Fanny, his American-born wife, began indulging them with her tasty chicken dinners. Before long, the sustenance became as popular as the bubbling spring. A public dining room was added to the family's home, now called the Virginia House, named for the Virginia creeping ivy that once covered the exterior. Word spread in all directions, and Schneitter Hot Pots enjoyed a good reputation for many years.

In 1951 one of the six Whitaker brothers from Heber visited the resort while on a fishing trip. Scattered in various parts of the country pursuing their varied careers, the Whitaker boys, on hearing of the plan to purchase the resort from the ancestors of

— continued on next page

Photo: The Homestead Resort

The Homestead Resort has been a summer and winter retreat
for locals and travelers for more than a century.

Simon Schneitter, all rallied to the idea of buying the place and landed on the doorstep of a new business venture.

Undaunted by their lack of experience in the hospitality business, the siblings went about changing the name and restoring the run-down property. In a short time, the Whitaker's had created a first class resort. They brought just enough sophistication from the outside world to make the resort appealing to both local and foreign gentry yet kept true to their Mormon roots. Their friendly demeanor blended well with their neighbors in Midway, mostly Swiss immigrants of the LDS faith.

The Whitaker's added more sleeping rooms and stables, cultivated the trails, took to the practice of lawn games in summer and expanded the restaurant services to include Fanny's Grill and Simon's Fine Dining, namesake's of the original owners. By the mid-'50s the Homestead was a thriving resort where movie stars and other celebrities, farmers, college students and families with children bobbed about together in the warm springs and shared a laugh or a song in the resort's gathering room. The Whitaker tradition continued for three more decades until 1986 when Great Inns of the Rockies Inc. purchased the historic resort.

A recent $2 million renovation project has added more luxury rooms, bringing the total number of guest rooms to more than 100. The stables have been renovated and a lighted tennis court has been added along with an 18-hole championship golf course with a five-tee-per-hole system. Guests now enjoy an exercise facility, and business travelers go about the business of commerce from the resort.

The new owners have gone to great lengths to enhance the history of the property while integrating modern conveniences with the resort's historic grace. They have kept up the tradition of summer hayrides and winter sleigh rides, and Sunday brunch is still a big event. The property has grown tremendously over the years promising future generations unforgettable summer and winter holidays with special considerations for a new turn-of-the-century crowd.

But it's still the Homestead, and many Insiders hold a multitude of cherished memories of this place that will last a lifetime.

Park City Municipal Golf Course
1451 Thaynes Canyon Dr., Park City
• 649-8701

This challenging public course located at the base of Park City Mountain Resort at the corner of Thaynes Canyon Drive and Utah Highway 224 offers hilly terrain, abundant lakes, firs and aspens on an 18-hole, 6400-yard, par 72 public course, rated 69.7 — perfect for all golfers. Greens fees are $29 for 18-holes and $14.50 for nine. Cart rentals are $22.50 for 18 holes and $13.50 for nine. Spikeless golf shoes are required. The course features a clubhouse, a driving range, a chipping green and club rentals. Tee times are taken seven days in advance.

The Homestead
700 N. Homestead Dr., Midway • 654-5588, (800) 327-7220

Designed by Bruce Summerhays and built in 1990, this 18-hole, 7000-yard, par 72 public course has a clubhouse, a driving range, a chipping green and a practice bunker. Located 20 miles from Park City, The Homestead accepts tee times seven days in advance. Greens fees on Monday through Thursday are $30 for 18-holes ($40 with a cart), and Friday through Sunday fees are $40 for 18-holes and $10 for cart rental.

Wasatch Mountain State Park
750 Snake Creek Rd., Midway • 654-0532

A 25-minute drive from Park City puts you at this spectacular public course with 36 holes, 6322 yards and par 72 with a White rating of 69.2. The "Lake 9" and "Canyon 9" can be combined for a complete 18 holes of golf or you can play the challenging "Mountain 18." A clubhouse, a driving range, a chipping green and a putting green are available. Tee times are taken seven days in advance. Greens fees are $17 on weekdays and $19 on weekends. Cart rental is $9.

Mountain Dell
3287 Cummings Rd., Salt Lake City
• 582-3812

Don't be confused by the Salt Lake address. This course is in Parleys Canyon, about 20 minutes from Park City. The East and the West courses make for a wonderful round of golf on this 36-hole, 6150-yard public course with a rating of 68. The facility offers a clubhouse and a putting and chipping green. Tee times are taken on Monday, Wednesday and Friday. Greens fees on Monday through Thursday for nine holes are $9 to walk and $14 to ride; fees for 18 holes are $18 to walk and $28 if you ride. Friday, Saturday and Sunday the fees are $10 to walk and $15 if you ride for nine holes and $20 to walk and $30 if you ride for 18 holes.

Mountain Biking

Spring in the mountains is a glorious time. One day the ground is blanketed with snow then the season seems to turn on a dime, the anxious green grass flourishing almost over night. It's time to tune up the bikes and head for the hills. From mid-June to mid-September, weather permitting, mountain biking is a great Park City sport. Bikers, from beginner to advanced can enjoy both scenic hills and heart-pumping thrills over 45 miles of single- and double-track trails.

The free "Park City Bike/Hike Guide," complete with descriptions of mountain bike rides and trail maps, is available at various locations throughout Park City and Salt Lake City. To order a copy of the free guide call (800) 453-1360.

Deer Valley Resort
2250 Deer Valley Dr. S., Deer Valley
• 649-1000

Deer Valley offers a biker-friendly lift that whisks riders up Bald Mountain via chairlift from Silver Lake Village, a midmountain resort. The chairs have hooks installed during the summer months to accommodate bicycles. The lift accesses all trails and is open Wednesday through Sunday and holidays from 10 AM to 5:30 PM, weather permitting. The lift operates on weekends only after Labor Day. The cost of the ride is $15 per person for an all-day pass or $6 for a single ride. Children and senior citizens ride for $5. The cost is $6. The trails are also open to bikers who prefer to cycle up the mountain. There's no charge for this strenuous exercise. Helmets are required for all cyclists. The ticket office and bike rental shop are at the base of the Sterling Lift. McHenry's Restaurant in the Silver Lake Lodge is open for quick lunches Wednesday through Sunday.

The Mountain Bike School, 649-1000, (800)

424-3337, at Deer Valley offers both group and private cycling lessons for beginners through advanced riders.

Park City Mountain Resort
1320-1425 Lowell Ave., Park City
• 649-8111, (800) 222-7275

Park City Mountain Resort has 20 miles of trails open to mountain-biking enthusiasts at no charge. The resort opens the King Road, a former mining route, each summer. Old mining buildings and historic structures and relics are visible from the trail. The trail is accessible from the south end of the resort just up from Main Street's historic district. Skilled bikers will enjoy the challenge of the Sweeney Switchbacks and the Shadow Lake Loops trails. A free summer trail map is available at the resort. Call for information.

Guided Tours and Rentals

Several companies as well as the resorts offer guided mountain biking tours and special children's, ladies and senior citizen programs for mountain bikers. The cost ranges from $10 to $40 depending upon whether you want instruction and need to rent a bike. Following are several touring companies you can call them to make arrangements: **Deer Valley** (lift-served mountain biking), 649-1000, (800) 424-3337; **Mountain Biking at Park City Mountain Resort**, 649-8111, (800) 222-7275; **Mountain Biking at The Canyons**, 649-5400; **Sport Touring Ventures**, 649-1551, (800) 748-5009; and **White Pine Touring**, 649-8710.

Many Park City sports stores and bicycle shops rent bicycles and helmets. Prices for bike rentals range from $15 for a half-day to $25 for a full day. Some companies offer tours and others group cycling adventures. Contact one of the following businesses for information: **Christy Sports**, Mont Cervin Plaza, Deer Valley, 649-2909; **Cole Sport**, 1615 Park Avenue, Park City, 649-4806; **Jans Mountain Outfitters**, 1600 Park Avenue, Park City, 649-4949; **Silver Lake Lodge**, Deer Valley, 649-4601; and **White Pine Touring**, 201 Heber Avenue, Park City, 649-8710.

Several hotels also rent bikes to their guests. Ask the concierge or reservationist if your hotel has bikes available.

Scuba Diving

The Homestead
700 N. Homestead Dr., Midway • 654-1102, (800) 327-7220

Believe it or not, you can scuba-dive in the mountains near Park City. The Homestead Resort's crater offers the only warm-water scuba diving in the United States. Lessons are available and you can get an introduction to scuba diving without certification. To find out more about the Homestead's crater and the warm mineral rich waters, see the Close-up on The Homestead in this chapter.

Sleigh Rides

Gliding through the freshly fallen snow in Park City and nearby areas is a real treat in a horse-drawn sleigh. Some of the companies listed below offer group rides with a minimum of 10 people as well as cutter sleigh rides for two. Rates range from $10 per person and higher.

Here are two places to call to arrange your excursion: Homestead Resort Sleigh Rides, 645-1102, (800) 327-7220; and Snowed Inn Sleigh and Carriage Company, 647-3310.

Wagon Rides

Blue Sage Recreation
1 mile west of Wanship off I-80
• (801) 268-2020

We call this a hay ride, but Blue Sage doesn't use hay anymore because too many people had allergies. This fun adventure takes you in a wagon on a 15- to 20-minute ramble to a large old building in a rustic area filled to the brim with old Western artifacts. You can ogle a genuine restored Conestoga wagon and try to imagine what it was like to travel west with without air conditioning or other modern conveniences. Horseshoes and a volley ball court are available for sporting fun and to help you work up a big appetite. You'll need it. The fixin's are pretty good. Chicken and ribs, old-style baked beans, corn-on-the-cob, salad and rolls are served at an all-you-can-eat spread. The amphitheater is the scene of some great country music. You get a song book and are encouraged to sing along. If you've got a banjo or git-tar, bring it along. You can join in with the musicians.

The cost for the wagon ride to and from the site and dinner is $19.95, not including tax and tip. Give them a holler and they'll give you directions. The outings require 30 or more people so you can book a group or ride along with friendly strangers.

The Homestead
700 N. Homestead Dr., Midway • 654-1102, (800) 327-7222

The Homestead's wagon rides cover the grounds of the resort and the lower river road. This is a fun outing but not quite the same as the old hay rides of yesteryear. Rides are $5 per person with a $30 minimum. This is a great way to see the Homestead property. The wagon rides depart from the livery at 5, 5:45 and 6:30 PM seven days a week.

Kidstuff

Park City Mountain Resort
1320-1425 Lowell Ave., Park City • 649-8111, (800) 222-7275

The resort offers a myriad of fun things for kids to do during the summer. You'll find the following activities at the foot of the resort.

Little Miners' Park mini-amusement park has a Ferris wheel, carousel and other rides for small children including boats, airplanes and a train. Each ride is $1.75, or you can purchase a book of 10 rides for $15.

The Big Air Trampoline is a ton of fun for kids! Not your average trampoline, this is like being inside a giant air bag. You wear a harness and bungee cord, height and weight appropriate, and the compressed air allows you to safely do back flips and all kinds of cool acrobatics. Children must weigh 30 pounds or more to bounce on the trampoline. The cost is $6.25 per person.

Silver Putt Golf will allow kids and adults to have a great time getting into the swing of summer. The miniature golf course is adorned with reminders of Park City's beginnings as a silver mining town. The cost is $5.25 per person regardless of age.

Pony rides are available for buckaroos 6 and younger, making the little ones feel mighty grown up. The cost of the ride is $5.

Hours for all these activities are noon to 10 PM on weekdays and 10 AM to 10 PM on weekends and holidays.

City Park
1354 Park Ave., Park City • 645-5152

Fun and games are available at the park including sand volleyball and a large playground. The park has covered picnic areas available for rent. This is a great place for families. The Parks and Recreation Department offers several children's summer programs and a few fun activities in the fall and winter, all held at City Park. To find out more about these, call 645-5100.

Arts and Annual Events

As befits a tourist town, Park City has plenty of festivals and artistic activities that jazz up the daily scene. No matter what you fancy, you'll find a dizzying array of events, concerts and artistic happenings to enrich your day. And with so much going on, you'll feel your energy level skyrocket the minute you get into town.

The tough part is deciding what to do. Will it be a tour of Park City's art galleries? A concert by the Muir String Quartet? How about a play in the Historic Egyptian Theatre? Music is especially popular in Park City, and venues all over town reverberate with the harmonious strains of every imaginable genre of music, from Bill Monroe bluegrass to Beethoven string quartets. Many of the music festivals go on for a month or two, with performances once or twice a week. Another plus is the gorgeous scenery, which makes the outdoor events all the more charming. Since skiing takes up much of the town's energy in the winter, you'll find many of the activities — especially the musical events — taking place during the other three seasons. Events are free unless otherwise noted.

We've divided this section into a seasonal calendar of events and a short tour of galleries and art organizations to help you pencil in a full itinerary for your visit to this charming city.

Annual Events

Spring

Chocolate Festival
1880 Park Ave., Yarrow Hotel, Park City • 649-4230

Come and enjoy yummy delicacies in the company of helpless chocoholics such as yourself. The aroma is overwhelming, the colors creamy and soothing, the choices dizzying — in short, you'll dive in feet first and depart with a feeling of bliss unattainable by any other means known to humans short of illegal narcotics. The event is sponsored by Planned Parenthood of Utah, Summit County Chapter. The event takes place on a weekend in mid-April. Admission is free, but you have to buy the chocolate.

Annual Easter Egg Hunt
Park City Mountain Resort, Park City • 649-6100

See the Easter Bunny on skis! Bring your camera, because you'll want plenty of photos of the floppy-eared rabbit slaloming down the slopes, throwing goodies and charming visitors during this two-day event. The kids will go crazy trying to find the hundreds of eggs hidden on the slopes. The hunt is held the weekend of easter and is free, although you'll have to pay to ride on the chairlifts.

Earth Day Celebration
Various locations • 649-9698

Most Park City residents are proud of the physical beauty of their town and take vigorous steps to protect the environment. For these reasons Earth Day April 22 draws big crowds of concerned citizens who build trails, clean up, plant trees and participate in other activities that enhance and protect Park City's ecosystems. Feel free to pitch in and help preserve and beautify this lovely mountain town.

Summer

Park City Pedalfest
Various locations • 649-6838, (800) 649-6100

Park City is emerging as a bicycling hotspot for mountain and road bikes. Bicyclists from kids to seniors will love this two-day event. Some of the activities include tours, clinics, exhibitions, skill-training workshops, a kids race and the Summer Solstice 200, a noncompetitive, 200-mile road race through scenic mountains and wide-open valleys. The cost is $25 for adults and $5 for kids younger than 12. All proceeds go to the Mountain Trails Foundation, a nonprofit organization that promotes public trail access in the Park City area. It's usually held the third weekend in June.

Park City International Music Festival
Various locations • 645-8825

The sweet strains of classical music mix with the elemental beat of the blues and jazz during the seven weeks of the annual festival, which begins in July and lasts until the end of August. Recitals and master classes for aspiring musicians are just some of the activities you can enjoy at many locations around Park City. Be it Bach, Beethoven or Howling Wolf, you'll easily find music that fits your taste. Tickets to all concerts are $10 for general admission.

First Security Mountain Concerts in the Park
Park City Park • 649-6100

Sponsored by First Security Bank, Park City radio station KCPW and the Park City Chamber/Bureau, this popular festival features music ranging from bluegrass to classical. All concerts take place in the Park City Park Bandstand on Wednesday nights at 6 PM. The concerts are free and held throughout the summer.

Utah Music Festival
Various locations • 752-5781, 658-2800

This two-month festival, which takes place in June and July, presents more than 30 concerts, ranging from chamber music to jazz and folk. Ticket prices vary.

Sundance Film Festival

In 1978 a few cinema buffs, fired with enthusiasm by the extraordinary achievements of the American film renaissance of that era (think of *The Parallax View*, *Five Easy Pieces* and *Nashville*), organized the Utah/U.S. Film Festival. The seven-day festival was held in Salt Lake City and presented retrospective programs, seminars and panel discussions. The highlight of the festival was a competition for American independent films.

Successful and growing, the festival moved to Park City in 1981. Instead of retrospectives, the festival emphasized independent films and documentaries and held seminars on filmmaking and video. A competition for documentaries was added in 1982.

The festival received a huge boost in 1984 when Robert Redford's Sundance Institute agree to sponsor of the festival. This meant a year-round staff, financial help and — most important of all — the cachet of Redford's name and his immense influence in the movie business. The Sundance Institute was organized in 1981 by Robert Redford and others interested in film with the goal of encouraging emerging screenwriters and directors and helping them exhibit their work.

The Sundance Film Festival is now recognized as one of the preeminent film festivals in the world and attracts more than 12,000 visitors to Park City every January.

— continued on next page

Photo: Trish Empey

The Sundance Film Festival always draws huge crowds eager to watch the latest in innovative film from talented young directors.

Members of the entertainment industry attend the festival to find new talent and discover films that transcend the artistic cliches and overworked themes of Hollywood.

Park City changes overnight from a bustling but pleasant ski town of 7,000 people to a happening place crammed with beautiful people armed with cell phones, black attire and obsequious personal assistants. The invasion produces enormous logistical hassles, and it becomes next to impossible to drive, park or find a place to eat. A few residents grumble about the disruption to the town and the arrogance of the movie moguls, but most accept the inconvenience for a chance to be witness firsthand some of the most innovative and ground-breaking cinema in the world.

The festival has a number of categories, including the American Independent Dramatic and Documentary Competition, Premieres and Short Films. The category Sidebar Screenings honors creative filmmakers from around the world. The Grand Jury Prize, which is awarded to dramatic films and documentaries, is a coveted honor guaranteed to earn the film and its director an incredible amount of media attention with the possibility of national distribution. The success of many films first screened in Park City show how important the festival has become for launching successful careers in the film industry. The Cohen brothers, whose film *Blood Simple* won the 1985 Grand Jury Prize, are widely regarded as the most important serious film makers in the country. Steven Soderbergh, who made a splash with *sex, lies and videotape*, followed up with the equally riveting films *Kafka* and *King of the Hill*. Robert Rodriguez, who made the amazing and exuberant *El Mariachi* for a few thousand dollars, went on to direct *Desperado*, a sequel to El Mariachi, and the gruesomely inventive and offbeat thriller *From Dusk Till Dawn*.

The festival also discovered many compelling documentaries that illuminate hidden corners of American life and the national psyche. *Crumb*, directed by Terry Zwigoff, is an uncompromising portrait of the talented cartoonist Robert Crumb, his strange family and his views on America. *Hoop Dreams*, directed by Steve James, shows the heartbreaking lives of two black teenagers in Chicago, both of whom think basketball will lift them from a life of poverty and oppression.

The "Arts and Annual Events" section has information on ticket prices and the date of the festival.

Park City's Old-fashioned Fourth of July Celebration
Main St. and the Park City Park • 649-6100

Come join the crowd and enjoy a patriotic parade down Historic Main Street, great food in the Park City Park and an impressive fireworks display at dusk. This event always draws a good-size crowd.

Writers at Work
1800 Park Ave., Yarrow Hotel, Park City • 292-9285

This nationally renowned conference brings some of the most talented storytellers in America to Park City. Aspiring writers learn their craft in workshops, panel discussions and lectures, all directed by successful authors, publishers and agents. Call for fees and the lineup. The conference usually takes place in mid-July.

Founders Title Company Folk and Bluegrass Festival
Snow Park Lodge at Deer Valley • 339-7664

This festival, held on a sunday in mid-August, grows in stature and popularity every year. With a superb lineup of stars, a gorgeous mountain setting and a mellow crowd out to have fun, this daylong celebration of American music is a required event for fans of folk and bluegrass.

Among the talents who have played at this festival are Greg Brown, a great raconteur, poet, dharma bum, fly fisherman and probably the greatest songwriter in folk since John Prine and Bob Dylan. If you've wondered who the Woody Guthrie of our time might be, Greg Brown is as close as anybody. Brown is a fantastic musician, charismatic performer and hilarious storyteller who never gives a bad show.

Other talents you might see at the festival are bluegrass diva Alison Krauss; Peter Rowan, a fabulous mandolin player and singer; Kate MacKenzie, whose sweet and plaintive voice can be regularly heard on Prairie Home Companion; and the witty Austin Lounge Lizards. Tickets are $17 in advance and $19 at the gate. Coolers are welcome, but dogs aren't.

Park City Arts Festival
Historic Main St. • 649-8882

Now in its 29th year, this flamboyant and friendly arts festival has become one of the most successful in the Intermountain West. You'll experience sensory overload as you gape at the displays of hundreds of artists, smell the fabulous food from Park City's best restaurants and groove to music that ranges from jazz and salsa to rock and blues. Youngsters will go gaga over a Youth Art Yard and other entertainment geared toward children. To see art in action, go to the Demonstrating Artist Stage, where you can see artists actually creating art.

As you wander up and down Historic Main Street, the savory smells emanating from dozens of food booths and restaurants are sure to entice you to dig in and enjoy the myriad variety of food. For the lover of fine brew, a beer garden sells the wonderfully hoppy and aromatic locally brewed Wasatch beers.

Be prepared for crowds — more than 100,000 art lovers crowd the cozy confines of Park City's Historic Main Street during this weekend day festival. During the festival, traffic on Main Street is restricted. Admission is $5. It's usually held the first weekend in August.

Utah Symphony Summer Series
Snow Park Lodge at Deer Valley
• 533-6683

The accomplished musicianship of the world-renowned Utah symphony makes the Deer Valley hills ring with melody during this annual series, a favorite of Park City residents. Bring a blanket and munchies and enjoy both light and classical favorites. Concerts take place on selected evenings in August. Ticket prices vary.

Park City Music Festival
Various locations • 645-8825

The festival, held in July and August, goes on for a couple of months and fills Park City with all variety of classical music from a number of orchestras, string quartets and other musical groups. The music is sublime, and the venues scenic. The group puts on one or two concerts a week. Ticket prices range from $10 to $15.

The People Make the City Festival
Snow Park Lodge at Deer Valley
• 649-6100

It's full-tilt boogie when Park City's abundant supply of talented local musicians are put on center stage during this all-day outdoor concert. Each year a committee chooses performers from a number of musical genres, including choral music, jazz, gospel, pop and bluegrass. You won't find a better outdoor venue, the music gets white hot and the crowd is cool. Bring food and drink, but leave your pooch at home.

Last year's concert was held the last weekend in August. Tickets are $10 in advance, $12 the day of the show.

Autumn

Winter White Ball
1895 Sidewinder Dr., Olympia Park Hotel, Park City • 649-6100

Each year a different theme, such as a 1950s sock hop or 1930s big-band jitterbug, sets the tone for this annual ball, now entering its 20th year. The ball includes a sit-down dinner, dancing, door prizes and awards for best

costume. the event takes place the first weekend in November. Tickets are $25.

Winter

Tour de Suds Mountain Bike Race
The Mountains around Park City
• 649-4035

This uphill challenge has been a favorite of
local mountain bikers for years. It's a great race
with good friends through pine-clad hills, mountain meadows and scenic byways. The race
draws both professional bikers who compete for
prizes and amateurs with potbellies and bursting lungs. Both the svelte and the tubby have
fun, and their effort is amply rewarded with a big
party, beer galore, food and general hilarity.

The course runs from Park City Park to
Bonanza Flats, climbing 1,700 feet over the 7-
mile course, and concludes back at the Park.
The tour gets on the road in mid-September.

Norwegian School of Nature Life's Annual Halloween Bash and Fundraiser
Steeps, Park City Mountain Resort
• 649-5322

This bash will shake the cobwebs out of
your system. Dress up in your spooky best
and come and get the scare of your life at this
great party and fundraiser. With music by local hot bands, a silent auction, a costume contest and dancing, what better way to have
some ghoulish fun? All proceeds benefit the
Norwegian School of Nature Life, a nonprofit
organization dedicated to teaching people to
better understand and respect themselves,
others and nature through outdoor experiences. No one younger than 21 is admitted.
It's held on Halloween. The bash costs $12 in
advance and $15 at the door.

Nouveau Beaujolais Festival at Deer Valley
Silver Lake Lodge at Deer Valley
• 649-1000, (800) 424-3337

Quaff a beaker of good red wine at this
annual festival the last weekend of November
sponsored by Mountain Food and Wine Society. Patterned after festivals in France, the
Nouveau Beaujolais Festival celebrates this
light, fresh, fruity vintage from Burgundy. Along
with the wine, great food and music compete
the picture. Tickets are $45.

Christmas in the Park Christmas Tree Lightning Ceremony
Park City Park • 645-5177

On the second Wednesday of December,
Park City comes alive with holiday cheer as
the city Christmas tree blazes to life. You can
get into the holiday spirit with roasted chestnuts, hot chocolate and cider. Caroling and
Santa's arrival top off the evening.

Christmas Eve Program
Park City Mountain Resort • 649-8111

A breathtaking torchlight parade and
candlelight caroling make for a magical Christmas on the snowy slopes of Park City Mountain Resort. Watching the sinuous line of skiers snaking down the mountain, each carry-
ing a torch, can really give you the shivers.
Saint Nick leads the parade, and Mrs. Claus
also makes an appearance. It's held on Christmas Eve.

Sundance Film Festival
Various Locations in Salt Lake City and Park City • 328-3456

Since 1984 Robert Redford and the
Sundance Institute have labored to create a
forum for new, independent dramatic and
documentary film. Now recognized internationally, this 11-day festival brings cinematic
moguls from all over the world to see what's
new and hot (see the Close-up in this chapter).

the curtain rises in the middle of January.
Tickets go on sale a few days before the festival begins. Prices range from $6 to $16 per
show, and shows sell out quickly.

Annual Coca Cola Winterfest and Snow Sculpture Contest
Park City Mountain Resort • 649-6100

Park City turns into an outdoor sculpture
garden during this annual event, now going
into its 27th year. Skilled sculptors with
chainsaws and axes turn huge mounds of
snow into spectacular frozen works of art. In
past years sculptors have carved bears on
skis, alligators, Snoopy, sharks eating boats,
dogs and every other imaginable figure of

whimsy or sentiment. Hey, we're talking winter wonderland here.

Along with the snow sculpture contest, a Winterfest celebration takes place in the afternoon. Activities include dogsled rides, snow-cave building, snowshoeing and avalanche safety clinics. Prize drawings liven up the day, with winners taking home great stuff like snowboards, bikes, and lift tickets.

It's held on the third weekend in February and costs $25 to enter a sculpture, although admittance is free.

Art Organizations

The Institute at Deer Valley
Various locations • 645-6981

Formerly known as the Snowbird Institute of Arts and Humanities, the Institute at Deer Valley still follows the same mission of fostering excellence in music, dance and the humanities. Established in 1975, the Institute directs its energy to providing artists a retreat where they can create new works in dance and music. The Institute is also involved in arts education and broadening and strengthening the audience for the humanities. Emerging artists and scholars are supported through career-development opportunities, as well as by technical and financial assistance. Humanities programs have included seminars on a just society, Japanese economics and the state of education in America. Some of the world-renowned musicians and dancers who have performed at the Institute include the Muir String Quartet, American composer Jean Tower and the Ririe-Woodbury Dance Company. Ticket prices for concerts and events vary.

Park City Performances
328 Main St., Historic Egyptian Theatre, Park City • 649-9371

This recently renovated gem of a theater is a wonderful venue for an intimate theater experience, be it drama, comedy or musical. The Egyptian Theatre was built in 1926 for vaudeville and silent movies and is on the Register of National Historic Landmarks. Plays range from toe-tappin' musicals like *The Fantasticks* to comedies like *Greater Tuna*. In addition, the Park City Film Series shows art films and independent films each week throughout the year. Call for a schedule and prices.

Art Galleries

Artworks Gallery
461 Main St., Park City • 649-4462

This gallery emphasizes contemporary American crafts such as leather, drums, wood, pottery and stained glass. They also sell custom jewelry designed by Juddy Summer.

Coda Gallery
804 Main St., Park City • 655-3803

Emerging artists from all over the country fill this gallery with unique paintings, sculpture and furniture. The glittering hand-blown glass art is a must-see here.

F. Marks Collectables
Corner of Swede Alley and Heber Ave.
• 655-2820

You'll find the crème de la crème of glass art in this distinguished gallery, including Kosta Boda, Hermes of Paris and Utah's only Mackenzie Childs Ltd. collections. You'll also find Rigaud candles from Paris, painted porcelains and tasteful recycled paper goods.

Images of Nature
556 Main St., Park City • 649-7579

This gallery showcases the work of Thomas Mangelsen, a well-known artist who specializes in the scenery and wildlife of the Rocky Mountains. His bear paintings are particularly evocative.

INSIDERS' TIP

The late J.E. Jenkins, better known as Pop Jenks, was a well-known Park City character and photographer during the early 1900s. Thirty-two of his photographs with text have been compiled in a book that you can view or buy at the Park City Historical Society and Museum.

Kimball Arts Center
638 Park Ave., Park City • 649-8882

One of the oldest and best galleries in Park City, Kimball's has been at the forefront of the Park City art scene for decades. Along with sponsoring the Park City Arts Festival and assisting with the Sundance Film Festival, Kimball puts on numerous institutes, workshops, art classes and other educational opportunities in the arts. The exhibits are eclectic and wide-ranging, varying from bird decoys, quilts and traditional landscapes to photography and sculpture. The shows are wonderfully imaginative and presented with exquisite taste. Two exhibit halls feature new shows monthly. The gift shop sells local art including ceramics, jewelry and other media.

Meyer Gallery
305 Main St., Park City • 649-8160

Folks come here to see the contemporary Southwestern art of Malcolm Furlough as well as the work of Kent Wallace, a landscape impressionist. You can also find bronze sculpture, Native American pottery and jewelry.

Richard Thomas Galleries
715 Main St., Park City • 655-7600

One of Park City's newest fine-arts galleries, Richard Thomas features sculpture and painting for the educated connoisseur. Among the 50 artists represented are Jiang, Henry Peeters, Yuri Gorbachev, Csaba Markus and S. H. Lee.

Valline Gallery
1101 Park Ave., Park City • 649-8102

This longtime Park City gallery specializes in Bev Doolittle prints and is a certified Greenwich workshop dealer. They also specialize in custom framing.

Index of Advertisers

Index

ing Somewhere?

_ublishing Inc. presents 48 current and upcoming titles to popular destinations all
_the country (including the titles below) — and we're planning on adding many more. To
order a title, go to your local bookstore or call (800) 582-2665 and we'll direct you to one.

Adirondacks	Minneapolis/St. Paul, MN
Atlanta, GA	Mississippi
Bermuda	Myrtle Beach, SC
Boca Raton and the Palm Beaches, FL	Nashville, TN
Boulder, CO, and Rocky Mountain National Park	New Hampshire
Bradenton/Sarasota, FL	North Carolina's Central Coast and New Bern
Branson, MO, and the Ozark Mountains	North Carolina's Mountains
California's Wine Country	Outer Banks of North Carolina
Cape Cod, Nantucket and Martha's Vineyard, MA	The Pocono Mountains
Charleston, SC	Relocation
Cincinnati, OH	Richmond, VA
Civil War Sites in the Eastern Theater	Salt Lake City
Colorado's Mountains	Santa Fe
Denver, CO	Savannah
Florida Keys and Key West	Southwestern Utah
Florida's Great Northwest	Tampa/St. Petersburg, FL
Golf in the Carolinas	Tuscon
Indianapolis, IN	Virginia's Blue Ridge
The Lake Superior Region	Virginia's Chesapeake Bay
Las Vegas	Washington, D.C.
Lexington, KY	Wichita, KS
Louisville, KY	Williamsburg, VA
Madison, WI	Wilmington, NC
Maine's Mid-Coast	Yellowstone

Insiders' Publishing Inc. • P.O. Box 2057 • Manteo, NC 27954
Phone (919) 473-6100 • Fax (919) 473-5869 • INTERNET address: http://www.insiders.com